Democracy and the Media

This book presents a systematic overview and assessment of the impacts of politics on the media, and of the media on politics, in authoritarian, transitional, and democratic regimes in Russia, Spain, Hungary, Chile, Italy, Great Britain, Germany, Japan, the Netherlands, and the United States. Its analysis of the interactions between macro- and micro-level factors incorporates the disciplinary perspectives of political science, mass communications, sociology, and social psychology. These essays show that media's effects on politics are the product of often complex and contingent interactions among various causal factors, including media technologies, the structure of the media market, the legal and regulatory framework, the nature of basic political institutions, and the characteristics of individual citizens. The authors' conclusions challenge many forms of conventional wisdom concerning the political roles and effects of the mass media on regime support and change, on the political behavior of citizens, and on the quality of democracy.

Richard Gunther is Professor of Political Science and Executive Director of International Studies at Ohio State University. He has served as cochair of the Social Science Research Council's Subcommittee on Southern Europe and as Director of the West European Studies Program at Ohio State University. He is author of *Public Policy in a No-Party State* (1980) and coauthor or coeditor of other volumes, including *Spain after Franco* (1986), *Elites and Democratic Consolidation in Latin America and Southern Europe* (1992), *Society and Democracy: The Case of Spain* (1993), *The Politics of Democratic Consolidation* (1995), and *Parties, Politics and Democracy in the New Southern Europe* (2000).

Anthony Mughan is Professor of Political Science and Director of the Undergraduate International Studies program at Ohio State University. He formerly held positions at University College, Cardiff in Wales, and at the Institute for Advanced Study at Australian National University. He is author and editor of numerous books, including most recently *Senates: Bicameralism in the Modern World* (1999), *Media and the Presidentialization of Parliamentary Elections* (2000), and articles in leading international journals.

COMMUNICATION, SOCIETY, AND POLITICS

Editors

W. Lance Bennett, *University of Washington*

Robert M. Entman, *North Carolina State University*

Politics and relations among individuals in societies across the world are being transformed by new technologies for targeting individuals and sophisticated methods for shaping personalized messages. The new technologies challenge boundaries of many kinds – between news, information, entertainment, and advertising; between media, with the arrival of the World Wide Web; and even between nations, with CNN, MTV, and the like being broadcast to every continent.

Communication, Society, and Politics is a new series that will probe the political and social impacts of these new communication systems in national, comparative, and global perspectives. It aims to lead a transition toward new, rigorous, empirically grounded theoretical perspectives. The series will adopt an inclusive definition of politics: the exercise of power within and between nations. It will explore power in the new communication order through interdisciplinary and critical approaches to the social, cultural, and economic underpinnings of politically significant communication. While the series will strive for a diversity of methods and views, it will emphasize works that address questions about democracy, equality, justice, and other normative concerns.

Democracy and the Media

A COMPARATIVE PERSPECTIVE

Edited by

Richard Gunther   Anthony Mughan

The Ohio State University

CAMBRIDGE
UNIVERSITY PRESS

PUBLISHED BY THE PRESS SYNDICATE OF THE UNIVERSITY OF CAMBRIDGE
The Pitt Building, Trumpington Street, Cambridge, United Kingdom

CAMBRIDGE UNIVERSITY PRESS
The Edinburgh Building, Cambridge CB2 2RU, UK   http://www.cup.cam.ac.uk
40 West 20th Street, New York, NY 10011-4211, USA   http://www.cup.org
10 Stamford Road, Oakleigh, Melbourne 3166, Australia
Ruiz de Alarcón 13, 28014 Madrid, Spain

First published 2000

Printed in the United States of America

Typeface Minion 11/13 pt.   *System* QuarkXPress 4.04 [AG]

A catalog record for this book is available from the British Library.

Library of Congress Cataloging in Publication Data
Democracy and the media : a comparative perspective / edited by Richard Gunther,
Anthony Mughan.
p.   cm. – (Communication, society, and politics)
Includes index.
ISBN 0-521-77180-3 (hb) – ISBN 0-521-77743-7 (pb)
1. Mass media – Political aspects. 2. Democracy. I. Gunther, Richard. II. Mughan,
Anthony III. Title. IV. Series
P95.8 .D394 2000
302.23 – dc21   99-053841

ISBN 0 521 77180 3 hardback
ISBN 0 521 77743 7 paperback

MERSHON
CENTER
Additional support provided
by the Mershon Center,
The Ohio State University

For our incomparable children
Elizabeth
Siân and Tomos

Contents

List of Contributors

Cees van der Eijk is Professor of Political Science at the University of Amsterdam. He was principal investigator of a series of Dutch Parliamentary Election Studies, and of European Election Studies conducted since direct elections to the European Parliament were introduced in 1989. He is the author or coauthor of seven books, among which are *Choosing Europe* (1996), *In Search of Structure* (1998), and *Electoral Change in the Netherlands* (1983), and of numerous articles on Dutch politics, electoral behavior and campaigns, European integration, and comparative politics and methodology.

Richard Gunther is Professor of Political Science and Executive Director of International Studies at Ohio State University. From 1990 to 1998 he served as cochair of the Social Science Research Council's Subcommittee on Southern Europe. Among his publications are *Public Policy in a No-Party State* (1980), *Spain after Franco* with Giacamo Sani and Goldie Shabad (1986), *Elites and Democratic Consolidation in Latin America and Southern Europe* with John Higley (1992), *Politics, Society and Democracy: The Case of Spain* (1993), *The Politics of Democratic Consolidation* with Nikiforos Diamandouros and Hans-Jürgen Puhle (1995), and *Parties, Politics and Democracy in the New Southern Europe* with Nikiforos Diamandouros (2000).

Max Kaase is Professor of Political Science and Comparative Survey Research at the University of Mannheim, Germany. He has been on leave from that position since October 1993 and currently holds a Research Professorship at Wissenschaftszentrum Berlin für Sozialforschung. He has published widely in the fields of comparative politics, electoral sociology, and mass communication.

Ellis S. Krauss is a professor at the Graduate School of International Relations and Pacific Studies, University of California, San Diego, where he specializes in postwar Japanese politics and political economy, and U.S.–Japanese relations. He has authored or edited several books on Japanese politics and published many articles, including a number on the mass media and politics in Japan. A forthcoming book entitled *Broadcasting Politics in Japan: NHK and Television News* looks at the interrelations of television news and politics.

Carlo Marletti is Professor of Sociology in the Faculty of Political Sciences and Dean of the Department of Political Studies at the University of Turin. His current interests are in political sociology and the relationship between the media and politics. He is cofounder of the Osservatorio-Archivio della Communicazione Politica at the University of Turin. His most recent books include *Politica e società in Italia* and two volumes about the Italian political transition.

Ellen Mickiewicz is the James R. Shepley Professor of Public Policy Studies and Director of the DeWitt Wallace Center for Communications and Journalism of the Terry Sanford Institute for Public Policy at Duke University. Her latest book is *Changing Channels: Television and the Struggle for Power in Russia* (1999).

José Ramón Montero is Professor of Political Science at the Universidad Autónoma de Madrid at the Centro de Estudios Avanzados en Ciencias Sociales, Instituto Juan March, Madrid. Among his many published works are *La CEDA: El catolicismo social y político en la II República* (1977), *El control parlamentario* (1985) with Joaquín G. Morillo, *Crisis y Cambio: Electores y Partidos en la España de los Años Ochenta* with Juan Linz (1986), and *El régimen electoral* (1996) with Richard Gunther and others.

Anthony Mughan is Professor of Political Science and Director of the Undergraduate International Studies Program at Ohio State University. His books include *Party and Participation in British Elections* (1986), *Political Leadership in Democratic Societies* (1992) with Samuel C. Patterson, *Senates: Bicameralism in the Contemporary World* (1999) with Samuel C. Patterson, and *Media and the Presidentialization of Parliamentary Elections* (2000).

Thomas E. Patterson is the Bradlee Professor of Government and the Press in the John F. Kennedy School of Government at Harvard University. His books include *Out of Order,* which was labeled "the most important political book of the year" by a leading national commentator; *The Mass Media Election* (1980), which received a Choice award as Outstanding Academic Book, 1980–1; and *The Unseeing Eye* (1976), which was selected by the American Association for Public Opinion Research as one of the 50 most influential books of the past half century in the field of public opinion.

Franca Roncarolo is a Lecturer in the University of Turin's Department of Political Studies and teaches in the Faculty of Political Sciences. Her research interests lie in the relationship between government and the media, election campaigns, and gender problems in Italian political communications. She is the author of *Controllare i media* (1994) and coauthor of *I media come arena elettorale: La campagne elettorale 1996 in TV e sui giornali* (1997).

Holli A. Semetko is Professor of Audience and Public Opinion Research and the Chair of the Department of Communication Science at the University of Amsterdam, where she also teaches in the international Ph.D. program of the Amsterdam School of Communications Research (AS-CoR). Semetko's research interests include cross-national comparative studies on media content and effects and political communication. Her most recent books are *On Message: Communicating the Campaign* (1999) with Pippa Norris, John Curtice, David Sanders, and Margaret Scammell and *Germany's Unity Election: Voters and the Media* (1994) with Klaus Schoenbach.

Miklós Sükösd received his Ph.D. in political science from the Hungarian Academy of Sciences and currently teaches political communication and media policy in the Department of Political Science, Central European University, Budapest. He has coauthored or edited nine books on the media and political theory, most recently *Media Law and Media Policy in Hungary* (1999) with G. Cseh. He has also edited ten special issues of journals dealing with election campaigns in Hungary.

Guillermo Sunkel received his Ph.D. from the Centre for Contemporary Cultural Studies, Birmingham University, England, and is Professor in the School of Journalism, Social Science Faculty, Universidad de Chile. He is the author of *Razón y pasión en la prensa popular.*

Eugenio Tironi is Associate Professor in the Institute of Sociology at the Universidad Católica de Chile. He was Director of Communication in President Patricio Aylwin's administration. His latest book is *El régimen autoritario: para una sociología de Pinochet* (1990).

José Ignacio Wert has been President and CEO of DEMOSCOPIA since 1987. He has been Deputy Director of the Centro de Investigaciones Sociolócias, and Director of Research Services in, and Member of the Board of, Radio Televisión Española. He has also been a Madrid city councillor and a member of the Congress of Deputies. He has directed more than 500 market and opinion research surveys and has authored or coauthored several books and numerous articles on sociology, public opinion, and market research.

Acknowledgments

This book would not have been possible without generous grants from the Battelle Endowment for Technology and Human Affairs and The Mershon Center for National Security and Public Policy at The Ohio State University. With their support, our collaborative project was initiated with a conference on Mass Media Technologies and Democracies held at Ohio State University on October 9–11, 1992. We are grateful to Daniel Schorr for opening this conference with a stimulating keynote address.

Paul Beck played a crucial role in initiating this massive project and serving as codirector during its first two years. His critical comments throughout this project have contributed significantly to improving the quality of its ultimate product, this volume. We would also like to express our appreciation to Felipe Agüero, Richard Hamilton, Judith Kullberg, Bradley Richardson, and Goldie Shabad for serving as discussants on the initial drafts of these chapters.

Most important, we want to express our thanks to our wives, for their tolerance during this protracted endeavor.

CHAPTER 1

The Media in Democratic and Nondemocratic Regimes: A Multilevel Perspective

Anthony Mughan and Richard Gunther

The mass communications media are the connective tissue of democracy. They are the principal means through which citizens and their elected representatives communicate in their reciprocal efforts to inform and influence. Despite the widespread acknowledgment of the paramount importance of this "political communications" function, however, the literature in political science is notable for the general absence of rigorous comparative analyses of the mutually influencing interaction between the flow of political information, on the one hand, and the basic democratic character of political regimes and individual political attitudes and behavior, on the other. As one student of politics and the media has recently bemoaned: "The state of research on media effects is one of the most notable embarrassments of modern social science" (Bartels 1993, 267).

An important obstacle to a deeper understanding of the relationship between the media and the democratic political process has long been the lack of an integrated research agenda. Compartmentalization and fragmentation have resulted not only from the scattering of scholars among different academic disciplines (mainly sociology, political science, social psychology, and communications) that rarely interact with one another, but also from a puzzling and seemingly unnecessary bifurcation into distinct schools of analysis. One scholarly approach has been for media analysts to adopt a micro perspective in their focus on the questions of how, and in what ways, the media matter. They have restricted themselves to investigations of the individual-level effects of political communications, usually during election campaigns. Do the media change political attitudes and behavior or do they just reinforce them? Do they differ in their political impact? Are all individuals equally susceptible to media influence? These are among the many micro-level foci of analysis in this important school of research.[1] A second and contrasting tendency has been for scholars to be more distinctively macro in focus, studying the structure of media *systems* and how these systems affect politics. Among the systemic characteristics usually examined are patterns of government regulation, of media ownership, of program content, of audience structure, and of viewership. Some scholars have employed this approach in the study of communications media in nondemocratic regimes, while others have sought to draw inferences about how the structural characteristics of the media system affect the distribution of political power in democracies, or to bemoan the normative implications of the allegedly "liberal," "conservative," or "capitalist" bias of the mainstream media.[2]

Few published studies, however, have combined these macro and micro perspectives to examine the reciprocal relationship between the media and the politics of democracy and democratization. As a result, our understanding and appreciation of the complexity of this relationship are underdeveloped. This book steps into this void by offering a synthesis of the macro and micro perspectives in ten single-country studies. It explores the relationship between the communications media and democracy from a variety of perspectives and in widely varying political settings. It shares with the majority of published works in this field a concern with the ways in which political communications influence the attitudes and behavior of citizens and affect the quality of political life in established democratic systems. But in developing these themes in the contexts of Britain, Germany, Japan, the Netherlands, and the United States, an effort is made to enrich this micro-level perspective by systematically examining macro-level or structural characteristics of these media systems, as well as the interaction between the micro and macro levels.

Other chapters in this volume broaden the traditional geographical and thematic bounds of empirical studies in this field by examining the media's contribution to processes of political change, particularly democratization, in political systems that have been fundamentally transformed over the past decade or two. Studies of Chile, Hungary, Russia, and Spain assess the extent to which government-initiated liberalization of political communications helped to undermine support for authoritarian or posttotalitarian regimes, as well as the contribution of the media to the transition to, and consolidation of, political democracy in these countries. In the case of Italy, we examine the roles of the communications media in a different but no less dramatic kind of political

2

change, from one kind of democratic regime to another with decidedly different characteristics. From several perspectives, the scope of this volume is quite broad, and it opens up a series of important questions that have barely been explored comparatively.[3]

This introductory chapter sets the scene for the change-oriented focus of the individual country studies by reviewing the theoretical background, empirical findings, and evolution of the literature on the media and politics since its initial appearance in the 1940s and 1950s. Familiarity with the early classic studies is important, since they effectively framed popular understanding of the relationships between politics and the media for decades. An overview of more recent research is also desirable, insofar as this information should help the reader to understand the causal mechanisms that underpin processes of political change in the single-country studies that follow.

THE MACRO-LEVEL PERSPECTIVE

THE MEDIA AND REGIME TYPE

Throughout the twentieth century, the mass communications media were central to the dynamics of the relationship between governors and the governed in all types of political regime. Initially because of the spread of literacy and subsequently because of advances in communications technology, the media – and particularly television in today's world – have increasingly become the principal source of political information for the mass public as political discussion within, and information flows through, family, community, and other intermediary organizations have declined in frequency and importance. While the extent to which (and the processes through which) the media actually influence the way in which citizens structure their attitudinal and behavioral orientations towards politics will be discussed later in this chapter (and throughout the remainder of this volume), suffice it to say at this point that political elites widely, if not universally, believe that the media are of paramount importance in shaping these orientations. For this reason, they have been very sensitive to the power of information and have developed media policies to suit their economic, social, and political purposes, although, in practice, government regulation of the mass communications media has varied greatly in both scope and substance. The starkest contrast, in this respect, is rooted in the differing roles of the media in democratic and nondemocratic political systems.

The traditional view has been that the media are schizophrenic in

3

character and play contrasting roles in the establishment and maintenance of political order in authoritarian/totalitarian regimes and in democracies: the media have been depicted as manipulative and subversive of individual freedom and political choice in the former and as guarantors of political liberties and government accountability in the latter (Neuman 1991, 22–47; see also Kinder and Sears 1985). Stated more fully, the defining characteristic of the authoritarian/totalitarian model is strict governmental control of the media to achieve objectives set by self-selected, unaccountable political elites and widely promulgated by virtue of their "unconstrained and pervasive power" over their media systems (Neuman 1991, 31). These unaccountable elites are seen not only as setting the policy agenda, but also as carefully structuring the information they convey to the public through their "puppet" media, with the objective of forming and manipulating nonelite attitudes and behaviors. Beyond this similarity, however, authoritarian and totalitarian regimes differ in the nature of the specific goals pursued. According to Juan Linz's classic typology (1975), authoritarian rulers are primarily concerned with demobilizing and (when necessary) repressing their subject populations with a view to imposing social and political order while maintaining themselves in office. Totalitarians, in contrast, have social-revolutionary objectives. In their efforts to create the "new person" in a radically transformed society, they manipulate the media in an effort to reshape the hearts and minds of nonelites, thereby enforcing the disciplined conformity necessary for mass mobilization in support of a revolutionary ideology and the construction of a utopian society. Such marked divergences in ultimate objectives notwithstanding, however, totalitarian and authoritarian regimes do not differ in their relationship to the mass media (Linz 1974, 1496–7). Both are characterized by strict censorship, repression of journalistic liberty, and heavy-handed efforts to structure highly selective flows of information to the general public.

The political communications process has been portrayed very differently in democratic societies. The media, through the information they convey to the mass public, serve as key guarantors of elite accountability and popular control of government in democracies, since "a broadly and equitably informed citizenry helps assure a democracy that is both responsive and responsible" (Delli Carpini and Keeter 1996, 1). Two characteristics of democratic media systems are held to ensure that political information disseminated by the mass communications media serves to constrain, or check, government power rather than magnify it. The first is that constitutional guarantees or conventions assure citizens of free access to political information. Freedom of the press, of speech, and of assembly provide for a wide diversity of political communications and points of view. These freedoms also give citizens the right to take issue publicly with their government and its goals and to remove it from office through free and competitive elections if its actions or inactions are unacceptable to enough of them. The second is that the media are protected from the arbitrary exercise of government power, and media pluralism is institutionalized. Not only are the media free from direct political control but, in addition, legal frameworks are established to promote and sustain a diversity of media forms and outlets. Democracy is strengthened and its integrity ensured by the free flow of information and competition among public and commercial media articulating (often under force of law) a variety of political viewpoints to educate the public and allow it to make informed choices, particularly at election time.

To be sure, this association of democracy with a free press and authoritarianism/totalitarianism with a media enslaved is overdrawn and has never been fully convincing. The media in nondemocratic regimes, for example, never enjoyed the pervasiveness, penetration, or omniscience popularized in George Orwell's *1984* (Pool 1973b; Mickiewicz 1981). In the same vein, the media in democratic societies have never been fully free of government control. In Britain, for example, the government can stop the publication of stories that it unilaterally determines to be prejudicial to national security through a system of so-called D-Notices (May and Rowan 1982). More dramatically still, the broadcast media in France, was actually a state monopoly from the early twentieth century until the 1980s (Palmer and Tunstall 1990). Nonetheless, social scientists' understanding of the relationship between the media and politics has been fundamentally shaped by these sharply divergent ideal types.

To some extent, the simplistic view that the media in nondemocratic regimes were associated with the suppression of popular, accountable government, while contributing importantly to its healthy functioning in democracies, was largely rooted in a Cold War mentality that saw the world divided into the "forces of light" (read democracy) and the "forces of darkness" (read authoritarianism/totalitarianism). Rhetorical overstatement notwithstanding, this dichotomy enjoyed some superficial plausibility and credibility; the media did seem to be associated with the differing political objectives of elites in the two types of regime. As the West rebuilt itself economically and politically after the devastation of

World War II, democracy seemed to prosper under governments' relatively laissez-faire approach to the media. Indeed, a free and competitive media system was widely credited with playing a key role in the socialization of the post–World War II German and Japanese populations to democratic norms and values (Verba 1965; also see the chapters by Kaase and Krauss in this volume). The totalitarian Soviet Union also seemed to go from strength to strength economically and politically, but it advanced under the aegis of a massive and relentless media campaign mounted to discredit the democratic world and resocialize Soviet citizens into the values of communism, thereby making possible the mobilization of their support behind its ideological goals (Neuman 1991, 22–47). Economic success, regime stability, and the absence of large-scale manifestations of popular discontent all seemed to vindicate the Bolshevik media strategy.

As plausible as this conventional wisdom about the nature of the relationship between the media and political-regime type may have seemed in the postwar years, however, developments in the late 1980s and 1990s posed serious challenges to its validity. The strength of the relationship between rigid state control of the media, on the one hand, and nondemocratic political regimes, on the other, was called into question by what was perhaps the most important and unexpected political change of the late twentieth century – the "global resurgence of democracy" (Diamond and Plattner 1993). The seemingly worldwide retreat of more authoritarian forms of government certainly suggests that state control and manipulation of the media have been notably unsuccessful in sustaining nondemocratic forms of government the world over. Even the "darkest force" of all, the Soviet Union, collapsed and disintegrated into a number of independent states, most of them aspiring to democracy, at least in principle. This implies that the regime's ability to translate its control of the media into compliant and lasting mass-level attitudes and behavioral norms was by no means as great as initially estimated. Indeed, even more damaging to the conventional wisdom about the political role of the media in nondemocratic regimes is that this development took place at the very time when vast technological improvements in the communications media, the deep penetration of regime-controlled information flows into society, and the high level of sophistication of their content implied that such regimes should have become more, not less, able to entrench themselves by enhancing their legitimacy in the eyes of their populations. Why did the opposite transpire? Why were expectations concerning the seemingly limitless antidemocratic potential of media manipulation so totally contradicted by the contagion of worldwide democratization in the 1980s and 1990s?

Similarly, the traditional stereotype of the uniformly positive contribution to democracy by free, unregulated communications has come under increased scrutiny and criticism. In contrast with the traditionally positive image of the media in the established democracies, some journalists and broadcasters in these countries have been charged with undermining representative democracy rather than buttressing and reinforcing it. As we shall see in subsequent essays of this book, this trend is not apparent in all or even most Western democracies (emerging, therefore, as an important but heretofore largely unexplored subject for comparative analysis), but in some prominent cases there has been a growing disillusionment over the extent to which the media present to the electorate an unbiased flow of a plurality of viewpoints, or even an adequate volume of the kinds of information that democratic theory implies should be available to voters. In the United States, for example, it has been argued that journalistic cynicism, coupled with trivialization and personalization of media coverage of politics, has undermined the possibility of the kind of healthy and substantive political debate that democratic government requires. The complaint is increasingly heard that the American media in general, and television in particular, now undermine democracy by equating news with entertainment and deemphasizing coverage of serious, substantive political issues. Instead of broadcasting policy-relevant information to help to create and sustain an informed electorate, the media are accused of devoting undue attention to ephemeral, nonsubstantive matters like current public opinion poll standings and the personalities, character, and foibles of the leading political figures.[4] Voters are seen as increasingly obliged to reach conclusions and make choices on the basis of criteria that are unrelated to the real business of government. Their choice among competitors for public office is trivialized, and the accountability of public office holders is thereby weakened (Ranney 1983; Bennett 1988; Entman 1989; Iyengar 1991; Patterson 1993; Fallows 1996). "Talk radio" is a good example: rather than facilitating a two-way flow of responsible dialogue between citizens and their elected representatives, it has too often interjected into the public discourse an unprecedentedly venomous stream of malicious, often unsubstantiated rumors and personal insults (Kurtz 1996). As one study put it, "the talk-show culture too often exchanges only the mutual ignorance of listeners and hosts who share mainly a taste for ranting and raving" (Diamond and Silverman 1995, 141). There is even evidence of disillusionment with democracy itself, as this type of coverage of politics encourages public cynicism (Cappella and Jamieson 1997) and as the negative advertising that is the norm in U.S. election campaigns encourages not citizen participation but the *de*mobilization of voters (Ansolabehere and Iyengar 1995).

To some extent, this wave of pessimism may have emerged in reaction to the largely uncritical assessment of the relationship between the media and democracy that was prevalent in the first few decades of the postwar era. The positive contributions of the media to the development of democratic political cultures in Germany and Japan stood in stark contrast to the tightly controlled media in the repressive regimes of the Soviet bloc. At the micro level as well (as will be seen later in this chapter), early studies seemed to indicate that the impact of the media on political behavior and attitudinal development or change in established democracies was limited and benign. In general, such studies concluded that the media served to educate and inform the electorate, but could not be used to manipulate the attitudes and behaviors of citizens in such a way as to undermine the practice, as well as the principle, of government accountability. In this regard, they were seen as vehicles of communication that perfectly served the purposes of electoral democracy.[5] With further technological advances, the television medium even came to be regarded by some as heralding a "new dawn," making possible the transition from representative to participatory democracy (Grossman 1995; Budge 1996).

The current wave of pessimism may turn out to be as transitory as the idealized view of the media and democracy of that earlier era. But what is clear is that it cannot be ignored; a reassessment of the role of mass communications systems in contemporary democracies is long overdue. An explicitly comparative study is particularly timely insofar as numerous cross-national differences are apparent that raise important and interesting questions. Why have the American media, for example, been criticized for excessive cynicism, trivialization, and personalization in their coverage of politics, while such trends are largely absent in other established democracies or, at worst, present only in an incipient form? A reexamination of the media's political role under nondemocratic regimes is also long overdue, as is assessment of the role played by print and broadcast media in their recent democratization. Were the initial ideal types simply wrong or have changes in media technology, the structure of media systems, or the structures of these societies themselves overtaken the old models and made them irrelevant? These are among the many questions that will serve as the foci of analysis in the following chapters.

Our strategy in this volume is to deliberately combine the general and the idiosyncratic in country-by-country examinations of the relationship between democracy and the mass media. The idiosyncratic in each chapter focuses on country-specific considerations like political culture, electoral law, historical legacy, type of social structure and party system, style of executive leadership, and the like. Our more theoretical concern is with the general – with the identification of common media trends making for similar political outcomes, be they in the area of democratic transitions from authoritarianism or in influencing popular attitudes and behaviors in established democracies.

Two important macro-level variables substantially affect the nature of the relationship between the media and the politics of democracy and democratization: the structure of the media system in each country and the pattern of government regulation. As we shall show in the following chapters, these have been configured quite differently in the cases examined in this book, and with important political consequences. And in the last chapter, we will reach a conclusion strikingly at odds with a well-established conventional wisdom: key characteristics of a functioning, healthy democracy are not necessarily enhanced by minimizing government regulation. While we shall defer to the individual country chapters for the presentation of information about the structure of their respective media systems, it is timely at this point to survey the different approaches adopted by democratic governments to the regulation of the communications media.

GOVERNMENT REGULATION OF THE MEDIA

A change of fundamental importance over the last 40 years or so has been the more or less worldwide emergence of television as the preeminent medium of political communication and information. Together with the other broadcast medium, radio, democratic governments treated it differently from the printed press right from the outset. Newspapers and magazines were normally granted virtually unlimited freedom, whereas radio and television were subjected to the close regulation reminiscent of the way authoritarian governments respond to all media.

Respect for, and guarantees of, freedom of the press have long been regarded as among the fundamental tenets of democracy since the unhindered flow of political information was recognized as integral to holding governments accountable for their (in)actions. Accordingly, governments were to interfere as little as possible with the free flow of information through the print media. Among the consequences of this hands-off approach was that newspapers could determine their own partisan stance, the level at which they would pitch their appeal, and the style and type of story that would constitute their hallmark. It followed that the audiences for different newspapers tended to vary substantially in their educational levels, political sophistication, and partisan preferences. The result was the emergence of two de facto models of print journalism in democratic societies. One, typified by several continental European countries, is characterized by a highly partisan press in which newspapers openly publicize their preferences for their respective parties. In the other, exemplified by most American newspapers in the late twentieth century, newspapers display no obvious partisan preferences in the political coverage that appears in their "national news" sections, even when their editorial pages contain endorsements of specific candidates (Dalton et al. 1998).

With regard to the broadcast media (radio and later television) that began to emerge in the early decades of the twentieth century, by contrast, democratic governments had no choice but to take a more interventionist stance, if only because they were obliged to resolve the problem of wavelength scarcity by awarding broadcast licenses on the basis of criteria they themselves had to formulate. Two modal regulatory philosophies emerged. Typified by the initial responses of the governments of the United Kingdom and the United States, these may be labeled respectively the "public service" and "commercial" models. The principal distinction between them is that public service broadcasting is characterized by an emphasis on news and public affairs, features and documentaries, art, music, and plays, whereas commercial radio and television broadcasting stress general entertainment more heavily (Williams 1974, 78–86). The oversight role of the state is decidedly different in the two models.

The British Broadcasting Corporation (BBC) is perhaps the best-known and most influential example of the public service model.[6] From the birth of radio in the 1920s, British governments (of whatever party) regarded the broadcasting media as a public utility that the state had to control in the public interest. Two especially important benefits were seen in the ability to broadcast nationwide. First was the opportunity to rise above the partiality of newspapers and provide common access to a wide range of public events, ceremonies, and national occasions, thereby bringing all classes of the population together and strengthening national social solidarity. Second, in a country where the franchise had only recently been extended to all men and was imminent for all women, radio was seen as harboring immense potential for helping to create the educated, informed, and enlightened electorate widely deemed necessary to a healthy pluralistic democracy (Scannell 1989, 1990).

Thus, when the BBC was created in the early 1920s, it was granted both a broadcasting monopoly and financial and political independence from government through the imposition of an annual license fee paid by all radio (and later television) owners. The BBC was answerable to a nonpartisan regulatory body; its reciprocal obligation was to remain impartial in its coverage of political affairs. In practice, impartiality has manifested itself in balanced coverage of the major parties and guarantees of their equal access to the broadcast media (Burns 1977).[7] Even when commercial television (financed not through a license fee, but through paid advertising) was created by an act of Parliament in the mid-1950s, it too was mandated by law and under pain of losing its broadcast license to inform and educate as well as entertain. The public service ethos remained alive and well.

Regulation was strengthened during the highlight of the democratic calendar: election campaigns. The expectation of impartiality remained in force. In addition, to ensure media independence as well as impartiality, paid political advertising, even on commercial television, was forbidden in favor of a system whereby political parties with enough support received free television time in which they were able to broadcast programs of their own devising. Moreover, at least until 1979, these programs were broadcast on all channels simultaneously to maximize their chances of reaching voters as a whole.[8] The media's role in local contests was also minimized by the imposition of stringent spending limits at the constituency level.

The "commercial model," as best typified by broadcasting in the United States, is based on a sharply contrasting philosophy. In keeping with the country's traditional liberalism and governing ethos of minimal interventionism, governments opted for a largely private, regionalized, and unabashedly profit-oriented broadcasting system. The Radio Act of 1927 may have established "public interest, convenience and necessity" (a phrase borrowed from public utility legislation) as the discretionary yardstick for the licensing of radio stations, but no effort was made to establish a financially independent public broadcasting sector with an explicit public service mission. Indeed, special provision was not even made for noncommercial educational stations in the distribution

11

of transmission frequencies and broadcast licenses. The result was that the 600 educational stations that reached 40 percent of all U.S. households in 1930 soon shrank in number under the twin assaults of the Great Depression and the popular predatory commercial networks that were being formed to link stations across the country (Katz 1989, 195–7). Reaction against the excesses of commercialism's broadcasting hegemony eventually led to the establishment in 1967 of the Corporation for Public Broadcasting as a federally chartered, nonprofit, and nongovernment body to oversee the public broadcasting service as a "free-standing institution, like other nonprofit corporations created to serve the public interest" (quoted in Katz 1989, 197). Given its explicit public service mandate, it was placed under a regulatory structure quite similar to that of the BBC. However, public broadcasting in America has remained very much the "poor relation" of commercial stations, in part because it is not allowed to air advertisements or to charge a license fee and in part because it attracts far smaller audiences than the commercial radio and television networks (Katz 1989; Boddy 1995).

The overwhelmingly commercial nature of American television does not imply that no attention was paid to concerns over partisan balance. As mandated by the Communications Act of 1934, radio broadcasters had to satisfy general public interest and equal time standards. In the face of ever greater wavelength spectrum scarcity in an increasingly crowded broadcasting world, broadcasters' public obligations were tightened with the passage of the Fairness Doctrine in 1949. Thenceforth, broadcasters were required to be nonpartisan, to give air time to controversial news and public affairs programs, and to provide reasonable opportunities for the presentation of contrasting viewpoints (Donahue 1989; Lichtenberg 1990, 252). As we shall see, however, this doctrine was abolished in 1987, with significant implications for the kinds of political communications reaching voters.

In addition to these differences in regulatory norms and philosophies, political communications in the United States and the United Kingdom differ starkly because of the role of money in elections in the two countries. From the outset, the United States allowed unlimited and unregulated paid political advertising on the broadcast media, both at election time and throughout the year. Nor was the right to purchase advertisements restricted to candidates competing in the election. Instead, political parties, interest groups, and, later, political action committees were able to air advertisements with or without the permission of candidates and for or against them. Candidates, in turn, have always had to devote much of their energy to fund-raising, a need that has intensified with the rise of the primary election, the decline of party loyalty among voters, and the increasing tendency to fight elections on television. The upshot is that money has always played much more of a role in U.S. elections than in those of other democracies (Alexander and Shiratori 1994).

One factor that helps to explain Americans' attachment to the commercial model is that the interventionist role of the state central to the public service model is incompatible with the suspicion of strong government that is embedded in the American political culture. Intervention can also be confused with the manipulation of the media that exists in authoritarian and totalitarian political systems. Indeed, the rationale underpinning both is derived from an awareness of the importance of political communications and of the state's ability to control their flow in pursuit of societal objectives. And even when the notion of government regulation of the media does not conjure up images of nondemocratic behavior, many Americans oppose an active regulatory role for the state because of their fear (justified or not) that state intervention will encourage corruption and partisan manipulation on the part of incumbents. Indeed, the example of Gaullist manipulation of French television in the 1960s suggests that this fear is not entirely groundless (Kuhn 1998, 29). What insulates the ideal-type public service model from the dangers of partisan manipulation, however, are strict guarantees of partisan balance that are institutionalized in carefully crafted regulatory structures. These nonpartisan or broadly representative interparty oversight structures clearly differentiate the democratic public service model from the direct government control found in authoritarian and totalitarian political systems.

DEREGULATION: Deregulation of the broadcast media was widespread throughout both democratic and nondemocratic political systems in the 1980s and 1990s. This diminution of the state's role in broadcasting occurred for different reasons and with very different political consequences. Deregulation took two forms. One was a liberalization of political control, and the other was the opening of the airwaves to private sector, commercial broadcasters with few or no public service obligations.

Liberalization was the principal form of deregulation in authoritarian political systems where it proceeded at uneven rates and for different reasons. In some cases (e.g., Chile), media liberalization was an unintended by-product of the Pinochet government's commitment to free-market economics and the consequent commercial pressures to provide the more open and entertainment-oriented content valued by consumers in an essentially demand-based economy. In other cases, liberalization of the media was regarded as part of an intentional strategy for the achievement of other, more highly valued political objectives. During the *glasnost* era in the Soviet Union, for example, Mikhail Gorbachev relaxed the state's stranglehold on both the print and electronic media in order to mobilize public support for his assault on the bureaucratic ossification and entrenched self-interest that were stultifying society and crippling the economy. In both instances, however, once unleashed, the liberalized media played significant roles in the processes of political change that brought these nondemocratic regimes to an end.

In established democracies, media deregulation has been part of a broader neoliberal reaction against government intervention in social and economic life. The market came to gain greater acceptance as the proper adjudicator of what was offered to the public and what it, in turn, chose to consume. This did not necessarily imply a withdrawal of government support for public service television. Indeed, the member states of the European Union (EU) formalized their commitment to it at their June 1997 Amsterdam summit by clarifying that government funding for public television does not violate EU rules on fair competition. The most consequential form of deregulation has been the opening up of the established and licensed television sector to competition from private cable and satellite broadcasters that are unabashedly commercial in character and not subject to the same "inform and educate" strictures as their longer-established counterparts. While common to established democracies worldwide, telecommunications deregulation has probably gone furthest in the United States, unhindered by a strong public service broadcasting tradition. Not only has cable and satellite television been encouraged, but also, in 1987, the Reagan administration repealed the Fairness Doctrine, arguing that the proliferation of channels meant that the original condition giving rise to the need for regulation – spectrum scarcity – no longer applied (Donahue 1989; Lichtenberg 1990). Accordingly, the major networks (the American Broadcasting Company [ABC], the Columbia Broadcasting System [CBS], and the National Broadcasting Company [NBC]) – the bastions of what little public service tradition existed in the American popular television sector – responded to increased competition for audience ratings and advertising revenue by downplaying their serious news programming (Bennett 1988, 1–19; Patterson 1993). This trend has reached such an extreme point that the new Fox network has been able to mount a serious challenge to the three broadcasting giants even though it does not air a national news program.

The proliferation of channels resulting from deregulation has enabled viewers to select more entertainment-oriented programs that tend to portray politics (when they deal with politics at all) as merely a "horse race" between competing personalities or parties, or to avoid political or news programs altogether. The net effect has been a reduction in coverage of and exposure to the programmatic positions taken by the candidates and parties, and their displacement by the daily drama of "who's ahead," by campaign trivia dressed up with attractive visuals, and by gaffes or scandals. Seen in this light, deregulation may have compounded the so-called media logic (Altheide and Snow 1979; also see Ranney 1983) whereby television, by its nature, has an inherent propensity to emphasize candidates and their personalities over parties and their programs, and to compress the presentation of information into brief "sound bites," at the expense of more complex, policy-relevant information. In the words of one vociferous critic of the medium, "The primary purpose of television . . . is to amuse rather than to edify the viewers; it is a medium which presents information in a form that renders it simplistic, nonsubstantive, nonhistorical and noncontextual; that is to say information packaged as entertainment" (Postman 1985, 141) As such, it infringes on one of the key criteria that we and our contributing authors employ to assess the quality of political communications in democratic systems. In our view, the quality of the performance of the media in democracies should be assessed in light of the extent to which they impartially present factual information about candidates, programs, and policies that is adequate enough in volume and content to enable citizens to make informed voting choices and hold governments responsible for their actions.[9] Concerns over media satisfaction of this criterion have been articulated most frequently in the United States. As this volume will show, however, the same concern over the substance and style of television's coverage of politics is becoming more common in countries like Germany, Great Britain, and the Netherlands as well.

At the same time that political coverage in the media has experienced some "dumbing down," there have been developments at the level of individual citizens and politicians that potentially leave voters more open to persuasion, perhaps manipulation, than used to be the case. In other words, what accounts for change in the relationship between the media and the politics of democracy and democratization is the *interaction* between macro- and micro-level developments.

MICRO-LEVEL MEDIA EFFECTS

In a manner quite parallel to the preceding discussion of the media and regime type, assessments of the power of the media to influence individual-level behavior and attitudes have undergone substantial evolution over the past decades. Initial alarm over the power of the media grew out of the interwar period in Western Europe, when numerous democratic systems collapsed and were replaced by authoritarian or totalitarian forms of government. Since this development coincided with the emergence of radio as a major form of mass communication, it is not surprising that this technological development was ranked high among the causes of democratic breakdown. The new breed of demagogic dictators and the unprecedented appearance of truly totalitarian regimes, were both linked to the emergence of a new medium that enabled despots to communicate directly and frequently with their subjects, and thus to control their thoughts and behavior by manipulating the flow of information. Accordingly, the potential power of the media was seen as nearly limitless, and the alarm was raised concerning the emergence of a "brave new world" of totalitarian systems in which a "big brother" could use communications media to dominate a society and change the way its citizens think (Kinder and Sears 1985, 706; Neuman 1991, 87).

Subsequent empirical research, however, roundly debunked the myth of the broadcast media's totalitarian potential. Assessments of their impact on the political attitudes and behavior of individuals lurched to the opposite end of the continuum, and minimal or negligible effects were found in a new round of research (e.g., Klapper 1960). Experimental and survey studies alike found that individuals' attitudes and values were likely to be reinforced rather than changed by media exposure (see Roberts and Maccoby 1985, 541). Moreover, the behavioral effects that were identified in this research were modest and benign: while not persuading voters to change, media exposure did make voters more informed and knowledgeable, as well as more likely to turn out to vote. "The more exposure to the campaign in the mass media," a classic study concluded, "the more correct information the voters have about the campaign and the more correct their perception of where the candidates stand on the issues" (Berelson et al. 1954, 252; see also Trenaman and McQuail 1961, 187–90).

Both of these sets of contradictory findings have subsequently been subjected to criticism. The initial "totalitarian" interpretation is now commonly regarded as in error in part because it was based on a sim-

16

plistic stimulus–response psychological model. Its basic operating assumption was that such influence is direct and unmediated. As Neuman (1991, 87) puts it, "We need only hit the target (a particular audience member) to have the intended effect." The "minimal effects" literature, meanwhile, was faulted for establishing all-or-nothing tests of the totalitarian hypotheses (in which the standard for assessing media impact involved a change in fundamental attitudes), for ignoring more subtle manifestations of the impact of the media on individuals, and for not taking into consideration characteristics of human beings that enable them to resist efforts at manipulation and maintain their initial attitudinal predispositions (Roberts and Maccoby 1985, 541; Neuman 1991, 87). These studies also ignored structural characteristics of the communications media themselves, especially the fact that most of the time individuals are exposed to mixed, if not contradictory, signals from multiple media sources, the net effect of which would make it appear as if the media lacked the ability to influence individual attitudes and behavior (Bartels 1993, 275–6).[10]

In light of such considerations, the media, particularly television, have come to be recognized for their contribution to persuasion as well as learning. They may not change fundamental political attitudes and behaviors directly, but they do have more subtle, indirect effects that nonetheless amount to political persuasion, which itself can be defined as "instances in which individuals alter their preferences for a candidate, policy, or some other object or idea in response to a particular message" (Ansolabehere et al. 1993, 146). Three such effects have been identified – mainly in studies of American presidential contests. The first of them is agenda setting, whose essence is perhaps best captured in the following statement: "The press may not be successful much of the time in telling people what to think, but it is stunningly successful in telling its readers what to think about" (Cohen 1963, 13; see also McCombs and Shaw 1972 and Weaver, et al. 1981).

Aside from influencing individuals' political agendas, the media can "prime" the responses of citizens to those agenda items by changing the criteria that people use to evaluate presidential candidates (Iyengar and Kinder 1987, 63). Priming "refers to the capacity of the media to isolate particular issues, events or themes in the news as criteria for evaluating politicians" (Ansolabehere et al. 1993, 148). If television coverage of an American president, for example, focuses overwhelmingly on alleged weaknesses in the incumbent's character, then voters will tend to evaluate him or her on the basis of these personal failings rather than on such dimensions as a record of accomplishments in foreign or domestic policy. The priming effect is especially strong when the media directly attribute responsibility for the state of national affairs to specific politicians (Iyengar and Kinder 1987, chapter 9).

A third type of media effect that has been extensively explored in the American literature is "framing" – that is, the manner in which news stories allocate responsibility for action or inaction on issues and problems that concern them. If television presents unemployment, poverty, and homelessness, for example, as problems with individual rather than social causes, then viewers tend to blame them on individuals rather than on political parties, politicians, policies, or societal factors. "Policy preferences, assessments of presidential performance and evaluations of public institutions are all powerfully influenced by attributions of causal and treatment responsibility" (Iyengar 1991, 127). Thus, by shifting the analytical focus to processes such as agenda setting, priming, and framing, rather than to wholesale changes in individuals' fundamental attitudes, media exposure has been shown to have a significant influence on individuals.

Another substantial departure from the simple stimulus–response model is that most studies see the political impact of the media as interacting with a host of micro- and macro-level factors that are not uniform across either individuals or national electorates. An example of the importance of individual-level factors is McGuire's (1968) "two-factor theory," according to which persuasion is dependent first on people being exposed to the message and second on their accepting it (also see Converse 1964, 1975; Zaller 1992). Thus, the potential impact of media messages is complex and contingent: some factors may enhance reception but at the same time impede acceptance. For example, individuals who are strong partisans, well informed about and deeply involved in politics, have deeply rooted attitudes and are less likely to change their opinions in response to new information; in other words, acceptance of the message is less likely (Patterson 1980a, 6; Iyengar and Kinder 1987, 60). At the same time, those who are completely ignorant of and uninterested in politics are unlikely to be exposed to (or cognizant of) the influence-bearing message; hence, reception is unlikely. Thus (as is confirmed by the findings of the chapter on Spain in this volume), those with moderate interest and involvement in politics are the subgroup of the population most likely to respond to media influences (Converse 1964, 1975; Zaller 1992).

Macro-level factors can also influence the media's ability to persuade.

It is noticeable, for example, that the research revising the minimal effects model has mostly been carried out in the United States, with its presidential political system and extraordinary dependence on television advertising as the principal focus of electoral campaigning. Priming effects may be unusually important, if not unique, to this setting due to the sheer volume and intensity of these communications, to the ability of the candidates to completely control their content, and to the greater potential volatility of attitudes toward an individual candidate (who might not be well known at the beginning of a campaign) than toward a collective governing entity like a coalition government in a parliamentary system. Another consideration is the extent to which the media disseminate mixed, heterogeneous messages: the more the media tend to converge on a single opinion or orientation, the more homogeneous the environment in which attitudes are formed or altered and the greater the likelihood of significant media effects (Kinder and Sears 1985, 713; Bartels 1993, 275–6). The character of the media market will also have implications for the media's political effects. That is, the greater the extent to which citizens depend on one particular medium, the greater the ability of that medium to mold public opinion; by contrast, when citizens have a number of information sources from which to choose, they are less susceptible to the potential influence of any one of them. For example, the Argentine electorate in the 1989 presidential election was largely unfazed by extensive television-based campaigns, largely because reading newspapers was almost common as following the campaign on television (Zuleta-Puceiro 1993, 74). Conversely, three different studies of the 1989 Brazilian election concluded that in that country (where two-thirds of the population are illiterate or semiliterate and where only 3 million newspapers are sold daily to a total population of 140 million), manipulation of a completely dominant private television network was decisive in electing the previously obscure Fernando Collor de Mello president (da Silva 1993; de Lima 1993; Straubhaar et al. 1993).

Attempts by governing elites in nondemocratic political systems to manipulate or reshape public opinion can also be affected by their larger social and political context. Thus, when a regime's messages are at odds with contemporary social reality, their impact may be very different from that intended but politically significant nonetheless. Media messages, for example, have to be credible to be persuasive, but as Sükösd shows in Chapter 4 of this volume, the lack of credibility of the media in Communist regimes had the perverse effect of undermining their legitimacy. Similarly, as the following chapter on Spain will suggest, heavy-handed efforts by the Franco regime to disseminate antidemocratic, Spanish nationalist, and traditionalist Catholic values among the population were so discordant with the modern, increasingly affluent, and rapidly secularizing Spanish society of the 1970s that they not only failed to move the country's modal values in the intended direction but may have effectively "immunized" Spaniards against the appeals of the antidemocratic right for decades to come.

In light of such findings regarding the contingent nature of media effects, we argue that important changes in the structure of the media, as well as changes in the social context in which they operate, significantly affect the degree to which media effects can have an impact on politics. While by no means an exhaustive list, there are several such transformations that are worthy of mention at this point, if only because they characterize so many new and established democracies in the world today. The first is that television has come to dwarf other mass media in terms of being the major, most credible, and most trusted source of information for the majority of citizens. The second is that contemporary viewers tend to be less deeply anchored than those of a generation or two ago in social and community groupings, identification with which effectively served to bind them to a political party and to insulate them against the blandishments of discordant political messages. Thus, their resistance weakened, they are more vulnerable to media persuasion today. The third change lies less in the realm of individual citizens and more in the greater sophistication of politicians and political parties increasingly reliant on the media to attract popular support, especially at election time. Let us briefly speculate about the nature of each of these changes.

THE RISE OF TELEVISION

It is too easily forgotten that, at the time of the early political communications studies, television was a new medium to which most voters, especially outside the more technologically advanced United States, had limited access (at best) during election campaigns. The two election campaign studies that were perhaps most influential in establishing the conventional wisdom of "minimal effects" – that the media reinforce political attitudes and behavior but do not change them – were *The People's Choice* and *Voting,* conducted during the 1940 and 1948 U.S. presidential elections. Both studies analyzed the impact of campaign coverage by newspapers, radio, and magazines; television was not even considered (Lazarsfeld, et al. 1948; Berelson et al. 1954, 240–5).

A subsequent study carried out during the 1959 British general election – the first in which television played a major campaign role – found that television was "equal in penetration . . . to the press" and had displaced radio "as an instrument of political communication." Still, at the time of this study, only 75 percent of British households had a television set, and four years earlier this figure had barely exceeded 50 percent (Trenaman and McQuail 1961, 81). Today, by contrast, there are very few households in any advanced industrial democracy without at least one television set.

In most democratic societies today, television is the most widely used, credible, and trusted source of political information (Dalton 1996, 23). Ranney (1983, 13–17) has suggested four reasons why this is true, albeit in the particular context of the United States, with its distinctive media structure and style of television journalism. First, the messages television conveys in its political programming (not advertisements) are nonpartisan. Second, these messages do not generally question viewers' deeply held beliefs. Third, compared with reading a newspaper or attending a political meeting, watching television is a relatively cost-free means of acquiring political information. Finally, television is unique for conveying its messages through the mouth of a human being whom viewers can see, like, and trust, not least because television networks go to great lengths to choose news anchors who exude precisely these qualities. The media environment of voters, in other words, was very different in the early days of media-effects research from what it was at the end of the twentieth century and the beginning of the twenty-first. The same can be said for the voters themselves.

VOTER DEALIGNMENT

A particularly important social reality underpinned the conclusion of early studies that the media reinforced, but did not alter, political attitudes and behavior. In the 1940s, when these classic studies were undertaken, strong group loyalties based largely on social class or religion were pervasive. This contributed to strong attachments to political parties protecting and advancing group interests in the electoral arena.[11]

As late as the 1960s, the basic parameters of democratic party politics were commonly thought to have been set in stone by national cleavage structures that showed little sign of change over long periods of time. In the famous words of Lipset and Rokkan (1967, 50): "The party systems of the 1960s reflect, with but few significant exceptions, the cleavage structures of the 1920s." Steadfast loyalty to party manifested itself in a number of ways, including highly stable voting patterns, low swings in aggregate levels of support for parties, and established party systems insulated against the threat of new parties emerging to disturb the political status quo (Daalder and Mair 1983). But more important, from our perspective, it also left citizens less open to media persuasion by insulating them from discordant messages. Three psychological mechanisms were identified as instrumental in this process: selective exposure, selective perception, and selective retention (Lazarsfeld, et al. 1948; Klapper 1960). In other words, strong partisan loyalties meant that individuals tended to expose themselves to, take in, and remember media messages that did not threaten their previously established political attitudes.

By the 1980s and 1990s, group loyalties had weakened considerably. Study after study has shown that objective and subjective social group identifications do not predict political attitudes and behavior as strongly as they once did. "One thing that has by now become quite apparent is that almost all of the countries we have studied show a decline during our period in the ability of social cleavages to structure individual voting choice" (Franklin et al. 1992, 385; also see Gunther and Montero 1994). As a result, electoral behavior at both the individual and aggregate levels has become more volatile, and party systems have become more unstable as old parties decline and new ones arise (Crewe and Denver 1985; Dalton 1996, 196–219). These developments have enhanced the potential for media influence – especially short-term influence – and a compelling argument can be made that "the emergence of television as the main mass medium of politics has made the short campaign period – and the issues, people and events it brings into prominence – a more powerful determinant of the vote" (Crewe 1983, 190).

INCREASED SOPHISTICATION

At the same time that voters' stabilizing attachments to parties and secondary organizations are weakening in many democratic countries, the use of television by politicians has become much more sophisticated as a result of its having become the dominant medium of election campaigning and political communication. In the 1940s and 1950s, television was still a new medium for politicians and they tended to approach it with caution, preferring more traditional methods of communicating with the public and getting out the vote. Seeing it largely as one more way of communicating with the party faithful, they tended to treat it as a means of mobilizing political support rather than as one of attacking the political opposition to undermine its credibility. A good example is the Party Election Broadcast in Britain. Television slots are awarded to the major political parties during election campaigns, and in the absence of paid political advertising, they provide the only opportunity for the parties themselves to control the image they convey to voters. Until 1970, the parties adhered strictly to a "talking head" format, whereby the head and shoulders of a leading party politician, interspersed with occasional illustrative footage, filled the screen and he held forth on his own party's policy for the whole ten-minute broadcast. The Conservatives changed this format in the 1970 campaign when they introduced striking graphics to criticize the performance of the Labour government. Labour's poor record on inflation, for example, was vividly demonstrated by a pair of scissors attacking a pound note, with a voice in the background simultaneously drawing attention to the sharp decline in its buying power.

This example is symptomatic of a new style of election campaigning that has taken hold in democracies worldwide. Television is at its center, and politicians have called on the services of marketing experts, advertising agencies, actors, film directors, and other media professionals to cash in on its potential for the mobilization and conversion of popular support. Entertainment, not policy debate, is increasingly the hallmark of election campaigns. Rather than emphasizing their policies and promises, parties parade their leaders in a never-ending series of contrived settings, sound bites, and walkabouts. Sketchy policy pronouncements are made not at party meetings or in speeches before distinguished audiences, but in news conferences and "appropriate" settings on the road and in front of the television cameras – always in time to catch the evening news. Television is a key resource in the propaganda war. Parties have increasingly devoted substantial effort and sometimes staggering sums of money to using it to maximum effect (Kaid and Holz-Bacha 1995). If the electoral law forbids them from purchasing advertising time on it, they go to great lengths to stage events that television producers will deem worthy of coverage in news programs. Instead of spending time on the road mobilizing support in the constituencies, party leaders go from television studio to television studio giving interviews that reach a wider national audience. Television and political marketing strategies pioneered in candidate-centered elections in the United States are now at the heart of political parties' strategies to be elected and reelected worldwide (Bowler and Farrell 1992; Butler and Ranney 1992; Swanson and Mancini 1996).

In terms of both quantity and quality of usage, then, television today is simply not the same medium of political communication and mobilization that it was even 25 years ago – let alone in the 1940s and 1950s, when the thesis of the media's minimal political effects was formulated.

CONCLUSION

This introduction was not intended to arrive at conclusions about the nature of the relationship between the media and the politics of democracy and democratization at the turn of the millennium. Instead, we have attempted to set the stage for a reassessment of this relationship in light of important changes in both the media environment of politics and the political environment of the media dating from about the early 1980s. Some of the more important of these changes (both at the macro and micro levels) have been identified, and emphasis has been placed on the need to study them in their interaction if their potential political implications are to be fully investigated and understood. For example, television's potential influence, fully recognized by a new generation of "media-friendly" political leaders, can be hypothesized to have increased not only because of government deregulation, but also because individuals' political attitudes and behavior are not as deeply rooted in enduring group loyalties as they once were. It should be noted that we are not claiming that all countries have experienced these changes to the same degree or that certain changes will have the same implications for the style and substance of democratic politics in all countries. Rather, the changes and their impact are a matter for investigation and evaluation in individual cases. Only then can more general conclusions be drawn about the relationship between the media and the quality of democracy in new and established regimes.

This is precisely the purpose of this volume. Chapters 2 through 5 present studies of the role of the communications media in the transition to, and consolidation of, democracy in formerly authoritarian and totalitarian regimes. Conventional thinking would lead us to believe that state control of political communications in these regimes was more or less comprehensive and, consequently, that the media were the enemy of democratic advance. As these chapters demonstrate, however, the reality turns out to be more complicated. State control of the political messages reaching citizens may have been close to comprehensive in the totalitarian Soviet Union, but it was far from complete in its Eastern European satellites, let alone in the final years of the authoritarian regimes in Chile and Spain. As we shall see, authoritarian controls over communication flows were relaxed in all of these countries, albeit for a variety of reasons. The net result was a diversification of the political messages and cues reaching citizens so that the media – a substantial degree of continued state control notwithstanding – ended up playing a surprisingly significant role in subverting the legitimacy of nondemocratic regimes. The picture that emerges is the more striking for filling large gaps in a highly influential literature on democratization that pays little or no attention to the role of the media in precipitating the breakdown of authoritarianism, thereby ignoring the puzzle of how authoritarian regimes could have collapsed so easily if they substantially controlled the official flow of political communications to, and loyalty of, a manipulated citizenry. These chapters then analyze the roles of the media in the democratic regimes that subsequently emerged in each country.

Chapters 6 through 11 look at established democracies. The findings here are no less surprising. The minimal effects hypothesis is challenged by empirical studies documenting a significant impact on electoral behavior and outcomes, on the nature of parties and election campaigns, and on important characteristics of the political cultures of these democratic societies. A more striking departure from the dominant conventional wisdom involves varying patterns of relationships between the broadcast media and the state or other public institutions. Two different roles are relevant here: one derives from a direct role in producing and broadcasting programs through public-sector media; the other pertains to the extent to which public organizations engage in oversight of public- and private-sector broadcasting media. It is often argued that democracy and the free flow of politically relevant ideas can be enhanced by reducing state or public sector intervention to a bare minimum – that both the overall volume of a wide variety of political viewpoints and their impartial dissemination among the general public can best be achieved by establishing an unrestricted free market for mass communications, and that unrestricted democratic participation by citizens can be maximized when state control or regulation is minimized. The empirical studies presented in this volume suggest that the reality is much more complex than this conventional wisdom implies. Indeed, we will identify and analyze certain pathologies in specific established democracies that relate to this public-sector involvement in surprising ways. Some of these involve a diminution of the quality of democracy in certain countries derived from a reduced volume of policy-relevant information flowing to voters; from a shift from substantive issues to a focus on the personalities and foibles of politicians, to the "game" of politics and the excitement of the electoral "horse race," and, more generally, the ephemera of politics; and from gratuitous editorializing by reporters. Consequences of some of these trends include widespread cynicism toward politics and politicians, low levels of political knowledge among broad sectors of the electorate, withdrawal of psychological and behavioral involvement with politics, and the increased tendency to avoid political news altogether. Fortunately, even though these trends are increasingly apparent in several of the countries examined here, they are far from universal or inexorable phenomena. By comparing the countries where these pathologies are most pronounced with those where mere hints of such trends are apparent, we venture an explanation of these developments. That explanation involves a significant reconsideration of the role played by the state in the "free market" for political ideas. We also contend that the trends outlined earlier must be assessed in interaction with an array of legal, cultural, and institutional factors that, in several countries, form a barrier against the spread of these tendencies. Accordingly, both their public-sector and commercial broadcast media have largely avoided the sensationalistic, personality-centered, and cynical style of coverage that, as in the United States, can undermine popular respect and support for the institutions and processes of democracy.

One of the central objectives of analyses of established democracies in this volume, then, is to explore in detail various alternative configurations of media structures, journalistic norms, and political-reporting practices. It is hoped that both governments and journalists can reflect on the success stories of broadcast journalism (including the profound transformation of political cultures in countries previously incapable of sustaining stable democracies), as well as its failures and shortcomings, and can fashion regulatory frameworks and journalistic norms that can help new democracies in their efforts to consolidate and stabilize the new political order, and help established democracies promote informed electoral choice and democratic accountability.

NOTES

1. Classic studies that have adopted this approach include Berelson, et al. 1954; Katz and Lazarsfeld 1955; Klapper 1960; Butler and Stokes 1974; and Iyengar and Kinder 1987.
2. See, for example, Miliband 1962; Postman 1985; Lichter et al. 1990; Bagdikian 1991; and Dye 1995.
3. Notable exceptions are Swanson and Mancini 1996; Graber, et al. 1998; and Randall 1998.
4. Ranney 1983, 74–87; Bennett 1988; Entman 1989; Iyengar 1991; Patterson 1993; and Fallows 1996.

5. This conclusion of politically neutral media does not apply, of course, to more radical thinkers, like Marxists, who see the media as instruments of class oppression. See, for example, Miliband 1962.

6. The broadcasting philosophies and structures of a number of countries, including the United Kingdom and the United States, are described in Avery 1993.

7. This is not to say that it is uniformly perceived to be objective in its content. The fierce debate over whether or not television news is biased is summarized in Goodwin 1990. Also see Mughan 1996.

8. The U.K. public service model should be regarded as located at one end of the continuum. The media systems of other countries share some of its characteristics but not others. Canada, for example, allows paid political advertising and provides parties with free air time (see LeDuc, et al. 1996, 45–8).

9. The complex relationship between political information and political democracy is impressively analyzed and discussed for the United States in Delli Carpini and Keeter 1996.

10. Bartels (1993, 267) further argues that the methodological shortcomings of these studies also contributed to their negative or minimalist findings.

11. France of the early Fifth Republic was a notable exception. Here, party loyalties were shallow and the party system was changeable. See Converse and Dupeux 1962.

CHAPTER 2

The Media and Politics in Spain: From Dictatorship to Democracy

Richard Gunther, José Ramón Montero, and José Ignacio Wert

Few Western European polities underwent as many dramatic changes in the mid-twentieth century as Spain, and yet succeeded in establishing stable, fully consolidated democratic systems. Spain developed a fully democratic regime in 1931, the first in its long history. But this government was extremely unstable and collapsed in a bloody civil war just five years after its founding. An interlude of nearly four decades of authoritarian rule followed. A transition to democracy began in 1975, but in a very short period of time Spain was able to establish a stable, consolidated parliamentary monarchy indistinguishable in many ways from many other Western European democracies. Thus, over the course of just six decades, Spain underwent an extraordinarily broad array of political experiences: from polarized, unstable democracy, to civil war, to authoritarian repression, to uncertain transition, to successful democratic consolidation.

Even this overview, breathtaking as it may be, fails to do full justice to the scope of the political, social, economic, and cultural changes that Spain has undergone. Indeed, between Franco's death in 1975 and the mid-1980s its political system underwent *two* transitions: one from authoritarianism to democracy, the other from a highly centralized state to one in which considerable political power and fiscal resources devolved on autonomous regional governments. The magnitude of the social-structural change has been equally impressive. From a situation of semi-peripheral underdevelopment, Spain transformed itself into a country whose social and economic characteristics were comparable to those of other advanced Western European societies in less than 20 years, compared with the five or six decades required by most other European countries to develop economically.

The Spanish communications media have also undergone an extraordinary transformation, especially with regard to freedom of information. After nearly four decades of authoritarian rule that systematically suppressed the free flow of information, established a rigid system of censorship, and denied freedom of expression, a media structure emerged that is characterized by extraordinarily high levels of pluralism and complete liberty, solidly rooted in the democratic constitution of 1978. The structure of the mass communications system was profoundly transformed by the shift in dominance from the print media to television as the public's principal source of information about politics. And the size and composition of media audiences have changed considerably, from a small, attentive public to mass consumption, particularly of the broadcast media.

Given the multidimensional changes that Spain has experienced over the past six decades, it is an ideal laboratory for the examination of a wide variety of ways in which the communications media influence – and are affected by – politics. Three different periods in Spanish political history will be distinguished and examined separately, since the structure and political functions of the media were decidedly different from one period to another. The first period is the dictatorship of Generalísimo Francisco Franco. Our examination of this period will focus on the structural constraints imposed on the media by this authoritarian regime, its efforts to use the media to solidify its position in power, and, in the last decade of authoritarian rule, its tentative liberalization and relaxation of control over some of the media. The second period spans the transition to democracy, in which some important segments of the media played significant roles in establishing a new political regime and in disseminating to the general public new democratic values and behavioral norms.

Finally, we explore some of the subtle and interactive ways in which the media affect electoral behavior in contemporary Spanish politics. Although this overview will cover significant media-related political developments up to the time of this writing, the bulk of our analysis shall focus on the 1993 parliamentary election. This is done to take advantage of a massive multimethod study of the 1993 elections that we undertook as part of the Comparative National Elections Project, which includes pre- and postelection panel surveys of Spanish voters (using questionnaires including numerous items designed to tap into "media effects") and parallel content analyses of political news coverage by television and newspapers.[1]

FRANQUISMO: CONTROL OF THE MEDIA
UNDER AN AUTHORITARIAN REGIME

The political system established in 1939 by Francisco Franco was, along with the Salazar regime in neighboring Portugal, one of the longest-lasting dictatorships in Western Europe. It was the quintessential authoritarian regime (Linz 1975), characterized by limited and nonresponsible political pluralism, political demobilization, a leader who exercised power within formally undefined but clearly recognizable limits, and the absence of an elaborated ideology. While these regime characteristics remained more or less constant, an overview of four decades of *franquismo* must make note of four distinct periods. From the victory in the civil war in 1939 until the mid-1940s, its totalitarian aspirations, its association with Hitler and Mussolini, and the recency of the war led to harsh repression, the presence of military officials among its governing elite, and efforts to establish a powerful quasi-fascist party. The regime during the 1950s was quite different: totalitarian aspirations abandoned, the party and its ideology were progressively watered down; and international isolation, stark poverty, and an attempt to implement an autarkic economic development strategy had far-reaching effects on society. Over the following decade, however, the complete abandonment of economic autarky contributed to one of the most rapid and sustained rates of economic growth in the world (7.3 percent between 1961 and 1973, second only to Japan; Gunther 1980, 63), transforming Spain into a relatively modern, affluent, urban society and forging ever closer social and economic links with the rest of Europe. This socioeconomic modernization was accompanied by additional political changes, most significantly the virtual disappearance of the official party as a significant political actor and the making of most government decisions by a new, technocratic elite. These changes notwithstanding, the regime remained fully authoritarian throughout all four periods, and whatever limited pluralism did exist was restricted to those conservative to ultraconservative political factions and those upper-stratum social and economic groups that supported the regime. Limited as these changes may have been, however, they had a significant impact on the communications media.

Totalitarian and authoritarian regimes do not differ greatly with regard to control of the communications media (Linz 1974, 1496–7). Despite the gradual disappearance of the regime's totalitarian features in the 1940s, its press restrictions did not change significantly. With some variations, these same policies were applied to radio and, beginning in the 1950s, to television. Only during the final ten years of *franquismo* were privately owned newspapers able to benefit from some liberalization, enabling them to play an important role in the crucial period immediately preceding the death of Franco and throughout the democratic transition. Strict government control of radio, television, and the state-owned press, however, remained unchanged throughout the life of the regime.

THE PRESS LAW OF 1938: CENSORSHIP AND ORDERS

The basic framework for the franquist regime's communications policy was established by the Press Law of 1938. Although established on a provisional basis during the civil war, it remained in effect for nearly three decades. Its markedly totalitarian provisions were modeled after fascist legislation enacted in Italy in 1923 (Terrón 1981, 55–6). The law required state authorization for publications of any kind and provided for the suspension of any publication without appeal. In addition, it enabled the state to intervene in the appointment and dismissal of newspaper managers and editors, even in the case of the privately owned press. Journalists were under especially strict control. Many were purged following the civil war, and all had to be officially registered with the government, belong to specific associations, and submit their reports for daily inspection to eliminate any information regarded as harmful to the dictatorship (Abellán 1989; Sinova 1989a). Not even advertising was exempt from this scrutiny. The criteria applied in this censorship process were inconsistent, however, changing in light of international circumstances and the current political proclivities of the regime. This introduced an element of arbitrariness, capriciousness, and even silliness in actual practice.[2]

A second means by which the state sought to dominate the flow of information was by issuing "orders" – obligatory instructions to interpret news events in a particular way or to avoid coverage of certain themes or events altogether. These orders were so detailed as to involve specific arguments to be included in editorials, the size of headlines, and even the position of photographs (Pizarroso 1989, 241–2; Sinova 1989b, 266). Press censorship and the issuance of orders remained in effect until well into the 1960s (Terrón 1981, 83–157).

The franquist regime created a substantial journalistic empire of its own, although, in contrast with some other nondemocratic systems, it did not establish press or radio monopolies. The so-called Prensa del Movimiento (operated by the franquist National Movement, formerly the Falange) was created during the civil war out of publishing facilities confiscated from parties, trade unions, and business firms that had supported the Republic. This made the state the principal newspaper publisher in Spain and one of the most important in Europe, at least in terms of the total number of newspapers published (Montabes 1989, 24). By 1948, these state and Falange-operated enterprises owned a press agency and were publishing 38 daily newspapers, 8 weekly magazines, and five monthly magazines. But despite the enormous state-subsidized infrastructure at their disposal, their circulation was significantly less than that of the private press. In 1950, for example, the state press published only about one-third of the 1 million daily newspapers sold and its market share subsequently declined, culminating in nearly complete collapse in the final years of *franquismo* (Sinova 1989b, 270–1).

The diversity of the franquist coalition (which included *falangistas,* Catholics, monarchists, and Carlist traditionalists) largely explains the survival of private-sector journalistic enterprises, the most important of which were owned by Catholic or monarchist groups. At the end of the 1950s, the Catholic press included 34 newspapers (most of which were linked to the Asociación Católica Nacional de Propagandistas – ACNP – a lay organization that had exerted considerable influence on Spanish political life since 1909), with an average daily circulation of 340,000. The ACNP controlled a press agency and five newspapers, among them *Ya,* whose daily circulation exceeded 100,000 (García Escudero 1984; Hermet 1985, 195–9). Various monarchist groups published five newspapers, the most important of which was *ABC,* whose circulation exceeded 200,000 daily (Iglesias 1980). Even though there was a large number of private-sector publications, the controls imposed on the press by the authoritarian regime precluded the development of a diversity of ideological or political orientations. These newspapers could only differ from one another with regard to secondary or marginal issues, always within the overall framework of continued support for the regime. Accordingly, in a 1964 survey,[3] 49 percent of newspaper readers in Madrid thought that all newspapers had the same political orientation, and 65 percent claimed not to believe the news they read (IOP 1965b, 196).

Despite the large number of newspapers, their aggregate circulation was remarkably low. A comparison with other Western countries in 1964 showed that the number of newspapers sold per thousand persons in Spain (71) was not only the lowest among the 16 countries surveyed, but was also far behind even the next lowest country in this survey, Italy (where newspaper sales averaged 123 per thousand). By comparison, in

France, the United States, West Germany, Japan, and Britain, the number of daily newspapers sold per thousand persons ranged between 242 and 573 (IOP 1964, 17). The uniformity and resulting monotony of domestic news coverage alienated the public from the print media and help to explain the low levels of both newspaper readership and trust in the press (Sinova 1989a, 13 and 17; 1989b, 270).

Newspapers devoted more space to commercial advertisements than to any other type of material (IOP 1964; 1965a, 147). "Political news" was limited to official press releases concerning ceremonies, appointments, and inaugurations written in a rhetorical style charged with triumphalism, adulation, and sectarianism. In coverage of local news, some minor criticisms were tolerated, although these sometimes resulted in conflicts with the local authorities and the imposition of sanctions against the offending newspaper. In sharp contrast, coverage of international news was remarkably balanced, and was often so extensive as to dominate the news segments of the newspapers (Beneyto 1965, 22; Pizarroso 1989, 248). Openness and balance in coverage of international news were especially notable among those newspapers that could afford to have their own foreign correspondents.

THE PRESS LAW OF 1966: CONTROLLED LIBERALIZATION

Several developments came together in the mid-1960s to create pressures for the enactment of a new Press Law. For some time, the Catholic factions within the regime had favored a less rigid and bureaucratic system of control (Terrón 1981, 135–53; Tusell 1984, 344–59). Their position within the franquist coalition was strengthened after 1957 by the influx of Opus Dei technocrats into the government and by repudiation of the Falangist economic policies of economic autarky. Economic liberalization and the more open, international orientation of these largely apolitical technocrats substantially undermined support for the heavy-handed, nationalistic propaganda long disseminated by the Movimiento and imposed by censors, and created conditions favorable to an increased liberalization of the press.

The most decisive steps toward press liberalization were taken by Manual Fraga Iribarne, who assumed responsibility for regulation of the communications media in 1962. At first, Fraga merely relaxed the most repressive aspects of censorship and the issuance of orders, leaving the Press Law of 1938 unreformed. These modest steps made possible a certain intellectual liberalization within university circles that subsequently spread to the print media.

The Press Law of 1966 (commonly referred to as the *Ley Fraga*) carried this process much further. Its most important innovations were the elimination of prior censorship and relaxation of direct controls on newspapers and publishing houses. Publishing firms were also allowed to appoint their own managers and editors (although their job security was made conditional on their publications not incurring three or more formal sanctions a year). The state also retained the right to punish publishers for what it considered violations of ill-defined norms, whose interpretation was solely at its own discretion. This led to the emergence of new forms of self-censorship that, in combination with state-imposed sanctions based on arbitrary and poorly defined criteria, led to confusion and occasionally harsh repression, including heavy fines, confiscation of newspaper and magazine issues, and, on occasion, the closure of offending publishing houses. Thus, this reform was always regarded as an *apertura* (an opening up, or partial liberalization) vis-à-vis the heavier and more narrow constraints of the preceding era, rather than as the establishment of the press freedoms and regulations characteristic of Western democracies.[4]

The most significant impact of the 1966 Press Law involved the quality of reporting on political news. A certain ideological differentiation was allowed among private-sector periodicals, particularly magazines, stimulating a rise in their modest levels of circulation.[5] Public confidence in the press increased significantly: between 1960 and 1973, the share of Spaniards polled in surveys who expressed confidence in the press rose from 33 to 47 percent, while the share of those expressing of distrust fell from 65 to 30 percent (IOP 1975a, 305). State-run publications, however, which remained subject to strict government vigilance and rigorous political control, did not evolve in this manner. As a result of their continuing monotony and lack of credibility, their circulations declined precipitously in the mid-1970s (Montabes 1989, 38 and 46).

The *Ley Fraga* played a significant role in undermining *franquismo*. While it did not establish freedom of the press, it did increase freedom of expression, which, in turn, expanded the audience of the print media and stimulated greater popular interest in the news (Sinova 1989b, 270). Some newspapers and magazines, especially those based in Madrid and Barcelona, took considerable advantage of increased government tolerance and the greater fluidity of Spain's rapidly modernizing society by markedly broadening and liberalizing their news coverage, including reports on formerly taboo subjects such as strikes, student protests, and critical alternatives to policies adopted by the government (Barrera 1995,

107–8). As Terrón has written, "Newspapers began … to perform a moderately critical role, and magazines were converted in many instances into outlets for political opinions and ideologies distinct from and sometimes contrary to those of the regime" (1981, 217).

RADIO AND TELEVISION: CONTINUING NEWS MONOPOLY

Like the press, radio emerged from the civil war as an instrument of government propaganda. The franquist Nuevo Estado seized pro-Republican broadcasting stations while allowing many other networks and stations to remain in the hands of private business enterprises. As with the print media, a 1939 decree (which would remain in effect for the next 38 years) established a system of prior censorship for all commercial radio broadcasts. Coverage of general news, both national and international, was reserved exclusively for the official network, Radio Nacional de España (RNE). Private-sector broadcasters were required to retransmit RNE news broadcasts twice each day. In general, radio did not undergo the same liberalization that the print media enjoyed under Fraga's reforms of the mid-1960s.

The structure of radio broadcasting, however, did change considerably, mainly to consolidate and regulate the explosive and seemingly chaotic expansion of the 1960s. In 1963, there were 471 broadcasting stations throughout the country (over four times the number existing two decades earlier), 71 percent of which lacked the requisite broadcasting licenses (Multigner 1989, 274–5). Under Manuel Fraga, the Ministry of Information and Tourism reversed this proliferation of stations, reducing their total number to about 200 and grouping them into six broadcasting networks. About half of these stations were state-run, and the other half belonged to the COPE network (operated by the Catholic Church) and various commercial chains, the most important of which was the Sociedad Española de Radiodifusión (SER) (IOP 1970, 169–70).

Throughout the franquist era, radio coverage of politically relevant developments was subjec-ted to severe restrictions. Although the practice of prior censorship was phased out, private radio networks were prohibited from broadcasting their own news programs until after Franco's death and the onset of the democratic transition. Spaniards thus had no alternative but to receive the news through the official broadcasts of RNE. And in describing those broadcasts, González Seara (1972, 781) writes:

> aside from the pompous style of the reporters, the news was broadcast in a solemn tone such that the description of [Franco's] ap-

Table 2.1   *Percentages of Survey Respondents Who*
Have Television Sets and Watch Television

	1966	1967	1969	1973	1975
Have television sets	33	36	68	—	81
Usually watch television[a]	54	54	81	91	—

[a]This figure is greater than the percentage who own television sets because of access to television in public bars, tele-clubs, the houses of friends and relatives, and so on.
Sources: For 1966, IOP 1967 (60–3); 1967 and 1973, IOP 1975b (265); 1969, IOP 1969 (338–42); and 1975, Wert 1976 (124).

pearance at an inaugural ceremony was read almost like a recital from Shakespeare. . . . The news was full of exaltations of the patriotic virtues and the progress of our society, all according to orders.

During the two decades preceding the transition to democracy, radio audiences shrank considerably, and radio was rapidly overtaken by television as the principal electronic communications medium. While 86 percent of Madrid residents had reported in a mid-1960s survey that they listened to the radio every day, by 1974 only 33 percent of nationwide survey respondents claimed to listen to the radio every day or several times a week (IOP 1975a, 308–15). Thus, radio was not in a position to play a significant role in liberalizing Spanish society or initiating the political transition.

Regular television broadcasts began in 1956. Less than two decades later, over 90 percent of all Spaniards were regular viewers (see Table 2.1). Television quickly overtook radio as the principal entertainment medium and surpassed the print media as the principal source of political news, especially with regard to international political developments. As recently as the mid-1960s (see Table 2.2), more people relied on the press than on television as a news source. But by 1973, this situation was completely reversed. A poll conducted in that year revealed that 31 percent of Spaniards regularly read a newspaper, 42 percent listened to radio, and 75 percent watched television every day (IOP 1975b, 272; also see IOP 1976, 401). Given some evidence that survey respondents exaggerate the frequency with which they read newspapers, it is probable that the gap separating television from the other news sources is even greater

Table 2.2   *Medium through Which Spaniards Received*
Information on Selected News Events

Event	Newspapers	Radio	Television	Other People
British elections (1964)	40%	25%	33%	2%
U.S. elections (1964)	30	32	34	4
Italian elections (1965)	52	15	30	3
Vatican concilium (1965)	38	23	30	2
U.S. space flight (1965)	29	19	49	3
Soviet space flight (1965)	36	23	31	10
Spanish referendum (1966)	13	19	34	7

Source: González Seara 1967 (40).

(Wert 1976, 129–35) and that, for a large segment of the Spanish population, television had become the *only* news source. Regarding television as a valuable tool for socialization and propaganda, the Ministry of Information extended the reach of television even to those not owning sets by setting up "tele-clubs" in rural and suburban areas. By 1972, these clubs had attracted over 800,000 members (de Bergareche 1976, 1056).

Government control over the new medium was tighter and more direct than over radio and the press, and television news broadcasts functioned as a propaganda tool at the service of the regime until after Franco's death in November 1975. González Seara (1972, 783–4) characterizes the nature of television news broadcasts as dominated by

> a Manichean conceptualization of the universe characterized by generally evil and negative developments abroad and peace and progress at home. . . . An example of how Televisión Española presented the news can be seen the sequence of items covered in its program *24 Hours:* killings in Vietnam, massacres in Dacca, protests in Warsaw, disturbances in Belfast, students stoning the police in Milan, layoffs at Volkswagen, accusations against the Minister of the Interior in the French National Assembly, parliamentary crisis in Italy; then [following this string of foreign disasters], the opening of a new hotel in the Balearic Islands, the closing ceremony of the Auto Show in Barcelona, the gala banquet for recipients of national cinema and television awards, a speech before the Chamber of Commerce . . . and, to conclude, a local festival, accompanied by cheerful bagpipe music.

Despite the authoritarian regime's more direct control and heavy-handed, propagandistic manipulation of television than of any other medium, Spaniards regarded television as the most trustworthy medium and the best source of news. Repeated surveys undertaken in the 1960s and 1970s revealed that about half of those polled regarded television as the medium that provided the most complete and interesting news, compared with 19 percent who preferred the print media and 15 percent who preferred radio broadcasts (IOP 1967, 204; 1975b, 273; 1976, 409). Two-thirds of those interviewed in a 1973 survey said that they trusted television "a great deal" or substantially, compared with only 57 percent who similarly evaluated radio and 47 percent who rated newspapers as trustworthy (IOP 1975b, 274). This striking inconsistency between the reality of state manipulation of television, on the one hand, and widespread feelings of trust and confidence in that same medium, on the other, constitutes a puzzle to which we shall return later.

THE MEDIA AND AUTHORITARIANISM: AN ASSESSMENT

Throughout the first three decades of franquist authoritarianism, the impact of the media on politics was relatively uniform and completely supportive of the regime. The regime regarded the communications media as propaganda tools in the service of the state (Sinova 1989a, 276–7), irrespective of whether a particular medium was state property or privately owned. But in accord with the basic nature of the authoritarian Franco regime, the primary result of media control was to secure the *passive acquiescence* of the Spanish population rather than to resocialize the citizenry into active participatory roles. In contrast with the role of the media under a totalitarian regime – whose objective is to mobilize the population in an effort to remake society in accord with an official ideology – the nonrevolutionary (indeed, reactionary) political and social objectives of *franquismo* meant that the overriding political function of its communications policy was to demobilize and depoliticize Spanish society. This was particularly true of the period following the end of the Second World War.[6] Regime maintenance was facilitated by communications policies that effectively bored most Spaniards into passivity and acquiescence and deprived them of stimuli that might have triggered political mobilization. The dissemination of apolitical, antipolitical, and antidemocratic messages was of particular political significance during the processes of rapid social modernization that began in the early 1960s.

In effect, it helped to postpone the political mobilization of a population whose levels of literacy, urbanization, and education were rising rapidly.

While we lack sufficient empirical evidence concerning the linkage between media consumption habits and political values during the 1960s and early 1970s to substantiate claims of causality, it is important to note that these characteristics of the Spanish media under *franquismo* are entirely compatible with fundamental characteristics of Spanish political culture at that time. The absence of a clearly defined regime ideology and mobilizational intentions meant that no identifiably franquist political culture would be inculcated into more than a small minority of the population, but marked apoliticism and cynicism toward politics were widespread (Montero and Torcal 1990). Studies conducted in the late 1960s indicated that most of the population (50 to 55 percent) had only the most simplistic political attitudes; they looked on politics with distrust and fear; they responded to political stimuli in a defensive and authoritarian fashion; and they would eventually emerge as a passive segment of the electorate (López Pina and Aranguren 1976, 63–72; López Pintor 1982, 78–80). Alongside this majority segment of the population were two politically aware minority groups. About 15 percent of the population actively identified with the Franco regime and shared its authoritarian values, its dogmatism, and its intolerance. At the other extreme, about one-quarter to one-third of the population held entirely different values and were alienated from the regime.

In the absence of survey data from the 1960s that would provide direct evidence concerning the linkage between media exposure and basic attitudes toward politics, a comparison between the passive majority and those minority sectors of Spanish society that were actively in opposition suggests that this relationship interacts with other social and political determinants of mass behavior. Beginning in 1956 but especially in the 1960s, workers in certain parts of Spain and university students occasionally mounted protest demonstrations. These were especially frequent and massive in the late 1960s. Maravall's excellent study (1978) of political activists in the late 1960s revealed that, although workers and students occupied very different positions in Spain's stratification system, they shared one attribute: they were immersed in subcultures that exposed individuals to information and values incompatible with the official doctrines of the regime and that served as stimuli for protest activity. Both militant workers in heavy-industrial centers in the north of Spain and students in university communities (which several varieties of Marxism flourished and often represented the dominant ideological orientation) were highly atypical of most Spaniards insofar as they were frequently confronted with flows of information that undercut the credibility of franquist propaganda. The majority of Spaniards residing outside of these subcultural milieus, on the other hand, were not exposed to this conflicting information, and were therefore predisposed to behave in conformity with the cues disseminated by the regime.

A broader implication of these findings is that the type and basic characteristics of the nondemocratic system may have an important impact on the effectiveness of state control of political information. Both totalitarian and authoritarian regimes dominate the mass communications media, and the two types of regime are indistinguishable from one another with regard to their use of the media as channels for propaganda. Authoritarian regimes, however, are characterized by a shallow penetration into the interstices of society, thus allowing significant subcultures to retain considerable autonomy. We hypothesize that within those pockets of society, independent flows of information may be so incompatible with the regime's messages that even the minimal objective of deterring protest behavior may be out of reach. The greater the penetration by a nondemocratic regime into its society, and the fewer the pockets of society with subcultural autonomy, the more likely the regime's messages will go uncontested, and therefore that it will effectively discourage protest or perhaps resocialize the population.

The basic thrust of the messages the regime sought to disseminate was also increasingly inconsistent with the realities of Spain and of Western Europe of the 1960s and 1970s. Franco's efforts to resurrect traditionalist values and marry them to a corporatist-authoritarian political structure were doomed to failure by the country's substantial and rapid modernization in the 1960s and 1970s. The passivity, deference to authority, narrow religiosity, and antiliberalism that were central components of franquist propaganda simply did not ring true in a modern, urbanized society set within the context of a stable, prosperous, democratic Western Europe. This inconsistency was made highly visible to many Spaniards as the result of the internationalization of the Spanish economy beginning in the late 1950s. The temporary migration of 2 million Spanish workers abroad (most of them to affluent, peaceful, democratic Western European countries) and the annual influx of 40 million tourists, almost all of them from rich democracies, exposed many Spaniards to the values of democracy, provided many of them with models for emulation, and destroyed the credibility of the regime's anachronistic propaganda. All of these factors exposed Spaniards to flows of in-

40

formation that were either internally inconsistent or simply did not fit with easily observable reality.

This is not to say that the regime's propaganda had no lasting impact on Spanish society. While the regime completely failed to institutionalize a significant antidemocratic, right-wing party or movement that could survive in the democratic era,[7] depoliticization and cynicism toward competitive-party politics – central themes disseminated by Franco's communications media, and by the formal "civics" training provided by the severely underfunded and underdeveloped education system – represent distinguishing characteristics of Spain's political culture today. Since the end of the 1980s, levels of interest in politics have consistently been among the lowest of all European countries. A 1993 survey revealed that only 4 percent of the Spanish electorate claimed to be very interested in politics, another 21 percent were somewhat interested in politics, and only 9 percent said that they discussed politics "often" with their friends.[8] The frequency of reading about politics in the newspapers and in news magazines was also substantially lower than that of other industrialized societies (as we shall see later in this chapter), as is turnout at general elections. While the overall level of support for democracy is as high as the average among European Union countries (Montero and Gunther, 1994), levels of party identification are the lowest of any Western European country, and cynicism toward parties and politicians is widespread. Surveys have shown that, when asked to describe their feelings about politics, most Spaniards use terms such as "distrust," "indifference," and "boredom," while their own relationships with the political system are characterized by lack of subjective competence and inefficacy (Montero and Torcal 1990; Montero and Gunther 1994). This suggests that one unanticipated legacy of *franquismo* was a cluster of political cultural attributes – political indifference, cynicism, and apathy – that somewhat diminished the quality of Spanish democracy through at least the 1980s (Montero et al. 1998).

THE ROOTS OF CHANGE

The incompatibility between Fraga's press liberalization and the continuation of authoritarian rule had become increasingly apparent by the early 1970s. A growing segment of newspapers and magazines took advantage of Fraga's partial liberalization by expanding the informational content of their news reporting, adopting a new language of cautious (sometimes coded) political discourse, and reporting on the increasingly frequent internal conflicts and external developments that weakened the regime's hold on power (Maravall and Santamaría 1989, 192–6). Some private radio stations behaved similarly, breaking the news monopoly that had been granted to the official RNE (Martínez de las Heras 1989, 430).

One particularly interesting and politically significant practice was to use international news events as vehicles for the education of Spaniards about the workings and merits of democratic politics and prospects for political change.[9] While clashes between political ideologies or the basic nature of parliamentary democracy could not be openly discussed with specific reference to Spain, press coverage of elections or parliamentary struggles in Italy, France, or Britain was relatively free from censorship and thus could be used to teach Spaniards about the underpinnings of democratic politics. The higher levels of affluence and long traditions of democratic stability of Spain's European neighbors enhanced their attractiveness as models for emulation (López Pintor 1974; Moral 1989). One indirect measure of this vicarious learning process can be seen in the findings of a survey conducted in 1973, prior to the death of Franco, in which 29 percent of those polled stated that they identified themselves with one of the major Western European "political families" – Christian Democratic, liberal, social democratic, socialist, or Communist (Linz et al. 1981, 14). Three years later (but still one year before the first democratic elections), that figure had risen to 58 percent (Jiménez Blanco et al. 1977, 121). Even larger numbers of Spaniards were able to place themselves and various Spanish political actors on the left–right scale, based on terminology and concepts that had been banned from Spanish political discourse over the previous decades. In two polls conducted in 1976, seven out of ten were able to do so.

The scope and pace of fundamental changes in the political orientations of Spain's citizenry are impressive and challenge some common notions about political socialization. Rather than conforming to the conventional wisdom that basic attitudes toward democracy, political parties, democratic institutions, and so on are largely fixed by early adulthood and are not easily amenable to pressures for change, the Spanish citizenry demonstrates fundamental shifts occurring in a remarkably short period of time. Between 1966 and 1974, for example, the percentage of Spaniards stating in public opinion surveys that they favored freedom of expression increased from 40 to 74 percent (IOP 1967, 222; Gómez-Reino et al. 1976, 1168). As Table 2.3 shows, a number of other attitudes incompatible with the basic tenets of *franquismo* – regarding freedom of religion and trade union affiliation in particular – were also

Table 2.3   *Support for Different Kinds of Freedoms,*
by Selected Variables, 1974

			Support for Freedom of		
	Press	Religion	Trade Unions	Political Parties	N
Gender					
Male	82%	77%	66%	43%	1,969
Female	68	67	52	32	2,431
Size of community					
Less than 2,000	67	64	50	33	1,006
More than 100,000	85	84	70	47	855
Age					
15 to 19	79	77	71	47	559
20 to 24	85	81	71	52	491
50 to 54	75	71	54	29	403
Over 54	65	63	49	28	806
Education					
Elementary	70	67	53	31	2,597
University	89	84	72	59	225
Social class					
Upper and upper					
middle	86	84	71	56	231
Middle	82	79	67	46	1,630
Working, poor	65	63	49	28	1,631
Overall Population	74	71	58	37	4,399

Source: Adapted from Gómez-Reino et al. 1976 (1191–6).

widespread among Spaniards one year before Franco's death. Similarly, in May 1976, after a decade of press liberalization but one year prior to Spain's first democratic elections, fully 78 percent of those polled favored the popular election of government officials, up from just 35 percent in 1966 (López Pintor 1982, 84). Since the greatest shift was from the "don't know" category in 1966 to support for democracy a decade later, this resocialization function appears to have primarily involved the inculcation of democratic attitudes into a population whose political opinions were inchoate, poorly anchored, and sometimes contradictory.[10]

Since the formal socialization imparted by the regime through its control of the educational system remained antidemocratic until the end, the principal sources of prodemocratic socialization (except for relatively affluent elites and those Spanish workers who migrated abroad for temporary employment) were messages and information disseminated by the media. Liberalization of the press thus appears to have contributed to the democratic transition by facilitating a significant (but incomplete) transformation of Spanish political culture. Fundamental democratic principles were disseminated through increasingly free and critical news reporting and journalistic commentaries, and through the appearance in the press of intellectuals, representatives of clandestine parties and trade unions, or the "alegal" or tolerated opposition. Greater media pluralism also contributed to democratization over the long term by delegitimizing the franquist regime, by providing a platform for the discussion of alternatives to *franquismo,* and by serving as the principal channel for the resocialization of the "attentive public." A reemergence of civil society, featuring much greater ideological pluralism, also resulted (López Pintor 1982, 90). To some extent, this reemergence was facilitated by the preservation and intergenerational transmission of democratic attitudes that predated the Franco regime (Maravall 1978), but the public articulation of these values in the press during the late 1960s and early 1970s appears to have significantly reinforced this attitudinal contagion and crystallization.

DEMOCRATIZATION

During the first six months after Franco's death, the government of Spain was led by the ultraconservative Carlos Arias Navarro. This was a time of extreme political and social tensions, especially between late January and early May 1976. During this period, the regime maintained its rigid control over television news broadcasts and, to a lesser degree, over radio, but the print media (sporadic government crackdowns notwithstanding) enjoyed considerable freedom regarding both news coverage and the expression of editorial and op-ed opinions. While there was no change in the legal statutes that regulated the media during this period, those statutes were interpreted more permissively. Overall, this period should be regarded as merely an extension of that initiated with Fraga's Press Law.

By this time, only a handful of publications and a few dozen journalists had assumed clearly democratic positions. Other journalists were divided between fervent, sycophantic supporters of *franquismo* and a much larger number of those who were characterized by "complicity, docility, indifference and passivity" vis-à-vis the regime (Santos 1995, 57). The press of the Movimiento, the extreme-right press, and the ultraconservative monarchist daily *ABC* remained hostile to political change.

44

Within two years, however, the print media were transformed, with nearly all of the press supporting democratization (Aguilar 1982). This transformation was facilitated by the disappearance from newsrooms of the older generation of editors (Santos 1995, 60–1) and by the appearance of new newspapers and magazines. By far the most important of these was the daily *El País,* which began publication in May 1976 and served as a vehicle for disseminating the opinions of progressive reformers within the regime, as well as those of representatives of the moderate opposition groups (liberals, social democrats, and Christian Democrats). Its principal stockholders included representatives of all of the political families that would govern during the transition to democracy. From its very first issue, it was clear that *El País* represented an important change in Spanish journalism. It functioned as if there were no restrictions on freedom of the press. With regard to both its news coverage and its editorial opinions, it behaved like any other Western European news daily, without recourse to the tricks others employed to sidestep the obstacles presented by the Press Law. *El País* appeared at a key moment in Spain's political development, when it became clear that the political option presented by Arias Navarro had failed to meet even the most minimal reformist demands. It quickly became the country's leading newspaper and a model for emulation by other dailies (Imbert 1988), particularly with regard to its commitment to democratization and its dissemination of a broad array of political opinions. The breech opened by *El País* in the regime's system of information control helped to accelerate the pace of political and media change (Cebrián 1980; Gaitán 1992).

It was not until Adolfo Suárez was appointed prime minister in July 1976 that one could speak of a true process of political transition.[11] Indeed, the first significant act of the democratic era was enactment of the Law for Political Reform in the autumn of 1976. This law – the centerpiece of the regime-transition strategy formulated by Suárez and his collaborators – established an array of basic democratic freedoms, called for free democratic elections within six months, and initiated a series of sweeping changes regarding the structure and control of the communications media. During this early phase of the transition to democracy, many segments of the media served as conduits for information about the strategy for political change being implemented by the reformist Suárez government, as well as platforms for the articulation of political demands by newly emerging political and trade union organizations.[12] Once the transition was well underway and the institutions and behav-

Table 2.4   *How Readers of Three Major Newspapers Voted in 1993*

	Newspaper Read Most Frequently		
	El País	*ABC*	*El Mundo*
Voted for PSOE	36%	13%	10%
Voted for PP	14	74	38
Voted for IU	24	3	21
Voted for other party	7	5	2
Did not vote	19	5	29

Source: 1993 Spanish CNEP survey.

Table 2.5   *Opinions of Readers of Three Major Newspapers*

	Newspaper Read Most Frequently		
	El País	*ABC*	*El Mundo*
Believe the government wastes a large amount [*gran parte*] of the taxpayers' money	28%	61%	61%
Believe that there is much corruption in Spanish public life	34	58	55
Believe PSOE is more corrupt than the other parties	28	42	60
Believe that Felipe González is "honest" [*honrado*]	66	32	26

Source: 1993 Spanish CNEP survey.

ioral norms of the new democratic regime began to take shape, the communications media began to play a second crucial role: to explain to the general public the new rules of the game and the basic values and orientations underpinning democratic politics, thereby completing the political resocialization that had been set in motion a decade earlier.

These changes in the political orientations and behavior of the media were accompanied by significant structural changes.

TELEVISION

By the end of the franquist era, television was by far the most popular communications medium, as well as the one most heavily subjected to government control. Prior to the first democratic election in June 1977, there was no change in the structural relationship between TVE and the government: its two channels remained under the direct control of the Ministry of Information, and the content of news coverage was subjected to political oversight down to its finest details. In terms of the substantive biases of television coverage, however, there was a fundamental change following Suárez's appointment as prime minister: television was transformed into a voice supporting processes of democratic transformation. Of particular significance was that it was used as a medium through which the nature of political change could be explained to newly enfranchised citizens and through which newly legalized political parties could appeal to voters.

The fact that the liberalization of this period did not include a reform of the structural relationship between the government and TVE, however, led to predictable political controversies: questions regarding the partisan objectivity of the state's television network soon became salient. Rival parties complained that TVE tilted its news coverage in favor of Aldofo Suárez's Unión de Centro Democrático during the 1977 election campaign. The first institutional response was the creation, following the 1977 elections, of a Council of Vigilance and Control, composed of members of Parliament. It was practically inoperative, however, during its brief existence. This was followed by much more substantial institutional reforms enacted through the Organic Law of 1980. As we shall see, those structural changes had a substantial impact on the objectivity and balance of political coverage through the public broadcasting media, but they did not put an end to opposition party complaints about partisan bias.

THE PRESS

Contrary to all expectations, the establishment of full freedom of expression did not lead to an increase in newspaper readership. To be sure, the total number of newspapers in circulation increased by about 30 percent (Wert 1980, 40–1), but the expectation that the winds of freedom would scatter the seeds of interest in the press and lead to a broadening of readership was not realized: in 1974, 32 percent of Spaniards reported that they read newspapers every day; by 1979, that figure had fallen to 29 percent (Wert 1976, 119; 1980, 39). In other respects, however, the press evolved in a manner that one might have anticipated following the demise of an authoritarian regime: readers shifted to the emerging democratic press, and those newspapers that had supported the franquist regime virtually disappeared.

During the transition (1976–9), a number of periodicals reflecting a variety of political orientations came into existence. Within a few months of the birth of *El País,* a new newspaper, *Diario 16,* was created by the publishing group that produced the prodemocratic news magazine *Cambio 16.* This new daily provided a liberal[13] counterpoint to the social democratic *El País.* Similar initiatives were launched in Barcelona and some other provinces, leading to a substantial expansion of the democratic press, previously represented by a handful of publications, including *Informaciones, Ya,* and a few others. The principal impact on the size of the reading audience, however, was limited. Much of the increase in circulation reflected the reading of multiple daily papers by an informed and interested minority of the population. More important, the new publications crowded established newspapers out of the market. Three Madrid dailies, for example, had played important roles in disseminating democratic viewpoints during the final years of *franquismo:* the morning newspapers *Ya* (published by the Editorial Católica) and *Nuevo Diario* and the evening daily *Informaciones.* These newspapers suffered such severe financial difficulties that the latter two disappeared,[14] while *Ya* (whose potential readership has continued to shrink as a result of the substantial secularization of Spanish society over the past two decades – see Montero, 1993) fell from its position as the most widely read Madrid daily to last place in terms of circulation (Edo 1994, 83–95). A general indicator of this process can be seen in the evolution of the total number of newspapers in existence at various stages in the transition: when Franco died, there were 115 newspapers; within two years, this figure rose to 143 as new publications flooded the market; but by 1979, following the financial collapse of many uncompetitive newspapers, the total was reduced to 103 (Wert 1980, 34–5), and by 1989 it had fallen to 84 (Montabes 1994, 66). Meanwhile, the newspaper with the highest circulation in 1979 was one that did not even exist four years earlier: *El País.*

MAGAZINES

In the final years of the franquist regime, magazines had been the medium through which political criticism could be most easily channeled. Given their more limited circulation, less rigorous state oversight was exercised than with regard to daily newspapers, and they were in a better position to articulate democratic values and provide a public forum for once clandestine opposition groups (Sunkel 1994, 169). During the course of the transition era, however, daily newspapers began to enjoy the same freedom from government control, and news magazines found themselves increasingly unable to compete for adequate shares in the print media market. The major national newspapers adopted a style that posed a direct competitive threat, since their high-quality, general-information format provided more national and international news than most avid readers could keep up with on a daily basis, and their extensive, glossy Sunday supplements left little room for competitors. Thus, paradoxically, such magazines as *Cuadernos para el Diálogo* and *Triunfo*, which had valiantly struggled under *franquismo* to keep alive the flame of democracy, began to experience irreversible financial crises just as their goal was achieved.[15]

The only successful entries into this tough market were hybrid publications that mixed political news coverage and commentary with sex (sometimes pornographic) and sensationalism. The most successful of these odd publications was *Interviú*, born in 1977, which juxtaposes in-depth political interviews and provocative photos of attractive nude women, and whose circulation in 1979 reached 3 million per week (Wert 1980, 42–3). But even this publication declined in circulation over the following decades, falling to just over 1 million by 1994 (*Anuario El País 1995*, 202). Other news magazines suffered more serious declines in circulation and political influence. In its better days, *Cambio 16* (with over 170,000 weekly sales at its peak in 1981) had a devoted following among the politically informed and active sectors of the population. In the early stages of the transition period, it had played an important communication function within the politically informed strata of Spanish society. By the mid-1990s, however, it had undergone a serious decline in circulation (down to just over 90,000 in 1993),[16] prestige, and influence.

News magazines, which had played an important opposition role under the Franco dictatorship, became much less important politically after freedom of the press was secured. Among respondents in our 1993 Comparative National Elections Project (CNEP) survey, 87 percent said that they read news magazines less than once a week (23 percent) or never (64 percent). With these small readership levels, their political impact is most likely quite limited.

Radio

In this same period, radio was undergoing its own transformation. With the substantial growth of television during the 1960s and 1970s, both its share of the media market and its role in Spanish society were on the wane. During the transition, however, radio underwent a significant rebirth as a source of news. This was facilitated by the fact that government oversight, control, and censorship of radio had always been more relaxed than for television, in part because of the existence of a sizable private broadcasting sector.

With the onset of the transition in 1976, the legal framework regulating radio was relaxed (Santos 1995, 133–6). First, private radio stations were released from the obligation to retransmit the state's news broadcasts. By 1977, private radio networks were allowed to develop their own news services completely free of state control. The gradual expansion of their news-reporting activities, which began with news coverage of sports and nonpolitical events (train wrecks, etc.), spread to reporting about local news developments, and eventually included coverage of national and international political news. The style and format of news broadcasts also changed. In contrast with the solemnity and excessive restraint of RNE news broadcasts, private radio (led by the SER network) initiated a more informal and less irritating style and, unconstrained by the kinds of rigidity in scheduling that limited television's flexibility, was more responsive to the immediacy of news developments. Subsequently, even state radio networks were urged to keep up with the competition by taking on a more independent role as a source of information. Thus, liberalization of the public sector of radio began, and stations soon exhibited substantially greater pluralism and less progovernment bias than was characteristic of state-run television, even prior to enactment of a statute that institutionalized external oversight of public radio designed to guarantee its pluralism and objectivity.

This qualitative change was accompanied by a rapid increase in the size of radio audiences. The segment of the population listening to radio news programs increased from only 7 percent in the final years of *franquismo* to 20 percent during the transition (Wert 1976, 126–7). And audiences for all kinds of radio programs also expanded considerably, from 35 percent of the population in 1973 to 50 percent in 1979 (Wert 1980, 49–51).

THE MEDIA AND POLITICS DURING THE TRANSITION

In general, the transition was a period of effervescence in the media – of political involvement and more real change in the structure and behavior of the media than might be suggested by the relatively modest reforms in their regulatory framework. They adapted to the newly emerging democracy, but they also played a role in contributed to that process of political change.

Perhaps the most important political function performed by the communications media during the transition period was to help to re-socialize Spain's adult population to acknowledge the legitimacy of the new regime and to internalize fundamental norms of democratic behavior. Given the shallow penetration of party organizations into Spanish society, coupled with the weakness or absence of other secondary organizations with explicit ties to political parties, the media served as the principal channels for the flow to citizens of partisan cues, democratic values, political information, and norms of tolerance of differing political views. Television, radio, and the press helped to teach these norms and values largely by example: they were the most visible arenas in which individuals could debate and disagree with one another civilly. This informal and indirect dissemination of pluralistic attitudes and norms of tolerance undermined many of the central tenets of franquist political culture, among them the notions that liberal pluralism and individual freedom inevitably culminate in destructive conflict and that a single enlightened ruler could somehow translate absolute truths into policies that were in the interests of all members of society. The media also placed a variety of important reforms on the agenda and served as forums for political dialogue, which were necessary for the development and eventual institutionalization of political pluralism. In general, the media contributed to democracy by spreading the belief that a continuation of *franquismo* was untenable and that democracy was the only viable alternative to that discredited political system. They presented a realistic and attractive model for the exit from authoritarianism based on pacts and transactions, on gradualism, and on the adaptability of the demands of political actors and social forces to greatly altered circumstances (Wert 1986, 168).

The media's positive role notwithstanding, we must remain skeptical about the exaggerated claims commonly made by journalists and broadcasters concerning their heroic roles as the "Paladins of liberty" in this process of political transformation (e.g., in Maxwell 1983). They were merely one set of actors among many who contributed to the eventual success of the democratization of Spain, and their principal function was to channel to the mass public messages that originated among political elites.

THE MEDIA AND POLITICS TODAY

The beginning of the current era of Spanish politics dates from 1982, by which time the transition had been completed and Spanish democracy consolidated (Gunther 1992a; Gunther et al. 1995). In this period of normalcy, we can focus our attention on questions involving the relationship between the media and politics, and the contribution of the media to the quality of Spanish democracy, without having to take into consideration the particular and extraordinary demands of the democratization and consolidation processes. By 1982, the Spanish party system had taken on a relatively stable configuration. Following the disappearance of the Unión de Centro Democrático (UCD) (Gunther 1986; Linz and Montero 1986; Gunther and Hopkin in press), partisan politics at the national level came to be dominated by a very moderate, social democratic Partido Socialista Obrero Español (PSOE) and a center-right to right Alianza Popular (renamed the Partido Popular [PP] in 1989). Finally, the structure of television broadcasting in Spain was transformed as the central government's former monopoly was brought to an end, first by the devolution to the new regional levels of government the right to establish their own public television networks and then by allowing private-sector firms to establish their own nationwide broadcasting networks. This concluding section of the chapter will therefore be an exploration of "politics as usual" in Spain and the role of an evolving media structure in Spanish democracy today.

THE PRINT MEDIA

Between the mid-1970s and 1998, the proportion of Spaniards over the age of 14 who read newspapers every day increased from 32 to 36 percent. Nonetheless, Spain continues to lag far behind most other Western European countries, whose average daily newspaper readership was 61 percent in 1994.[17] Two important reasons for this lag are Spain's late economic development (which began in earnest only in the 1960s) and the franquist regime's highly inadequate educational system. This is evident in the frequency of newspaper readership among our 1993 CNEP survey respondents, broken down into subcategories according to age and education. A relationship of moderate strength (tau-B = .13, sig. at .000) emerged when newspaper readers were broken down by age: 42 percent of those over age 50 (whose childhood socialization took place prior to the economic takeoff of the 1960s) stated that they never read newspapers, compared with only 30 percent of those under age 50. But this relationship is explained

52

entirely by the fact that older Spaniards had far more limited educational opportunities than have younger Spaniards. When education is introduced as a control variable we find that, among the college educated and those completing secondary education, older Spaniards read newspapers somewhat more frequently than do those under age 50. The strength of the relationship between educational attainment and newspaper reading is substantial within both groups: the tau-B among those over age 50 is .39, and among younger Spaniards it is .27. This would suggest that as the older generation of less well educated Spaniards is gradually replaced by cohorts whose educational achievements are comparable with those of other advanced postindustrial societies, this distinguishing characteristic of Spanish political culture should fade.

Even when we take into consideration late industrialization and lagging educational opportunities, however, Spaniards read newspapers less frequently than other Europeans, presenting us with a puzzle. The same number of daily newspapers were being sold in Spain in 1980 as in 1931 (Alférez 1986, 225). But in 1931, Spain had 23 million inhabitants, between 30 and 40 percent of whom were illiterate and over half of whom lacked formal schooling. Today, in contrast, Spain's population is nearly 40 million, illiteracy has virtually disappeared, and education is free and compulsory up to age 16. Clearly, something other than education explains these reading habits.

The boredom and monotony of the press during the decades of *franquismo* may simply have discouraged many Spaniards from regularly reading daily newspapers, and shifted their attention to the more lively and entertaining new medium of television. Over time, this may have become a behavioral norm with a life of its own. Another possible explanation has to do with a structural characteristic of the Spanish media, especially the daily press. In many respects, the inability of newspapers to attract large audiences among the lower and lower middle strata of society is a product of the lack of a popular press whose language and news content might make them more accessible and attractive to persons with relatively little education. The major national newspapers in Spain are modeled after the small handful of quality newspapers found in Western democracies, and their relatively demanding vocabulary and detailed presentations of often complex issues make them inaccessible to many citizens. With the shift to the democratic press, some newspapers with the ability to appeal to the lower social strata (such as the daily *Pueblo*, run by the franquist corporatist trade union system) disappeared and were not replaced by others with a similar style.[18]

With regard to the overall structure of the newspaper market, Spain lies somewhere between Britain (dominated by newspapers with nationwide circulations) and the United States (where local papers predominate). The great majority of the 123 daily newspapers published in 1994 were local or provincial papers with geographically restricted circulation. A second group of newspapers are regional, some of which articulate regional-nationalist concerns, while others (in regions lacking nationalist parties or movements) merely focus their attention on regional issues.[19] However, newspapers with nationwide circulations (which account for over one-third of all daily sales) have by far the greatest impact on national politics. Indeed, the country's political discourse is largely dominated by a handful of newspapers published in Madrid. Outside of three areas with their own languages and cultures (Catalonia, Euskadi, and Galicia), the regional and provincial press consists of minor, low-quality publications with extremely low circulation levels.

The most significant press development since the end of the transition period has been the birth of a new Madrid daily, *El Mundo,* whose sensationalist attacks on the PSOE and the government of Felipe González have had a major impact on Spanish politics. This paper quickly attracted a following and assumed a prominent position in the newspaper market, previously dominated by the center-left *El País* and the right-wing *ABC,* with *Diario 16* occupying a relatively small market niche ideologically sandwiched between the other two. By 1994, *El Mundo*'s reported sales and readership roughly equaled those of *ABC* and greatly exceeded those of *Diario 16,* although *El País* easily retained its position as the leading daily.[20]

The political stance of *El Mundo* is quite distinct from that of its two principal rivals, as indicated by data from our 1993 CNEP survey (corroborated by the findings of a much larger survey of 30,000 Spanish citizens[21]). *El País* was perceived by 62 percent of its readers ($n = 95$) as objective and not favoring any particular party, but the great majority of those who perceived bias (30 of 36) believed it favored the governing PSOE. *ABC* has a much more clearly partisan profile, with 60 percent of its readers ($n = 38$) regarding the conservative daily as having a partisan bias and with half of its readers specifying that the PP was the favored party. These biases were confirmed by a systematic evaluation by a trained coder of newspaper articles dealing with the 1993 campaign.[22] *El Mundo* appears at first glance not to have any partisan biases: only 16 percent of its regular readers ($n = 42$) said that it favored any party. Instead, its bias is manifested not in support for a particular party, but in its aggressively hostile stance toward González and his PSOE government. With its aggressive, muckraking journalism (in which scandals involving government and party officials were headlined almost daily), it quickly filled a previously unoccupied niche in the relatively staid national newspaper market. In several instances, it uncovered important scandals involving unconscionably corrupt behavior by prominent government appointees (such as the governor of the Bank of Spain and the commander of the Civil Guard) and involvement in illegal counterterrorist activities by the minister of the interior.[23] A useful journalistic function was thus performed by helping to purge corruption from a system that perhaps had been dominated by a single party for too long. But in other respects, the lack of a distinction between news reports and journalists' own opinions, the frequent lodging of unfounded allegations against the PSOE, and behavior that sometimes seriously violated the ethical standards of journalism revealed an excess of antisocialist zeal.[24] In the end, *El Mundo* succeeded in making corruption in public office the most salient issue throughout the period from 1993 to 1996, contributing to the PSOE's electoral defeat in that year. Unfortunately, its attacks and its indiscriminately shrill and rancorous tone have also helped to give Spanish politics a nastiness and an unsavory character that had been largely lacking during the transition – when the "politics of consensus" prominently featured civilized and restrained clashes between opposing party representatives and a deeply entrenched sense of mutual respect, which contributed substantially to the consolidation of the new democracy (Gunther 1992a).

The three newspapers' biases are reflected in the ideological orientations and electoral preferences of their regular readers.[25] The mean self-placement on the left–right continuum (with 1 representing the far left and 10 the extreme right) of *El País* readers was a center-left 3.8, while that of *ABC*'s followers was a right-of-center 6.1. Interestingly, *El Mundo*'s readers placed themselves at 4.6 – a center-left position that is close to the mean placement of the PSOE on the left–right continuum by our CNEP respondents. Nevertheless, as Table 2.4 shows, *El Mundo*'s readers gave far less electoral support to the PSOE (10 percent) than did the Spanish electorate as a whole (38 percent). This represents a very significant departure from the least-ideological-distance principle, which has been an accurate predictor of the vote in all previous Spanish elections (Gunther et al. 1986; Linz and Montero 1986). While the small number of regular newspaper readers in our CNEP survey reduces the statistical reliability of these relationships, we should note that, once again, these findings are corroborated by other studies[26] and by the consistency of findings across a large number of indicators. Overall, these findings suggest that reading a particular newspaper is closely associated with holding specific attitudes either directly or indirectly relevant to partisan preferences. As Table 2.5 clearly illustrates, the regular readers of these three papers were clearly differentiated from each other by their opinions concerning whether or not they believed that the government wastes "a large portion" of the taxpayers' money, that there is much corruption in public life, that the PSOE was more corrupt than other parties, and that Felipe González was honest.

TELEVISION

The structure of television broadcasting has been substantially altered during this era of "democratic normalcy." A new statute for Radio Televisión Española (RTVE) was incorporated within an Organic Law, passed in 1980 (see Maxwell 1995, 37), that established new democratic mechanisms for regulating state-owned broadcasting media. But despite the new Radio and Television Statute's commitment to impartiality, pluralism, the separation of news from editorial opinion, and the promotion of democratic values, creation of these new regulatory bodies did not end partisan tensions over the alleged progovernment bias of these media (Sinova 1983, 29–42). This is perhaps the logical outcome of one continued institutional linkage between the incumbent government and the country's largest television network: the director general of TVE remained a government appointee. Despite numerous other institutional changes, and the fact that partisan biases in coverage of politics on TVE are (as we shall see) quite modest, the continuation of this linkage (rather than replacing the government-appointed director with a strictly nonpartisan governing body, like those that control the British Broadcasting Corporation or the American Public Broadcasting System) has led to charges by opposition parties of political favoritism by the public television network. No matter which party has been in control (the UCD from 1977 to 1982, the PSOE from 1982 to 1996, and the PP today), opposition parties have complained about bias in news coverage by the state-owned television network.

Initially, incremental reforms were implemented in an attempt to ensure greater objectivity and partisan balance in broadcasting by the state television network: oversight of the two state-run channels (TVE-1 and La 2) was institutionalized through the creation of a commission whose members are selected by a two-thirds majority vote in Parliament. In the

1980s, more far-reaching structural changes were implemented, including the creation of regional broadcasting systems and several private-sector television networks. In the end, what had been a government monopoly, subjected to sometimes heavy-handed political control, was replaced by a highly pluralistic arrangement that, in the aggregate, provides for a high level of partisan balance in television coverage of political news.

Accompanying Spain's transition to democracy was an equally profound transformation that replaced the rigidly centralized and hydrocephalic franquist state with a highly decentralized political system (the *Estado de las Autonomías* – a regionally varying, quasi-federal system). This decentralization was a recognition of the cultural and linguistic pluralism of Spain's population[27] and a response to demands by powerful Catalan and Basque nationalist parties for the reestablishment of extensive self-government rights. Decentralization of the television system was an integral part of this larger transformation. In reaction against the franquist regime's linguistic and cultural intolerance, as well as concerns that the spread of Spanish-language television broadcasts posed a grave threat to the everyday use of the regional languages, Catalan and Basque political leaders placed the right to create their own regional television networks near the top of their political reform agendas. The new Catalan and Basque regional governments, established in 1980, moved quickly to create their own broadcasting systems. The end result is that viewers in these regions have two additional regional stations to choose from – TV3 and Canal 33 in Catalonia and ETB1 and ETB2 in Euskadi. Regular broadcasting in Catalan and Euskera complements the respective regional governments' policies promoting the everyday use of their regional languages.[28] This partial decentralization of television broadcasting has spread to other regions as well. The nationwide networks are complemented by Canal Nou in Valencia, Televisión de Galicia, Canal Sur in Andalucía, and Telemadrid in Madrid.

More recently, media pluralism has been reinforced by enactment of a 1988 law permitting the establishment of private television channels to compete nationwide with the state-run stations.[29] In 1989, Antena 3 Televisión was the first private station to begin broadcasting. The Italian media magnate Silvio Berlusconi was the next to enter the field, initiating broadcasts by his Tele 5 in 1990. In 1994, Canal Plus España (modeled after its French parent) began entertainment broadcasting to those who pay annual subscription fees, in addition to unscrambled broadcasts of its news programs free of charge. Satellite television viewers (about 3 percent of the population) were presented with a still wider array of options.[30] By 1995, viewers in over 90 percent of Spain could receive all four of the nationwide free-television channels, in addition to the unscrambled portions of Canal Plus broadcasting. The overwhelming majority of the population (residing in the populous regions of Madrid, Catalonia, Andalucía, Valencia, Galicia, and Euskadi) could also receive one or more of the regional channels.

Spaniards are heavy consumers of television broadcasts. Over 90 percent of the population watch television daily, and 67 percent of our 1993 CNEP respondents said that they followed the news on television every day (with another 12 percent watching television news broadcasts three or four times a week). The number of viewing hours has increased steadily since the introduction of private television in 1990: by 1994, the average Spaniard was watching about three and one half hours of television per day. In terms of audience shares, TVE-1 and Antena 3 Televisión were the leaders, attracting about 25 percent of the viewing audience each. Tele 5 followed, with between 18 and 20 percent, La 2 regularly attracted about 10 percent of viewers, and Canal Plus another 2 percent. Regional television channels averaged about 16 percent of their respective geographical segments of the viewing public, ranging between the 25 percent of the Catalan audience that regularly watched TV3 to 5 percent of Basque viewers tuned in to ETB1 (which broadcasts in Euskera, which is not an Indo-European language and is spoken by less than 30 percent of the population of Euskadi).[31]

In terms of news broadcasts (whose typical length is 30 minutes), TVE-1 remains the preferred channel by a wide margin, with a share of 32 percent of the viewing audience for its lunch-time Telediario (3:00 P.M.) and a 27 percent share for its 9:00 P.M. news broadcast. Despite their comparatively limited technical and news-gathering resources, the private channels have quickly mounted a strong challenge to TVE-1. A recent survey found that, out of a total average daily exposure to television news of 38 minutes, TVE-1's share was 13 minutes, and the shares for Tele 5 and Antena 3 were 8 and 7 minutes, respectively. Information consumption through regional channels amounted to an average of eight minutes, while Canal Plus and La 2 (the second public broadcasting channel) had just one minute each (Sofres 1997).

In contrast with the strongly biased and censored television news coverage under the franquist regime, Spanish television in the mid-1990s was broadcasting the news in a reasonably objective manner. Our 1993 survey data, for example, reveal that very large majorities of the regular viewers of news broadcasts on each of the three major networks regarded those broadcasts as impartial. Seventy-five percent of the regular viewers of TVE-1 news broadcasts ($n = 668$) agreed that those programs did not favor any particular party, as did 76 percent of Antena 3 viewers ($n = 254$) and 86 percent of Tele 5 viewers ($n = 130$). When asked which party was favored by the news broadcasts of each of these networks, 22 percent of the regular viewers of the state-run TVE said, not surprisingly, the governing PSOE. Balancing this perceived progovernment bias, 16 percent of Antena 3's regular viewers said that the news broadcasts they most frequently watched favored the Partido Popular. Eleven percent of the news broadcast viewers of the other major private channel, Tele 5, however, said that their preferred network favored the PSOE, while just 2 percent said that it was biased in favor of the opposition PP.

These survey findings are, by and large, consistent with other CNEP data based upon coding of media broadcasts by trained observers. During the course of the 1993 election campaign (including both the official campaign, which lasted from May 21 to June 6, and six days of the preceding "precampaign"), a total of 335 television news broadcasts were taped and their content was analyzed. Of the 5,536 news segments broadcast, 1,921 dealt with politics and were coded using a detailed system (which generated over 100 different variables for each of those 1,921 news items).[32] The several different indicators of bias built into the coding scheme clearly reveal that partisan favoritism exists, but also that these biases are quite moderate and uneven across various indicators and that, in 1993, the preferences of one network were balanced by the contrary orientations of another. Thus, in the aggregate, there was a high level of pluralism in Spanish television coverage of this election campaign, providing Spaniards with a wide and relatively balanced variety of viewpoints.

One indicator involves the ability of a political actor to initiate a news article and thereby influence the agenda of the election campaign. In this respect, there was almost no difference among television networks: they all allowed the governing PSOE to initiate a larger number of news items than the major opposition party, the PP, although the difference was not substantial. The PSOE initiated 15 percent of all news items dealing with political matters, compared with 9 percent for the PP. When one realizes, however, that an additional 7 percent were initiated by the left-wing Izquierda Unida (IU), and another 15 percent by other parties, the ability of the governing party to dominate the content of television news broadcasts appears to be marginal. The visibility of political figures in this coverage reveals a wider margin in favor of the PSOE and again does not vary greatly from one network to another. In the course of 335 news broadcasts, leaders of the six major parties were mentioned by name a total of 1,117 times; 47 percent were references to PSOE representatives, compared with only 17 percent for the PP, 13 percent for Izquierda Unida, 8 percent for the Centro Democrático y Socini (CDS), and 5 percent each for the Catalan Convergència i Unío (CiU) and the Basque Partido Nacionalista Vasco (PNV).

Similarly, the amount of time that political leaders spoke on television gave a significant advantage to the governing party over its closest rival, the PP, particularly during the precampaign period.[33] This was true with regard to all channels, both public and private. This advantage is offset, however, by the multiparty character of Spanish democracy. When the time devoted to coverage of all opposition party spokespersons is summed, messages by PSOE leaders are roughly balanced by others criticizing its performance in office during the precampaign. During the official campaign, the amount of time devoted to opposition-party messages significantly exceeds those of the government on all television channels.[34]

These indicators, however, do not tell us whether the news coverage was favorable to the principal object of the news segment or was critical. Three indicators of evaluative biases of television reporters and anchors give a much clearer picture of the extent of network partisan favoritism. One item asked coders to count the number of evaluative statements made by the reporter in each news segment (up to five such statements per news item) and to indicate whether these statements were positive or negative toward the relevant parties. Over the course of 1,921 news segments, reporters made a total of 97 statements favorable to the PSOE and 151 casting it in a negative light. There were also 51 positive references to the PP and 127 unfavorable statements. The most striking conclusion to emerge from these data is that Spanish television reporters and anchors generally shy away from making evaluative statements about parties: the combined total of all positive and negative statements concerning the two largest parties amounted to just 426 out of the 1,921 news segments covered – that is, an average of one evaluative statement out of every five political news items. As Díez Nicolás and Semetko (analyzing these same data) have written: "The immense majority of statements ... were descriptive, neutral, without evaluative judgments concerning the actors in the news" (1995, 286).

When evaluative statements are broken down by network and steps are taken to estimate the net balance of these assessments by each news organization, several points emerge clearly. The first is that, like television journalists in the United States, Spanish reporters and anchors of all networks tend to make more critical than favorable comments about politicians and parties in general (see Table 2.6). With the exception of Tele 5, the results presented here are consistent with those derived from the perceptions of our survey respondents. The governing Socialists did benefit in the 1993 election from more positive statements about the PSOE and more negative evaluations of the PP on TVE-1. This was largely offset by the net balance of evaluative comments about the PP broadcast by all the other channels surveyed, including (by a tiny margin) TeleMadrid, which was operated by the PSOE government of the region of Madrid. The partisanship implicit in these figures, however, is most restrained. No network was seriously biased in favor of one or the other major party.

A similar mixed picture emerges when we examine a second variable: expressions of disdain toward political parties. Coders were asked to identify reporters' comments that reflected cynicism toward a particular party. In this instance, TVE-1 emerges as the most balanced of the network news broadcasts: in only 3 percent of the 525 news items covered by TVE-1 was disdain expressed toward the PP, as compared with 2 percent toward the PSOE, giving the PSOE a net advantage of 1 percent. The most partisan stand was taken by reporters and anchors of Antena 3, who made 4 percent more snide remarks about the PSOE than about the PP. The other channels ranged between these extremes: Tele 5 journalists were more negative toward the PSOE by a net margin of 1 percent, while Canal+ and TeleMadrid reporters made more cynical remarks about the PP, by net margins of 1 and 3 percent, respectively. In general, such expressions of disdain were very infrequent, and more commonly involved cynical remarks referring to all parties than to any one of them in particular.

An equally mixed picture emerges from an examination of data derived from a third indicator, in which coders were asked to use a scale from 1 to 7 indicating how favorable or negative reporters' remarks were toward each party's national leader. When the mean of all such ratings were calculated for each network and the negative scores were subtracted from the mean of the positive evaluations, Felipe González was seen as favored by TVE-1 (a mean of 0.5 point), TeleMadrid (1.5 points), and Antena 3 (0.4 point). PP leader José María Aznar benefited from more favorable coverage on Canal+ (0.5) and Tele 5 (0.2) broadcasts.

Overall, the Spanish television media were quite pluralistic and inconsistent in their patterns of bias. The slight progovernment bias of the

Table 2.6   *Balance of Positive and Negative Evaluative*
Comments about Political Parties, by Network

	Net Evaluative Comments Toward[a]		
	PSOE	PP	Overall Balance[b]
Public Television			
TVE-1	−0.2	−4.4	+4.2 PSOE
Telemadrid	−5.3	−5.2	+0.1 PP
Private television			
Tele 5	−5.5	−3.2	+2.3 PP
Antena 3	−2.4	−2.1	+0.3 PP
Canal+	−5.2	−4.5	+0.7 PP

[a]This figure was calculate by subtracting the total number of negative evaluative statements about each party on each network from the total number of positive evaluative statements about that party and then standardizing by dividing the resulting figure by the total number of evaluative statements on both the PSOE and PP that appeared on news broadcasts by that network.

[b]This figure was calculated by subtracting the absolute value of the net of evaluative statements about the less favored party from the absolute value of the net of such assessments about the more favored party.

Source: 1993 Spanish CNEP media content analysis (see Díez Nicolás and Semetko, 1995).

state-operated TVE-1 was effectively canceled out by the antigovernment sentiments articulated more frequently on the other networks.[35] Clearly, no "pack journalism" was apparent, in which a climate of opinion among journalists decisively favored one party or the other (unlike the situation in the 1992 American presidential election, in which a significant anti-Bush sentiment was apparent in both newspaper and television coverage of the campaign,[36] or in the 1994 congressional election, following two years of hostile media criticism of Democratic incumbents). Just as important, the biases that were exhibited by the various television networks were quite restrained. Overwhelming majorities of our survey respondents believed that their preferred news broadcasts were impartial, a finding that is entirely consistent with the extensive content analysis of news broadcasts during the 1993 campaign itself.

The relative lack of bias exhibited by Spanish television journalists appears to be, at least in part, the product of a particular broadcast journalism style that limits opportunities for the infusion of personal bias and editorial comment by reporters. In sharp contrast with American television, where sound bites allowing politicians to state their own positions have been reduced to an average of 9 seconds, and where the great bulk of each news broadcast is devoted to the reporter's own interpretation of what was said or meant by a politician or news event, Spanish television is largely restricted to a straight news format. Spanish reporters rarely pontificate or reinterpret statements or news events. The actual protagonists in the news are the political elites themselves, rather than reporters, anchors, or commentators. Spanish politicians were allowed to speak, uninterrupted, for an average of 24 seconds during the course of the 1993 campaign ($n = 2,067$ sound bites timed by our coders). Indeed, only 13 percent of Spanish politicians who appeared on television were allotted the American *average* sound bite of 9 seconds or less. Moreover, a much larger portion of these news broadcasts was devoted to the actual policy proposals of the respective parties than is typical of American election coverage. Fully 32 percent of the 1,921 political news items studied by our coders dealt with public policy issues.[37] Finally, contrary to the American model, very little attention was paid to the so-called horse race aspects of the campaign, in which polling data concerning who is ahead at each stage of the campaign serve as the principal subject of the news story. Only 2 percent of the 1,921 news items broadcast during the 1993 campaign focused on which party was in the lead at that point in the race.

THE ELECTORAL IMPACT OF TELEVISION BIAS: Despite the fact that most Spaniards regarded their favorite news broadcasts as unbiased, our 1993 survey data suggest significant media effects on their voting preferences. At first glance, these effects would appear to be substantial: among regular TVE-1 news broadcast viewers, 58 percent ($n = 295$) voted for the PSOE in the 1993 election, and only 30 percent ($n = 153$) voted for the PP; among viewers of the other channel seen by viewers as favoring the governing party, Tele 5, 57 percent ($n = 47$) voted for the PSOE and 32 percent ($n = 26$) supported the PP; in sharp contrast, among Antena 3 viewers, only 35 percent ($n = 61$) cast ballots for the PSOE, while 55 percent ($n = 97$) supported the PP. On closer inspection, however, we must conclude that these media effects are more modest, since some viewers tend to select television news broadcasts that largely conform to their own partisan or ideological biases.[38] When left–right self-placement was introduced as a control variable, this relationship between viewing habits and electoral support decreased considerably. Indeed, among those with a marked ideological preference for the left (positions 1, 2, 3, or 4 on the 10-point left–right continuum) or the right (7, 8, 9, or 10), there was no significant relationship at all: irrespective of which channel one watched, persons with clear-cut ideological stands were not about to abandon the party to which they were closest on the left–right scale. Among those at the center of the political spectrum, however, viewing habits appear to have made a difference electorally. If we examine only those who placed themselves at position 5, the center of the political spectrum, we find that among TVE-1 viewers ($n = 69$), 75 percent voted for the PSOE in the 1993 election, while only 22 percent cast ballots for the PP. In contrast, among regular Antena 3 viewers in that same left–right category ($n = 22$), 50 percent supported the PP and 45 percent the PSOE (findings significant at the .05 level).

These data suggest that media effects are most likely to *interact* with other attributes of voters. One of these attributes is the initial ideological stance of the individual: among voters with firm political ideas and preferences, media effects will most likely be negligible, but among those near the center of the political spectrum, whose political attitudes may be mixed, weakly held, or nonexistent, even subtle biases in news coverage may have a measurable impact on electoral preferences. What is particularly significant about this finding is that in Spain, as in many other countries, the ability to attract large numbers of votes from the moderate center of the political spectrum is the key to electoral success. Thus, the individuals who are the key swing voters in close elections are precisely those who may be most susceptible to media influences of the kind under examination here.

Consistent with this swing voter hypothesis, there is some evidence that the erosion of electoral support for the PSOE since the previous election may have been somewhat increased by the way television channels presented news events during the four intervening years. Among those who had voted for the PSOE in 1989 and who regularly followed the news on TVE-1 ($n = 305$) during the 1993 campaign, over 78 percent voted for the Socialists again in that contest. But among those 1989 Socialist voters ($n = 78$) who watched the anti-PSOE Antena 3 (which did not exist in 1989), only 57 percent did so again in 1993, with 30 percent shifting to another party and another 13 percent not voting. Since we can conclude that some prior partisan predisposition did not lead these respondents to opt for one television network over the other (since all of this subsample had voted for the Socialists four years earlier), we can lay to rest doubts about the direction of causality underpinning these statistical relationships.

Overall, the effects of media bias on electoral behavior in Spain are only moderate and are interactive with other determinants of the vote, such as initial ideological or partisan predisposition. It is important to note, however, that the moderate strength of these relationships is consistent with the relatively restrained nature of television network bias in Spain. One is tempted to speculate that if TVE-1 had not been subject to democratic controls by the interparty oversight body, and that if the official campaign period did not impose additional restrictions designed to enhance fairness, the government's broadcasting network might have supported its reelection campaign more overtly and effectively. And it is undeniably true that termination of the state's monopoly over television broadcasting has greatly increased of pluralism in the political information market. Voting behavior in democratic systems where such safeguards have broken down (such as occurred briefly in Italy, where the Berlusconi government completely dominated both public and private television networks) is much more likely to be substantially affected by media biases.[39]

THE MAIN EVENT: GONZÁLEZ VERSUS AZNAR: Media effects should be most clearly observable in analyses of panel data collected prior to and following an election campaign. It is during election campaigns that individuals are asked to make unequivocal choices among various partisan alternatives on the basis of a flood of information presented to them through the media. Our 1993 survey was based on a panel design that makes such analysis possible. We were particularly fortunate in focusing our attention on that campaign, since it is the first in over a decade to produce an outcome different from preelection expectations. And it was the first Spanish election that featured the quintessential television campaign event: a face-to-face debate between the leaders of the two major parties. But before presenting an analysis of panel data intended to estimate the impact of this debate on the outcome of the 1993 Spanish election, a brief description of the basic structure of television coverage of election campaigns is in order.

Perhaps the most important differences between television coverage of electoral competition in Spain and the United States are the complete ban on advertising (on both public and private networks) and the allocation on both public television and radio public networks of free air time for all political parties.[40] Unlike American election campaigns – where candidates use television commercials to mold images and attract "buyers" in the same manner as toothpaste and under-arm deodorant are marketed, and where facile slogans are all that can fit into 15- or 30-second slots – Spanish parties and candidates appearing on television are placed in a setting where they actually have to say something about where they stand on issues. All parties fielding candidates in at least 75 percent of the provinces receive a free broadcasting slot of 10 minutes, and larger parties (in accord with their shares of the vote in the previous elections) receive more free air time ranging up to 40 minutes each for the two largest parties. (Purely regional parties are also given 15 minutes of free air time, if they received over 20 percent of the vote within their respective regions.) Fairness in the allocation of these time slots is guaranteed by strict oversight by the Radio and Television Committee of the Junta Electoral Central.[41] This format does not by any means guarantee the veracity of the claims made by parties and candidates, nor does it force party representatives to stick to the "high road" of discussion of policy alternatives, but it does establish a context in which mere slogan-mongering would look foolish. Similarly, although the public networks' allocation of slots to political parties does systematically favor the larger parties over the smaller ones (with prime time reserved for those parties with the largest percentages of the vote in the previous election), this source of bias pales in comparison with those arising out of the necessity in American campaigns to purchase time for expensive television commercials in order to be elected, thereby giving an enormous advantage to wealthy candidates or those with special access to well-heeled and well-organized special interests.

A second noteworthy feature of the regulations governing Spanish election campaigns is that the Junta Electoral Central strictly oversees and regulates the behavior of both the broadcast media and the parties during election campaigns. Parties are prevented from campaigning before the start of the official election campaign 15 days prior to the vote, although controversy always arises concerning de facto campaigning (i.e., in which parties portray themselves in the most favorable light, but without actually asking citizens for their votes) during the precampaign. There is little ambiguity, however, concerning oversight of the broadcast media during the official campaign period: the Junta Electoral Central exercises the strictest vigilance over the public media ("stopwatching" coverage of the various parties on news broadcasts, for example) in an effort to guarantee neutrality and objectivity.

The 1993 election was (to date) unique in that it featured a face-to-face debate between the candidates of the two leading parties. The creation of private networks (which are not constrained by the same equal-time provisions as the state networks) allowed for two such debates between Felipe González and José María Aznar during the 1993 campaign, as well as a series of debates among second-ranking party representatives. While the debates among minor party luminaries had low ratings (less than 7 percent of our 1993 survey respondents reported that they watched one of these secondary debates), the clashes between the leaders of the two largest parties drew enormous audiences: 70 percent of our respondents stated that they saw at least one of the two debates, and 49 percent said they watched both. Among other things, the much greater audiences for the Aznar–González debates are indicative of a "presidentialization" of electoral politics in Spain.[42]

These debates were without precedent and emerged as the main events of the 1993 campaign (Wert 1994). Unlike American presidential debates (which are a succession of short speeches by candidates rather than true clashes of opinion), these involved a great deal of give-and-take. In accord with the opinions of expert observers, our survey respondents thought that Aznar won the first debate, by a margin of 31 to 15 percent, over González. Their opinions were also consistent with the view that González won the second debate more decisively, with 38 percent believing that he emerged victorious from that encounter compared with only 7 percent who thought that Aznar won.

Most observers had expected that the PSOE would be swept from power in 1993. A decade after its triumphant 1982 victory (in which the PSOE attracted 48 percent of the popular votes and 58 percent of the seats in the Congress), the Socialist government of Felipe González was showing signs of having worn out its welcome. The Spanish economy was slumping badly after having expanded at the fastest rate of growth in the Economic Community from the middle to the late 1980s. The election was held in the midst of the worst economic crisis in three decades, with gross domestic product falling by 1 percent, unemployment reaching over 22 percent, and the peseta being devalued by 22 percent (the third devaluation in one year). The climate of public opinion was made even more negative by a series of scandals involving financial practices of the governing party and outright corruption of some of its more distinguished members. In combination with the usual erosion of public support that occurs after more than a decade in office, these circumstances made the PSOE's prospects for continuing in government quite dim. Indeed, the final published poll revealed that just one week prior to the official start of the two-week campaign, the PP had nudged ahead of the PSOE in terms of stated voting intentions, leading the government party by a margin of 35.5 to 33.9 percent.[43] There were widespread expectations that the election would culminate in the formation of a new government under the PP's youthful leader, José María Aznar (Sinova 1993). Instead, the PSOE was returned to power and attracted over 1 million more votes than in 1989, although, given the higher turnout (of over 3.5 million more voters), this represented a modest decline of 1.5 percent in its share of the popular vote. Controlling 45 percent of the seats in the Congress of Deputies (compared with 40 percent for the PP), the PSOE formed a single-party minority government supported de facto by the Catalan CiU. The PP did make spectacular gains, increasing in popular votes by 3 million and in the share of the total vote by 8.5 percent (from 26.3 to 34.8 percent), but in spite of all preelection forecasts, the PSOE was able to form a homogeneous and stable government for the fourth consecutive time. Thus, a prima facie case can be made that this was one election in which the campaign itself made a significant difference.

Some preliminary studies have argued that this unexpected electoral outcome was the product of changes in partisan preference by many voters during the campaign itself (e.g., López Pintor, et al. 1994, 611–12), while others have asserted that it was the result of the mobilization during the campaign of habitual nonvoters, attraction to the PSOE of a disproportionate number of undecided voters, and retention of former PSOE voters who were contemplating a shift to the IU or abstention (Arango and Díez 1993; Wert et al. 1993; Díez Nicolás and Semetko 1995). Most commonly cited as a decisive factor in the Socialist Party's victory was the second televised debate between González and Aznar, in which the prime minister succeeded in reversing the momentum of the campaign (Wert 1994).

If González's victory in the second televised debate was as decisive in determining the outcome of the election as these observers have claimed, then we should expect to find that a disproportionate number of those who regarded González as the winner should have shifted their support to the PSOE after that event. Our panel data reveal that 23 percent of the 416 respondents who were undecided on the preelection wave of our study eventually voted for the PSOE, while only 14 percent chose the PP; 41 percent apparently remained undecided and reported in postelection interviews that they did not vote. Given that 29 percent of those interviewed in the preelection round fell within this undecided category, the magnitude of this electoral shift during the course of the campaign is significant. It represented a net gain for the PSOE (over preelection statements of voting intention) of 4 percent of all votes eventually cast – a figure that is remarkably close to the difference between the 33.9 percent that the final preelection Centro de Investigaciones Sociológicas (CIS) poll predicted for the PSOE and the 38.8 percent it actually received on election day.

Our panel data indicate that the second televised debate between the two candidates was decisive in bringing about this shift. Among those who were undecided at the time of the preelection panel survey and who eventually voted for either the PSOE or the PP ($n = 104$), 68 percent thought that Gonzalez was the clear winner, while only 12 percent regarded Aznar as the victor. Among the initially undecided voters who thought that González had won, 82 percent eventually voted for the PSOE and only 18 percent supported the PP. Conversely, among the much smaller number who thought Aznar had won the debate, all 12 respondents cast ballots for the PP. These data are not only statistically significant (at the .001 level) but also, given the crucial role of these swing voters in determining the outcome of the election, they represent clear evidence that television coverage of a key campaign event can have considerable political significance as well. This kind of "media effect" is different from that resulting from partisan bias on the part of journalists, insofar as the politicians themselves are the only protagonists in the drama, but it is one in which an altered outcome would probably not have materialized if news about this event had been channeled to voters through any medium other than television.[44]

Radio

Radio listening has undergone a remarkable comeback in Spain between the 1970s and the 1990s. In 1973, only 35 percent of Spaniards over the age of 14 reported that they listened to radio daily; by 1994, that figure had climbed to 55 percent. Most of this increase occurred during the transition, but there has been a steady expansion of the radio audience since then as well. Of particular significance is the proliferation of highly politicized talk shows, in which reporters and journalists engage in often lively arguments about political matters (Santos 1995, 136–42). SER, COPE, and Onda Cero each broadcast three such programs during the day, which attract an estimated daily audience of 3 million. The tone of these debates is often quite contentious and goes well beyond the bounds of what would be tolerated in the print media.[45] Given these and other types of programs, radio has become a much more intensely politicized medium than television. The regular audience following political news on the radio, however, is much smaller than that of television. In our 1993 postelection survey, 82 percent of respondents said that they had followed the campaign by watching television news, but only 33 percent claimed to have listened to radio news broadcasts about the campaign.

The largest radio networks are the SER chain (owned by the PRISA group, which also publishes *El País*), with 34 percent of the market; the COPE network (owned by the Catholic Church and some private investors), with 24 percent; Radio 1 (a state-run conventional radio station), with 17 percent; Onda Cero Radio (owned by ONCE, the parastate organization that provides various forms of support for the blind), with 15 percent; and the state-run, all-news Radio 5, with 7 percent of the radio audience. The programs with the largest followings are the morning broadcasts of SER (with nearly 2 million listeners) and COPE (with over 1.5 million).

When asked whether their preferred radio station favored a political party, the responses given by regular radio listeners perfectly paralleled those of the television viewers described earlier: the great majority (ranging from 68 percent of COPE listeners to 87 percent of the RNE audience) said that their respective networks were impartial in covering the news and did not favor a political party. Nevertheless, among regular listeners who acknowledged bias by their favorite stations, unequivocally clear pictures of partisan favoritism emerged: Antena 3, and especially COPE and Onda Cero, were perceived as favoring the PP, while SER and RNE were regarded as supporting the PSOE.[46] Given the relatively small number of regular radio listeners in our sample, the necessity of introducing control variables into the analysis, and the remarkably comparable partisan compositions of the regular audiences of COPE, Onda Cero, and Antena 3, on the one hand, and those of SER and RNE, on the other, the following analysis will be based on a division of regular radio listeners into those two camps.

As in the case of television, an initial glance at the relationship between radio listenership and the choice between the PP and the PSOE in the 1993 election would give a misleading impression of an extraordinarily strong relationship. When the sample is further divided to include only those who voted for the PSOE or the PP in 1993, we find that two-thirds of the regular listeners of Antena 3, COPE, and Onda Cero (hereafter the "conservative channels") voted for the PP in that election, while three-quarters of RNE/SER listeners supported the PSOE, producing a tau-B of .42 between the two variables (significant at the .0001 level).[47]

To a much greater extent than among television viewers, however, it is clear that radio listeners chose stations compatible with their ideological preferences, with right-wing and/or religious Spaniards opting for the conservative channels and those to the left of center listening to RNE or SER stations.[48] Thus, it is necessary to introduce ideological self-designation as a control variable. To a greater extent than among television viewers, this leads to the complete disappearance of any significant relationship among those on the left (who located themselves at positions 1, 2, 3, or 4 on the 10-point scale) and right (7, 8, 9, and 10). For these individuals, the political biases of their respective radio stations were insufficient to overcome their standing attitudinal convictions and cause them to support a party on the other side of the left–right cleavage. As among television viewers, however, those at the center of the political spectrum appear to have been quite responsive to these media biases. Among those who placed themselves at position 5 on the left–right continuum, 86 percent of those who regularly listened to RNE/SER ($n = 22$) news voted for the PSOE compared with only 50 percent of those who listened to the conservative stations ($n = 18$, tau-B = .39, sig. at .01). Among those who placed themselves at position 6, 91 percent of those who followed the news on the conservative stations ($n = 21$) voted for the PP compared with only 46 percent of those who listened to RNE/SER ($n = 11$, tau-B = .49, sig. at .005). If we were to combine categories 5 and 6 into one centrist cell (which is standard practice but in this case conceals a significant difference between the two scale positions), we would see that 76 percent of those falling into this ideological category who regularly listened to RNE/SER ($n = 33$) voted for the PSOE, while 72 percent of COPE/Onda Cero/Antena 3 listeners ($n = 39$) supported the PP in 1993 (tau-B = .47, sig. at .0001).

Thus, as in the case of television viewers, it would appear that media effects are most notable among centrists, whose attitudes are more malleable, than among those who clearly locate themselves on the left or the right. Also consistent with our findings concerning television viewership, those most susceptible to the influences of media biases may also be the swing voters who can determine the outcome of election campaigns. Among those who had voted for the PSOE in 1989 and who were regular radio listeners ($n = 135$), 94 percent of those who followed the news on RNE/SER remained loyal to the Socialist Party four years later, while among those who regularly listened to one of the conservative stations, 23 percent defected to the PP in 1993 (tau-B = .24, sig. at .005).

THE MEDIA AND POLITICS IN SPAIN TODAY:
AN ASSESSMENT

An assessment of the impact of the media on Spanish politics today must begin with an awareness that the media system has been dominated by television since the 1970s. The preponderance of television as the principal channel of political communication in contemporary Spain is consistently revealed in surveys of the Spanish electorate. The CNEP survey of the 1993 election, for example, included three different measures of the frequency with which respondents followed political news through each communications medium. One was a question in the preelection interview asking how frequently the respondent followed political news through newspapers, magazines, television, and radio. The second was a postelection survey question asking how often the respondent had followed political news during the recent election campaign. The third item was more specific, asking each respondent which newspaper/magazine/television news broadcast/radio network he or she had read, watched, or listened to about politics during the previous campaign. As Table 2.7 shows, the resulting data are remarkably consistent. Except for some exaggeration of the frequency with which politics was followed through magazines and radio reported in the more general preelection question, these data indicate that, by wide margins, Spaniards follow news about politics through television, while extraordinarily few respondents read about politics in news magazines. These data make it clear why television was regarded as the most influential medium by 82 percent of our respondents compared with 7 percent who selected radio, 5 percent who so regarded newspapers, and less than 1 percent who placed news magazines in this category. While levels of television viewership in other industrialized countries are comparable to those found in Spain, the relative political importance of television is greater than in most established democracies due to the weakness of Spain's other communications media.

Other data indicate why television has been selected as the preferred medium of mass communication by most Spaniards. Table 2.8 presents responses to three questions asking respondents to identify the medium that is most credible, most informative, and most easy to understand. As can be seen, television was selected by pluralities or majorities of respondents as the answer to each of these questions.

The emergence of television as the preferred medium in response to each of these questions is worthy of some additional comment. First, we

Table 2.7   *Frequency with Which Politics Was Followed through*

Medium	Preelection	Postelection	
	First Item[a]	Second Item[b]	Third Item[c]
Magazines (once/week or more)	13%	3%	5%
Newspapers (three times/week or more)	32	28	27
Radio (three times/week or more)	47	29	28
Television (three times/week or more)	79	73	83

[a]This item asked respondents, "Could you tell me how frequently you follow political information through . . . [newspapers, general-information magazines, television, and radio]: Every day or almost every day, 3 or 4 days a week, 1 or 2 days a week, less frequently, or never or almost never?"

[b]This item was nearly identical to the preceding question, except that it referred specifically to the election campaign that had just ended: "During the election campaign, how frequently did you follow political information through . . . [newspapers, etc.]?"

[c]Data in this column summarize responses to probes (asking how many days per week or, in the case of news magazines, how many days during the campaign) following these questions: "During the past election campaign, which newspaper [or news magazine] did you read the most?", "During the past election campaign, did you listen to information bulletins or news broadcasts in general on a radio station?", "What is the name of the broadcast network on which you heard the news?, "During the past election campaign, did you watch the news on television?", and "Can you tell me the name of the television network on which this news appeared?"

Source: 1993 Spanish CNEP survey.

should recall that television was also regarded as the most credible medium under the Franco regime, even though it was the most closely controlled and most heavily censored medium. It would appear that many viewers place a certain blind faith in television that may, in some instances, be unwarranted. Second, our respondents' decision that television is the most informative medium does not hold up well in light of other data supplied by these same individuals. A political knowledge score was constructed out of responses to four of our CNEP questionnaire items in which respondents were asked to identify four prominent public figures.[49] A clear positive association was found between the frequency of newspaper reading and the respondents' scores on this political information test even after education was controlled for. The Pearson's *r* correlations for each educational subgroup (primary education or less, complete secondary education, and higher education) ranged

Table 2.8   *"Which Medium Is the Most . . ."*

Medium	Credible	Informative	Easy to Understand
Magazines	1%	1%	1%
Newspapers	17	20	8
Radio	27	27	19
Television	33	44	64
None of the above	16	2	3

Source: 1993 Spanish CNEP survey.

from .30 (among the least educated) to .37 (among high school- and college-educated respondents), and all of these measures of association were significant at the .0001 level. A relationship of moderate strength emerges between the frequency with which political news is followed on the radio and the political information score: correlations ranged from .16 to .28 among the three educational subgroups (the significance level for the two less educated categories was .0001, while for the smaller college-educated group it was .05). In short, the more one follows political news on the radio, or especially in the newspapers, the greater is one's political knowledge. The frequency with which political news was followed on television, however, was more weakly associated with respondents' levels of political knowledge, despite the fact that Spanish television news has a much denser public-policy content than American television news: correlations within the two less educated subgroups were .16 and .17, respectively. Among those with a college education, however, there was no statistically significant relationship between the frequency of television news viewing and political knowledge. Thus, the less well educated acquire some factual information about politics from television viewing (but much less than from reading newspapers or following the political news on the radio), but the incremental political knowledge gained by better-educated citizens is negligible. In accord with a commonly hypothesized but rarely tested notion (e.g., see Ranney 1983), television does not appear to be a good medium for conveying factual information, and it certainly pales in comparison with the effectiveness of regular newspaper reading.

These data suggest that television is the preferred medium among most Spaniards because it is the easiest one to understand, and therefore is the medium that disseminates political information at the lowest cost (in terms of time and effort) to the viewer.[50] Verbal and often graphic presentations of news about politics appear to be more readily accessible to the less well educated majority of the mass public than does the often dense and confusing presentation of political information in the print media. Since the major national newspapers are classified as high-quality media (using the distinction first developed in Britain), Spaniards with little education have no recourse to a popular or tabloid press and thus rely predominantly on television for information about politics. This does not necessarily have negative implications for the quality of Spanish democracy: in contrast with the unconscionable bias and sensationalism of the British tabloid press, both public and private television in Spain do a reasonably good job of presenting a considerable amount of political information to their viewers in a relatively balanced (or at least subtly, not blatantly, biased) way. On a world scale, they are closer to the television news broadcasts of the British Broadcasting Corporation than to those of the major American television networks (Miller 1991).

This empirical study of the 1993 parliamentary election has uncovered some evidence of media effects on Spanish politics. The most significant example of the influence of a news medium was that of the second televised debate between the country's leading political rivals. In this television era, it would appear that the personal campaign performances of a few prominent individuals can have a significant impact on electoral outcomes. In this sense, it is clear that the personalization or presidentialization of politics, even in parliamentary systems, is becoming an important feature of campaign politics in the modern era (also see Sartori 1998).

We have seen that the relatively modest political biases of news coverage by newspapers, radio, and television have had some impact on Spanish politics, but their capacity to affect voting decisions appears to be largely restricted to those near the center of the political spectrum – including both "true centrists," with moderate, nonideological orientations toward politics, and "false centrists," who locate themselves near the center largely by default, lacking well-defined attitudes toward most political issues.[51] Another factor that makes the aggregate political impact of the media relatively modest is that the predominant behavioral norm among television journalists is conducive to straight news reporting and the avoidance of editorializing, at least compared with their counterparts in the United States. In addition, overall, there is a great deal of pluralism among information sources in the Spanish media market – with *El País*, TVE-1, Tele 5, the RNE stations and the SER radio network perceived as favoring the PSOE in 1993 and the conservative opposition benefiting from the partisan biases of Antena 3 television, the COPE and Onda Cero radio stations, and such newspapers as *ABC* and *El Mundo*. In this respect, the quality of democracy in Spain has been reasonably well served to date.

But what of subsequent elections and the future? A study of the media in the 1996 Spanish parliamentary election revealed the same patterns of relatively balanced and restrained coverage of the campaign by television, but it also provided some crucial insights into the factors underpinning these patterns. Basing their analysis largely on newsroom observation and interviews with the editors of the two major networks (TVE-1 and Antena 3) during the official campaign, Semetko and Canel (1997) concluded that the public-service broadcasting ethic that guided the behavior of the TVE-1 news editors led to "a constant determination to achieve an appropriate balance in the electoral block of coverage. . . . Election news on TVE-1 in the official campaign was largely descriptive, with little or no evaluative comments from reporters. . . . Election news was 'straightjacketed' into the formula called the electoral block, which was rigidly 'balanced,'. . . to such an extent that on a day when there were no rallies to report, news professionals actually called the parties to ask them what they wanted covered that day!" (475). Only election coverage by television in Japan appears to have been guided by such a concern with partisan balance (see Chapter 8 by Krauss in this volume). And in contrast with the confrontational and disdainful stance often adopted by American reporters when interviewing candidates, the TVE-1 bureau chief who interviewed all the party leaders described his aim as "to be 'respectful' and 'let them speak' to viewers about what they were interested in" (Semetko and Canel 1997, 475).

But the Semetko and Canel study also "showed that there were profound differences in attitude and approach taken by the two main competing news organizations. . . . News professionals at Antena 3 would have found it anathema to call the parties and ask them for their most important story of the day. Instead, reporters and producers there made a special effort to initiate news via analysis and interpretation. . . . News on Antena 3 was also ironic and critical, occasionally disdaining and frequently entertaining. There was some sacrifice of substance for style. Instead of focusing on the substantive issues addressed in a speech at a rally, for example, Antena 3 reported on the style or tactics of the leader, or offered a humorous piece on how the leaders move – Felipe's feet or José

Marías hands. . . . The aims of the young Antena 3 were everything that TVE-1 was not" (476).

This presents us with decidedly different scenarios for the future. Will the entertainment orientation, gratuitous and disdainful editorializing, and low information content that have progressively crowded hard news coverage out of nightly news broadcasts on television in the United States increasingly characterize the newsroom orientation at Antena 3 or perhaps spread to other television networks in Spain? Will the "straight-jacket" that TVE-1 journalists had strapped on be cut loose, allowing the incumbent government to manipulate campaign coverage more blatantly than in the past? It is already clear that the change of government that occurred as a result of the 1996 election (bringing to power a PP minority government) has shifted the overall partisan balance in the television sector: the new government immediately replaced the director general of TVE-1, who, in turn, replaced the network's editors and bureau chiefs. Without doubt, this channel's modest pro-PSOE biases in the past have been reversed, although no content analysis of TVE broadcasts have been undertaken in an attempt to quantify this shift. Will other changes take place in the future, possibly shifting TVE-1 from the core tenets of public-sector broadcasting? The question of how to combine some editorial freedom for journalists with the need to provide balanced and unbiased information on issues poses obvious questions regarding governance and regulation, particularly concerning the public sector of television broadcasting. An independent structure of administration, based more on professional expertise than on political patronage and government intervention, would probably provide better opportunities for presenting the political information necessary for well-informed public opinion. These and other matters pertaining to the long-term evolution of the relationship between politics and the media in Spain remain open questions.

NOTES

1. The Comparative National Elections Project involves teams of researchers who utilized a "common core" of questionnaire items in studies of nationwide elections in Bulgaria, Chile, Germany, Great Britain, Greece, Hong Kong, Hungary, Italy, Japan, Chile, the United States, and Uruguay. The Spanish study (under the direction of José Ramón Montero, Richard Gunther, José María Maravall, Ludolfo Paramio Francisco Llera, and Francesc Pallarès) involves analysis of data derived from a survey of the attitudes, social characteristics, and electoral behavior of a sample of 1,440 Spanish citizens, supplemented by oversamples of the Basque and Catalan regions and by

a "snowball" sample of 500 friends and family of the primary respondent, as well as analysis of data derived from a detailed coding of all coverage of the campaign by the print and broadcast media. This panel survey was carried out in two waves by DATA, S.A., one prior to the start of the 1993 election campaign and the other immediately after the election. The authors wish to acknowledge the generous financial support from the Comisión Interministerial de Ciencia y Tecnología that made this survey possible, as well as the extraordinarily important collaboration of Juan Díez Nicolás and Holli Semetko, who carried out the coding of television broadcasts throughout the campaign.

2. Reports on the Madrid stock market, for example, were sometimes suppressed on the ground that they were "depressing." On many occasions, newspaper articles based exclusively on information published in official government publications, were suppressed (see Sinova 1989a, especially 77–82).

3. The 1964 survey was conducted by the Instituto de la Opinión Pública (IOP) in July based on a sample of 1,408 Madrid residents.

4. Indeed, Fraga regarded his reform as a "third way" between the press freedoms of most Western countries and the old system of control first adopted in 1938 (Terrón 1981, 188). Between 1966 and the death of Franco in 1975, the application of the *Ley Fraga* served as the legal framework for filing 1,275 legal actions against publishers and imposing 405 formal sanctions, most of which were directed against newspapers and magazines published in Madrid and Barcelona. Initially, these sanctions were related to publication of sexual materials (all forms of nudity were banned from movies and published photographs, while all forms of cinematic violence were cheerfully allowed by the regime's censors), but they were later extended to criticisms of the regime or expressions of support for protest demonstrations against the Franco dictatorship (Terrón 1981, 202–10).

5. The circulation of general information magazines (of which there were eight in 1974) was far smaller than that of women's and sports magazines, whose weekly circulation totaled over 2 million (González Seara 1972, 777–8; de Bergareche et al. 1976, 1068–9; Wert 1976, 111–6).

6. For a relatively brief period, from the end of the civil war until about 1943, the regime had some totalitarian aspirations. But the extraordinary importance of the Catholic Church for both domestic and international legitimation of the regime, the impending defeat of the Axis powers, the drastic downgrading of the Falange within the franquist coalition, the lack of social revolutionary aspirations of General Franco, and the absence of any consensus within the franquist elite concerning a regime ideology led to the abandonment of all such aspirations and the development of the regime as a quintessentially authoritarian system.

7. In the 1996 parliamentary election, all extreme right-wing parties combined received just 17,000 votes, or .02 percent of all votes cast.

8. Source: Spanish CNEP survey.

9. The retirement from politics of General De Gaulle, for example, gave journalists an opportunity to make somewhat veiled allusions to the disappearance from power of Generalísimo Franco. A few years later, the coup and the beginning of the democratization process in Portugal were used by newspapers as pretexts for calling for the replacement of *franquismo* by a democratic regime.

10. An example of this inconsistency was that most Spaniards in 1973 favored some form of democratic elections, but only 37 percent of those polled at that time favored "freedom of association for political parties" (i.e., the legalization of competitive parties). Nonetheless, just four years later, nearly 79 percent of Spaniards were casting ballots for one party or another in competitive elections.

11. It is interesting to note that this key step in the establishment of democracy was badly misinterpreted by the independent and opposition press. The most famous example of this misunderstanding is the oft-cited article by Ricardo de la Cierva in *El País,* published on the day after Suárez's appointment, titled "What a Mistake! What an Immense Mistake!"

12. These functions have been variously described as those of a "resonance chamber" for the voices of political change (Sunkel 1994, 163) or of a "paper parliament" for the presentation and discussion of political alternatives (Montabes 1994).

13. "Liberal" in the European sense. In the misleading American terminology, this newspaper was liberal on social issues and "conservative" on economic matters.

14. In the case of *Informaciones,* this was the product not only of the entry of new dailies into the market, but also of the more widespread crisis confronting afternoon newspapers everywhere.

15. See Montabes (1994, 57) for the lament of the editor of *Triunfo,* one of the news magazines that played a significant role during the transition but that faced, in his view, "Darwinian" extinction in the 1980s.

16. Sources for circulation data: *Anuario El País 1988,* 216; *Anuario El País 1995,* 210.

17. Sources: Spanish data from the October–November Estudio General de Medios, based on 13,285 interviews nationwide; West European data from *Zenith Media Worldwide,* 1994.

18. In 1991, a new newspaper, *Claro,* was launched with the stated intention of appealing "to those readers who do not read." A joint enterprise of the Prensa Española (publishers of *ABC*) and the Axel Springer group of Germany, the paper survived only four months before disappearing (Edo 1994, 133–7).

19. Among the more politically significant of these regional papers are: in Catalonia, the high-quality, centrist Catalan daily, *La Vanguardia, El Periódico,* and the more aggressively Catalan nationalist *Avui;* in Galicia, the moderately conservative *La Voz de Galicia;* and in Euskadi, the moderately conservative *El Correo Español–El Diario Vasco* and a plethora of dailies reflecting the political fragmentation of the regional party system that existed, including the PNV-owned *Deia* and the pro-ETA, pro-Herri Batasuna *Egin* (Coca and Martínez 1993).

20. In 1994, *El País* reported an average daily readership of 1.5 million, *ABC* and *El Mundo* both about 1 million, and *Diario 16* about 400,000 (as reported in the Estudio General de Medios, a regular survey of the general public's reading, viewing, and listening habits). In terms of daily sales, *El País* averaged over 400,000 per day compared with 322,000 for *ABC* and 269,000 for *El Mundo* (*El País,* June 16, 1995, 39). These shares of the reading audience remained stable over the following five years, with one significant exception. The most recent survey (for 1997) indicates that *El País* had approximately 1,572,000 daily readers, *ABC* had 952,000, and *El Mundo* had 926,000. This survey also indicates that circulation figures for these three dailies remained relatively stable, with *El País* selling about 440,000 copies each day, *ABC*

300,000, and *El Mundo* on average 285,000. The major change over this period was the collapse of *Diario 16*, whose readership fell below 100,000 – a decline of over 75 percent in just four years (Source: Oficina de Justificación de la Difusión).

21. A May 1993 Demoscopia–El País survey directed by José Ignacio Wert included interviews with over 30,000 Spanish citizens, creating a data base large enough to include 1,524 regular readers of *El País*, 712 of *ABC*, and 403 of *El Mundo*. A comparison of data derived from that survey reveals that our much smaller CNEP sample was remarkably representative, as the presentation of data later in this chapter will reveal.

22. Using a coding scheme developed by the German CNEP team, all of the news articles dealing with the campaign published on randomly selected days during the campaign were assessed according to 95 different criteria. A total of 131 articles were coded in this manner. Sixty percent of the articles appearing in *El País* and 58 percent of those appearing *ABC* were classified as including no evaluative statements or biases. But of those perceived as including biased evaluative statements, the PSOE was regarded as being more favorably treated by *El País* and the PP was favored by *ABC*. The mean score of all evaluative comments (with highly negative comments scored as 1 and highly favorable statements as 7) regarding the PSOE was 4.3 in *El País* (somewhat positive) and 3.0 in *ABC* (somewhat negative), while the PP received mean evaluative scores of 3.4 in *El País* and 4.7 in *ABC*. The authors wish to express their heartfelt thanks to Ms. Archana Dheer for volunteering her services in this project.

23. *El Mundo* played a leading role in uncovering evidence of the involvement of high-ranking Interior Ministry officials in financing and organizing state terrorist activities against ETA (the Basque terrorist organization) by the so-called Gruops Antiterroristas de Liberación. In 1998, after a very complicated investigation, the Supreme Court found José Barrionuevo, minister of interior from 1982 to 1986, and Rafael Vera, deputy minister for security, among other high-ranking officials guilty of kidnapping a Basque citizen living in France in 1983. They were sentenced to ten years in prison, although the government, following a recommendation of the Supreme Court, partially pardoned them and released them from jail three months later.

24. As *El Mundo*'s most popular cartoonist stated in explaining his resignation from the newspaper, "Everything is now oriented towards [reporting on] corruption. I think that this kind of news should be reported, but it is really not affecting the average Spaniard to this degree. . . . This newspaper is not balanced, ideologically speaking." (Statements by Antonio Fraguas, reported in *El País*, February 14, 1995, 31.) Under the PSOE, both *El Mundo* and *ABC* indiscriminately mixed news coverage and editorial comment critical of the government (see statements by Luis Carandell and Soledad Gallego-Díaz in Santos 1995, 163). *El País* was also guilty of this practice under the UCD governments, but largely (and not surprisingly) desisted after the PSOE came to power. (Also see Roca 1989, 97–8; Santos 1995, 187–208.)

25. The reader should be cautioned that, because of the extremely low level of newspaper readership in Spain, the number of cases on which the following analyses are based is low: there were only 95 regular readers of *El País* among our 1,448 survey respondents, 42 regular readers of *El Mundo*, and 38 *ABC* readers. We are well aware of questions that may be raised concerning sample size and representativeness. Thus, we have taken care to present levels of statistical significance of our findings, when-

ever relevant, and have couched our conclusions in very cautious language. We should also note that our data are perfectly consistent with the results of the Demoscopia/*El País* survey of newspaper readership among a nationwide sample of 30,000 Spaniards: the mean self-placement of *El País* readers in the Demoscopia survey was 3.8 – exactly the same as in our survey; Demoscopia's *El Mundo* readers were located at 4.2 (vs. our 4.6); and *ABC* readers were located at 5.6 and 6.1, respectively.

26. For example, among the 1,524 regular *El País* readers polled by Demoscopia in May 1993, 46 stated that they intended to vote for or were sympathetic toward the PSOE, 10 percent for the PP, and 16 percent for IU; 23 percent of *ABC* readers were disposed to vote for the PSOE, 52 percent for the PP, and 4 percent for IU; and only 11 percent of *El Mundo* readers included in the Demoscopia sample favored the PSOE, while 26 percent were predisposed to support the PP and 22 percent IU.

27. While virtually everyone can speak Spanish, about 41 percent of Spaniards also use Catalan, Gallego, Basque, Valenciano, Alicantí, Mallorquín, Menorquín, or Ibizenco as a first or second language (Linz 1985).

28. Reversing a decline that occurred under the Franco regime, by 1994, 74 percent of the population of Catalonia were able to speak Catalan and 22 percent more understand it. Only 4 percent say they do not understand it. Among Basques, these same figures are 31, 15, and 54 percent, respectively. (See Siguán 1994, 19.) This increase in knowledge of the regional language is particularly striking in the Catalan case. In 1981 (at the start of what the regional government calls its "linguistic normalization" program), 80 percent of those in the region said that they could understand Catalan. By 1993, that figure had risen to 96 percent of the population. This increase was particularly pronounced among those born in other parts of Spain who migrated to the region: from 65 percent in 1981 to 88 percent 12 years later.

29. This process is different from the one that took place in France under the first "cohabitation" government under Jacques Chirac. In France, part of the public television system was simply transferred to the private sector. The González government, in contrast, maintained the existing two state channels but allowed for the creation of new private-sector competitors. Hence, the Spanish process was not really one of "privatization" in the strict sense of that term.

30. These include the English-language Cable News Network (CNN), the National Broadcasting Company's (NBC) international channel and The Sky Channel, Mexico's Televisa, the French Tele 5, Italy's Radiotelevisione Italiana (RAI), and the German-language Deutsches Sport Fernehen (DSF).

31. The source for these television audience estimates is *Anuario El País 1995*, 220.

32. We are greatly indebted to Holli Semetko and Juan Díez-Nicolás, who are undertaking an exhaustive analysis of the content of news broadcasts during the 1993 campaign. They have generously made available to us data sets based on the exhaustive coding of tapes of those broadcasts. For a preliminary report of their findings, see Díez Nicolás and Semetko 1995.

33. During the official campaign period, broadcasts by the TVE network are subjected to careful scrutiny by an interparty oversight commission in order to encourage fairness in coverage by the public stations.

34. Spokespersons for the governing PSOE spoke for 3,062 seconds during the precampaign broadcasts coded by Díez Nicolás and Semetko (1995) compared with 2,858 seconds for all opposition-party leaders combined. During the official campaign,

PSOE leaders spoke for a total of 6,040 seconds compared with 8,821 seconds for the opposition. (Calculated from data presented in Table 10 of the Díez Nicolás and Semetko piece. It should be noted that, although they base their analysis on the same data that they made available to us, we reach somewhat different conclusions.)

35. It should be noted that Díez Nicolás and Semetko reach somewhat different conclusions, largely in the direction of perceiving greater pro-PSOE bias than does our analysis. These differences are due to the fact that their estimates of bias are based on analysis of only the first (out of a possible total of five) evaluative statements made during the news article, while our analysis is based on all such evaluative statements, up to the maximum of five per article that were coded.

36. See data based on the American CNEP content analysis and survey reported in Dalton et al. 1998, 1995. Of those polled in the American survey ($n = 1,290$), 28 percent said that television favored Clinton in the 1992 campaign, while only 3.5 said that Bush was favored by this medium.

37. While the American CNEP did not include a comparable measure, the American coauthor of this chapter estimates that American television news has a much lower public-policy-relevant content.

38. Among those regular television news viewers on the left (who placed themselves at position 1, 2, 3, or 4 on the left–right scale), 82 percent followed the news on TVE 1 or Tele 5 and only 18 percent watched Antena 3 news broadcasts. Among those on the right (Position 7, 8, 9, or 10 on the left–right scale), 34 percent watched Antena 3 and 66 percent followed the news on the still-dominant TVE 1 or Tele 5. Another study, using a different methodology (logistic regression analysis), confirms our findings about the significant but relatively modest impact of media bias after the effects of other variables have been taken into consideration. See Belén Barreiro and Ignacio Sánchez Cuenca, "Análisis del cambio de voto hacia el PSOE en las elecciones de 1993," *Revista Española de Investigaciones Sociológicas*, 82, 1998, 191–211.

39. Indeed, empirical evidence supports this assertion. One study (Luca Ricolfi, "Politics and Mass Media in Italy," *West European Politics*, 20, 1997, 135–56) estimated that the combined electoral impact of the three RAI networks (which were, comparatively speaking, relatively muted in their political biases) "explained" about 5 percent of the aggregate vote, while the three channels of Berlusconi's Fininvest (which were much more blatant in their partisan bias) accounted for about 13 percent of the vote. With regard to vote shifts, the impact of exposure to the campaign through RAI was minimal, while Berlusconi's channels led to a shift of 4 percent from the Partito Democrática della Sinistra (PDS) to the center-right coalition.

40. It should be noted that advertising for political parties and candidates is permitted on private radio networks and newspapers, while the public radio networks are subject to the same controls as public television.

41. The Junta Electoral Central (JEC) is composed of eight Supreme Court justices (selected by lottery) and five professors of political science or constitutional law nominated by political parties with parliamentary representation. The strong presence of prestigious and impartial jurists on the JEC (rather than partisan politicians, as in many other countries) substantially reinforces its ability to guarantee fairness and balance in the conduct of election campaigns.

42. Another measure of this phenomenon can be seen in the increasing domination of news coverage by the top leader of each party at the expense of other party candi-

dates. During the 1993 campaign, 121 of 189 references in news broadcasts regarding PP elites referred to Aznar; 85 of 150 references to IU candidates focused on the leader of that coalition, Julio Anguita; and 66 of 87 references to CDS candidates dealt with party leader Rafael Calvo Ortega. The domination of electoral politics by the presidential candidates has reached such an extent that virtually all of the television news coverage of the final days of the 1995 *regional and municipal* election campaigns focused on the national leaders of each party. The actual candidates for the offices at stake (mayors, presidents of regional governments) were virtually absent from the television screens, and purely local issues were almost never mentioned. Instead, these local elections were portrayed as a referendum on the PSOE national government. (For a full general statement of the "presidentialization" thesis, see Bean and Mughan 1989.)

43. This poll of 2,500 Spanish citizens was conducted by the Centro de Investigaciones Sociológicas between May 16 and 19. The results were leaked to and published in *Diario 16* on May 26, 1993. For similar data concerning voting intention at various points during the campaign, see Díez Nicolás and Semetko 1995.

44. The detailed multivariate analysis undertaken by Barreiro and Sánchez Cuenca (1998, 205) confirms our findings about the decisive impact of this debate on the outcome of the 1993 election.

45. As a journalist stated, "You grab anything that comes along, any rumor, you throw it out through the radio, and there is no consistency at all. What sells best is to brand as a jackass the prime minister, the Governor of the Bank of Spain, or anybody else that you can use as a punching bag.... Talk shows are part of a plan of attack against the [PSOE] government, and the closer you get to election day, the more virulent they become." (See Santos 1995, 141–2.)

46. COPE was perceived as favoring the PP by 96 percent of its listeners, who perceived bias ($n = 23$), Onda Cero ($n = 17$) by 88 percent, and Antena 3 ($n = 6$) by 67 percent. Among RNE listeners who perceived bias ($n = 12$), 83 percent thought that RNE favored the PSOE, as did 82 percent of SER listeners who perceived bias ($n = 11$). Expressed as percentages of all regular listeners to these networks, these figures are reduced to the following, more modest levels: those who perceived pro-PP bias included 29 percent of all COPE listeners ($n = 76$), 23 percent of the total Onda Cero audience ($n = 65$), and 9 percent of regular Antena 3 listeners; 10 percent of all SER listeners thought that their network was pro-PSOE, as did 9 percent of the regular RNE audience. It should be noted that COPE and Onda Cero were regarded as much more biased than the other radio networks.

47. These empirical findings are very similar to those derived from the massive Demoscopia survey of 30,000 Spaniards undertaken just prior to the 1993 election.

48. Among regular radio listeners on the left (position 1, 2, 3, or 4 on the left–right scale), 71 percent listened to RNE or SER, while 72 percent of radio listeners on the right (position 7, 8, 9, or 10) preferred COPE, Antena 3, or Onda Cero. We should recall that among television viewers on the right, although they were much more predisposed to follow Antena 3 news broadcasts than those of TVE 1 or Tele 5, fully 64 percent watched the news regularly on those generally pro-PSOE channels.

49. These individuals were the minister of finance and economics, the leader of the Comisiones Obreras (the trade union that is closest to the Spanish Communist Party), the speaker of the Congress of Deputies, and the president of the Confed-

eración Española de Organizaciones Empresariales (CEOE) (the most important association of big-business employers). Scores on this "information test" ranged from 0 to 4, with 1 point given for each individual correctly identified.

50. As Ferejohn (1990, 14) has observed, "Because information acquisition is costly, individuals will generally not choose to be completely informed about anything. Our argument shares with "rational choice" scholars in American politics this concern with the costs of information seeking but comes to a different conclusion. Americanists in this school (see Ferejohn and Kuklinski 1990 and Popkin 1991) argue that because of the cost of information seeking, most voters choose to be well informed about very few issues (if any). While we would not disagree with this argument, we focus on the significantly different costs of information seeking through different communications media.

51. In an analysis of the 1990 German elections, Rüdiger Schmitt-Beck finds strong evidence that the "bandwagon" effect of the campaign was much more pronounced among independents and less sophisticated voters. (See "Mass Media, the Electorate, and the Bandwagon: A Study of Communication Effects on Vote Choice in Germany." *International Journal of Public Opinion Research*, 8, 1996, 265–91.)

CHAPTER 3

Institutional Incapacity, the Attentive Public, and Media Pluralism in Russia

Ellen Mickiewicz

The Russian mass media, and particularly television, have been associated in recent years with changes that have a profound significance for democracy. Post-Soviet Russia is a huge, complex, turbulent country where mass media, penetrating the farthest reaches of a vast territory spanning 11 time zones, abruptly shifted from one structural design to another in the space of only a few years. The changes wrought over this period tell us much about the interaction between media systems and political change. The reforms introduced by the last leader of the Soviet Union, Mikhail Gorbachev, resulted in reduced regulation and ultimately the erosion and implosion of institutions of power. Space was thereby made for the birth of pluralism. In post-Soviet Russia, problems attendant on the development of new institutions to buffer editorial autonomy from political and commercial power have produced a peculiar paradox: the most impartial and comprehensive public-interest programming comes from commercial media organizations.

Market pressures made the establishment of a brand imperative in an increasingly competitive media sector, and the legitimacy of commercial structures as purveyors of news had to be built up and consistency displayed. Thus, to enter the news business credibly, a commercial news organization had to be perceived as bringing a new set of values and techniques to the Russian public. NTV, the largest commercial network in post-Soviet Russia, achieved this branding during the first war in Chechnya. Competition led the new commercial network to differentiate itself in terms of sophistication, balance, accuracy, and production values. The introduction of genuine choice into news and public affairs programming also set in sharp relief the different norms and practices of jour-

I thank the Markle Foundation for its support of this research.

nalists, some of whom retained elements of the old approach and some of whom appeared to follow other, foreign examples. Throughout this chapter, the tension between old and new ways surfaces. The media are central to questions of generational change and cultural identity. Control over media, in turn, is seen as control over the shaping of fundamental Russian values and identity in the post-Soviet period, when the very definition of the country is at issue.

These basic issues remained unresolved precisely because the wrenching shift from Soviet to post-Soviet regimes required time and resources to allow the development of shared values and institutions. Resolution was attempted frequently through *nine* national elections and referenda over the course of just *eight* years (1989–96). Russians went to the polls repeatedly and turned out in large numbers in an effort to bring about systemwide change, but the electoral process in itself was not sufficient to create institutions; it became obvious that it would take time to forge patterns of shared interests and interactions. That parliamentary debates were often harsh and strident and control over television was a zero-sum game, reflecting the still powerful cleavages rending the system. Moreover, the frequency of elections that purported to alter the very nature of the political system and solve the continuing constitutional crisis put enormous pressure on television, the medium that was accorded near-magical powers of persuasion from the days of the Soviet rulers to post-Soviet Russia.

The Soviet economy was badly suited to reform. Its huge state-owned production infrastructure was largely obsolete and was uncompetitive in the world market. Its skewed dependence on military production had created numerous communities in which no other employment was possible as that sector declined in the post-Soviet world. No nearly adequate safety net existed to moderate the effects of this dislocation on the health and welfare of the population. The breakup of the Soviet Union also meant that the regional specialization and division of labor necessary for a great deal of production and distribution no longer existed, and production now took place in foreign countries. In the media sector, the absence of credible and effective government regulatory structures or, for that matter, the absence of a legal culture and judicial institutions, left the media market without rules that could be applied impartially across the country. The crash of the economy in 1998 exacerbated political and economic tensions in an already fragile society. The failure of the Russian economy was partly due to circumstances beyond its borders: an oil glut, plummeting oil prices, and economic problems in Asia and worldwide. But part of the problem also had to do with the privatization model the country adopted. The television industry – especially its music and entertainment components – as part of this economy was certainly vulnerable to corruption. The question was, to what extent, if at all, could a news operation with professional and ethical journalistic norms take root in such an environment?

As will be seen, even with all of its troubles, the market did provide for the emergence of such a news operation, which, together with the other, more government-dependent channels, offered viewers a choice.

Soviet and then Russian leaders often underestimated the public. In Soviet times, official theory dictated that the public was the target, not the cocreator, of media messages and was presumed to be malleable. It is true that the public's choice of information sources was severely restricted and that most media consumers – unlike their leaders and the privileged – had fairly limited knowledge of Western political, economic, and social alternatives. They could compare what they saw and read with what they experienced in their lives, but they lacked access to each other's views. As Timur Kuran (1995) has shown, the expression of unpopular or politically unacceptable views depends very much on the ability to know that others both hold these views and are willing to express them. Large numbers of people may hold unpopular views but express them only when they know it is safe to do so. It is for this reason that sudden, very large shifts in public opinion appear to occur when the tipping point has been reached. In Soviet times, simply keeping quiet and failing to support the system actively was considered unacceptable, which is why the term "spiral of silence" is less accurate than "spiral of prudence" (Kuran 1995). By eliminating secondary associations and controlling much of the content of large-scale mass media, the making of this critical connection between individual attitudes and group attitudes could, the regime estimated, be prevented. One of the great changes wrought by the post-Soviet Russian media has been to convey a variety of views to the public by reporting on public opinion surveys and charting dissenting elite voices on political issues. This was most dramatic during the first war in Chechnya (Mickiewicz 1999). For the first time, popular dissatisfaction with government policy – significantly, though not, of course, uniquely – the result of television coverage, led to changes in Boris Yeltsin's election strategy and to the consequent conclusion of the war by General Alexander Lebed. The larger constitutional questions regarding secession were not resolved, and political and economic order did not ensue.

In 1999 a second full-scale war in Chechnya began. In this one, the Russian military choked off access to reporters except under its own supervision, while on Chechen-controlled territory, journalists were prey to kidnapping and extortion, which were routine now that any semblance of real government had vanished. As a result, news of the war – its conduct and its consequences for civilians in Chechnya – was far thinner than it had been three years before. In the first few months of the war, Russia's bombing campaign limited Russian casualties; the military said it was following the script of NATO's bombing of Kosovo. That relatively "cost-free" strategy for the armed forces (as compared to the first Chechen war, at least) and the fear and insecurity produced by the *casus belli*, the terrorist bombing of large apartment buildings in Russia and an armed incursion into neighboring Dagestan, resulted in strong approval ratings for the action. At the same time, only a third of the Russians polled in nationwide surveys said they were getting adequate information about the war from the media. Another third said the media were not providing enough information about the war, and a third said they didn't know.

While the post-Soviet Russian public has gained something new from the media – a much larger information universe and knowledge of others' views – it has also retained the culturally specific skills that, as Soviet viewers and readers, they had brought to the consumption of media messages for many decades. This chapter draws on new research with focus groups to illuminate the particular way Russian viewers evaluate the news and the strategies they adopt for amplification and correction. The legacy of their political culture has made them extraordinarily sophisticated media consumers, especially as television viewers. Their cognitive complexity is as impressive in the high school- as in the college-educated populations. Although levels of information and number of sources differ, the heuristics employed are derived from a common experience (Mickiewicz 1999).

THE MEDIA BEFORE GORBACHEV

Political communication in Russia may be analyzed on different planes: the microenvironment of journalists; the organizational disposition of the media, including their economic, technological, and programming resources; and policies regulating the media system (Epstein 1973; Schudson 1978; Tuchman 1978). Superimposed on these analytical perspectives is the larger context of a media system shaped by the Stalinist period of the Soviet system, then by the liberalization of that system in fitful spurts until the Gorbachev administration, then by the *glasnost* and *perestroika* policies of Gorbachev, and, after the dissolution of the country, by an environment of contested power and weak institutions. All of these dimensions are interrelated, and they have much to tell us about the nature and effects of fundamental systemic political change and the uneven course of building democracy.

The rapidly escalating series of events that ended the Soviet Union began with the introduction of *glasnost* shortly after Mikhail Gorbachev came to power in 1985. That this radical policy took the shape fundamentally of a reform of the media attests to the central importance Soviet political elites attached to communication and information. To understand the changes in the media system in the Gorbachev era, one must see them in the light of continued dissent and finally disorganization within a ruling elite that considered the media, and particularly television with its powerful political mobilizational potential, a unique resource. This same elite, however, displayed little consensus on the values underlying the utilization of that resource. The breakdown in consensus along a softline–hardline axis produced the sorts of cleavages within the elite itself that have generally been important for transitions from authoritarian rule (O'Donnell and Schmitter 1986).

For the leadership emerging in 1985, reform required a substantial liberalization of mass media policy (*glasnost*) if the credibility that would make the media an appropriately powerful instrument of persuasion was to be achieved. Trust, after all, is essential to the acceptance of information (Page et al. 1987). In addition, the unique capacity of the media to embrace broad masses of viewers (and, to a lesser extent, readers) was used by Gorbachev-era reformers to make their reform virtually irreversible. Such mobilization has been noted in other cases of transition from authoritarian rule, where liberalization "usually produces a sharp and rapid increase in general politicization and popular activation" (O'-Donnell and Schmitter 1986, 19). A related effect – that the policy helped to undermine the foundations of the Soviet regime itself – was an unintended consequence of the original reforms.

Soon after the Bolshevik victory in the Russian Revolution, Lenin, recognizing that a revolution required resocialization and remobilization, and also understanding the twin problems of illiteracy and dispersion of population across a vast territory, decreed the rapid development of the new technology of radio. Together with the reinforcement provided by interpersonal "agitation" (the amplification of Communist Party policies and goals via personal interaction in the workplace), the new electronic medium would carry the message of Moscow's new leadership to a largely rural and ethnically heterogeneous country. Stalin then transformed the media system into a highly centralized and uniform set of interrelated structures and sharply curbed the profusion of modernist revolutionary styles, punishing their practitioners and insisting on a standard of expression that would be widely intelligible in a traditional, rather Victorian fashion. Since the explicit purpose of the media was socialization of the audience to the values and rules of the regime, it was considered inappropriate to assess audience demands, much less to be driven by them. The innovative public opinion survey research that flourished shortly after the 1917 revolution was prohibited by Stalin and only partially restored by Nikita Khrushchev and Leonid Brezhnev (Shlapentokh 1970a; Benn 1989).

But gossip and rumor easily evaded the official filter. In addition, party ideologists were concerned about the permeability of international borders and the practical impossibility of keeping out messages that for some recipients filled the vacuum left by the failure of domestic media to deal with politically controversial events. Border areas were difficult to isolate and essentially porous; Estonians, for example, regularly watched Finnish television. Even though the Soviet government allocated considerable resources to a massive jamming effort, Western radio broadcasts reached substantial audiences. It is estimated that in 1982 there were about 40 million shortwave radio sets in the country (Benn 1992). Foreign information sources were widely used during officially imposed information blackouts of such extraordinary events as the shooting down of Korean Airlines flight #007, the Chernobyl catastrophe, and the attempted coup of 1991.

The Stalinist pattern functioned until the liberalization initiated by Mikhail Gorbachev loosened its strictures. The most important features of the Stalinist model were the centralization of media organs and personnel, Communist Party control (through the use of government levers and budgets) of information, and saturation. Centralization was effected by subordinating the media to the dual authority of a government ministry or state committee (such as the State Committee for Television and Radio Broadcasting – Gosteleradio) and the Ideological Department of the Central Committee of the Communist Party and, ultimately, to the "second secretary" – the second most powerful individual in the ruling Politburo. The *nomenklatura* system also served to centralize the media by requiring that leading positions in prominent media organizations be filled by Party members agreed on by the Politburo (Terekhov 1991). Glavlit (Chief Administration for the Affairs of Literature and Publishing Houses) was founded in 1922 to censor domestically generated messages.

By the time Gorbachev came to power in 1985, those in responsible media positions had internalized the norms, and the system operated largely on the basis of self-censorship within the media organizations themselves. The exception was television, which had always been controlled more tightly by the Soviet leadership. When television went out live, the censors had a more difficult problem preventing slips, both intended and accidental. Later, when videofilm and videotape were introduced and programs could be previewed, live television declined rapidly until only the news was broadcast live. TASS, the official wire service, was the uniquely valid source for breaking news. Official attempts to control newer forms of communication – such as photcopying, faxing, and electronic mail – turned out to be deleterious to the economy and were embedded in a tangle of regulations and restrictions that eventually proved obsolete and largely unenforceable.

Newspapers in the Soviet period were printed and distributed in huge numbers, particularly national newspapers published in Russian (such as *Pravda, Izvestia, Komsomol Pravda, Trud,* and *Red Star*). Altogether, by the mid-1970s, 8,000 newspapers of all kinds were published, with a total circulation of almost 170 million copies annually. Newspaper editors, even within the pattern of oversight and restrictions previously noted, enjoyed considerably more discretion than television officials in crafting messages and shaping an individual identity for themselves. *Literary Gazette,* for example, regularly featured a page of veiled satirical notes that its highly educated readers understood to be politically provocative. As in all countries, better-educated people are more likely to be newspaper readers, and even the most popular newspapers have circulation figures that are only a fraction of the television audience. In Soviet times, party officials called newspapers "small caliber." Given their more narrow, relatively well-educated range of readers, their impact was less likely to trigger reactions in the masses. It was television that officials considered to be "large caliber."

Television developed rather late in the Soviet Union. It was not until the first communications satellites were launched in the late 1960s that it became possible to penetrate the enormous country. In 1960, only 5 percent of the Soviet population could watch television, but by 1986, the second year of Gorbachev's administration, fully 93 percent were viewers, and the prime-time audience for the nightly news was estimated at about 150 million people. Like newspapers, television was organized at the central (all-Union) republic, regional, and city levels. Two national channels (Channels, or Programs, One and Two) broadcast in Russian to Russia and the 14 other republics of the Soviet Union. From the standpoint of the leadership, no program was more crucial than *Vremya* (*Time*) – the 9:00 P.M. news broadcast – and no station anywhere in the country was permitted to broadcast anything else in that time slot.

It is remarkable how quickly television toppled newspapers from their venerable perch at the top of the media-consumption ladder. From the 1920s through the 1960s, the newspaper was the leader in providing information to the Soviet public (Shlapentokh 1970b). Then, as elsewhere, the introduction of television sharply altered traditional time use patterns, increasing the passive behavior that was at odds with the official values of activism and collectivism. Movie- and theater-going, reading, visiting friends, participating in sports, hobbies, and civic volunteer work all declined, even though the function and organization of the media remained, for the most part, unchanged during this period. It was clear from the start that television possessed its own dynamic and its own appeal to the most heterogeneous audience of any medium.

Unexpectedly for Soviet officials, it also appeared that rising levels of education – which they thought would benefit the program of official resocialization – instead provided awareness of alternatives and a more analytic perspective. In the late 1970s, it was found that college graduates were most critical of books by contemporary Soviet writers, that the better educated were most dissatisfied with television programs in general and most interested in, yet least satisfied with, political and news analysis programs on television (Mickiewicz 1981). A large-scale survey of Soviet citizens who emigrated to the United States in the late 1970s found, similarly, that "the long-term growth of educational attainments works to undermine support for established institutional practices" (Silver 1987, 132).

Those present at the creation of Mikhail Gorbachev's *perestroika* program trace the roots of that liberalization to the 1960s, when the intelligentsia experienced "a swallow of freedom" (Zaslavskaya 1990). That was the time when Communist Party leader Nikita Khrushchev made changes referred to as the "thaw," which involved the extension of the range of permissible subjects of discussion, including the delegitimation of the Stalin cult. The Stalinist constitution, though, was left untouched, so there were no guarantees that reform would last (Roeder 1993). With

Khrushchev's son-in-law at the helm, the newspaper *Komsomol Pravda* boldly pushed for the provision of livelier information, especially to the young. Alexander Solzhenitsyn published his pathbreaking *Day in the Life of Ivan Denisovich*, and Grigory Shakhrai directed a new genre of humane, nuanced films. Still, this top-down liberalization was not intended for all audiences. Religion was severely constrained, people's militias and courts unconcerned with legal procedure were created, and "parasites" (those who were living on unearned income, including unofficial creative artists) were subjected to summary sanctions. The subsequent Brezhnev chill (including trials of dissidents, use of psychiatric hospitals for political deviants, and the broad application of libel and slander laws) instilled in many members of the "generation of the 1960s" the commitment to irreversible reform at the next opportunity – though their goals would later appear to be too limited for younger activists. In sum, before Gorbachev, liberalization was initiated and terminated by the leadership, making the issue of reversibility a central concern for the generation of the 1960s and creating expectations about what could be done in the future if and when a more reformist leadership came to power.

An international political shift also served to heighten Soviet concern about the media before the liberalization of the Gorbachev period. The aggressive communications policy of the Reagan administration resulted in a major effort to penetrate the "evil empire" through an increase in transborder communications facilities. Konstantin Chernenko and Mikhail Gorbachev viewed this effort as "imperialism" and "intervention" and were pressed to consider more urgently the effectiveness of their own media, as well as that of the increasingly competitive media of hostile foreign powers, though they had insufficiently rigorous methods for assessing media effects (Mickiewicz 1988). An explicit acknowledgment that saturation of official messages did not spell assimilation, and that underreporting did not necessarily remove events from the public's field of information, this countercommunication agenda necessarily put a much greater emphasis on media effects. Competition with foreign media sources was now prominently on the agenda.

This concern with media effects, together with the growing recognition that the Soviet public, especially the well educated and young, were alienated from their communications sources, was part of a more generalized understanding of the problems of widespread alienation and national economic decline. The secret, and widely leaked, memorandum prepared by sociologist Tatyana Zaslavskaya for Soviet leader Iury Andropov detailed for the party leadership the deep divisions and dissatisfactions in Soviet society (Zaslavskaya 1984). Western observers have written extensively about the secular decline of the Soviet system and the failure of its institutions, especially in relation to the effects of modernization and the inability of elite-recruitment processes to incorporate the interests or participation of increasingly well-educated, professional, urbanized populations. This political stultification was accompanied by economic decay and a progressively greater inability to achieve growth through the diffusion of technology. The war in Afghanistan and the capacity (largely unchecked by the Brezhnev regime) of the military to absorb resources further constrained the ability to invest in and reform the deteriorating system.

These conditions of systemwide erosion notwithstanding, it was ultimately the decisions taken by the Gorbachev leadership that launched the drive for change and determined (at least initially) the sectors and sequences of liberalization. First among them were the mass media.

LIBERALIZATION IN THE GORBACHEV ERA

Mikhail Gorbachev had risen swiftly through the Communist Party hierarchy, and in March 1985 he took over the reins as general secretary, the most powerful position in the Soviet Union. He was a candidate on whom the small circle of the Politburo at the apex of the party could agree, since all were convinced of the need for change, even though they disagreed on its shape and certainly on its depth and scope. Gorbachev's drive for radical reform was more profound than the numerous abortive policies of past leaders. It exceeded the more conservative expectations of his colleagues on the Politburo and, in the end, even his own expectations. His exact intentions have been the subject of much discussion (Aslund 1991; Buckley 1993; Brown 1996; Gorbachev 1995). Politburo member Alexander Yakovlev, the architect of *glasnost,* foresaw genuine democratic elections with limited competition in which the Communist Party would lose its monopoly on nominating candidates and a small number of political parties would be allowed. This position was not shared at the time by fellow liberalizer Eduard Shevardnadze or by Mikhail Gorbachev himself. Yegor Ligachev, at the time number two in the Politburo, advocated reform of the Communist Party, but he "did not see any other force in the country that could sufficiently reform society" (Ligachev 1991, 11).

As noted by DiPalma (1990), struggles between, on the one hand, those favoring modest reforms and, on the other, those with more radical agendas typically culminate in unforeseen results. In the Gorbachev era, intraelite divisions arose over, first, the instrumental use of *glasnost* to reform and retain the fundamental system and, second, the more far-reaching aim of some measure of democratization. This elite dissensus – both in the period of liberalization and then in the attempts to consolidate post-Soviet democracy, especially in Russia – was an important element in the capacity of the media to support political change.

Television was one of the most strategic battlefields on which intraelite conflict over control of the agenda took place. These divisions, initially within the Politburo itself and later with different, more confrontational political actors (less accommodating to previous doctrinal values and elite status norms), became rooted in alternative institutional power bases. Thus, an increasingly fractured institutional base ultimately served to strengthen media pluralism and autonomy. As a consequence, individual media officials, generally at the level of newspaper editor or television department chief, were able to advance more radical or more conservative agendas by entering into working alliances with Politburo patrons of their own political hue. In the television sector, this meant dramatically different programming policies in the different divisions seeking the protection of different Kremlin authorities. For the reformers, situated most prominently in the Department of Youth Programming, it was a high-wire act that often failed but still served to push the envelope in tense confrontations that an entire nation watched. The youth department was especially interesting for two reasons. First, its leadership was bold and believed in reform; second, new ideas and new formats for youth were needed to make domestic messages more competitive with Western media messages. Western popular culture – expressed in jeans, rock music, new vocabulary, and new attitudes – had become very attractive to Soviet youth.

Increasingly, the small-caliber/large-caliber distinction was drawn. Politburo members watched television closely, noting how events were covered, how the news was presented, what other programs went out over the air, and how prime-time programming differed from late-night programming. Even Raisa Gorbachev was involved in evaluating programming and advising her husband; when change occurred on the large-caliber medium, television, there were instant reverberations at the summit of power (Mickiewicz 1999).

Glasnost was a policy designed to enhance media credibility and engage a detached audience, most of all the young – the replacement generation noticeably alienated from Soviet norms. Establishing the credibility of the media, in turn, required a reduction in party control, the airing of subjects previously off limits, packaging messages in new and attractive forms, and, not least, determining audience demand through public opinion surveys. Newspaper editors newly appointed by the reform political leadership distinguished their papers from the standardized fare; ran stories sharply critical of the armed forces, the KGB, and previous Soviet regimes; and reintroduced to the Soviet population such figures as Leon Trotsky, Nikolai Bukharin, and Tsar Nicholas II and his family. Their subscriptions soared. Television, always closer to the center of power, and with a much larger and more heterogeneous audience, took advantage of the openings provided by *glasnost* more slowly at first, but perhaps with wider impact. It had, by this time, begun to function as the primary source of news and information for Soviet citizens. New television programs provided candid criticism of officials by dissatisfied youth, electronic graphics and previously banned rock music, and the return of large numbers of live programs much less amenable to the censors' control. Uninterrupted live coverage of the contentious sessions of the first largely competitively elected legislature introduced an astounded and attentive audience to unprecedented debate of the most divisive political issues. Although procedurally chaotic and stormy, these sessions probably did more to diffuse information about democratic free speech than anything previously seen.

Foreign policy discourse was also increasingly affected by *glasnost*. Televised debates about foreign policy issues were joined by "space bridges" (interactive live television programs with large studio audiences in other countries). The new policy of access to American viewpoints, even if adversarial or hostile, was initiated in a television program in January 1986 and was followed by a rapidly increasing flow of American views, including the startling Phil Donahue/Vladimir Pozner space bridges and the later "Congressbridges." By incorporating policy conflict into messages on state-run communications systems, the leaders hoped to deprive foreign communicators of their assumed impact. It was logical that the cessation of jamming followed shortly (in 1987 for the British Broadcasting Corporation [BBC] and the Voice of America and in 1988 for Radio Liberty).

As the dynamic of change began to spiral out of control, Mikhail Gorbachev attempted to rein it back in. In the fall of 1990, he appointed a hardline chief of television who canceled a number of the daring new programs. Early the next year, when Soviet forces seized the Lithuanian television center by force to halt the growing secessionist movement, television was heavily censored and some of the medium's most popular journalists were fired. Boris Yeltsin had been elected chief of Russia, the largest of the 15 constituent republics of the Soviet Union. In this capacity, he had an institutional claim on Channel Two, and after much delay, he won six (noncontiguous) hours of the broadcast day. First in order was the inauguration, in May 1991, of an alternative 8:00 P.M. news program, on which Soviet viewers saw some of their favorite faces anchoring and reporting the news; they had come over from the repressive Channel One.

In a matter of months, all news was shut down. Mikhail Gorbachev was put under house arrest at his vacation home in the Crimea, and an "Emergency Committee" took over the mass media. It was an inept, poorly planned coup d'etat by Kremlin leaders (including military and internal security officials) opposed to the impending decentralization agreement with the republics. During three days in August 1991, the Emergency Committee attempted to take over the country. But it failed to prevent Boris Yeltsin from mounting a counterdemonstration and barricading himself and his supporters inside the White House, where the Russian Parliament met. It failed to secure an information monopoly, and uncontrolled information flowed in and out through new channels – fax, computer, and (mainly for political elites) Cable News Network (CNN). But, more important, the nationally televised *domestic* newscasts managed to slip in visual proof of opposition to the Emergency Committee.

When the Emergency Committee gave up and Gorbachev returned, the balance of power effectively shifted. Boris Yeltsin was now in control, and at the end of the year the Soviet Union was gone. As leader of one of the new countries, the Russian Federation, Yeltsin appointed a reform-minded head of state television. In 1993, the second year of the Russian Federation, two commercial television stations – TV-6 and NTV – began broadcasting from Moscow. TV-6 began as a collaboration between Turner Broadcasting and a Russian group headed by Eduard Sagalayev, the former head of the youth department of Soviet television, then its news chief, and then, after the attempted coup, the head of Russian state television. TV-6 was a family channel featuring youth programs, especially entertainment. The partnership with Turner was later dissolved, and TV-6 became wholly Russian owned. NTV, financed by banker Vladimir Gusinsky, was the creation of a trio of former Soviet television officials: Igor Malashenko, who had been in Gorbachev's apparat and briefly headed state television; Oleg Dobrodeyev, who had been in charge of news at Channels One and Two; and Evgeny Kiselyov, the most popular anchor on television.

Unlike TV-6, NTV, from the beginning, stressed its focus on news and built a large and professionally expert corps of reporters. By the end of 1998, about two-thirds of the country could receive NTV, and it and TV-6 were expanding beyond large cities into smaller population centers. Four large networks dominated the Russian television landscape. Channel One, called Russian Public Television (ORT), was 51 percent owned by the Russian state and 49 percent by private institutions. The largest private stockholder was the automobile company Logovaz, owned by Boris Berezovsky, and he was the most influential decision maker at the station. He used his power there to push his private economic and political agenda. The government and Parliament both battled over what that 51 percent of ownership actually bought them, since neither could contribute substantial and badly needed continuing subsidies to the station. The Russian government had a clearer position with Channel Two, which it directly controlled, and appointed and fired its presidents. NTV and TV-6 both offered a mix of news and entertainment, although the former was clearly the leader in news and public affairs. In addition, there were other channels more limited in the range of their penetration, both in Moscow and in the provinces.

DEMOCRATIC MEDIA SYSTEM ATTRIBUTES
IN POST-SOVIET RUSSIA

A democratic media system is one that is characterized by pluralism (how much pluralism representing how broad a range of views is a key question), is protected as much as possible from interference with editorial news decisions (traditionally defined as independence from government interference but increasingly concerned as well with the influence of commerce), and has the economic means for survival. For such a system to operate most effectively, it should be shaped by the journalistic values and norms of accuracy, fairness, and responsibility. The notion of the media system as essential to the democratic process is often likened to the familiar marketplace of ideas. If, the theory goes, this marketplace functions efficiently, citizens will be informed enough of varied political points of view to be able to perform their roles adequately as citizens and especially as voters. A corollary is the idea of the press as a check on the abuse of power. Quite apart from the marketplace notion, an arena of free speech can also be seen as important to an individual's development, to fulfilling his or her need for self-expression (Kuran 1995). No media system fully meets the ideal standards of the perfect marketplace. Certain players and a certain range of views are privileged, but technology has the potential to expand the opportunities for choice as the number of television channels multiplies in the digital age. The Internet allows still greater access to opinion group that lack the resources to compete effectively in larger television arenas. Indeed, the very notion of "mainstream" or "national" news becomes less valid as publics fragment into customized narrowcasts and niches.

This picture of an explosion of choice does not yet fit post-Soviet Russia. The choice available to citizens certainly has increased exponentially, but from an extremely narrow base. In larger cities, such as Moscow, viewers can access many channels, and some can even get CNN and BBC teletext. Channels One and Two continue to cover the entire Russian territory, and NTV and TV-6 are expanding. Direct broadcast satellite, cable, and ultra-high-frquency (UHF) options exist as well. Internet connectivity is more common in big cities and is spreading, but it is still limited in scope. The crash of 1998 fell heavily on a rapidly expanding television sector and restrained its brisk growth. However, television remains central to the democratic process, and especially elections, in view of the public's increasing informational dependence on it – from an already high plateau. The rest of this chapter therefore focuses on television and issues of democracy.

Pluralism

By 1997, television properties counted among the most desirable investments in Russia, and business was booming. The advertising market was driving growth and doubling in size every year. Advertising agencies had gone beyond the national stations to seek profits in the provinces and, for the first time, local stations became attractive for their own markets. Moscow-based networks began to expand into the provinces, buying smaller stations outright or concluding agreements to provide them with programming for part of their broadcast day. Local stations were multiplying. About 1,200 licenses had been awarded, and about half of the stations were on the air. Nor was the favorable market confined to broadcasters. Cable television was an early entrant into the market, gaining viewers initially with pirated foreign films and then converting to more stable and legal fare. As well, NTV, the largest commercial national network, led the way into the world of direct broadcast satellite services with NTV+.

Not all of these options offered significant news capabilities. Some local stations were still state-owned and -run, and often under the influence of local political leaders. For their part, many of the much more numerous local commercial stations had limited news-gathering resources, relying instead on a mix of Moscow-based programming and home-grown music and entertainment shows. Some larger ones, such as Afontovo in Krasnoyarsk and Volga in Nizhny Novgorod, did offer professionally competitive local news shows. Although the newspaper market was slightly buoyed by the growth of the regional press, it was still fragile. The crash of 1998 dealt it a severe blow. Thus, television continued to be by far the primary source of news and entertainment for this vast country. Moreover, with broadcast television costing viewers nothing and with incomes contracting because of nonpayment of wages and the devaluation of the ruble, television watching grew.

The numbers suggest that, before the crash, a reasonable television market was developing, one that included a large number of media organizations that were structurally independent of the government. Structural diversity was apparently developing, and the first condition of pluralism, ownership, appeared to be in place. The second condition, content diversity, however, is a vexing issue since it requires an entity to monitor and rule on content. Over time, this role has been progressively abandoned by the Federal Communications Commission in the United States. In Russia, there has been a continuing battle between Parliament and the president over television content, an issue I discuss at length later on.

Was there sufficient structural diversity, then, in the Russian market? Was it in fact open to new entrants? There were formal procedures governing licensing (in two stages – for the frequency and then for the right to broadcast) and largely nominal competition. The biggest commercial networks, TV-6 and NTV, for example, had no competitors for their frequencies. Cross-ownership and monopolies were also virtually unregulated. Thus, one of Russia's richest men, Boris Berezovsky, was the largest private stockholder (or rather his company was) in the hybrid state–private partnership that owned Channel One (ORT), the biggest television network in Russia. He had also become a majority investor in the commercial station, TV-6, and controlled newspapers (for example, *New Izvestia* and *Independent Newspaper*), as well as a large-circulation magazine, *Ogonyok*. The Uneximbank empire, run by Vladimir Potanin, included such media properties as the newspapers *Izvestia, Komsomol Pravda,* the Prime news agency, *Expert* magazine, and the Europe Plus radio station. The natural gas industry, the huge Gazprom, with which former Prime Minister Viktor Chernomyrdin had been associated, acquired its own media properties, investing in the daily newspapers *Trud* (*Labor*) and *Workers' Tribune,* the magazine *Profil,* and the private NTV's direct subscription DBS operation. Vladimir Gusinsky grew rich with his MOST bank, which controlled NTV. In the winter of 1997, he moved over to head the MOST media group, an amalgam of the big commercial network NTV and all its spin-offs, such as NTV+ (the DBS service) and TNT (called THT outside Russia – the network made up of regional stations). In addition, Gusinsky controlled the newspaper *Segodnya,* the radio station Moscow Echo, the magazine *Itogi,* and the program guide *7 Days.* In the fall of 1998, NTV launched its own U.S.-built satellite, providing substantial digital television transmission capacity. This event marked the first time that satellite signal dissemination capability was in private hands.

Yury Luzhkov, mayor of Moscow and presidential hopeful, had municipal funds to invest since Moscow was the vigorously growing center of foreign investment and business until the crash. Luzhkov, like all the other leaders and contenders for power, understood the value of media properties to a political career. He converted the local television station into a new channel, TV-Center; he invested in the struggling commercial station REN-TV; and he had the power to influence all the other media outlets of which the city was part owner: the Moscow radio station and a newspaper group that included *Evening Moscow.* He had some shares in TV-6 and went looking for alliances with politically compatible regional television stations outside Moscow. The 1998 crash reined in the exuberant expansion, but not the ambitions.

Finally, the Russian government was still a very big player in the post-Soviet television system. It directly controlled a number of electronic communications properties, including 51 percent of Channel One (although Boris Berezovksy was the principal decision maker there because of his financial stake in the station), Channel Two (Russian Television and Radio – the second largest Soviet-era channel), big radio stations such as Radio Russia and Mayak, 2 big news agencies, and over 100 state-owned radio and television properties in the provinces. In the fall of 1997, the Yeltsin government converted the St. Petersburg Channel (broadcasting throughout European Russia, with very low ratings and inferior programming) into the Culture Channel.

It is true that media concentration was proceeding apace all over the world. In the United States, 80 percent of viewers receive their television programs from six cable companies, while seven companies control 70 percent of the programming on cable. In the music industry, five international companies control over 60 percent of the world market in music sales. In the European Union, the top ten European publishing conglomerates control 50 to 70 percent of the market.

Although the field of owners was far broader than in Russia, the adverse consequences of concentration had long worried American observers about their own media system. In the United States, Ben Bagdikian warned as early as the 1960s that "if executives of dominant media corporations are personally silent about dangers of concentrated ownership, it is not surprising: the process benefits them in terms of both money and power. But the media they control are also silent" (Bagdikian 1992, 22). In Russia, some voiced their concerns, but others, such as Sergei Dorenko, one of the most opinionated television news personalities, openly pushed his owner's agenda, saying, "Yes, I never criticized a single stockholder of ORT, including Berezovsky . . . I have not yet touched a single commercial structure belonging to stockholders" (Varshavchik 1997, 23). Using the argument of external diversity, he further argued that his weekend news analysis/opinion program was just one of three on television, and "together with my colleagues on the various channels, we present viewers with the entire spectrum of the political rainbow." His point is that no single channel need ensure representation of all salient points of view if there is reasonable diversity across the channels available to viewers. But this argument requires that viewers sample broadly, which represents a significant commitment of their scarce time resources (Downs 1957). It imposes a heavy responsibility on a public whose time is limited and who must calculate the trade-off between acquiring information and relaxing with entertainment.

Given the high degree of media concentration in the post-Soviet media system, was there sufficient pluralism to convey a reasonable diversity of views? The newspaper market did display a wide range of views, but its problem lay in the economics of the marketplace and the tremendous decline in circulation overall. To be sure, government subsidies to individual newspapers did prevent some bankruptcies, but they also introduced a degree of dependence into the relationship. What about the television market? In time of crisis, it was the national television networks to which Russians turned. This was true during the first war in Chechnya and again during the crash of 1998 (Mickiewicz 1999). Were Russian viewers presented with an adequately diverse range of views on the national news programs? Three national networks had established prime-time news programs and weekend analysis/review programs. In certain time slots, some of them competed. However, NTV had two editions of its evening news program, and since the crash of 1998, across the national stations there was an upsurge in public affairs discussion shows. Viewers could – and did – tune in to more than one version of the news and compare the results. Two more networks, TV-6 and Moscow's TV Center, were building a news capacity.

The daily news programs on the three big stations were quite different from the weekend opinion programs. The latter were anchored by a big star, whose personal stamp reflected his approach; and NTV's program, hosted by Evgeny Kiselyov, was the clear leader. When owners pressed their interests, it was done most openly on the weekend shows. The daily programs, on the other hand, tended to be less personalized (unless Sergei Dorenko was anchoring), covered a far greater range of subjects, and resulted in a much broader universe of news stories. On some important national questions, such as the first war in Chechnya, the paralyzing miners' strikes in 1998, and Alexander Lebed's campaign for governor of Krasnoyarsk (and the first stage of his run for the presidency), the coverage offered by the three networks was substantially different. Ultimately, however, the key test of television pluralism is related to the way viewers consume the news. To the degree that they use more than one source and to the degree that they bring critical skills to their viewing, they expand the amount of usable pluralism. To the degree that they are passive and light consumers, they are more disadvantaged by media concentration. As we shall see, Russian viewers exhibit an extraordinary degree of media literacy and active engagement with news messages.

AUTONOMY

In addition to pluralism, a democratic media system requires editorial autonomy, or protection from interference with editorial news decisions. In the United States, that autonomy has been defined as freedom from government control or censorship. A broader definition might also include making editorial decisions independently of owners' interests. With regard to government, freedom from interference in post-Soviet Russia has been lodged in very fragile institutions. Over 100 television stations are owned by a state that is also the major shareholder in the country's largest station, Channel One (ORT), and the direct owner of the second largest, Channel Two (RTR – although its ratings have slid badly). No effective mechanisms were put in place to protect the stations from the state. Thus, for example, the head of Channel Two could be summarily appointed or dismissed with no recourse, as happened when Oleg Poptsov was sacked for broadcasting stories critical of President Yeltsin. The story was the same when presidential advisors changed and their favorites were installed or removed.

Direct government ownership also meant that the definition of "government" would be contested. When the presidency and the Parliament were in conflict over still unresolved basic issues of power and authority, television was a key target of the clash. Each side repeatedly sought to create boards or councils to monitor content and impose moral and political standards. The struggle for control of television has been a constant feature of post-Soviet Russia because power seekers attributed to the medium a near-magical persuasive power. This was true in Soviet times and it continued to be true thereafter, especially during election campaigns. One prominent Russian observer called television "a propaganda apparatus of monstrous 'thermonuclear' force, *mass medium number 1*" (Klyamko 1993; emphasis in the original). Being in part a function of the continuing weakness of other channels of mobilization, this faith in television was understandable. The fight for control of it sometimes broke into violence and civil strife. During the spring of 1993, for example, opposition forces of the Communist left and the nationalist right laid siege to the television center at Ostankino on the outskirts of Moscow and hurled invectives, especially anti-Semitic ones, at employees braving the gauntlet they had set up. In the fall of that year, Yeltsin's parliamentary opponents and their supporters broke out of a besieged White House to try to take Ostankino by force. After the battle was over, scores of persons lay dead on the concrete apron in front of the blockwide building. Control of television was seen as a zero-sum game, so that whoever held power was loath to share it.

The government's control of its television properties was by no means total, since it lacked the resources to support the assets it owned. Before the crash of 1998, Channel Two complained of receiving only 12.5 percent of its scheduled support, noting as well that this figure had not risen above 20 percent for several years. Mikhail Shvydkoi, the head of Channel Two in 1998, claimed that the state had given him only 7.5 percent of its promised budget for programming before the crash and nothing at all immediately afterwards. Advertising had to make up the difference, even though it too was in short supply after the crash. Advertising and ratings shaped programming choices even on state-run channels. Audiences and their interests now mattered, as they had not in Soviet times.

In addition to government-owned stations, there were fully commercial ones. TV-6 was the first of them, and then came NTV and dozens of smaller stations in both Moscow and the provinces. Foreign broadcasters had also bought into the Russian market, albeit on a much more limited scale than in Eastern Europe. The market structure did enable these commercial stations to be reasonably independent of government interference, but the autonomy that they enjoyed depended not on the legal protections that private property afforded, but rather on the political clout of the few very rich and powerful owners. During the first war in Chechnya, the Yeltsin government exerted strong pressure on NTV to cease its vivid and accurate reporting on that disaster. The commercial station resisted the pressure, but was constantly made aware of its vulnerability and knew that its license could be revoked. Another example occurred with the miners' strikes of 1998. Yeltsin heavily criticized NTV's coverage of the threat posed by the strikes but backed down when publicly rebuked for his interference. There was no legal authority compelling him to desist. Whatever the protection the station enjoyed was afforded by its market position and international recognition. The market, however, had dangerously weakened, and after 1998, political pressure in the form of a financial squeeze was much more likely to occur. Loans taken out in heady times were now due, and NTV, in particular, was at risk, especially at election time, when so-called information war pitted stations against each other and the Yeltsin government against its critics.

In short, the commercial television sector displayed a greater degree of independence than did the state sector, but its relative autonomy rested on the power and influence of the media moguls, not on legal guarantees. It could be argued that had these resources been more widely dispersed, there might not have been enough of them for any station to be able to counteract an intrusive government. In addition, television is a very expensive operation. Unlike radio and newspapers, the technology and personnel costs are extremely high. While I do not minimize either the very restrictive limits on entry into the television market, especially after the 1998 crash, or the dangers of collusion among the media "oligarchs" or between them and the government, it is nonetheless true that there was little else to sustain the autonomy of the commercial channels, an autonomy that was impressively exercised at many important junctures.

SURVIVABILITY

What were the prospects for survival of the newly pluralized Russian television industry? Before the crash, they looked good, not least because foreign investments were trickling in. NTV, for example, was on the verge of making an initial public offering in New York when the economy faltered. When it did, the question became one of triage. What would fail and with what consequences? When the advertising market collapsed, the few big agencies that controlled the market registered a 70 to 80 percent drop in business (Likhina 1998). Since the television industry, including state television, was heavily dependent on advertising, the fallout devastated the whole industry. Many workers were not paid, others received pay cuts, and many others were fired. If all else failed, the broadcast day would have to be cut back. The Russian economic disaster made foreign imports substantially more expensive. Advertising prices were discounted to attract buyers and these discounts went deep, as much as 80 percent off the published price list. But even these inducements were not enough to attract the many foreign products that were now priced out of reach. The movies viewers loved were in shorter supply. Because talk shows, both as entertainment and as public-affairs programs, were the least expensive of all to make, viewers were subjected to many more of them. More made-in-Russia programs were created, a consolation for some.

The government, for its part, was becoming increasingly worried by the prospect of dependence on the commercial stations in the run-up to the 1999 parliamentary and 2000 presidential elections. Even before the crash of August 1998, the Russian Federation's government had ceased to control the messages sent by the Moscow-based television network. The president's "story," together with its desired spin, could be assured of coverage only on RTR (Channel Two), the national channel his government controlled directly. This was an increasingly unattractive outlet, however, since it was losing viewers to other stations. With its typical lurching response to dilemmas, the Yeltsin government issued a decree on May 8, 1998, designed to prop up the state television sector's influence. Under the terms of the decree, all local state stations and government-owned technical facilities (such as transmitters) were placed under the sole authority of Channel Two. Previously, the huge Ostankino transmitters on which Moscow-based state and commercial broadcasters relied had been under a ministry, but they were henceforth to be in the hands of one of the competitors in the television market. Clearly, the creation of this new Holding Company, as it was called, was a potential political asset to the government as elections approached. It could, for example, choose to charge preferential rates or to impose punitive measures on the various users of the resource. The handwriting on the wall said that in the future, technological independence would be no less important for opposition forces than rules regarding censorship.

JOURNALISTIC NORMS

Elsewhere, I have analyzed the role that journalists played in the development of democratic practices in Eastern Europe and the former Soviet Union (Mickiewicz 1998). Television journalists especially played to huge audiences and their support was enlisted to implement the Gorbachev policy of changing the Soviet system. Programs were developed to make end runs around calcified institutions and sclerotic bureaucracies. Journalists ran for office and gained parliamentary immunity to push their agendas, many of which, but not all, were reformist. As I noted earlier, this process of attacking rotting institutions was far more effective than later attempts to create new ones.

The journalist-politicians did not abandon their media jobs, so that many deputies during the waning days of the Soviet Union were well-known television personalities. For example, all of the youthful hosts of the hit program *Vzglyad* (*Viewpoint*) became deputies. Their late-night show was a bold challenge to the Soviet system, and it was often suspended or canceled. Parliamentary immunity strengthened their position, as it did for Bella Kurkova, St. Petersburg's feisty creator of the innovative and daring program *Fifth Wheel*. Perhaps not surprisingly, it was generally the antireform journalists who questioned the ethics of using the television podium to advance personal political careers. Nonetheless, it was a serious ethical issue, and the more obvious forms of the practice were substantially curbed in post-Soviet Russia.

Still, other issues of journalistic norms surfaced. The question of subjectivity and objectivity in the news was one. In Soviet times, subjectively reported news was for many the first bold step in the direction of unbiased coverage and a challenge to the state-dominated message. Opposing the news reader's dry presentation of the official party line were bold young reporters and anchors who voiced their own views and their own generation's values. Usually they were exiled to safer late-night slots since the political leadership was convinced that viewership would, as it had always been, be low at that time. They had not counted on the ability of viewers to change their behavior and to choose new programming options that they found more satisfying. How well suited this legacy of subjective reporting was to the construction of an independent, credible, modern media system remained very much at issue in post-Soviet Russia.

Nonetheless, journalists' political activism endured. What constitutes objectivity in news reporting is a thorny issue, not least because the principle of selection always privileges some institutions and groups over others. The real question, however, is not whether true objectivity can be achieved in news reporting, but rather the *degree* to which the broadcaster's editorializing and opinions should frame stories designated as news. This remained an open question in Russia, and different stations approached it differently. NTV's programs, more than those of any other channel, relied on the provision of fact-based, multiple-sourced stories. Its news teams routinely swept Russia's highest award for excellence in television, the TEFI. Its reporting on the first war in Chechnya, which I have treated in detail elsewhere (Mickiewicz 1999), shattered the Soviet-style information policy by presenting comprehensive and reliable on-location stories that were always supported by pictures. The Russian government was unprepared for the choice its citizens had in news programs and for their newfound ability to compare official propaganda with other news sources and viewpoints. That was in 1994–6. The second war in Chechnya was very different. The Russian government had learned both to exclude reporters from the war zone and to provide them with information from a centrally controlled information bureau specially set up and staffed by a civilian specialist in public relations. Reporting of this was was heavy but insufficient. The national stations differed in their coverage, but none had a great deal of access to the war zone and none made the huge flow of refugees their central focus. NTV did hold a remarkable televised session with Russian and foreign reporters, ordinary people, military spokesmen, and correspondents from the front to address the adequacy of Russian news coverage. There were patriotic voices urging total censorship to protect the military operation and critics, including Russian ones, urging fuller disclosure. The bombing of a busy market in Chechnya came in for intense criticism all around, for the deed itself and for its obfuscation by the military.

Yet, the NTV format was seen by some as an imported model that did not fit Russia's news culture. As one observer put it:

> Our "lighthouse" has become NTV. [It is] a superbly professional channel. [It is] beyond state, beyond popular, beyond ethnic. It is done intelligently and professionally, and with determination it destroys the state domination and mentality of the people in order to

create a new state and a new people. But this is idealism. And strangely, even Bolshevism. The Bolsheviks tried to change the nature of the Russian person and created a generation of Soviet people. The new Bolsheviks are doing just about the same thing. They think we – this provincial, undisciplined, unnecessarily emotional, unable to organize ourselves – people need to adopt a western intellect and then Russians finally will learn how to live, work, think and feel, as they do in America. (Kuchin 1996, 12)

THE CONUNDRUM OF ELECTIONS

The increasingly important role television plays in elections in post-Soviet Russia has been analyzed in considerable detail elsewhere (Oates 1998; Mickiewicz 1999). Television's rise to prominence is rooted in a number of factors. Russia stretches across a large landmass with uncertain transportation facilities, especially during bad weather, so that campaigning nationally presents immense logistical difficulties; the party system is young and is characterized by large numbers of highly personalized parties fragmenting, re-forming, and renaming themselves; the official campaign period is extremely short – only one month; and, finally, other forms of campaign information dissemination, such as newspapers, are failing economically. In addition to these reasons for the importance of television in election campaigns is the deep-seated belief of many Soviet and post-Soviet politicians that the medium has an almost unlimited capacity for persuasion. Therefore, in the absence of a system of rules and legal institutions to ensure fairness and impartiality, television became a hotly contested prize in the battle for political power and control.

In April 1993, a national referendum was held to resolve the constitutional problem of the distribution of power between the president and Parliament, with Yeltsin holding the presidency and the opposition controlling Parliament. The political system was deadlocked, and political cartoonists portrayed it as the national symbol of the double-headed eagle whose heads savagely tore at each other. Television played a central role in the run-up to the vote in the referendum, and two important dimensions of the role it played had implications for subsequent elections. First, limiting the opposition's television access to interviews with hostile journalists, the Yeltsin government refused it any opportunity to communicate with voters in an unmediated setting. Second, political advertising was allowed only for the Yeltsin government, which used spots contributed by an American firm. These remarkable ads skillfully framed the choice as going backward into the grainy, combative, black-and-white harshness of Communist rule or forward into a sunlit future characterized by blossoming opportunities for children and families. The referendum brought victory to the Yeltsin camp but failed to resolve the fundamental issues in dispute.

Because of its exclusion from television, the parliamentary opposition vowed to take over the medium and tried to do so violently later that year. In the fall, Yeltsin suspended the intransigent Parliament and surrounded it with troops. When the opposition deputies and their supporters broke through the cordon, they proceeded to the television center to take it by force and announce their takeover of the government on television. In their view, television had the ability to confer legitimacy and power. The planned violent takeover failed; the Parliament was attacked by the army, and a number of opposition parties were proscribed for the coming parliamentary elections later that year.

During those anxious hours when the television center was besieged, the army of two minds, and outcomes uncertain, television played a historic role. When the head of Channel One suddenly shut it down to avoid what he erroneously judged to be an imminent takeover, Channel Two came up on the same frequency to assure the public and maintain a thread of legitimacy for the government. All night long, in an improvised studio with gunfire audible in the background, television stars, stage and film actors, and public officials came to speak spontaneously to, and reassure, an anxious public. It was this extraordinary civic connection that led Boris Yeltsin to say that "the Russian channel, the only one that stayed on the air was what saved Moscow and Russia" (Yeltsin 1994, 275).

The rules governing television's role in election campaigns changed markedly after the violence. Free time was allotted fairly to all registered parties; journalists were ordered to cease partisan or subjective coverage; and political advertising became open to purchase by all parties. These changes were possible in part because extremist parties had been proscribed and the government was more confident. Approval of a new constitution was on the ballot as well, and the Yeltsin government, keen to have it passed, wanted an electoral process that would be considered fully legitimate. Moreover, after the bitter storming of Parliament, the government was anxious to assure the Russian public that it could govern under the new constitution. Under these circumstances, the appearance of a more equitable resolution of disagreements with political opponents, and even a degree of conciliation, seemed to be called for. The rules for free time and paid advertising became the model for subsequent campaign coverage regulations. The rules about journalists were another matter. Their room for maneuver was now so restricted that they had become little more than faceless moderators. Any attempt at analysis or serious questioning was forbidden, so that candidates, especially the nationalist rabble-rouser Vladimir Zhirinovsky, could speak as irresponsibly as they liked without fear of contradiction or penetrating questions. In the next national election, journalists again refrained from analysis, and it was not until the 1996 presidential election that they joined the fray. In this contest they took an actively partisan position, supporting Yeltsin's candidacy.

In Western electoral experience, political parties have become increasingly detached from their social roots, and candidate-based campaigning (largely through television) has tended to replace the party-generated patronage of the past (Aldrich 1995). The Russian parties are also socially detached but, importantly, without having first established grass roots. Television might, it was thought, substitute for parties' historical function of aggregating local demands and loyalties into a national fabric of party identification. The prominent exceptions, the closely allied Communist and Agrarian parties, exploited the old structures and economic levers of the Soviet system. They did so by continuing, wherever possible, to monopolize or adapt instruments of local power. Some parties spent heavily on political advertising and did not pass the 5 percent threshold necessary to be allowed parliamentary representation. The Communists, in contrast, spent nothing, relying instead on their grass-roots loyalists to get out the vote. This strategy reaped great rewards, with the party proving especially popular among older citizens and in rural communities – people and places most fearful of and least adaptable to the risk-laden future. Vladimir Zhirinovsky proved a shrewd campaigner, tailoring his ads to traditional issues, eschewing Western advertising models, and introducing an entirely new mode of discourse – emotional, direct, and relishing such hitherto taboo subjects as nationalism, religion, and sex. He did very well in the vote and was particularly successful in appealing to Russians who felt threatened by newly foreign states peopled in the Soviet era by cocitizens. The government-favored candidates spent heavily and had the added advantage of dominating the news coverage of the election. Many of them were incumbents, and their numerous official appearances were designed, as is so often the case, to attract coverage, but the disporportionately heavy coverage was also the result of the television stations' partisanship. These candidates did not, however, have an advantage in effectively communicating with viewers. Many of them were politically tone-deaf, did not appreciate the living conditions of ordinary people, and pitched their ads to Moscow yuppies. Others were didactic and unable or unwilling to speak plainly and simply. With this election, political advertising, together with public opinion surveys, public relations firms, and political consultants – both homegrown and foreign – came of age in Russia and continued to gain importance in future elections.

Two years later, Russians again went to the polls to vote in national parliamentary elections, this time with 43 parties competing for seats. A study by British scholars found that because of the fragmentation of parties and the threshold requirement, about half of the voters supported parties that ended up failing the 5 percent test. They concluded: "[T]he 1995 Duma produced the most disproportional election result of any free and fair proportional election" (White et al. 1997, 227). Parties in that election spent most of their campaign funds (about 57 percent) on television and radio, while only a quarter of those resources was spent on newspapers. The big parties spent much more, nearly 80 percent, on electronic media advertising. The Communists, with their infrastructure of local activists, spent far less on their campaign (Oates 1998). As before, candidates and parties close to the government dominated the news, but all parties had the same amount of free time, randomly assigned.

With economic problems burgeoning and Chechnya, bombed to ruins, still unpacified, Boris Yeltsin's approval rating had dropped to 4 percent by December 1995 and was up to only 8 percent in early 1996, just months before the presidential election. He was remote and barely visible. When he did venture out of the Kremlin, he was surrounded by officials, just as old-time Soviet leaders had been. The Communist Party had become the dominant party in a legislature of limited authority and its candidate, Gennady Zyuganov, was heavily favored to beat the dozen or so other candidates and win the presidency, where the true power lay. The real issue in this contest was the unfinished business left over from the April 1993 referendum: whether Russia should revert to communism or break with it. The two parliamentary elections in between had not resolved this fundamental question, and only the capture of the presidency could advance the agenda. It would be difficult to overestimate the importance of this election for Russians.

Television was partisan throughout the contest, and in both Russia and the West, bitter recriminations occurred. It must be said, though, that the issue of objectivity and partisanship in the 1996 presidential election is not simple. Television's partisanship was based on the perception that a Communist return to power meant the return of a regime seeking monopoly power and likely to eliminate free electoral choice, not simply the installation of a basically democratic administration with a populist or social welfare complexion. The Communists denied that this was their intention, but their party was actually an alliance, some of whose more extreme members repeatedly and publicly advocated anti-Semitic and coercive nationalization policies. Faced with the looming threat the television organizations and the government perceived – the return of Communism and the potential shutdown of speech pluralism – what should a free press do? The traditional democratic answer is to oppose free speech with free speech, since only in times of crisis can this basic right be qualified by restrictions on "hate speech" that causes immediate and specific harm.

There were important differences among the networks in the way they covered the campaign, but unbiased coverage was not among them. All four of the Moscow-based television networks coordinated their offerings to maximize Yeltsin's chances. The president of NTV, Igor Malashenko, became the president's media campaign manager, and his first order of business was to prove that Yeltsin was physically strong enough to be a candidate. Television, with the credibility attached to visual evidence, was his prime weapon. Yeltsin suddenly became a barnstorming campaigner, going down into mines, talking to schoolchildren, dancing, and orating. He was the very model of a vigorous incumbent, dominating news broadcasts with a new initiative every day. When the opposition questioned his fitness for office, Yeltsin's team could tell them to just watch television and see how dynamic the president was. The newly energized president led an impressive campaign, but it also took its toll on him. Between the two rounds of the election, Yeltsin suffered a series of heart attacks, which were concealed by the networks and presented instead as mere colds.

The networks' partisan collaboration was not a full return to the 1993 referendum situation in which Yeltsin's opponents were almost completely denied television coverage. Free-time rules were in force and fairly applied. Paid political advertising was still an option and was generously used by the president's campaign managers, as well as by most of his competitors in the first round. NTV, although it was a major part of the Yeltsin campaign, offered the Communist Party's opponent, Gennady Zyuganov, considerable time for live interviews (each one lasting over 20 minutes) and its news broadcasts covered the competing campaigns. But while NTV was tough in its coverage of Zyuganov, it did not turn the same spotlight on the president's generous campaign promises, decrees, and projects or his precarious health. Boris Yeltsin and Gennady Zyuganov finished the first round with only 3 percentage points separating them, with the result that the networks' strategy for the second round was more combative and negative. Yeltsin's television advertising strategy shifted from "positives" – warm and reasoned testimony of ordinary people praising new ways – to a confrontational attack campaign. Some new spots showed old black-and-white footage of labor camps and mass hunger and urged voters not to allow Russia to return to those troubled times. Others showed old footage of brother against brother in civil war and newer clips from the 1993 violence in Moscow, all the while urging voters not to let it happen again. As always, Zyuganov's approach was sober and deliberately uncharismatic as he shunned the trappings of "Americanized" campaigning.

Yeltsin won decisively in the second round. There are many reasons for his victory, including voters' judgments of the past and the future, their attitudes toward the market, and their ideological preferences. The newly reelected president soon underwent a multiple heart-bypass operation and was vulnerable to illness thereafter. His erratic, unpredictable style of governing, his increasing absence, and recurring and ever-growing crises weakened the political system and the fragile economy. NTV hoped to regain its reputation for balance and news professionalism, while Channels One and Two were going through cycles of changing leaders as their owners decreed.

Television has been a key factor in the Western world's changing pattern of campaign politics in particular. In Russia, the medium has assumed perhaps even greater political prominence because of the deterioration of the national newspaper market and the weak organization of most political parties at the local level. These conditions have contributed to making television the primary vehicle for the dissemination of political information, including perhaps most importantly the critical flow of information about candidates, parties, and elections. This primacy has, in turn, made control of television an invaluable asset in the campaign and has placed it squarely at the center of the struggle for power.

RUSSIAN VIEWERS READ THE NEWS

The intensity of the Russian political elite's struggle for power over television rested on assumptions about the medium's ability to persuade, and these, in turn, were predicated on assumptions about how the public processed televised information. Other than ratings, elites knew very little about the way people actually watched the news – what their thoughts and emotions were and whether they were interested enough to spend time and energy engaging the issues. In the West, economic models of information acquisition tell us that the likelihood of citizens accessing and digesting large amounts of political information is quite low (Downs 1957; Hamilton 1998). We know that in the United States, most people are often characterized as poorly informed, as indicated by their performance on tests that pollsters use to see if they know who their representatives in Congress are, the level of U.S. foreign aid, or the geography of the world. There has been found to be a significant gap between people who have the ability to process large amounts of information and those who do not, but that this ability is not simply reducible to the level of formal education. Other kinds of learning – from various types of experience – also expand the individual's ability to process information (Iyengar and Kinder 1987; Graber 1988; Zaller and Hunt 1994, 1995; Zaller 1996). It is also evident that people make up for their lack of information about issues or events that matter to them by taking mental shortcuts that rely on both emotion and reason. These shortcuts are commonly called "heuristics" (Sniderman et al. 1991). Because the patterns by which viewers make sense of the news in post-Soviet Russia were formed during the Soviet period, I refer to them as "Soviet-era" heuristics.

The foundation of the Soviet-era heuristic was skepticism. For decades, television news was rationed, centrally controlled, and confined to a single authoritative source. Viewers questioned the credibility of the source even as they watched attentively, since the limited volume of information could contain vitally important cues about coming threats or opportunities and had to be carefully and skillfully mined. That skepticism, together with strong interest in news, creates the basis for today's exceptionally media-literate Russian viewer. That said, I do not mean to imply that Russians simply reject everything they see on the news as meaningless rubbish. They do not. Their strategies enable them to tease out what is important for them and to correct for methods of news coverage they find troubling. It is a continuous process of discovering and refining. These are subtleties and dynamics that the mass public opinion survey can rarely capture, but they are particularly well suited to studies based on focus groups. Research based on focus groups in Russia also yields insights into reactions drawn not just from memory, but also from actual viewing of specially designed news excerpts (Mickiewicz 1999).

Three of the most important elements of the Soviet-era heuristic are suspicion of broadly generalized good news, attention to sources of news as potential beneficiaries, and evaluation of internal inconsistencies in the news. Viewers are keenly aware of overly positive messages that make grand generalizations and claims. Since Soviet news programs were intended to inspire and lead the public to a desired policy goal, stories were frequently about hoped-for rather than actual progress. Small gains were exaggerated into large-scale achievements on the theory that the future was tending in that direction in any case. As a result, post-Soviet viewers deflate stories of excessive optimism.

Considering who might benefit from a news story is also part of the critical apparatus ordinary Russians bring to their consumption of the news. They pay attention to sources of news stories and to possible bias in them. Inconsistencies in news content set off warning signals in viewers. It may be a matter of facts appearing to contradict each other or, more subtly, a disparity between the anchor's previously displayed level of intelligence and subsequent material he or she presents. As a result of these tensions and evaluations of imbalance or dissonance, Russian citizens employ a system of correctives. Some of the correctives involve accessing their own real-world experience and that of others whose opinions they know to be close to their own. It is not at all unusual to hear stories about people contacting friends and relatives about interpretations of individual news stories. Nor is it at all uncommon to hear viewers compare "how it is on the street" with how it is on the news.

Education makes a difference. College-educated Russians consume more political information and typically use more sources, including media in general and newspapers in particular. They are also more skilled at articulating the steps in their reasoning strategies. However, both high school- and college-educated viewers in Russia employ the same basic strategies, and both groups bring sophisticated critical perspectives to their news watching.

Russian viewers employ both active and passive strategies to deal with issues of objectivity and bias in the news. The active strategy is to change channels or turn off the set. In larger cities, there are more choices and channel surfing is more common, especially among the well educated. Viewers are able to watch different news programs and to compare them. Especially during times of crisis – for example, the first war in Chechnya and the crash of 1998 – that is exactly what they do. During both of those (protracted) events, ratings for all stations shot up, with NTV gaining most.

Russian viewers also come to the news consumption process with cultural baggage. Just as they bring Soviet-era tools of analysis, they also bring the habit of staying with news programs. Among both high school- and college-educated viewers, most continue to watch a news program in which they have lost trust. But as they continue to watch, their attitude changes. The mental process is vividly described by two members of a focus group:

Evgeny: I do not switch if there's a theme that interests me. . . . I'm interested in *how* they do it. . . . Do they lie well or skillfully? Will they lie dazzlingly? Will they lie disgustingly, vilely?

Katya: Even if you don't like something, you have to know your enemies; that is, you have to know how the other side is presented. That's why it pays to see it and stay abreast of things.

Because this passivity may not affect ratings, it goes unnoticed by television and political officials. This disconnect adds to the misperceptions elites hold about ordinary Russian citizens. Elites apparently do not understand that media publics bring to their consumption of news and public-affairs programs the willingness and habits to engage actively with the news. They may not change the channel and therefore the ratings. Nonetheless, behind their apparent passivity lies a very active challenge to the news. It is a warning to politicians, television station owners, and anchors alike that viewers do not appreciate stories in which the deck is stacked and the public is held in contempt.

INSTITUTIONAL INCAPACITY AND PLURALISM

In looking back over the rocky road to a democratic media system in Russia, a key element of the journey's dynamic has been institutional incapacity. In important ways, the inability of the old institutions to continue to impose Soviet-style patterns of behavior made it possible for reformers and innovators to institute new approaches, as well as to attack the institutions themselves. In the interstices of failing structures, new shoots could push their way up. To put it differently, to the degree that government demands of television have been diffuse and unfocused, network and station officials have been able to parry them or ward them off. Before the breakdown of the Soviet system under Gorbachev, political elites' demands were concentrated, ordered by specific officials, and presented as a unified program to state television. There was a strict order of precedence, and sequences of individuals and stories were carefully monitored. Any deviation was symbolic and freighted with political meaning. There was little room for experimentation on television since it reached the largest audience of any medium. Newspapers were less subject to this institutional conformity. As the institutions of power generally, and the Communist Party in particular, decayed, demands were no longer concentrated. Thus, institutional incapacity provided the space for nascent pluralism. To the degree that the demands for authority over personnel, news coverage, spin, and direct access for key leaders are numerous and the structures making the demands fragmented, there is a measure of protection for press autonomy. But this autonomy is fragile because it is neither institutionalized nor supported by a strong, independent, and impartial judiciary. It would, of course, be far preferable to embed protection for press freedom in the legal system, but during democratic transitions, however long they may be, such guarantees are largely absent.

The inability of the Russian state to provide substantial or even adequate funding for its own media properties meant that the traditional notion of public-service or public-interest television could not be based on state or public revenues. Subscription fees or new taxes would strain already reduced personal income and deprive the public of its principal source of news and information. Because other revenues were simply not available, cultural offerings, documentaries, and programs to serve minorities and regions could not easily gain a place on television networks that depended so heavily on advertisers and therefore on ratings. The Culture Channel was begun precisely to fill this void and, eschewing advertising, was content with low ratings and with catering to underserved groups. Its funding, inevitably, was always precarious. Television analyst Vsevolod Vilchek thought that the channel was a "still birth," not because its public-interest mandate was unimportant but because Russia could not afford the BBC model. "Every democracy," he said, "looks out for and protects the rights of minorities, and cultural minorities ought to be served by the state budget" ("Interviu . . ." 1998).

Nor did Channels One and Two, closely tied as they were to the government and fiercely contested by Parliament, provide the in-depth political information and independent viewpoint commonly associated with the public-service model of television. Rather, as some Russians remarked, it was the commercial stations that approximated this model more closely. The irony is that in today's Russia, it is a commercial station large enough and strong enough to maintain a comprehensive newsgathering and broadcast capacity that best fulfills the medium's public-service obligations. Channel One is called Russian Public Television, but function and title are very different things. Comparing Russia with Western democracies, Vsevolod Bogdanov, head of the Russian Union of Journalists, told a meeting of the Russian National Association of Broadcasters: "Eduard [Sagalayev – founder and head of TV-6 and of the Association] and I went to Atlanta, Vienna, and Salzburg [for meetings of the nongovernmental organization, the Commission on Radio and Television Policy] and we discussed and discussed public and state television and how they differed from each other. And right now, living in our wild market, we understood that the most public television we have, strange as it may be, is commercial" (Ukhlin 1998, 13).

The capacity of language to address issues of political importance is essential to the development of democracy, and television in Russia contributed significantly to a revolution in political discourse. Mikhail Gorbachev started a revolution in speech, and it was communicated through television. For over seven decades of Soviet history, the stuff of politics was forbidden. Out of bounds for ordinary people, it was the domain of the country's self-selected leaders. Accordingly, speech was transformed into abstract ritual that only the political priesthood could modify. Mikhail Gorbachev began to close this gap with his direct and plain – if long-winded – television appearances. It was a rhetorical invitation to bring in the public and rally around his notion of citizenship the energies of an alienated, passive, and subject population.

Although unaware of the full import of the changes they promoted, leading television figures did self-consciously and deliberately use the medium to effect change. They had a better bully pulpit than Gorbachev or Yeltsin because they, unlike their masters, were skilled in and totally comfortable with the medium. Several of the most influential of them used it to enter Parliament. The television stars could then directly shape the course of the country and, in the process, acquire another key political commodity: legal immunity. Only gradually did the law attempt to regulate this obvious conflict of interest, but the stars continued to see themselves as kingmakers. Television news also picked out the most dramatic figures to cover. At first, they were the democratic reformers. The old guard still spoke in the wooden, abstract Soviet style, while the new reformers appeared genuine and unaffected. Very soon, the nationalist Vladimir Zhirinovsky and then the fierce anti-Semites, Viktor Anpilov and General Albert Makashov, understood that their firebrand style made for gripping television. Some of the messages were clearly and obviously illegal under the Constitution and under other legal acts prohibiting speech that arouses or exacerbates ethnic tension. The problem was that institutions did not exist to enforce these rules. It was the democrats who were, by contrast, pale and dry. The lessons of television effectiveness – dramatic narratives, sound bites, a focused message, and a clear image – were available for all to learn, not only the democratically minded.

The profound changes that shook the Soviet Union and then post-Soviet Russia were telescoped into a relatively brief slice of time and powerfully affected a population of tens of millions of people distributed across the world's largest landmass. In many important ways, the thread connecting them was television. It was so during the uncertain days of civil violence in October 1993, and it remained so as other connecting threads became weaker.

Television, even if imperfectly, succeeded in a very short time in allowing the post-Soviet Russian public to access multiple sources and points of view in the news. Some stations – notably NTV – did this with more balance and professionalism, and during each crisis, its ratings climbed. Television also allowed viewers to understand what had not been possible to convey during Soviet times: that other individuals and groups held similar views, many of them dissenting ones. During the first war in Chechnya, viewers saw some military officers condemn the action and others support it, some elected deputies criticize the president and cabinet ministers defend him. One regional governor collected a million signatures protesting the war. Only television could amplify and extend that message. Viewers compared what human rights advocates said they saw in ruined Chechnya with what footage from the front showed. Such opportunities for independent verification were few in the second Chechen war, and the public clearly knew that it was not getting the full story of what was happening inside that ruined region. As noted earlier, public support for what it saw as a low-military-casualty operation to stem the projection of terrorism into Moscow and elsewhere in Russia was based on a different calculus.

If institutions guaranteeing autonomy were largely absent from the Russian scene, there was a wobbly market that was nonetheless strong enough to support commercial television stations that could compete with, and challenge, governmentally managed news. Media concentration shored up the ability of the commercial stations to do so, especially in the sagging postcrash economy. It also reduced the number of station owners, while economic difficulties increased incentives to purchase news – news as infomercials for corporate interests or political hopefuls. But the likelihood of success of attempts to buy the public outright had to be considered in the context of the way Russians consumed news and public-affairs programs. Here were people who had acquired over many decades an approach to news watching that made them sophisticated, active, subtle, and critical analysts of what the stations put before them. Perhaps future generations would look more like Western media consumers, forgoing the hard work of carefully watching and deconstructing the news and making comparisons across newscasts. The Soviet method of news watching would likely fade in time, but until it did, there would be surprises in store for elites who confidently pushed their messages in ignorance of the public's ability to evaluate them.

Television could not remake Russia; it could not eliminate the profound cleavages and solve the unanswered constitutional questions. It could and did substantially alter the information environment of ordinary people and elites alike and afford them a genuine, if limited, choice. This was perhaps the most singular and profound achievement of a controversial, disputed, and flawed transition plan. The market, even in its greatly weakened condition, has been the main prop of news diversity, and keeping that choice alive is the most important public service that television has performed.

CHAPTER 4

Democratic Transformation and the Mass Media in Hungary: From Stalinism to Democratic Consolidation

Miklós Sükösd

Television images from 1989–90 will haunt many of us for the rest of our lives: German youths in colorful dress dancing and waving flags on top of the Berlin Wall; massive prodemocracy demonstrations in Leipzig, East Germany; Václav Hável announcing the victory of Czechoslovakia's Velvet Revolution at Prague's Wenceslaw Square; Imre Nagy, prime minister during the 1956 Hungarian Revolution, is finally buried with full honors in Budapest. These unforgettable images were seen by over a billion people around the world, including millions of citizens of Central and Eastern Europe. These citizens, who became key players in these events, were motivated by the information and visual images they received from the media daily about the collapse of the status quo in the Soviet-dominated parts of Europe. Undoubtedly, the mass media played important roles both in the breakdown of these Communist regimes in 1989–90 and in the radical transformation of the region since then.

An analysis of the impact of the mass media on the dramatic events of 1989–90 and the subsequent democratization of Central and Eastern Europe requires that we first examine the roles played by the media under the former Communist regimes. Institutions rarely change overnight, and mass media institutions are no exception. Significant parts of anti- and post-Communist media activities during and after 1989–90 occurred within an institutional framework that had been built by Communist one-party regimes several decades earlier. Although the contents of the official propaganda media had softened during the 1970s and 1980s in some countries, the basic institutional framework remained intact throughout the region until as late as 1990.

The functioning of the media in the Communist one-party systems was fundamentally different from their role in any Western democracy. In the classic Communist model, exclusive party-state ownership, tight political control, institutionalized censorship, informal party directives, and unbounded propaganda made the media the instruments of Communist parties' ideological mass persuasion. The structure, political roles, and effects of the media in the posttransition era differ radically or at least substantially from those of the Communist period. During the 1990s, the most important challenges faced by democratic political elites, media entrepreneurs, and journalists were to make the media systems of the region more independent, pluralistic, and democratic – and this has been far from an easy task.

With democratization, the new Central and Eastern European countries have come to differ considerably in the extent to which their political and media structures have been transformed. After 1989–90, the area that had been usually defined in the West (especially in the United States) uniformly as "Eastern Europe," gradually evolved into three major regions as deeply rooted historical boundaries between regions reemerged (Szucs 1988). After peaceful transitions to pluralist rule, the countries of Central Europe (including Poland, Czechoslovakia [after its split, the Czech Republic], Hungary, Slovenia, and former East Germany as a special case) established stable pluralist democracies and capitalist economies and soon became associate members of the European Union (EU), with the goal of full EU membership. (Slovakia differs somewhat, given abuses of power by the government and the secret police between 1993 and 1998, as well as limitations on minority rights.) In a further step toward European integration, the Czech Republic, Hungary, and Poland became members of the North Atlantic Treaty Organization (NATO) in 1999.

The transformation of the Southeastern European countries (including Albania, Bulgaria, Romania, and the newly independent republics that emerged out of the former Yugoslavia) and the Eastern European countries (Belarus, Russian, and Ukraine) has proceeded at a slower and more uneven pace. In several Balkan cases, Communism was ended by bloody revolutions, to be followed by severe ethnic conflict and war. In some Eastern European countries, post-Communist democracies remain unstable, while in others, authoritarian semidemocracies or pseudodemocracies have emerged. Political pluralism and competition remain somewhat limited, elections often have been biased, some governments use political violence, and legislatures pass fewer postcommunist laws. In some countries, ex-Communist authoritarian leaders such as Serbian President Slobodan Milosevic or Belorussian President Alyaksander Lukashenko have not been removed since the

Communist period. I will differentiate among the regions in my terminology. When referring to the region as a whole, I will use the term "Central and Eastern Europe."

This chapter analyzes the political roles of the media in Hungary's democratic transformation from a Central and Eastern European comparative perspective. It includes background information concerning patterns of media ownership, institutions of control, the legal environment, and the typical political uses of the media in different periods. However, I will focus primarily on the changing effects of the media on politics, including the role of the media in the (de)legitimization of Communist and post-Communist regimes, agenda setting, citizens' mobilization, voters' orientation, political identity formation, and party building. I will also analyze the role of the media in the consolidation of post-Communist democracies.

This analysis will be broken down into three distinct periods: the Communist period, 1948–88; the transition, 1988–90; and the consolidation of democracy, 1990–9.

THE MEDIA IN THE COMMUNIST PERIOD, 1948–88

From 1948 to 1988, the uniform postwar Stalinist regimes and propaganda systems of the Central and Eastern European region developed into different political and media systems. Thus, in discussing the classic Communist period, I will focus on common features in political uses and effects of the media; when discussing the later periods, I will increasingly emphasize the distinctive features of the Hungarian case.

CLASSIC PROPAGANDA MEDIA: 1948–58

The totalitarian aspirations of newly established Communist regimes had a profound impact on the patterns of ownership, control, and legal environment of the media in Central and Eastern Europe. The Soviet annexation of the region after World War II created radically new and uniform political structures characterized by extreme centralization and control. The media served a common purpose too: they were made the exclusive channels for institutionalized mass communications. Any form of public discourse, from social or political issues and policy debates to entertainment, was defined and dominated by Communist authorities. The party-state monopolized the ownership of all print media, news services, radio, newsreel, film, and record production companies. Although some newspaper publishers (e.g., publishing houses of trade unions or the Communist Youth League) remained formally independent of the state and the Communist Party, close party control led to the same effect. This classic Communist media system had no alternative channels, either legal or illegal, for institutionalized social communications. It was exclusive and absolute: it was meant to be total.

Hungary, an ally of Nazi Germany in World War II, was liberated and occupied by the Soviet Red Army during 1944–5, along with other countries in the region. After a short period of multiparty democracy after 1945, a Stalinist one-party dictatorship, led by Mátyás Rákosi, was established in 1948. The Communist Party (Magyar Dolgozók Pártja – MDP) soon established a publishing monopoly by banning all printed materials, broadcasts, newsreel, movies, and records that had been published by the democratic parties and independent media ventures in the short-lived pre-Communist democratic period. Economic control, including a publishing monopoly and a monopoly of access to printing presses and paper, radio studios, and other communication technologies, formed the context for political control. But as in the rest of the region, censorship offices were not the main instrument of this control. Instead, control was achieved by five institutions that together were more effective and far-reaching than simple censorship.

The first was the *nomenklatura* system, which effectively gave the departments of the party's Central Committee the right to nominate, appoint, or veto individuals for all leadership positions in significant social, political, economic, and cultural institutions. The Department of Agitation and Propaganda of the Central Committees and local branches of the Communist Party effectively controlled the media through nomination and appointment of the media *nomenklatura*, that is, chief editors and other senior decision makers (Szakadát, 1993), even though this practice was not publicly acknowledged or regulated in legal codes. In Hungary, the *nomenklatura* system remained in effect from 1948 until as late as 1989.

Regular informal interventions by Communist officials in the everyday work of editors reinforced this *nomenklatura*-based control. Special direct phone lines tied editorial offices with leading party and state officials, including the top party secretary (Lendvai 1981). Through these lines, party officials banned coverage of events and determined the type of coverage a news event would receive. Often they ordered the publication of materials that had been previously prepared by specialized party agencies for propaganda purposes (e.g., in the case of Stalin's or national leaders' birthdays or party purges).

A third control mechanism was a special government agency (in Hungary, the Central Communication Office) that kept secret files on every journalist. These files were consulted by agents of the political police before members of the media *nomenklatura* and rank-and-file journalists were nominated or appointed to their posts. The office was directly linked to the personnel departments of newspaper publishing houses, which also collected political and other sensitive information about journalists.

Party control of journalism schools was another mechanism for dominating the media, since employment by the mass media usually required graduation from such institutions. In accord with the Leninist philosophy of the press, journalists were taught to be "the sharpest weapon of the party" (Lendvai 1981). Ideological indoctrination was especially effective since holding a top media post usually required membership in the Communist Party. Party membership, in turn, required the journalist to obey and execute party directives. In Hungary, generational change and mobility of the new graduates into key positions was especially rapid since many older journalists left the country in successive waves of emigration (in 1944, 1945, 1948, and 1956), while others left the field because they were fired or their papers were banned.

Political terror was the fifth means of control of the media world. Obedience was reinforced by regular purges and political show trials that could result in punishment (including prison, torture, and even death sentences) for journalists who did not actually commit any crime. Thus, pervasive terror, in combination with the other mechanisms of political control, led to extremely centralized control of the media throughout Central and Eastern Europe by Communist parties that were, in turn, under the control of Moscow.

The principal objective of this control was to legitimize one-party rule by popularizing and mobilizing support for party-state political decisions (domestic as well as international). This function could be defined as one of overall political socialization and Sovietization. The media, together with the subjugated educational system, were to convince citizens of the wisdom of the new Communist policies and that the road to a classless society ran through forced industrialization, the collectivization of agriculture, the Sovietization of culture, and the personality cults of Stalin and domestic Communist leaders. In geopolitical terms, media propaganda fed Western intelligence with misinformation and mobilized public opinion against Cold War enemies, especially the United States, Western European NATO countries, and Josip Tito's nonaligned Yugoslavia.

In accord with the totalitarian aspirations of the regime, one of the central objectives of Communist propaganda was the active mobilization of the population at the grass roots. Propaganda penetrated everyday life at the workplace, where lecture series were organized for party members and everybody else. Employees, for example, were obliged to study the central party's paper for 30 minutes after the work day ended. Local cultural centers repeated the messages, inundating citizens with propaganda about many aspects of everyday life (Lendvai 1981), propaganda reinforced by ritualistic media coverage modeled after that in the Soviet Union.

Media entertainment also became politicized. High and popular literature, movies, and even popular music (stressing working-class marches and translations of Soviet songs) had to express ideological "truths." Western popular culture, including jazz, rock and roll, and Hollywood movies, was condemned as a pestilence spread by the Central Intelligence Agency. Antisocialist, decadent hooligans harassing Stakhanovite factory workers, as well as other villains in propaganda movies, often had Elvis haircuts with sideburns, wore striped rock-and-roll jackets, and listened to jazz as indications of mental degradation and political corruption.

The key objectives of this propaganda in Central and Eastern Europe were to politicize and homogenize all message content, to promote Communist indoctrination; to mobilize the population behind the domestic and foreign policies of the new regimes, the Soviet Union, the Warsaw Pact, and the COMECON trading bloc to legitimize party leaders directly through a cult of personality; and to criticize Western democracies. These objectives had a direct and substantial impact on political news coverage by the media.

The rationale for and basic structure of the Soviet totalitarian propaganda system were artificially transplanted to East Central European societies after World War II. This model was imposed without taking into account regional variations in socioeconomic development (including higher levels of industrialization and modernization), class structure (including a larger and historically rooted urban population, bourgeoisie, professional and working classes), national cultural traditions (among them the historically grounded drive for national independence and respect for national culture), the diverse pre–Communist Party systems, and related intellectual discourses and ideologies (among them strong traditions of anticommunism, nationalism, and social democracy).

THE 1956 REVOLUTION AND THE MEDIA

This lack of fit laid the groundwork for the rebellions that shook the Yalta system (which divided Europe into Eastern and Western blocs) over the following two decades. A series of anti-Communist and anti-Soviet revolts included an outburst of workers' dissatisfaction in East Germany in 1953, large-scale political demonstrations in Poland in 1956, the Hungarian Revolution in 1956, and the "Prague Spring" in 1968. These outbursts cast severe doubt on the thesis that Communist states had been successful in atomizing and reeducating their subjects (Friedrich 1964). In Hungary, the participation of all major social groups (intellectuals, students, workers, and rural residents) in the 1956 revolution clearly indicated that the majority of the population rejected the Communist system. Although Soviet troops eventually crushed the Hungarian Revolution, over the course of its 13 days several democratic parties of the pre-Communist period (among them the Smallholders, the Social Democrats, the Christian Democrats, and the Peasants' Party) reorganized themselves, thereby recreating a pluralist party structure for a new democratic system. Joining the revolution, and declaring neutral status for Hungary and its official withdrawal from the Warsaw Pact, Prime Minister Imre Nagy and other reform Communists established a new, democratic Socialist Party and promised to preserve pluralism until democratic general elections could be held. The rapid reorganization of the pluralist political scene, along with the widespread formation of workers' councils in factories, provide striking evidence that democratic consolidation could have followed if the Soviets had not intervened to crush the revolution.

Several features of the 1956 revolution are relevant for the analysis of media effects in the process of democratization. First, the revolution provided evidence of a dual temporal character of media effects in the Communist institutional framework. Communist propaganda communicated to a rebellious population may be counterproductive in the short run. Hungarian society not only resisted the six-year-long attempt at Stalinist brainwashing, but also organized itself successfully for insurgent action. There is also ample evidence that at the beginning of the revolution controversial radio broadcasts in support of the status quo in fact had an unintended countereffect, fueling anti-Stalinist sentiment, turning public opinion against the regime, and mobilizing listeners to participate in revolutionary action.

The revolution and its aftermath, however, also illustrated the ability of the propaganda state to influence social value systems in the long run, as well as the ability of censorship to close off channels of crucial information for the audience. Socialist values took deep root in the six years between 1948 and 1956. The strength of the new nationally organized workers' councils supports this claim. During the revolution, these workers' councils took control of factories and other production units and resisted attempts at privatization. Taken together with the reorganization of the Socialist Party, the establishment of these councils suggests that non-Stalinist socialism had very strong support among both workers and intellectuals. Indeed, among intellectuals, different branches of socialism became mainstream, hegemonic political orientations from the 1950s until the 1980s. In the 1970s, the first opposition voices articulated Marxist or Maoist discourses. The hegemony of Marxism was at least partly a long-term effect of the Socialist-Communist monopoly of political discourse. Another long-term effect of censorship was that citizens behind the Iron Curtain had little factual information about everyday life in Western capitalist societies. Later interviews with postrevolutionary refugees indicated that Hungarians, especially young people who grew up under Communism, developed misconceptions about life in the West. In this sense, Communist propaganda and censorship proved effective in the long run.

A third notable media-related feature of the revolution was that it began on October 23, 1956, as a fight for control of the national radio headquarters in Budapest, with an insurgent crowd demanding that their grievances and demands be aired. Thus, in contrast with the classic scenario of eighteenth- and nineteenth-century political revolutions – which focused on traditional power centers (such as parliament) or hated symbol of oppression (such as a prison) – the 1956 rebellion in Hungary was triggered by the struggle for control of a broadcasting station. This pattern was repeated during the Romanian revolution in 1989 in Bucharest and during the 1991 and 1992 coup attempts in Moscow. These events indicate that, in severe political crises in the late twentieth century, the media are widely seen as the real power center, as the decisive mobilizing resource and major source of legitimacy.

Both the audience for and the mobilizational capacity of Radio Free Europe (RFE) grew dramatically during the 1956 revolution in Hungary (Benkô 1993a, b). RFE broadcasts had a well-documented effect on audiences by hinting that Western military intervention was pending, thereby giving rise to expectations of military victory and persuading many Hungarians to join armed revolutionary fights against Communist government forces and Soviet tanks. This suggests that in periods of open political crises, propaganda from a trusted media source may have a greater impact on political behavior than it does under stable and peaceful conditions.

The fourth point is that the mass media became crucial institutions in the reorganization and articulation of a pluralist political society, providing crucial information not only about the quickly changing political and military situation, but also about the newly emerging democratic forces. These forces included pluralist parties, their national leaders and local chapters, street fighters' revolutionary groups, the revolutionary national militia, and other organizations. Party newspapers published calls for former members of democratic parties to rejoin, invited new members, and printed the addresses of national party headquarters and local branches. The media, in other words, contributed directly to party building, the rapid reconstruction of civil society, the quick reestablishment of a pluralist party system, the legitimation of revolutionary government, and the strengthening of other democratic institutions.

Although the revolution was soon suppressed, the memory of political pluralism, a free press, and uncensored media remained an important political experience for later generations. In many families, collections of 1956 newspapers became treasures of family archives, to be shared and studied in secret with trusted friends and young family members. The experience of a truthful, pluralist, and uncensored press in not-so-distant history enhanced Hungarian society's ability to resist coming decades of softer Communist media propaganda and had a lasting impact on the country's collective memory.

In a sense, then, the Hungarian revolution triumphed, at least partly. After crushing the uprising, the Soviet leadership appointed as new Communist Party secretary János Kádár, a moderate, non-Stalinist Communist. After two years of bloody repression (1956–8), Kádár's policies shifted to promote national reconciliation, depoliticization, and the cooptation of non-Communist professionals and intelligentsia. This political strategy initiated far-reaching changes, among other fields, in media policy and the interrelationship of media and politics.

SELECTIVE REPRESSION AND THE MEDIA, 1958–76

Together with anti-Communist revolts in East Germany (1953), in Poland and Hungary (1956), and in Czechoslovakia (1968), de-Stalinization and Khruschev's "decade of euphoria (1954–64) led to a considerable moderation of direct Soviet repression and propaganda in Central and Eastern Europe. As a result, domestic political and social forces played an ever-growing role in shaping national political and media systems as different governing Communist parties chose different paths to regime consolidation after a period of unrest and uncertainty. Both popular and elite media culture became more Westernized, pluralistic, and open to national traditions. Yugoslav media from the 1960s and Romanian media during the 1970s became especially open. In Hungary and Poland, where repression became more selective and restrained, liberalization of elite and popular culture had unintended subversive consequences.

The background to the weakening of state control of the media in Hungary was the policy of liberalization (however cautious, gradual, and selective) introduced a few years after the revolution,[1]which received a major impetus in 1963 with an amnesty for participants in the revolution. This liberalization was intended to achieve political consolidation through demobilization. In what came to be described as "goulash Communism," the new government sought to consolidate itself by making life more bearable, even pleasant, and by promoting a limited consumer culture that at first involved products made mostly in socialist countries. Holiday travel to other Communist countries also became widely available, and even travel to the West became possible every third year. Against a background of increasing affluence and consumerism, political control of the media in the region tended to ease as well.

CLIENTELISM AND (SELF-)CENSORSHIP IN THE MEDIA

In the post-Stalinist era, the pattern of party-state control of the media in Central and Eastern Europe became more subtle. As in the past, the *nomenklatura* system and the state Information Offices remained in existence, journalism schools retained their role of educating for the role of propagandist and screening politically dangerous applicants, and party and state officials continued to guide and advise media personnel (chief editors and journalists) about the party line at regular weekly and monthly consultations. But at the same time, the main instruments of media control became censorship, self-censorship, and journalists' clientelist dependence on the media *nomenklatura*. In this "velvet prison" or "culture of censorship" (Haraszti 1987), self-censorship became a commonly accepted and internalized norm among intellectuals, journalists, and authors, reinforced by the belief that the divided Europe of the Yalta system would remain in place for at least one or two generations.

Selective liberalization did not stretch to political journalism, which remained severely restricted throughout the region. News reporting remained extremely centralized. Newspapers, as well as radio and television, were obliged to use the news coverage provided by the central wire service (MTI in Hungary), so that the political contents of different newspapers remained uniform no matter which institution formally published them. News programs were just as uniform across radio and television channels, not least because state broadcasting (gradually coming to comprise three radio and two television channels in Hungary) enjoyed monopoly status. Radio and television censorship in particular remained very tight. Several basic political taboos could not be broken, including the need for the one-party system itself; the correctness of decisions by any central party, state leader, or office; potential splits in the leadership; the domestic and foreign policies of any Warsaw Pact country; and COMECON economic policies. Independent domestic or foreign political reporting was completely impossible, as was endorsement of any sociopolitical alternative to the existing socialist system.

In terms of foreign policy, frequent ritual repetition of slogans such as "proletarian internationalism" and "the leading role of the Communist Party" in the member countries of the Warsaw Pact was required from journalists. The only sources they were allowed to use to cover other Communist countries were official news by national wire services and central Communist Party dailies that were the equivalent of Pravda. In terms of international politics, no Central or Eastern European communications medium (except in pro-China Romania and Albania and independent Communist Yugoslavia) ever criticized Soviet foreign policy. They all had to closely follow, if not repeat word for word, Soviet communiqués and evaluations.

Political news coverage was ritualistic, repetitive, dull, and extremely boring. Depoliticization, alienation, cynicism, and disbelief were the response on the part of the audience. Cultural media content, by contrast, was allowed to become varied and interesting as the result of specific policies intended to coopt intellectuals, academics, and young people in Hungary.

INTELLECTUALS, ACADEMICS, AND ELITE MEDIA CULTURE

After the 1963 amnesty, a number of intellectuals who had participated in the Hungarian Revolution obtained employment in cultural institutions like publishing houses, newspapers, weeklies, journals, the national news services, libraries, and, to a smaller degree, radio and television. The Hungarian policy of cooptation and liberalization differed markedly from that of Czechoslovakia, where intellectuals who had participated in the Prague Spring were blacklisted and could only find menial manual employment.

Some Hungarian intellectuals subsequently became decision makers, even *nomenklatura* members, and used their positions to slowly liberalize their respective fields from the inside while remaining committed to the new regime (although not necessarily to Communist dogma). This cooptation of intellectuals involved in the democratic revolution was part of a larger strategy to broaden the Kádár regime's support base by promoting a new legitimizing ideology that exploited professional academic discourses. Disbanding the feared and autonomous AVH (the Hungarian KGB) and the special Communist guard units that had been used to restore order in 1956–7, the regime shifted its instruments of power from pervasive terror to softer measures. The regime's emphasis on a "scientifically grounded" official ideology (based on a mix of Western scientific concepts and Marxism-Leninism) enhanced the importance of the scientific community to the regime and placed it in a stronger bargaining position than before.[2] One unintended consequence was that some scientists used their privileges, and their positional and intellectual capital, to slowly formulate independent professional discourses and later to criticize the regime.

The new regime selectively liberalized elite media culture as well. From the mid-1960s on, a limited number of new journals and, later, publishing houses were permitted to review and publish the works of Western European and American writers and scientists. Contemporary Western concepts and discourses were introduced into Hungary during the 1960s, 1970s, and 1980s by journals such as *Valóság* and *Kritika*. The representatives of party-minded ideological arts and sciences were challenged and a space was created for public debate, even if it did move only slowly outside the framework of official discourse, using mostly Marxist-Leninist phraseology. Inevitably, however, the different interpretations of Marxism diluted this discourse's official character, and it gradually became interspersed with Western terminologies.

YOUNG PEOPLE AND POPULAR CULTURE

The Kádár regime also gradually liberalized youth culture from the 1960s on in an effort to conciliate, depoliticize, and demobilize the younger generation. In practice, however, the Western pop and rock music to which they were exposed became an important form of symbolic resistance to the Communist regime. Some Hungarian bands (especially the popular group Illés) raised, between the lines of their songs, themes of national independence, national cultural heritage, resistance to Soviet domination, and sex as a form of generational symbolic cultural resistance. In this way, a sensitive dynamic of cultural politics gradually developed, based on the symbolic resistance resulting from a shared generational language and set of understandings. An unintended consequence of the liberalization of popular culture, therefore, was that, in the long run, it created a counterculture involving millions of young citizens that competed effectively for their loyalty with the Pioneer Association (the Communist organization for teenagers) or the Communist Youth League. Even the Communist Youth League began to organize rock concerts and disco parties to attract young people.

At the same time that popular commitment to official culture was declining, the availability of Western alternatives was increasing. One important result of officially sponsored socialist consumerism was the opening of the East Central European mass market to home electronics products. During the 1960s, televisions, record players, and tape recorders became widely available; in the 1970s, it was the turn of color televisions and stereos; and in the 1980s, of videocassette recorders (VCRs), dish antennae, and cable television. This technological infrastructure encouraged consumption of a growing proportion of imported entertainment programs (first from COMECON and later from Western countries), which in turn contributed to the depoliticization of previously overpoliticized media offerings. Most visible was the gradual Westernization of entertainment programs on television. Successful domestic radio call-in and order-a-song shows were also subversive in their own way insofar as they encouraged audience participation.

In short, as part of the regionwide de-Stalinization initiative, both elite publications in the arts and sciences and popular culture were gradually subjected to fewer ideological constraints in Hungary and other Central and Eastern European countries. At the same time, ideological indoctrination and aggressive penetration into the private sphere disappeared. Political news coverage, by contrast, was still extremely centralized, continued to communicate a wide range of public taboos, and, by repeating party slogans and Soviet media messages, remained ritualistic.

LIBERALIZATION AND THE DUAL MEDIA SYSTEM, 1976–88

I have chosen 1976 as the starting date for this period because this was approximately the time when the party-state communications monopoly was broken as a growing number of independent sources and channels of media communications surfaced in Poland, Hungary, and Czechoslovakia. A significant proportion of these independent communications networks functioned illegally, creating a "second public sphere" of independent and foreign media. In Poland, Hungary, and Czechoslovakia, illegal networks of intellectuals who exchanged uncensored typewritten or mimeographed papers emerged from the mid-1970s on. The first original typewritten *samizdat* (literally meaning "self-published" in Russian) volumes were published in Hungary in 1976. At the next level of organization, illegal publishing houses were created in Poland in the late 1970s, and in Hungary in the early 1980s. This progressive dilution of state control of mass communications was accelerated in the 1980s by the private importation of new media technologies from the West, including VCRs and satellite dish antennae.

In East Central Europe's state-socialist societies, a new, oppositional, and largely illegal political elite emerged to challenge traditional Communist elites. Organizations like Poland's KOR (Workers' Defense Committee) and Solidarity, Czechoslovakia's Charter 77, and Hungary's democratic opposition ultimately emerged as part of the new political elite in the post-Communist democracies, and by creating a rival, largely illegal media system, they broke the Communists' longstanding communications monopoly and fundamentally changed the dynamics of political communications.

Two distinct dimensions can be distinguished within these dual media systems. One differentiates official from illegal channels of information flow, while the other juxtaposes overtly political against entertainment (not openly political) communications.[3] On the basis of these two dimensions, we can distinguish four types of media: official versus illegal political communications and official versus illegal entertainment programs. Within each of these sectors, key characteristics of the media (regarding ownership patterns, control mechanisms, legal status, agendas, the quality of information, the tendency toward bias, and political uses and effects) interacted in different ways. This pattern of complexity meant, effectively, that the state's monopoly had ceased to exist. I will proceed by analyzing each sector separately.

THE OFFICIAL POLITICAL MEDIA: These media continued to be owned and controlled in large part by the party-state. At the same time, however, the liberalization of elite culture proceeded apace, with the result that the extent of state censorship became dependent on the size of the potential audience and the type of medium. The larger the audience for a particular medium or message, the more heavily censored it remained. Prime-time news programs on television and radio fell into this category: daily *nomenklatura* directives, self-censorship, and other old mechanisms of control continued to define their required modes of coverage. To a somewhat lesser extent, large-circulation dailies also preserved their official monolithic value system, centralized structure, and tight political control.

Conversely, the smaller the circulation of or audience for the newspaper or television program, the freer of censorship it became. Late-night discussion programs on television, radio talk shows, and programs for specialized audiences (for example, literature or social science programs) became relatively autonomous. Several low-circulation, elite cultural book series, journals, and newsletters were also established during the 1980s. Their publishers included not only state-owned publishing houses, but also universities or university departments, semiautonomous college dormitories that offered educational courses (*szakkollégium*), semi-institutionalized cultural groups, and even some Communist League organizations

In Hungary, the pluralistic values and opinions originally characteristic of only the smaller-circulation media slowly infiltrated the mass media over the course of the 1980s as the frontiers of what could be said publicly were pushed further back each year. One expansionist strategy was for some journalists and editors in the large-circulation media to cover issues on the fringes of legality by referring to topics that had been discussed in the lower-circulation press, on talk shows, and so on. The structural opportunity for such expansionism was provided by the gradual liberalization of elite culture by a Communist regime that assumed that its clientelist patronage would coopt cultural elites and keep liberalization within well-defined limits.

The erosion of taboos and self-censorship that accelerated from the mid-1980s on was due mostly to Gorbachev's policy of *glasnost,* which invited discussion of topics like economic stagnation, organized crime, drug abuse, the misuse of power by local functionaries, the Afghanistan war, and historical personalities such as Trotsky and Bucharin. Once such discussions were allowed in the Soviet Union, it became impossible for media *nomenklatura* in Central and Eastern Europe to continue their oft-voiced claim that they could not transgress Moscow's rigid censorship norms. The way was opened to criticize aspects of socialism as it was practiced, to discuss different political alternatives, and to offer less bounded analyses of international affairs and domestic social problems. The eventual result was a structural criticism of state socialism in both Hungary and Poland.

THE ILLEGAL POLITICAL MEDIA: The emergence and rapid growth of an illegal political media network from about 1976 on included clandestine publication of written, visual, and audio materials in Poland, Czechoslovakia, Hungary, the Soviet Union, and Romania. Despite their low circulation, their regular reports on human rights violations and independent political programs became well known among a wide range of social groups during the 1980s (Bugajski 1987). Western radio broadcasts, especially the U.S.-backed Radio Free Europe/Radio Liberty that broadcast in all Eastern European languages, often quoted or repeated them, thereby increasing the audience for and impact of the illegal political media. Democratic oppositions were thus able to create a new public discourse beyond the limits of the party-states' control. They formed a critical public sphere, in the true Habermasian sense that democratic and even openly oppositional values could develop and be popularized, and opposition personalities and political experts could be introduced to the general public (Habermas 1989). Western diplomatic and economic pressure on the Polish and Hungarian governments also contributed significantly to the continuation of political liberalization policies, since both countries faced an international debt crisis and needed new loans to finance their debt.

Not surprisingly, changes in the number of *samizdat* publications did not go without an official response. In Hungary, editors of illegal journals found themselves the objects of intensive political police surveillance, regular phone tapping, frequent home raids, short-term detainment, trials, fines, and threats. All these actions clearly indicated that the regime recognized that, in the long run, illegal media activities, along with other forms of opposition activism, posed a great potential threat to its power, even though illegal publications reached a relatively small, elite audience. In Poland and Czechoslovakia, political repression was harsher and included long prison terms for such leading activists as Adam Michnik and Václav Hável.

The creation of the dual media system closely reflected political, social, and economic changes in East Central European societies, that is, the reemergence of civil societies and their later transformation into political societies. The underground *samizdat* media sector played an important role in setting a democratic agenda, the most important issue of which was human rights violations. Illegal political media also served as a catalyst for the development of opposition organizations, democratic discourse, programs, and political alternatives. Finally, they selected and made known potential new leaders who, as well as being trusted, excelled in theoretical insight, political program building, and/or organizational skills and capacities. Leaders and readers formed networks linked by communication media and underground organizations. Over the course of the 1980s, the illegal media's influence was strengthened in both Hungary and Poland by the gradual development of links with the official media. This development progressed in stages, gradually evolving from increased attention to issues raised initially in the illegal sector, to direct citation of illegal publications in the official media, to outright legalization of those publications.

THE OFFICIAL ENTERTAINMENT MEDIA: The domestication of Western radio and television genres defined late Communist media culture as party policy makers mixed propaganda and entertainment in an effort to coat the pill of political messages. Television and radio targeted specific audience groups (consumers, children, teenagers, car lovers, pop and rock music fans, etc.) with informative and entertaining programs (Lévai 1987, 54). Audiences were presented with direct political propaganda and cultural favorites in the same program, while the medium itself was legitimized by the apparent trustworthiness and friendliness of the programs and their hosts.

From the early 1980s on, westernization characterized the popular culture scene in East Central Europe as Western, and especially American, popular culture flowed into the region, eventually to become mainstream. In a program environment dominated by party-state policies, the broadcasting of Western cultural products clearly resulted from decisions taken at the highest political levels to allow further liberalization of popular culture as a means of depoliticization. Liberalization was especially evident in Yugoslavia, Hungary, Poland, and, to a lesser extent, Czechoslovakia. (In East Germany, much stricter cultural policies did not prevent a significant part of the population from regularly watching West German television.)

An audience poll conducted in 1983 in the ethnically mixed region of southern Slovakia (see Andras 1984, 13–14) presents striking evidence of both the extent of transborder media communication and the overwhelmingly greater popularity of Western-made entertainment programs over East European- and Soviet-made ones. In this region, over 90 percent of the population could receive Czech television channels, around 80 percent could get Hungarian ones, and just over 50 percent could get Austrian ones (Eduard 1984, 8). A clear preference for Western popular culture was apparent: American, French, Italian, and British programs were consistently preferred over those produced in the Eastern bloc. Among the various ethnic groups represented in this survey sample, preferences for American programming ranged from 55 to 82 percent, 49 to 81 percent liked French programs, Italian shows were preferred by 47 to 71 percent, and 43 to 66 percent liked British programs. In sharp contrast, preferences for Soviet programs ranged from 14 to 33 percent, Czechoslovak shows were preferred by 24 to 40 percent, programs made in Poland by 8 to 18 percent, and those from Bulgaria and Romania lagged even farther behind. Only Hungarian minorities in Slovakia departed slightly from this pattern, with as 43 to 57 percent watching Hungarian programs, but even among this group, Western shows were much more popular (with preferences for British, Italian, French, and American programs ranging between 57 and 82 percent). These data reflect the deep dissatisfaction with the East bloc–made entertainment programs and represent a rejection of the international state-socialist culture industry, despite its decreasing propaganda content and its heavy state subsidization.

The effort to gain political legitimacy by allowing a greater privatization of lifestyles through access to private entertainment clearly failed, and at least part of the reason for this failure is that the official entertainment media remained state-owned, politically regulated, and censored. Censorship norms may have slowly relaxed with liberalization, but certain genres, like pornography and violent action movies, remained absolutely taboo for Communist policy makers and were not shown. A vacuum was thereby created, and a black market in certain entertainment genres grew up to fill it. In this way, the official importation of Western popular culture resulted in a spiraling of demand for the forbidden fruit that, in turn, encouraged the growth of an illegal entertainment sphere.

THE ILLEGAL ENTERTAINMENT MEDIA: The dual media system of East Central Europe included an illegal entertainment sector whose ownership structure, control mechanisms, contents, and functions were different from those of the three other sectors just characterized. Illegal entertainment activities all over the region included profit-motivated smuggling, copying, distribution, and consumption of those popular culture products not available officially. Illegal networks circulated such banned genres as pornography, horror, vampire, zombie, and action movies on videocassettes. The illegal video business was especially lively in Poland and Hungary. Its main actors were black-market entrepreneurs who were also involved in other businesses such as boutique fashion or small-scale export-import. In the illegal entertainment sector, private ownership was dominant, and this sphere was controlled exclusively by illegal market rules. (As a result of economic reforms, private video rentals were gradually legalized around 1990.)

Thus, it is important to distinguish among four sectors in analyses of the media systems in Hungary and Poland in the 1980s. The official media remained basically state-owned, state-controlled, subsidized, and censored, while the independent media became privately owned, uncensored, and partly market-oriented. The main political goal of the official political media was to secure political consolidation, and to support and legitimize the party-state as well as Soviet domination. The cooptation of reformist intellectuals into this subsector in Hungary, however, partially subverted this goal and allowed the publication of more pluralistic values and criticism. In contrast, the illegal political media criticized the existing dictatorial power structures, exposed abuses of power, and documented human rights violations. They also introduced and crystallized political alternatives. The official entertainment media sought to encourage regime stability by depoliticizing and demobilizing the general public. This required the legitimation of party-controlled radio and television institutions by presenting them as trustworthy sources of audience-friendly entertainment and valuable information. And in the fourth media sector, illegal entrepreneurs simply wanted to secure a profit – a new element in the media history of state socialism.

DEMOCRATIC TRANSITION AND/BY THE MEDIA 1988–90

Several important changes paved the way for the transition from Communism in East Central Europe in the late 1980s. The key event was Gorbachev's relaxation of Soviet oversight of the region beginning in the mid-1980s. After his meeting with U.S. President George Bush in Malta in 1989, the possibility of Soviet withdrawal from the occupied countries frequently figured in public discussions in the region. Ruling Communist parties reacted differently to the new Soviet moderation. Two basically different paths were followed in their countries' transitions to democracy – negotiation and revolution. Poland and Hungary took the first path, with face-to-face (or roundtable) negotiations between delegations of the Communist party-state and the democratic opposition clearing the way for pluralist elections (Bruszt 1992; Bozóki and Sükösd 1993). These negotiations took place in April 1989 in Poland and between May and September 1989 in Hungary. The revolutionary path was followed in the winter of 1989 in East Germany, Czechoslovakia, and Romania, and later in Albania, where unrest and mass mobilization swept away the Communist regimes.

In Hungary, standing differences between reformers and hardliners led to a split in the Communist Party leadership and its breakup into separate socialist and Communist parties. This began at a stormy party congress in 1988 with the removal of János Kádár by a short-lived coalition of party hardliners and reformists. An open fight soon broke out between the two factions, which had sharply different policy plans for overcoming Hungary's deepening economic and political crisis. The result was a schism in October 1989 in which the Hungarian Socialist Workers' Party was dissolved and transformed into the reformist Hungarian Socialist Party.

Between 1988 and 1990, independent political organizations, including parties, legally established themselves, competed openly for power with the Communist Party, and prepared for free elections. Communist censorship ended,[4] partial privatization of the press took place (especially in Hungary), and both governments allowed the state broadcasting system to cover independent organizations. Previously clandestine political, economic, and cultural activities had become legal and legitimate in both countries.

In the course of both the Polish and Hungarian 1988–90 transitions, then, bottom-up political democratization meshed with top-down liberalization of the press, including the abolition of censorship. A large independent press (especially news weeklies and local papers) emerged, although the vast majority of high-circulation newspapers, as well as national television and radio, remained under weakening party and government control. Nonetheless, the power vacuum presented an opportunity for many journalists to assert themselves as advocates of pluralization and democratization, while others remained faithful to the old regime. In terms of media content, the unrestricted political agenda of *samizdat* surfaced in the legal (official) public sphere and the two formerly separated public spheres merged into one.

Three changes were of particular importance in the radical liberalization of the media that took place between 1988 and 1990. First, the privatization laws passed by the last, reformist Communist Parliament opened the way for the large-scale private ownership of the print media for the first time in 40 years. Second, the abolition of the *nomenklatura* system in 1989 freed the media from official control, and the liberated media jettisoned practically all political taboos that had constrained them previously. Third, the ownership structure of the press was radically transformed. New, for-profit and privately owned dailies and weeklies were established following replacement of the licensing system by a simple registration process. Of the roughly 3,000 registered periodicals that existed in 1992 (including dailies, weeklies, journals, and book series), almost two-thirds had been established after 1988.[5] The overwhelming majority of these new newspapers and periodicals had local Hungarian owners, typically private entrepreneurs, local branches of state-owned firms, and editors and journalists. Many cable television networks were established and operated by municipal governments, local entrepreneurs, and editor-turned-managers or joint ventures of these actors.

Privatization of party-controlled newspapers also made way for the entry into the Hungarian media market of foreign investors, mostly European multinational corporations, attracted by the sizable networks of advertisers and subscribers of those papers. They radically changed the ownership structure of the Hungarian media system. Initially, multinational media moguls were allowed to buy only a minority share of the newspapers. Another minority bloc of shares was kept by the state or the party, and the third (smallest) portion went to the editors. In the later stages of privatization, economic pressures by multinationals enabled them to acquire majority ownership.

Rapid privatization was in the interests of the *nomenklatura* and the incumbent editors, in part because it allowed both to escape from the party-state while at the same time avoiding dismissal by the incoming anti-Communist government. In addition, former *nomenklatura* clients of Western investors were offered top managerial positions for their help in effectuating a smooth and profitable transfer from party-state ownership to private ownership. Economically powerful Western owners could also offer a promise of economic stability and competitive salaries and could underwrite the modernization of the technologically backward newspaper industry (which, until 1990, even lacked computers).

Unlike its treatment of the press, the government neither privatized the state-owned broadcast media nor distributed frequencies for new, private ventures. The period leading up to the 1990 election campaign focused attention on the issue of political control over broadcast media still monopolized by the state. Especially sensitive was the issue of media access for the opposition parties. The two national television channels and three radio stations had been under strong party-state control, but the national roundtable negotiations between the Communist Party and opposition organizations represent a turning point in national media policy. In their wake, Communist ideological directives and political taboos rapidly disappeared in both Hungary and Poland. The way was opened for democratic, pluralist elections. Agreement could not be reached in Hungary, however, on a new media law or other legal mechanisms to ensure the independence of the public media. The only outcome they were able to produce was a general statement on the "Principles of Impartial Mass Communication" for the Hungarian News Agency, Hungarian Television, and Hungarian Radio as "national public service institutions." The statement declared that different political forces, actions, and statements would be treated equally and that journalists would refrain from letting their political leanings influence their reporting of the news.

Party elites were unable to reach agreement, however, on the composition and structure of a Committee for Impartial Communications that would monitor media performance during the election campaign. This stimulated numerous intraorganizational conflicts in which members of the old media *nomenklatura,* as well as reform-minded or opposition journalists, allied themselves openly with different political leaders and parties. The national media did not come close to the Western ideal of objective, nonpartisan coverage.

Top party leaders also struggled for control over the content of television's coverage of political matters. Although Imre Pozsgay (the reform-Communist state minister responsible for media affairs and later Socialist Party presidential candidate) gradually loosened central control and ideological censorship, the opposition removed him after the roundtable negotiations. As the result of a political deal between the (ex-Communist) Socialist Party and the moderate opposition Hungarian Democratic Forum (HDF) – which won the subsequent elections – Posgay's protégé, István G. Pálfy, was appointed chief editor of key news programs. As part of the Socialist-HDF deal, the two parties tried to limit coverage of the rival opposition party, the then radical anti-Communist

Free Democrats. Campaign coverage was influenced to a minor degree, but prearranged advertising time gave the other parties and independent organizations significant opportunities for media exposure.

MEDIA EFFECTS AND THE TRANSITION TO DEMOCRACY

In this period, characterized by rapid political pluralization, democratization, party formation, and preparation for democratic elections, the media played several extremely important roles. The first involved *democratic agenda setting.* By telling readers, listeners, and viewers "what to think about" (McCombs and Shaw 1972), the media define certain social and political issues as important, creating a context that helps the audience to order and organize the political world. This was an especially important role for the media in an Eastern Europe where crucial topics had totally evaded public discussion for four (or, in the Soviet Union, seven) decades. When combined with the public's hunger for information about these topics, the media's ability to fill this vacuum meant that their agenda-setting role was much more pronounced and sharply evident than it is in established democracies, where such topics are covered regularly. By expanding their scope of news coverage and opinion pieces to cover hitherto taboo topics, the media contributed to the setting of an open-ended, democratic, and pluralist political agenda. Moreover, it was an agenda that helped the opposition forces, partly because it largely overlapped with their reform agenda and partly because many of the issues on this agenda could be viewed as valence issues overwhelmingly favorable to them (such as national independence, calls for further democratization, criticism of the failures of state-control of the economy, and one-party rule) rather than position issues on which voters can take pro or con stances.[6] The party disadvantaged by the new democratic agenda throughout East Central Europe was the ex-Communist Party. No matter how deeply committed to change ex-Communist leaders declared themselves to be, and no matter how much they publicly expressed regret for some of their earlier actions, voters well remembered their record and their unchanging positions on many crucial issues not previously open to public debate. More generally, media freedom contributed substantially to the delegitimation of the regime.

The *development of civil society and political parties* was also facilitated by the media during this crucial period. In response to gradually decreasing dictatorship and terror, hundreds of civic groups emerged onto the political scene between 1987 and 1988. These groups quickly obtained legal status and developed into a web of civil society that was the prerequisite for the emergence of political society. Among them were groups that would subsequently become political parties, such as the HDF, which first emerged as a social movement in 1987 but subsequently won the first election, to become the senior governing party between 1990 and 1994. Others included the Network of Free Initiatives, which later became the liberal Alliance of Free Democrats and formed a minority government between 1994 and 1998, and the Alliance of Young Democrats, which won the 1998 election. Other civic groups born during this period included independent trade unions, democratic discussion clubs, and ecological groups. Journalists played a key role in the legalization of civic groups by presenting them in an impartial and sometimes even a sympathetic manner, in sharp contrast with the old Communist practice of labeling them as criminals. The media also increasingly reported on their events and disseminated their political communications to the public, not only giving them a public presence, a public identity, and an opportunity for interested citizens to join, but also contributing to the legitimation and pluralization of civic groups and the strengthening and development of civil society. In effect, the Hungarian media helped to rescue the democratic opposition from the small and relatively closed "intellectual ghetto" to which it had been relegated over the preceding decades. Eventually, the media played a crucial role in making the political programs, policy alternatives, and leaders of the new parties known to the emerging Hungarian electorate. Some newspapers offered free space for classified advertising of the meetings of parties, their addresses, the names of contact persons, and so on. A special wire service (Országos Sajtószolgálat, the National Press Service) was established exclusively for conveying the messages and statements of parties and other political and civic organizations. Coverage of party meetings, rallies, and mass demonstrations also helped to mobilize the population for participation in the new democracy and its first pluralist election, and to resocialize them to embrace democratic values.

A *personalization of politics* also resulted from media coverage of politics. Most of Hungary's parties were founded by individuals (including writers, law students, and academics) previously unknown to the general public. The last pluralist elections had been held in 1947, with very few of the democratic political leaders of that era surviving the 40 years of Communism. By presenting the new generation of leaders to the public, the media helped to "personalize" politics in the positive sense of introducing hitherto unknown individuals to voters as potential new political leaders; linking them to parties, programs, policies, statements,

145

and symbols; and bestowing greater authority and responsibility on them.[7] For example, Viktor Orbán, leader of the Young Democrats, became widely known through coverage of his fierce anti-Communist speech in 1989 at the reburial ceremony of the revolutionary Prime Minister Imre Nagy (who was executed after the 1956 revolution). Both television (which broadcast live coverage of the speech) and the press (which reflected on Orbán's speech for weeks) played important roles in this process. The media also personalized politics through their roles in the candidate selection process, providing voters with important information about candidates and the groups that supported them. This candidate selection process was sometimes affected by media coverage of factional struggles within parties and their ultimate (re)organization and consolidation. Some party leaders (like Anna Petrasovits of the Social Democrats) proved unable to solve internal leadership crises and were effectively "deselected" by the media and the public. The final role of the press in personalizing politics had both positive and negative implications for popular support for the new democracy. Exposeés of the opulent lifestyles of the former Communist elite by new tabloid newspapers produced a populist backlash against the growing inequality in Hungarian society at the same time that it (rather paradoxically) helped to legitimate glamorous consumer capitalism and to redefine success.

Finally, by covering crucial political events of great symbolic importance, the mass media reinforced and legitimized the *symbolic appropriation of the national past* and democratic traditions by the new democratic parties. The most important of these were live coverage in 1989 of the reburial ceremony for Prime Minister Nagy, the March 15 rallies commemorating the anti-Habsburg revolution and war of independence in 1848, and the October 23 demonstrations in memory of the 1956 revolution (Dayan and Katz 1992)

The symbolic and real impact of the media in the Hungarian transition is perhaps best illustrated by its role in an event that transpired in 1990. Not only did news coverage of political scandal help to dislodge the post-Communist government from power, helping to complete the transition to democracy, but it also stood as a symbol of how far political change in Hungary had progressed. Indeed, it would not be an exaggeration to assert that media coverage of government scandals can occur only in democratic contexts. The appearance of such coverage in Central and Eastern Europe was a clear indication that democratization was underway and indicated that the Communist regime did not have enough power to control its own media or avoid the establishment and empowerment of truly independent new media. More broadly, the significance of some media campaigns for processes of political change (such as in Italy and Japan) suggests that "scandology" deserves a place in the broader field of "transitology."

The scandal in question broke in early 1990. In the winter of 1989, at the height of the first democratic election campaign period, a high-ranking secret service official leaked information to a journalist indicating that the political police still monitored the activities of democratic opposition leaders, and that government members (leaders of the Socialist Party) still received secret service reports about their opponents, including information on their election strategies. This was illegal and contradicted both the spirit and the letter of the national roundtable agreements. The official then smuggled the journalist and a cameraman into the cellars of the national secret-police headquarters, where they videotaped documents showing the illegal information-gathering practices. The press conference at which the videotapes were presented was widely covered by the media, and the case remained a top story for weeks. The resulting criticism not only discredited the Socialist Party but was formulated in systemic terms. It was widely argued that a one-party system without checks and balances inevitably produce such practices. The media framed the case in terms of "constitutionalism versus Socialist Party hegemony" and "old moles' repression of the democratic opposition." It should not be forgotten that, at this time, Hungary still had a one-party Parliament. In this situation, the media alone played the role of the major democratic institution. And they played it well. As a result of this scandal (called Danubegate – *Dunagate* in Hungarian), the interior minister resigned, indicating that a major change had taken place: the rule of law had prevailed over that of the party-state. The scandal also helped to swing public opinion from the ex-Communist Party to the democratic parties just before March 1990 election.

ELECTIONS AND DEMOCRATIC CHANGE

Hungary's first democratic election of the 1990s was not only a relatively rare event (the only other truly free vote of the postwar era occurring in the 1945 election), but it they also carried much greater weight than elections in established democracies. The very rules of the political game and the constitution and structures of the new democratic system had yet to be worked out, and these would be significantly affected by the outcome of the first two elections of the 1990s. Indeed, the path of future political development would be largely defined by the winners of these first democratic contests. Among the important structural features of the new democracies that would be decided were the choice between the presidential and parliamentary forms of government and the basic features of the electoral law and the party system. The stakes were thus extremely high.

The two major electoral contests of the Hungarian transition to democracy were the referendum of November 1989 and the first parliamentary election in the spring of 1990. The referendum was to resolve four issues. The first largely determined whether Hungary would adopt a presidential or parliamentary system. Voters were asked to answer the following question: "Should the president of the Republic be elected only after parliamentary elections?" The other three referendum votes involved a reduction in the power and autonomy of the Communist Party. Ballot items dealt with the withdrawal of party organizations from workplaces, disbanding of the Workers' Guard, and a call for the Communist Party to give a public accounting of the property it owned and managed. The fact that the referendum was called was itself a significant political development, indicating that the Communist Party was no longer capable of determining the country's political agenda: it was initiated largely by two radical opposition groups – the Free Democrats and the Young Democrats – and it posed a radical alternative to the partial democratization that might otherwise have resulted. Indeed, the Free Democrats and Young Democrats demonstrated impressive organizational skills by gathering the necessary 100,000 signatures in less than a month, indicating that there was substantial public support for radical democratization and popular participation in systemwide change.

The three referendum items reducing the power of the Communist Party were each overwhelmingly endorsed by about 95 percent of the voters. In contrast, the referendum on the timing of presidential and parliamentary elections was decided by the razor-thin margin of 50.07 versus 49.93 percent in favor of holding parliamentary elections first. This was an extraordinarily important vote because it precluded a likely election victory by the ex-Communist Imre Pozsgay, who might have used his power as president to constrain the subsequent course of the country's political evolution. The referendum's outcome delegitimized Communist rule and the possibility of partial democratization. It also had the long-term effect of institutionalizing a parliamentary system in Hungary – in sharp contrast with the presidential and semipresidential forms of government adopted in most of the other post-Communist countries of Central and Eastern Europe.

The mass media served as central institutions in the public debate over the referendum. While coverage in news and discussion programs was somewhat biased in favor of the positions advocated by the Socialists (which is not surprising, since the electronic media were still state-controlled), television granted free air time to newly organized parties (to all registered parties on the first round of broadcasts and to only those parties presenting candidate lists on the second round) and allowed the purchase of air time for political advertisements. The national television network provided professional assistance on request but did not interfere with the content of the party-sponsored programs. The Free Democrats made the most of the pay-for-air-time option and produced commercials (the first TV ads in the country's history) featuring popular actors like Iván Darvas (who had been imprisoned for his active participation in the 1956 revolution) and pop singers to appeal to the baby boom generation. Television coverage was of considerable significance in this referendum campaign. Since voters had no previous party record or past performance on which to base their decisions, they had to rely to a much greater extent than in established democracies on the televised campaign itself.

DEMOCRATIC EDUCATION BY THE MEDIA

During the transition to democracy, the media played a central role in disseminating democratic values, concepts, and skills. Both abstract democratic concepts and the everyday procedures and reality of pluralist democracy were presented to audiences in advance of what was, for most Hungarians, the first democratic election in their lives. Given the general lack of such participatory experience, the media's presentation of information about democratic practices and information about political alternatives, new parties, and their leaders was of considerable importance in forging a new democratic culture.

The resocialization of the Hungarian population had several distinct dimensions. First, citizens generally came to understand that pluralism is preferable to one-party rule, that democracy is morally superior to dictatorship, and that pluralism and democracy could become a reality in their country after decades of Communist rule. Second, they were made aware of what strategies the major parties were advancing. During the 1988–9 period, for example, ex-Communist Party leaders increasingly talked about introducing democracy, but what they really had in mind was a limited form of pluralism based on a strategic alliance with satellite parties of the moderate opposition under a strong socialist president in a presidential system. Public discourse in the media revealed the true nature of these intentions and presented to voters the more truly democratic alternative that the radical democratic opposition was proposing. This was particularly important with regard to discussions of institutional alternatives leading up to the referendum. Thus, voters gained a clearer understanding of the fundamental constitutional issues that were at stake. The media also helped to educate the public by giving them practical information concerning their roles as voters: previously, they had been unfamiliar with details relevant to the electoral law, party lists, the structure of electoral districts, candidate selection procedures, and even basic information about how to vote. Finally, publication of historical accounts of democratic movements, parties, and personalities from previous periods in Hungarian history (especially in 1918, 1945–7, and 1956) gave citizens a vision of history that differed distinctly from that presented under the former regime. In short, the newly democratized media provided an opportunity to reevaluate and rewrite history from a democratic and pluralist perspective.

DEMOCRATIC CONSOLIDATION AND/BY THE MEDIA 1990–7

Different evolutionary paths have been taken by Central and Eastern European countries during the post-Communist period. Hungary's is unique in terms of both politics and media economics. One significant difference is the relative stability of the Hungarian party system and the composition of the Hungarian Parliament. This is the only country in the region (aside from the exceptional case of East Germany) where the first democratically elected government remained in office until as late as 1994. Throughout the first full decade of Hungarian democracy, moreover, there was little change in the structure of the party system or the identity of the leading parties. This party-system stability is partly a product of the fact that parties had the opportunity to establish themselves over a two-year period (1988–90) prior to the first election. In contrast with the first partisan contests in several Eastern and Central European countries, this relatively long evolutionary period gave parties sufficient time to establish themselves, set up organizations, select leaders, formulate public identities, crystallize their respective party programs, and mobilize voters. In other post-Communist countries, party formation typically began *after* the first pluralist elections at which large umbrella organizations (the Solidarity trade union, popular fronts, or loose movements) represented the opposition.

Three distinct periods of Hungarian democratic consolidation can be identified: 1990–4, 1994–8, and after 1998. The 1990 elections were won by the HDF (which had by then evolved into a center-right conservative party), with the Free Democrats finishing second. Three conservative-national parties formed a majority coalition government headed by HDF Prime Minister Josef Antall. The two liberal parties (the Free Democrats and the Young Democrats) and the Socialist Party remained in opposition. This low level of party-system fragmentation and government stability stands in contrast with the situation in some neighboring countries.[8] While these structural features augured well for democratic consolidation, the government introduced and pursued authoritarian media policies that represented a challenge to the consolidation process and to the basic quality of the emerging democracy.

This situation changed significantly after the 1994 election, which was won by the Socialists, who formed a center-left coalition with their former opponents, the Free Democrats. Authoritarian media policies were discontinued, and in 1996 a media law was finally passed. I will argue that the media played a significant role in the consolidation of democracy by resisting government pressures between 1990 and 1994, by disseminating democratic values, and by legitimating consumer capitalism. This positive influence of the media had a broad impact – on civil society, political society, the rule of law, the state apparatus, and the economy (Linz and Stepan 1996, 14). Since 1998, under the Young Democrats' government, the media have played an important role in resisting majoritarian democratic pressures and encouraging discussion of public affairs in a manner that bodes well for the quality of democracy in Hungary.

PRESS PRIVATIZATION BY GERMAN AND AUSTRIAN INVESTORS

Hungary differs from all post-Communist countries in that its media market has the highest proportion of foreign ownership in the region. Between 1990 and 1994, the print media were privatized almost completely. In the case of national newspapers that had been partially privatized during the previous period, foreign minority owners (including the Bertelsmann, Murdoch, and Maxwell firms) gained majority ownership. As for the regional press, in 1990–1 most of the 19 ex-Communist dailies were taken over from the Socialist Party by foreign investors, including

Axel Springer (who bought nine regional dailies in Central Hungary), the *Westdeutsche Allgemeine Zeitungsverlag* (four newspapers in the Western region), and the Austrian *Funk, Verlag und Druckerei* (three papers in the East). Two other foreign investors (Nice Press and Associated Newspapers) acquired one regional newspaper each. Only one regional daily was nationalized by the state, and a tabloid and several weeklies are owned by Postabank (partially owned by Hungarian state and multinational banks). Most of the Hungarian-owned small local papers that were established during the press boom of 1988–9 did not survive the competition with the newly privatized, large-circulation ex-Communist dailies. Thus, most of the print media, including the major national newspapers, are owned by Western investors. This economic dependence raises questions concerning control of Hungary's print media by foreign investors who may be more interested in profits than in quality journalism.

On the positive side, however, majority foreign ownership has made these publications independent of potential government interference – which became significant in 1990–4 when the center-right government attempted to control the media and compel the state-owned press to take a progovernment stance. This media strategy led the editors of a number of Hungarian papers to leave state-owned publishing houses in 1990. Western ownership provided protection against government and party interference.

Media War: The Struggle over Government Control of Broadcasting, 1990–4

National public channels completely dominated the radio and television broadcasting systems until 1997. Indeed, until that time, there were no national commercial television stations and only four large commercial radio stations – two of them entirely or partly state-owned. A few private studios rented air space from the two national public channels for the production of morning news programs, talk shows, and entertainment programs, but by and large, the public media retained a near monopoly of the air waves. Beginning in 1989, a number of entrepreneurs (including media giants like Silvio Berlusconi) expressed interest in applying for licenses to operate television or radio stations, and they lobbied legislators to pass a media law that would allow for the issuance of new frequencies to the private sector. However, media legislation was not passed during the first democratically elected Parliament. The government distributed a few local frequencies in a constitutionally and legally questionable way (on the basis of Culture Ministry decrees), leading to the establishment of local and regional radio and televisions stations during the mid-1990s. Most local TV stations were sponsored by city governments, although local radio stations also became commercial.

Considerable efforts were also initiated to reform the state-owned national broadcasting system and make it resemble the public-service networks of such established Western European democracies as the British Broadcasting Corporation and the German public media. Following the first democratic elections in the spring of 1990, the six parties represented in Parliament agreed on the appointment of new presidents of the public media systems. Accordingly, sociologist Elemér Hankiss and political scientist Csaba Gombár – both prominent democratic intellectuals and public figures – became the heads of the public television and radio systems, respectively. Their main tasks were "to steer a middle course between the governing parties and the opposition and ensure the impartiality of the two media institutions" (Hankiss 1996, 245). Both new presidents initiated profound changes in the internal structure of public media so as to transform them from party-state media to Western European-type public media. Hankiss reduced the number of television employees and created a system of independent producers selling programs to public television at a market price. He also separated the two channels in order to stimulate programming diversity and innovation and to encourage them to compete for advertising. Likewise, Gombár separated the three public radio stations (Kossuth primarily for news and public affairs programs, Petőfi for entertainment, and Bartók for classical music and highbrow culture) and appointed new station directors. These changes evoked a storm of criticism from the government, and Hankiss and Gombár (acting in the absence of a new media law) were accused of overstepping their authority.

These were the first volleys of a war that was to turn into a long, bitter, and divisive political conflict over control of the post-Communist media. Indeed, between 1990 and 1994, the most heated and continuous political debate centered on control of public media and the press. Controversy erupted over the government's right to interfere directly in the broadcasts and organization of public media and over the supposed hostility and liberal bias of journalists.

Soon after the first democratic election, it became obvious that the new coalition government and its leading party, the HDF, was extremely sensitive to press criticism. Its members, from rank-and-file to top leadership, railed against the press in general and certain privatized papers in particular, labeling them oppositional, antigovernment, ex-Communist or "Judeo-Bolshevik-liberal." This reaction reflected the HDF's underlying philosophy that the major newspapers and public media should serve the democratically elected government since it represents the majority of voters. Accordingly, Prime Minister Antall repeatedly attempted to remove the two media presidents, but he was consistently foiled by President Arpad Göncz's veto. The battle did not stop there, however. In the spring of 1992, Antall succeeded in appointing vice-presidents of national television and radio to limit the presidents' independence. Debate continued to rage concerning the relative authority of the prime minister and the president to appoint and fire media presidents. The Constitutional Court made five decisions in the case, but none of them was sufficiently conclusive to quell the open conflict between the president of the Republic and the prime minister or to fill gaps in media regulation.

Open bias was apparent in television news programs edited by government supporters, especially the Sunday night weekly political program, A Hét (The Week). Several independent content analyses have demonstrated that coverage was regularly partisan and confrontational, that individuals critical of the government received little or no air time, and that anchors made negative comments about opposition leaders. While he was able to discipline partisan editors, television president Hankiss was unable to dismiss them because they enjoyed the support of the government. Even his introduction of a second news program in 1991 to balance the progovernment, right-wing news programs that were the norm on television had little effect. In the 1994 election campaign, television news programs were clearly biased in favor of the HDF. Some programs used anti-Semitic hints and remarks in their aggressive antiliberal campaign. A historical series entitled "Illegal Socialism" equated the Socialist Party with Stalinism. Bias in radio broadcasting was equally evident. Direct attacks on the opposition, the independent press, and the heads of public television and radio were common.

At the same time, government influence was also exercised through financial pressure. Tight budgetary constraints were imposed on the public media. In the 1992 budget debate, for example, the governing majority voted to withhold 1 billion HFTs (then worth approximately $13 million), which represented most of the state subsidy for public television. Great pressure was put on the television president to pursue a less independent line, but he responded by introducing more advertising. The use of public funds to create progovernment newspapers was another attempt to shape public opinion and another source of controversy. The launch of the progovernment, conservative *Új Magyarország* (*New Hungary*), a semiofficial daily, was made possible by government pressure on six partly state-owned banks and other state concerns to provide capital for Publica, the newspaper's newly created publishing house. The few papers that remained state-owned also turned strongly progovernment. Nor did individual journalists escape this struggle as a progovernment faction split off to form its own association opposed to press freedom.[9] The debate over press freedom even spilled into the streets. In September 1992, 15,000 progovernment supporters demanded the public television president's resignation, but a counter-rally of 60,000 people denounced their attacks and accusations, expressed solidarity with President Göncz, and supported, among other things, media freedom (Hankiss 1996, 252). Still, government pressure on the media continued.

Such disputes highlighted the inability of the government and the opposition to reach agreement on all aspects of media law. During the early 1990s, they had been able to do so on such major issues as the regulation of sponsorship, limits on advertising, the establishment of community or "public access" media, and quotas for Hungarian- and European-made programs. A consensus was also reached on the setting up of a new Radio and Television Commission (RTC) responsible for frequency allocation to commercial broadcasters and oversight of the media. The two sides, however, proved unable to resolve the question of how appointments were to be made to both the RTC and the public-service media. Government supporters argued that such appointments should be the prerogative of the prime minister, while the opposition argued that to avoid appointees' direct dependence on the government, the premier's nominees should receive the endorsement of either two-thirds of parliament or an independent supervisory board.

The government's position on the question of media freedom demonstrated clear authoritarian leanings, even though its actions were not always illegal in the strict sense of the word. The paradox was that, while the first post-Communist government and its supporters were committed to ridding Hungary of the practices of the Communist past and, at least verbally, to the separation of powers and fair and equal electoral competition, they were, in fact, relying on the former regime's techniques and regulatory decrees to further their own objectives. Thus, the first democratically elected Hungarian government's majoritarian view of democracy gave way to nondemocratic authoritarian practices regarding the media. The absence of regulation provided great opportunities for government intervention.

The opposition parties regularly criticized the government's media policies and called for enactment of a media law that would shield media organizations from government pressures and allocate frequencies impartially to commercial broadcasters. Many journalists (even within the public-sector media system) also resisted these authoritarian tendencies. Indeed, even though they often bowed to government pressure, the press and some broadcasters increasingly played the role of government watchdog. Journalists polarized between progovernment and opposition camps, with independent papers and broadcasts criticizing the authoritarian leanings of the government and providing news coverage of opposition parties and leaders. While this split in the journalistic elite provided the public with a broader array of views and opinions in the aggregate, it also entailed a progressive abandonment of journalistic objectivity.

Television and radio presidents Hankiss and Gombár openly resisted the prime minister's attempts to control public broadcasting. They also struggled to retain their jobs in the face of government pressure. Hankiss — accused of violating media regulations, commercializing and Americanizing Hungarian television, allowing journalists and editors to express overt criticism of the government, and ruining the old production workshops through his reorganization program — was required to defend his actions before Parliament's Culture Committee. The hearings were widely covered by television and newspapers. Instead of appearing defensive and victimized, Hankiss stood his ground and used the occasion as a civics lesson for the country. As he described it:

> It was an interesting exercise in learning about democracy. It was almost moving to see how governing party deputies, or at least some of them, struggled with their consciences – to see how they tried to squeeze their party interests (and their antipathies for this meddlesome television president) into the forms and strait jacket of legal rules. By that time, almost the whole country was watching. (Hankiss 1996, 251)

The minutes of the trial were published in a form and under circumstances reminiscent of the good old days of *samizdats*, and they became a best-seller overnight. Actors in a Budapest theater read passages of the minutes, with the audience roaring with laughter and indignation. The Media War became a political tragicomedy (Hankiss 1996, 255). More important, it served as a model for resistance of civil society against government interference with freedom of expression. Thousands of citizens participated in protest rallies organized by Democratic Charter (a political action committee), and civic and journalistic organizations were mobilized against the government's attacks on freedom of the press.

Those who watched may have understood, for the first time in their lives, that democracy was not an abstract construct comprising a few sublime ideas but simply a well-defined set of rules of the game. This "civics lesson" clearly indicated that a democratic polity needs well-defined rules accepted by all interested parties, as well as the willingness of its citizens to observe these rules even at the cost of their short-term interests. Coverage of these parliamentary debates significantly contributed to the diffusion of democratic values. Public opinion polls indicated that, even though many citizens dismissed the floor debates as fruitless, this intensive coverage disseminated knowledge about democratic procedures, important political issues (including tasks to be performed in the construction of a post-Communist democracy), and the policies and leaders of the various parties.

At the same time, however, this live coverage appears to have had the somewhat negative unintentional effect of demonstrating to members of Parliament that television coverage of these debates could be used as a publicity event. Instead of focusing on substantive policy discussions, they spoke to their media audiences and constituents. They learned the value of bon mots, rhetorical phrases, and even a body language developed especially for the cameras. Phrases were carefully crafted for inclusion as sound bites in the evening news.

LEGITIMATION OF PRIVATIZATION
AND CONSUMER CAPITALISM

Related to their role in the transformation of the Hungarian and East Central European political systems, the media also contributed to the legitimation of the economic transition to capitalism. Government-sponsored privatization generally enjoyed positive coverage by the media. Economic journalists, news reporters and opinion writers framed privatization and Western investment as the only viable alternative to bankruptcy under the inefficient state-controlled economy. The transition to a capitalist system was neutrally dubbed "economic modernization." Such anomalies as privatization-related corruption, and the lack of regulation and transparency of privatization, were rarely mentioned. Although social problems like the general impoverishment of society, decreasing real value of pensions, problems of economic survival for families with children, homelessness, and unemployment were often discussed, they were not linked to systemic changes in the economy. By framing economic reforms in this manner, media coverage generally supported and legitimized privatization and the transition to capitalism.

Advertising on television and radio, and in the press (which grew dramatically from the 1980s and especially during the 1990s), reinforced this legitimation in a more subtle way as well. A wide array of goods and services that had been unavailable under Communism, except as symbols of the Western lifestyle, were attractively presented as available consumer options. Audiences were bombarded with images and sounds of happy families, and colorful and successful lifestyles, all based on buying and consuming. Indeed, for a few years, Western-style ads became a real sensation in every Eastern European country: audiences watched them with the same attention they paid to regular programs. Later these ads became an ordinary experience, but by that time, the explosion of advertising had contributed to the positive framing and legitimation of consumer capitalism during the period of democratic consolidation.

MEDIA AND THE QUALITY OF DEMOCRACY, 1994–9

Despite biased, progovernment television and radio news programs, the popularity of opposition parties grew and far exceeded that of the government in the run-up to the 1994 election. Aggressive anti-Communist, antisocialist, and antiliberal propaganda backfired and, along with economic and other factors, helped turn the tide of public opinion in favor of the Socialist Party and the Free Democrats. After the 1994 election, these two parties formed a coalition government supported by a substantial parliamentary majority. Thus, alternation in government took place, removing would-be hegemonic parties from power and improving the prospects for democratic consolidation. In this period, a media law was finally passed that paved the way for the large-scale introduction of commercial media. Journalistic professionalism increased, and a new law on freedom of information offered greater transparency in government.

The media law that came into effect in 1996 elaborated an extremely sophisticated system of regulation ensuring the independence of public-service media, as well as a liberal distribution of new broadcasting frequencies to private firms. Remembering its own suspicion of government interference, the new Socialist-liberal government supported a bill that included strong guarantees of freedom of the press. Henceforth, the public media would be overseen by bodies in which parliamentary parties as well as civic groups were represented. Within this body, interparty consensus was facilitated by a representation formula that gave the opposition as much voting power as the governing parties. The membership-selection and decision-making formulas were the same in the National Radio and Television Commission (NRTC), the agency that regulates and oversees the media. The law also mandated public-service content quotas, and regulation of advertising and anticoncentration measures, and it liberalized registration of satellite, cable, and new network broadcasting systems (Cseh and Sükösd 1999).

Profound change in the Hungarian media structure quickly followed. As soon as the legal mechanism was established for the allocation of broadcasting frequencies, bids were accepted for the creation of two national commercial television networks and two national commercial radio networks. In 1997, all four began broadcasting. (The two national commercial channels, TV2 and RTL Klub, are owned by European consortia. The commercial radio stations, Danubius, Juventus, and Sláger, are owned by both European and American investors.) This competitive challenge induced the public channels to change as well, leading them to make their programming much more commercial.

Structural change has also significantly affected the journalistic ethos and practices. Although the factionalism of the journalistic profession inherited from the transition to democracy still exists, partisan bias in the mainstream media has significantly decreased. Norms of objectivity and impartiality are now enforced by a Complaints Board set up by the NRTC to investigate alleged cases of biased coverage. During the first year of its operation in 1997, most complaints were submitted by opposition parties arguing that their policy positions and press conferences had not been covered adequately. The board has found in favor of the complainants in several noteworthy instances. Some journalists have argued, however, that in a parliamentary system of seven parties it is impossible to present all party positions on all issues; that party publicity events and press conferences should not be covered mechanically; and that it should be their professional responsibility to judge what is newsworthy. Discussion of these competing demands on the media is underway, but it is less politicized and more professional than in the 1990–4 period.

Between 1994 and 1998, the drive for journalistic independence was also evident in the fact that even liberal and center-left newspapers heavily criticized the governing Socialist and liberal coalitions and exposed their wrongdoings. Similarly, after the 1998 election of a Young Democrats government, the illegal business activities of its appointee as Internal Revenue Service director were investigated and criticized by the otherwise sympathetic mass-circulation daily *Népszabadság*.

Nonetheless journalistic performance still leaves something to be desired in Hungary and the whole Eastern European region. Informative, high-quality news analysis is hard to find, while subjective opinion journalism rich in metaphors abounds. Very little is reported about the process of legislation, not even concerning such important issues as privatization, reform of the pension system, or major public-health issues. Ephemeral political issues, especially personal conflicts, dominate the public sphere. Financial corruption in public television has affected entertainment and sport programs in particular, with kickbacks regularly paid by private-sector producers to encourage the airing of their unreasonably expensive programs. This practice was made possible by lack of regulation of the public media (and broadcasting as a whole) until 1996. While enactment of a new media law subsequently led to attempts to clean up these irregularities, these reforms have been held back by the precarious financial condition of many stations, which are perched on the brink of bankruptcy.

CONCLUSION

The "mediatization" of politics is a neglected aspect of studies of democratization in Eastern Europe. The clear conclusion to emerge from this chapter is that the media played a central role in maintaining Communist regimes, as well as in the democratic transformation of post-Communist states and societies. While the media did not cause the former communist regimes to break down or trigger the transition to democracy, they did play crucial roles in determining *how, when, and to what degree* democratization took shape in both the transition and consolidation periods. The media operated just as they were supposed to – that is, as forces mediating political change. Their importance derives from their roles in channeling information about alternative programs, policies, and personalities from parties to citizens and, more generally, in linking elites to the other social strata, especially in the early phases of democratization. Media literati – politicians, journalists, public intellectuals – also played key roles in setting public agendas and mobilizing citizens for democratic participation. Our understanding of the complex processes of political change remains incomplete if we fail to take into account how the electorate receives information about elite-level developments, who performs the crucial role of gatekeeper, and what frames of reference are conveyed to the public for the interpretation of these events.

One of the most crucial developments in East Central Europe during the Communist era was the progressive loosening of party-state control over the official media. While the media were still far more heavily censored than any Western media system, the way was opened for symbolic resistance and the expression of non-Communist values in the context of a dynamics of cultural politics characterized by mass distrust and disbelief of the official political media and a vast appetite for depoliticized entertainment. As the official media became more varied, pluralism in public discourse increased, even in the official sector. In Hungary, the regime's decision in the early 1960s to liberalize the media opened the way for the importation of Western elite discourses and popular culture, resulting in a substantial increase in pluralism despite heavy political controls that persisted until the late 1970s. The influx of Western movies and rock music, as well as advertisements, contributed to the erosion of Communist dogma, the pluralization of identities, the cultivation of personal beliefs and lifestyles, and the desirability of consumerism. Liberalization of the official media, in other words, became a major source of the "detotalization" of the Communist system.

The illegal democratic-opposition media that developed in Poland, Hungary, Czechoslovakia, and the Soviet Union, and among ethnic Hungarians in Romania, had a similar effect, setting a democratic agenda, crystallizing opposition discourse strategies, and providing an unrestricted public sphere. *Samizdat* media also contributed to the organization of opposition groups and to the emergence of new leaders who would play important roles in the democratic era. The role of the media was no less significant once democratization was set in motion. They familiarized the public with new parties, their programs, and policy alternatives, especially during the first democratic election campaign; they mobilized the population to attend rallies and symbolic transforming events; and they set a new public agenda by providing coverage of the wrongdoings of former Communist governments. It is important to note that these functions were performed in all Eastern European countries, irrespective of their transition trajectories. The principal difference among them was that these media roles gradually emerged in those transitions that unfolded through negotiations, but they materialized abruptly following revolutionary political changes.

The democratic role of the media did not stop with the transition to democracy. The nature of the emerging post-Communist regimes was affected by the media – especially the official media. In some countries, the media remained the creatures of authoritarian governments and contributed significantly to blocking democratic consolidation. In the case of Hungary, the "media wars of independence" played a key role in the consolidation of the new democracy, as is reflected in Elemér Hankiss's memoirs:

> In their stubborn fight for autonomy, Hungarian Television and Radio became the major actors of a society protesting against the centralizing and authoritarian efforts of the government.... [We] had to learn that democracy cannot be ... established overnight by a first and single free election. It may be generated only in the course of a long and tedious learning process in which everybody has to take part and has to take up his or her responsibilities ... The fact that two fragile public institutions, which could rely only on the letter and spirit of the law, were able to protect their newly won autonomy against extremely strong pressures and attacks coming from the side of the Government and the governing parties, proves that all the main political actors observed, at least until the last act, the rule of law, and have accepted the basic rules of the democratic game. (Hankiss 1996, 256–7)

Individual responsibility and civil courage, the learning process of democracy, the relative strength of the democratic polity, autonomy, and the rule of law are the key concepts highlighted in the struggle for control of the media in the first phase of democratic consolidation in all Eastern European countries and in the achievement of media independence in the second period of consolidation. All these relate to the five major dimensions of the consolidation of democracy (Linz and Stepan 1996, 7–15). On each of these dimensions, Hungary's democracy can be regarded as consolidated.

With regard to the development of civil liberties and civil society, freedom of association was fully achieved in the 1988–90 transition to democracy. Freedom of communication was more difficult to secure; it emerged by the mid-1990s as the outcome of a long media war. In the second arena, political society, free and inclusive elections have been already held several times and have gradually become fairer; the majority of the media show no favoritism among the competing parties. In the third arena, the rule of law and constitutionalism, even the media war was conducted legally in the sense that constitutional and legal interpretations were invoked to legitimize the actions of antagonists. Subsequently, enactment of a new law regulating the media guaranteed media freedom and the rule of law (as has also been the case in Poland and the Czech Republic). With regard to Linz and Stepan's fourth dimension, rational bureaucratic methods of media regulation took over in Hungary in 1996 with the establishment of the NRTC and its Complaints Board. Ministries and other state institutions may still strive to bias democratic communications in their favor by financing media programs and exerting influence over those public media still owned by the state, but countervailing forces have gradually emerged in the form of legal guarantees of freedom of information and transparency of government, stronger professional norms among journalists, and greater financial security of their employers. Finally, in the area of economic society, private commercial media have been established, and media competition takes place within a regulatory framework conforming to EU standards in Poland, Hungary, and the Czech Republic.

The one note of pessimism in this picture stems from the entertainment orientation of even the public media in these countries. The casualty is detailed, high-quality coverage of international and domestic politics, especially regarding major legislative initiatives and institutional reforms. In this regard, the Eastern Central European media are following much the same path as many of their Western counterparts. The big difference is that the older media systems developed during an era when the public-service ethos was strong, while the newer East European media developed in the late 1980s and 1990s, when privatization and deregulation were the international mantras. It remains to be seen how the media will contribute to the quality of democracy in these regimes in the general absence of the political information and democratic socialization that had been provided by the public-service media of postwar Germany and Japan, which played such significant roles in the consolidation of democracy in those two countries.

NOTES

1. Détente did not occur until 1958. In the two previous years, large-scale political terror suggested that totalitarianism had returned after the revolution. Police crackdowns on participants in the revolution were common, as were massive imprisonment of democratic activists, labor leaders, and former street fighters, the execution of revolutionary leaders and government members (among them Prime Minister Imre Nagy), and the renewed use of the media for party-state propaganda purposes.
2. This is why social and natural scientists, along with Western-oriented representatives

of the humanities, were among the first dissidents in all Communist countries. The cultural capital that allowed them to become outspoken critics of the regimes resulted from several factors, including the elite positions they occupied in these scientifically administered societies, their scientific achievements, the compatibility of their specialized knowledge with that of Western scientific communities, and membership in the global scientific community. In Russia and China, dissident nuclear physicists like Andrei Sakharov and Fang Lizhi are cases in point. In Hungary, where no cutting-edge war technology research was conducted, young leftist philosophers, students of the Marxist philosopher György Lukács, formed the first opposition circle in the late 1960s.

3. Narratives, characters, visual images, and so on in entertainment programs may also carry implicit and explicit political messages and may function differently in various sociopolitical contexts. An American television series or action movie, for example, with a scene set in a supermarket containing shelves filled with attractive consumer goods, may carry a powerful implicit political message to viewers in shortage-ridden Eastern Europe. Thus the previous distinction between politics versus entertainment refers only to the explicitly and directly political character of some media genres.

4. In Poland, censorship offices were still functioning during the summer of 1989. Their effectiveness, however, was completely undermined by the publicity they received when their decisions were appealed and struck down by the courts. This happened in several cases during the May–June 1989 electoral campaign.

5. This number may be somewhat inflated, since several owners of papers that fail in the market, hoping to start again, do not report when they stop or suspend the publication of their papers. Exact data on the number of periodicals in print are unavailable.

6. As described by McCombs and Shaw (1993, 65–6). "A valence issue is simply a proposition, condition, or belief that is positively or negatively valued by all (in fact, most of) the voters. . . . To the extent that the press (via its agenda-setting function) has a direct impact on the outcome of a particular election, it is likely to be through the medium of valence issues which directly accrue to the advantage or disadvantage of one political party."

7. It should be noted that in the Eastern European context, the term "personalization" does not reflect an extreme emphasis on political personalities and human interest stories (at the expense of issues or policies), as it often does in the critical Western literature. It refers primarily to the more positive function of introducing hitherto unknown persons to voters, linking them to parties, programs, policies, statements, and symbols, and conveying authority and responsibility to them.

8. In comparison, in Poland, three democratic elections were held in the early post-Communist period. After the second election, Parliament was fragmented among more than 15 parties.

9. Addressing the new association, its honorary president, professor of psychology Istvan Benedek, stated: "The fact of the matter is that we do not want press freedom. Because a free press leads to an abusive press, that freedom is intolerable. We do not want freedom of speech because freedom of speech leads to hatred. We want honesty of press and we want honesty of speech!" (quoted in Sükösd 1992, 71–2).

CHAPTER 5

The Modernization of Communications: The Media in the Transition to Democracy in Chile

Eugenio Tironi and Guillermo Sunkel

Translated by Richard Gunther

> The weapons that served the bourgeoisie in bringing down feudalism will now be used against the bourgeoisie itself.
>
> Karl Marx and Friedrich Engels,
> *The Communist Manifesto*

This chapter explores the various roles played by the mass communications media in the reestablishment of democracy in Chile and in the current process of democratic consolidation. These roles involve such functions as undermining popular support for the regime of General Augusto Pinochet, preserving political-cultural traditions and partisan identities, and, more recently, establishing a basic consensus in support of a pluralist democracy and a free market economy.

It is clear that the relationship between the communications media and the political process is not unidirectional. The media have an impact on the political process but, at the same time, changes in the political-cultural and socioeconomic spheres have a significant influence on the field of communications. The reciprocal character of this relationship acquires particular relevance in a society like Chile, which in a short period of time changed from an authoritarian to a democratic regime, as well as from a closed economic system strongly regulated by the state to an open market economy.

The prevalent view of the Chilean communications media under the authoritarian regime emphasizes restrictions on freedom of expression and the mechanisms used by the regime to control the content and flow of information. In essence, this view focuses on the impact of the political system on the communications system, particularly concerning re-

165

pression and ideological conformity. But this same traditional view also draws attention to the effects of the communications media on politics insofar as it highlights the contribution of some media (particularly those close to the opposition to the Pinochet regime) to the unleashing of the political transition. Some opposition media played the role of protagonist in the so-called battle for the freedom of expression, in undermining support for the authoritarian regime, and in encouraging mass mobilizations in favor of democracy. Other media, in contrast, were *oficialistas* insofar as they abided by the restrictions placed on them by the regime instead of participating in the democratization process.

In this chapter, we argue that it would be insufficient to focus on political variables alone in understanding the role of the media under authoritarianism. Certainly, the dynamics of the political and ideological controls that were quite strong in the first years of the authoritarian regime should not be overlooked, nor should one ignore the media's efforts (sometimes heroic) to defend freedom of expression. But a focus on political dynamics alone would not explain the evolution of the media system during the 17 years of authoritarian rule. Nor is it possible to account for the participation of the media in the democratization process exclusively in terms of political liberalization. Endogenous factors related to internal modernization of the mass communications media, in the context of a growing free market economy, are crucial for understanding the evolution of the democratic transition and consolidation processes.

This chapter is divided into five sections. In the first, we present a general background discussion of the evolution of the media in Chile prior to General Pinochet's seizure of power in 1973, and we explore the impact of the military coup on the media system. The second section examines roles played by the opposition media in the democratization process. As we shall argue, however, the opposition media were not alone in undermining support for the Pinochet regime and in paving the way for the transition to democracy. More subtle processes of change were set in motion by a fundamental transformation of the media system itself. In the third section, therefore, we explore the less salient but highly significant modernization of the communications media under the authoritarian regime. In the fourth section, we analyze the liberalizing impact that resulted from this modernization through an examination of two landmark media events of the transition: the visit of Pope John Paul II and television broadcasts by the two opposing sides in the 1988 plebiscite. In the final section, we examine developments within the communications field during the process of democratic consolidation that began in 1990.

GENERAL BACKGROUND TO THE CHILEAN MEDIA SYSTEM

The structure of the mass communications media in Chile prior to 1973 is quite heterogeneous, with each medium (press, radio, and television) having its own distinctive characteristics. The print media, the oldest of the modern communication media, emerged in the nineteenth century as a vehicle for the efforts of certain political groups to influence the course of the nascent Republic. The link between the print media and politics was maintained throughout most of the twentieth century. In fact, until 1973, each significant party in the Chilean political system either owned or was closely linked with a newspaper or magazine.

This did not impede the emergence of independent journalistic enterprises, which established a predominant position in the print-media market beginning in the first decades of the twentieth century. Among the daily newspaper firms, the country's leading (and oldest) was El Mercurio, S.A. Owned by the Edwards family since its founding at the beginning of the twentieth century, it published the Santiago dailies *El Mercurio, La Segunda,* and *Las Ultimas Noticias,* as well as a network of regional newspapers. Its principal competitor was the Consorcio Periodístico, S.A. (COPESA), founded by the Picó-Cañas family in the 1950s, which published the daily newspaper *La Tercera.* Another firm of some importance published the popular daily *Clarín* until it was closed in 1973.

Between 1940 and the end of the 1960s, these independent journalistic enterprises underwent considerable expansion, securing preeminent positions in the market but not rendering insignificant those media more openly tied to political parties. In fact, the political press retained considerable importance until 1973, especially the "press of the left" and the "Christian democratic press." During this period, for example, the Communist Party published the daily newspaper *El Siglo* and the magazine *Principios;* the Socialist Party published the magazine *Arauco* and the daily *Las Noticias de Ultima Hora;* and the Christian Democratic Party published the daily *La Tarde* and the magazine *Política y Espíritu.* During this period, one could also speak of a "press of the right," since this political sector maintained indirect but close ties with such publications as *El Mercurio* and *El Diario Ilustrado.*

Around the end of the 1960s, and especially when Salvador Allende's Unidad Popular government came to power in 1970, the political press increased significantly in importance. Alongside the more traditional ideological-doctrinaire media, there emerged a cluster of publications clearly oriented toward political confrontation. These sentiments were articulated by magazines on the left such as *Punto Final* and *Chile Hoy,* as well as the daily *Puro Chile,* and, in the Christian democratic camp, by the daily *La Prensa.* This process was also manifested in the appearance of a militant and more explicitly partisan right-wing press. The magazines *Sepa* and *Tizona* and the daily newspaper *Tribuna* were clearly part of this tendency toward political confrontation.[1] In short, while the development of the print media received a strong push from the private sector, it is clear that its configuration until 1973 was also shaped by its close relationship with the political world.

In contrast, starting with its first broadcasts in Chile (1922), radio has always been commercial in character. The great force behind the development of radio in Chile was the private sector, which quickly saw the advertising possibilities offered by this medium, as well as the market that had been created for the sale of radio receivers. These factors determined the emergence of the first radio stations as small-scale commercial enterprises that subsequently grouped into networks, broadening their coverage to include the entire country. Radio was conceived principally as an entertainment medium and, to a much lesser extent, as an information medium. For this reason, contrary to what happened with the print media, radio broadcasters had much less extensive or close ties to political parties, and the ties that did develop were limited to those periods when there was an intensification of political conflict.[2]

It should also be noted that in radio, as with the press, nonprivate types of ownership – such as university or state ownership – were marginal and did not have great influence over the general evolution of either medium. In the 1950s the state published a daily newspaper – *La Nación* – but it had limited circulation and influence, despite the efforts of successive governments. A few university radio stations also appeared, primarily devoted to the broadcasting of classical music; but these also failed to have a major impact on mass culture. In 1974 the military government created Radio Nacional de Chile, which succeeded in becoming the largest broadcast network in the country, with shortwave international transmissions as well.

The evolution of television in Chile was significantly different from that of the press and radio. Among its distinguishing characteristics was that the private sector did not secure legal authorization to operate television channels until the early 1990s. Instead, universities (and later the state) were the principal developers of the medium, playing a pioneering role with the first experimental broadcasts in the late 1950s.[3] It is noteworthy that rejection of the concept of private television was reinforced in the 1960s following a debate that involved actors from across the political spectrum. This debate focused primarily on the medium's responsibility to advance the common good, a task that many thought it would be better able to perform if left in the hands of the universities and the state. With the coming to power of the Christian Democratic government in 1964, a broad political consensus (which included Christian Democrats, the left, and part of the right) was established rejecting private television on the grounds that it could not fulfill the basic educational and cultural objectives that were currently being met by existing university stations and the state television network.

This political consensus, which legitimized the so-called university-state system, was manifested in the first General Law regulating television, enacted in 1970. Three aspects of the legal framework it established are of great importance. First, the law defines the objectives that are to be met by television. Among these are affirmation of national values and the dignity of the family, support for the development of education and culture, and the provision of objective information about national and international events. With regard to the last key function, it is important to note that the law specifies that "television will not serve any particular ideology, and will maintain respect for all the various viewpoints expressed by the Chilean people." Second, the law modified the structure of television ownership by creating Televisión Nacional de Chile (TVN). While the state television channel had begun broadcasting in 1968, prior to promulgation of the General Law, the 1970 legislation enabled the state to take greater advantage of television by making TVN the only network authorized to extend its coverage throughout the country. TVN was established as a public corporation linked to the state through the Ministry of Education. Finally, this law created a new body, the National Television Council, charged with responsibility for "overseeing the proper functioning" of the medium, with full authority to establish norms regulating programming and advertising on all channels, but without directly or peremptorily interfering with the content of programming.[4]

THE MEDIA UNDER PINOCHET

In September 1973, a military coup overthrew the constitutional government of Salvador Allende, breaking with a democratic tradition that had lasted for several decades (Valenzuela 1978). The coup had a great impact on the media. The most profound and immediate change was the severing of ties between some media and political parties. Radio stations, magazines, and newspapers belonging to the parties in the left-wing coalition, Unidad Popular, were confiscated by the military authorities and subsequently transferred to the state or sold to private firms. Those that belonged to the Christian Democratic Party, while not closed down at first, were burdened with continuous and increasing restrictions and censorship. Before long, these constraints, in combination with a failure to attract sufficient advertising revenues, culminated in the closure of these media as well. Finally, with the decision by the main party of the right to dissolve, its allied media were also obliged to close. Various political groups that supported Pinochet, however, created new communications media or established preeminent positions within existing media, which they then used to try to influence the political and economic decisions of the military government.[5]

The television channel that was most immediately affected was the state network, TVN. In the immediate aftermath of the coup, the military occupied its facilities, arrested scores of its officials, and destroyed films and tapes. This intervention was given legal sanction in October 1973 through a decree dismissing the network's directors and placing all of its facilities under a new director general appointed by General Pinochet. In 1974, through another decree, TVN was transferred from the Ministry of Education to the General Secretariat of the Government, which was charged with responsibility for all of the government's political communications, as well as control of the body charged with censorship and control of the press, the Dirección Nacional de Comunicación Social.

But the military government's presence was not limited to the state network. It extended to all of television, since the other channels operated by the universities were submitted to control by government-appointed university presidents. The principle of university autonomy (which had been an integral and zealously maintained part of democratic politics in Chile) was thereby suspended,[6] and all television communications were placed, directly or indirectly, under the political control of the military government. Mechanisms designed to safeguard the autonomy, independence, and pluralism of media both in the state network and in the university stations were suppressed almost instantly, leading to a period of "emergency," after which television became very different from what it had been prior to September 1973.

Relations between the military government and the communications media were adapted to the regime's policies of strict control. These policies were oriented toward the demobilization and depoliticization of the population, typical of authoritarian regimes, and not toward the kind of active mobilization that characterizes totalitarian systems (see Chapter 2 in this volume). During the initial phase of installing the authoritarian regime, this logic led to the elimination of the political press, direct intervention in television, the detention of journalists, and the imposition of censorship. Subsequently, some civilian groups supporting the government created their own media or assumed prominent positions in those already established, using these outlets as platforms for influencing the political and economic policies of the new regime. In 1974 Radio Nacional de Chile was created. It became the largest broadcast network in the country, with international shortwave broadcasts in several languages. Its objective was to propagate the regime's ideas and counter the "anti-Chile campaign" in the international arena. TVN, meanwhile, was dominated by the government throughout the authoritarian regime and was under the leadership of ideologues who wished to use it for propaganda purposes.

The regime continued to maintain its control over the communications media throughout its institutionalized phase in the 1980s,[7] but this control ceased to be the only, or even the principal, dynamic governing the evolution of the communications system. One important development during this latter period was the emergence of alternative media – some opposition daily newspapers and an assortment of radio stations and magazines that operated legally but that were backed (from behind the scenes) by political actors. Another development was the consolidation of the predominant position of the private sector in the communications system in a manner consistent with the regime's economic liberalization policies (Foxley 1983). This occurred first with regard to radio and the press, where the disappearance of the party-owned media following the coup served to strengthen the already dominant position that had been secured by private firms prior to 1973. This dominance of the private sector was further reinforced by subsequent processes of economic liberalization and internationalization (Portales 1981).

In the case of television, as we have seen, the private sector was excluded from ownership until the beginning of the 1990s. Nevertheless, this did not prevent it from participating in the medium's development. Originally, the dominant conception was that of university television financed solely by the educational institutions themselves. This conception was soon abandoned, however, once university stations found that the only way to meet increasing expenses and continue to grow was to accept advertising.

Recognition of this reality had been reflected in the General Law of 1970, which permitted, but regulated, commercial advertising on television. At the same time, this law established public financing, with funds to be distributed in inverse proportion to a station's commercial income. This mixed system of financing, however, was ended by the military when it abolished the wealth tax that had served as the fiscal basis of television subsidies. Then, in 1977, all existing restrictions on commercial advertising were eliminated, enabling the private sector to expand its role in the development of the medium. The paradox of university channels financed by the private sector was thus created.[8] This situation was solidified at the beginning of the 1980s, during the so-called economic boom, with its accompanying increases in consumption and advertising. Finally, to all of this activity must be added the authorization of private television in the final days of the military regime, leading to the establishment of two commercial channels.

THE MEDIA IN THE STRUGGLE FOR DEMOCRACY

As we have seen, the initial impact of the 1973 coup on the communications system was the suppression of ties between several media and parties or other political organizations. Radio stations, magazines, and newspapers owned by parties of the left were confiscated by the military authorities, and those linked with the Christian Democratic Party were pushed rapidly toward closure.

The reemergence of political-ideological pluralism in the communications media occurred initially through the establishment of alternative communications media by opponents of the military regime. This process began timidly around the end of the 1970s and reached its zenith during the institutionalized period of military rule in the 1980s. Its principal antecedent was the dissident and clandestine culture that first appeared in the early days of the Pinochet regime to give voice to opposition to the "official world" and the repressive and exclusionary practices of the military government (Brunner et al. 1989).

The alternative media of the 1980s, however, had two characteristics that set them apart from earlier clandestine efforts. First, alternative outlets in two of these media, radio and public affairs magazines, succeeded in establishing themselves legally and publicly, implying an abandonment of clandestinity and illegality. The magazines acquired legal status and the right to publish by following legal procedures established by the regime.[9] Alternative radio stations, however, emerged through a more evolutionary process by redefining their basic functions.[10] The second difference from the earlier clandestine efforts was that these media were not direct outlets or advocates of political parties; instead, they attempted to articulate a multiparty opposition that, at that time, had no means of public expression.

While the alternative media were not the voices of political organizations, it is clear that they had a more or less organic relationship with parties that, at that time, were still illegal. Indeed, the main impetus behind the establishment of these alternative media was political: politically active groups and leaders took the initiative in founding these media, fighting for their existence through legal means, recruiting their top personnel, establishing their editorial policies, and frequently acting as commentators. These media managed to maintain themselves only through financial support regularly contributed by actors (foundations, cooperative agencies, political parties, etc.) deeply involved in the democratization process. This financial support was essential for nearly all of them, since they were incapable of surviving through market mechanisms alone; neither advertising nor circulation revenues would have been sufficient.[11]

These alternative media played their opposition roles in two different ways. One involved complete rejection of the authoritarian regime and the market regime by operators of media outlets who perceived themselves as marginalized and excluded (Brunner et al. 1989). It implied a position of moral superiority and the defense of ideological purity against all contamination. This *alternativismo de base* (alternativism of the base) was the dominant conception of those who expressed themselves through the micro-media of the Catholic Church, trade unions, neighborhood associations, and young people. This was also the dominant stance of mass-culture radio stations and magazines located on the left of the political spectrum. A second approach was taken by radio broadcasters and magazine publishers located closer to the political center. They set forth an *oferta alternativa* (alternative offering). Their stance was not one of total rejection of the system but, rather, the notion that it is necessary to participate in the debate by taking positions within the mainstream of the media system. It was an alternative approach that attempted to influence everyday mass culture incrementally.[12]

From the time that the alternative media secured a visible presence at the beginning of the 1980s until the period preceding the presidential plebiscite of 1988[13] – which marked the beginning of the transition to democracy – they played significant political roles. Apart from helping to preserve the historical memory of Chile's preauthoritarian democracy, four of these roles are particularly important. The first was in the struggle for freedom of expression, whose reestablishment (however imperfect) represented a precondition for a successful transition (Sunkel 1992). This "battle for freedom of expression" – as it was called by these media – began with the formal application for authorization to disseminate printed matter, which eventually permitted the (partial) reintroduction of pluralism within the communications system. The battle then moved to the Courts of Justice for a long period as the military government sought to prosecute opposition journalists and broadcasters.

The second significant role was that of interlocutor. Since those opposition elites who had not been removed from the scene altogether were not allowed to express themselves publicly, the basic interlocutory function shifted from the political arena to the mass media (Contreras 1983). In taking on this new role, the media were not seeking to perform a political representation function; instead, they sought to open up opportunities for communication to those political actors who had none. The presence of political and social leaders as frequent contributors to alternative magazines was one manifestation of this interlocutory function.

The third role played by the media was that of disseminating the values of a democratic culture. During the period prior to the transition, the alternative media not only defended the right of freedom of expression, they also worked to defend other rights that had been violated and spoke out on behalf of values (such as political freedom, social justice, and solidarity) that were absent from the ideological framework of the regime. The media thereby played an important role in the reconstitution of a democratic political culture.

The final and related role was that of introducing political themes and language to the public arena. In fact, until the dynamics of the presidential plebiscite were set in motion in 1988, the alternative press provided the infrastructure for the articulation of viewpoints that included radical criticism of the authoritarian regime. In general terms, and notwithstanding variations among these media, this criticism emphasized three themes: human rights, poverty, and political activity (Sunkel 1991a). Violations of human rights by officials of the military regime's security forces were denounced. Abuses and arbitrary actions were condemned in the name of those most directly affected – the victims of repression. The alternative media also launched a criticism of the regime's economic philosophy and denounced the too often ignored poverty in Chilean society, a theme that ran counter to the self-congratulatory rhetoric of the military regime's supporters. Finally, these media attempted to relegitimize political activity per se in a context in which parties were still legally proscribed.

Without doubt, the political roles played by the alternative media in the period prior to the democratic transition were highly significant. Nevertheless, it should be noted that these media – especially the magazines – were able to reach only a restricted audience despite efforts to enter the mainstream of commercial distribution. Their problem was that, insofar as these magazines worked within the framework of alternative communications, they were incapable of establishing a presence among the mass public. Instead, their audience was limited to the politically sophisticated sector of society, mainly among the middle and upper strata; it was there that their political influence was highly significant.[14]

This elitism was particularly characteristic of those media that completely rejected the system. In effect, they tended to restrict their reach to the segment of the public that identified itself with the opposition, thereby confining itself to a kind of ghetto through its use of certain symbols, vocabulary, forms of expression, and the reelaboration of a particular historical memory. Thus, even though such media utilized commercial distribution networks, they never reached a mass public. Instead, through a rite of collective self-identification, they tended to represent – or to constitute themselves as – an opposition subculture. Greater penetration of the Chilean public was achieved by those media that presented alternative offerings and that, although fewer in number than their "complete rejection" counterpart, attracted a massive public audience. In these cases (such as the magazine Hoy and Radio Cooperativa), exposure – and therefore political influence – were not limited exclusively to those segments of the public that already had a strong political identification with the opposition.

Finally, we must consider the opposition daily newspapers that emerged in the early stages of the political transition, such as La Epoca and Fortín Mapocho, both of which first appeared in early 1987. Like the alternative media, these dailies received their main inspiration and support from the political arena, with one of their central identifying characteristics being a strong commitment to the struggle for reestablishment of a democratic regime. In contrast with the alternative media, however, these opposition dailies sought to attract mass audiences in the mainstream communications market. *La Epoca*, for example, tried to reach an "enlightened" public "cross-cutting all social strata," while *Fortín Mapocho* was directed to the mass public.[15]

The opposition dailies certainly reached a larger audience than the alternative magazines, but readership of the dailies was also delimited in political terms (Sunkel 1991b). Accordingly, the typical reader of *La Epoca*, for example, was of the center and the left, with a much smaller audience among those on the right, while readers of *Fortín Mapocho* were exclusively of the center and the left. This political distribution of the reading public was closely related to the manner in which these dailies structured their respective images: *La Epoca* was perceived by the public as "more serious," while *Fortín Mapocho* was regarded as a "more politicized" newspaper.[16]

During the election campaigns of 1988 and 1989, in the midst of the democratic transition, the opposition dailies played roles that had previously been the preserve of the alternative media – defender of freedom of expression, interlocutor, and rebuilder of a democratic political culture. These roles were performed, however, in a changed setting, given the development of the political process.

As soon as the principal opposition forces signed the agreement to participate politically within the institutional framework created by the authoritarian regime (with the objective of defeating General Pinochet in the 1988 plebiscite), the opposition dailies played significant roles in mobilizing the electorate, operating as the voices of the opposition alliance. In the context of electoral competition, given its confrontational character, these dailies responded to increased demands for political information, providing accounts of the various activities of the opposition alliance. But their response was not merely to pass on information, as if it came from somewhere external to the media themselves; in fact, they involved themselves actively in the contest, adopting the opposition's political-electoral strategy and publicizing its positions. During this period, they widely disseminated the messages of the opposition alliance: the notion of the plebiscite as an opportunity for restoring dignity, calls to register to vote as a means of recovering true political citizenship, calls for widespread participation in the various campaign activities of the opposition, and so on.

THE MODERNIZATION OF THE MEDIA SYSTEM

Paralleling the struggle for survival of the alternative media, as well as efforts to restore freedom of information and opinion, another process – more general and less analyzed – unfolded beneath the surface under the authoritarian regime. This was the modernization of the country's communications system, which took place mainlyduring the 1980s and was largely part an indirect consequence of the authoritarian regime's free market economic philosophy. The gradual transformation of the communications system from one based primarily on the print media – which were highly dependent on the state and heavily concerned with politics – to a more mass-oriented system largely dominated by television, increasingly in private hands and decisively oriented toward the market, preceded changes in the political sphere. In the following discussion, we will refer only to those characteristics of the modernization process that are relevant to the analysis of the media's political impact on the transition.[17]

One aspect of this modernization was an increase in the reach of the media, largely involving a massive diffusion of the infrastructure for receiving communications broadcasts. In this sense, the key was the spectacular growth of television: ownership of television sets increased sixfold between 1970 and 1983.[18] By 1983, almost 95 percent of Chilean households had at least one, and during the 1980s this medium moved into first place in terms of cultural consumption by the population.[19]

A second characteristic of modernization was the increasing economic importance of the communications system. Growth in advertising spending is a good indicator of this change. In 1983, during an economic recession, total advertising expenditures amounted to $127.6 million (U.S. dollars). This figure steadily increased beginning the following year and reached $188.6 million in 1988, thereby regaining the spending levels prior to the 1982–3 economic crisis. Between 1989 and 1993, advertising spending increased from $231.5 million to an estimated $391.9 million. Of the latter total, 43.5 percent was spent on television advertising, 37.3 percent on newspapers, 10.7 percent on radio, and 4.4 percent on magazines.[20] These figures clearly reflect the economic importance of the communications system. Within this system television has seized the dominant position, displacing the daily press, which had been the most important recipient of advertising revenues until 1982.

A third aspect of this modernization process was that, during the 1980s, most of the communications sector became part of the market system. As we saw earlier, this occurred first in the radio and press, where the elimination of political-party ownership of media following the coup helped to consolidate the leadership position of private-sector firms. It also occurred in television, where the private sector expanded substantially once restrictions on advertising were eliminated. It grew further following the appearance of private television in 1990. It is interesting to note that the authoritarian state, in accord with its general political-economy orientation, imposed a policy of self-financing on its media. The media were thus led to operate according to the logic of the market, and the state ceased to be the dominant actor in the communications system. The exceptions to this general tendency were the alternative media, which, as we saw, were highly politicized and occupied a marginal position within the communications system.

A fourth characteristic of the modernization process was the dominant position acquired by television. This was manifested, as we saw, in television's rapid rise to first place among the public, becoming the fundamental component of daily mass culture. It was also manifested in television's dominant position with regard to revenues from advertising (accounting for 43.5 percent of all such spending in 1993), making it the "most dynamic sub-sector of the culture industry" (Brunner et al. 1989).

How did the modernization of the communications system that took place under the authoritarian regime contribute to the political transition? We contend that this modernization, promoted by the regime's own economic strategy, had a liberalizing impact much more profound than that of the marginal opposition media. This was due in large part to the fact that the impact of the opposition media was always limited to particular political clienteles, while the impact of the formal media – especially television – was more massive, setting in motion forces that culminated in the transition to democracy. These forces were not the product of any firm democratic convictions on the part of these media; instead, they resulted from characteristics of the market, that is, from dynamic processes within the communications media system itself. In fact, beginning in the mid-1980s, the media encountered great difficulty in maintaining their commitment to modernity and progress – which they maintained before to the public – without distancing themselves from the incongruities between liberties in the economic sphere and harsh restrictions in the realm of politics. The media therefore exerted pressure on the regime to lift its political controls, which had weakened the credibility of the media and reduced its possibilities for expansion.

TELEVISION VERSUS AUTHORITARIANISM

The liberalizing impact of the modern communications media, television in particular, is best seen in two landmark events. The first involved television broadcasts of the visit of Pope John Paul II in 1987; the second was the series of broadcasts by the opposing sides in the plebiscite campaign of 1988.

THE POPE ON TELEVISION

The April 1987 visit by Pope John Paul II (the first time a Roman pontiff had ever visited Chile, a profoundly Catholic country) stimulated massive public interest and enthusiasm. No large public meetings had been permitted by the regime; clearly, the events surrounding the pope's visit would change that situation. Organized down to its smallest details by the Catholic Church, the visit lasted for five days and involved 24 public events in Santiago and other major cities. For the Chilean Catholic Church, this intense program was intended to serve as an act of "communication with [the pope's] personal presence, thought and great love for the Chilean people."[21] From this perspective, television was called on to guarantee that the various public meetings and ceremonies of the pope would be opened up to the whole country, permitting the great majority of Chileans to understand his gestures and hear his words. Toward this end, an agreement was reached concerning the official television broadcasts, with each channel assigned some function in covering the visit.

For the church, this agreement represented an assurance that television would perform this role in an efficient manner, with respect for the images and words of the pope and without succumbing to the temptation to distort the meaning of these vivid events. The question that some persons asked during and after the pope's visit was whether television had fulfilled its commitment to cover the visit in "an opportune, clean, integral and uninterrupted manner," as indicated in the agreement. Some studies evaluating the way television covered the pope's visit reached a decidedly negative conclusion (Portales et al. 1988). Those channels most closely tied to the military government (basically, TVN and the Universidad de Chile's channel) were roundly denounced for distorting the meaning of the events by "manipulating" them and "using them for political purposes." Nonetheless, as Sergio Contreras, the secretary general of the Episcopal Conference, acknowledged, "Television performed its important role, permitting the great majority of Chileans to enjoy . . . these vivid events during five unforgettable days" (Portales et al. 1988, 10). It is noteworthy that the general public appears to have responded to the government's efforts at media manipulation by not watching those channels that censored these public events (TVN and the Universidad de Chile's channel), thereby giving the largest audience share to the free and open coverage provided by the Universidad Católica's Channel 13.

All of this is important for the transition insofar as the pope, in the course of his visit, issued a fervent call for reconciliation and recovery of Chile's democratic traditions. The result was to legitimate an ethos antagonistic to the authoritarian regime, an ethos that would eventually serve as the basis for the victory of the "No" side in the 1988 plebiscite (Tironi 1990). At the same time, the pope, in all of his public acts, listened to painful testimonies of humble Chileans who had never before had access to the communications media. Television, despite its many shortcomings, was the principal vehicle for conveying these messages to a mass audience.

The visit of the pope thus marks the beginning of *apertura* (opening) in Chilean television and thereby in the authoritarian order itself. One study noted that

> Channel 13 took advantage of the papal visit to create an *apertura*, a moderate pluralism. Alongside the broadcast of complete, uncensored ceremonies, it established a daily prime-time slot for conversations and debate devoted to analysis of the Pope's visit. On the panel of commentators, opposition politicians shared in this *apertura* with government officials." (Portales et al. 1988, 100–1)

The pope's presence served to justify the appearance of opposition political leaders on television and initiated a dialogue among them. Indeed, it was the first time since the 1973 coup that representatives of the various political groups met around the same table. This type of roundtable program became increasingly common in the period prior to the plebiscite of 1988, and created a climate of dialogue and mutual tolerance that was propitious for the transition to democracy.

The papal visit was not only a great television event, it also marked the turning point in the history of authoritarianism in Chile. Public statements and the pope's private meeting with General Pinochet presented Chileans with a peaceful alternative to the seemingly intractable conflict between the regime and the opposition: on the one hand, it effectively committed Pinochet to the 1988 referendum and to respecting its results; on the other hand, calls for reconciliation and rejection of all forms of violence restrained the opposition and led it to accept, for the first time, the legitimacy of the plebiscite (provisions for which were set down in the authoritarian regime's constitution of 1980) as a viable means of conflict resolution. More generally, these television broadcasts changed the political atmosphere, leading Chileans to see themselves as a community capable of eschewing violence, living in peace, and replacing the previous skepticism with hope for the future. Television, one of the products of the regime's modernization policies, helped make this "miracle" possible.

"WITHOUT FEAR, WITHOUT HATRED, WITHOUT VIOLENCE": THE 1988 PLEBISCITE CAMPAIGN

When the military regime faced the plebiscite of October 5, 1988, it was obliged to accept a package of guarantees to ensure its fairness and consequent democratic legitimacy. Decrees regulating this event established a free television slot of 30 minutes daily throughout the 30 days prior to the plebiscite – 15 minutes for each side at a time (11:15 P.M.). These slots were not expected to attract large audiences. However, they had a great impact on the election, the outcome of which triggered the transition to democracy.

Let us begin by exploring the principal characteristics of both sets of slots, those for "Yes" (in favor of continuing under General Pinochet) and for "No" (in favor of convening elections). An analysis of these broadcasts by María Eugenia Hirmas characterized the "Yes" ads in the following terms:

> There is no doubt about the strategy of the "Yes" campaign on TV. There were months of propaganda on television ... [that] pointed to the economic success of the military government, as well as its social and institutional accomplishments. In August, a new campaign ("Yes, you decide") was launched which had a very different look from its predecessors. This began with a campaign of fear, in which the object was not to "seduce" the voters, but rather to frighten them into voting "Yes" as a rejection of all that the "No" option stood for. Its slogan was, "Yes, you decide if we will continue to move forward or return to the UP" [referring to the leftist government of President Allende, 1970–3]. The ad then explored the two alternatives, but with a clear emphasis on aggressive and ter-

rorizing propaganda.... Part of the 15-minute slot was devoted to claiming that Chile was a "winning country . . . of champions," which had left the rest of Latin America behind. The remaining time was spent attacking the "No" alternative, discrediting opposition leaders in an effort to enhance its own credibility.... It insisted that a victory for the "No" option would imply a return to the past, to government by the UP, with which . . . it associated only negative images. This threat was reinforced by a series of film-clips from 1973 which showed scenes of violence, destruction, disorder, long lines and shortages. It fell back on testimony from victims of violence, making morbid use of their misfortunes to emphasize its frightening aspects. (Hirmas 1989, pp. 121–4).

The "No" campaign was based on the notion that Chilean society had just passed through a prolonged period of disintegration and that the tacit demand of Chileans was for strengthening the bonds of social integration (Tironi 1990). Thus, the "No" campaign strategy basically articulated messages and symbols that, instead of reinforcing the conflictual and disintegrative tendencies dominant in Chilean society over the preceding years, responded to repressed desires for national reconciliation and social cohesion. The public opinion surveys on which the campaign was based revealed that Chileans longed for several fundamental changes: first, an open and tolerant society that would stress security, and not fear; second, respect for individual rights and dignity and an end to the humiliating abuses visited on citizens by the state and other powerful groups in society; third, the opportunity for progress and social mobility for all members of society, such that some would not be condemned to a frustrating marginalization, deprived of the benefits of economic modernization; and fourth, the opening up of channels of political participation, thereby making possible an end to alienation and a revival of citizenship and a sense of membership in a political community – the Chilean nation.

The "No" campaign did not attempt to change public opinion, since the majority was already favorable to this option in principle. Instead, its objective was to overcome the widespread feelings of resignation and despair, born out of fear and skepticism, so that individuals would act in a manner congruent with their opinions and aspirations. This campaign sought to identify itself with such values as social cohesion, historical continuity, national unity, and normalization. In contrast, the "Yes" campaign was automatically identified with the abrupt break in 1973 with historical traditions, internal war, and a prolonged period of convulsions that most Chileans wanted to leave behind.

The "No" television broadcasts were the principal tool for carrying out this strategy. The plebiscite was presented as an opportunity for Chileans to overcome the present situation, and mobilize in support of their aspirations. The team that produced the "No" ads was made up of independent producers and directors, some with experience in television and others trained in documentary filmmaking and advertising. This team, in response to proposals formulated by the technical committee of the "No" command center,[22] designed a television program that was broadcast over the course of 27 days. This team itself reflected the modernization of the Chilean communications media in the 1980s, since all of its members were professionals with considerable experience and success in the media field. In other words, without the previous modernization of the communications system, there would have been no such "No" programming.

A public opinion survey undertaken at the time these programs were being broadcast – in September 1988 – clearly shows that the "No" television slots were very positively evaluated by viewers, while the "Yes" ads failed abysmally. This can be seen in Table 5.1. The much greater effectiveness of the "No" campaign was enormously important, since the outcome of the plebiscite was far from certain; indeed, the indecisive results of numerous public opinion polls carried out during the months prior to the election indicated that its outcome was very much in the balance. A June 1988 Centro de Estudios Públicos survey, for example, revealed that 37 percent of respondents favored the "Yes" option, 41 percent favored the "No" alternative, and about 20 percent were undecided. Indeed, the undecided segment remained quite large right up to the time of the plebiscite, making it practically impossible to predict the outcome with any certainty. In the end, however, Pinochet's plebiscite preference was rejected by a substantial margin: 54.7 percent of Chileans voted "No," 43 percent voted "Yes," and 2.3 percent cast blank or null ballots.

What were the factors that changed this apparent deadlock by swinging most of the undecided voters to the "No" side and thereby producing its electoral triumph? Several events took place in the months prior to the plebiscite that had some influence; among these was the designation of General Pinochet as the sole presidential candidate in August 1988, as well as the intensification of the various political campaigns.

Table 5.1   *Public Assessments of Television*
Campaigns in the 1988 Plebiscite

	"Yes" Campaign	"No" Campaign
"Which ad did you regard as . . ."		
More entertaining	16%	62%
Closer to the people	19	60
More motivating	21	58
Clearer and more understandable	25	57
More dynamic	22	56
More optimistic	24	55
More credible	24	52
More appropriate for a political campaign	23	47
Projecting a greater capacity to govern		
the country	29	43

Source: Roberto Méndez et al, "¿Por qué ganó el NO?." In *Estudios Públicos*, no. 33, Summer 1989, p. 93. These data were collected in a survey by the Centro de Estudios Públicos and Adimark.

Nevertheless, as several analysts have concluded, the decisive factor that produced this electoral outcome was the publicity campaign waged on television (Méndez et al. 1989).

Admittedly, it is difficult to determine with precision the degree to which the "Yes" campaign undermined support for its political option and provoked a flight of undecided voters to the "No" side or, conversely, the extent to which the "No" programs succeeded in converting voters who had not made up their minds. What is clear is that the presence of the opposition on television screens, during prime time and on numerous television channels, by itself had an enormous impact. It is also clear that the basic design of the "No" program, intended to show that political change was possible without major upset or breakdown of the socioeconomic order, succeeded in modifying citizens' perceptions of the political forces in opposition to General Pinochet. This program positioned the opposition as a political force identified with change and, at the same time, with order – that is, it presented the opposition as having the ability to initiate a substantial change in Chile while reestablishing social cohesion.

It is interesting to note that both of these key television events – coverage of the pope's visit in 1987 and the "No" campaign in the 1988 plebiscite – projected the same message of national reconciliation and consensus. The same message and the same style characterized Patricio Aylwin's triumphant 1989 presidential election campaign, as well as the following period of democratic consolidation (1990–3). In the pivotal 1987 period, television opened up new possibilities and helped to reorient national politics.

THE MEDIA AND DEMOCRATIC CONSOLIDATION

Having examined those media-relevant events that contributed to the installation of a democratically elected government, let us return to our examination of how the communications media evolved in Chile. We shall refer to the period that began in March 1990, with the formation of a government by the Concertación de Partidos por la Democracia headed by Patricio Aylwin, as one of "democratic consolidation" in order to differentiate it from the previous period of electoral mobilization, which some would regard as a period of "transition."[23]

In contrast with other countries – such as Spain, Portugal, and several Eastern European countries – Chile experienced no discontinuity or dramatic change in the media system following the end of the authoritarian regime and the beginning of democratic consolidation. The change of political regime did not imply the overturning of the communications system established in the previous period, nor did it create a new framework for the communications media. The fundamental reason is that, prior to changes in the political realm, the communications system had already completed its own transition: the process of modernization transformed it from a system based on the printed word, dependent on the state, and strongly politicized to one based on television, in private hands, self-financed, and oriented toward entertainment or news. In Chile, therefore, we do not find in the political transition factors conducive to change in the communications system; indeed, the opposite occurred, and modernization of the media system was an important factor that helped to unleash the political transition.

This is not to argue that no changes took place during democratic consolidation; however, these changes occurred in a manner consistent with the system that had taken shape by the second half of the 1980s. One such change involved the structure of the media system: under the new democratic government, the media became completely dominated by the private sector, continuing the process set in motion under the authoritarian regime.

Three factors led to the complete privatization of the media. First, a multifaceted crisis (involving economic difficulties, declines in audience, and a loss of direction) beset those media (the press, in particular) that had been most heavily politicized. Especially hard hit were those media that were unable to distance themselves from the political realm at a time when the public was increasingly viewing politics in negative terms. Some of them (including the daily *Fortín Mapocho* and the magazine *Cauce*) disappeared altogether, while others (such as the daily *La Epoca* and the magazines *Hoy* and *Apsi*) found it necessary to reposition themselves in the late 1990s, differentiating themselves from their competitors according to nonpolitical criteria.

Second, the state media were privatized (e.g., Radio Nacional in 1994) or transferred from government control to autonomous public bodies, thus reducing the government's involvement in the communications system. In this sense, we should note that the communications policy of President Aylwin's government had as its principal objective the instauration of pluralism, both among the various media and within each medium (Secretaría de Comunicación y Cultura 1990). From this perspective, the continued existence of government media with certain privileges and guarantees would clearly have interfered with this goal. The most important of these transformations was the conversion of TVN into an autonomous public entity headed by a board of directors approved by the Senate. Its structural autonomy enabled it to design and carry out its own administrative policies, management practices, and programming free from government interference. And with regard to finances, the privileges previously enjoyed by the state media – subsidies, special grants, and so on – were eliminated. The result was that TVN had to compete with other television networks on an equal basis.

The third change was the opening up of television to private enterprise, which occurred only in the final months of the military government. In response to criticism from the political opposition, the Consejo Nacional de Televisión initiated the process of granting very-high-frequency (VHF) wavelengths to private firms in 1989.[24] The first two private stations to be authorized were Megavisión and La Red. Megavisión – owned by an economic group with interests in various sectors of the economy (shipping, industry and agriculture) in association with the Mexican firm Televisa – began broadcasting in October 1990. La Red–owned by an economic group with strength in the banking sector that controls one of the two most important journalistic syndicates in the country, COPESA–took to the air waves in May 1991. In March 1993, the Universidad de Chile sold 49 percent of its television station to the

Table 5.2 *Sources of Political Information*

Magazines (once a week or more)	14%
Newspapers (three times a week or more)	27
Radio (three times a week or more)	45
Television (three times a week a or more)	73

Source: Chilean CNEP survey, 1993.

Venezuelan consortium Venevisión, and in 1994 Canal 2 was born, linked to Radio Cooperativa.[25] Privatization and internationalization were two important tendencies in the evolution of the Chilean media.

Thus, these three developments – the crisis of the political media, the transformation of government media into autonomous public corporations, and the authorization of private-sector television ownership – greatly contributed to the establishment of pluralism within the communications system. A striking paradox thus emerges: all three of these processes were set in motion by the authoritarian regime of General Pinochet, but by undermining government control over the flow of political information to the general public and by promoting the development of pluralism in Chilean public opinion and society, these same processes contributed directly to the demise of the authoritarian regime itself.

Not all of the changes in the media system in recent years are continuous with those earlier transformations, however. Two new developments, in particular, stand out: the dominant position achieved by television and the depoliticization of the media image in the eyes of the general public. To be sure, the beginnings of television's commanding position in the advertising market and in the entertainment and cultural spheres, can be traced back to the early 1980s. The novelty with regard to television's current role primarily involves its status as the principal channel of political information.

A panel survey of public attitudes and behavior at the time of the 1993 general election[26] included a number of questions about how frequently citizens received political information through the various communications media. The resulting data revealed that over 70 percent of Chileans follow the political news principally through television (see Table 5.2). The dominance of television as a source of political news is consistent with the fact that 78 percent of respondents in this survey regard television as the most influential medium. In sharp contrast, only 10 percent

Table 5.3 *Amount of Attention Paid to Political Information in Various Media*

	Much	Some	Little	None
Magazines	8.7%	21.2%	23.1%	44.2%
Newspapers	11.5	27.7	49.8	11.3
Radio	9.6	20.9	53.4	15.1
Television	8.2	21.9	54.2	14.5

Source: Chilean CNEP survey, 1993.

Table 5.4 *Perceptions of the Media*

	Most Credible	Most Informative	Easiest to Understand
Magazines	3%	2%	1%
Newspapers	14	16	9
Radio	20	19	13
Television	44	54	72
None of the above	15	3	2

Note: The question was: "Could you tell me which of these media is . . . , in your judgment?
Source: Chilean CNEP survey, 1993.

regarded radio as most influential, 7 percent cited newspapers, and 1 percent mentioned magazines. Nonetheless, while television clearly emerges as the preferred source of political news, it must also be noted that, in general, few Chileans pay much attention to politics, whatever the source of the news. This general lack of interest in politics can be seen in the data presented in Table 5.3.

The centrality of television as a source of political information is linked with a second phenomenon: the positive perception of television as a news source. As Table 5.4 indicates, a majority of respondents consider television to be the most believable and most informative medium, as well as the easiest to understand. (Even more striking are other data indicating that *all* of the communications media are held in very high regard by Chileans. In a survey undertaken in March and April 1995 by the Dirección de Estudios Sociológicos of the Universidad Católica, the communications media were the most highly evaluated of all Chilean institutions – far higher than the Catholic Church, the police, the armed forces, private businesses, local and national levels of government, the

Table 5.5   *Perceptions of Partisan Bias of the Media*

	Yes (Biased)	No (Not Biased)	No Answer
Newspapers	29%	69%	3%
Radio	29	67	4
Television	23	74	3

Note: The question was: "Do you think that any of these . . . [newspapers, radio stations, television networks] favored any party or candidate?
Source: Chilean CNEP survey, 1993.

judiciary, Parliament, and political parties.) Television's current prestige stands in sharp contrast with attitudes toward the media under the authoritarian regime and during the transition, when radio was selected (by 41 percent of respondents in a 1987 poll by Flacso-Ceneca) as the most credible medium, far outdistancing both newspapers (18 percent) and television (14 percent).

Another characteristic of attitudes toward politics and the media that breaks sharply with the past concerns perceptions of partisan bias. Traditionally, Chilean society was highly politicized, and Chileans were actively involved in politics, and were accustomed to communications media that were explicitly linked to specific parties or political options. Nevertheless, the great majority of Chileans today regarded the media as neutral even in the course of an election campaign. As Table 5.5 shows, between two-thirds and three-quarters of those polled in our 1993 CNEP election survey regarded the three principal communications media as not favoring any particular party or candidate. It is also interesting to note that, of those who thought that the media were biased in favor of one political option or another, most thought that they favored the Concertación por la Democracia coalition and its candidate, Eduardo Frei. This is surprising since the great majority of the media are controlled (by ownership or management) by persons linked to the right and the former authoritarian regime. It is likely that the widespread perception of the media – especially television – as impartial has contributed significantly to their highly positive evaluation by Chileans. We suspect that this perceived neutrality has contributed so significantly to the high prestige of the media today in reaction against the superpoliticization of society and the media under Chile's preauthoritarian democracy, in combination with the largely successful depoliticization efforts of the Pinochet regime.

Table 5.6 How Often Did You Talk about Politics with . . . During the Campaign?

	1993	1996
Family		
Often	17.0%	11.5%
Sometimes	27.6	24.2
Almost never	27.7	26.0
Never	27.7	37.4
No answer	.1	.9
Friends		
Often	13.7%	7.9%
Sometimes	24.0	20.2
Almost never	19.9	20.1
Never	38.7	50.6
No answer	3.8	1.0
Coworkers		
Often	12.1%	9.8%
Sometimes	15.8	14.8
Almost never	14.3	18.2
Never	38.9	54.3
No answer	19.0	3.0

Sources: 1993 Chilean CNEP survey, and 1996 DESUC-COPESA survey of greater Santiago.

This shift toward greater partisan neutrality implies a significant change in a basic political function performed by the media. As they did during the transition to democracy, the media continue to play a significant role in the democratization process. But unlike that earlier period, when the media actively promoted change, their current function is to contribute to the stability of the new regime through various efforts to modify public opinion in accord with the requisites of democratic normalcy. Various public opinion surveys have revealed that, since the first year of democratic government, the polarization of political attitudes and the intensity of political involvement of most Chileans have declined to levels characteristic of stable, established democracies. One manifestation is the low and decreasing level of political discussion among Chileans, which can be seen in Table 5.6. Chileans are no longer moved by the great conflicts characteristic of the pre-coup era or of the transition to democracy. The several conflicts that led to polarization earlier appear to have evaporated, and the political space they previously occupied in terms of public attention has been filled by a multiplicity of small conflicts or issue-problems. The time of high centrality of politics has ended, and the great epics have been displaced by chronicles of daily life (Tironi 1991).

The communications media – first television and radio, then the print media – have adapted to and helped mold this new state of public opinion. Just as the media had earlier been pushed by the "invisible hand" of a public demanding political liberalization and the democratic transition, they now – still following public opinion – are distancing themselves from political and ideological conflicts, thereby contributing to democratic consolidation. This trend continued throughout the 1999/2000 presidential campaign and was greatly facilitated by the pragmatic election strategy of the conservative Joaquín Lavín, in which the candidate sought to distance himself from Pinochet and the former regime, and presented himself as a problem-solving populist. This has further contributed to Chile's democratic consolidation.

CONCLUSIONS

The thesis we have developed in this chapter can be reduced to four central points. The first is that under the authoritarian Pinochet regime, especially during the 1980s (a time of great socioeconomic change), an important modernization of the communications media took place. Among the characteristics of this process were the subordination of the media to the dynamics of the market and the spread of the associated market logic throughout the communications system; the expansion of the privatization and internationalization processes; and the increasing centrality of television among the media.

The second key point is that this modernization of the media had a great impact on the political system. This process helped to free the media from authoritarian control. Liberalization and increased pluralism within the media were largely products of the logic of the market system (specifically, the necessity to be in tune with the aspirations of the audience) rather than the result of a political commitment to liberty or democracy. Similarly, the contradiction between the expansion of economic freedom inherent in the Pinochet regime's free market philosophy, on the one hand, and restrictions in the political sphere, on the other, became unsustainable. These factors, among others, led the mass media to contribute decisively (sometimes without knowing it) to the broader processes of political liberalization and *apertura.*

The third point refers to the role in this process played by the opposition media – which had strong political ties but which occupied a marginal position within the communications system. These media served not so much (as has been believed) to exert massive pressure for liberalization as to introduce to the political realm themes, terminology, and personalities that until that time had been absent from public life. In other words, they mainly helped to reconstitute the political culture.

Finally, and in contrast with the media in other countries that have passed from an authoritarian regime to democracy, the Chilean media did not experience dramatic changes or breaks with the past; instead, most of the restructuring of the media system began under the authoritarian regime. The only media affected by the transition process were the politicized media that had opposed the authoritarian regime; faced with a general public increasingly indifferent to politics and strongly favoring greater impartiality, all of them disappeared (with the exception of Radio Cooperativa) after the fall of the regime against which they had struggled.

As we have argued, the continuity in the structure of the Chilean mass communications system reflects the fact that the media – with the exception of the opposition media just mentioned – were forced to rely for financial support on the market, severing their former dependent and tutelary relationships with political forces. In short, the transformation of the communications media – their modernization and emancipation from political control – had already taken place prior to changes in the political scene, so that the political transition did not bring about an abrupt break with the past.

NOTES

1. For an analysis of the daily newspaper market, see Portales 1981. For a survey of the magazine market, see Munizaga 1984.
2. Thus, for example, it was during the Unidad Popular period that parties of the left became proprietors of some radio stations. This was the case with Radio Portales, purchased by persons tied to President Allende, the Socialist Party's Radio Corporación, and the Communist Party's Radio Magallanes. For an analysis of radio in Chile, see Lassagni and Edwards 1988.
3. The experimental stage for university channels lasted from 1959 to 1962. At that time, the expansion of channels of the Universidad Católica, the Universidad de Chile, and the Universidad Católica de Valparaíso began. (See Hurtado 1989.)
4. For an analysis of this legal framework, see Munizaga 1981. For a study of the evolution of television in Chile, see Hurtado 1988.
5. For an analysis of the impact of the military government on the print media, see Navarro 1985.

6. Respect for the autonomy of universities (including the inviolability of campuses and university properties) had been an integral part of democratic politics in Chile and was zealously maintained for decades.

7. During the first seven years of military rule (a period referred to as "dictatorship"), Chile was governed under the provisions of temporary constitutional acts passed by the Junta. In 1980, a constitutional committee appointed by General Pinochet approved a constitutional draft that was subsequently submitted to a referendum. Through an allegedly fraudulent process, the constitution was ratified. Nonetheless, and despite the authoritarian nature of the constitution, the regime was bound by its own constitutional rules. Thus, the period following 1980 is known as the "institutionalized phase."

8. The case of TVN was different since the state continued to contribute financial support, offsetting its persistent annual deficits.

9. The first of these magazines to appear were *Apsi* (which received authorization in 1977 as an international affairs bulletin, and which subsequently transformed itself into a political news magazine), *Hoy* (which emerged from a schism within another magazine in 1977 growing out of a labor dispute), and *Análisis* (which was born under the protection of the Academia de Humanismo Cristiano and the archbishopric of Santiago). The magazine *Cauce* appeared in 1983 and scored several journalistic coups through its aggressive investigative reporting.

10. The main example is Radio Cooperativa, owned by a company whose directorate is made up mainly of persons close to the Christian Democrats. This radio station achieved prominence in 1980, when it redefined its functions as those combining commercial and informational radio. See Lassagni and Edwards et al. 1988.

11. The precarious financial state of the magazines *Análisis* and *Apsi* was particularly precarious. In 1980 they obtained just .21 and .17 percent, respectively, of all advertising income. The magazine *Hoy* received much more advertising income – 24.64 percent of the total. The situation is similar with regard to circulation: in 1980 *Análisis* and *Apsi* accounted for just 3.28 and 4.21 percent, respectively, of total annual magazine sales, while the circulation of *Hoy* reached 33.99 percent. See Catalán 1981.

12. The media that best represent this conception are the magazine *Hoy* and Radio Cooperativa, both linked to the Christian Democrats.

13. For a more extensive discussion of this plebiscite, see LASA International Commission 1989.

14. For a study of the audience for such magazines, see "Preferencias de lectores de revistas e imagen de revista Apsi," 1986. (Santiago: DIAGNOS, January 1986).

15. *La Epoca* competed with *El Mercurio*, attempting to attract a portion of its "enlightened" public. *Fortín Mapocho* was locked in competition with the dailies *La Tercera*, *La Cuarta*, and *Las Ultimas Noticias* for a share of the mass/popular audience. See Ossandón and Rojas 1989, 41–2.

16. These data (cited in Sunkel 1991b) were derived from a poll on "Reading Habits and the Images of Newspapers" undertaken by the survey-research firm Diagnos in 1987.

17. We shall leave aside other characteristics of the modernization process that are important for understanding the evolution of the communications system itself but that did not have a direct impact on the political process. Therefore, we will not deal with the internationalization of communications, the segmentation of audiences, professionalization, and a host of technological changes.

18. While there were 53 television sets for every thousand persons in 1970, this figure increased to 121 in 1974, to 205 in 1980, and to 302 in 1983. See Brunner and Catalán 1989.

19. In a survey of cultural consumption undertaken by FLACSO-CENECA in 1987, 91.3 percent of those interviewed stated that they had watched television in the last few days. This was followed by radio (79.6 percent), books (21.1 percent), movies (22.2 percent), and newspapers (21.1 percent). See Catalán and Sunkel 1990.

20. Other recipients of advertising revenues were public billboards (with 3.8 percent of the total) and movie theaters (.3 percent). Source: Time-América Economía, *The Chilean Market 94/95: Marketing and Financial Statistics,* Santiago, 1994.

21. From Contreras (secretary general of the Episcopal Conference of Chile) 1988. The following discussion is based largely on Portales et al. 1988.

22. The Comité Técnico was the body charged with designing strategic alternatives for the campaign on which the political directors would base their decisions. It was created in November 1987 and was composed of social scientists with access to a broad array of public-opinion survey data.

23. Guillermo O'Donnell speaks of two transitions: the first ends with the installation of a democratic government and the second with the consolidation of democracy. The consolidation process involves the elimination of "tutelary powers" of "non-elected elites," disappearance of "reserved domains" in which elected governments were precluded from acting, and correction of distortions in the electoral system. Beginning in 1990, the Chilean political process was characterized by democratic consolidation, with advances in all of these respects. (See Valenzuela 1992.)

24. The Consejo Nacional de Televisión, created by the Ley de Televisión of 1970, has as its function "oversight of the correct function of the medium." With changes in this law introduced in 1989, at the end of the authoritarian regime, the Consejo was given the authority to grant new concessions of television wavelengths to private entities.

25. These four television networks have met with very different fates. Megavisión achieved third place position behind TVUC (the network of the Universidad Católica) and TVN; the other three never took off and have encountered severe financial difficulties.

26. This study is part of the Comparative National Elections Project (CNEP), in which teams of scholars based in Germany, Great Britain, Italy, Japan, Spain, the United States, and Uruguay used questionnaires including a battery of common questions. In Chile, the survey was carried out by the Dirección de Estudios Sociológicos of the Universidad Católica. The panel consisted of a preelection wave (undertaken in October and November 1993), and postelection follow-up interviews carried out from February to March 1994. This was based on a quota sample of 1,305 Chilean residents over age 18 living in the Greater Santiago area.

CHAPTER 6

Media Influence in the Italian Transition from a Consensual to a Majoritarian Democracy

Carlo Marletti and Franca Roncarolo

Foreign observers tend to view the Italian political scene as a kind of puzzle, as complicated as it is fascinating and incomprehensible. One French expert on Italian issues, for instance, has rather maliciously noted that his fellow countrymen tend to look on Italian politics as "strange, mysterious, paradoxical, Byzantine, irrational, illogical" (Lazar 1995, 231). These kinds of opinions can only have been strengthened by a 1994 election that saw the sudden emergence of important new political parties and the demise of old ones that had governed Italy for decades. A protracted series of center to center-left coalition governments gave way to a clear triumph of the center-right, including for the first time the postfascist Alleanza Nazionale–Movimento Sociale Italiano (AN–MSI) as a full coalition partner[1] and a new party, Forza Italia, headed by an individual with no previous experience in elected office, the television magnate Silvio Berlusconi. The winning coalition also included the Lega del Nord (Northern League), a recently formed party emphasizing localism and capitalizing on the protest of the Po Valley regions against the Roman bureaucracy and government centralization. In addition to the wholesale replacement of majority parties and party leaders, the basic formula of government formation was altered. Indeed, the magnitude of these political changes was so substantial as to lead some to refer to this process as giving birth to a "second republic," whose fundamental features are decidedly different from those of the previous five decades of the post–World War II era.[2] While this was certainly a dramatic change, it did not represent a complete break with the past, since political instability continued, and the magnitude of electoral change varied significantly from region to region.

A few months later, the Lega del Nord provoked a government crisis and abandoned its allies on the center-right. The election that followed in April 1996 was won by a new coalition, the Ulivo coalition, that included centrist parties such as the Christian democratic Partito Popolare Italiano (PPI) and the Partito Democratico della Sinistra (PDS, which emerged out of the majority segment of the former Communist Party), with the PDS being the strongest, if not the dominant, party in the alliance. For the first time since 1947, politicians with Communist backgrounds became government ministers. Thus, only two years after turning to the right, Italian politics changed again, shifting to the left.

But this did not end political instability in Italy. The center-left government headed by the Ulivo leader Romano Prodi also experienced difficulty in transforming a broad electoral alliance into an effective governing coalition and had to deal with problems resulting from its slim parliamentary majority. The Prodi government fell in October 1998 and was replaced by a a reconfigured coalition located closer to the center, with PDS leader Massimo D'Alema as prime minster. This government crisis and the ensuing changes had the effect of increasing political fragmentation. Divisions within and between parties increased, complicating government policy making and undermining the majority coalition's ability to deal with serious domestic and international crises.

The role played by the mass communications media in this protracted transition is one of the most hotly debated questions among political observers and commentators. One group of scholars regards the impact of the media as dramatic and decisive, viewing the 1994 election in "catastrophist" terms and arguing that it reflected the conversion of Italy into a "teledemocracy" – a political regime in which parties were replaced by television and traditional models of parties gave way to the media-party founded by Berlusconi.[3] Others, however, advance a more complex and conditional interpretation, bringing into the equation a number of social-structural, institutional, and cultural changes that evolved over a longer period of time. While recognizing the impact of the media on the 1994 electoral campaign, they regard the resulting party-system change as the product of exceptional circumstances, probably unrepeatable, relating to the crisis provoked by an unprecedented wave of scandals and by the transition from party government to majoritarianism.[4] What is clear is that a substantial change in the nature of party–media relations occurred during the 1980s and early 1990s that helped to undermine mass support for the old order. Parties that previously counted on certain media outlets for support (following the establishment of an elaborate quasi-consociational system in the mid-1970s) found in the 1990s that increasingly influential segments of the media, especially television, were exposing their misdeeds and subjecting politicians to unprecedented levels of critical scrutiny. Not only did the media play this role in toppling the old order, but the most powerful player in the communications industry, Silvio Berlusconi, parlayed his nearly complete domination of commercial television broadcasting into a successful campaign for national political leadership.

In addition to playing a key role in bringing about massive political change, television in Italy has become a subject of controversy, since its political role poses new problems for democratic theory and ethics. Following his election as prime minister, Berlusconi was in a position to control the public broadcasting system as well. In a dramatic break with the consensual *lottizzazione* practices of the 1980s – in which each of the major parties had its own share of the public broadcasting system, Radiotelevisione Italiana (RAI, which originally stood for Radio Audizioni Italiane) – Berlusconi and his coalition allies (Gianfranco Fini of the Alleanza Nazionale and Umberto Bossi of the Lega del Nord) adopted majoritarian winner-take-all policies in appointing directors and overseers of the RAI broadcasting empire. Thus, one set of partisan elites was in a position to dominate both the public and private sectors of television broadcasting, raising serious questions regarding the quality of Italian democracy.

This chapter focuses primarily on the relationship between television and partisan politics in Italy. To some extent, the distinguishing features of this relationship derive from processes that are found worldwide but that, despite Italy's sociocultural modernization and media development, were delayed by a very fragmented, quasi-consociational party system. These processes include the growing predominance of television as the principal medium of political communication in combination with what we shall refer to as the "media logic" (Altheide and Snow 1979). The latter concept refers to the tendency of the media (especially television) to "spectacularize" the events and themes of politics in order to attract mass audiences. This involves a degree of personalization of politics and an increasing tendency to regard coverage of political news as entertainment rather than political communication per se.

But the relationship between politics and the media is also a product of important structural attributes of the Italian sociopolitical and sociocultural systems. This relationship has been profoundly affected by Italy's fragmented and polarized party system. By the mid-1970s, a quasi-consociational set of practices had come into being as a means of coping with conflict, instability, and potential polarization.[5] Party colonization of television became an important element of the politics of the old order. Television served as a particularly important medium of political communication in Italy because of certain aspects of Italian culture, especially its low levels of newspaper and periodical readership. This linkage was weakened beginning in the mid-1970s, however, given the persistent gap between the political class and the masses, the rapid and unregulated growth of the media, and the increasing inability of parties to contain the democratic struggle. In short, the party system ceased to represent the myriad social identities and economic interests in a rapidly changing and ever more complex society. Sociocultural changes, driven in large measure by economic growth and the expansion of mass consumption, combined with the political crises provoked by political corruption scandals and dissatisfaction over the state of the economy, led to widespread demands for political and institutional change. The media played a significant role in delegitimizing the old party system and bringing about a shift to the new order.

In short, our argument is that the media have had a marked impact on politics but also that politics affects the media as well. This reciprocity is seemingly generic, if not universal, but what has to be explained is the particular way in which, in the Italian crisis, the interplay between media and parties occurred. This requires an exploration of the relationships linking the media and the political and institutional characteristics of Italy both before and after the transformation. As we shall see, just as the old order was underpinned by partisan control of sectors of the public broadcast industry, in the incompletely institutionalized and increasingly majoritarian winner-take-all game of partisan competition in Italy today, the changing role of the media, their deregulation, and the control exerted by private groups over television networks and the press have assumed great importance as a crucial challenge to Italian democracy.

THE BACKGROUND TO CHANGE

Since 1946, Italy has been a stable democracy founded on an unstable political equilibrium. No other major European nation has the same long tradition of short-lived governments, whose average life span has been about ten months. This instability notwithstanding, Italian democracy has survived a very rapid, intense, and socially dislocative process of modernization without experiencing dramatic institutional change or authoritarian reaction. Agriculture still played a dominant role in the national economy as late as the end of World War II, but today Italy is one of the world's major industrialized countries (Bagnasco 1996). It has survived terrorism of both the right and the left, including the terrorist kidnapping and murder of former Prime Minister Aldo Moro, and yet has had to place fewer restrictions on personal freedom than, for example, the United Kingdom, Germany, and, more recently, Spain (Della Porta and Pasquino 1983).

The key factor explaining the nature, successes, and failures of Italian democracy is the relationship between the political regime and civil society. The fragmented and polarized multipartyism that has been characteristic of party government (Sartori 1966) has most commonly been singled out as a serious inadequacy of Italian democracy, particularly insofar as it contributed to the development of particularism, favoritism, and political corruption. At the same time, however, it created a vast web of interest mediation networks that served to mitigate the impact of social conflicts and to permit the growth of individual freedoms in the context of a pluralism of social identities.

During the late 1940s and early 1950s, Italy's political system had been highly polarized between a dominant Christian Democratic Party (DC) and its religious and moderate subculture, on the one hand, and the Marxist Communist (PCI) and Socialist (PSI) parties and their radical subcultures, on the other. Conflict between "Reds" and "Whites" was mitigated and successfully managed, however, through several aspects of party ties to civil society. Farneti (1976; 1983) first argued that the way in which parties performed their intermediation functions allowed for the coexistence of potentially conflicting political subcultures. Graziano (1979, 729) built on this notion and pointed to the quasi-consociational nature of the Italian party system, which, although based on a "permanent division of society," fostered integration through the construction of overlapping memberships involving religion and class, and through bargaining and logrolling between workers and owners. Even the highly particularistic forms of interest intermediation in the south (particularly by the DC) served this integrative function.[6] Cassano (1979) and Morlino (1991) have pointed to the way in which Italian parties performed their "gatekeeping" function – that is, the manner in which parties exchange electoral support for interest representation (also see Hine 1993 and Calise 1994) – helped to mitigate and regulate potential conflict. The high point of quasi-consociational interparty accommodation was the strategy of *compromesso storico* (a "historic pact" between the majority centrist parties and the leading party of the opposition, the PCI), launched in 1972 and culminating in the so-called governments of national solidarity of 1977–8.

The communications media played a key role in stabilizing interparty relations and depolarizing political conflict, although the nature of party–media relations emerged only gradually. Initially, there was only one television network, RAI, a public entity that was effectively controlled by the governing DC. The television monopoly's first stance on partisan politics was largely to ignore it – its first broadcasts in 1954 to those at the end of the decade being notable mainly for the absence of overtly political communication. Indeed, the first program featuring party representatives was *Tribuna Politica* (*Political Forum*), which began during the 1960–1 season, following the failure of an attempt to form for the first time a center-right government coalition with external support of the neofascist MSI. Subsequently, the formation of the first center-left coalition to include the PSI in 1962 led to an early form of a quasi-consociational system that helped to facilitate accommodation among party elites. This was accompanied by the emergence of the *lottizzazione* system, in which sectors or "lots" of the broadcasting media were controlled by the various parties. Establishment of a second RAI channel in 1961 meant that, over time, one of the public stations (RAI-1) would be controlled by the DC and the new RAI-2 would publicize the viewpoints of the other parties in the government coalitions of the 1960s – the PSI, the Social Democrats (PSDI), and the Republicans (PRI).

In 1979, the DC's inability to form a government with its usual coalition partners brought the *lottizzazione* system to full fruition. Given its dependence on the once vilified PCI for parliamentary support, the minority DC government agreed to a series of unprecedented concessions. The PCI was given the chairs of several parliamentary committees, as well as the presidency of one of the two houses of the legislature. At the same time, a third public television station was created and made available to the PCI. Thus, throughout the 1980s, partisan pluralism within the public broadcast media was rigidly institutionalized through adoption of quasi-consociational practices. The DC was allowed to dominate RAI-1, the PSI largely controlled RAI-2, and the PCI made its views known through RAI-3. This sharing of the public communications media helped reduce the Red–White polarization that had characterized Italian politics since the late 1940s, although serious objections can be raised to the appointment of broadcasters on the basis of party patronage rather than merit.

It should be noted that partisan biases in news coverage and political broadcasting by the three public networks were somewhat restrained. This occurred largely because the institutional and political frameworks for television broadcasting were considerably different from those of the other communications media. The press was allowed to be partisan and opinionated in its political coverage, for example, but television was held to strict standards of impartiality by oversight boards whose members included representatives of all the major parties. While almost all the big national newspapers had been privately owned since the prewar years, television was under monopolistic and strict state control from the very beginning. Apart from reducing the potential for partisan distortions of television news coverage, these structural differences also had a marked impact on journalistic careers. It was very difficult to start a career in a newspaper and then switch to television or vice versa. This is still the rule today, albeit to a somewhat lesser extent.

While the structure and communications function of television helped to mitigate the polarization that characterized partisan politics following World War II, it failed to reduce a political cleavage of another kind. One of the persistent characteristics of Italian political culture, dating back to the founding of the Italian state, has been a significant separation between ordinary citizens and political elites. The Italian unification process, the Risorgimento, was led by elites isolated from, and not responsive to, the wishes of the mass public. This continuing cleavage has sometimes been characterized as separating the "legal country" from the "real country" – the institutions and laws of the regime, on the one hand, and the attitudes and behaviors of the citizenry, on the other.

The cultural gap between elites and masses was all the wider for the low level of literacy in Italy throughout the nineteenth and early twentieth centuries compared with countries such as Britain, France, and Germany. Indeed, illiteracy remained widespread in Italy until the end of World War II. Book and newspaper reading was then, and has remained, the preserve of a fairly small and atypical section of the public.[7] Even today, the country is close to the bottom of the European ladder for newspaper sales – just above Spain and Greece – and below Spain in book reading.

The introduction of radio, the first electronic means of communication, did little to change this picture. Soon after the beginning of regular public broadcasting in the 1920s, the number of radio-set owners in the United States increased in a short period from 100,000 to over 1,500,000 and in Britain from 36,000 to 1,130,000. Italy, by contrast, counted just

10,000 owners in 1925 and about 98,000 in 1929. Their number topped 1,000,000 only in 1939, some ten years later than other industrialized Western countries (Papa 1978, 7 and 26).

In sharp contrast, the introduction of television in 1954 produced a dramatic change in media consumption habits, as its audience soared almost immediately to between 7 and 10 million people. By the beginning of the 1960s, television broadcasts were available throughout virtually the whole of the country, and viewership of television encompassed almost all citizens within a few short years. Today, 99.6 percent of households (more than 20 million families) own a television set, and Italy has a very complex and articulated television system, richer than those of other European countries with regard to the number of stations, quantity and variety of broadcasts and formats, and perhaps quality as well.[8]

The omnipresence of television viewing has produced remarkable changes not only in mass behavior and attitudes, but also in the spoken language. Before television, regional dialects were spoken by the majority of Italians, while the Italian language was little used and badly spoken except among elites. Exposure to television broadcasts in a single form of Italian has contributed substantially to a nationwide standardization of the language (De Mauro 1973; Berruto 1988; Dardano 1994).

But this standardization of the Italian language did not lessen the separation between the masses and their political leaders. Readership of newspapers and magazines has always been a middle- and upper-class pastime; the chosen medium of the masses is television. Nonetheless, despite its potential for bridging this gap, television actually reinforced the cultural division between elites and masses.

The opening of television to partisan politics in the 1960s failed to meet the expectations aroused by broadcasting, for the first time, debates over public issues before the entire citizenry. After initially attracting mass audiences, the main political programs, *Tribuna Politica* and *Tribuna Elettorale* declined significantly: while television news and entertainment programs in the 1970s reached audiences of over 10 million, these political programs had audiences that rarely exceeded 500,000 to 700,000 except during electoral campaigns (Cipriani 1962; Jacobelli 1971; Mazzoleni 1992, 132–40 and 181–96). In part, this was the result of the party leaders' tendency to speak to each other in these televised encounters using the jargon and abstract concepts of political elites, rather than communicating with ordinary citizens using language and ideas that they could more readily understand. Paradoxically, the creation of this new political communication format – with its capacity for making direct contact with millions of ordinary citizens – merely reinforced the growing dualism between elite and mass political cultures. The cultural and political consequences of this divide have been enormous.

The traditional mass–elite cleavage in Italian society has been linked to a second source of conflict that was relevant to the collapse of the old order in the early 1990s: the growing competition between party politicians and media chiefs. Politicians wanted to maintain their traditional control over political communications, whereas media chiefs were intent on attracting large audiences by providing entertainment programming. This conflict was an important factor undermining the quasi-consociational elements of Italian politics and moving it in the direction of institutional majoritarianism.

Consociational and majoritarian politics differ significantly with regard to the relationship between politics and the media. In majoritarian systems, direct appeals to public opinion as a means of resolving controversial partisan issues are common and are accepted as normal arenas for the articulation of conflict (Marletti 1995b). The clear demarcation between majority and opposition allows such issues to be presented in accordance with a media logic whereby the press, radio, and television simplify, dichotomize, and play up the entertainment value of political events, themes, and personalities to attract the attention of the mass audience. Under multiparty systems and especially consociationalism, however, direct appeals to public opinion occur relatively infrequently, and their political impact is seldom decisive. The reasons are three. First, multiparty systems develop their own internal mechanisms, some formal and some informal, for accommodating economic and social interests and resolving controversial issues. Moreover, the parties commonly prefer these conflict management mechanisms to those offered by the media because they do not entail the same risk of loss of control that is associated with going public. Second, multiparty systems of the consociational type often lead to an overrepresentation of pressure groups and to a segmentation of collective identities because they offer these groups a plurality of channels as outlets of expression. This occurs when, for various reasons, party-system fragmentation increases, resulting not only in a larger number of parties, but also in the formation, within the major parties, of groups organized as "wings." These subparty organizations weaken the interest-gatekeeping function of parties and make it less selective by multiplying the points of access to the decisional system and the forms of exchange among parties, party wings, and interest groups

(Pasquino 1980 and 1988; Dente 1985; Regonini 1994). All this is reflected in the media, which, being *lottizzati,* highlight certain themes and events for partisan reasons and launch campaigns in favor of one or the other political or economic group. This, in turn, intensifies the struggle for control over the media and for access to coverage. Third, multiparty systems by definition encompass and represent many voices that are organizationally distinct from each other. These voices cannot be easily condensed into a small number of choices and presented in simplified form to the public for its arbitration. The needs of governments concerned with complexity, and the needs of media concerned with simplicity and drama, are directly at odds under these circumstances. An additional source of tension between party and media elites in systems adopting quasi-consociational appointment and promotion procedures, such as the *lottizzazione,* derives from the fact that this "spoils" method implies the preferential allotment of managerial posts on the basis of partisan loyalty rather than merit or professional qualifications. With the professionalization of the broadcast media, resentment over party intervention was bound to increase.

Generally speaking, therefore, politicians in multiparty systems seek to control the behavior of the media and to keep controversial political issues out of the public domain. But in the Italian case they failed, and the conflict between their needs and those of the media exploded onto the political scene, delegitimizing these quasi-consociational practices and party government under the old order. One reason was that, as the media grew in size and complexity, so did the influence of associated, independent bodies of mass communications professionals, pollsters, and marketing experts. This development both complicated and dislocated the traditional web of formal and informal linkages between political parties and interest groups. The political elite responded to the dislocation by trying to restrain the media's development and limit their influence, initially by maintaining a state monopoly over television broadcasting, intervening directly in programming decisions, and using overt political censorship. The adoption of *lottizzazione* practices only served to modify the nature of partisan intervention, although it did allow (in the aggregate) for greater pluralism (Monteleone 1992; Pellegrino 1993).

Maintenance of control, however, was made increasingly difficult by conflict and cross-pressures within the parties, by the instability and short life span of coalition governments, and by the cumbersome and protracted decision-making processes typical of a fragmented multiparty system like that of Italy. The large number of organized political groups (each with the right of voice, institutional representation, and access – often in competition with each other – to lobbies) significantly slowed decision-making processes, both because of the large number of participating actors and because of their recourse to the mutual veto. These problems have beset the appointment of RAI officials[9] and, more generally, virtually all decisions concerning communication policies. Thus, the ability of political parties to control mass communications has been progressively weakened by fragmentation and political cross-vetoes.

Prior to the mid-1970s, the traditional relationship between parties and the media was based on the use of specific media outlets as allied or dependent channels for partisan political communication. Until at least 1983, television exercised little influence on politics that was independent of party control, despite the growth of a large and differentiated mass communications system. But by this time, the partisan subcultures within which the media functioned had been eroded away by modernization and secularization processes, and by the emergence of a mass culture that was isolated from, if not cynical toward politics. In addition, cross-pressures within the media meant that the communications system entered a hotly contested phase of deregulation in which mass culture become an important political resource for those outside the party system.

THE STRUGGLE FOR ECONOMIC AND POLITICAL CONTROL OF THE MEDIA

As we have already seen, throughout the first two decades of television broadcasting (which began in 1954), the government exercised monopoly control over the medium. In 1976, however, the Constitutional Court declared this monopoly unconstitutional, thereby allowing the emergence of private-sector broadcasting. It is important to note that the beginning of this second phase in the development of Italy's communications media coincided with the electoral weakening of the largest party and centerpiece of all postwar governments, the DC. As a result, coalition governments became more unstable, the weight of the smaller parties within them grew, and conflict within the governing majority increased. Thus, the DC, as noted earlier, was obliged to forge a more collaborative relationship with the PCI and to allow its entry into the quasi-consociational *lottizzazione*.

Against this background of political uncertainty and change, the

Table 6.1   *Average Television Audiences, 1987–93*

	RAI	Fininvest	TMC and Others
1987	45.1%	44.8%	10.1%
1988	46.7	39.2	14.1
1989	48.4	38.0	13.6
1990	51.4	36.8	11.8
1991	48.2	41.5	10.3
1992	47.3	43.4	9.3
1993	49.1	43.7	7.2

Source: Auditel data elaboration from Brigida *et al.,*1993.

structure of the television industry changed substantially. The end result was the emergence of a duopoly pitting the three RAI channels against a private-sector television empire dominated by a business tycoon from Milan, Silvio Berlusconi.

At first, the 1976 Constitutional Court decision encouraged a proliferation of independent local stations. Over time, however, an enormous number of these stations were acquired by Berlusconi's holding company, Fininvest. By the end of the 1980s, Berlusconi had come to dominate, unchallenged, the private sector of television broadcasting. The three largest private networks were his (Canale 5, Retequattro, and Italia-1), and his closest competitor (Telemontecarlo) lagged far behind. The RAI and Fininvest networks all but monopolized the Italian television audience, as can be seen in Table 6.1.

Thus, in the late 1970s and early 1980s, the television industry was a battlefield on which two struggles were being fought simultaneously: a political struggle over partisan control of the public sector and an economic fight over audience share between RAI and Fininvest-Publitalia. These two struggles often overlapped and became entangled, especially as the interparty fight for control of public television intensified. At first, Berlusconi's private networks remained above the struggle between the majority parties, maintaining good relations with all of them. Subsequently, however, they shifted to open support of the PSI, led by Bettino Craxi, who had become premier after the 1983 election. Craxi repaid this support by quickly passing two decree-laws revoking the blackout that magistrates had imposed on Fininvest channels several times between 1984 and 1985.[10]

It was in this context that political scandals began to rock the dominant parties and their leaders. As we shall see, commercial television and adversary-journalism campaigns in the press both played significant roles in the "destructuration" and ensuing crisis of the Italian political party system.

THE CHANGE OF POLITICAL SUBCULTURES IN THE 1980s

The massive political change that occurred in the early 1990s was the product of both long-term and short-term factors. Socioeconomic modernization and secularization progressively undermined the old order by weakening the subcultural and institutional underpinnings of the parties that had dominated Italian politics since World War II. The aforementioned gap between masses and elites led to the lack of potentially stabilizing attachments, as well as to a pervasive cynicism about parties and politicians (Sani and Segatti 2000) and dissatisfaction with the perceived low efficacy of Italian governments (Morlino and Montero 1995). Short-term causes of the breakdown of the old order included the massive corruption scandals that involved prominent leaders of most of the major parties, as well as the simultaneous occurrence of an economic crisis. The emergence of a new, adversarial form of journalism also played a decisive role in bringing about this transformation.

For over 30 years, the stability of voting patterns had been a defining characteristic of the Italian party system.[11] Even if the vote share of individual parties varied from election to election, the distribution of the total vote among parties falling into right-, center, and left-wing groupings remained more or less constant. Indeed, both Italy's intrabloc volatility score (measuring net shifts of votes among parties within the same ideological bloc) of 6.4 and its interbloc volatility average of 1.6 between 1953 and 1987 were both considerably lower than the 8.1 and 2.9 averages for the rest of Western Europe during this time period (Morlino 1995, 318 and 320). The main reason for this constancy is commonly held to be the persistence of subcultural cleavages underpinning the Italian party system (see Gunther and Montero 2000).

Throughout the first republic, the Italian party system was characterized by fragmentation and polarization (Sartori 1966). This ideological polarization was less the product of social-structural cleavages than of political factors outside the party system – namely, the historical legacy of the fascist past and the confrontation between East and West during the early stages of the Cold War. Two major fault lines were created. The first differentiated parties committed to the republican constitution, on one side, from monarchical groups, and above all from the MSI, a party sympathetic to the fascist regime, on the other. This fault line separated the parties of the center and moderate center-right from the antisystem parties of the extreme right. The second cleavage divided the other constitutional parties from the PCI, the major left-wing party. Branded as an antisystem party, the PCI was never allowed to enter the government, although in the late 1970s it helped sustain in office a minority DC government. As a result of these ideological fault lines, coalition governments could not form on the basis of purely strategic or programmatic considerations; coalition formation could take place only within clearly defined ideological limits. While numerous efforts were made to transcend these boundaries (especially the PCI's desire to enter government by forging a *compromesso storico* [historic compromise] with the DC), these ideological cleavages continued to divide parties throughout the life of the first republic (Farneti 1976; 1983).

Nonetheless, long-term processes of social change were eroding some of the foundations of this electoral stability. Parties began to lose the symbiotic relationships with their respective subcultures and started to transform themselves into political machines whose cohesion depended mainly on networks of underlying interests.[12] The DC was the first party to suffer this fate. The country's largest party for almost 40 years, it had participated in (if not dominated) every government coalition and had produced all but two of the first republic's prime ministers. The key to its success was its close association with the Catholic subculture, transformed into a "bulwark against Communism" following the outbreak of the Cold War. It is important to note that the identification of Catholics with the DC was primarily the product of a political, not a social, cleavage (Farneti 1976; 1983). It emerged shortly after World War II and was fully manifested first in the 1948 election campaign, when the DC enjoyed the open support of the Catholic Church, enabling it to reach people even in isolated rural parishes. Bishops and parish priests exhorted their parishioners to vote for the DC and against the Communist peril (Prandi 1968), and religious associations such as the Azione Cattolica and the Comitati Civici mobilized support for the DC in nearly all Italian cities. The media also played a significant role in the DC's campaign: "friendly newspapers" backed the anti-Communist campaign and published the appeals of these civic committees;[13] radio broadcasts (such as those by the so-called God speaker, Father Lombardi) echoed the same themes; and even movies were used for electoral propaganda.[14]

In the 1960s, however, the subcultural basis of the DC's support began to erode, partly as the result of the long-term secularization of Italian society[15] and partly in response to a change in the church's stance on politics. The direct intervention of the church in Italian politics had continued throughout the papacy of Pius XII. But under Pope John XXIII, and in particular after the Vatican Council II, the church publicly distanced itself from politics while maintaining a privileged relationship with the DC (Poggi 1974). The DC's ties to the mass communications media were also transformed. Until 1976, it had derived a remarkable electoral benefit from the government's monopoly over radio and television broadcasting. Following the development of the *lottizzazione,* its direct control was narrowed to RAI-1 (the most important public station, with the largest audience), although it also continued to exercise some influence over the entire public broadcasting sector through its appointment of the sector's general director (Marletti 1988a).

While the religious base of DC support weakened progressively over time, it never completely disappeared. The PSI, by contrast, had lost its ties to its subculture almost completely by the end of the 1980s. One reason is that, while the White (Catholic) political subculture remained essentially unitary and tied to a single party (the DC) for more than 40 years, the Red (PSI) political subculture was divided from the very beginning among several parties that were mostly in competition with each other. Particularly salient was the division between the more radical wing, which by and large identified with the PCI, and the more reformist wing, for the most part linked with the PSI. For a variety of reasons, the PCI expanded its base of support within the Red camp, at the expense of the PSI. Its greater organizational ability, derived from its strongly centralized party structure, proved to be a substantial asset in this regard. The PSI's shift toward the government bloc, and specifically its decision to enter into a coalition with the DC beginning in 1963, also caused socialist activists and supporters to defect to the PCI. By the late 1970s, many observers predicted that the PSI would eventually be completely absorbed by the PCI. Craxi reacted against this tendency and, in alliance with the centrist wing of the DC, clashed with PCI leader Enrico Berlinguer over the PCI's efforts to bring about a *compromesso storico.* Craxi's strategy and alliances with the DC had the effect of redefining the basic orientation and electoral base of the PSI, progressively alienating it from its traditional supporters on the left: it became much more center oriented, and it was increasingly transformed from a mass workers' party to one representing the middle class. What is more important, interest groups came to dominate the party to such an extent that it lost all sense of its electoral clientele and became a vehicle for the (often corrupt) pursuit of organized-group or merely personal interests (as illustrated by the indictment of former Prime Minister Bettino Craxi).

In contrast with the DC and PCI, the PSI did not enjoy close and durable ties with newspapers apart from the party's own *Avanti!*. In the 1960s and 1970s, the party was generally supported by some daily papers, such as *Il Giorno* (which for a while ranked fourth among Italy's newspapers – Murialdi 1972 and Table 6.2), by magazines such as *L'Espresso*, and by some other periodicals appealing to the reformist, laic middle class. But this support disappeared in the 1980s following Craxi's turn toward the center. *L'Espresso* even launched a campaign strongly critical of the PSI. The PSI continued to control RAI-2, the second public television station, on the basis of quasi-consociational agreements with the DC. In the aggregate, Craxi transformed the PSI into an "opinion party" in which the charismatic personalization of its leader and direct appeals to party activists and voters through the television counted more than a capillary mass organization.[16]

The PCI was more successful in maintaining its subcultural links than most other parties. Excluded from government due to the continuing Cold War and the resulting cleavage between Communist and anti-Communist parties, it depended more heavily on its own supportive infrastructure and was not ensnared in the networks of interests that surrounded the governing parties. The PCI needed a strong mass organization to maintain the loyalty of its electorate and to mobilize the masses for political action. It also relied more heavily on its own channels of political communication and propaganda. Most important among them was the party's newspaper, *L'Unità*, with a normal daily circulation of just over 100,000. In addition to being sold at newsstands, however, it was distributed directly by party activists on special occasions, usually on Sundays or at mass demonstrations, which pushed its circulation to up to 1 million. Until the late 1970s, the party also counted on mass demonstrations as a channel of political communication. In addition to election rallies, these included national strikes, which assembled hundreds of thousands of protesters, and the Festival of L'Unità. These festivals (which are still held throughout the country, albeit on a smaller scale) include trade fairs, dances, fast-food vendors, and entertainment, accompanied by cultural and political debates, visits of foreign delegations, and so on.[17] The party's success in maintaining its own mass communication and propaganda channels of this kind was also due to the fact that coverage by the broadcast media and independent press was

Table 6.2   *Daily Average Circulation (in Thousands) of the Eight Largest Newspapers (Excluding Sports Papers) and Their Political Orientations in 1971 and 1991*

1971	
Corriere della sera (moderate, center)	504
Stampa (liberal, center)	420
Messaggero (liberal, center)	274
Giorno (liberal, center to left)	244
Nazione (moderate, center to right)	219
Resto del Carlino (moderate, center to right)	218
Tempo (moderate, right)	205
Paese Sera (liberal to radical, left)	154
1991	
Repubblica (liberal, left)	677
Corriere della Sera (liberal, center to left)	674
Stampa (liberal, center to left)	406
Il Sole – 24 ore (liberal, center)	274
Messaggero (liberal, center to left)	269
Resto del Carlino (moderate, center to right)	234
Nazione (moderate, center to right)	202
Giornale (moderate, right)	160

Source: Based on Murialdi (1972) and Pucci (1996). Data were not available for *L'Unità* in 1971.

limited and was insufficient to reach a mass audience. Only after 1979 did the PCI control its own public television station, RAI-3 – a product of its support for "national solidarity" and the related quasi-consociational agreements with the DC. Aside from RAI-3, the PCI (and subsequently the PDS) could only count on the support of a small number of local television and radio stations. Nonetheless, by maintaining its own traditional channels of propaganda and political communication, the PCI was better able to preserve a closer bond with its supportive subculture than were the government parties.

Beginning in the 1980s, internal divisions began to appear within the PCI, based on ideological differences and interest-group ties (such as with the Lega delle Cooperative, which represents the interests of small and medium-sized businesses), as well as a gradual distancing of the party from its traditional bases of support and the aging of its militants. In 1986, for example, the PCI still had a strong mass organization (with 1.6 million members), but only 3.2 percent of its members were young people, while retired persons had grown as a share of total membership from 17.3 percent to 21 percent in less than ten years (Mammarella 1995). The transformation of the PCI into the PDS at the twentieth party congress in 1991 produced a new schism, with a minority of its members departing to form a rival party, Rifondazione Comunista. Thus, the Red subculture was no longer unified, greatly complicating the tasks of interest representation and the advancement of ideological and programmatic objectives.

Beginning in the mid-1980s, there were increasing signs that the apparent stability of electoral behavior (in terms of low levels of interbloc volatility) masked an increase in the actual number of voters who were shifting their support among parties. While interblock volatility remained remarkably low in 1983 and 1987 (0.3 and 1.1, respectively), there was a substantial increase in the number of voters switching from one party to another, as reflected in the increase in total volatility scores from 5.3 in 1979 to 8.5 in 1983 and 8.4 in 1987 (Morlino 1995, 318 and 320). This situation was characterized as "mobility without change" (Corbetta et al. 1988). It was initially dismissed by many observers as yet another anomaly characteristic of Italian political life. Instead, it should have been interpreted as a signal that, beneath the apparent stability of voting patterns, a substantial pool of floating voters was emerging whose behavior could be influenced by communications media that were no longer effectively controlled by the established political parties.

THE EMERGENCE OF ADVERSARY JOURNALISM

An important qualitative transformation of the Italian political system occurred in the 1980s with the replacement of a system in which parties dominated their own respective channels of political communication by one with a preponderance of private commercial communications media (Marletti 1984). One important requisite for democracy is pluralism in the flow of political information to voters. At a minimum, this requires that politically significant parties and movements gain access to the media so that their electoral options can be fairly presented to the general public. It also implies that the independent media (particularly the major newspapers and television networks) should disseminate a variety of opinions without censorship and with a minimum of bias. Significant departures from these principles can raise important questions about the quality of democracy in a political system.

The Italian media have never performed this function very well, largely because of their submission to the control of parties or economic groups. This was a particularly serious problem during the first two decades of Italian democracy, when television was initially restricted to a single publicly owned channel that the governing parties used to privilege their points of view. It was not until 1979 that the creation of RAI-3 made it possible for the PCI, the largest opposition party, to disseminate its opinions and programs through what had become the most important medium of mass communication, television.

The structure of the newspaper industry also significantly restricted pluralism in the flow of political information to the electorate. Since the end of World War II, over 75 percent of national newspapers have been under the control of powerful economic groups with generally conservative political values. Hence, center to center-right viewpoints were much more extensively disseminated than were those of the left. At the beginning of the 1970s, 29 of the country's 93 national daily newspapers were biased in favor of the center-right to right, while 53 had a moderate and center to center-right political orientation and only 12 leaned to the left (Murialdi 1972). Considering that the great majority of the last group included party newspapers with limited circulations, one can appreciate the extent to which the major mass communications media (both television and newspapers) conveyed politically biased information to the public. The predominance of a center to right-wing press bias in the 1970s can be seen in the daily circulation figures reported in Table 6.2.

The media picture started to change in 1974, when the DC had to grapple with the highly emotional issue of divorce. This issue represented a special problem for the DC because of the party's close relationship with the Catholic Church, which was implacably opposed to divorce. The church – the party's principal channel of communication with voters and means of mobilizing support – and fundamentalists in the party's own ranks insisted that a referendum be held on a divorce law that had been passed by Parliament. By this time, however, the secularization of Italian society had proceeded to the point where only a minority of the public opposed divorce on religious grounds. Support for legalized divorce exceeded 70 percent of those polled in such important regions as Piemonte, Liguria, and Emilia-Romagna, and even in the most antidivorce regions, nearly half of those polled supported the law (Grossi 1976). The DC thus found itself in a quandary: its antidivorce stand was at odds with the positions of the other governing parties, as well as with public opinion. In the referendum campaign, the majority of newspapers, including the most widely read and influential moderate to liberal papers, favored keeping the divorce law, while some radical to liberal intellectual and elite magazines (above all, *L'Espresso*) had considerable influence in molding public opinion on this important issue (Mannheimer et al. 1978; Mancini 1980).

Television was a different story. The DC tried to use the main public network channel to disseminate antidivorce propaganda. As noted earlier, however, RAI's policy was to broadcast as little as possible about politics, thereby frustrating the DC's attempt to use television for its own political purposes. This was somewhat ironic, since this policy had been imposed by the DC itself as part of its effort to keep the political struggle away from the mass public. In addition, the governing party's own electorate was divided on this issue. Divorce was an issue that divided supporters of all parties, but the DC was especially affected because of its weakening bond with its subcultural clientele. The net result was that the prodivorce law forces carried the day, suggesting that in this instance the press might have been a more effective medium of political communication and persuasion than television.

Given their lack of success in using television in this campaign, coupled with the Constitutional Court's ruling that the public television monopoly was unconstitutional, leaders of the majority parties, particularly the DC, were persuaded to open the way for private-sector television. The ensuing government instability and fierce fights within the majority led to complete deregulation of the system. Television stations sprang up everywhere: by 1977, 188 private stations had come into existence; by 1980, shortly before the Berlusconi group started to acquire many of these stations for its own networks, this number had risen to 500.

Television's potential as a medium for political communication was not immediately realized even though there were some initial indications of its possibilities during the 1979 election campaign – the first in which paid political advertising appeared on the screen (Marletti 1984, 105–16; Mazzoleni 1992, 131–40). Instead, the most notable innovation during this period was a sharp politicization of the press. Previously, newspaper readership was limited and confined almost exclusively to the elites, except for the PCI's *L'Unità* and a few others. The period from 1968 through the early 1970s, which was characterized by sharp social conflicts, witnessed a substantial political mobilization of the middle and lower classes. This increased political participation, especially among young people, stimulated demand for more political information and led to an expansion of newspaper readership beyond its traditional bounds.

A turning point occurred in 1976, when the birth of *La Repubblica* popularized an adversarial style of journalism that had first appeared a decade or so earlier in elite liberal magazines like *Il Mondo* and *L'Espresso*. The prime mover of this development was Eugenio Scalfari, editor of *La Repubblica*, who came out of the liberal journalistic tradition and had been among the protagonists in the fight over the divorce law. *La Repubblica* broke with the media tradition of ignoring the PCI, the leading opposition party, and began to give it regular and generous coverage. Gradually, other national newspapers were forced to follow suit. Soon afterward, the PCI became a member of Italy's quasi-consociational "club," and in 1979 it was given control over the third public television network. This represented a substantial change that laid the groundwork for the emergence of a new situation in which both the majority and opposition parties might obtain access to nonpartisan communications media. Initially, this transformation of the media into an open arena in which parties and leaders could address the public directly was only partial, since the public networks continued to follow the consensual practices of *lottizzazione*. The spread of independent journalism to public television was delayed by the persistence of a spoils system, which placed usually reliable "party men" in key managerial and journalistic positions. As a result, television broadcasters continued to shy away from controversial political issues, and they were reluctant to develop independent stands that were not in keeping with their respective networks' partisan orientations. To this was added the bias of Berlusconi's networks in favor of the majority parties, particularly the PSI of Bettino Craxi.

In a direct reaction against the absence of universalism and openness in the television system, the adversary journalism of *La Repubblica* and *L'Espresso* became overpoliticized. The newly established *La Repubblica* began this trend by subjecting the political class to constant scrutiny in its effort to renew Italian political life by breaking down the fault lines that fragmented the party system and made alternation in government impossible. Its program (as described by Scalfari himself in *La Repubblica*, 14, 1, 1996) was to demolish the two "ideological parishes [Red and White] that constrained Italian society" and to approximate the open style of democracy found elsewhere in Europe. Exposure to this more critical and independent flow of political information was largely limited to a minority of the population (totalling no more than 3 to 4 million people, or between 7 and 10 percent of the electorate). Its readership, however, was an influential minority, better educated and including a disproportionate share of professionals and students who were more politically active and informed than the general public. The "opinion leaders" reached by *La Repubblica* also tended to be more liberal and included a large number of PCI supporters. Television's much more massive audience was largely unexposed to the adversarial style of journalism that was emerging in Italy. But while the size of this newspaper group's audience was too small to account for the tectonic shift in mass political attitudes that would eventually take place, it was sufficient to stimulate more lively debates and opinion campaigns that had important repercussions within the political elite.

Given *La Repubblica*'s limited audience, it was incapable of substantially affecting electoral outcomes or the level of popular support for parties or individual politicians. Accordingly, the editors and writers of *La Repubblica* modified the journalistic role they wished to play. Instead of serving as a watchdog outside of the party system, the newspaper became an important channel of communication within the established system, enhancing the ability of the political elite to interact and communicate with one another. This led some critics to accuse *La Repubblica* of acting as an interest group or "covert party."

Such controversies apart, *La Repubblica* rejuvenated political journalism in Italy and stimulated public interest and involvement in political affairs. It also denounced political corruption and launched investigations of several economic and political issues that television and most other newspapers either handled cautiously or neglected altogether. Among these were campaigns against the excessive power wielded by large state corporations, their managers (called the "owner race" by Scalfari) and their corrupt practices that enlarged the public debt, terrorism, the Mafia, the P2 (a renegade Masonic lodge that posed a serious threat to Italian democracy in the 1970s and 1980s), RAI's *lottizzazione* practices, and the growing control exercised by Berlusconi over commercial television and the advertising market (Marletti 1984; Murialdi 1986). However, in the end, *La Repubblica* failed to have the desired impact on the political elite and to initiate serious reforms. Its adversary style of journalism also encouraged the Italian press to adopt a more sensationalistic style of reporting on economic and political news based more on gossip than on reliable information. *La Repubblica* has also become very commercial in recent years. Weakening its original commitment to being a high-quality conduit in the Italian information system, it ended up being almost indistinguishable on occasion from the popular tabloids. This led to an increase in readership, and in 1991 *La Repubblica* had the largest circulation of any newspaper in Italy, initially competing favorably even with Milan's authoritative and influential *Corriere della Sera* (see Table 6.2), although its years of success were followed by stagnation and slight decline. Regrettably, the commercial war between these two newspapers and their heightened concern over increasing market share had the unfortunate consequence of weakening their commitment to serious, high-quality journalism. Moreover, by the mid-1990s, total readership in Italy had fallen below 7 million daily (Murialdi and Tranfaglia 1994). These developments facilitated the emergence of television as the most important channel of political communication (Bosetti 1994; Cardini 1994).

THE EMERGENCE OF TELEVISION IN ELECTION CAMPAIGNS

The national press was the principal channel of political communication between elites and public opinion until the mid-1980s, but its preeminence had already been seriously challenged by television by the end of the 1970s. The rapid growth of television's mass audience had set the stage for its emergence as the dominant medium of political communication. Television, however, is more suited to entertainment programming than to the serious presentation and discussion of complex political issues. Thus, the growing importance of television was accompanied by a substantial transformation of the style of political communication. This change was already apparent in the 1979 election.

The private television stations (most of them local) that had emerged over the previous five years were not subject to the same rigorous regulation as the public networks. They were therefore able to experiment with new, more direct, entertainment-oriented forms of political communication. For the first time, paid political advertisements were broadcast, mainly in support of candidates of the majority parties. While these ads were initially rather amateurish and had little obvious impact on the electorate, they set the stage for a far greater use of television as the principal medium for electoral mobilization (Mazzoleni 1992).

Television played a much more prominent role in the 1983 election campaign. By this time, private television had become far more developed, and Silvio Berlusconi's Fininvest had established itself as an important force in broadcasting. Color television had arrived and audiences continued to expand, as did television coverage of politics. For the first time, an election was a "media event" (Grossi et al. 1985; Marletti 1985).

Since the new forms of propaganda and electoral mobilization required a type of expertise that traditional party activists did not have, commercial advertising agencies, pollsters, and media consultants also made their debut on the Italian political scene. While paid television advertising was restricted to the private networks, its use increased massively. The PSI was particularly enthusiastic in embracing commercial advertising and new political marketing techniques during the campaign. Altogether, candidates and parties spent a total of 25 billion lire (about $1.7 million U.S. dollars) for 1,023 spots broadcast on national networks during the 30 days of the campaign – an average of 34 per day.[18]

Italy's political elite, however, was still unfamiliar with the new medium and was insufficiently skilled in its use to realize its full potential. It continued to use television in much the same way it had used the press for years, thereby failing to tailor its television messages to suit the needs and wants of a mass television audience. Instead, media messages appeared to be oriented more to other political elites than to the mass public. The abstract and self-referential language they used was better suited for interelite negotiations than for the persuasion of a vast, heterogeneous, and often politically unsophisticated television audience. This had the perverse effect of further increasing the gap between masses and elites that had characterized Italy's political culture throughout its modern history.[19] This disjuncture between candidates and the mass audience worsened in the 1987 and 1992 campaigns. To a considerable extent, this situation was due to the tradition of quasi-consociational practices in which political elites had been obliged to make mutual accommodations among themselves and to avoid appealing directly to public opinion to make choices or resolve conflicts.

Analysis of data derived from election surveys conducted by Perugia's Osservatorio-Archivio della Comunicazione Politica in 1983, 1987, and 1992 suggests that there are three different ways in which electoral communication styles in consociational and majoritarian democracies differ.[20] Using terminology derived from Patterson (1980a), Perugia's Osservatorio della Comunicazione Politica has classified these as follows: (1) party-oriented versus opinion-oriented; (2) party-centered versus candidate-centered (focusing on the candidate's appearance, lifestyle, professional or political abilities, etc.); and (3) political issue-oriented (i.e., regarding the generic themes of ideology, relations among parties and factions, and coalition formation) versus policy issue-oriented (i.e., concerning concrete policy proposals relating to the economy, housing, public health, schools, environment, education, the public debt, etc.) (Cheli et al. 1989, 15 and 87). The introduction of a direct link between politicians and voters via television within a context of polarized multi-partyism meant that campaign communications became an uneasy mix of two styles. The amount of television time allocated to parties and candidates, for example, increased progressively, but party elites still adhered to old styles of political discourse. They continued to disregard policy issues and to focus mainly on political issues, neglecting the opportunity to use television as a means of describing to the mass electorate their proposed solutions to the country's problems. Television also reinforced the tendency of the Italian candidates to campaign separately from their parties, which derived from the rivalries among the various factions within the governing parties (especially the DC and PSI), on the one hand, and the preferential ballot provisions of Italy's proportional representation electoral system, on the other.[21]

At the same time, Italian print journalism failed to perform its watch-dog and agenda-setting functions effectively. It tended to react to the political agendas set by parties rather than try to set the agenda itself. It proved no more adept in doing so in the era of television-based campaigning than it had in the earlier newspaper era. This failure of the press to seize the initiative favored the emergence of television as the dominant medium of politics in the 1983, 1987, and 1992 campaigns.[22]

The personalization of party politics during the campaign is a more complex phenomenon (Cavalli 1994; Fabbrini 1994). Italian multiparty government had long discouraged the emergence of a special role for the party leader in electoral politics. Instead, personalism in Italian politics was manifested in particularism, favoritism, or outright bossism, giving birth to political machines controlled by a patron in a personalistic patron–client network. Personal power of this kind was kept hidden from the public as much as possible. The rise of television as the dominant campaign medium placed complex and sometimes conflicting demands on party leaders, culminating in a mix of the new and the old. As a visual medium, it transformed party leaders into the public face of the party, and elections began to evolve into contests between highly visible individuals, some with charismatic appeal. President Sandro Pertini and Marco Pannella (leader of the small Radical Party) were particularly effective in this respect. At the same time, however, Italian politics in the 1980s continued to be based primarily on networks rooted in personal loyalties and particularistic interests. Thus, the initial impact of television was more apparent than real – more of style than of substance. In the aggregate, television failed to do away with the particularism and hidden power relationships of the old order.

THE DEVELOPMENT OF LOCAL MEDIA
AND SUBNATIONAL IDENTITIES

Changes in the communications media, especially the development of local media outlets, affected Italian politics in two important ways in the late 1980s and early 1990s. The first concerns the fragmentation and particularism of political relations that, as noted earlier, had led to favoritism and personal control of party machines by bosses and local notables. The second concerns the reemergence, once the ideological subcultures had begun to weaken, of a center–periphery cleavage and territorial identities dating back to the Italian nation- and state-building processes. This cleavage has surfaced periodically throughout Italian history. In the second half of the 1980s, it took the form of resentment in the northern industrial regions against state bureaucracy, centralism, and the high cost of social welfare programs and subsidies that mainly benefited the less developed south, as well as resentment against the patron–client politics and corruption that northerners saw as characteristic of that region.

These resentments culminated in the emergence of a new localistic political movement, the Lega del Nord, whose electoral success contributed substantially to the collapse of the old style of party government and the traditional political elite. The Lega del Nord was able to establish itself in spite of the fact that the major national media – television networks and national newspapers – largely ignored it, effectively shutting it out of national political discourse. The movement relied on interpersonal local communication networks and resorted to traditional propaganda channels that others parties had by then deserted or neglected (such as mass meetings and popular festivals), built a strong electoral following, and eventually (after the 1994 election) entered the center-right governing coalition in Parliament. More important, the Lega del Nord capitalized on the growing prominence of territorial identity[23] – following the collapse of the traditional political subcultures – as a basis of social cohesion and as a decisive political resource.

The potential sociopolitical impact of local media is a function of several factors, among which are the nature of political contestation in a particular region and the extent of media pluralism in that area. A notable characteristic of the Italian communications media, in this respect, is that ownership and control are highly concentrated at the national level (especially within the television and newspaper media), while at the local level the system is quite fragmented.

This high local fragmentation is most characteristic of the radio sector, whose daily audience is very large: over half of the Italian population listens to the radio at least once a day. Between 5,000 and 6,000 radio stations are licensed to broadcast in Italy – one for every 8,000 to 10,000 citizens – a ratio unequaled in Europe. While most of these radio stations exist only on paper, more than 1,000 do broadcast daily. From one perspective, this high level of fragmentation weakens the impact of radio on Italian politics and threatens the economic viability of many stations. A recent survey, for example, found that only 40 percent of these stations had a substantial audience, and just 35 out of 600 stations surveyed had at least 100,000 listeners daily.[24]

Fragmentation also characterizes the local television and newspaper sectors, although to a lesser extent. The local press and television markets are quite dynamic at present. Deregulation of the communications media made possible the proliferation of local stations. Although market rationalization and higher levels of ownership concentration will probably continue to reduce the number of independent stations, considerable pluralism is likely to remain at the local level, since the majority of local newspapers and magazines are profitable and can count on stable audiences and advertising revenues (Brigida, et al. 1993; and Marletti 1988b). Sociocultural and political factors have also contributed to the growth of local media, providing citizens with information on local affairs that national TV networks and newspapers ignore. This pluralism of information channels is particularly important during election campaigns and in the process of building political agendas for parties and governments alike.

The 1992 election gave some hint of the important role that local media could play in Italian politics, and it marked a definite transition toward a more candidate-centered campaign (Roncarolo 1993 and 1995). This was due not only to the general tendency of television to personalize politics, but also to the introduction of an important change in Italy's electoral law (Pasquino 1993; Morlino 1995). Previously, voters were presented with lists of candidates in multimember districts. While they could indicate their preference for individual candidates, few voters chose to do so. The 1992 election took place under a modified electoral law that substantially increasing the candidate-oriented character of electoral competition and decreased the ability of parties to control their candidates.

Data collected by Perugia's Osservatorio revealed remarkable differences between local political communication in industrial northern regions and in the South; they also documented the importance of the local media to electoral politics in the 1992 campaign (Mancini 1993). The North was characterized by high levels of pluralism and competition, with old forms of propaganda giving way to new forms of political communication. Campaign politics in that region was characterized by a much greater concern with directly addressing public opinion than with the old-style debate among parties and elites. The campaign was more centered on policy issues, although party-political issues remained important. In the South, in contrast, electoral appeals on local television appeared to be of little importance. The great bulk of campaign activity focused on mobilizing interest groups and patron–client networks. One key factor helping to account for this dramatic difference between the two regions is that the local media system in the South has not yet reached the degree of development and pluralism that it has attained in the North.

These findings suggest that the basic modes of political communication are changing, both because of the transformations occurring in civil society (i.e., the passage from industrialism to postindustrialism, accompanied by growing individualism, the crisis of ideologies, and the reemergence of territorial identities) and because of the development of local media. These changes in political communication were even more pronounced in the municipal elections of June 1993. But by far the greatest change in Italian electoral politics occurred in 1994, with the irruption onto the political stage of Silvio Berlusconi and his supportive media empire.

THE ELECTORAL EARTHQUAKE OF 1994

Using Lijphart's well-known distinction between "Westminster" and "consensual" democracies (Lijphart 1984), we can argue that institutional differences can bring about relevant discrepancies even on the level of political communication. Political elites in consensual democracies, particularly in fragmented multiparty systems such as that of Italy, differ from their counterparts in Westminster democracies because they tend not to appeal directly to public opinion through the mass media in order to resolve conflicts over controversial issues. They prefer to utilize the vast range of mediation and communication channels within the party system, whose delicate balance could be upset by bringing an unpredictable public into the mutual accommodation process. Thus, elites try to control the media by limiting their development and by ignoring or repressing demands to involve the public in the debate over political issues. The Italian case suggests that these practices can easily be upset in rapidly modernizing societies with rapidly evolving mass communications systems. Under these circumstances, the elites' inability to control the media (especially the increasingly important television medium) can facilitate the emergence of new challenges to the established order, if not a serious crisis of the political system, particularly when internal and external events interact and call into question the efficacy and probity of the system. This is especially likely to happen if the new challengers to the established order understand the full potential of the new communications system. Such a crisis erupted in Italy between 1992 and 1994, culminating in the complete breakdown of the established parties and the quasi-consociational system that they had created.

There were numerous grounds for dissatisfaction with the old style of politics. Magistrates in Milan began investigations of political corruption within the highest ranks of the PSI in 1992. A few months later, in the first of four elections to be held within less than two years, the Lega del Nord made spectacular electoral gains, securing 20 to 27 percent of the vote in several important northern cities (see Table 6.3). The Lega, a political movement completely outside of the old party structure, articulated a strong critique of government practices – indeed, of the structure of the Italian state itself. Its startling success signaled the beginning of the crisis.

The scope of the corruption scandals continued to broaden, variously referred to in the media as *mani pulite* (clean hands) and *Tangentopoli* (Bribesville) investigations. Both the DC and PSI, as well as their traditional coalition allies, were implicated. Inflamed by the adversarial journalism campaigns in the press, now accompanied by reports broadcast on both public and private television, public disgust with Italy's governing elites increased dramatically. In a political culture long characterized by cynicism toward parties and dissatisfaction with government efficacy, these new accusations contributed greatly to the growing delegitimation of Italy's style of party government. Opposition parties on both the left and the right added fuel to the fire, hoping to obtain electoral advantage from the governing parties' crisis, while subsequent press campaigns demanded the resignation of the government.

Table 6.3   *Increase in Electoral Support for the*
Lega del Nord from 1987 to 1992 in 12 Cities

	1987	1992	Difference
Bergamo	7.3	27.6	+20.3
Brescia	—	26.4	—
Varese	7.2	25.9	+18.7
Vicenza	4.5	24.9	+20.4
Como	6.3	24.9	+18.6
Treviso	3.8	24.5	+20.7
Verona	4.1	23.7	+19.6
Belluno	2.7	21.9	+19.2
Sondrio	4.7	21.7	+17.0
Pavia	—	21.3	—
Cuneo	5.1	20.6	+15.5
Vercelli	5.0	20.7	+15.7

Source: Our elaboration from Diamanti 1993, 33.

In April 1993, Italians were again called to the polls to vote on a number of referendum issues, the most important of which involved the elimination of proportional voting for the Senate. This proposal was approved by 87.2 percent of the voters, and it cleared the way for the introduction of majoritarianism into Italian democracy. The municipal elections held that same year revealed further evidence of the deteriorating support for the governing parties. Not only did opposition parties (especially the former PCI) win control of many important cities, such as Torino and Catania, but the PSI was completely obliterated from its traditional power bases in Milan by the candidates of the Lega del Nord.

The crisis came to a head in the parliamentary election of March 27, 1994. This election, conducted under a new electoral law in which three-quarters of the seats in both houses were allocated to those receiving a plurality of the votes in single-member districts,[25] culminated in a massive change in the Italian party system. Parties that had dominated Italian governments for decades, including the DC and the PSI, disappeared completely. It is no exaggeration to say that the traditional party system collapsed. Even the newly transformed Democratic Party of the Left (PDS – formed by the reformist majority faction of the PCI in association with non-Communist leftists) failed to enjoy the success it had anticipated on the basis of its strong performance in the 1993 municipal elections.

The real victor in 1994 was a new center-right coalition, the Polo della libertà ("Freedom Pole"), formed by Forza Italia (FI), a party created by television magnate Silvio Berlusconi in coalition with the Lega del Nord and the now postfascist MIS. The principal outcome of this election was that FI had become the largest party, with 21 percent of the vote, and its leader, who had never held political office before, was the new prime minister.

Amid the rubble of the traditional party system, a common question the day after the election was whether television could determine the outcome of elections. In light of Berlusconi's meteoric political rise, had Italy become a teledemocracy? In the vast and complex debate on this question that followed, it is important to distinguish between the dramatized, often hyperbolic judgments of commentators and journalists and the evidence derived from systematic empirical research.

Fortunately, several important studies of this election focused on precisely those factors that were most directly relevant to the teledemocracy question. A study conducted by the Perugia group found that the seven public and private television networks had broadcast twice as much election-related coverage during the 1994 campaign (14,000 total minutes) as they had throughout the parliamentary election held just two years earlier (Mancini and Mazzoleni 1995, 72), representing a dramatic culmination of a long-term process of increasing television campaigning. This same study revealed that Berlusconi's Fininvest stations broadcast more than twice as many election-related programs as did the public RAI networks – a finding in accord with that of another major study (Mancini and Mazzoleni 1995, 92–4; Morcellini 1995).

Perhaps more important, there were substantial qualitative differences in the use of television during the campaign between Berlusconi and his political rivals and between Berlusconi's television stations and those of the public sector. A study by the Pavia Osservatorio found that Berlusconi departed dramatically from the manner in which Italian party leaders had previously used television by relying heavily on advertising on his Fininvest stations. The style of those televised spots, moreover, broke totally away from the restrained and elite-centered discourse that had characterized the old political elite. As described by Giacomo Sani (1995, 5): "Most of the spots had a commercial-style jingle and a slogan associating Forza Italia with the promise of a 'New Italian Miracle,' and they all featured Berlusconi addressing the voters in various settings (his study, garden, etc.)." Thus, Berlusconi followed what we have referred to as the media logic, and capitalized on the abilities of television as a medium well suited to the personalization of politics – a characteristic, moreover, that was entirely compatible with a campaign against the established parties.

To this point, nothing had been said about ethical questions relating to the propriety of running for office and, at the same time, controlling the vast majority of the private sector of national television broadcasting. The fact that Berlusconi and FI bought more ads or used of television more skillfully to appeal to a broader sector of the Italian electorate clearly suggests that Berlusconi had a better understanding of the potential influence of this medium than most other Italian politicians. But the story does not stop there. There is considerable evidence that the Fininvest stations exhibited a marked bias in favor of FI, while the three RAI networks were more impartial in allowing the various parties to present their appeals to the voters. The Pavia media project included precise measures of how long representatives of the various parties were allowed to appear on screen and present their electoral appeals on the regular newscasts of the three RAI and the three Fininvest networks. The results of this analysis can be seen in Table 6.4, which shows that the three Fininvest stations gave FI candidates far more opportunities to speak for themselves than they did any other party. Conversely, the candidates of the former DC center (PPI and Patto), from which Berlusconi hoped to draw most of his votes, were almost absent from the screen, receiving less than 10 percent of the time candidates were allowed to speak for themselves. The three RAI channels, in sharp contrast, were much more balanced in their coverage. While Fininvest channels allocated 65 percent of these blocs of time to Berlusconi's FI and his future coalition allies (AN and the Lega), compared with 16 percent to the parties of the left and less than 10 percent to the former DC center, the RAI channels gave 38 percent of this time to Berlusconi's Polo della libertà coalition, 24 percent to the parties of the left, and 29 percent to the center (Sani 1995).

When the three RAI stations are examined individually, the same general conclusion can be drawn. To be sure, RAI-1 (traditionally dominated by the DC) gave somewhat more coverage to the centrist PPI and Patto (44 percent of the time that this network dedicated to the campaign) than it did to the right-wing Polo parties (34 percent) and the parties of the left (18 percent), but the other two RAI stations appear to have been scrupulously balanced in their news coverage (in this respect, at least). Indeed, RAI-3 gave as much coverage to FI candidates as it did to the PDS (22 percent each), despite the fact that under the old quasi-consociational arrangement RAI-3 was regarded as the PCI's media out-

Table 6.4   *Percentage of Time Party Representatives Were Allowed to Appear on RAI and Fininvest Television News Broadcasts*

	Television Network	
Party	RAI	Fininvest
Alleanza Nazionale	5%	5%
Forza Italia	23	50
Lega del Nord	10	9
Partito Popolare Italiano	14	5
Patto per l'Italia	15	4
Partito Democratico della Sinistra	19	11

Source: Sani 1995, 10. The figure presented in the table for each party/network is the mean of the three figures (for each of the three channels in the broadcasting system) indicating the percentage of the total amount of time that representatives of parties appeared on screen and were allowed to speak for themselves. For example, the Forza Italia/Fininvest figure of 50% is the mean of the three separate percentages for each of the three Fininvest channels (68% for Rete-4, 30% for Canale-5, and 53% for Italia-1); the 23% figure for Forza Italia coverage on the RAI network is the mean of the 22% for RAI-1, 26% for RAI-2 and 22% for RAI-3. While the presentation of these mean figures conceals a bit of channel-by-channel variation (e.g., RAI-1 devoted only 14% of on-screen time to PDS candidates compared to 22% for RAI-3), these channel-by-channel differences are insufficient to justify the cluttering of this table that would result from presenting separate figures for each channel.

let (Sani 1995, 13). In short, there is overwhelming evidence that Berlusconi used news coverage by his three television networks to systematically favor FI candidates and to deny the DC's successor parties adequate media exposure.

But what was the impact of this media bias on the behavior of Italian voters? Measuring media effects of this kind is always difficult and, at a minimum, requires a public opinion survey with a panel design. Fortunately, Luca Ricolfi and his collaborators at the University of Turin undertook such a study, using a nationwide panel of 3,500 respondents to track the impact of television exposure on changes in voting intention during the campaign. The initial partisan predisposition of each panel respondent was established in a May 1993 survey, and, beginning in mid-February 1994, was reexamined every 15 days by means of a Nielsen-Cra electronic polling system. In addition to measuring the evolution of voting intentions, each respondent's exposure to television coverage of political events, and the extent of his or her cognitive structuring, were re-examined at regular intervals until after the election. The sophisticated multivariate analysis of these data established a positive relationship between television exposure and vote shifting (Ricolfi 1994). It was found that 13.7 percent of these respondents (which, through extrapolation, would be equivalent to 5.5 million voters nationwide) changed their votes as a result of something they saw on television. Berlusconi's networks, with their highly partisan campaign, were particularly influential, shifting some 4 million votes. RAI, by contrast, with its more pluralistic and neutral political content, appears to have shifted only 1.5 million votes. As Table 6.5 shows, these changes in voting intention played a decisive role in determining the outcome of the 1994 election. Ricolfi (1994) concluded that without the unbalanced coverage in its favor, Berlusconi's center-right coalition would not have won.

A second finding of this study was that those who changed their vote through exposure to television had above-average education and obtained above-average scores on the survey's cognitive tests, which measured the respondent's ability "to structure the relevant situation in meaningful, integrated ways" and the "tendency to organize and evaluate abstract information" (Ricolfi 1994, 1046). Contrary to what might have been expected, it does not appear that the less knowledgeable and uninvolved sectors of the electorate were most susceptible to persuasion by television. The probable explanation is to be found in the notion of "instrumental rationality." The campaign provided voters with a real choice. The left-wing parties continued present their traditional message of the need for austerity in hard times and sacrifice for the common good. The right, by contrast, promised relief from hard times and personal sacrifice through a Reagan-style program of deep tax cuts and cutbacks in social welfare expenditures. Berlusconi's networks packaged this program very attractively and peddled it incessantly to receptive viewers. Those who thought they would benefit from such a program seem to have been persuaded by it.

In short, the right won for three reasons. First, it proposed policies that appealed to middle class voters tired of big government, high taxes, and an expensive welfare state. Second, it articulated this message in an understandable and persuasive manner, using language quite distinct from that of the traditional pattern of elite discourse in Italy – and one still used by the left in 1994. Third, it used the private sector of television to give disproportionate coverage to its own message, both by out-

Table 6.5   *Estimate of the Net Impact of TV on Partisan Preferences*

	Votes Shifted by RAI	Votes Shifted by Fininvest	Net Gain by TV influence
In favor of:			
Right	−0.1%	+8.8%	+8.7
Center	+1.4	−4.2	−2.8
Left	−1.3	−4.6	−5.9

Source: Our synthesis from Ricolfi's 1994 elaboration.

spending its rivals on television advertising and by its manipulation of news coverage on the majority of private stations that Berlusconi owned.

TOWARD MAJORITARIANISM IN POLITICAL COMMUNICATION?

Following his electoral victory in 1994, Prime Minister Berlusconi was well placed to strongly influence political communication through the public sector of television broadcasting as well. Abandoning the quasi-consociational principles that had prevailed over the previous two decades, he capitalized on this opportunity in a manner that poses serious questions for the quality of Italian democracy.

Beginning in 1992, laws governing the public broadcasting sector provided for the appointment of RAI's governing board by the speakers of the two houses of the legislature. This meant that the board was appointed by one representative of the governing DC and one representative of the PDS. Also, in accord with long-standing quasi-consociational principles, both government and opposition parties were represented on the board. The Berlusconi government completely abandoned these practices and switched to winner-take-all majoritarianism. Consequently, both houses of Parliament would be led by members of the governing coalition, one from FI and the other representing the Lega. The end result was a purge of the RAI management. General managers, news directors, and other top-ranking personnel of the three RAI stations were replaced by individuals allied with Berlusconi (Gundle and O'Sullivan 1996, 217–18).

Although this majoritarian packing of the RAI governing board and key management positions did not produce as complete a break from the consensual practices of the past as the center-right government had hoped,[26] it does appear to have had an impact on news coverage by the public television stations. The Pavia research team undertook the same kind of survey of the 1995 regional election covreage as it had of the 1994 national election, making it possible to compare of the extent of coverage of individual parties both before and after the changes in RAI management under the Berlusconi government. While in the 1994 contest (before the management changes) FI received by a slight margin the largest amount of coverage across the three RAI channels (28 percent of the total time devoted to coverage of parties and candidates compared with 22 percent given to the PDS), by 1995 FI's dominance of news coverage had strengthened considerably. During this campaign, 35 percent of all campaign coverage was devoted to FI and its candidates, while coverage of the PDS fell to 16 percent of the total (Sani 1995, 18).

The right-wing coalition parties looked forward to the April 1995 regional elections with great optimism, given their previous victory and their increased strength in both the private and public television broadcasting systems. Electoral outcomes, however, are determined by a variety of factors, not just favorable television coverage. On election night, Berlusconi's supporters – in particular, Rete 4 anchorman Emilio Fede – loudly proclaimed victory on the basis of partial returns and exit-poll projections. But they were bitterly disappointed by the final results available the following morning. The center-left coalition had won in 9 of 15 regions and the Polo in only 6. Even more significant was that the center-right, which expected to gain over 50 percent of the votes, barely exceeded 40 percent of the total, while the PDS overtook FI and became the leading Italian party, with 24.6 percent of the votes – 2 percent more than Berlusconi's FI. Unlike the previous general election, the Lega del Nord ran independently of the center-right coalition and obtained just 6.6 percent of the votes cast nationwide, although it retained its strength in small towns in Lombardy and Veneto, maintaining a 24 percent share of the total votes in these areas.

Berlusconi recovered from this setback with a victory in the June 1995 referendum. Three ballot issues directly concerned his dominant position in commercial television and in the advertising market, while another concerned privatization of RAI. While the center-left parties mounted a relatively quiet campaign, Berlusconi heavyhandedly used his networks to campaign against referendum proposals that would have forced him to divest part of his television empire. Nearly 90 percent of the ads (many of which featured popular singers and famous actors) broadcast by Fininvest networks opposed those ballot issues and favored another measure that would have privatized RAI. Berlusconi won on all of these referendum issues, with 55 to 57 percent majorities.

A new parliamentary election was scheduled for April 1996, following the failure of efforts to reach interparty agreement on several institutional reform proposals (ranging from adoption of a French-style semipresidential system to a more majoritarian parliamentary system like that of Germany). Now in opposition, FI and its center-right ally, Alleanza Nazionale, pushed aggressively for new elections, while the center-left coalition supporting the Lamberto Dini government approached the renewed electoral competition more cautiously. In contrast with 1994, television played a much less decisive role in this campaign for at least three important reasons. The first was that a very restrictive equal-time rule had been imposed on all networks to equalize coverage of each party, its leaders, and its propaganda. This rule had been introduced by the Dini government prior to the 1995 regional elections and was supported by the parties of the center-left (Bettinelli 1995). It was not fully respected by Fininvest in that campaign, although it did limit the use of propaganda ads on local channels. In the 1996 election, however, the equal-time rule did play an important role by reducing partisan bias and restoring greater equality of access to television audiences among the various parties (*Panorama*, April 25, 1996, 144).

The second factor reducing the electoral impact of television was the increasing rivalry between the center-right coalition parties and their leaders, Silvio Berlusconi and Gianfranco Fini. Preelection polls had shown that Fini's growing popularity might give him more votes than Berlusconi and convert Alleanza Nazionale into the main party in the Polo. Berlusconi proclaimed that his networks would not broadcast paid political ads in protest against the alleged complexity of the equal-time rule. In reality, he did not want to broadcast spots favorable to Fini or Dini (his former treasury minister, who became prime minister with the support of the PDS and other parties of the center-left). Fininvest's renunciation of paid political advertising substantially reduced the electoral weight of television and had a spillover effect on all political communication and information programs.

The third reason for the decline in the political impact of television is rooted in the media logic itself, particularly the extent to which the attraction of large audiences or their conversion to one side or another of an issue requires some degree of novelty. In 1994 Berlusconi was a novelty, but in 1996 he was not. Indeed, as his own political marketing experts and pollsters have suggested, his excessive presence on television may have produced a boomerang effect. In any case, during the campaign, Berlusconi's popularity gradually decreased, while that of Romano Prodi increased. Prodi, a professor of economics with origins in the left wing of the DC, was nominated as the center-left coalition's candidate for prime minister. Adopting a low-profile strategy, he appeared on television with a rather careless look and an image of a "good and tranquil guy." In contrast with Berlusconi's charismatic posture as "savior of the country," Prodi spoke softly and without stigmatizing his rival, although showing firmness, resolve, and the ability to cope expertly with concrete problems.[27] Initially, Prodi seemed unsuited for political communication on television, but later he captured the audience's attention and, in a face-to-face debate toward the end of the campaign, appeared more convincing than Berlusconi, who still enjoyed a high degree of popularity, according to the polls.

On the eve of the election, most observers anticipated a deadlock between the two coalitions, with a subsequent return of government instability and a renewal of efforts to reach interparty agreement on basic institutional reforms. Instead, the center-left bloc, the Ulivo (Olive Tree) coalition, reversed the tide of the 1994 election and scored a decisive victory. It fell short of an absolute majority in the Senate by just one seat (compared with the Polo's 37 percent of the seats), while in the Chamber of Deputies it also had the largest bloc of seats (44 percent compared with 39 percent for the Polo and 9 percent for the nonaligned Lega del Nord). With the external support of Rifondazione Comunista, a radical left-wing party founded after the dissolution of the PCI (which received 3 percent of the seats in the Senate and nearly 6 percent in the Chamber), a center-left government was formed in which the PDS was the major party, allied with PPI (with origins in the left wing of the former DC). This situation led some scholars to observe that Prodi's was neither a majority government nor a classic minority government (D'Alimonte and Nelken 1997). To be a majority government, it would have had to have shared a legislative program with the Rifondazione (which rejected the government's plans). Instead, it preferred to enter into specific agreements on individual parliamentary proposals. But it also lacked the flexibility of minority governments to seek allies on both the left and the right in support of its legislation.

It would be premature to conclude that the tumultuous period of change in Italian politics has come to an end and that the basic features of partisan politics have become fixed. Indeed, some aspects of this process of change have been quite surprising. Contrary to the initial objectives of the reform of the electoral law reform, for example, the fragmentation of the Italian party system has actually increased.[28] This has further complicated policy making and has given effective veto power to small parties. Assessments of the impact of the media on politics must also remain tempered and balanced. While television remains a strong influence on political life, contrary to initial impressions it can be regulated and limited, and it does not necessarily represent an advantage for the right wing. As Gundle and O'Sullivan (1996, 219) have observed: "it should be emphasized that it was not 'television' but rather the highly particular model of relations between political power and press and television owners as it developed in the 1980s that created the premises for the emergence of Berlusconi as a political player in his own right."

CONCLUSIONS

Our principal thesis is that the Italian case, although unusual, should not be interpreted as an anomaly, but rather as the product of interactions among social, political, and cultural cleavages, technological changes within the media system, and political leaders and institutions. The elite-led nation- and state-building process has not succeeded in bringing about a unitary civic culture, but rather has created a gap between the political cultures of the masses and the elites, accentuated by the centralism of the Italian state. Italy remains a fragmented and pluralistic country, with various territorial identities and political subcultures, in which state centralism is only a heavy superstructure. It was in this context that multiparty government based on a model of consensual democracy and quasi-consociational practices between the governing majority and the opposition developed. This style of government emerged not only as a product of efforts to reduce polarization between left and right, but also because (given East–West confrontations and the Cold War) the major opposition party, the PCI, was excluded from government for more than 40 years and there was no alternative majority to the centrist coalitions headed by the DC.

Italy's particular type of party government did favor the process of democratic consolidation, but it also encouraged various forms of political corruption among party elites. Given its proportional electoral system – adopted with the aims of safeguarding all minorities and of maintaining a certain balance of strength in the relations between the majority and the opposition – the number of parties proliferated, greatly complicating the policy-making and implementation processes. The result was a diffuse sense of public discontent with the parties and politics in general.

Within a highly fragmented multiparty system, as we have argued, political elites try to avoid direct appeals to public opinion through independent mass media in resolving controversial issues. They prefer to rely on numerous channels of private communication and on intra- and interparty bargaining in pursuit of mutual accommodation. An unfortunate side effect of this style of politics is that it favors the development of cynical attitudes among the political elite, as well as a cryptic and self-referential political discourse. In Italy, this language and style of communications characterized not only officialdom but also the press, whose adversarial style of journalism was initially intended to narrow the divide between parties and civil society.

The emergence of television as the most popular, credible, and persuasive communications medium increased this gap between elite and mass cultures and presented the multiparty regime with a real challenge. The political elite attempted to control the medium's independent development first through the state's broadcasting monopoly and censorship and then through *lottizzazione* practices. For several reasons, these control efforts became increasingly ineffectual. One was inherent in the politics of fragmented multipartyism and quasi-consociationalism itself: paralyzed by cross-vetoes, the elite was incapable of subordinating television to its control. The second was the erosion, in the 1980s, of the political subcultures underpinning the political and ancillary organizations of the major parties, due not only to secularization and modernization processes but also to growing cynicism at both the elite and mass levels of the polity. This resulted in the reemergence of territorial and anticentralist identities in the northeast regions, as well as the emergence of a more volatile floating electorate that, tending to choose on the basis of instrumental rationality, could be influenced by the media. The third reason was Berlusconi's powerful multimedia empire and its near monopoly over commercial television broadcasting in the late 1980s and early 1990s. This monopoly gave him the power to control most of the advertising market and put him in a strong position to compete with the public RAI networks. It also provided him with a powerful tool for shaping collective behavior in such a manner as to raise serious questions for the quality of Italian democracy. The final and perhaps most important reason was the fall of the Berlin Wall and the end of the East–West confrontation. This event profoundly altered the context of Italian politics, making possible an alternation in government between left and right, making obsolete the DC-dominated centrist coalitions that had governed Italy for over 40 years, and replacing the consensual and quasi-consociational practices of that period with a more majoritarian style of democracy. Majoritarianism, however, exposed the political elite to increased scrutiny (sometimes with sensationalist overtones) by the media. It also implied that elites needed to be more aware of the so-called media logic, and learn how to go public on important issues.

One individual who realized the potential of these new styles of political communication was Silvio Berlusconi. While the "clean hands" crisis of the early 1990s was the product of judicial investigations covered in great detail by a left-wing adversarial press, it was capitalized on by a television magnate of the right. Widespread feelings of political disaffection and disgust with the older generation of politicians were juxtaposed to the atmosphere of optimism and escapism spread over several years by the commercial Fininvest TV networks, allowing Berlusconi to mobilize moderate voters with an aggressive political marketing campaign depicting him as the savior of the nation. Under conditions of political crisis, an aggressive television campaign based on populist appeals can be decisive in mobilizing social resentment and bringing about radical change. But the story does not stop here. As the political victory of the center-left in 1996 suggests, television may enable certain individuals to acquire great popularity in a very short time, and it may play an important role in dismantling an aged and corrupt political system and installing new leaders in power, but it cannot endow them with the ability to govern effectively or maintain a political consensus. This is as true for the right wing as it is for the left. It also suggests that excessive reliance on the media logic can be counterproductive. Romano Prodi's victory in the 1996 election shows that very different kinds of personalities can be successful on television: charismatic and populist appeals can be successfully countered by an understated message of competence and seriousness.

Prodi's government initiated a period in which the right reduced its aggressive polemical attacks on parties of the left through Berlusconi's private television networks. At the same time, the left came to understand the importance of television and put great efforts into the modernization of its political communication staff. Prime Minister Massimo D'Alema, of the Democratici di Sinistra (as the PDS was renamed in 1997), has created a staff of political consultants and spin doctors to improve his command of television. His strategy of going public is designed to soften his image as a hard and somewhat arrogant man. He has sought to create a more conciliatory image of himself as an open and popular leader who loves sailing and Italian cooking. These efforts involve frequent television appearances on talks shows and on programs with pop singers,[29] which has significantly increased his popularity with the electorate – raising his approval rating by over 10 percentage points between summer and autumn 1998 (*Corriere della Sera,* November 2, 1998), and he continues to be more popular than his government (*La Stampa,* March 2, 1999). In several respects, his communications strategy is similar to that of Britain's Tony Blair.

D'Alema's more attractive image, his status as leader of a socialist government participating in the EU's monetary union, and his skills as a negotiator have produced some important political victories. The first was the appointment of Romano Prodi as the president of the European Commission. This not only fostered a reconciliation with Prodi (relations with whom had been damaged by the government crisis that toppled him from power) but also further strengthened D'Alema's political standing and authority.

Meanwhile, Berlusconi's efforts to take control of RAI were halted and reversed under the Prodi and D'Alema governments. In the aftermath of sometimes contentious new appointments to the RAI board of directors, that body issued a "Directive on Pluralism" in January 1997 that promised all political forces in the country access to public television. In June 1998, the board approved the nominations of the directors of the RAI TV channels and news programs, applying selection criteria that to some journalists appeared reminiscent of the old *lottizzazione.* The failure of the bipartisan effort to reform the constitution and the electoral law, however, precluded resolution of this issue, which remains an open partisan question. These matters have been further complicated by the increasing presence of multinational media conglomerates (such as that of Rupert Murdoch and his massive empire) and of EU regulations that open the door to new privatization policies.

The weakest link in the Italian political communication system is the printed press. The percentage of regular newspaper readers in Italy is still among the lowest in Europe (surpassed only by that of Greece), and the big dailies have been unable to increase their readership. Relations between the left-wing government and the press (especially *L'Espresso*) have worsened as a result of attacks on D'Alema. Even the government's relations with *Repubblica* have been strained. This situation has not been helped by D'Alema's preference for going public on television – a medium that enables him to speak directly to the public without the need for journalistic intermediaries or interpreters. At stake are both freedom of the press and the ability of journalists to take control over the political agenda away from the self-interested political parties. And this, in turn, has direct implications for the quality of democracy in Italy.

NOTES

1. The traditional classification of coalitions in Italy distinguishes among the following phases: centrism (1948–62); center-left (1962–73); "historic" compromise and governments of national solidarity (1974–80); and pentaparty (1981–91). (See Pasquino 1980, 87; Pasquino 1995, 68 and 355–6; and Fabbrini 1995b, 391.) From the end of World War II until 1994, only one attempt was made to form a center-right coalition between the DC and the post-fascist MSI. This occurred in 1960 under the leadership of the DC's Ferdinando Tambroni, who formed a government with the external support of the MSI. It provoked strong negative reactions, however, not only from the opposition but also from the traditional governing parties and even the DC itself. Within a few months, in the aftermath of violent riots in Genoa and Reggio Emilia (where police shot and killed several demonstrators), Tambroni was forced to resign and was replaced by Amintore Fanfani, opening the way to the formation of a center-left government (Mammarella 1995, 203–4).

2. The expression "second republic" was coined by the press and is frequently used by both political elites and the general public. Many scholars, however, reject this terminology as a "symbolic construction of reality" imposed by the media, since the 1947 republican Constitution has not been changed (Di Giovine and Mastropaolo 1993; Calise 1994; Warner and Gambetta 1994). The only important change in the institutional framework of Italian politics involved the electoral law (note 20). Other scholars disagree, pointing out that a "material" if not a "formal" change has occurred (e.g., Fedele 1994 speaks of a "referendum democracy"). For others, the expression "second republic" does not imply such specific meaning but is useful for referring in general to these political changes (Mazzoleni 1993; Mannheimer and Sani 1994; Livolsi and Volli 1996). For a critical discussion of the implications of these changes in party government for the Italian Constitution (including the adoption of presidentialism or semipresidentialism), see Fabbrini 1995a and 1996; Ceccanti et al. 1996.

3. See Catanzaro 1993; Berardinelli 1994; Calise 1994–5; Gamaleri 1994; Rodotà 1994; Statera 1994; and Losano 1995. Ricolfi (1994) initially attributed decisive importance to the influence of television on the victory of the center-right coalition and Berlusconi, but he subsequently adopted a more cautious and prudent view (see his interview in *Panorama*, April 25, 1996, 144).

4. See Diamanti 1994a; Diani 1995; Lazar 1995; Marletti 1995a and 1995b; Gundle and O'Sullivan 1996; Livolsi and Volli 1996. For discussions of media influence in the 1994 election, see Morcellini 1994 and 1995; Maraffi 1995; Novelli 1995; Porro 1995; and Follini 1996.

5. The growth of quasi-consociational practices between the majority parties and the left-wing opposition occurred in two phases. The first stage corresponded to the formation of the center-left coalition in the early 1960s, which allowed the PSI to enter the government for the first time; the second occurred in the mid-1970s, with the "historical compromise" and the formation of "national solidarity governments" backed by the PCI (Fabbrini 1995b).

6. Tarrow 1967; Caciagli 1977; Calise 1978; Cassano 1979; and Gribaudi 1980.

7. In 1960, daily newspaper circulation averaged 104 copies per 1,000 inhabitants, with considerable differences between southern Italy and the other regions: in the northern and central regions, newspaper circulation averaged 145 and 155 per 1,000, respectively, while in the southern region and the islands, it averaged only 24 and 41 per 1,000. Only 4 daily newspapers published more than 200,000 copies, and 13 exceeded 100,000 (Weiss 1961). By comparison, 165 families per 1,000 owned television sets that same year. Newspaper readership did not change appreciably over the following decade, but the number of television owners increased by 50 percent, totaling 25.3 percent of all families (Pinto 1980). This trend has remained: in 1991 newspaper circulation averaged just 119 per 1,000 inhabitants, while virtually all families owned a TV set and 42 percent had more than one (Brigida, et al. 1993).

8. In 1983, the Unites States accounted for 53 percent of television broadcasting worldwide, amounting to about 5.6 million hours of broadcasting per year. Italy was second worldwide (ahead of Canada and Japan), with 1.5 million hours of television broadcasting per year. Only eight countries offered more than 100,000 hours per year; among them, they account for 93 percent of the world's television broadcasting. The first European country after Italy was France, with only 30,000 hours per year (Pilati 1987, 121–2; also see Morcellini 1986; Zollo 1987; Murialdi 1990; Menduni 1996).

9. The appointment of Enrico Manca (PSI) to a three-year term as president of the RAI Administrative Council in 1986, for example, had been deadlocked for three years (see Marletti 1988a).

10. In three Italian regions (Piemonte, Lazio, and Abruzzo), a lower court judge in 1984 ordered the blackout of the Fininvest networks for infringements of the law. This measure was strongly opposed by Berlusconi. His protest found support among the government parties, especially Craxi's PSI. On October 16 the PSI obtained approval for a first decree that allowed the Fininvest networks to resume broadcasting. When that decree expired, another one was issued on December 6 and later converted into Law #10 of February 4, 1985, which legitimized Berlusconi's claim. Berlusconi used this law to maintain his monopolistic position against competitors, in particular TMC (De Santis and Ferrigolo 1990, 501–2).

11. Barbagli et al. 1979; Fedele 1979; Novelli 1980; Pasquino 1985; Biorcio and Natale 1986; Corbetta et al. 1988.

12. See Martinotti 1978; Pasquino 1978; Sani 1980; Mannheimer and Sani 1987.

13. Aside from the party's journal, *Il Popolo* (read only by party activists and a few executives), the DC indirectly owned some important papers and enjoyed support from many centrist "friendly papers." In addition, it derived considerable benefit from a vast network of information bulletins and diocesan journals belonging to the Federazione Italiana Stampa Cattolica. At present, this organization publishes 123 periodicals, only one of which, however, is a daily newspaper – *L'Avvenire,* an outlet for the Bishops' Council.

14. See Facchi 1960; Poggi 1963; Brunetta 1978; Isenghi and Lanaro 1978; Urettini 1978; and Bonini 1990.

15. On the effects of secularization process, see DeSandre 1965; Burgalassi 1968; Rusconi 1969; Sivini 1971; Carbonaro 1976; Parisi 1979; Calvaruso and Abbruzzese 1985; Garelli 1991; Diamanti and Gianni 1992.

16. On this cultural and organizational transformation of the PSI, see Cazzola 1970 and 1985; Merkel 1987; Statera 1987; Tamburrano 1990; Sabbatucci 1995.

17. Despite the existence of a vast literature on the PCI as a political party, there are few studies (see Bechelloni and Buonanno 1981; Marletti 1984; and Mancini 1987) of the PCI's use of mass demonstrations as a propaganda and political-communication conduit. The PCI's peculiar organizational characteristics, compared with those of other European parties, are described in Belligni 1983. Electoral trends, the PCI's base, and its identification with the party electoral trends are analyzed in Mannheimer 1987 and Mannheimber et al. 1978.

18. Source: AGB 1983, cited in Mazzoleni (1992, 156). Until 1983, electoral spots were broadcast only on local stations, so no precise data on expenditures in previous electoral campaigns are available. Nonetheless, Mazzoleni (1995, 15) estimates that about half a billion lire were spend on electoral advertising in the 1980 administrative election.

19. On the political language of party elites, see Facchi 1961; Eco 1973; Costantini and Moltedo 1976; Pallotta 1991. For an analysis of self-referential practices in media–party relationships, see Marletti 1985.

20. The Osservatorio-Archivo sulla Comunicazione Politica, established in 1990 and currently located at the University of Perugia, is a consortium among three universities (Perugia, Salerno, and Torino), and includes individual scholars from the universities of Catania, Florence, and the Università Cattolica di Milano. Its archives include parallel data sets (based on a common research design and questionnaire content) for all elections since 1983. While other research centers (most importantly the Osservatorio of the University of Pavia and Mediamonitor at La Sapienza University in Rome) have studied electoral communications in the 1994 and 1996 elections, the Osservatorio of Perugia is unique insofar as its archives include data spanning 15 years of electoral campaigns in Italy. Its studies are regularly published by the RAI-Verifica Quallitativa Programmi Trasmessi (VQPT) and in *COMPOL,* the bulletin published by the Osservatorio itself (Grossi, et al. 1985; Marletti 1985; Cheli et al. 1989; Mancini 1993; Mancini and Mazzoleni 1995; Marini and Roncarolo 1997).

21. The multiple preference vote allowed each voter to give three or more preferences for specific candidates in multimember districts. While originally intended to make the proportional-representation system more democratic by giving voters greater control over the election of their parliamentary representatives, it became a tool for vote trading that developed among the leaders of the main party factions, their local representatives, and the voters (the "exchange vote"). In practice, not only did this corrupt the electoral process but, especially in the South, it increased the ability of local bosses to manipulate the voters. (See Mazzoleni 1990.)

22. See Tinacci and Cheli 1986; Statera 1986; Mazzoleni 1987a and 1987b; Pasquino 1990; Notarnicola 1994.

23. Bagnasco (1996) claims that regionalism and more "municipalism" have been constant characteristics of Italian history, and that their reemergence today can explain many so-called anomalous aspects of Italian society and the present political change. Similar arguments are also advanced in Diamanti's 1993 and 1994b analyses of the emergence of localistic movements in the northeast. (Also see Mannheimer 1991; Diamanti 1992).

24. Source: 1988 *Audiradio* survey. Also see Fenati 1993; Menduni 1994.

25. The new electoral law represented a compromise between majoritarian and proportional-representation principles (Pasquino 1995; Warner and Gambetta 1994;

Pizorusso 1995). Accordingly, three-quarters of the members of both the Senate and the Chamber of Deputies are elected by receiving a plurality of the votes cast in single-member districts. The remaining seats are awarded according to modified proportionality rules. With regard to the Senate, ballots cast in the single-member districts are aggregated to the regional level to determine the partisan distribution of the remaining parliamentary seats (to be filled by candidates who failed to secure seats on the first round). The balance of the Chamber's seats are determined by casting a separate vote; seats are allocated to parties receiving at least 4 percent of the vote, which distribute the seats among their candidates on separate national-level lists. In order to compensate parties that do poorly in the single-member-plurality round, a "proportional recuperation quotient" (the *scorporo*) transfers votes from the first round's victorious parties to the losing parties in determining the allocation of additional seats in both the Chamber and the Senate. This procedure significantly reduces the majoritarian biases of single-member-district balloting, especially for the Senate.

26. Between the 1994 and 1996 elections, the news continued to reflect the previous *lottizzazione* insofar as RAI-3 continued to offer more coverage to the PDS and other left-wing groups, while RAI-1 continued to be controlled by former DC factions. The major change occurred at RAI-2, where the disappearance of the PSI (which had controlled it previously) allowed the center-right governing parties to gain more favorable coverage.

27. Even the symbols adopted by Prodi and his allies were consistent with this image. The emblem of the coalition – an olive tree – is a symbol of peace and is widely used in religious services on Palm Sunday, the first day of the campaign. The bus Prodi traveled in throughout the campaign stood in sharp contrast with Berlusconi's luxury jet. Photographs picturing him while riding his bicycle in the countryside on weekends recalled the simple life and popular pastimes in contact with nature, as opposed to frantic life in large cities and the ever-increasing, polluting automobile traffic. If in 1994 Berlusconi won with a strategy based on status symbols that played on the relative deprivation felt by the middle classes, in 1996 Prodi played on understatement and on the working classes' need for well-being and the quiet life.

28. In the so-called first republic, voters were typically presented with a choice among about ten party lists. In the 1994 elections this number rose to 14 and in 1996 to at least 20.

29. Two examples typify this great exposure through television. The first occurred in January 1997 and sparked criticism from the majority's coalition partners. In the initial broadcast of a new series of political programs (TG3 Prima Sera), then Prime Minister Prodi remained in his government office, connected electronically to the television studio, for two hours, but was allowed to speak for only nine and a half minutes; the PDS leader D'Alema, however, took advantage of his status as a studio guest and dominated the discussion throughout the entire program (*Corriere della Sera,* January 11, 1997). A second example involves back-to-back television appearances on February 17, 18, and 19, 1999, first on an RAI-1 political news program, then as a guest on a musical program on a Mediaset channel, and finally as a participant in a popular talk show on the most widely followed Mediaset channel.

CHAPTER 7

The United States: News in a Free-Market Society

Thomas E. Patterson

News is a construct. It is not, as some journalists like to say, a mirror held up to reality (Mickelson 1972). News is the product of conventions – a set of informal and subjective rules that guide the decisions of those who gather, produce, and transmit the news (Lippmann 1922; Davis 1995). In the United States, these conventions have developed in the context of a press that is decidedly commercial and adversarial in its orientation. This orientation has intensified in recent decades, accentuating what was already a distinctive construction of the news. The values at stake in political conflict and society's underlying problems, for example, are not conspicuously aired in the news. On the other hand, political failings and disputes are prominently displayed, as are the strategic actions of top officials.

The basic theme of this chapter is that the key to understanding the political role and impact of the U.S. news media is contained in the media's commercial and adversarial orientation. From this perspective, the emergence in recent decades of broadcast and cable television as important news sources is important primarily for their impact on tendencies that already existed in U.S. news journalism. Television and print news differ in style and mode of presentation, but they are based fundamentally on the same model of journalism.

This chapter is divided into six sections. The first discusses the U.S. conception of press freedom and is followed by sections on the commercial and adversarial orientation of the U.S. news media. The fourth and fifth sections explore two major tendencies in U.S. news: game-centered coverage and negativity. The final section examines the issue of whether the U.S. news media have the capacity to organize public opinion and debate in a substantial and meaningful way.

A FREE PRESS

In comparison with other news systems, the U.S. press is one of the freest. Its mandate is provided by the First Amendment, which reads: "Congress shall make no law . . . abridging the freedom of speech, or of the press." Despite its language, the First Amendment does not provide a guarantee of absolute freedom from government regulation. Press freedom can be denied, for example, if it is obscene, endangers national security, or damages the reputation of another. Nevertheless, the American press has always been relatively free of government regulation and in recent decades has achieved an extraordinary level of autonomy.

Libel law is an example. Although a public official can sue a publisher or broadcaster for reporting false or damaging information, the prospect of success is remote. In *The New York Times v. Sullivan* (1964), the Supreme Court held that a *Times* advertisement that accused Alabama officials of physically abusing African Americans during civil rights demonstrations was not libelous. The Court ruled that libel of a public official requires proof of "actual malice," which was defined as a knowing or reckless disregard for the truth with intent to damage the official's reputation. This imposing standard of proof remains essentially intact today. It is extremely difficult to prove in a court of law that a news report was motivated by malice rather than, say, by a desire to expose an abuse of power. No federal official has won a libel judgment against a news organization in the three decades since the *Sullivan* ruling (Robinson 1993).

The press is also almost completely free of government censorship. Although national security interests can be a basis for restrictions, the burden of proof is on the government. In *The New York Times v. United States* (1971), the Supreme Court ruled that the *Times*'s publication of the Pentagon Papers (secret government documents revealing official deception about the progress of the Vietnam War) could not be blocked by the Department of Justice, which claimed that public disclosure would harm the war effort. The documents had been illegally obtained by antiwar activists, who had turned them over to the *Times* and other news organizations. The Court concluded that "any system of prior restraints" on the press is unconstitutional unless the government can provide compelling reasons for the restriction.

In granting freedom of the press, the framers of the Constitution were intent on protecting the expression of opinion. The production of information was not at issue; in 1791 there were no full-time reporters and no daily news coverage. The printer and the pamphleteer constituted the press, and nearly any citizen who wanted to join its ranks could do so.

A century later, publishing was a privilege enjoyed only by a few. Newspaper ownership was beyond the financial reach of the political parties, much less the average citizen. Social and technological changes had made possible a press system centering on the wire services and mass-circulation newspapers. The twentieth century brought further transformations in the form of radio and television networks and a pattern of chain ownership that would eventually embrace three-fourths of the nation's dailies (Bagdikian 1992). The journalist A. J. Liebling noted the contradiction between the theory and practice of Americans' rights: "We have a free press today. . . . Anybody in the ten-million dollar category is free to buy or found a paper in a great city like New York or Chicago and anybody with around a million (and a lot of sporting blood) is free to try it in a place of mediocre size like Worcester. As to us, we are free to buy [a copy of today's] paper or not, as we wish" (1961, 15).

This situation could justify a positive conception of press freedom under which media owners are required to provide other interests with reasonable opportunities to present their views. In 1919 (*Abrams v. United States*), Justice Oliver Wendell Holmes argued that the First Amendment was in fact intended to foster a "free trade in ideas," which, in an industrial age, could reasonably be said to exist only if all groups were afforded the means to express their views broadly and forcefully.

This view has never been widely accepted in the United States, and the news media have opposed policies that would compel them to share their power in defined ways with other groups. The "Fairness Doctrine" is a case in point. The Federal Communications Commission (FCC) held that broadcasters, because they control a scarce public resource, are obliged to air important issues of public concern and to provide opposing sides on these issues with a reasonable opportunity to present their views. This regulation did not prevent broadcasters from airing their own views, but it did prevent them from censoring the views of others.

Nevertheless, broadcasters assailed the FCC's position as an unacceptable restriction on their First Amendment rights. The FCC's policy was upheld, however, by the Supreme Court in *Red Lion Broadcasting v. FCC* (1969): "It is the purpose of the First Amendment to preserve an uninhibited marketplace of ideas in which truth will ultimately prevail, rather than to countenance monopolization of that market, whether it be by the Government itself or a private licensee." Yet the Court did not go so far as to grant citizens the right of direct access to the broadcast media. Broadcasters retained the power to decide who would be allowed to express a particular opinion and when it would be aired. Moreover, the regulation itself was not vigorously enforced; the FCC dismissed nearly all of the Fairness Doctrine complaints it received (Patterson 1987, 311). And in 1987, at the Reagan administration's urging, the FCC rescinded the Fairness Doctrine, declaring that the advent of cable broadcasting had negated the scarcity issue.

Broadcasters' response to the Fairness Doctrine typifies the media's self-referential interpretation of the First Amendment. News organizations have opposed, for example, any statutory provision that would give individuals an opportunity to rebut accusations leveled at them by a journalist. When the State of Florida enacted a right-of-reply statute requiring newspapers to publish the response of candidates whose personal character was attacked in their columns, the national media roundly condemned it. The Supreme Court upheld their position in *Miami Herald Publishing Co. v. Tornillo* (1974) by ruling that the Florida law violated the free press clause of the First Amendment.

The media's position on the First Amendment is also evident from a survey that asked U.S. journalists whether they think press freedom "is intended primarily to enable the news media to freely communicate the information and opinions they deem important [or whether it] is intended primarily to enable the many groups in society to freely express the values and beliefs they deem important." Only 24 percent of the respondents said that press freedom exists primarily for the benefit of social groups (Patterson 1992).

A COMMERCIALLY BASED NEWS SYSTEM

America's news media are not only among the freest in the world, they are also among the most commercial (Postman 1985). The United States has roughly 1,600 daily newspapers, 7,500 weeklies, 11,000 radio stations, 4 national television broadcast networks, 20-odd national radio networks, 1,000 local television stations, and 6,000 cable television systems. The vast majority of these organizations are privately owned. The business of news gathering and dissemination is almost entirely controlled by profit-seeking entities.

Early in the Republic, the profit motive was less basic to the functioning of the news system. The first newspapers had a partisan bent and were supported by government printing contracts and partisan subscribers. There was no mass audience to reach: the great majority of

244

Americans could neither read nor write. Even the large circulation papers had fewer than 1,500 readers (Mott 1962, 114–15).

Social and technological changes helped bring about the decline of the partisan press. After the invention of the telegraph in 1837, local editors received timely information from Washington, D.C., and their state's capital, giving them less reason to fill their papers with partisan argument. Another breakthrough was the rotary press, which made the printing process both quick and cheap. Benjamin Day's *New York Sun* was the first paper to pass on the benefit of high-speed printing to subscribers by reducing the price of a daily copy from six cents to a penny. The *Sun* also employed the country's first full-time reporter, an Englishman brought from London to cover the crime beat. The *Sun* aimed to sell newspapers through gossip and the human interest story, a strategy that was immensely successful. The paper's circulation rose to 5,000 in four months and reached 10,000 in less than a year (Mott 1962, 220–7).

The nation's rising literacy rate during the 1800s provided a steadily wider readership for the newspaper. By the 1890s, some big-city newspapers were printing 100,000 copies a day, which earned them high profits from advertising. A new type of reporting emerged as a means to boost circulation. "Yellow journalism" emphasized "a shrieking, gaudy, sensation-loving, devil-may-care kind of journalism which lured the reader by any possible means" (Emery 1977, 350).

Yellow journalism was as shameless as it was lucrative. In an effort to deflect mounting criticisms of their industry, newspapers turned to objective journalism, which required the journalist to report only the facts and to treat both political parties fairly. Objective journalism curbed some of the press's worst excesses, but it did not end its commitment to a form of journalism motivated more by the desire to attract a large readership than to create an informed public. The Commission on Freedom of the Press (1947, 8) complained that newspaper circulation was built on "practices which the society condemns." In the 1920s, radio intruded on the newspapers' monopoly of the daily news. By the end of the decade, a third of American homes had acquired radio receivers and hundreds of radio stations were in operation. Laissez-faire economics was the ideology of the 1920s, and the radio industry embodied it. Anyone with the money to start a radio station could do so, and broadcasters were free to transmit on a frequency of their choosing, even if it was already in use. The ensuing chaos prompted Congress to establish the Federal Radio Commission (replaced in 1934 by the FCC) to license stations and allocate frequencies. Yet Congress refused to allow the FCC to substantially regulate programming. The marketplace would determine nearly all of what Americans heard on their radios. Thus, at a time when Great Britain was forming the British Broadcasting Corporation (BBC) as a public-service corporation, the United States was laying the foundation for a commercial broadcasting system.

The 1950s was the decade in which television became a significant force in American life. By the late 1950s, more than 80 percent of U.S. households had a television set compared with less than 10 percent at the start of the decade. Because of high programming costs, television was organized around national networks. Their focus was entertainment programs. Television newscasts of the 1950s were brief, lasting no more than 15 minutes, and relied on news gathered by the wire services and leading newspapers.

In 1963 the Columbia Broadcasting System (CBS) expanded its evening newscast to 30 minutes in an effort to overtake the National Broadcasting Company's (NBC) lead in audience ratings (White 1982, 172–3). The popularity of President John F. Kennedy's televised press conferences had convinced CBS executives that the American people wanted more news programming. NBC and the American Broadcasting Company (ABC) followed suit, and the audience ratings of all three networks rose. Simultaneously, the networks greatly expanded their news-division staffs. Since their audience spanned the nation, the networks focused on national events and soon established themselves as the principal medium of national politics (Robinson 1981).

Like radio, television developed as a commercially based system. Public television was not established until the commercial networks were solidly entrenched, and they lobbied successfully against a strong public-sector component. Commercial stations held the more powerful very high frequencies (VHF) while public stations were assigned ultra high frequencies (UHF), which most of the television sets of the 1950s were not equipped to receive. The consequences of these early policies linger to this day. The nightly news audience of the Public Broadcasting System (PBS) is presently only one-twentieth of that of the four commercial broadcast networks (ABC, CBS, NBC, and Fox).

In other ways, too, the advent of television solidified the news system's commercial base. When the networks expanded their news operations in the early 1960s, they did not try to match the newspapers in the tone and depth of their coverage. The networks sought a livelier form of presentation that emphasized strong visuals within a fast-paced format, accompanied by a narrative style of reporting (Epstein 1973).

Unlike radio news, which had whetted people's appetite for news and contributed to increased newspapers circulation (Davis 1995, 96), television news competed directly with the newspaper for audience share. The first casualties were the afternoon papers, which faced direct competition from the evening newscasts. Dozens of afternoon papers closed or merged with morning papers. Although the overall circulation level of newspapers has declined only slightly since the 1960s, the percentage of households that receive a newspaper has dropped from 70 to 50 percent.

When the Roper Organization initiated its annual survey of the news audience in 1959, television and newspapers had a nearly equal share, followed closely by radio. Radio's share fell off rapidly thereafter, while the newspapers' share shrank more gradually. Today, according to the Roper Poll, three times as many Americans rely on television as on newspapers as their main source of news, with radio a distant third. (It must be noted that these ratios are somewhat misleading; more than half of those who cite television as their major news source do not watch its newscasts regularly, while a large majority of those who rely most heavily on the newspaper read it almost daily.)

In the 1980s, cable television achieved national prominence. In this decade, the Cable News Network (CNN) began its 24-hour news coverage; cable subscriptions increased from less than 25 percent of American homes to more than 50 percent; and cable channels captured a third of the broadcast channels' prime-time viewing audience. Cable television has a public component (for example, C-SPAN and public-access channels) but, like other U.S. media, it is for the most part a commercial medium.

Cable has altered the size and composition of the news audience. Before cable, Americans who turned on their television in the early evening had almost no alternative but to watch a newscast. The three networks broadcast their news simultaneously and had a combined audience share of nearly 90 percent. Cable provided viewers with a choice between news and entertainment, and the networks' audience share during the evening news hour fell below 50 percent by 1999.

Although cable has fostered a core of "news junkies" who immerse themselves in CNN and C-SPAN, its more significant effect has been to contribute to a steep decline in the overall size of the news audience, which has heightened the competition among news providers. Television newscasts now include more human-interest stories, shorter sound bites, and more dramatic visuals, while both television and newspaper stories have become shorter, more conflict-ridden, and more storylike, a news formula that is believed to have more appeal to viewers and readers than alternative formats (Adatto 1990; Hallin 1992).

Commercialism in the American press results in a remarkably homogeneous version of the news. The great number and freedom of news organizations may be expected to result in wide variation in the national news that Americans receive. And certainly the argument for a free press is typically based on the assumption that the absence of regulation will produce a robust "marketplace of ideas." Nevertheless, most Americans receive a relatively uniform rendition of the news. Of course, news organizations differ in how they tell a given story. Broadcast news tends to be, in essence, headline news with pictures. The reporting styles of newspapers vary in that some present the news in a straightforward manner, while others tend toward sensationalism. Such differences, however, do not disguise the fact that, each day, newspapers and broadcast stations from coast to coast are likely to highlight the same national news stories and to interpret them in similar ways (Patterson 1996).

A variety of terms – "pack journalism," "groupthink," "media concentration" – have been used to describe this phenomenon. It is due in large part to the objective model of journalism that prohibits news reporters from inserting their own partisanship into news stories. Guided instead by a set of professional values that they share, journalists tend to find significance in the same things (Barber 1980).

Of course, reporters do sometimes differ on which facts, events, and issues are the most important, but these polite disagreements are a far cry from the disputes and diversity that characterized the nineteenth-century American press. In the presidential election campaign of 1896, the *San Francisco Call* devoted 1,075 column-inches in photographs to the Republican ticket of McKinley-Hobart and only 11 inches to the Democrats, Bryan and Sewell (Lippmann 1922, 214). Competition in the U.S. news system today is mainly an issue of timing and imitation. All news organizations want to be the first to break an important story, and none of them wants to miss a story that others are covering (Gans 1980).

AN ADVERSARIAL PRESS

Not only is the American press freer and more commercial than most other news systems, it also has a more adversarial relationship with the officials it covers.

The media see themselves as a "fourth branch" of government, with the responsibility to act as a check on the executive, legislative, and judicial branches. This position has no clear basis in the original constitutional intent. During the early years of the Republic, newspapers were closely aligned with the political parties. The fourth-branch theory blossomed during the early 1900s, when the Progressives crusaded against self-serving party bosses and special interests. By then, newspapers were a mass medium and wielded substantial power in their own right. This power merged with the Progressive agenda in the form of muckraking journalism, which sought to expose abuses of political and economic power (Ranney 1983, 52–5).

Muckraking was eventually quieted by its own excesses and by the emerging rules of objective journalism, which held that reporters should refrain from expressing their opinions in news stories. Criticisms of politicians and the political process were relegated to opinion columns and editorial pages.

Straightforward reporting became the dominant style. The journalist's guidelines were the five W's: who said what to whom, when, and why. The focus was on the facts of an event rather than the underlying political situation. Since the "facts" were often based on what politicians had said or done, they greatly influenced the tone of the journalist's coverage. A standard formula for a news story was a descriptive account of what politicians said and to whom they said it. News accounts did not ordinarily delve into why they said it, for that would take the journalist into the realm of subjectivity. At the very least, journalists took pains to separate the facts of an event from their interpretations of it.

Today, facts and interpretation are freely intermixed in news reporting. Interpretation provides the theme, and the facts illuminate it. The theme is primary; the facts are illustrative. As a result, events are compressed and joined together within a common theme. Reporters routinely question the actions of politicians and commonly attribute strategic intentions to them, giving politicians less of a chance to speak for themselves (Andersen and Thorson 1989).

Interpretive reporting is nearly as old as journalism itself but has only recently become the dominant model of news coverage. When the television networks changed from a 15-minute to a 30-minute format and began to generate most of their own news, they increasingly relied on an interpretive style of reporting (Weaver 1972, 67–9). The inverted pyramid form of the traditional newspaper story was not well suited to television. This form trailed off as it proceeded from the most salient fact of an event to the least important, which allowed the newspaper editor to cut the story almost anywhere in order to fit it into the available space. On television, however, this form gave the appearance of a news story that had lost its punch. Network executives sought a more dramatic style of reporting that was built around storylines rather than facts. The president of NBC News, Reuven Frank, instructed his correspondents: "Every news story should, without any sacrifice of probity or responsibility, display the attributes of fiction, of drama. It should have structure and conflict, problem and denouement, rising action and falling action, a beginning, a middle and an end" (Robinson and Sheehan 1983, 226).

Newspapers pursued the interpretive style less as an attempt to imitate television than as an effort to establish a separate niche in the news market. Unable to compete with television as a source of fast-breaking news, the newspapers migrated toward reports designed to explain or embellish yesterday's events. The extent to which this interpretive form of reporting has taken over newspaper coverage is evident in *The New York Times*. Between 1960 and 1992, the proportion of interpretive reports on its front page increased tenfold, from 8 percent to 80 percent (Patterson 1993, 82).

The interpretive style empowers journalists by giving them more control over the news message. Whereas descriptive reporting is driven by the facts, the interpretive form is driven by the theme around which the story is built. Facts become "the materials with which the chosen theme is illustrated" (Weaver 1972, 67–9). The descriptive style places the journalist in the role of an observer. The interpretive style requires the journalist to act also as an analyst. The journalist is thus positioned to give shape to the news in a way the descriptive style does not allow.

An indicator of the change is the journalists' prominence in today's news. Whereas they were once the relatively passive voice behind the news, they are now as active and visible as the newsmakers they cover. In few respects is this trend more evident than in the "shrinking sound bite" of election campaigns. In 1968, when presidential candidates appeared in a television news story, they were usually pictured speaking; 84 percent of the time, candidates' images on the television screen were accompanied by their words. The average "sound bite" – a block of uninterrupted speech by a candidate on television news – was 42 seconds. By 1988, the 42-second sound bite had shrunk to less than 10 seconds and has remained there (Adatto 1990; Hallin 1992; Center for Media and Public Affairs 1996).

The voiceless politician is commonplace on television news. For every minute that the presidential candidates spoke on the network evening newscasts during the 1988, 1992, and 1996 campaigns, for example, the journalists who were covering them talked six minutes (Center for Media and Public Affairs 1992 and 1996). Newspaper coverage has followed the same trend. In 1960, the average continuous quote or paraphrase of a presidential candidate's words in a front-page *New York Times* story was 14 lines. By 1992, the average had fallen to six lines (Patterson 1993). On television and in the newspaper, the politician's views are now often subsumed in a narrative devoted primarily to expounding the reporter's view of politics.

At nearly the same time that interpretive journalism was working its way into the news system, the Vietnam War and the Watergate scandal soured the relationship between journalists and politicians. The deceptions perpetuated by the Johnson and Nixon administrations convinced reporters that they had failed in their duty to the nation by taking political leaders at their word. Although politicians such as William Fulbright, Eugene McCarthy, Sam Ervin, and Howard Baker played pivotal roles in the downfall of Johnson and Nixon, journalists saw themselves as the real heroes. "The press won on Watergate," declared Ben Bradlee, executive editor of the *Washington Post* (Kampelman 1978, 18). The *New York Times's* James Reston said much the same thing about Vietnam: "Maybe historians will agree that the reporters and the cameras were decisive in the end. They brought the issue of the war to the people, before the Congress and the courts, and forced the withdrawal of American power from Vietnam" (Reston 1975, 41).

Vietnam and Watergate brought power and prominence to the press and changed the way journalists operated. They claimed for themselves a broader and more aggressive role. "[Our] chief duty," the newscaster Roger Mudd declared, "is to put before the nation its unfinished business" (Kampelman 1978, 19). This outlook was new but not altogether surprising for a press that had a watchdog tradition. "Our habits of mind," the *Washington Post's* Paul Taylor notes, "are shaped by what Lionel Trilling once described as the 'adversary culture'. . . . We are progressive reformers, deeply skeptical of all the major institutions of society except our own" (Taylor 1990, 23).

Even as late as the early 1970s, however, the old rules of journalism maintained a powerful hold on reporters. The press attacked Johnson and Nixon, but only when the charges could be substantiated. Thus, the Watergate story developed slowly, gathering strength only as incriminating facts and credible allegations came increasingly to light. The *Washington Post* uncovered most of the Watergate story and did so while maintaining the strict rule that no allegation would be published unless it was confirmed by two independent and credible sources. The *Post* was nearly 50 stories deep in its Watergate coverage before it carried a story that was later discovered to include a major factual error (Bradlee 1995).

The press was unable to sustain this exacting scrutiny. Investigative journalism requires time and knowledge that journalists do not routinely possess. It ordinarily takes a great deal of effort to determine the validity of a politician's claim or to uncover the full range of motives behind it. The pressures of the 24-hour news cycle make it nearly impossible for journalists to engage in this type of reporting on a regular basis.

By the mid-1970s, the media had settled on a substitute for true investigative journalism. They began to use a politician's opponents as the basis for undermining his claims. When a politician made a statement, they turned to his adversaries to attack it. Conflict, always an element of political coverage, became the predominant theme (Sabato 1991).

By the 1980s, attack journalism had come to include reporters as direct participants; they regularly worked their own criticisms into their interpretive reports. These attacks are circumscribed in that journalists seldom contest the values inherent in political conflict. But they constantly question politicians' motives, methods, and effectiveness. This type of reporting looks like watchdog journalism, but in most instances it is not. It is ideological in its premise: politicians are assumed to act out of self-interest rather than also from political conviction. Journalists routinely claim that politicians make promises they do not intend to keep or could not keep even if they tried. Most bad-press stories criticize politicians for shifting their positions, waffling on tough issues, posturing, or pandering to whichever group they happen to be facing (Robinson 1983, 2).

If journalists had once been the "lap dogs" of the politicians, they were now "attack dogs." And nothing puts them on the attack more quickly than the whiff of political scandal. Moreover, the increased speed of the news cycle – a function of 24-hour news networks such as CNN and MSNBC – has made it increasingly difficult for them to hold their attack until they can verify the accuracy of an allegation. The Clinton-Lewinsky scandal, for example, developed at breakneck speed. It surfaced on a Saturday evening on the Internet, was picked up Sunday morning on a network talk show, and was front-page news in Monday's *Washington Post*. Over the next several days, rumors and unsupported allegations dominated news stories. The former journalist Marvin Kalb noted: "Many news organizations dropped the unofficial industry-wide practice of requiring two solid sources for information and others used flimsy, questionable sources, such as the reports of other news organizations or anonymous individuals, whose bias or identity was almost never characterized" (Kalb 1999, 11).

The Committee of Concerned Journalists conducted an analysis of news sourcing by major news organizations during the first two weeks of the Clinton-Lewinsky scandal. The committee found that only 1 percent of the stories were based on two or more named and independent sources. Another 25 percent were based on a single named source. The remaining 74 percent were based on anonymous sources who in most cases were identified as a single source and described in an opaque way: "A source today told our news organization that . . ." (Committee of Concerned Journalists 1998).

In the months that followed, "Monicagate" was far and away the top news story. It received more coverage than the next five top stories combined. The coverage was predictably negative in tone, and the attacks on Clinton were made primarily through sources. But reporters also joined the attack. Nearly 90 percent of reporters' unattributed statements about Clinton were negative in tone. After a Clinton news conference, for example, ABC correspondent Sam Donaldson remarked: "The President might have answered the key question as to whether he intends to stick to his story, but in the Rose Garden today, he deliberately chose not to" (Center for Media and Public Affairs 1996, 5).

NEWS DIMENSIONS AND EFFECTS, PART I: THE GAME

The commercial and adversarial orientations of the U.S. news media profoundly affect political coverage, mainly in ways that reduce the media's capacity as instruments of public information and debate. The chief goal of the media is not to foster a free marketplace of ideas but rather "to attract and hold a large audience for advertisers" (Jamieson and Campbell 1988, 4). The media's concern with novelty, for example, is predicated on the notion that news audiences are drawn to what is new and surprising and turned off by what is familiar and predictable. The significance of issues and events is defined less by their importance to society than by their recency. *The New York Times*'s James Reston described reporting as "the exhilarating search after the Now" (quoted in Taylor 1990, 25).

Of the many effects of commercialism on news content, none is more consequential than the media's tendency to report politics not as an issue but as a game in which individual politicians vie for power. "The game is a competitive one and the players' principal activities are those of calculating and pursuing strategies designed to defeat competitors and to achieve their goals," Paul Weaver (1972, 69) notes. "[T]he game takes place against a backdrop of governmental institutions, public problems, policy debates, and the like, but these are noteworthy only insofar as they affect, or are used by, players in pursuit of the game's reward." This conception of politics, which emerged when the nineteenth-century press shed its partisan ties, allows news organizations to appeal to the broadest audience possible. News reporters seldom take sides in political debate because to do so consistently would reduce their audience to those who hold the same values (Semetko et al. 1991).

The dramatic structure of the political game also enhances its newsworthiness. The struggle for power "is a naturally structured, long-lasting dramatic sequence with changing scenes" (Barber 1978, 117–18). The game provides the running story in which today's developments relate to yesterday's and, likely, tomorrow's events. Since it can almost always be assumed that officials are driven by a desire to gain advantage, their actions can hence be interpreted as an effort to acquire power or votes. The game is thus a reliable source of fresh news material.

The game also embodies the conflict that American journalists prize in their news stories, what Jules Witcover labeled the "I said – he said – I said" type of dispute (Barber 1978, 117). In journalists' game paradigm, the focus is on a few individuals, the politicians, rather than on the broader interests they represent and the broader political forces that shape their choices. Politics can then be portrayed as a struggle for personal advantage (Lang and Lang 1968; Owen 1991; Kurtz 1992). For example, in her study of the debate surrounding President Clinton's proposed restructuring of the nation's health-care system, Kathleen Hall Jamieson (1994) found that print and broadcast coverage focused overwhelmingly on who was winning the health fight rather than on the substance of the debate or the policy consequences. Jamieson found that political strategy accounted for about two-thirds of the health-care coverage and most of the headlines.

Reporters are, of course, aware of the larger issues that drive politics. Nevertheless, U.S. journalists do not easily deal with the values that are at stake in issues, since they would have to take sides in order to do so. The game, on the other hand, can be reported and evaluated without invalidating the reporter's claim to impartiality. In 1980, for example, the news media presented seven times as many stories on President Jimmy

Carter's problems with the activities of his wayward brother Billy as on the Strategic Arms Limitations Talks between the United States and the Soviet Union (Robinson and Sheehan 1983, 57). By the standards of news, Billygate was a more manageable issue than SALT II.

To expect the press to ignore the gamelike aspects of politics and report solely on enduring questions of national policy and leadership is to suggest inaccurately that the substance of politics is all that matters (Freedom Forum Media Studies Center 1992, 28). Strategy has always been an important part of politics, and has become more so as political parties carry less of the burden of mobilizing support and the individual politician carries more of it. Compared with times past, tactics and imagery are a larger part of American politics today (Ansolabehere, et al. 1993, 3). Nevertheless, the game looms much larger in the news than it does in political life.

For reporters, controversy and conflict are the real issues of politics. The press deals with charges and countercharges, rarely digging into the details of political positions or social conditions underlying policy problems. It is not simply that the press neglects issues in favor of the strategic game; issues, even when covered, are subordinated to the drama of the conflict generated by the opposing sides.

Clancy and Robinson's study (1985, 29) of the 1984 campaign indicates how fully political controversies can dominate the news. They used a broad definition of these issues ("short-term concerns about how *candidates* and their campaigns should behave") and found that they accounted for a larger part of the coverage than did policy issues ("enduring disputes about how *government* should behave"). The controversies ranged from George Bush's offhand remark to a New Jersey longshoreman that he had kicked "a little ass" in his vice-presidential debate with Geraldine Ferraro to Ronald Reagan's suggestion that the 1983 Beirut bombing that killed 241 U.S. marines was somehow former President Carter's fault. The 1984 election campaign had the dubious distinction of being the one in which the most intensely reported issue – Ferraro's refusal to make public her family's tax returns – was neither a policy issue nor one that involved a presidential nominee. As Murray Edelman (1988) noted, there is a tendency in news coverage for dramatic incidents involving prominent individuals to displace policy issues.

The effect of this type of coverage on the public is substantial. To a large degree, the power of the press works through its capacity to frame events, to interpret them in one way rather than another (Iyengar 1991). The news media's tendency to frame politics in gamelike terms serves to depoliticize issues, presenting them more as political tokens in the struggle for power than as objects of serious debate (Levy 1981). Although citizens sometimes take an interest in political infighting, it is not a central concern. For example, viewers and readers have fewer reactions to and less recall of game-based news stories than those based on issues (Patterson, 1980a). It is also the case that, when given a chance to frame the agenda, citizens tend to focus on issues. This tendency was evident, for example, in the 1992 presidential campaign, when voters had the opportunity through television call-in programs to interrogate the candidates directly. Their questions were problem-oriented, as opposed to the strategy-oriented questions that reporters tend to ask candidates at press conferences (Berke 1992; Patterson 1993).

In some cases, game-based stories draw citizens into an issue and provide information that is useful in making choices (Graber 1988; Neuman et al. 1992). But such stories mainly draw a passive response from citizens. When they encounter game-centered stories, people behave more like spectators than participants, responding, if at all, to the status of the fight, not to what the combatants represent. For example, a study discovered that when news stories discuss "serious social problems," people are inclined to advocate action to address the problems, but when stories discuss the game, people are less involved (Graber 1988, 203 and 206). Another study found that game-based stories were 30 percent less likely to draw an active response from readers or viewers than issue-based stories (Patterson 1980a, 90).

When citizens do respond to game-centered news, their reactions are often negative. Graber (1984, 141) found that even people who trust politicians tend to discount what they say when their actions are framed in a game context. Jamieson (1994) found that strategy-based coverage tends to confuse citizens about the substantive significance of issues and heightens their mistrust of political leaders and institutions.

The transition from newsmaker-centered to journalist-centered news has undoubtedly heightened the public's sense that politics is mainly a struggle among self-interested and self-serving politicians. An election study by the Center for Media and Public Affairs found, for example, that candidate communication in all its forms (speeches, advertising, debates, etc.) is framed primarily within the context of policy issues (1993b). Politicians pursue strategies but, unlike journalists, their public statements are framed mainly in policy terms. However, as the voice of the politician has faded in the news, so have issue-based messages. The Center for Media and Public Affairs' study (1993b) found that 75 percent of all issue references in the news are communicated by a single sentence. Fewer than 10 percent of the references contain enough substance to make their policy relevance readily apparent to an attentive member of the news audience.

Game-centered news is a reason why, despite extraordinary technological advances in mass communication in recent decades, the public's issue awareness has not increased dramatically (Mondak 1995) and by some indicators has even declined (Times-Mirror Center for the People and the Press 1994). Limited issue awareness is the almost certain consequence of news that contains infrequent, embedded, and fleeting issue references (Patterson and McClure 1976; Gitlin 1980; Popkin 1991). On the basis of a study that compared news content over a recent 20-year span, Catherine Steele and Kevin Barnhurst conclude that "rather than providing more information, journalists appear to provide less, and the context for the shrinking sound bite becomes not deeper, hidden fact, but a growing embroidery of journalistic opinion" (1995, 16).

NEWS DIMENSIONS AND EFFECTS, PART II: NEGATIVISM

The game-centered tendency of news coverage has its roots in the media's commercial orientation. A second tendency – negative news – has its roots in the media's adversarial stance.

Today, most of what happens in the political arena is viewed skeptically by the press. The accomplishments of the U.S. House of Representatives in 1995, for example, were historic in scope, but one would never have guessed that from the tone of the news coverage. Although the initiatives in the Republicans' "Contract with America" moved rapidly through the House, evaluations by network reporters and their sources were 65 percent negative. The Senate coverage was even harsher: 71 percent negative. Nor was the blistering attack on Congress confined to television. According to the Center for Media and Public Affairs (1995, 2 and 5), coverage of the early weeks of the 104th Congress in major newspapers was nearly as negative as network television's. Major targets for the media's criticism were the Republicans' top congressional leaders – Newt Gingrich, Robert Dole, and Richard Armey. Each received more negative than positive news, and their combined coverage was more than 60 percent unfavorable.

Some analysts would attribute this negative coverage to the allegedly liberal bias of the news media. According to this theory, the national press "tends to be strongly biased in favor of the Democratic-liberal-left axis of opinion and strongly biased against the Republican-conservative-right axis of opinion" (Efron 1971, 47). The problem with this thesis is that it does not fully fit the facts: during the first 100 days of the 104th Congress, Democrats (82 percent negative) received worse coverage than Republicans (68 percent negative). Democrats got substantially less attention from the press than the Republicans but were more soundly criticized when they were covered (Center for Media and Public Affairs 1995, 2).

The inadequacy of the liberal-bias theory of national news coverage is also apparent in the media's treatment of Bill Clinton's presidency. Although Clinton was the first Democratic president in 12 years, he did not even get the "honeymoon" period that newly elected presidents might expect from the press. Clinton's coverage was only 43 percent positive during his first two months on the job. Six months into his presidency, Clinton's numbers were worse – only 34 percent of news evaluations were positive. His press coverage improved somewhat in the closing months of 1993, when Clinton's successful fight to enact the North American Free Trade Agreement (NAFTA) was a leading news story but, overall, his first presidential year was characterized by negative coverage (Center for Media and Public Affairs 1994).

The liberal-bias theory fails because it ignores the checks and balances within the news system. Although journalists are disproportionately liberal and Democratic in their personal beliefs (Weaver and Wilhoit 1986), the norms of their profession include a commitment to the balanced treatment of the two parties, a code that is enforced by the layer of editors who oversee the work of reporters.

The norm of impartiality does not, however, include a restraint on criticism. Reporters have a negative opinion of politicians, whether liberal or conservative, and of the political process within which they work. More than anything else, it is this view that accounts for the news media's rough treatment of Clinton and the Republican Congress.

The absence of effective restraints on this attitude is reflected in the fact that political leaders and institutions are likely to be criticized almost regardless of what they do. The Democratic-controlled 103rd Congress (1993–4) was derided by the press as a do-nothing legislature that would not tackle the budget deficit, welfare, and political reform issues. An analysis by the Center for Media and Public Affairs found that television coverage of that Congress was 64 percent negative (1995, 2). When the Republican-controlled Congress took on each of these issues, the news media changed their tune but not their tone. Now Congress was faulted for being too aggressive and, as we have seen, the balance of this coverage was also negative.

President Clinton's first year in office also provides an instructive study in the press's tendency to criticize irrespective of the situation. No news theme was more persistent than the notion that Clinton was reneging on his policy commitments. This theme surfaced in the first weeks of his presidency, when Clinton broke a campaign promise to open the nation's shores to the Haitian boat people, and continued throughout the year. The fact is, however, that Clinton kept far more campaign promises than he broke. Among the promises kept were a tax increase on higher incomes, an end to the ban on abortion counseling in family-planning clinics, a family-leave program, banking reform, NAFTA, a college-loan program, the Brady bill, and a youth training program. He also proposed numerous programs, including health-care reform, that were still working their way through Congress as 1993 ended. Clinton's relationship with Congress was extraordinary. Since 1953, *Congressional Quarterly* has kept track of Congress's support of legislation on which the president has announced a position. Congress backed Clinton's position on 88 percent of contested votes in 1993, a level exceeded only twice in 40 years – by Dwight Eisenhower in 1953 and Lyndon Johnson in 1965. Even in their best years, John Kennedy, Richard Nixon, Gerald Ford, Jimmy Carter, Ronald Reagan, and George Bush did not achieve the level of congressional support that Clinton attained in 1993 (Center for Media and Public Affairs, 1994, 3620).

The news media's preference for the negative is well documented by scholarly studies (Jamieson 1992). In their content analysis of television coverage of the 1980 presidential campaign, Robinson and Sheehan (1983) found that negative images of the candidates predominated. "Network reporters," they observed, "do seem to want to make the public more aware of the frailties and inadequacies of their elected leadership." Although most news stories were neutral or ambiguous, television gave the candidates about three times as much "bad press" as "good press." The study concluded that reporters "seemed to be turning some motherly advice inside out – the correspondents said something critical or they said nothing at all."

The notion that "bad news makes for good news" has long been a part of commercially based journalism, but the media have raised its significance in recent years. Figure 7.1 shows the good news–bad news distribution for the major-party presidential nominees between 1960 and 1992. Bad news escalated during this period. Candidates of the 1960s got

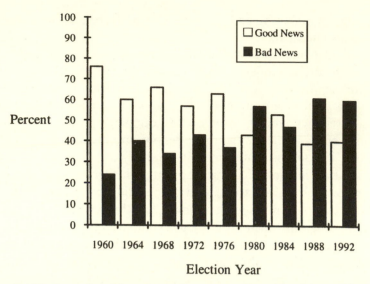

Figure 7.1 "Bad news" and "good news" coverage of presidential candidates, 1960–92. Source: Patterson 1993, 20.

more favorable coverage than those of the 1970s, who in turn received more positive coverage than those of the 1980s. The change is dramatic. Of all reporters' evaluative references to Kennedy and Nixon in 1960, 75 percent were positive. In 1992, only 40 percent of reporters' evaluative references to Clinton and Bush were favorable. The critical span of time in terms of an explanation of the trend is the 1976–92 period. Although Watergate and Vietnam receded with each election, the news coverage of presidential candidates became progressively less favorable. In three of the last four elections, bad news has outweighed good news. If Vietnam and Watergate marked a time when the press turned *against* the politicians, the recent period represents a time when the press has turned *on* them.

This development has heightened Americans' disenchantment with their political leaders and institutions. By the time the 1992 presidential race had narrowed to Clinton, Bush, and Perot, for example, polls indicated that most voters were unhappy with the candidates; all three had high negative ratings, and more than half of those surveyed said they wished they had other candidates from whom to select. In 1988, voters went to the polls to choose what they saw as the lesser of two evils. George Bush and Michael Dukakis were both viewed more negatively than positively by the electorate as a whole. On Election Day, more than three in five voters said they would have preferred someone else. The 1988 situation resembled that of 1980, when the choice was among Ronald Reagan, Jimmy Carter, and John Anderson. Half of the electorate interviewed in a poll said they were dissatisfied with the major-party nominees. Although Reagan won, opinion surveys indicated that he was the least popular presidential winner since polling began in the 1930s (Patterson 1993).

The electorate's discontent is without precedent. The Gallup Organization first asked voters their opinions of the presidential candidates in 1936. Through the 1960s, Barry Goldwater in 1964 was the only candidate with an overall negative rating with the voters. Since then, *most* candidates have had a negative rating. Moreover, the public's declining view of presidential candidates has coincided almost exactly with the increasingly negative tone of their coverage. The press's bad-news tendency is not the only reason why voters' impressions of presidential candidates have been so negative in recent elections, but it is clearly a major factor (Goldfarb 1991; Patterson 1993).

The same pattern holds true for Congress and the presidency. Since the late 1980s, news coverage of both Congress and the president has been extremely critical, and the public's perception of Congress and the president during this period has been largely unfavorable. The Center for Media and Public Affairs tracked the relationship between the tone of President Clinton's news coverage and his public approval rating. The two trends were closely parallel, with declines in Clinton's approval rating lagging slightly behind increases in his negative coverage, an indication that the public was responding to the tone of the news.

It could be argued that the press is merely "telling it like it is," that public officials are an ineffective and untrustworthy lot. Perhaps, as the press's election coverage implies, candidates routinely make promises they have no intention of keeping, and that are made not only to deceive the voters, but also to trick them into supporting actions that are contrary to their interests. The press makes such deceptions appear to be the norm. Candidates are said to change their positions as they campaign in different regions or talk with different groups, make promises they plan to break, and make commitments that cannot be honored even if they try. Cynical manipulation is the story that is told of politicians' efforts to woo the public. The story fits the press's game conception of politics, but is it accurate?

The importance of this question to the integrity of the democratic process has prompted scholars to investigate it. This research has involved extensive analysis in which winning candidates' campaign promises have been systematically cataloged and compared to what they did as presidents. At least four such studies have been conducted, each spanning a minimum of seven presidencies. Each of these studies discovered the same thing: presidents kept the promises they made as candidates. Pomper's exhaustive study of party platforms in nine presidential elections found that victorious candidates, once in office, attempted to fulfill nearly all of their policy commitments and succeeded in achieving most of them. When they failed to deliver on a promise, it was usually because they could not get Congress to agree or because policy conditions had changed (Pomper with Lederman 1980, chapter 8). Krukones (1984) reached the same conclusion after comparing the campaign speeches and in-office performances of 11 recent presidents. In a third study, Budge and Hofferbert (1990, 111–32) found "strong links between postwar (1948–85) election platforms and governmental outputs." In a fourth study, Fishel (1985, 42–3) concluded that presidents in the 1960–84 period signed executive orders or submitted legislative proposals corresponding to a large majority of their campaign pledges; in the case of legislative proposals, Congress enacted most of them (Johnson's 89 percent was the high, Nixon's 61 percent was the low).

The public has few psychological defenses against the news media's claim that political leaders are self-interested and inept. Unlike messages that attempt to change issue attitudes (such as editorials that take a position on abortion policy), the claim that an officeholder has a devious motive or lacks ability does not contradict any deeply held belief. Moreover, because the media speak with one voice, the message appears to be factual rather than what it really is, mere opinion. The media, television in particular, present "news without ambiguity, equivocation, or uncertainty" (Iyengar and Kinder 1987, 126).

Of course, politics is sometimes plagued by officeholders' deceit and myopia, and the media should inform the public about it. Democracy requires a degree of skepticism if it is to operate properly. Bennett talks about "degradation rituals" in politics, which, through the process of subjecting political leaders to close scrutiny, affirm the principle of accountability (1981, 311–13). But the press has gone way beyond the point of responsible criticism, and the effect is to rob political leaders of the public confidence that is required to govern effectively. Leaders must have substantial latitude if they are to pursue policies that will serve the public interest in the long run. The discontinuous, fluid, and transient form of politics that the press generates works against such leadership.

It is a politics of shifting standards and fleeting controversies, spurring citizens to demand immediate solutions to stubborn problems, which in turn encourages politicians to pursue short-term and ultimately self-limiting policies and strategies.

Research indicates that negative news coverage heightens the public's mistrust of government (Cappella and Jamieson 1997). This effect has been found for both newspaper readers (Miller et al. 1979) and television viewers (Robinson 1976; Patterson 1991). The effect is all the more remarkable in view of the fact that citizens who pay attention to the news have a higher sense of political efficacy than those who do not. Those who feel efficacious are more likely to have an interest in politics and therefore are more likely to follow the news. This exposure, however, reduces their confidence in government when the messages are relentlessly negative.

It is also likely that negative news misleads the public about social trends. A 1996 survey found that, by two-to-one margins, Americans wrongly believed that crime, inflation, unemployment, and the federal budget deficit had each increased during the previous five years (Blendon 1996). What would account for this extraordinarily high level of public ignorance except stories that day after day highlighted political scandal, wrongdoing, and incompetence? When negative stories overwhelm positive ones, the public can hardly be faulted for thinking poorly about the performance of government and the condition of society.

The presidency is particularly affected by a hypercritical press (Smoller 1988). Much of the president's authority derives not from constitutional grants of power, but from the public force that is inherent in the president's position as the only official chosen by the whole nation (Lowi 1985). When the president's public approval ratings are high, Congress is more responsive to presidential leadership. When approval ratings are low or in decline, which has now become the norm, congressional resistance intensifies (Brody 1991).

THE LIMITS OF MEDIA-CENTERED POLITICS

Changes in communication and in politics during the past few decades have placed an extraordinary burden on the press. It is increasingly expected by critics and apologists alike to organize public opinion and debate. Reporters often claim that they can fill this role. Even if the media did not want the job, the responsibility is in part theirs by virtue of their daily contact with audiences and a political system built increasingly on entrepreneurial leaders, floating voters, freewheeling interest groups, and weakened political parties.

Nevertheless, the press is much less adequate as a linking mechanism than is commonly assumed. The problem is that the press is not a political institution and has no stake in organizing public opinion. The media are in the news business, and their inadequacy as a linking mechanism becomes obvious once the nature of news is understood. The news simply is not an adequate guide to political choice. Its major themes are dictated by journalistic values, not political ones.

Decades ago, the journalist Walter Lippmann (1922, 229) concluded that the press's traditional concern with novelty was itself sufficient to disqualify it as an adequate link between the public and its leadership. "The press is like the beam of a searchlight that moves restlessly about," he wrote, "bringing one episode and then another out of darkness into vision. Men cannot do the work of the world by this light alone. They cannot govern society by episodes, incidents, and interruptions." In May and early June 1994, for example, front-page stories spoke of a pending nuclear showdown between the United States and North Korea. News reports projected a "day of reckoning" that would be President Clinton's "moment of truth." Then suddenly the issue disappeared from the front pages, not because it had been resolved, but because it was displaced by the breaking story that Nicole Brown Simpson had been murdered in Los Angeles (example from Fallows 1994, 32).

Recent trends in news coverage have further weakened the press's capacity as an effective political intermediary. To be sure, technological innovation has expanded the amount and range of news coverage. But the news itself is not a suitable basis for political choice. The media provide a narrow and biased version of political reality, one that focuses on the political game and political shortcomings and that weakens rather than strengthens the relationship between the American people and their political leaders and institutions.

The news, at best, is a workable compromise between the economic need of news organizations to attract and hold their audiences and the polity's need for a public forum. In this respect, the shift in recent years toward interpretive reporting is a step in the wrong direction. Interpretive journalism rests on the fiction that journalists are in a position to evaluate politics in a way that suits the public's needs (Lichter and Noyes 1995). Except when they play a genuine watchdog role, journalists are not an appropriate vehicle for the articulation of the values at stake in political conflict. Their interest is the riveting news report rather than the compelling public issue.

If the news is to better serve the public's needs, the political leaders who are the carriers of policy messages must be given more opportunities to express their views. There is, for example, no justification for news coverage that allots six minutes to the journalist for every minute that a presidential candidate speaks. The trend toward interpretive reporting has diminished the voices of those who are involved in the expression of values and has thereby weakened their connection to the public they represent (Rosen 1991). Theirs must be the larger voice if the news is to provide the type of marketplace of ideas that serves democracy's needs.

CHAPTER 8

Japan: News and Politics in a Media-Saturated Democracy

Ellis S. Krauss

Two related questions lie at the heart of the mass media's relationship to democracy in postwar Japan. The first is why the medium of television for most of the postwar period seems to have had less impact on politics in Japan than in many other industrialized democracies. I shall argue that television until recently only complemented, not supplanted, newspapers as the important medium of political communication in Japan; that its primary role had been the conservative one of reinforcing authority and dampening conflict; and that it had only a limited impact on elections and political leadership. Newspapers, in contrast, contributed more to promoting democratic norms, providing a check on those in power, and setting the political agenda. Further, I will argue, understanding the differences in the development and function of these mass media in post–World War II Japan will also help explain one important and distinctive characteristic of postwar Japanese democracy; why for most of the postwar period the mass media's enormous influence did not seem to lead to greater political instability. Speaking from the vantage point of the early 1990s, the efforts of the American Occupation (1945–52) to establish democracy, including a free and thriving fourth estate, were clearly successful. A central paradox of Japanese political development, however, has been that the extensive mass media penetration of society led to a citizenry that was politically highly informed, involved, and cynical, while the larger political system remained quite legitimate and stable. One major theme of this chapter is how the two media's journalistic organization and norms, in tandem with the organization and strategies of political authority, helped to give Japanese democracy this distinctive character.

The second question is the obverse of the first: why did the role of television in politics suddenly increase enormously in the early 1990s? This change was so great that the 1993 electoral campaign came to be called the first "television election." Broadcast journalism has become very controversial, and television news probably contributed first to a wave of reformist sentiment and then to a growing sense of political cynicism and malaise about Japanese politics. Television seems to have come into its own as a major force for the first time. Why and how did this change occur? Was it actually such a sudden transformation? Thus, if first we need to explain television's relatively secondary role compared to newspapers for most of the postwar period, we must also explain why this role appears to have changed precipitously in the last decade.

Because part of my conclusion is that the development and function of newspapers and television have been different in Japan, the two media will initially be treated separately, with the first few sections of this chapter dealing with newspapers: their context, functions, and impact. The following sections follow much the same format for television. I will conclude with an overview of the relationship between the media and democracy in contemporary Japan.

NEWSPAPERS

The media had high priority in the American Occupation's plans to accomplish the twin goals of democratization and demilitarization of postwar Japan. Most fundamentally, the new Constitution of 1947, echoing the American model, clearly guaranteed freedom of speech and the press.[1] The Occupation authorities also made extensive use of newspapers and radio to propagandize the value and practice of democracy in an effort to socialize Japanese to the new political system. It is doubtful that this enormous experiment in political acculturation would have had the success it did without the diffusion of information about the nature of democracy supplied by the mass media. In the words of one astute observer of Japan's early political development, a "free press has come to be an important democratic influence in contemporary Japanese life, at least partly in consequence of the reforms wrought by the Occupation" (Kawai 1960, 211). The press freedoms initiated by the Occupation eventually produced a diverse, thriving, and lively multitude of unrestricted printed media compared to the immediate prewar period (Nomura 1981, 107; Beer 1984, 315–30).

Today Japan has over 150 newspapers, with average daily circulation reaching 575 papers for every 1,000 persons – the highest per capita newspaper distribution rate in the world. It is particularly noteworthy that newspaper circulation rates have substantially increased over time: while only one newspaper was distributed for every 5 Japanese in 1945, there was one for every 2.5 of them by 1985.[2] Japan's newspapers range from local to regional to national in character. The national papers, though, account for slightly over half of the total newspaper circulation (Yamamoto and Fujitake 1987, 30) and are thus the most influential. These national newspapers include the so-called Big Three: the *Yomiuri* (1998 morning circulation, 10.2 million per day), the *Asahi* (8.3 million), and the *Mainichi* (4 million), each of them being among the largest newspapers in the world. In addition to these morning editions, there is the unique Japanese practice of each major newspaper publishing an afternoon edition with completely different content. The circulation of these afternoon papers is about half that of the morning editions (Nihon Shimbun Kyokai 1998, 103, 66, 93).

Competition in the newspaper market is fierce, in part because of highly leveraged financing, mostly internal ownership, and substantial dependence on sales for income (Lee 1985, 75–8; Westney 1996). There is, nonetheless, little variation in content or format among Japanese newspapers because of their homogeneous audience. Because they are national media, their readership is not segmented by region (as with many papers in the United States), or by class or educational level (as with many papers in Britain). Nor are their audiences politically segmented (as with many European papers) (Lee 1985, 82). These audience characteristics weaken the temptation to use journalistic or political sensationalism to increase sales, the fear being that some part of the audience would be offended and lost if such a tactic were tried. The scrupulous attention to impartiality on the news pages undoubtedly reflects these commercial realities (Lee 1985, 83; Westney 1996). In many ways, the Japanese newspapers resemble television in other countries in their broad audience spectrum and consequent orientation toward the impartial and conventional. Yet, Japanese newspapers manage to combine mass appeal with elite standards of quality.

Japanese newspapers do not continue news stories on separate pages: an entire news story is always completed on the page where it starts. Further, newspapers have a fixed and specific organization so that the reader always knows where to find particular categories of news.[3] Amid this predictability, politics always gets its fair share of coverage. A random survey (by the author) of all articles appearing in the Big Three national newspapers one day about every other year between 1975 and 1984, for example, indicated that, out of 15 different categories of story, articles about "politics, politicians, and bureaucracy" comprised an average of about 5 percent of the total. This was slightly less than society, economics, and foreign news, but it represented a substantial volume of political news reporting. Eliminating the advertising that comprises about half of the newspapers would make the share of politics in the "news hole" closer to 10 percent (Yamamoto and Fujitake 1987, 35). In addition, political news has always been considered by Japanese newspapers to be important "hard news" and has appeared on the front pages where attention warranted it. Perhaps this is why, according to the results of one recent survey, 36 percent of citizens say they "always read" political news third among 13 types of article (when sports and television and radio listings are excluded). Only articles about society and local events are read more frequently, with articles on other topics (such as the economy, foreign news, culture, the family, and entertainment) being followed less regularly (Yamamoto and Fujitake 1987, 37).

As to the nature of press coverage of politics, the conventional wisdom about journalists, especially among ruling Liberal Democratic Party (LDP) politicians, is that they have a leftist bias and tend to favor the opposition Japan Socialist Party. This may be the result of the lingering legacy of the newspapers' role in the crisis surrounding the 1960 U.S.–Japan Mutual Security Treaty, in which the press was severely critical of the government and some American observers accused the press of one-sided support for the government's opponents (Whittemore 1961; Packard 1966). Other analysts, however, have argued that the national elite press actually was not so unbalanced or biased (Lee 1985, 162–3). The leftist stereotype paints a misleadingly simple picture of journalistic bias. A survey of 177 journalists working for the five largest newspapers in 1973 indicated that they were more moderate than their image, were similar to the opposition parties on some controversial domestic issues but more pragmatic than the left on security issues, and were likely to dislike all political parties, including those of the left. Thus, Japanese newsmen may have been critical of the perennially ruling LDP and may have disagreed with it on some major issues, but this is not to say that they always supported the opposition parties (Lee 1985, 89–120; Feldman 1993, 175–7).

Another journalistic political cliché in Japan is that the national newspapers each reflect a very different political point of view. Accordingly, the *Yomiuri* is said to be right of center, the *Mainichi* relatively centrist, and the *Asahi* left of center. These images do reflect the different editorial stances of the newspapers to some limited degree, but differences in the news articles are more subtle, such as slight variations in the selection and placement of the articles on page 1, vague language, or the treatment of a particular country in the foreign news, as in the *Asahi*'s notorious policy of noncritical reporting on the People's Republic of China in the 1970s (Gibney 1975, 246–58). Otherwise, the three papers usually have remarkably similar news content each day, and their political stances can barely be detected in the substance of their coverage (Thayer 1975).

There are two basic reasons why Japanese newspapers verge on the indistinguishable in this regard. The first is that journalistic norms emphasize strict neutrality in coverage of stories. Given the limited space available in the newspaper for each type of story and the inability to carry stories over from one page to another, it is not surprising that most articles in the Japanese press are concise, oriented almost exclusively toward factual presentation, and largely devoid of interpretation, sensationalism, or even argumentation. Indeed, a recent study of coverage of three areas of disagreement in U.S.–Japanese trade relations found that the press covered the tension between the two countries in a relatively balanced and objective fashion but that their method of achieving that balance differed markedly. Whereas the American press tended to cite arguments from both sides, the Japanese newspapers tended to ignore arguments altogether and present instead short, factual accounts (Budner 1992, 10–14; Krauss 1992, 9–11).[4]

The second, and more important, reason for the uniformity of Japanese newspapers is the rather unusual method of news gathering in Japan. Most of the reporters for each major national newspaper are stationed in a specialized *Kisha Kura-bu* (reporters' club). To be sure, in many democratic countries, at least part of the press corps is assigned to specific agencies of government, and norms, rules, and procedures, governing relationships between journalists and their official sources have developed. The British "lobby" system and the American White House press corps are examples of the formal ways of organizing these relationships, while unwritten rules governing remarks made "off the record" or "not for attribution" by government sources represent more informal codes of conduct. What makes the Japanese system distinctive is that the reporters' clubs are so extensive and pervasive that, to a very large extent, they characterize the entire news-gathering system itself, and they are quite rigid and formal in their exclusivity and organization.

Reporters' clubs are found in almost every major institution – from government agencies and political parties to large businesses and labor federation headquarters – and their members provide full-time coverage of that organization, its leaders, and its policies. The clubs range in size from ten or fewer members to huge organizations such as the Nagata Club, located in a building next to the prime minister's office, whose nearly 300 reporters cover the prime minister and the Cabinet. Generally, reporters from only the major national and local newspapers and broadcasting companies may join. Magazine reporters, freelance reporters, and political party, trade, union, and religious papers, as well as foreign journalists until 1993, are uniformly denied membership (Thayer 1975, 296–300; Lee 1985, 62–6; Ooiwa 1991, 18; Feldman 1993, 67–74). Ostensibly only social clubs for reporters, they are actually important middlemen between reporters and their sources. Each club has written regulations governing the release and publication of information, and it is the clubs that sponsor the formal press conferences between journalists and sources. Violations of rules can lead to expulsion from the club, and thus denial of access to information for the reporters and/or their paper (Thayer 1975, 297; Kim 1981, 47; Lee 1985, 64–5).

This system of reporters' clubs has profound consequences for the nature of journalism in Japan for a number of reasons. First, almost all observers agree that it encourages conformity in the subjects covered and in journalists' approach to them (Gibney 1975, 245–6; Thayer 1975; Feldman 1993). The constant daily interaction of reporters from different news organs produces essentially similar news values, priorities, and approaches to a story. This is analogous to the "pack journalism" that some observers of American politics have claimed results from cooping up reporters on the same press bus during the course of election campaigns (Crouse 1972), a practice that stands in sharp contrast with the aforementioned stereotype of each major newspaper having a particular political tendency. Second, the clubs offer reporters the opportunity to gather a tremendous amount of information about the workings of government. As a result, Japanese newspaper readers can follow the process and progress of policy making from recommendation through formulation to enactment in the Diet. Information about the executive branch of government (the prime minister, the Cabinet, and especially the government bureaucracy), in particular, is provided to a degree rarely found in other countries. The close proximity of reporters to their news sources, however, has an important negative implication for the content and tone of news coverage since reporters' clubs encourage journalists to form dependent relationships with officials. Assigned to these specialized "beats" for two or more years, the reporters must rely on the leading officials of bureaucratic agencies to do their jobs and cannot afford to alienate them.

Further, background information is provided to the reporters in informal settings, subject to rules of release set by the officials themselves. It is customary, for example, for reporters to go each night on "night rounds" (*yomawari*) or "night attacks" (*youchi*), in which they visit the homes of the political or bureaucratic heads of the particular agency to which they are assigned. These officials are expected to provide the reporters with food and drink, and to spend time filling them in on the background to the formal news releases and other information they were given earlier that day. Through the intimate contacts the reporters' clubs and these night rounds provide, reporters often develop dependent relationships and friendships with the officials and politicians they cover, which can, in turn, enable the news sources to manipulate reporters and discourage critical reporting (Thayer 1975, 299–300; Kim 1981, 52–4; Lee 1985, 64). This tendency has led skeptics inside and outside the media community to criticize the reporters' clubs for transforming journalists into "news announcement organs of officialdom" (*yakusho no nyu-su happyô kikan*) (Koitabashi and Onose 1986, 85).

One consequence of this system is that, generally speaking, the elite press is not particularly investigative in orientation or searching in its coverage of party and government officials. When they unearth a political scandal, however, they can and do pursue it vehemently once the information becomes public.[5] This seems to have been the pattern in most of the important postwar political scandals, from the Tanaka and Lockheed scandals of the early 1970s through the influence-buying of a business entrepreneur in the "Recruit scandal" in 1987 to scandals in the early 1990s involving the stock market and financial contributions to powerful politicians of a trucking firm with connections to organized crime (Farley 1992, 25–41; 1996).

In order to free themselves from the constraints of the club system, some elite press reporters have occasionally slipped information and scoops to weekly magazine reporters that their own newspaper could not publish without alienating their sources. And many newspapers have sought to mitigate the effects of the system by establishing a separate category of reporter, the *yûgun*, a military term that literally means something like "forward scout" but in this context is best translated as "troubleshooter." These reporters are not assigned to clubs, and are therefore free to pursue and develop their own news stories. Series of such stories (running to over 50 articles) are sometimes used as part of a newspaper's campaign to pursue a particular issue or cause and regularly appear on one of its first pages. Journalists vary in their attitudes toward the role of *yûgun:* some aspire to this position because it gives them the freedom to develop their own stories; others try to avoid such assignments because they require far more hard work than being spoon-fed official information at a reporters' club (Kuroda 1985, 70–87).

THE FUNCTIONS OF THE PRESS

Perhaps the function most commonly attributed to a democratic press is the *watchdog* function, in which the press keeps government in its sights and exposes wrongdoing, corruption, and blunders. But this is only one of the important functions that the press can perform in modern democracies. To continue the canine metaphor, it can also be a *guard dog,* providing citizens with the information and guidance necessary to make political judgments and decisions and equipping them to participate in political life. And it can be a *guide dog,* educating and informing citizens about public affairs. Finally, often neglected is the important role of the media in allowing government to communicate with the public in order to mobilize its support for political authority, institutions, and policies. Call this the media as *lap dog.*

The effective performance of all these functions is essential to a healthy democracy. The record of the Japanese press in carrying them out, however, is spotty. It clearly did not play the watchdog role well in the past, although its recent coverage of scandals suggests that its performance may be improving. By contrast, there is no question that it has kept after the story – at the risk of overdoing the canine metaphor – like a pack of bloodhounds, and several postwar prime ministers and other influential politicians have been driven from office or had their ambitions for higher posts delayed as a direct result of the press's tenacity. In the Japanese context of a one-party dominant political system with opposition parties perennially shut out of power, the importance of this function for a healthy democracy is probably greater than elsewhere, although the cost may be a measure of cynicism in the public.

The Japanese national press has also been one of the outstanding *guide dogs* in the industrialized democracies. The range and depth of the daily information it provides to its readers about government, society, and the world is probably unparalleled elsewhere, and exposure to this information indirectly encourages political involvement and participation. This has been a particularly valuable service to the state, in its transition from authoritarianism to democracy, and to individual Japanese, in their transformation from subjects to citizens. The presentation of this information also has been impartial, by and large, and has consequently helped to inspire trust in the media.

Finally, the national press has played an ambivalent role as a lap dog. On the one hand, as we have seen, the reporters' clubs have given political and official elites ample opportunity to use and abuse the media in communicating to the public the information and views that they wish. On the other hand, the press's concentration on the misdeeds of politicians once revealed, its coverage of the message of mass movements (as in the 1960 antisecurity treaty movement), and, as I will discuss later, its potential to play an independent agenda-setting role in cases like the environmental issue have all helped to limit state power. If the national newspapers are lap dogs to the state in some respects, they remain creatures that can still sometimes bite the hand that feeds them.

POLITICAL IMPACT

If this is how the press has operated in Japan, what impact has it had on democratic political life? One extremely important contribution was that of helping to resocialize Japanese from subjects to citizens during and after the Occupation. Indeed, newspapers may have been the most important force for conveying to the general public the meaning of key concepts, including that of democracy itself. Most especially, the watchful eye of newspapers has constantly reminded political elites of the need to remain responsive to public opinion. The press has been especially crucial in this regard, since the uninterrupted rule of the LDP from 1955 to 1993 meant that the opposition parties and Parliament itself were not capable of limiting the actions of those in power and stimulating policy change. The threat of losing office, so effective a deterrent to the abuse of power, was simply not the limiting force in Japan that it has been in virtually all other established democracies. Under these circumstances, it fell to the press in particular to convey public sentiment to political elites and to hold those same elites accountable for their actions. The press, in other words, de facto performed part of the role of "loyal opposition" in Japanese politics.

The effectiveness with which it has filled this role is attested to by the views of other elites. When asked about the political power of the media in general, major political and societal elites in Japan – ranging from the LDP, opposition parties, and bureaucrats through business, farm, and labor elites to protest movements and intellectuals – ranked the media as the most influential group in society. Only media elites themselves disagreed with this judgment (Kabashima and Broadbent 1986, 335–40).[6] This is not to say, of course, that the media are the most influential group in any absolute sense. The more appropriate conclusion is simply that, in the absence of opposition parties and parliamentary institutions with the capacity to articulate and aggregate public opinion effectively, its expression through the media becomes a relatively more important touchstone for governments at perpetual risk of isolation, arrogance, and unresponsiveness.

At the same time that the press played this important political role of helping to resocialize the population to democratic norms and values, press coverage of political corruption and scandal seems to have contributed to public cynicism about political officeholders and alienation from them. Studies of Japanese political culture up to the 1970s pointed to the existence of a deep-seated disparity between the Japanese people's positive orientation toward democratic values and institutions, on the one hand, and their highly negative orientation toward politicians, on the other, including a large measure of cynicism about their responsiveness and political leadership (Richardson 1974, 65–82). Political socialization studies have replicated these findings. Japanese teenagers, although holding relatively positive attitudes toward political parties and elections, displayed highly negative attitudes toward politicians and political leaders, especially those in central government. Compared to their counterparts in other democratic countries, Japanese youth were more distrustful of their leaders in the government and the Diet and were more likely to see them as corrupt. These negative responses increased dramatically with age, particularly between the 8th and 12th grades (Massey 1976, 21–50).

Scholars analyzing these findings often attributed some degree of blame to the media. In particular, newspapers' concentration on the seamy side of politics in the form of corruption and scandals, together with holding Japanese practice to very high and idealistic democratic standards, was held to have contributed to public cynicism (Richardson 1974, 78–9). More recently, Pharr has concluded that media reports of officials' misconduct is the factor most associated with the Japanese public's mistrust of these same officials (Pharr 2000).

The third noteworthy impact of the press on politics in Japan involves its role in setting the policy-making agenda. Press coverage of government decision making in Japan is extensive, and citizens are given more information about how public policy is made than is usually available to the citizens of most other nations. The press therefore plays an important role in structuring relations between elites, and between elites and masses, by providing political and bureaucratic elites with a channel to send signals to each other, to impress constituents, to mobilize support or opposition to policies, and to float trial balloons. A recent analysis of the salient issues of administrative and political reform in the mid-1990s concluded that on these issues it was officials who set the agenda, not the newspapers. The press was more of an "agenda sitter" than an agenda setter; sometimes, and in subtle ways, it tried to protect the reform agenda by prodding officials to remain on course when they seemed to be backtracking on reform (Krauss and Lambert 1999). In a parliamentary democracy with a perennial majority conservative government, party discipline, and close bureaucratic involvement in the formulation of policy, the press rarely plays an independent and formative role in changing the policy agenda. There can be exceptions, however.

Perhaps the most important such exception was the role of the press in the protest against pollution in the 1970s. Beginning in the 1960s, a number of court cases brought by victims of pollution in various parts of Japan focused media attention on the costs of the rapid economic growth of the previous two decades, which led, in turn, to coverage of local citizen movements fighting against the location of polluting industries in their areas and the general problem of the environment nationwide. After a decade-long consensus among big business, the governing LDP, and the public on the desirability of rapid economic growth, widespread protests about the negative consequences of such growth emerged. The press was particularly instrumental in translating these disparate local protests into a nationwide public concern for the quality of life (Krauss and Simcock 1980, 193–5, 213). So profound was the shift in public mood that local governments and eventually the LDP itself had to take cognizance of it to the point that the national Diet passed many stringent antipollution laws in 1970 (Pempel 1982, 225–7).

The role of the press in the antipollution movements has been shown in various studies not to be a simple case of the media discovering or uncovering and then reporting the relevant facts. Instead, it involved a complicated relationship with sources that often featured mutual manipulation and bargaining. Nor was coverage always uniform. Some newspapers gave favorable coverage to the environmental issue. The *Asahi,* for example, created its own special pollution reporting group and reserved space for daily coverage of the issue. Other newspapers, in contrast, ignored it or covered it unfavorably (Reich 1984, 148–65; Groth 1996). These variations notwithstanding, the larger point is that sustained attention by the press transformed the environment into a legitimate political issue to which the government was eventually forced to respond, which it had been unwilling to do before.

A study of the rise and demise of another salient issue in the 1960s and 1970s, the "Old-People Boom" – regarding policies to aid the elderly – showed again how the media can either promote or undermine the placing of particular policy issues on the public agenda. Some bureaucratic actors were able to enlist the media in their efforts to attract public attention to their policy proposals, creating a "boom" of interest in the subject. The proposals of other officials regarding the same policy area were vociferously torpedoed by the media. Uneven coverage of this policy process, however, allowed still other officials to quietly push through their own plans without much attention (Campbell 1996).

Clearly, the press can sometimes play an important gatekeeping function in the Japanese policy process, introducing new issues to the policy agenda on behalf of one group or another, but at other times ignoring group demands, thereby preserving the routine policy agenda. It is noteworthy that in Japan it is the press – with its widespread distribution, conformist orientation, and eagerness to seize on an issue and convert it into the object of a "campaign" – that has occasionally played the lead agenda-setting role, rather than television.

TELEVISION

As was true of the press, fundamental norms regarding the broadcast media were also substantially modified under the Occupation to facilitate the establishment and consolidation of democracy. The Broadcast Law adopted in 1950 enshrines the legal principles of noninterference in content by any group outside the media organization, freedom of expression, and the "impartiality, integrity and autonomy of broadcasting" (Nippon Hôsô Kyôkai n.d. 1, 6). Licensing and regulatory functions were assigned to a unit within the Ministry of Posts and Telecommunications (MPT).

The keystone of the Japanese broadcasting system is the NHK (Nippon Hôsô Kyôkai, or the Japan Broadcasting Corporation) – one of the world's great public broadcasting services.[7] As part of their democratization effort, the Americans transformed the prewar government broadcasting service into a more independent public-service broadcasting agency, autonomous of the state but ultimately responsible to its democratically elected representatives, much like the British Broadcasting Corporation (BBC) in Great Britain. NHK's highest decision-making body is its board of governors, consisting of 12 persons appointed by the prime minister. The board, in turn, selects the president of NHK, its chief executive and the person primarily responsible for administering its huge organization of about 14,000 persons. NHK's revenues, like those of the BBC, come largely from viewer license fees, not from the state treasury. Despite some differences in fee collection and parliamentary supervision,[8] NHK's legal relationship to the state is similar to that of Britain's BBC, that is, both are "quasi-autonomous" (Burns 1977, 192).

In one respect, however, NHK developed very differently from the BBC and its European counterparts. Unlike public-sector networks in Europe, which enjoyed broadcasting monopolies until recently, NHK faced competition from a full range of commercial stations almost from the beginning, largely because of the American decision that Japan's media system should be "mixed," encompassing both a major public broadcasting service and commercial stations. In 1989, there were 106 television companies operating 6,718 stations in Japan (Yano Memorial Society 1991, 491), and the combined advertising revenue of the commercial stations surpassed NHK's revenues fourfold (Shimizu 1983, 129). Inhibiting the development of the private broadcasting sector to some extent, though, are regulations restricting the kinds of networks that the private broadcasting stations can form. Exclusive programming contracts are illegal in Japan. This has prevented the formation of the same kinds of commercial networks found in the United States, for example, as local stations often purchase programs from a variety of sources.

The restriction on exclusive programming contracts has also strengthened the newspaper sector in its constant struggle against television by encouraging the formation of a close relationship between newspapers and commercial broadcasters in providing the news. While purchasing entertainment programs from a variety of sources, many local television stations have an arrangement with a major Tokyo station to provide them with national news, in effect forming a de facto news network. Each of these Tokyo stations, in turn, has one of the major newspapers as a large shareholder (with a 10 percent upper limit on share ownership in a media company by a single individual or group for most of the postwar period, recently raised to 20 percent). In effect, there are five commercial news networks in Japan, each with a newspaper affiliation,[9] thereby extending the competition between national dailies into the realm of private broadcasting. Affiliation with a newspaper provides the commercial stations with some capacity for news gathering and story initiation, so that their news staffs are much smaller than NHK's huge news staff of over 1,400.[10]

Beginning in the 1960s, NHK focused its efforts on becoming the dominant broadcast-news source for Japanese citizens. Even today, 40 percent of the programming on its main general television channel consists of news and information, a figure double that of most of the other commercial flagship stations (Nippon Hôsô Kyôkai 1988, 247–8). In addition, the number and length of its news broadcasts are among the highest in the democratic world's news agencies (Terebi Hôdô Kenkyûkai 1981, 11). The closest rival to NHK in Japan is TV Asahi, the Tokyo flagship station of the Asahi News Network (ANN), with about one-quarter of its programming devoted to news (Hôsô Bunka Kenkyûkai 1991, 87). Thus NHK dominated the television news field for most of the postwar period. The Japanese commercial networks, however, have recently made a concerted effort to upgrade the quantity and quality of their news broadcasts, increasing their average news time as a proportion of all broadcast time by over 50 percent between 1970 and 1986 (Shigeru et al. 1987, 224).

The continued importance of newspapers in Japan notwithstanding, television has become a very important source of information. According to one source, with 587 television sets per 1,000 people, Japan is second only to the United States, with 811 sets per 1,000 people, in access to this medium (Yano Memorial Society 1991, 460).[11] The Japanese are also avid watchers of television, viewing it more hours per day (over three) than any other people in the world except the Americans. News and news shows receive the highest percentage of responses (77 percent) when surveys ask what types of programs viewers watch on a daily basis. Television viewing time, as well as the use of television for information rather than relaxation, tends to increase with age (Yoshida 1982, 126, 127, 133, 141).

By the early 1960s, television had surpassed newspapers when survey respondents were asked, "From which medium do you get your information?" By 1968 almost three times as many persons selected television over newspapers, and ten times as many preferred television over radio (Nippon Hôsô Kyôkai 1981, 2; Stronach 1989, 133). By the 1970s, moreover, television was preferred over newspapers and radio when citizens wanted to know information quickly. It was also the medium they most believed and the source from which they generally got their news. Newspapers were preferred only when the respondents wanted to know things more "deeply" (Nippon Hôsô Kyôkai Yoronchôsajo 1977). On the other hand, a 1976 survey of voters found that 95 percent read a newspaper regularly, while only 62 percent watched television news programs daily (Flanagan et al. 1991, 303). In short, television has become the news medium of choice, but newspapers remain a vital source of news and information for the Japanese people generally.

Consumers of the two media tended to have somewhat different profiles. Television viewing was associated with lower socioeconomic status, female gender, and less social integration. Reliance on newspapers instead of television for political information, by contrast, was associated with younger urban males who had more modern values, had an upper socioeconomic status, and were more socially integrated. Further, those who depended on the press for political information and who subscribed to national dailies tended to be the most exposed to political information in election campaigns, while those who relied on television and subscribed to local papers had lower exposure to such information (Flanagan 1991, 306 and 309).

The upshot of the Japanese pattern of media consumption appears to be that television was integrated into Japan's wide and deep newspaper audience without replacing print as a source of information but instead supplementing it.

To understand the political impact of television in Japan, though, it is not sufficient simply to look at patterns of viewership. The content of its broadcasts must also be examined, and here a simple fact emerges: Japanese television conveys a tremendous amount of information about politics and government to its viewers. A content analysis in the mid-1980s of NHK's flagship 7 P.M. news program indicated that more than half of the news items and more than half of the time were devoted to government and politics. Even when news segments were primarily about society and economics, they often also had a connection to public affairs (Krauss 2000). One of the few systematic studies comparing the content on NHK and the commercial networks found similar results concerning the high proportion of political content on NHK and the relatively little time devoted to such societal news as accidents, disasters, incidents, and so forth. When the networks were arrayed on the dimensions of "hard" and "soft" news produced by a factor analysis, NHK was close to the hard news end, while one of the commercial networks, Tokyo Broadcasting System (TBS), was closest to the soft news end, with the other networks in between (Kobaysahi 1982, 32–4). Although, as discussed earlier, commercial networks have tried in recent years to upgrade their news programs, it is still unlikely that they devote as much attention to political news as NHK does.

Turning to which political actors are portrayed most often and how, the content analysis of the NHK 7 P.M. news showed that the administrative bureaucracy or the advisory councils attached to it figured in some way in a remarkable 36 percent of news items. The combined total for the prime minister, Cabinet, political parties, and Diet did not even reach this figure! NHK's portrayal of the bureaucracy, moreover, was that of an active, paternal formulator of policy guarding the public's interest (Krauss 1996a; 2000). Kobayashi's content analysis of NHK and the commercial networks reiterates the importance of the bureaucracy in portrayals of domestic politics (Kobayashi 1982, 35).[12] His data indicate that the bureaucracy and advisory councils together were the second most thoroughly covered subject on NHK and Nippon TV and the third most thoroughly covered on the other three networks, generally following criminals and courts. Indeed, if we combined Kobayashi's categories related to government and politics, bureaucracy and advisory councils, government, the prime minister, elections, and the courts (excluding criminals), the bureaucracy alone, that is, without its advisory councils, would account for nearly half (48 percent) of NHK's coverage of domestic politics and public affairs and a little less (44 percent on average) than that of the commercial networks.[13]

Political parties and the legislature received much less coverage. An interesting question nevertheless remains: is the LDP's political dominance reflected in the attention it gets relative to the opposition parties? Recalculating Kobayashi's (1982, 35) data allows us to address this question. There is considerable variation among the networks with regard to the balance of coverage devoted to government and opposition parties. Only NHK comes close to giving the same coverage to the LDP that it does to the opposition and independent parties. The other networks, especially Asahi and Fuji, give disproportionate coverage to the LDP, and one of them, Nippon TV, gives no coverage at all to the independent parties. Indeed, combining all the independent parties into a single category masks a further disproportion among the networks; only NHK covers *all* the political parties. Every commercial network completely fails to cover one or more of the smaller opposition parties (Kobayashi 1982, 36). Clearly, NHK jealously guards its reputation for impartiality by showing no favoritism in its news coverage of Japan's political parties.

THE FUNCTIONS OF TELEVISION

To return to the canine metaphor used in the earlier discussion of the political functions of newspapers, it is clear that television has played the guide dog role well. The mixed system of quality public and diverse private broadcasters has probably provided Japanese citizens with as broad, deep, and plural a source of televised news as is possible.

Its performance of the watchdog function is less commendable, but it must be said that there are few countries where television oversees government effectively. With a small journalistic staff limited in its ability to gather news or uncover it directly, and largely oriented to brief items for which there are visuals, television news is not particularly well suited to investigative journalism; it is better at recording relatively uncontroversial "pseudoevents" and "medialities." Japan is no exception. Television does do somewhat better as a guard dog, however, joining the printed press in its coverage of wrongdoing once revealed, but the zeal and energy for the pursuit tend to come from the newspapers, not television.

Where television does seem to outdo newspapers is in its performance of the lapdog function. The combination of all the television networks' largely favorable focus on the bureaucracy, together with the commercial networks' connections to newspapers and their disproportionate coverage of the LDP, produce a style of television coverage that seems to buttress the authority of the state and the ruling party.

POLITICAL IMPACT

As in the discussion of newspapers, it is now time to consider the multifaceted political impact on television. One consequence of the structure, content, and tone of television coverage of government and politics has been its contribution to *political stability* in Japan. Television seems to have created and reinforced popular support for the state, especially the administrative state. The dependence on officialdom as its primary source of political news for television as well as newspapers has given the state bureaucracy a disproportionate share of largely favorable news coverage and, hence, great opportunity to mold public opinion. Television has been more supine than newspapers in this regard, as is indicated by the highly disproportionate attention even NHK has paid to the state bureaucracy, with the commercial stations being not far behind. With television as the most trusted and referred-to source of news for most Japanese, with the state bureaucracy being the most frequent and generally positive object of news coverage, and with the LDP being given more coverage than the opposition parties by commercial television stations, it is difficult not to speculate that television's buttressing of LDP-dominated regime support has been an important factor in the consolidation of Japan's democratic political system since the 1960s.[14]

Television appears to have exerted a somewhat different kind of influence over the policy agenda than has the press. If the print media were occasionally able to shape the policy agenda, as in the case of the environmental movement, television seems to have had an impact less on specific policies and more on the style of policy making. Overall, it seems to have played a role in dampening intense conflict in the electoral and legislative arenas.

Prior to the mid-1960s, Japan was racked by polarized confrontations between the left and the right over the highly salient issues of defense, foreign policy (especially the country's relationship with the United States), and domestic order. Inflammatory clashes over these issues led Joji Watanuki to refer to "cultural politics" in Japan as characterized by fundamental differences in values (Watanuki 1967, 456–60). Since then, these differences have not lost their ability to divide the parties and people, but they have become a lot less salient. Undoubtedly, the rise of middle-of-the-road parties since the 1960s, the transition to postindustrial society, and the simple passage of time have reduced the intensity of value differences rooted in the Occupation period. But it has been argued that television has also helped to dampen ideological conflict by shifting public attention from "position" issues to "valence" issues, that is, from issues dividing the public in the long term and on the basis of ideology to more ephemeral, election-specific image and morality issues on which there is general agreement, such as against pollution, crime, and scandal and for prosperity, safety, and honesty (Kohei et al. 1991, 279–82; Flanagan 1996).

There is reason to believe that television has also helped to reduce the intensity of parliamentary conflict. One consequence of the combination of a polarized political culture and young democratic political institutions was the eruption of intense and often violent confrontation in the Diet. During the 1960 treaty crisis, for example, there was pandemonium in the Diet, with fistfights breaking out at various points, and it was all covered on television. The undignified and sometimes uncivilized behavior of elected representatives during this ultimate postwar crisis had been brought directly to the public with an immediacy never seen in news coverage (Packard 1966, 279; Matsuda 1981, 131–86). While supportive hard evidence is lacking, it does seem that the negative public reaction to these and subsequent events in the early 1960s made Diet members conscious of their behavior, at least in the presence of television cameras. In this regard, television is, in all probability, one of the several forces that induced the Diet to develop better mechanisms for managing potentially disruptive partisan conflict (Krauss 1984, 243–93).

Another way in which television may have affected Japanese politics is through its apparent impact on the partisan preferences of citizens. As noted earlier, elite national newspapers, and especially NHK television news, have gone to great lengths to avoid giving the impression of partisanship or bias in their news coverage. Public perceptions reflect the success of these efforts. A recent survey found that 83 percent of the public viewed newspapers as accurate, 81 percent as trustworthy, and 58 percent as having balanced views. Television scored less well but still received majority (or close to it) public approbation on all three dimensions (*Japan Times* 1997). This degree of media credibility, especially in regard to newspapers, far exceeds that found in the United States (*Wall Street Journal* 1998). In a major study of Japanese voters in 1976, for example, only one-fifth of these respondents exposed to the media said that they could detect any partisan biases. It is also noteworthy that perceiving bias was not associated with disaffection from the political system: indeed, there was a positive relationship between perception of media bias, on the one hand, and strength of partisanship, interest in politics, and participation in political discussions, on the other. For the large, relatively uninvolved majority of Japanese voters, the media, with the exception of weekly magazines, were seen as balanced and, in consequence, greatly trusted (Flanagan 1991, 304–5).

Among those who did perceive a bias in the media, weekly magazines were seen to lean to the opposition, while those perceiving bias in television and newspapers were almost equally balanced between left and right, with "slightly more seeing the press as favoring the opposition and television as favoring the ruling party" (Flanagan 1991, 304). This finding is consistent with the earlier demonstration of how commercial television coverage tends to favor the LDP. The obvious question, then, is whether this perceived television bias has any impact on partisan support.

There is some indirect evidence that it might. One content analysis of news coverage by the various networks rank ordered them in terms of the amount of time devoted to the LDP compared to the opposition parties. Fuji television clearly emerged as the most favorable toward the governing party, followed in order by Asahi, NHK, TBS, and Nippon TV. A survey that happened to be conducted in Tokyo at the same time asked respondents to name the television channel from which they got their political news and also to say which party they supported–in other words, their party identification. The station whose audience included the highest percentage of LDP supporters was Fuji, followed by the other networks in exactly the same order that had emerged from the content analysis (Kobayashi 1982, 36). This evidence is suggestive rather than definitive, however. It is possible that a channel's bias in favor of the LDP led viewers to favor the governing party. Equally, however, it may be that LDP supporters chose to watch more frequently those stations that gave most coverage to their party of preference. In any event, it is clear that there is a relationship between a station's biases in news coverage and the partisan preferences of its viewers. But in terms of its impact on electoral choices made by voters, television appears to be quite limited. Before we discuss the medium's impact on election campaigns and outcomes, though, an overview of certain notable characteristics of Japanese electoral institutions and practices is advisable.

The Japanese electoral system for the House of Representatives in effect until the 1993 contest was rather unique. It was based on multimember districts with between two and six seats at stake, but the voter was allowed to cast only a single ballot. One consequence was that in many districts, candidates from the same party were pitted against one another. This intraparty competition, together with the small geographical size of the districts, placed considerable importance on the candidate's personality and individual appeal at the expense of party identification and issue differences between rival candidates. Such a candidate-centered system might be thought fertile ground for a television-based, individualistic, and presidential-style appeal to voters in the district. Access to television, however, was strictly regulated so as not to allow any one candidate to derive undue advantage from it. For one thing, television time cannot be purchased by candidates.

Television was used for the first time in an election campaign in 1969. The law allowed each candidate four television appearances of four and a half minutes each, all paid for by the government. These rules, with minor modifications, are still in effect today (Curtis 1970; 1988). These same rules also emphasize fairness and forbid production gimmicks to the extent of allowing only one camera, establishing a fixed location for candidates, and regulating the number of close-ups. In so doing, these rules have discouraged variability in the way the candidates present themselves to the electorate (*Asahi Shinbun* 1983, 22). The same scrupulous attention to equal access and advantage characterizes television news; a candidates' faces may appear on the television screen during a news segment only if those of their rivals do so too. Political parties, by contrast, have unrestricted ability to purchase media time and spots.

Only party policies may be advertised on these spots, however, and while party leaders and individual candidates may appear in them, it is illegal for them to mention or promote the candidacy of any individual (Curtis 1988, 168). Finally, the U.S. habit of negative advertising and campaigning more generally is still not found in Japan (Reid 1992, A16). For the first time since 1963, televised debates among party leaders occurred in the 1990 election.

The electoral system for the House of Councillors, the upper but less important chamber, provides for the election of a portion of its membership from local districts and the remainder from nationwide constituencies. Until 1983, the national candidates were elected by a direct ballot system in which the candidates with the most votes nationwide won. This system maximized national reputations, and many media personalities (what the Japanese call *tarento,* or "talent," candidates) were elected. In 1983 the system was "reformed" to elect the nationwide candidates by a proportional representation, party-list method. The result was that fewer media personalities and more serious candidates were selected by – and indebted to – the party leaders. Thus, the reform reduced the number and appeal of candidates who might have their own independent base of popular support through prior media recognition.

The Japanese electoral system and the strict regulation of media usage by candidates have had paradoxical effects on the electoral role of television. On the one hand, the House of Representatives' electoral system maximized the importance of the individual candidate's personality and minimized the importance of party loyalty in voting. At the same time, however, strict regulation inhibited the use of television to enhance the personal appeal of individual candidates while at the same time allowing the parties virtually unrestricted opportunity to get their messages across to voters. The House of Councillors' national constituency system, on the other hand, now maximizes the importance of party and party label in voting, but the party advertisements spend most of their time introducing the candidates the party has selected.

These paradoxes probably go a long way toward explaining why television's impact on Japanese voters has been limited for most of the postwar period. The most comprehensive survey-based study of Japanese elections, for example, found television to have little direct influence on the political attitudes and behavior of voters. For example, heavy exposure to television did not seem to weaken partisanship, increase voter volatility, or lessen interest in politics (Flanagan 1991, 316–18). Nor was there much evidence that either the print or broadcast media played a direct role in determining partisan preferences or candidate choice. A maximum of 8 percent of voters might have changed their evaluations of candidates as a result of exposure to one or another medium. But the change did not favor or disadvantage a single candidate and so had little net effect on the overall distribution of candidate evaluations or on the outcome of the election (Flanagan 1991, 328).[15]

Television may not have a great impact on candidate preference, but there is good reason to speculate that it has influenced how Japanese voters think about the parties. Richardson finds that party image has greater effects on Japanese voters than candidates' images or party identification, and he hypothesizes that this is because the Japanese electorate is more consistently exposed to information about parties than about candidates (Richardson 1988). It is entirely conceivable that his findings reflect the preferred access to television that parties are granted by the electoral law.

Research on televised campaign advertisements indicates they have some impact on the voting decision, but a limited one at best. One survey during the 1976 general election in four electoral districts found that about 86 to 88 percent of respondents had seen an election spot, mostly on NHK. Of this group, between 22 and 31 percent said it had reinforced their voting decision, whereas no more than 7 to 11 percent of them said that it had contributed to either deciding on a candidate or switching their vote. But even these figures may overstate the general impact of television since all four districts sampled had unusually high proportions of uncommitted or "floating" voters (Terebi Hôdô Kenkyukai 1981, 142).

A 1980 survey in an electoral district where all the political parties won part of the vote found that the desire to obtain information about candidates' thinking was the most important reason for watching television. Those who watched political advertisements tended to be LDP supporters, middle-aged, professionals, and housewives, with a generally high sense of political satisfaction and political efficacy. Those who did not watch the ads generally supported the Socialist Party or no party at all, were in their twenties, were workers, and had a low sense of political satisfaction and political efficacy (Senkyo to terebi kenkyûkai 1980, 11). Not surprisingly, given these differences, our tentative conclusion is that advertisements served mainly to reinforce voter's decisions and help sort out candidates, and had a greater impact on LDP supporters. They did not seem to have the same impact on opposition supporters, on those alienated from politics, or in stimulating vote decisions.

Television has not had the same impact on the practice and style of political leadership in Japan that it has had in many other democratic countries. This is largely because prime ministers, with one exception, did not have to use television to enhance their own popularity and political authority in their ascent to the top. An important reason lies in Japan's system of leadership recruitment, wherein factional politics essentially determined the selection of the LDP president, who, in turn, became prime minister by virtue of his party's majority of votes in the Diet. Who became the leader of each of the five major factions of the LDP was a function of seniority within the faction and the strength of his intrafactional support. Who became party leader, in turn, was a function of interfactional alliances. None of this had anything to do with popular appeal, and therefore the men who became prime minister were not, and did not have to be, particularly mediagenic. Once they assumed office, their ability to govern rested more on the same secretive, interfactional politics and the ability to manage a policy-making process that centers on intraparty and bureaucratic organizations (Krauss 1989, 45–50). Japanese prime ministers, therefore, have generally been colorless types with little personal appeal.

The glaring exception was former Prime Minister Yasuhiro Nakasone (1982–7). A longtime but relatively youthful (by previous Japanese prime ministerial standards) leader of one of the small LDP factions, he was the first postwar prime minister to intentionally exploit the media and public opinion to maintain himself in office. Reluctantly chosen as chief executive by the other faction leaders, he was studiously attentive to his public image, and used opportunities like television interviews and coverage of summit meetings abroad to make himself more popular with the public and indispensable to the party. He was able to continue as LDP president for two and a half terms (five years) after being allowed to stay on a half-term longer than party regulations allowed. In the previous decade, his six predecessors had not, on average, been able to last in office for a single term of two years (Curtis 1988, 105 and 159).

After Nakasone's departure in 1987, however, his immediate successors seemed to return to the mold of colorless faction leaders chosen primarily through backroom alliances. Nonetheless, Nakasone does seem to have raised the Japanese public's expectations of its prime ministers – expectations that probably added somewhat to the usual disaffection with LDP leadership and "politics as usual" by the early 1990s, setting the stage for the changes of 1993.

TELEVISION'S NEW ROLE: THE 1993 ELECTION
AND BEYOND

The year 1993 was a watershed year in postwar Japanese politics, witnessing the splitting of the perennially governing LDP and the crucial House of Representatives election that resulted in the formation of a seven-party coalition government headed by Prime Minister Morihiro Hosokawa, himself one of the several new, reform-oriented, and media-genic politicians prominent in that election. In general, television's importance seemed to expand dramatically prior to and during the course of the campaign. Two new types of program, both on the commercial stations, came to play important roles in that transitional year.

The first was the "news show," in which the entertainment and visual functions of the news play a greater role in the program and the anchor involves himself as a personality, not hesitating to make his own, often opinionated, comments on the news story. This stood in stark contrast with the traditional news program, especially NHK's 7 P.M. news, in which anchors were more like news readers and presentation involved straightforward, factual reporting, often with entertaining and dramatic visuals deemphasized (Krauss 1998).

The pioneer in this kind of program was Kume Hiroshi, the anchor of Asahi TV's late-evening "News Station" since 1985. Kume did not hesitate to introduce some of his own favorite issues and his opinions about them in discussing the news. Instead of avoiding controversy and affecting neutrality and impartiality as the anchor, he seemed to thrive on controversy and skepticism about those in power and often injected his personal opinions about events or the news (Schlesinger and Kanabayashi 1992; Krauss 1998). "News Station"'s unconventional style of journalism gradually built up a large audience of devoted viewers, and by the early 1990s it was the most popular news program in the country, with an average 20 million viewers per night. As many as three out of five Japanese preferred to watch it for political news, equaling and sometimes surpassing NHK (the choice of fewer than two of five viewers) as the dominant news source (Schlesinger and Kanabayahi 1992, A10; Altman 1996).

Kume and "News Station" soon spawned imitators at the other commercial stations. Once content to lead in entertainment programs and concede the field of news to NHK, commercial stations now saw that NHK's news dominance was vulnerable, particularly among young urban, salaried workers and women who returned too late from work and dinner with colleagues (as is customary in Japan) to watch early-evening news programs, and who found NHK's straightforward, uncontroversial, and serious news style to be staid and boring. They rushed in with their own later evening news shows featuring anchors and journalists willing to venture opinions.

Indeed, the extent to which television news journalism has adopted a more opinionated style can be partially gauged by a recent content analysis of news coverage over a period of seven months in 1992–3.[16] It found that in about 28 percent of the stories analyzed, an anchor or journalist expressed a personal opinion or comment (Budner 1994, 5). The proportion of such opinionated segments was much higher on the commercial stations' programs, including "News Station," than on NHK (Krauss 1994; 1996b, 263). Clearly, the early 1990s saw the arrival of a new and popular style of television journalism in Japan.

In the months leading up to the split of the LDP over issues of corruption and electoral reform, Kume's program focused special attention, often from a very cynical and openly critical viewpoint, on the scandals involving top LDP leaders and the endemic corruption involving the party. Moreover, in the period leading to the formation of new reform parties as well as in the election campaign, the program provided exposure for new politicians like Hosokawa, a former journalist and LDP governor, who had formed the Japan New Party (Nihon Shinseitô) to fight for reform and to seek election to the House of Representatives and ultimately the prime ministership (Altman 1996).

The other type of television program that had a sudden impact on politics was the live talk show. One in particular, "Sunday Project," also on Asahi TV, provided a freewheeling, unscripted, and informal opportunity for politicians to appear, but at the same time required them to respond spontaneously to difficult questions in front of the public. This is a rare format on television and in other Japanese institutions (even Diet parliamentary "debates" are usually extremely ritualized and not spontaneous). Thus, in contrast with traditional practices, the journalist–official relationship was not under the control of the source. The responses by politicians on live talk shows, moreover, could not be retracted, denied, or evaded later on. One of the most striking examples of this in the lead-up to the 1993 election occurred when Prime Minister Kiichi Miyazawa appeared on "Sunday Project" and was forced by the host's persistent questioning to commit himself to a promise of political reform during the current Diet session. When he could not live up to that promise, this commitment and the replaying of excerpts from that program undermined his credibility, ultimately contributing to the collapse of his government as well as the split of the LDP over the issue of political reform (Altman 1996).

In the subsequent election, the role of television was even greater, even though it was still forbidden by law to sell air time to candidates. Young candidates of the new reform conservative parties in particular challenged the diminished LDP, effectively using the television interview and opinion-centered news shows to establish name recognition and an image for themselves and their fledgling parties.

Few were better at this than Hosokawa. A member of one of Japan's oldest aristocratic families, the young, photogenic, and charming reform leader made an ideal candidate for the new television game. Just as important, as a former *Asahi* newspaper reporter, he was well aware of the structure and organization of the media, as well as the sources used by newspaper and television reporters to develop their stories. He used this knowledge to manipulate the media to his advantage (personal interview, 1994). Naturally, the portent of momentous political change – the LDP's loss of power after 38 years, and the emergence of new parties and a new generation of reformist politicians – also meant that the media had both unprecedentedly dramatic and interesting political stories to tell and a range of new sources who felt less constrained about expressing themselves publicly.

The new frenzy of "television politics" continued in the aftermath of the election, focusing on the cobbling together of a seven-party reformist coalition (which excluded the LDP) and Hosokawa's elevation to the post of prime minister. Hosokawa used televised press conferences, altering their previously innocuous and ritualized format to enhance his leadership image in a way that can only be compared to that of John F. Kennedy in the early 1960s. He was also the first Japanese prime minister to use a teleprompter in a broadcast to the nation (Altman 1996). Thus, the seeds of Nakasone's use of presidential-style television leadership bore full fruit a decade later with Hosokawa.

Television and its role in the election and in politics itself became a major political issue. The printed press and magazines debated the benefits and costs of television's new importance in elections and politics (Tahara 1993). Hosokawa's political ally and the mastermind behind the new coalition, Ozawa Ichirô, a veteran former LDP politician and leader of another reform conservative party, publicly criticized the reporters' club system and announced that he was no longer going to give exclusive, private briefings to the journalists assigned to him. Instead, he promised to hold open press conferences for all journalists, as was more appropriate for the new era of open debate in Japanese politics (*Japan Times Weekly International Edition* 1993, 17; Isaki 1993, 18; Altman 1996).

Most dramatically, the head of the news department at Asahi TV was accused of slanting the station's coverage of the election to try to topple the LDP. It was alleged, for example, that he explicitly instructed his staff to report the news in certain ways. This controversial accusation of television bias was then matched by an equally controversial move by the Diet to subpoena the Asahi news director and subject him to hours of televised questions about his thoughts and actions from LDP representatives who were stung by their loss of power and blamed biased television for it (Sanger 1993; Berger 1995; Altman 1996).

Within a year, Hosokawa's fragile coalition had collapsed following the desertion of the Socialists and another small party to a strange new coalition of former ideological rivals, including the LDP, which took power under a Socialist prime minister in 1994. Although the LDP was once more a governing party, much had changed since its previous 38-year period of continuous rule. First, television's more important and controversial role in politics continually reasserted itself. The year 1995 was a particularly salient media year, beginning with the devastating Kobe earthquake of January that dominated the news for months, including the media's unusual criticism of the government's slow response in providing disaster relief. Then in March, the murderous sarin gas attack on Tokyo's subway system by a deviant religious cult, Aum Shinrikyô, concentrated enormous media coverage on this event and its consequences. It is estimated that more than 500 hours of television coverage, with unprecedented ratings, were devoted to the sect and the incident in the two months after its occurrence on March 20 (Hardacre 1995, 4). Television news itself subsequently became a subject of controversy. One of the sect's leaders was assassinated while television cameras recorded the event, and the media frequently rebroadcast the gruesome footage. This and other aspects of coverage of the Aum Shinnrikyô investigation raised some serious questions about the propensity of television news toward sensationalism and trial by opinion (Hardacre 1995, 19–25). Then it was revealed that one commercial television station, TBS, had given videotapes to the sect of a lawyer involved in a suit against Aum Shinrikyô – a man who was later kidnapped and presumably killed with his wife and infant son in apparent revenge for his statements on the tape. This incident brought about the resignation of the network's chief executive and much soul searching in Japan about journalistic ethics in television news.

Second, one of the short-lived Hosokawa cabinet's accomplishments before its demise was to push through the Diet major electoral reform and campaign finance reform bills in response to public disgust with corruption. The electoral reform ended Japan's unusual multimember electoral district system, which had pitted candidates of the same party against each other and was perceived as encouraging personalist rather than issue-oriented elections, pork-barrel politics, and the need for massive funding that led to widespread corruption. In its place, a new electoral system was instituted for the House of Representatives, with three-fifths of its members elected by single-member districts, as in the United States and Britain, and two-fifths through a regional form of proportional representation, as in parts of continental Europe. The campaign finance bill had several complicated provisions, but its main thrust was to try to channel electoral spending to the parties. Both of these reforms, it was predicted, would strengthen party leadership and political parties at the expense of individual candidates and faction leaders.

Campaign advertising, however, was not part of the reform, and the stringent restrictions on campaigning and on candidates' use of media were continued. In the first test of the new electoral system in 1996, however, politicians once again used talk and debate shows to get around the limitations, and parties seemed to use their ability to purchase advertising more actively than in the past. With a strengthened party leadership and a parliament elected in both single-member and proportional representation districts rather than the old multimember districts, party advertising in elections may well involve a greater emphasis on party image as it acquires more importance for voters than candidates' personal appeal.

Finally, after the 1996 election, the media shifted attention from the corrupt practices of politicians to the previously impregnable elite bureaucracy. Various scandals involving civil servants erupted, including one in which government bureaucrats in the Ministry of Health knowingly made decisions that resulted in hundreds of hemophiliacs contracting the human immunodeficiency virus (HIV). Others involved the once powerful Finance Ministry. Civil servants' sins of omission and commission, the consequences of these errors for average citizens, and

calls for administrative reform of the ostensibly regulatory-mad bureaucracy have become prominent in news coverage over the last few
years.

TELEVISION AND THE PRINT MEDIA: COMBINED
EFFECTS, DIFFERENT FUNCTIONS

Empirical studies highlight the combined effects of print and television
media on citizens' political attitudes and behavior in Japan. Exposure to
Japan's serious, influential, and widely disseminated print and broadcast
media tends to increase citizens' political knowledge, issue consistency,
interest in politics, and political involvement. The media thus indirectly
stimulate political participation (Flanagan 1996). Although multivariate
analysis has revealed that media exposure has no direct effect on political participation, its indirect effect is stronger than that of many other
variables, including gender, a range of demographic variables, and partisanship. Media exposure is also associated with higher levels of discussion of politics (Feldman and Kawakami 1989, 280; Flanagan 1996).

The print and television media, however, seem to have performed
somewhat different functions in Japan's polity in the postwar era. Because of their conformity and the reporters' club system, national newspapers have not provided the diversity of opinion or realized their potential in performing the press's traditional watchdog function, leaving
these roles to magazines. Nonetheless, by providing a wealth of knowledge about government to citizens, stimulating political participation,
and largely substituting for the opposition parties in checking the power
of government and the ruling LDP, the press has played a critical, if ambivalent, role in the postwar consolidation of democracy. Television, in
contrast, until recently seems to have enhanced political stability by reinforcing authority, defusing conflict, and avoiding the volatility and dis-
ruption generally associated with personalized, individual leadership.
The recent apparent change in television's impact and its role in politics,
however, is belatedly helping to create more personalized, critical, and
cynical politics as well (Krauss 1998).

CONCLUSION

The recent and dramatic emergence of television as a factor in Japanese
politics may lead some to conclude that new media technologies drive
politics and that their impact, like the forces of nature, can only be coped

with, not managed. This analysis of the media throughout Japan's post-war democratic history, however, suggests that such a conclusion is both unwarranted and simplistic. To ignore the recent political changes would be foolhardy: the cork has been dislodged, and the television genie is out of the bottle. It would be equally foolhardy, however, to ignore the other interesting questions about the media and Japanese democracy: why has the genie been dormant for so long, and how did it finally get out?

The explanation of television's relatively secondary and dormant role in Japanese politics may be that the impact of media technology on attitudes and behavior is mediated by institutions and that its effects are contingent on institutional context. The political influence of, and the different roles performed by, the media are the products of interactions among media, political, and societal institutions, and some of the distinguishing features of political communications through the media in Japan result from specific characteristics of these institutional interactions. Indeed, the central media paradox in Japan – the pervasiveness of television but the surprising limits, until recently, of its ability to promote change in political life – is explained by the particular nexus of the institutions of state and society.

To a greater extent than in countries like the United States, television in Japan for much of the earlier postwar period complemented rather than replaced newspapers as a political news and information source. A superb precollege mass education system produced a literate citizenry well equipped and inclined to sustain a written rather than a visual news culture, which allowed newspapers to continue to attract a massive audience of regular readers. The nationwide distribution system of the main papers and their financial dependence on subscribers (rather than on advertising revenues), meanwhile, encouraged fierce competition over expanded readership, resulting in a diverse audience for the print media. The diversity of their audience, in turn, meant that newspapers attempted to maintain political neutrality and objectivity, precluding the formation of segmented political-journalistic subcultures. In this context, the popularity of television spread without undermining the public attachment to newspapers or trust in them.

Certain features of daily life in Japan also affected the audience structures of both broadcast and print media. The nature of Japanese companies, family gender roles, and an urban housing situation that prevents white-collar workers from returning home until relatively late at night (often following hours of train commuting) had a significant impact; the main television news programs were watched more frequently by the less educated, less urban, older population. The urban, educated population, which is more influential in setting the tone of Japanese political life, continued to depend on newspapers for their news in depth, particularly since long commuting hours provided considerable time for reading.

Other interactions between media organizations and the institutions of state and society either made television's influence supportive of authority or limited the medium's capacity to stimulate change. The reporters' clubs that so closely shape source – journalist relations in Japan, for example, have given politicians and government officials a greater ability than is usually found elsewhere to regulate the flow of information to the media.

Further limiting the autonomy of television was the dominance of the self-consciously impartial public broadcasting service in the gathering and dissemination of news. The fact that the public broadcasting service, NHK, was the unquestioned leader in television news for so many years, and the fact that the commercial networks seemed content to accept NHK dominance in this field, contributed to television's limited potential for change. NHK originally modeled its news editing and news gathering organization on that of the printed press, while commercial stations were closely connected to newspapers in their ownership and news gathering. As a result, television was no more autonomous of reporters' clubs in its news gathering than was the printed press. Indeed, because television, as a visual medium, is so restricted in its ability to undertake investigative journalism, it has a limited capacity for independent journalism, editorials, or "campaigns" to offset its reporters' club source dependence.

Regulatory restrictions on the formation and operation of commercial television networks seemed to diminish their ability to compete with NHK's overwhelming personnel advantage in providing a lot of news quickly. A superb provider of information it may have been, but the characterizations of the BBC as enjoying 'liberty on parole' and 'responsibility without power' (Burns 1977, 22, 13) apply equally to NHK. Indeed, NHK's vulnerability to the government may have been even greater than the BBC's because of the LDP's status as Japan's seemingly permanent government. Despite legal safeguards, the LDP repeatedly sought to influence NHK through informal control over the selection of its president and by delaying license fee increases needed by the broadcaster to bring its expenses into line with its revenues (Krauss 1998).

The need for a public broadcaster to satisfy both a heterogeneous audience and a government with considerable control over its budget reduced its capacity to question established power. NHK, much like the

BBC and other public broadcasters, propagates a corporate ideology of trust and reliability, but reliable news often turned out to be authoritative news, that is, direct from the political authorities (especially given the reporters' club system). Despite NHK's scrupulous attention to partisan balance in its news coverage, therefore, the generally positive and activist portrayal of the state, especially the bureaucracy, combined with a paucity of interpretive, critical reporting, led to what I have called elsewhere "video-legitimation" (Krauss 1996a) rather than the "video-malaise" described by Robinson (1976, 427–32) in the United States. Even in the early 1990s, the dominant position of NHK in satellite programming and high-definition television (HDTV), the fact that NHK has successfully competed against commercial channels for 40 years, and the relative weakness of cable alternatives (and the greater freedom of choice and consequent audience segmentation associated with cable TV) ensured that public broadcasting was still at least one of the cores of Japan's media and was still vital to a highly centralized information network.

As Gunther and Mughan suggest in the conclusion to this volume concerning the resocialization efforts of nondemocratic regimes, the more homogeneous the information flow to citizens, the greater the likelihood that it will be regarded as credible. A milder version of this hypothesis might also apply to democratic regimes, as illustrated by most of the postwar period in Japan. With television news dominated by NHK, and with that public network and the giant national newspapers all conveying news from official bureaucratic sources garnered through the source-dependent reporters clubs, Japanese citizens received a fairly homogeneous diet of political news based on official sources. In this situation, the similarity of newspapers and television – neither of which were particularly strong at investigative journalism – may well have helped relegate television news to a more supplemental and authority-reinforcing role in Japanese political life.

Finally, the electoral system, with its multimember districts and single ballots, tended to focus voter's attention on candidates. At the same time, however, individual candidates' access to television was strictly regulated and controlled, while that of the parties was relatively unfettered. An electoral law fostering candidate-centered competition, combined with media-access regulations making the parties the vehicle for television advertising, mitigated the impact on campaign politics of television, a medium normally well suited for the crafting and "selling" of candidate's images.

The net product of this set of linkages among state, society, and media was an informed and cynical Japanese citizenry that was also politically involved and supportive of political authority.

In the early 1990s, however, the system began a major transformation. What brought this transformation about? Certainly the institutions of reporters' clubs, public service broadcasting, electoral laws, and so forth underwent no change prior to the emergence of "television politics." But if institutions that inhibited television's influence did not change, what can explain the medium's greater political impact? Some tentative, if perhaps premature, speculations regarding the interactions among technology and democratic institutions offer plausible answers to this question.

I would argue that the new and seemingly sudden change in the role of television in politics in Japan was in fact not so sudden. Rather, it was due to a combination of evolutionary changes in the television industry and in politicians' strategies. In 1993, for the first time, the prospects for change in government served as a catalyst to bring about a manifestly different kind of political impact due to the interaction between the altered nature of television coverage of politics and the behavior of politicians themselves. One long-term transformation of the media that preceded this shift was the commercial stations' move in strength into television news journalism and the success of their opinionated news style. Only with the erosion of NHK's dominance in political news coverage could television begin to play a greater role in politics. Having decided in the mid-1980s to challenge this dominance, the commercial networks realized that they did not have the resources to compete with NHK in the gathering of news. Some stations, like Asahi TV, therefore concluded that they could establish a competitive advantage only by developing a different news-reporting style. As secondary players to a public broadcaster with a national but older and more rural audience, the commercial networks had much to gain and little to lose by using more controversial and entertaining news programming to attract a niche audience of younger, urban viewers. Here was a situation in which entrepreneurship and market forces partially undermined the established institutional relationships among the media, bureaucracy, and politicians (Krauss 1998). The success of Kume's "News Station" turned an experiment into the model for commercial television news. Its consequences, in retrospect, were a more diversified range of news program offerings and stimulation of audience demand for a more spontaneous, dramatic, and controversial style of political journalism on television.

The second longer-term transformation was the appearance of Japanese politicians who recognized the political potential of television. In the early 1980s, Prime Minister Nakasone was the first to use television to create an attractive public image for himself. He used his carefully crafted image of an international statesman to enhance his position in factional politics within the LDP. The subsequent return to a string of colorless backroom chief executives initially made Nakasone seem an aberration, but in retrospect he is more accurately seen as a pioneer. Hosokawa and the other politicians of the younger generation who skillfully used television in 1993 were in fact following a path already marked out by Nakasone. Hosokawa's unique contributions were to link the use of television to domestic politics and political reform and to use television directly to mobilize public support.

These two long-term transformations came together in 1993 and were facilitated by a final catalyst: the LDP's fragmentation and its resultant prospective loss of power. This is an oft-neglected dimension of the great media changes of 1993. Had the LDP stayed together and retained its aura as the perennial party of power, the changes discussed earlier certainly would not have occurred with the same dramatic intensity. But after it split, neither sources nor journalists had to worry about retribution from the party perpetually in government. Thus, the range of what sources could say without anxiety was expanded, as were the media in which they could say them. Also, the number of important sources was dramatically increased as the political world fragmented and a dominant party system began changing into a multiparty one. These political changes sparked the commercial networks' new style of political journalism and the new media styles of politicians.

Japanese viewers and readers have fortunately enjoyed a significantly higher level and a greater amount of political information in the postwar period from both their newspapers and their television journalists than have their American counterparts. This was the strength of the way Japan's journalistic institutions interfaced with its political institutions. Its weaknesses were the dominance of official sources and the lack of pluralist debate of opinions in the media.

Will the new role of television enhance media pluralism and offer citizens a wider variety of opinion than in the past? Undoubtedly. Events of the past five years point to the emergence in Japan of more controversial, if also more sensationalist – although not yet of the tabloid variety now found in many Western countries – television news coverage and also, more importantly, a new style of active, opinionated news by journalists and commentators and media cynicism toward the previously sacrosanct bureaucracy.. The institutional background to these changes is a revised electoral system in which television is gradually coming to play a role despite draconian campaign laws that prevent candidates from buying time or gaining an advantage over rivals through the use of commercials.

After an unusual quarter of a century in which television seemed tame and subservient to the powers-that-be, Japan during the past half-decade seems to have come to face many of the same issues of television journalism and its impact on politics that emerged in other nations much earlier. New developments in communications satellites and multimedia technologies that will dramatically increase the type and range of information accessible to individual citizens promise to accelerate these trends – and in the not too distant future. The genie cannot be forced back into the bottle.

On the other hand, the Japanese media will not soon resemble those of the United States. Many of the institutions that restrained the media's role in Japan previously – the reporters' club system, the financial and market relationships among the major national newspapers, restrictions on the formation of total networks, a public broadcaster still with a large audience, and the restrictions on candidates' ability to buy television time – are still in place. We should remember that the great transformation of 1993 represented not a destruction of the institutions that inhibited television's role previously, but the ability of key personnel in television and politics to find ways around them. If the genie is out of the bottle for good, political television will take a distinctly Japanese shape. Markets, technologies, and entrepreneurs ultimately cannot be completely denied, but they can be channeled and shaped by institutions created by political elites. If Japan's political and journalistic elites are careful and adroit, the country may be able to combine a high level of information with a high level of pluralist debate, through a combination of responsible and informative newspapers and public broadcasters with interesting and opinionated commercial-television news. Or it may find itself having the worst of worlds: information dominance by official sources and irresponsible entertainment news for profit.

NOTES

1. Article 21 of the 1947 states: "Freedom of assembly and association, as well as speech, press and all other forms of expression are guaranteed. No censorship shall be maintained, nor shall the secrecy of any means of communication be violated" (Ward 1978, 231).

2. Yamamoto and Fujitake 1987, 17–19; and Keizai Kôhô Center 1992, 95. It should be noted that these figures underestimate the distribution rate for Japan, which calculates such ratios differently that do most other countries. International comparative distribution rates count morning and afternoon editions separately even if they are produced by the same company, whereas in Japan they are counted as simply one paper if put out by the same company. Thus, the international distribution rate was about 68 million in 1985 but about 48 million as counted in Japan. The rate of 2.5 persons per paper is counted in the Japanese style, so this figure would be even lower if the international method had been used.

3. Typically, the top news stories from any field appear on page 1, page 2 always presents political news, page 3 deal with society and series, pages 4 through 5 include editorials and op-ed columns, pages 6 and 7 cover international affairs, pages 8 and 9 stocks, business, and finance, and so forth through culture, classified advertisements, family, sports, and local news, with television and radio listings appearing on the final page. (See Thayer 1975, 288.)

4. Balance was defined as giving "roughly equal representation to the substantive arguments and rebuttals being put forward by disputants in a controversy." This standard was applied to press coverage regarding three controversial issues: the struggle over the FSX fighter plane; negotiations over the Structural Impediments Initiative; and the purchases of Columbia Pictures and Rockefeller Center by Sony and Mitsubishi, respectively.

5. An important factor that made this change of heart possible is that, once identified as a scandal by others, a story falls under the purview of the society desk of the elite newspapers as well as the political desk. This makes possible greater aggressiveness in pursuing the story, since the society desk does not stand in the same close, dependent relationship to the government officials in questions.

6. Although the question did not distinguish between newspapers and television, it is most likely, given the leading role the printed press plays, that respondents were thinking more of newspapers.

7. NHK television broadcasts on one general channel, one educational channel, and two direct-broadcast satellite channels. NHK radio includes two AM channels and one on FM.

8. License fees are collected by the government in Britain and then reallocated to the BBC. NHK, in contrast, collects its own fees directly from the public, and they never pass into government hands. The National Diet (parliament), however, must approve NHK's annual budget, as well as any increase in the size of its fee, whereas the BBC does not need annual parliamentary approval.

9. For example, Nippon TV's network's flagship station has a relationship with the *Yomiuri* newspaper, the ANN Tokyo station with the *Asahi*, the TBS network with the *Mainichi* newspaper, the Fuji network with the *Fuji-Sankei* chains, and the Tokyo TV network with the *Nihon Keizai* newspaper.

10. Of the 14,654 people employed by NHK in 1990, approximately 1,429 were engaged in "news gathering–related" (*hôdô shuzai kankei*) tasks, both information and visual (Nippon Hôsô Kyôkai 1990, 70).

11. Other statistics often underestimate Japan's television ownership profile. For example, Japan's official number of sets per 100 persons is often given as less than 30, compared to more than 30 for most European nations and the U.S. figure of 83 (*Nippon*

Hôsô Kyôkai 1988, 277 and 283; Keizai Kôhô Center 1990, 90a). These statistics, however, are usually based on the number of households paying receivers' fees to NHK rather than on the actual number of sets in use.

12. In adapting the data, I combined several categories by putting government, prime minister, and elections together, merging Kobayashi's separate categories of criminals and courts, and combining all specific categories of other countries into a generic "foreign" category. Categorizations of items were mutually exclusive. (See Kobayshi 1982, 35.)

13. There are probably two reasons for this unusually heavy television coverage of the bureaucracy. The first concerns the role of the reporters' clubs in television news gathering and their institutionalized dependence on bureaucratic agencies for news and information. The second is NHK's constant effort to be seen as impartial in its political news coverage, an effort that leads it to value news that is authoritative and politically uncontroversial. News from official, especially bureaucratic, sources fits the corporation's requirements on both of these counts (see Krauss 1996a and 1998).

14. For other factors in the creation and maintenance of the LDP-dominated regime, see Pempel 1990, 189–259 and 282–305.

15. On the other hand, Flanagan attributes to the media some limited, indirect effects. Without distinguishing among the media, he finds that exposure to them was related to raising issue salience (in the case of the Lockheed scandal in the 1976 election). This media exposure, in turn, was associated with the tendency of some voters to vote against the incumbent party as long as they were not strong supporters of that party and had enough education and sophistication to make the connection between the scandal and LDP responsibility (Flanagan 1991, 322–7).

16. These findings are derived from a comparative content analysis of news reports dealing with the United States on Japanese television (including NHK and the four flagship stations of the commercial "networks" in Japan) and of reports on American television (the three major commercial networks, CNN, and PBS) concerning Japan. The period of time covered was mid-September to mid-December 1992 and mid-February to mid-June 1993.

CHAPTER 9

The Netherlands: Media and Politics between Segmented Pluralism and Market Forces

Cees van der Eijk

The notion that media and politics influence one another is hardly more than a truism. Of much more interest is the question of the circumstances under which the balance of influence shifts from one side to the other. The Netherlands is an almost exemplary case of how this balance can shift over the course of time.

In the closing decades of the nineteenth century, influence flowed mainly from the political realm to the emerging mass media. The same political conflicts that "pillarized" Dutch society shaped a media system that was to last for the better part of the twentieth century (Daalder 1966; Lorwin 1971). Then, between the late 1920s and the 1960s, influence flowed in both directions as the media and political systems influenced each other and reinforced their respective pillarized characteristics. Since the 1960s, however, the balance has shifted in the other direction, and developments in the media landscape have been cause rather than the consequence of the profound transformations in Dutch society and politics known as "depillarization." Indeed, starting in the late 1980s, the combination of rapidly developing media technology and the emerging transnational regulatory system of the European Union (EU) undermined the capacity of the Dutch state to influence, let alone shape, how the media system will evolve in the future. To an increasing extent, the world of Dutch mass media has become independent of politics despite the fact that its workings continue to have direct consequences for national political processes and outcomes.

This chapter first provides a summary picture of the evolution of the Netherlands into the pillarized society that was to persist for much of the twentieth century, and the role of the media in sustaining this pillarization is discussed in some detail. This is followed by a discussion of the developments – particularly those relating to the media – that undermined this sociopolitical order. The final part of the chapter focuses on recent developments and assesses their consequences for the interaction between the mass communications media and political democracy in the Netherlands in the 1990s.

THE EVOLUTION OF *VERZUILING*

The segmented structure characteristic of Dutch society for most of the twentieth century has its origins in a series of protracted political conflicts in the late nineteenth and early twentieth centuries. These conflicts not only dominated political life for almost half a century, but also involved the mobilization of common people on an unprecedented scale, thus giving rise to strongly organized cleavage groups that manifested themselves in multiple social domains that are commonly labeled *zuilen,* or "pillars" (Lijphart 1968).

Prior to the 1860s, the 12 percent or so of adult Dutch males entitled to vote favored liberal over conservative groups and had done so since the mid-1840s. To promote national and industrial development, the liberals advocated, among other things, the introduction of compulsory education and a system of state-subsidized public schools. This proposal provoked strong opposition in orthodox Protestant and Roman Catholic groups that insisted on equal state funding for private schools (Righart 1986; Hellemans 1990). The issue generated a tremendous and sustained mobilization of common people who had not counted politically up to that point, thereby laying the organizational groundwork for the first modern mass party in the Netherlands, the Protestant Anti-Revolutionary Party, and it was able to keep the "schools issue" on the political agenda until confessional demands were met in 1917.

Two other issues became prominent at about the same time: the extension of the franchise and the so-called social question. The piecemeal expansion of the franchise benefited the emerging Protestant and Catholic mass movements and the rising labor movement. It also undermined the numerical advantage of liberals rent by internal dissension between progressive and conservative factions. The liberals were gradually overwhelmed both numerically and organizationally. The associated increase in the political power of Protestants and Catholics enabled them to keep the schools issue salient until they achieved a satisfactory resolution of it. The social question concerned the conditions under which the working classes were to work and live, as well as the proper role of the state and other social and political institutions in this matter. The

Netherlands' relatively late industrialization meant that a socialist and labor movement acquired momentum only after Protestants and Catholics, through their struggles on the schools issue, had already successfully organized large segments of the working class and other ordinary people.

These political struggles produced modern mass-based and well-organized social movements of Protestants, Roman Catholics, and labor that, for ordinary people, gradually became objects of personal, social, and political identification. This process was facilitated by the protracted nature of the conflicts and by the gradual expansion of these movements as they created institutions and organizations catering to different aspects of their members' lives: labor unions, recreational clubs, schools, housing cooperatives, mutual insurance funds, media, and political parties. In 1917 the negotiated and conciliatory "Pacification of 1917" resolved in a package deal most of the issues that had dominated Dutch politics for decades. By that time, the social movements of the late nineteenth century had evolved into veritable subcultures with their own networks of organizations, or *zuilen*. Only the liberal groups did not evolve into a pillar of their own, although in a number of areas they did have their own organizations – mostly referred to as "general" to indicate their independence of what they considered particularistic subcultures (Daalder 1966; Lijphart 1968; Lorwin 1971; Ellemers 1984).

VERZUILING AND MASS MEDIA DEVELOPMENT

Mass circulation newspapers in the Netherlands developed at about the same time that the conflicts producing the system of *verzuiling* were at their height. The constitutionally guaranteed freedom of the press allowed the various subcultures to create their own newspapers as integral parts of their respective pillars. In this way, newspapers became linked to pillars and proved invaluable in recruiting and mobilizing supporters. Thus, by the beginning of the twentieth century, the newspaper industry had by and large acquired the form and structure that it was to keep until the 1960s. Albeit imperfectly, it also reflected the pillarized society in which it was rooted. A limited number of newspapers could be regarded as the authoritative voices of the Protestant, Catholic, or socialist *zuilen* or of the smaller liberal tendency in society. It was these newspapers that provided the public forum for national political debate. Other newspapers—and they were much larger in number—could be associated with one or another pillar or tendency, without any particular need to make such ties explicit. Finally, a smaller number professed to be apolitical, that is, not associated with any particular *zuil,* political party, or ideological tendency (Luykx 1978; Hemels 1979; Gosman 1993a).

Even though the newspaper industry was not completely pillarized, the part that was unequivocally linked to the different subcultures was sufficiently large and prominent to set the tone for the entire industry. It promoted the development of a style, even an ethos, of journalism that took pride not merely in reporting the news but also in providing readers with a clear point of view that was consciously intended to guide their interpretation and evaluation of the news and of the world in which they lived.[1]

Radio came to the Netherlands in 1919, and debate over its proper role and purpose remained intense throughout the 1920s. On one side were outspoken advocates of a nonpillarized, national structure providing radio programming for all groups in society. They were opposed by those who viewed a national broadcasting system as little more than the misguided claim that the various subcultures could prosper under a liberal banner. They regarded their identity and subculture as being sufficiently protected only under a radio system organized along pillarized lines. In 1930, the government imposed a regulatory regime that represented an almost unqualified victory for the advocates of *verzuiling,* and the broadcasting industry was turned into the most completely pillarized sector of Dutch society.

The regulations enacted started from the premise that broadcasting should be the province of private organizations that had to satisfy two requirements. First, they had to serve "manifest cultural or religious needs in the population," which meant, in effect, that they had to be associated with one of the pillars. Second, they had to provide comprehensive programming that satisfied a wide range of cultural, educational, and recreational demands. Only four private organizations were deemed to satisfy both criteria and so earned the right to broadcasting time: the Nederlandse Christelijke Radio Vereniging (NCRV, Protestant), the Katholieke Radio Omroep (KRO, Catholic), the Vereniging voor Arbeiders Radio Amateurs (VARA, social democratic), and the Algemene Vereniging voor Radio Omroep (AVRO, general). The relevant cultural tendencies in society were thus covered, with each organization being allocated 20 percent of the available time slots. The remaining 20 percent were reserved mainly for national programming, like daily newscasts, coverage of national festivities or ceremonies, and so on.[2]

Radio was regulated in this way to preserve the peaceful subcultural relations that had prevailed since 1917. Explicit political propaganda was prohibited, as were broadcasts undermining religion, morality, or public authority. Reflecting the philosophy that the cultural and religious needs of the population should be satisfied, advertising and other commercial uses of the medium were also banned. Inevitably, when television was introduced after 1948, its organization was embedded in this same pillarized broadcasting structure. In addition, the principles governing radio were applied equally to the allocation and prescribed uses of television broadcast time.

Thus, the political realm largely determined the structure and character of the emerging mass media in the Netherlands. The newspaper industry was strongly shaped by the struggles that gave rise to the pillars as organized cleavage groupings. Radio and, later, television were even more comprehensively pillarized than the newspaper industry as the result not of the same struggles, but of government regulation aimed at preserving the political structure that, since 1917, had pacified formerly antagonistic subcultures. *Verzuiling* was the dominant paradigm of social and political organization, and it enabled the entrenched pillars to restrict access to the new media of radio and television to their own associated broadcast organizations.

Pillarization itself lasted unchallenged until the mid-1960s. The pillarized media not only reported the divisions in society, but also gave them organizational expression and legitimized them. They were the mouthpiece through which the subcultural elites could tell their followers how to think on important issues of the day, thereby both reproducing the divisions separating the pillars and reinforcing the boundaries within which their respective members were safe. At the same time, the pillarized parties provided their own media with political patronage, safety from competition, and a clear sense of mission. Yet, this comfortable system of reciprocal reinforcement did come to an end, and abruptly.

How, why, and with what consequences are discussed next. The basic theme is that developments in the media that were altogether independent of politics helped to erode pillarization. The flow of influence from politics to the media, in other words, was reversed.

DEPILLARIZATION

The changes in Dutch society that became known as depillarization started in the mid-1960s and comprised three different but interlocking and mutually reinforcing phenomena. First, citizens became less loyal to their respective pillars, increasingly looking elsewhere for their newspaper, radio, and television programs, recreational clubs, schools for their children, and party to vote for in elections. Second, there was a decline in the *zuil* distinctiveness of organizations. The goods, services, and benefits provided by the various *zuil* organizations became less unique, making it harder for *zuil* elites to demand subcultural loyalty. Third, the internal cohesion of the pillars decreased. Formal and informal ties that bound subcultural organizations dissolved. Teachers, politicians, journalists, and others increasingly emphasized their professional independence over their subcultural identities. The result was that Dutch society at the end of the 1970s was quite different from what it had been in the early 1960s. *Verzuiling* belonged to an irrevocably lost past.[3]

But what caused the pillarized structure of the Netherlands to crumble, and what was the media's role in this process? In answering these questions, account must be taken of other contributions to depillarization so as not to overestimate the role played by the media. All of the most important general explanations of depillarization emphasize an eroded raison d'être for this form of subcultural organization (van Schendelen 1984; Lijphart 1989). One explanation holds that, because of its success in helping to integrate religious and ideological subcultures into a modernizing nation, *verzuiling* had outlived its usefulness and no longer contributed to continued modernization (Stuurman 1983; Ellemers 1984; Bax 1988). Another is that once *verzuiling* had satisfied subcultural groups' demands for social and political emancipation, it removed the reason for its existence. Yet another perspective emphasizes the role of pillarization in helping to contain and resolve group conflicts. With pacification, the need for groups and individuals to remain within their subcultures disappeared (van der Eijk et al. 1992a).

Bearing these general perspectives in mind, the question of the media's role in depillarization can now be addressed, as can the auxiliary question of depillarization's consequences for the media in the Netherlands.

THE MEDIA AND DEPILLARIZATION

Changes in the Dutch media landscape played an important part in bringing about and feeding depillarization. Ellemers (1984, 142) states the general argument nicely: "In particular, television made people aware of the ideas and values of other groups, and subsequently eroded existing cleavages. On the other hand it made people aware of . . . the new problems of the 1960s. . . . These developments were in many respects at variance with much that was once characteristic of *Verzuiling*." This diagnosis is accurate as far as it goes. But in addition to the *contagion* of television, *convergence* and *escape* were also important.

"Contagion" refers to the corrosive effects of communications and influences of subcultures other than one's own. Despite having been only incompletely pillarized, the printed press offered no more than limited opportunities for such contagion. Dutch people have traditionally obtained their newspapers through subscription, an act whose relatively public nature discouraged subscriptions outside of one's subculture. More overt pressures to conform were at work as well. Catholic priests, for example, used their regular visits to parishioners' homes to encourage appropriate readership (Bakvis 1981, 36–8).

The essentially private consumption of radio and, later, television represented a more dangerous and less easily controlled source of contagion. The lack of available wavelengths prevented each pillar from having its own exclusive frequency to which its followers could keep their receivers permanently tuned (although that would still have allowed them to listen to other stations had they desired to do so). But the necessity of different ideologies sharing alternating time slots on a single station exposed their respective followers to the risk of accidentally being exposed to communications from subcultures other than their own. Consequently, *zuil* elites strongly urged their followers to avoid the broadcasts of different subcultures by switching off their radio or television sets when these broadcasts began. Television was a particular source of contagion. The absence of alternative stations to watch, the somewhat addictive effects of this new medium, and the small number of hours it was on the air all conspired to thwart efforts to prevent the exposure of Dutch people to political and social views different from those with which they had been brought up. Radio also played its part, but television soon turned contagion into a widespread and inescapable phenomenon (van den Heuvel 1976, 13–53; Brants 1985, 106).

"Convergence" in content also contributed to depillarization insofar as the program offerings of the different pillars became increasingly similar. It was least marked in the core areas of subcultural identities, that is, ideological and religious commentary, symbolism, and reaffirmation of subcultural distinctiveness. But when catering to recreational and aesthetic needs, convergence was substantial. It was also an almost inevitable consequence of the small size of the pillarized media organizations and their lack of the resources needed to produce all their own materials independently. No Dutch newspaper, for instance, was ever large enough to employ its own network of domestic, let alone foreign, correspondents. Newspapers' distinctive profiles, therefore, derived much more from their commentary and interpretation than from the contents of the factual news they presented since the latter was derived mainly from a single common source: press agencies.[4]

Other factors also made for convergence. Strident reaffirmations of pillarized identities seemed more and more out of place in the media, as the subcultural conflicts from which the pillars sprang belonged in a continuously receding past. In addition, declining individual loyalties to the pillarized media encouraged catchall programming in the electronic media in particular as a way of keeping them viable. Thus, by the early 1960s, programs were much less colored by who offered them than they had been in previous decades. Paradoxically, the almost complete organizational pillarization of the electronic media had proved to be no guarantee of the subcultural distinctiveness of program content.

"Escape" refers to the opportunity to move outside pillarized structures and consume or produce nonpillarized communications. Escape has always been possible with the printed press since constitutionally guaranteed freedom of the press allowed the production of newspapers independent of the *zuilen*. Indeed, *De Telegraaf*, the highest-circulation national newspaper in the country since the turn of the century, has always enjoyed such independence, bearing witness to the latent demand for nonpillarized media. Radio and television, however, are another story. Because of the virtual broadcasting monopoly enjoyed, and zealously protected, by the *zuil* organizations from 1930 on, consumers could not escape (at least for programs in their own Dutch language) from the fare offered by the pillarized broadcast system. But this monopoly was never entirely uncontested. Business interests, for example, had repeatedly, but unsuccessfully, asked to be allowed to use radio, and later television, for commercial purposes. Their first success came in the 1960s, when technological advances made it feasible to resort to an extraterritorial escape route. Commercial "pirate" radio ships were moored in the North Sea just outside Dutch territorial waters, and broadcast pop music could be picked up on land. Preferring it to stolid pillarized radio, young people turned to it in massive numbers. This encouraged further commercial ventures, the most famous one being the attempt to set up a commercial television channel broadcasting from a platform in international waters just off the Dutch coast. This particular challenge was too dangerous for the established system to leave unanswered, and in little more than a year, the legal basis was laid for the seizure and confiscation of pirate stations. The legacy of this episode, though, was the transformation of the structure of Dutch broadcasting and the acceleration of depillarization.

OPENING UP THE CLOSED BROADCAST SYSTEM

In the face of such attacks on it, the broadcasting regulatory system was changed in two ways in 1965. First, advertisements were introduced into regular broadcasts to appease commercial interests and to help pay for the newly introduced second television channel. It was also hoped that this measure would make further extraterritorial ventures economically inviable. Second, the premise that the broadcasting organizations of the *zuilen* represented the full range of demand in the Dutch population – the cornerstone of the 1930 regulatory regime – was abandoned. Henceforth, the size of broadcast organizations' dues-paying membership would be the measure of the public demand for their programming, and broadcasting time slots would be allocated accordingly. In effect, room had been made for new broadcasting organizations, although the requirement that all licensed broadcast organizations offer a full range of programs remained in place.

The already existing broadcast organization that were linked to the *zuilen* enjoyed a head start and were able to retain the largest share of government-allocated time slots. Still, they could not prevent three new broadcasting organizations from acquiring a license: TROS (general and originally a little more conservative than the already operating other general organization, AVRO), Veronica (a former pirate radio station strongly geared toward a secular and hedonistic youth culture), and EO (evangelical, established partly in reaction to the already operating NCRV's loss of its clear religious orientation). But even more important than newcomers winning the right to broadcast was the inability of the traditional media organizations to justify any longer their large share of broadcast time merely by their association with one of the *zuilen*. They now had to compete with aggressive newcomers and with each other for broadcast time. They did adapt, but not quickly enough to prevent the rise and growth of new broadcast organizations. Moreover, the form their adaptation took was increasingly to deemphasize their particular subcultural identity, so that the Catholic, Protestant, and socialist broadcasting organizations soon lost their distinctive programming profiles.

Contagion, convergence, and escape, then, interacted with each other, just as they did with more general forces promoting for the depillarization of Dutch society. The overall effect was the transformation of Dutch politics and society, the political aspects of which will be discussed in more detail later in this chapter.

THE EFFECTS OF DEPILLARIZATION ON THE MEDIA

Depillarization had profound consequences for the media, as well as for Dutch politics and society in general. The regulated, noncompetitive media system gave way to market forces, and the stability and safety of partly captive markets gave way to the much harsher and less predictable world of intense competition for market share. Inevitably there were casualties, particularly in a newspaper industry that had to cope simultaneously with the economic slump of the 1960s and 1970s, with declining revenues as the result of competition from broadcast advertising, with declining consumer interest because of the rapid spread of television, and with the need to invest heavily in new technologies. Many newspapers disappeared, merged, or survived only as local branches of larger conglomerates of newspapers.[5] Broadcast organizations were not as hard hit, but the world had changed for them too. They could no longer rest on their laurels, but had to learn new habits and practices so as not to lose members and, in consequence, broadcast time.

To cope with this new environment, the media in general adopted two strategies. On the one hand, they broke away from *zuilen* and *zuil* organizations, most notably political parties, labor unions, and churches. On the other hand, and as a direct result of their loss of *zuil* identity, they gradually redefined their substantive profiles, a process that in some instances resulted in substantive distinctiveness and in others in an indistinct "catchallism." Most national newspapers opted for distinctiveness in order to appeal to audiences differentiated along left–right and lifestyle lines. The success of this move away from the old sociostructural cleavages was helped by the electorate's passing through a period of dealignment and realignment at much the same time (van der Eijk and Niemöller 1987; 1992). Catchallism, by contrast, was the main pattern in regional and local papers, as well as in broadcasting. In the latter industry, only three organizations developed something like a distinct lifestyle profile. The formerly modernist Protestant VPRO reoriented itself in a secular, nonconformist, and libertarian direction. The former pirate station, Veronica, remained loyal to its origins by emphasizing a secular, hedonistic youth culture, and the newly established EO kept to its goal of advocating evangelical and traditional Christian values. The remaining broadcast organizations became increasingly similar in their programming and public profiles.

These media developments in the 1960s and 1970s were not part of a conscious and coherent political strategy orchestrated by government, Parliament, or political parties. To the contrary, media developments catalyzed changes in the political and social structures of society that the traditional political institutions would have preferred not to take place. With the dissipation of the antagonisms between the subcultures and the reduced distinctiveness of each subculture (van der Eijk, et al. 1992a), the pillarized structure of Dutch society had become increasingly outdated. The processes affecting the media system – contagion, convergence, and escape – undermined its ability to support the country's outdated social and political structures of *verzuiling*. At the same time, these processes left politics increasingly less able to dictate the course of subsequent media developments – a story to be repeated in the 1980s and 1990s.

THE CURRENT DUTCH MEDIA LANDSCAPE

The broadcasting regulatory regime introduced in 1965 took some time to make its full effects felt. By the late 1970s, however, all the relevant actors and institutions had adapted to its demands. Broadcast organizations now competed for dues-paying members, whose numbers determined their share of scarce broadcast time and state funds. But competition was not yet cutthroat since increases in the number of channels, in the number of broadcasting hours, and in the number of advertisements on the air not only afforded time and funds to newcomers, but also increased the amounts of both going to the traditional broadcast organizations.[6] This win-win state of affairs could not last forever, though, and new media developments helped to usher in a new regulatory regime in the late 1980s.

The advent of cable television was particularly instrumental. By the early 1990s, over 90 percent of Dutch households were hooked up to cable, which brought viewers the existing Dutch radio and television channels as well as some from the neighboring countries of Belgium, Germany and Great Britain. One consequence of this increased choice was a reduction in the size of audiences for Dutch channels and in the commercial value of the advertisements aired on them. A major source of their income was threatened. The Dutch authorities reacted by forbidding the distribution by cable of foreign radio or television programs when dubbing or subtitles aimed their advertisements directly at the Dutch market. Amid some controversy, the European Community (EC) quickly struck down this action because it violated the free movement of products, services, information, and ideas.

Debate over the Dutch government's action was overtaken on another front as well. In 1989 an extraterritorial escape route was used once again to circumvent its regulatory authority. A commercial Dutch television channel was introduced under the name RTL4. Although programmed, produced, and commercially exploited entirely in the Netherlands, it was broadcast from a transmitter located in Luxembourg (as well as by satellite). International (particularly European) law and existing regulatory instruments required that this new channel be allowed access to cable distribution, so a fourth channel, free of Dutch government regulation, found its way into almost every household overnight. To rub salt into the wound, RTL4 became the most popular of all Dutch channels starting in 1992.

The Dutch media landscape, then, has come to look very different since the mid-1990s than it did in the past. Following is a brief overview of the contemporary situation.

PRINT MEDIA

Newspapers are the principal print medium and appear every day of the week except Sunday. The distinction between national and regional or local newspapers is important since the former, in particular, function as forums for public debate on social and political affairs. Political and other elites use the national newspapers to air their views or engage in discussion with one another, and politically interested citizens use them to keep informed, occasionally even intervening in elite discussions.

Of the total newspaper circulation, approximately 55 percent is accounted for by some 60 to 70 local and regional newspapers (down from almost two-thirds in the 1970s), with the remaining 45 percent consisting of a small number of nationals. Most local and regional papers have become part of a small number of publishing conglomerates, and those in the same stable usually produce their information on nonregional matters collectively, distinguishing themselves by their coverage of regional affairs. Their explicitly political coverage is geared far more to the national political arena than to the local or regional one. Even local and regional elections are usually reported as reflections of national politics (van der Eijk et al. 1992b).

National newspapers are few in number, and five stand out as the major ones for the general public. *De Telegraaf* is by far the largest of them, with a circulation of approximately 777,000 in 1997–8. Politically, it is center-right, but it is especially strongly geared to nonpolitical matters like sports and human interest stories. The second largest national paper is the *Algemeen Dagblad,* with a circulation of almost 390,000. It is politically centrist and has a comparatively strong emphasis on economic affairs. *De Volkskrant,* with a circulation of some 347,000, is probably the most distinctive example of change in substantive profile as a consequence of depillarization. Formerly strictly Catholic, it has evolved into a secularized, left-of-center newspaper with a particularly strong appeal to public sector employees. It is widely seen as a semiquality paper in part because of its comparatively strong emphasis on providing the background for national and international news, but even more so because its op-ed page has evolved into one of the foremost platforms for political debate among politicians, spokespersons of economic and social interests, and social movements. The 266,000-circulation *NRC-Handelsblad* is widely considered to come closest of all Dutch newspapers to the international notion of a quality paper. It is neoliberal-conservative politically, concentrates on politics, economic affairs, and the arts, and carries relatively few sports and human interest stories. Together with *De Volkskrant,* it offers the most influential platform for national political debate and is a preferred place for many political, economic, and social leaders of various backgrounds to publicize their views. *Trouw* (circulation approximately 112,000) is the smallest of the general national newspapers. It is progressive Protestant in inclination, a semiquality paper distinguishesd by its high-quality coverage of Third World affairs and religious news.

Two shared characteristics of the newspapers in the Netherlands deserve special mention. The first is their dependence on press agencies for material. As mentioned earlier, the Dutch market is, and always has been, too small and too fragmented to allow individual papers to employ large reporting staffs. Thus, newspapers are unusually dependent for content on the services of press agencies, especially the ANP (Algemeen Nederlands Persbureau), for domestic political, social, and economic news. Under these circumstances, newspapers tend to distinguish themselves less by the stories they run and more by the spin they put on them. This style of journalism served the papers well in the *verzuiling* era as well as after it.

The second characteristic concerns the relationship between economic and editorial control of the press. This relationship is weak. Be-

tween the late 1960s and early 1970s, editorial staffs were able to capital-
ize on the wave of democratization washing over all major social institutions to wrest guarantees of editorial independence from owners
throughout almost the entire newspaper industry (Gosman 1993a).
These so-called editorial statutes (*redactiestatuten*) were instrumental in
ensuring that concentration of ownership and production facilities
would not be followed by a commensurate decline in the substantive and
stylistic diversity of the industry. They also help to explain why depillarization did not leave the field open for the establishment of an all-out
commercial or tabloid press.

Electronic Media

The Dutch radio and television landscape has changed dramatically
in less than a decade. The number of Dutch television channels jumped
from three in 1989 to eight in 1996, not counting the manifold cable and
satellite offerings. Five of the eight are commercial channels, and the remaining three are the preserve of the private broadcasting organizations
that until 1989 jointly monopolized the public airwaves. Named Nederland 1, Nederland 2, and Nederland 3, these channels capture approximately 40 percent of the television audience, with the remaining viewers
being distributed over the various commercial stations.

Seven different licensees broadcast on the three public channels. Some
of them (VARA, KRO, NCRV, AVRO, and VPRO) were founded during
the *verzuiling* era, and the others (TROS and EO) came into being after
the regulatory reforms of the mid-1960s.[7] All cooperate (through the
federative Nederlandse Omroep Stichting [NOS]) in producing newscasts and coverage of major events, including sports. Whereas each of
them formerly enjoyed time slots on each of the public channels, they
now form teams that operate just one channel. This change was forced
on them by a government trying to prop up the competitiveness of the
public channels by encouraging them to develop their own clear and distinctive substantive profile, blended from the separate identities of the
formerly independent broadcast organizations. The result of these efforts is not yet entirely clear, but it seems unavoidable that for distinct
and coherent channel identities to emerge, the distinctiveness of the licensees that share a single channel must diminish.

Those licensees broadcasting on the public channels are required by
law to offer a specific mix of educational, informational, cultural, and
entertainment programs. Some of these programs they produce themselves, others are bought from independent producers, and still others

are bought on the international market. Production costs are covered mainly by license fees and advertising income. Membership dues paid to the broadcast associations contribute relatively little. The license fee is set by the national government and levied on every household owning a radio or television set. Advertising income is distributed among the broadcast organizations according to their allotted broadcast time, not their audience share or program ratings.

The situation in early 1999 was that the public channels competed for audiences with the five commercial ones that now exist: RTL4, RTL5, Veronica, SBS6, and NET5.[8] Transmitting from Luxembourg, RTL4 was the first commercial station and remains by far the most popular, enjoying an audience share of some 18 to 20 percent. It positions itself as a general station, aiming at a broad public and competing directly with the public networks in offering a variety of programs: news, background, human interest, and entertainment. Its affiliate, RTL5, is slightly more up-market but, with a stable share of less than 5 percent, has never attracted a large audience. Veronica started operating in 1994. This occurred at almost the same time that SBS6, a Scandinavian-American–owned enterprise, was set up to cater to the seemingly lucrative Dutch market. More than either RTL4 or RTL5, both of these channels are oriented to entertainment programming, with Veronica aiming at a slightly younger audience than SBS6. Both have achieved a market share of about 10 percent. NET5 started its operations in late 1998. It is owned by the same corporation as SBS6 but aspires to be somewhat more classy.

Radio has similarly developed into a mixture of public and private networks. As with television, the programs of the (five) public radio channels are produced by the broadcast organizations, but the attempt to develop distinct channel profiles by forcing the organizations that share time slots on a single channel into collaborative and coherent programming has succeeded much better than it has for television. Dedicated public radio stations exist for news and sports, for pop music, for classical music, and so on. Commercial channels have proliferated since European regulations forced the Dutch state to admit them to the airwaves and to cable. More than a dozen of them now operate, some on a national scale (mostly specializing in one musical genre or another) and some regionally (adding regional information to their musical appeals). Overall, though, radio audiences have become quite fragmented in the past decade, particularly in the music and entertainment area. The one station, public or private, specializing in the coverage of social and political affairs is the public station Radio 1. Its audience, however, is limited, especially compared to that of television; at its daily peak, it numbers no more than some 3 percent of the adult population.

MACROPOLITICAL EFFECTS

The political effects of the Dutch media take different forms. Some of these effects characterize developed democratic systems generally and so will not be discussed here. These include media influence on the public and the political agenda, or their framing or priming impacts. More relevant to this chapter are the distinctive ways in which the media influence the political process in the Netherlands. Two such influences will be discussed. The first is a very broad perspective on the different ways in which the media and the political realm have interacted over time. The focus will then shift to some specifics of media behavior and content, and their consequences and changes over time. In the following section, the (changing) role of media in election campaigns will be described.

INTERACTION OVER TIME

As described previously, the mass media have been most important by far for their effects on the sociopolitical structure of *verzuiling*. The relationship between the two has been dialectical in nature, with a gradual, inescapable change from positive to negative reinforcement and feedback. After being shaped by the emerging sociopolitical regime of *verzuiling* in the late nineteenth and early twentieth centuries, the media were highly instrumental in perpetuating this regime for over half a century. Yet they could only do so in a way that would ultimately undermine a regime built on a fundamental contradiction. On the one hand, the media assumed deep cleavages between subcultures and, on the other, de facto pacified relations between them. Inescapably, the media – as well as other ideological structures in society – experienced ever greater difficulty in reproducing the subcultural identities required for the legitimization of the existing order. In this respect, the substantive media offerings of the different pillars could not but converge.

Contagion was inescapable too, since it was impossible to cut members of one subculture off from the radio and television broadcasts of the other *zuilen*. As convergence progressed, subcultural identities based on mutual animosity were undermined. When this situation is taken together with the fact that pillarization had never been complete and had always had opponents in the first place, it is easy to understand why the media had lost their ability to perpetuate the ideology of *verzuiling* by the early 1960s. Worse still, the advent at much the same time of extra-territorial, nonpillarized broadcasting transformed the positive feedback between the sociopolitical and media realms into a negative one. Separating themselves from the political parties and other subcultural organizations to which they once were linked, the media, especially in their news production and information services, embraced independent rather than apologetic journalism. They thus accelerated whatever depillarizing tendencies already existed in society and at the same time endowed these tendencies with an unparalleled degree of visibility, credibility, and legitimacy in the public eye.

Today, little remains of this once strong relationship between politics and the media. The country's political (and economic) borders have simply become less relevant in this respect. Of more importance is the EU, which is increasingly constituting an economic, legal, and political system in its own right. Its influence is growing on media systems whose audiences are kept largely national by language differences. Elaborating on these influences exceeds the scope of this examination of the Dutch case, although some remarks on them will still be made toward the end of the chapter.

POLITICALLY RELEVANT CONTENT

During pillarization, the leading media organizations were clearly apologetic, conveying subcultural elite perceptions of friends and foes, of goals and aspirations, as well as their definition of pressing problems and how to deal with them. Whatever the media conveyed in terms of background and opinions was clearly grist to the mill, but this situation changed with depillarization. Independence put a premium on presenting commentary and opinion from ideologically different sources, and internal pluralism became the dominant journalistic norm. To the extent that media organizations showed political leanings – and, particularly in the newspaper industry, many did – these were now usually less toward individual political parties and more toward generalized political causes, value systems, or lifestyles. These kinds of political, yet not necessarily partisan, views are most distinctive in the major national newspapers. *Trouw,* for example, is clearly progressive Christian in character and makes much of its sympathy for Third World causes, environmental protection, and progressive theology. *De Telegraaf,* by contrast, is socially and politically more conservative in tone, even evincing a certain dislike for all political parties and their strategic and tactical maneuvering. Of the national dailies, the *Volkskrant* is most strongly oriented toward postmaterial values such as education, multiculturalism, and socioeconomic equality, in addition to having a positive fascination for the political world that it shares with the more conservative and academically oriented *NRC-Handelsblad*. In all these cases, though, the norm of internal pluralism means that inclinations or tendencies do not translate into blatant bias or partisan propaganda.

Political leanings in favor of a cause or value system are less pronounced in the case of Dutch radio and television. One important reason is that, via their federative organization, NOS, the different broadcast organizations produce the newscasts on the public channels jointly; consequently, these newscasts are unlikely to reflect the central values of any one of these organizations. Even political talk shows and current affairs programs have become less distinctive in their politically relevant (let alone partisan) viewpoints as a consequence of collaborative productions by different broadcast organizations that share the use of the same public channel.

The shift from *zuil* identification to professional independence had serious consequences for political parties and other groups that had grown accustomed to easy access to, and uncritical coverage from, related, and hence friendly, media organizations. In the late 1960s and early 1970s, the major parties representing the various *zuilen* in Dutch society were suddenly confronted with what they often took to be journalistic hostility. Many politicians at that time could not cope well in this new environment, and almost all parties were able to adapt to it only after a new generation of leaders had come to the fore. Small and new parties that had never enjoyed the advantages of an affiliated broadcast organization tended to benefit most from these changes as media organizations, anxious to prove themselves independent of established power centers, took them to be more newsworthy and gave them more coverage than before.[9] This improved access to coverage was extended not only to small or new political parties, but also to new social movements. It was only in the early 1980s that the novelty value, and hence media coverage, of these movements declined (Duyvendak, et al. 1992).

The political consequences of *zuil*-independent broadcasting go beyond the ease or difficulty political groups have in obtaining favorable media attention. While news value used to be defined by party- or pillar-driven criteria, it is increasingly a function of media-driven ones. In terms of bias, the operative criteria for news value often favor novelty over continuity and sensationalism over relevance (McQuail 1992, 200,

213–22). Moreover, news value thus defined seems to attract larger audiences, so that as channels proliferate and competition between them for audience share increases, journalistic styles change and novelty and sensationalism become more the broadcasting norm. The media become more active in what McQuail (1992) calls the "self-origination" of news. Rather than simply conveying information and perhaps some commentary, journalists become activists resorting to practices as diverse as investigative reporting, sensationalism, personalizing, and occasional attempts at muckraking. While this style of journalism is unlikely to favor any particular party, social group, or political cause consciously or consistently, it tends to be most harmful for dominant groups and most rewarding for any group or party presenting itself as whistle-blowing, novel, or different. If such bias became dominant, it would risk eroding diffuse support for the democratic political process, as the oversights, mistakes, or transgressions of prominent individuals or the major parties are increasingly the political diet that the media feed to their consumers. The argument to be made in the next section, however, is that, at least to this point in time, Dutch election campaigns and the media through which voters largely experience them perform the important function of restoring and reinforcing diffuse systemic support.

CAMPAIGN COMMUNICATIONS

Dutch parliamentary elections are conducted under a system of proportional representation in which the entire country serves as a single constituency. The number of seats at stake was increased from 100 to 150 in 1956 so that, today, winning no more than two-thirds of 1 percent of the votes cast suffices to obtain parliamentary representation. Large numbers of parties win at least a single seat, and even larger numbers compete in the election. Every election since 1956 has seen at least 15 and sometimes as many as 30 party lists presented to the voters. Moreover, never fewer than 7 and often as many as 12 or 13 of them have been successful in winning at least one seat. Parties control nominations by presenting an ordered list of candidates. Since it is very difficult to be elected out of list order via preferential votes, parties, and not candidates, are the focal point of attention in elections and campaigns. The major exceptions to this observation are the list leaders, who tend to personify their parties in the eyes of voters.

No single party can reasonably hope to acquire more than 35 percent of the vote, and hence of the seats in Parliament. Governments, therefore, are inevitably multiparty coalitions. These simple parameters define very specific tasks for the major parties. On the one hand, they must maximize their share of the vote in order to gain as many seats as possible. On the other hand, competition has to be restrained so as not to alienate prospective coalition partners.[10] The dilemma of how to navigate between the Scylla of waging too aggressive a campaign and the Charybdis of being too timid has been further complicated since the 1970s as a result of the largest party's being awarded an extra prize: the right to have the first attempt to form a coalition. Such considerations do not, of course, weigh on small parties that in all likelihood will not be part of whatever government is formed. Their problem is to convince voters that supporting them will not be tantamount to wasting their vote.

The Netherlands had compulsory voting for most of the twentieth century. Its abolition in 1970 had only a limited impact on the parliamentary election turnout, which remained around the 80 percent level (van der Eijk and Oppenhuis 1990; Oppenhuis 1996). Parties thus were able to pay less attention to getting out the vote and more to influencing voters' choice of party.[11] In the heyday of *verzuiling*, election campaigns were predominantly defensive and identity-reaffirming in character (Lijphart 1974; Bakvis 1981). With depillarization, however, parties found themselves confronted with increasing numbers of voters without set party loyalties but with rather stable multiple party preferences instead. The implication is that purely defensive electoral strategies are doomed to fail because they require that the potential voters for a party not be attracted to other parties, a condition that ceased to exist when *verzuiling* disappeared (van der Eijk and Niemöller 1984; Tillie 1995; Oppenhuis 1996).

In their efforts to mobilize supporters and convert waverers, parties find themselves heavily dependent on the free publicity provided by the media. Government regulations and the small size of their campaign chests combine to prevent parties from waging campaigns in which the paid advertising they control is of great significance. Political advertisements have never been allowed on public radio or television channels, and this situation is unlikely to change in the near future. Parties that have at least one seat in Parliament are provided by law with a small amount of direct and controlled access to radio and television, which is of equal size, regardless of the number of seats the party holds. During the 1994 and 1998 campaigns, this amounted to six three-minute television slots for each party. These party-controlled broadcasts attract very small audiences (2 percent on average in 1994) and are generally considered to be of marginal importance at best (Brants et al. 1995).

The introduction of commercial stations made it possible in principle to buy radio and television time for political advertisements, but the parties have barely availed themselves of this opportunity thus far. Plans for political advertising on the commercial RTL4 channel in the 1994 campaign were withdrawn by all parties on the urging of the cabinet minister for media affairs; she feared a deterioration of the quality of public debate if political advertisements were used. Some political advertisements were aired nonetheless for the first time in 1994 on a few small local and regional radio and television stations not subject to the same regulatory regime as the public channels. Still, the limited financial means of the Netherlands' political parties makes it unlikely that this is the beginning of a large-scale, irreversible trend. The major barrier to expansion is that parties' funds for waging campaigns come from their dues-paying members, and the years since the early 1960s have seen a dramatic decline in membership for almost all parties (Katz and Mair 1992; Koole 1992).[12] The resulting shortfall of income is unlikely to be made up by contributions from corporations or other organizations. While such funding is certainly legal, it is so controversial that so far all parties have refrained voluntarily from accepting even unsolicited contributions.

All in all, then, the shortage of funds makes Dutch election campaigns a relatively low-cost affair. The combined spending of all parties per voter fluctuates between $0.30 and $0.60, which is about a quarter of what parties spend in Italy or Denmark and barely one-twentieth of what German and American parties together spend per eligible voter (Koole 1992, 369–71).

The upshot is that the Dutch parties are heavily dependent on free publicity to reach voters. Their most important sources of this publicity are television, in the form of newscasts, current affairs programs, and political talk shows, and the national newspapers. Other media, such as radio or regional newspapers, are less important because they have smaller audiences and rarely set the agenda or tone of the campaign.[13] This kind of publicity was easily obtained in the pillarization era, when the major parties could depend on newspapers and broadcast organizations that were part of their respective pillars. For smaller parties not supported by a network of affiliated media organizations, it was then much harder to reach the electorate effectively through the media. Since the 1970s, however, the inequality of access has decreased (see note 9), and *all* political parties have had to work hard to win media coverage. The problem they always face, of course, is that they cannot guarantee that free publicity will be sympathetic in tone and content. Consequently, they have to invest heavily in damage prevention and, when necessary, damage control. This has contributed greatly to the professionalization and centralization of parties' election campaigns (van Praag 1992; Brants and van Praag 1995).

TELEVISION

Newscast exposure is particularly sought after by political parties since newscasters are the main source of political information for about two-thirds of voters. Moreover, many citizens regard television news as the most trustworthy source of information available. Even during pillarization, newscasts were nonpillarized in character, which has undoubtedly contributed to their lasting image as nonpartisan and honest. A single newscast used to reach a very large audience, but not so today with the proliferation of channels and the resulting audience fragmentation. As late as 1988, when the only channels available were the three public ones, the average daily audience for the 8 P.M. television news was almost half of the national electorate of slightly over 10 million. Since then, this figure has dropped sharply to about 1.5 to 2 million people, partly because of competition from the news programs on commercial stations (attracting almost 1 million people) and partly because of a proliferation of abbreviated versions of the major daily newscast aired at different times during the day on the public channels. Since 1995, the three public and four commercial channels together provide some 15 different newscasts per day.

In spite of this fragmentation, the reach of newscasts and their image of impartiality and objectivity still make them highly valued sources of free publicity. The strategies parties adopt to get newscast coverage are those used in other democracies as well; among other things, they stage campaign events deemed to be newsworthy, announce important speeches in advance, and schedule events so that they can be reported in a newscast while at the same time minimizing the time available for political opponents to react. In this struggle for air time, the large number of parties and their unequal size prevent broadcasters from applying simple rules of fairness and balance in coverage. The larger parties enjoy an advantage because of their greater political weight, but this does not mean that small parties are entirely neglected. Parties in government have a clearly higher publicity value because they are linked to actual policy and because they can stage events so that their leaders can don the mantle of caretakers of the common interest (attending international summit meetings, announcing new government policies, and so on). Opposition parties often get coverage because the media like to highlight the different sides of an issue by asking one of them to comment on government actions. For all parties, though, the sine qua non for gaining and making good use of this kind of free publicity is increasingly a strong, professionally run campaign organization.

Since the 1970s, public channels have throughout the campaign reserved a set amount of their broadcast time for election news. Their reporting style was rather like what Semetko et al. (1991) refer to as "sacerdotal" in the manner of the public-service British Broadcasting Corporation (BBC). Since 1994, election campaigns have also been covered in the news programs of some Dutch commercial stations, RTL4 in 1994 and RTL4 and SBS6 in 1998. To use the terminology of Semetko et al. once again, a more pragmatic style, such as that of the commercial National Broadcasting Company (NBC) in the United States, might have been expected from these commercial stations. Such a style means that there is no special campaign news desk, campaign stories have to compete with other items for inclusion on the basis of news value, and a much smaller staff is assigned to cover just the campaign. In fact, however, the differences between the Dutch public and commercial stations were not that great. To be sure, the public stations provided more extensive coverage of the six-week campaign, devoting 22 percent of their total newscast time in 1994 to it compared with the 15 percent of the commercial station (RTL4). Beyond this, however, there were some striking similarities between the two types of station in both 1994 and 1998. Both reacted to the parties rather than trying to initiate news stories, and both devoted considerably more time to the "hoopla" and "horse race" aspects of the campaign than to the discussion of its policy or issues. In addition, both paid considerably more attention to the larger parties than to the smaller ones, and both focused heavily on the list leaders of the parties, although this focus was itself partly the product of the parties' own decision to personalize their campaign strategies.

These similarities should not be seen as simply a function of convergence resulting from competition between public and private channels, however. They existed before commercial television was introduced into the Netherlands. A study of the four election campaigns from 1982 to 1994 uncovered a steady decline (from 60 to 35 percent of total coverage) in attention to policies and issues in public station newscasts. Moreover, the slack was taken up mainly by increased attention to the horse race aspects of the campaign (Brants and van Praag 1995, 164–5).

It would be incorrect, however, to assume that the differences are of the same degree between the public and *all* the commercial stations. In 1998, the commercial station SBS6 adopted a style of coverage that differed in important respects from from that of its competitors. Whereas both the public stations and RTL4 showed respect for the political process, SBS6 radiated skepticism, if not downright distrust, of parties and politicians. The result was an almost total neglect of the parties' campaign agendas or the horse race aspect of the campaign. Instead, the relationship between journalists and politicians was confrontational, and entertainment vied with substance in their interactions (van Praag and Brants 1999). This finding illustrates vividly that competition between stations (even commercial ones) does not necessarily lead to convergence in presentational styles and formats, but instead can result in a variety of formats that are (hoped to be) differentially attractive to different publics with different lifestyles.

Current affairs programs and various kinds of talk shows also offer the parties free publicity. Although the audience for each of these programs is smaller than that of newscasts, their combined audience is formidable, and together these programs offer more air time than newscasts. In contrast to newscasts, current affairs programs on public television are produced by the various broadcast organizations separately. But despite their efforts to remain nonpartisan, none of them rivals the newscasts in terms of having an aura of impartiality. Their constant need for interesting and newsworthy content turns them into valued targets for political parties that, as some of the principal providers of relevant stories, see opportunities to regain some influence over program content.

Over time, the increased competition for audience share in Dutch broadcasting has promoted a tendency to enliven and dramatize current affairs programs. One successful recipe has been to mix elements of entertainment and information, particularly in talk shows that emphasize the human interest side of politics. But although this "infotainment" trend has been clearly visible since the mid-1980s, the free publicity available to parties and politicians is still largely of the pure information kind. An alternative strategy for increasing audience share is to dramatize politics by emphasizing conflict, scandal, and disclosures from investigative reporting. This strategy, of course, increases the kind of publicity that the parties would rather avoid because it tends to exacerbate intra-party dissension and can lead to miscalculations and mistakes in damage control, sometimes with dire electoral consequences. An example involves the Christian Democratic Party (CDA) in the 1994 election. Entirely unconnected to his political position, Eelco Brinkman, the party leader, was commissioner of a commercial firm that was accused during the campaign of (minor) financial fraud. Although it was almost immediately clear that the CDA leader had no knowledge of or involvement in an affair that would otherwise hardly have been noticed, the story commanded almost exclusive media attention for many days, carrying the unmistakable, if implicit, message that there was more to it than met the eye, strong doubts were in order about the moral character of the CDA leader, and so on. To some extent assisted by Brinkman's poor damage control, this implied message became so strong that it exacerbated other (somewhat dormant) problems in the already faltering CDA campaign. The self-propelling nature of this process is best illustrated by a comment in *De Telegraaf*: if the CDA leader were to show himself able to walk on water, it would only be reported as his inability to swim. In earlier elections similar processes occurred, to the cost of the neoliberal conservative Volkspartij voor Vrijeid en Democratie (VVD–1986), the left-liberal D66 (formerly Democraten 66 – 1982), or the social democratic Partij van de Arbeid (PvdA – 1981). To be sure, the damage inflicted was in all cases also attributable to already existing intraparty conflict, strategic misjudgment, mistakes, poor crisis management, and so on, but the media's assumption of wrongdoing generated problems that would not otherwise have existed.

The fragmentation of audiences over different channels and over many different kinds of programs makes it difficult to assess the importance of any single program or type of program. The political importance of all of them combined, however, may be illustrated in two ways. First, current affairs programs and the like spend approximately three times as much time on items concerning politicians and parties as newscasts do. Consequently, parties cannot afford to ignore them as publicity outlets. Severe logistical problems are the inevitable outcome. Campaign strategy is increasingly dictated at the center, and the quality of parties' campaign organizations has become crucial for their ability to cope effectively with the problems and opportunities provided by free publicity. Second, current affairs programs often act as the primary definers and framers of what becomes newsworthy over short periods of the campaign. In this sense, they help to shape campaign dynamics.

What politicians say on television provokes reactions in the next day or two from opponents, which in turn encourages further debate as the truth, consistency, or viability of political statements and promises becomes subject to journalistic scrutiny. This autonomous media contribution to the dynamics of election campaigns has been documented for all campaigns after the era of pillarization (Brants et al. 1982; van der Eijk and van Praag 1987; Kleinnijenhuis and Scholten 1989; Brants and van Praag 1995; Kleinijenhuis et al. 1995a, b; 1998; van Praag and Brants 1999).

Debates

Televised debates are a major source of free publicity for the parties. Since the mid-1970s, it has been customary for the leaders of the major parties to confront each other in a debate that is usually held the evening before election day. The precise format of the debate has varied a little from campaign to campaign, but it consists basically of one or several political journalists questioning each of the participants in turn, with the other participants then being given the opportunity to comment on the initial answer. Arduous negotiations are necessary to solve anew in each campaign the biggest problem in mounting these debates: which parties to include or exclude. The larger parties like to keep the number small, implicitly conveying the message to viewers that only a few parties really matter. Working in the opposite direction, however, is the Dutch political culture's emphasis on consensus and tolerance. This puts the onus on all parties to avoid giving the impression of being intransigent and unreasonable.

Every campaign thus far has seen a different solution to this problem, partly because of shifts in the electoral strengths of the different parties (either in Parliament or as projected by opinion polls). A number of campaigns have been characterized by a three-way debate between the (leaders of) CDA, PvdA, and VVD. At other times, the leader of D66 (Democrats, left-liberal) was added as a fourth participant, and in 1994 and 1998 the leader of GreenLeft (left-ecologist) took part as well. Increasingly, the election-eve debate has been supplemented by additional debates earlier in the campaign, often between only two parties, one of which is usually a small party not included in the final debate. Up to this point, commercial television has altered these arrangements only insofar as yet another debate has been added to the campaign calendar. Televised debates, in particular the one on the day before the election, have always enjoyed large audiences; sometimes almost half of the electorate tunes in (van der Eijk and van Praag 1987; Brants and van Praag 1995).

PRINT MEDIA

The final source of free publicity for political parties is newspapers. Of these, the five largest national daily newspapers are generally considered to be the most important for the campaign and for public debate on politics. As argued earlier, nonpartisanship and internal pluriformity were depillarization's most significant legacy for the politically relevant contents of newspapers. Today virtually no newspaper is linked to a specific political party, and explicit partisan endorsements during campaigns are rare. Unlike the situation in the era of *verzuiling*, newspapers do not now see themselves as having a partisan advocacy role. Rather, they seek to contribute to the public debate between ideologies, creeds, values, and political opinions. Thus, their columns are opened up to politicians of different hues and to supporters of all kinds of parties, interest groups, citizen initiatives, and so on. In addition, interviews, solicited comments, op-ed pages, and the like are all used to present a variety of viewpoints rather than just one.

This is not to say, however, that reporting and commentary are neutral in their treatment of the various parties. Detailed analysis of their content shows the major national newspapers to be evaluative in three ways (Kleinnijenhuis and Scholten 1989; Kleinijenhuis et al. 1995a, b). First, differences in their explicitly stated political opinions notwithstanding, their implicit evaluations of the performance of parties and politicians, and of the success of policies, display striking similarities. This convergence is to some extent the result of all newspapers' tendency to concentrate on what is negative about the political parties much more than on what is positive about them. Second, all newspapers focus on power and its exercise, leading all of them to devote much more attention to government and large parties than to smaller ones. Equally, they focus heavily on the opinion poll standing of the major parties and on indicators of national economic performance, especially during election campaigns. These "objective" data thus constitute sources of stories and commentary that are identical for all media and that result in a surprisingly common portrayal of who is doing well and who is in trouble. Finally, while their evaluative content may be very similar, newspapers are still more critical of parties the more the political views of these parties, as expressed in left–right terms, are different from their own.

CONTROLLED COMMUNICATION

Not all political communications in Dutch elections are based on free publicity. The parties themselves directly control a small part of it. Most of this is traditional and designed to keep the parties in the public eye. Billboards and election posters fall into this category. They have the advantage of allowing parties to project what they see to be their strong points by using catchy slogans and eye-catching designs. Other popular forms of controlled publication are election and newspaper advertisements. On the whole, though, the meager financial resources of Dutch parties mean that the total amount of controlled communication in campaigns is small. Nonetheless, some interesting observations can still be made about it.

The first concerns the almost total absence of negative campaigning in the Netherlands. As noted earlier, parties hesitate to wage too aggressive a campaign for fear of alienating prospective coalition partners. Restraint even stretches to small parties that cannot realistically expect to be included in any coalition. No party can expect to ignore the cultural norms of conciliation and tolerance without impunity. The result is that their campaign messages rarely focus on the defects or failures of opponents, emphasizing instead, and often in quite general terms, their own strengths. The party leader, who is usually the list leader as well, may, for example, be the centerpiece of a highly personalized campaign strategy. Slogans may be designed to associate a party in the public mind with competent leadership – often with an added sense of urgency. In 1986, "Let Lubbers finish the job" was the CDA slogan when its leader, Ruud Lubbers, was riding high in popularity after his first term as prime minister. Even more personalized was the simple PvdA slogan in 1994, "Vote Kok."

A second observation is that parties strive in their communications to emphasize the strategic implications of voting one way or another. Major parties stress that voting for small parties is tantamount to wasting the vote, particularly when the opinion polls suggest that the race for first place, and the right to the first attempt at forming a coalition, is a close contest. Smaller parties counter by emphasizing their steadfastness in defense of particular values that cannot be entrusted to major parties whose behavior in office is necessarily more equivocal than their campaign promises. Along the same lines, parties try to shape the outcome of the election in their own favor by raising during the campaign the issue of the coalition government that will be formed. In 1981, for example, the VVD hoped to form a center-right coalition with the CDA, but could do so only if the two parties together won a parliamentary majority. This outcome, however, was threatened by D66's (left-liberal) obvious attractiveness at the time to potential VVD voters. The VVD responded with a newspaper advertisement spelling out the danger that voting for D66 risked putting Labor in power in a center-left coalition.

Such anecdotes notwithstanding, though, controlled communications are far less significant for Dutch election outcomes than is the far greater free publicity that the parties receive in the course of the campaign.

MEDIA EFFECTS

The effects, if any, that political communications through the media have on election outcomes remain difficult to establish definitively. What voters actually see, hear, or read during campaigns is virtually unknowable in nonexperimental situations. Moreover, not only is the electorate fragmented in terms of overall patterns of communication consumption, but also voters' media usage and exposure may vary from day to day. Finally, voters' selective reception and retention of campaign communications, as well perhaps as their active interpretation, acceptance, or rejection of them all, complicate the hypothesis of a simple linkage between specific communications and effects on political attitudes and behavior.

These qualifications notwithstanding, it must be said that survey-based research in the Netherlands has come to largely negative conclusions on the issue of media effects during election campaigns. Changes in voters' party preference, in the party for which they actually vote, or in their evaluation of party leaders are far more often than not unrelated to the use of specific media or to exposure to specific messages. As Brants et al. (1982) explain it, the situation is like a tug-of-war in which everyone pulls as hard as possible in different directions. The result is that nobody advances, but nevertheless no one can afford to stop since the first team to do so will lose ground to others.

To make this general observation is not to say that the media never influence election outcomes. They have been known to have a discernible directional influence in a number of instances. The 1986 election is a case in point. The VVD lost a record nine seats that year, which prevented most observers from recognizing that it was the only party to gain a significant number of votes at the very end of the campaign because of its leader's strong performance in the election-eve debate. Without the debate, the VVD's loss would have been two or three seats greater. Its gains were made at the expense of a party (D66) that was deemed too small that year to warrant a place in the debate. Interestingly, none of the other small parties that were excluded from the debate suffered large last-day losses (van der Eijk and van Praag 1987). These findings illustrate not only that debates occasionally have a differential effect, but also that not debating is not necessarily a setback, but only so under specific circumstances. Finally, it must be emphasized that the total differential impact of such effects on the overall results is quite limited. Two or three seats out of 150 is simply not a very large net movement.

The 1994 election campaign was heavily researched. It also happened to become an important election because of the unparalleled shifts in parties' vote shares. The CDA lost 20 seats and the PvdA 12, whereas the VVD and D66 gained 9 and 12 seats, respectively. There were also important changes affecting smaller parties, particularly the strong emergence of a party for the elderly that won six seats. Yet, these losses and gains are associated with particular patterns of media consumption or exposure only to a very limited extent. Weekly opinion polls show that support for the major parties changed considerably in the final months before the election. During that time, the position of the CDA declined continuously, D66 support remained more or less stable, and the PvdA and VVD improved their public standing. Were these changes the result of how the media covered the campaign and treated the various parties and their leaders? A single exception apart, they were not. Changes in the pattern of support for the parties were virtually the same for all voters, regardless of what (if any) national newspaper they read and whether they watched the news on public or commercial television. Evidently, then, whatever the differences between these information sources in news content, implicit or explicit evaluation of parties and party leaders, journalistic style, and so forth, they were inconsequential for the way voters' opinions and party preferences evolved during the campaign. The one important exception to this general finding involved the PvdA and its leader, Wim Kok. Support for this party grew much more among regular television news viewers than among voters who rarely followed the news on television. To be sure, PvdA support also increased in this latter group, but to a significantly lesser degree. For the other major parties, no such differences were found. Exposure to television news thus reduced PvdA losses, but not at the expense of any other major party in particular (Couvret et al. 1995).

The general conclusion of no systematic media effects is confirmed only when movements in support are correlated with content analyses of media treatment of the various parties (Kleinnijenhuis et al. 1995a and 1995b). This exercise makes it even more difficult to credit the media with any part in the explanation of why some parties prospered while others floundered. That is, some parties lost in spite of extensive and favorable media coverage, some gained (or lost) as many seats as others despite being treated very differently by the media, and so on.

But while media exposure may have little or no systematic effect on the vote, it generates strong effects in other ways. The same studies cited earlier found pronounced increases in positive evaluations of parties and their leaders over the course of the campaign. Since the media are virtually the only sources of political information and imagery for the large majority of voters, such changes may be plausibly labeled "communications effects." Interestingly, though, these effects are common to all voters, regardless of their patterns of media consumption or exposure to specific campaign communications. Such effects may be masked when interest focuses on the implications of differential exposure or media use for voting behavior, but they are no less real. Viewed from a systemic perspective, election campaigns in the Netherlands are indeed important for the general increases during them in popular esteem for virtually all mainstream parties and politicians. When the parties benefit equally, their relative strengths remain unaltered. When they do not, as in 1994, some (such as the PvdA and VVD) gain and others (such as the CDA) lose votes over the course of the campaign.

In general, then, the evidence suggests that Dutch election campaigns shore up the public standing of political parties and politicians, thereby helping to restore the diffuse support (Easton 1965) that erodes between elections simply as the result of governments making hard policy decisions that create winners and losers. This, of course, is not a necessary feature of election campaigns. Rather, it may be the particular result of the absence of negative campaigning and the restrained interparty competition that flows from parties' need to collaborate in the formation of a coalition government after the election.

THE FUTURE OF DUTCH BROADCASTING

The terms of debate on the structure and regulation of the Dutch broadcasting system have changed markedly since the late 1980s. Earlier, the virtues or drawbacks of a pillarized media structure were the focus of public debate, whereas now the respective (dis)advantages of a public or a commercial system are at issue. A change in discourse has occurred in which the term "public" has acquired a meaning quite different from the one it had in earlier times. Before the 1960s, "public" implied a nonpillarized national broadcasting system in the mold of the British BBC. But since the late 1980s, the existing system has increasingly been labeled "public." This is something of a misnomer since the broadcasting system consists of a collection of competing private organizations (the broadcast organizations) that are largely autonomous in their programming. The only public aspects of the system are the government's allocation of broadcast time and finances and its enforcement of general regulatory principles.

Of course, the current "public" system is obviously commercial too, in the sense that it derives a large part of its income from advertisements (see note 5), but it remains distinct from the private sector in two important respects. First, in the public system the private broadcasting organizations bear responsibility for programming, whereas the public agency is responsible for generating income from advertisements. This separation of responsibilities does not exist, or is weaker, in a commercial system. Second, the public system must devote a certain proportion of its broadcast time to educational, cultural, and informational programming, while this same responsibility is not placed on the commercial system.[14] In combination, these two differences are commonly thought to promote higher cultural, informational, or even moral value, as well as greater diversity in the viewpoints articulated on the public as opposed to commercial channels.

Regardless of the merits (or otherwise) of this argument, what is currently at issue in the Netherlands is the definition of the appropriate mix of public and commercial broadcasting, and at what cost to whom. The alternatives currently being debated can be situated between two poles. At one extreme is the containment by all possible means of commercial radio and television, preventing further growth of their market share. How this goal can be achieved is not immediately obvious, since both technological advances and European law make it impossible to prevent Dutch viewers from viewing commercial stations. One often discussed possibility is to enhance the quality and attractiveness of what the public channels offer, thus increasing their audience share and advertising income. The problem with this argument is that containment (and possibly even rollback) of commercial broadcasting is desired for reasons that by definition violate the conditions for success. The offerings of the public system should, according to this view, be distinct from the "lowest common denominator" fare that commercial stations offer in order to draw as large an audience as possible. But if public stations succeeded in offering other, more varied and distinctive programs, these would almost inevitably draw smaller audiences and produce less advertising income. The financial basis of the public system in its current form would thus be threatened and the containment, let alone rollback, of commercial stations would be made less likely. The alternatives to advertising income – increases in license fees or direct state subsidies – lack political support in the neoliberal political climate of 2000.

The other pole in the debate is the abandonment of public broadcasting altogether, the abolition of the license fee and the reduction of the government's role to one of guaranteeing fair play in the marketplace. In its extreme version, this proposal lacks political support, but a more moderate version, questioning the almost sacrosanct status of public broadcasting and advocating a larger role for the commercial channels, now looms large in the political debate. Political support for stubborn defense of the public system declined during the 1980s and 1990s, partly because of widespread, if often reluctant, recognition that the commercial broadcasting sector is here to stay and partly because of changes in Dutch politics.

Traditionally, the CDA and the PvdA were the staunchest defenders of the public system and the private broadcast organizations comprising it. Together with most of the smaller parties (orthodox Christians, left-of-labor groups and Greens), they emphasized the need to guarantee minority access, the virtues of ideological pluriformity, and the low quality of programming that commercial television was likely to bring. Starting in the late 1980s, the PvdA moved steadily away from this position, but without fully embracing its opposite – defense of consumer autonomy and the allegedly greater efficiency and lower costs of a commercial system subject to market forces. More consequential, however, has been the recent eclipse of the CDA's clout in Dutch politics. Its size and ideological positioning between the PvdA and VVD had always given the party an uncontested and, except once, leading role in any Dutch coalition government. It was politically emasculated, however, in 1994 when, following unprecedented electoral losses, a government of which it was not a member took office for the first time since 1917. Thus, the political force that was most strongly committed to the public system and the traditional broadcast organizations was not represented in government. The stage was set for a significant shift in broadcasting policy.

The 1994 social democrat–liberal government of the PvdA, VVD, and D66 was intent on maintaining a viable public system that nonetheless coexisted with commercial broadcasting. The commercial stations may transmit from other countries (as with RTL4 and RTL5 broadcasting from Luxembourg), from the Netherlands or the programs may be delivered directly by cable, with no actual signal emission. Stations based in the Netherlands, however, are subject to the same regulations governing the content of advertisements as the public channels. In contrast to the public channels, though, commercial broadcasters are not subject to rules governing the allocation of broadcast time to different types of program. The existing private broadcasting associations of the public system can choose to go their own way by acquiring commercial status, thereby gaining more freedom in programming but at the same time forsaking all right to revenues from the public system. Broadcast associations in the public system can get a five-year license on condition that they commit themselves to strong collaborative programming with the other licensed associations using the same channel. It is thus hoped that each of the public channels will develop its own clearly recognizable programmatic identity and that their loss of audience share to the commercial channels will be arrested. Licenses for commercial as well as public channels are granted for five-year periods, which gives governments the opportunity to revise broadcasting policy regularly. It also keeps pressure on the private associations in the public system to deliver on their grudgingly given promise to develop channel identities and engage in collaborative programming.

Radio broadcasting has already been reorganized along these lines. For television, reorganization got underway in September 1995. At the time of writing, it is too early to judge the fate of this new broadcasting policy. Success will be measured by the ability of the public channels to retain a sufficiently large audience share to be able to finance themselves from advertising revenue and license fees kept at their current level. If the policy is not successful, then the already existing pressure to reduce the number of public channels will undoubtedly increase.

In sum, it is clear that the Dutch media system, particularly the organizational structure of the electronic media, will remain in flux for some time. But whatever form it eventually takes, it will remain essentially a dual system of public and commercial channels, with a mixed financial system for public channels drawing on both license fees and advertising revenues. The currently existing fragmentation within each of the public channels is likely to decrease as the government forces the traditional broadcast organizations to give up their individual autonomy and develop collective channel identities instead. As such, the system will increasingly resemble the dual and mixed financing systems that exist elsewhere in Europe, such as in Germany, Spain, and Switzerland. At the same time, it will remain different from systems, like the American one, whose shape is overwhelmingly determined by the commercial broadcasting sector.

THE MEDIA AND THE QUALITY OF DUTCH DEMOCRACY

This review of the relationship between politics and the media in the Netherlands over the last century brings us to the question of where it stands today. Should it be evaluated positively or negatively? Do past trends portend a brighter or darker future for Dutch democracy? Bearing in mind that the answers to such questions will obviously be based on the author's own normative premises, and that these may or may not coincide with those of the reader, a number of propositions can be made.

When a number of traditional requirements for a functioning, healthy system of democratic government are examined, the future looks bright. Take the printed media. Freedom of press remains deeply entrenched and taken for granted. Despite a reduction in their number in past decades, citizens can choose from an assortment of daily newspapers that offer a meaningful choice between substantive profiles. None of them assaults its readers with blatant propaganda or one-sided partisanship; instead, all provide for the expression of different points of view in their columns. Literacy is almost universal, affluence is high, and newspapers are comparatively cheap, all factors that allow the large majority of citizens to use newspapers on a daily basis to inform themselves about the world around them. Add to newspapers the large number of other politically relevant print media (general public opinion weeklies, special interest group periodicals, etc.), and a vast supply of politically relevant information can be seen to exist and to be used regularly.

A similar abundance exists in the realms of radio and television. A large number of noncensored offerings is available to virtually all households in the country at low cost. The public channels are subject to government regulation, the main effect of which is to limit the amount of pure entertainment without affecting the style, tone, choice of topics, or evaluative contents of politically relevant broadcasts. Newscasts on the public channels have a long-standing and justified reputation for nonpartisanship and are broadcast several times during the day. There are plenty of politically relevant current affairs programs providing information and opinion, some of which are produced for special clienteles, such as foreign language minorities in the country or children and young adolescents. Commercial channels exist in addition to the public ones, providing additional newscasts and coverage of political affairs. Using cable or satellites, those who have sufficient passive mastery of other languages can also access American, British, German, Belgian, or French newscasts or current affairs programs. Virtually every household possesses television and radio sets and is hooked up to cable.

The open character of the society and the disappearance of cleavages that previously divided the population into stable and mutually exclusive segments both contribute to a kind of media competition that prevents any one source from systematically misleading or manipulating its audience. At the same time, diversity of programming allows for the airing of truly diverse viewpoints and values. What more, one might wonder, could one wish for in a real-world democracy? There are flaws in this picture, however. A critical perspective on how a media system enhances democracy is how well citizens

> understand the significance of what they are doing. Such a criterion does not require all voters to become fully acquainted with all party policies on all issues of the day. . . . [A] democratic test of a political communication system would be how far it enabled people to make choices in accord with the politics they wished to support, implying an availability of information on the basis of which they could grasp the policy goals and intentions that parties and leaders would pursue if given power. (Blumler 1982, 633)

The realization of this state of affairs would, for this author, require

> not unprocessed data resources but a well-armed set of informational agents, able to act effectively on our behalf as mediators who can (1) scan the information environment for us; (2) reduce and relate it to a coherent view of the main issues that society faces; (3) update that agenda of main issues as required; and (4) organize a coherent dialogue about how best to tackle them. (Blumler 1983, 633)

Seen from this perspective, not all recent changes in the Dutch media landscape are welcome. The competition for audience share between public and commercial television has promoted the emergence of media-driven criteria for news value – novelty over continuity, sensationalism over relevance, as well as a style of journalism referred to as "self-origination" – that often militates against both the articulation of coherent views on politics and engagement in a coherent dialogue between them. This situation has been worsened by the fragmentation of audiences, which may help political entrepreneurs and political consultants to target specific publics and tailor specific messages for them. At the same time, however, it undermines the notion of a single electorate (or, in more archaic terms, a polity) whose members are exposed to the same information and debates and make choices on the basis of their different values or priorities. In the specific case of the Netherlands, such a single polity was best approximated after depillarization and before the fragmentation of the media in the wake of the 1989 introduction of commercial broadcasting.

The most important shortcoming of the Dutch media system, though, comes not from changes in its operational structure, but from its failure to keep up with changes in the location of the political realm. Over the past two decades, the locus of political power has shifted, with clear implications for many of the policies affecting the daily lives of the Dutch people, as well as for the direction in which their country is moving in the long run. In many ways, the relevant political arena for the Dutch is now Brussels, the seat of EU power. To maintain their political relevance, the Dutch media should have reacted by providing greater coverage of this second arena, scanning it for information, structuring it in coherent ways, and relating new events to it in such a way as to encourage informed and coherent public debate on the interconnections between domestic and EU politics. In reality, however, this kind of EU media coverage is all but nonexistent. The amount of media-provided information on EU politics is extremely small and is rarely structured in ways that help citizens to understand its significance for, and impact on, their daily lives. Even less does it allow them to grasp how their national government and political parties are involved in EU policy decisions. Domestic political elites are thereby allowed to pursue short-term political strategies that, when convenient, enable them to hide from public scrutiny their own involvement in making EU policies, to claim credit for the benefits these policies appear to bring, or to blame others (unnamed "Eurocrats") for the costs associated with them.

By their neglect of EU politics and the role in them of domestic political elites, the Dutch media fail to make their essential contribution to democracy, that is, to illuminate who exercises power and thereby ensure that power holders account for their (in)actions in public debate and elections.[15] The fact that Dutch media are in this respect hardly different from those in other member states of the EU is little consolation (see Van der Eijk and Franklin 1996). The most important challenge for the media of all the member states of the EU is to help create an informed and structured public awareness of the interplay of EU and domestic politics. Only then will citizens be in a position to make choices that reflect their values and interests, and only then will the interactions between citizens and elites help to make those wielding power accountable for their (in)actions.

Notes

1. In spite of changes over the course of the twentieth century, including depillarization, this characteristic seems to have endured. Witness a perceptive recent comparison of the way in which American and Dutch newspapers cover foreign affairs, an observation that is equally valid for domestic affairs: "[A] significant part of Dutch press coverage of Dutch foreign affairs is interpretative rather than factual" (Cohen 1995, 108).

2. From this remaining 20 percent of time, a small part was allocated to minor broadcast organizations that were not considered to be one of the major cultural streams of society, yet were too entrenched culturally to be entirely disregarded. The major beneficiary of this was the Vrijzinnig Protestantse Radio Omroep (VPRO, nonorthodox Protestant). Originally, the VPRO used its time mainly for broadcasting religious services, expanded in the 1960s to include more comprehensive programming.

3. This is not to say that all organizations of the pillars disappeared. Quite often they remained in existence, albeit without their former ties to other *zuil* organizations and without the exclusive and loyal clientele of the people of that *zuil* (Hellemans 1993, 142–5).

4. In 1934 a single Dutch Press Agency, ANP (Algemeen Nederlands Persbureau), was created and owned collectively by the publishers of Dutch newspapers. Few attempts were ever made to pillarize this part of the communications industry, and none of them was successful. The ANP is not only unrivaled for distributing unprocessed news, it is also responsible for newscasts on the public radio channels. Nonpillarized newscasting (as opposed to current affairs programs, which are much more interpretative and evaluative, hence traditionally pillarized) has always characterized television newscasts as well.

5. The reduction in the number of independent newspaper owners/firms generated considerable political concern over the diversity of the press, which is considered to be indispensable to a vigorous democracy and had previously been guaranteed by pillarization. To counter this risk, the state supported newspapers by compensating them for the income allegedly lost because of the introduction of radio and television advertisements in 1967. From the beginning of the 1980s, this compensation was gradually reduced from 5.9 to 2.6 percent of gross radio and television advertising income (Gosman 1993a). Additionally, more targeted (but temporary) support was given to economically troubled newspapers to allow them to reorganize and regain their economic viability – a measure that was successful in some cases but not in others. These measures did not stop further concentration in the newspaper industry, but they did provide more time for newspapers to adapt to shifting markets and changing economic and technological conditions.

6. Between 1951 and 1964 television broadcasting increased from 3 to 30 hours per week. In 1964 a second channel allowed further growth to 121 hours per week by 1988, a number that, in turn, went up to 163 hours with the introduction of a third television channel in 1988 (calculated from Gosman 1993b). The introduction of daytime television in 1992 caused this number to grow still further. During this period, income from license fees rose dramatically as the number of households owning a TV set increased from barely 2 million in 1965 to over 5.6 million (out of 6.1 million, i.e., 92 percent of all households) in 1989. Between 1967, when radio and television advertising was introduced, and 1989, when the commercial channel RTL4 appeared, income from advertisements increased more than tenfold. Whereas in 1966 license fees accounted for almost all income for the broadcast system, by 1989 advertising income had reduced their share of total income to 59 percent (source: Central Bureau of Statistics, *Statistisch Jaarboek 1990*).

7. In addition, some minor licensees exist with narrower aspirations, like catering to foreign language communities in the country, providing educational broadcasts, and so on.

8. For a brief period a Dutch commercial station named Sport7 existed. Meant to focus exclusively on sports, and in particular on soccer, it operated for only six months in 1996. Lack of viewers, and hence of advertisement income, forced it into bankruptcy.

9. Although the playing field of media access and free publicity has become more even for political parties generally, it has not become entirely level. Being more likely to influence the course of political events, large parties are regarded as more newsworthy than small ones, and hence benefit from more coverage, free publicity, and easier access. This may, in the case of negative publicity, occasionally not be to their advantage, but small parties remain structurally disadvantaged by their comparative lack of exposure.

10. Starting in the mid-1960s and completed in the mid-1970s, depillarization was responsible for a realignment from cleavage-based voting to ideological voting along left–right lines. As a consequence, parties that are ideologically similar are paradoxically competitors for votes, as well as likely coalition partners (van der Eijk and Niemöller 1983; 1984; 1992). For the trade-off between vote maximization and coalition-building potential, see van Praag (1991; 1992).

11. More recently, turnout seems to be in decline, reaching an all-time low of 73 percent in the 1998 parliamentary election. Moreover, turnout in provincial, municipal, and European elections has fallen sharply to levels (at times far) below 50 percent. Even though these second-order elections generate less campaign activity, these low turnout levels spurred parties' efforts to get out the vote.

12. Political advertisements did become prominent in a 1997 local referendum campaign in the city of Amsterdam. In this case, however, it was not political parties that set the tone of the campaign, but rather the municipal government on the one side of the issue and well-endowed social movement organizations on the other (Neijens and van Praag 1999).

13. Local and regional media have become somewhat more important for the parties since the early 1990s. This is partly the consequence of parties' efforts to bypass the skepticism of journalists specializing in "Hague" politics, thereby maintaining more party control over the free publicity they win. Furthermore, the free publicity in gos-

sip magazines that was once ignored by party strategists increased significantly in the 1990s. It is evidently now more acceptable to parties and politicians seeking to maximize the media coverage they receive (Brants and van Praag, 1995).

14. The public channels (and the broadcast associations) were bound by government regulation to devote at least 25 percent of their time to nonentertainment programming in the arts, education, cultural affairs, and information. They also had to give broadcast time to organization-like political parties, religious groups, and so on.

15. The arguments in this section derive from extensive analyses of European elections and of political communication in that specific electoral process. Together with an appraisal of the political consequences of media neglect of the EU political arena, these studies have been reported by Van der Eijk and Franklin (1996).

CHAPTER 10

Great Britain: The End of *News at Ten* and the Changing News Environment

Holli A. Semetko[1]

Television and the press in Britain appear to exemplify the two extremes of a continuum from nonpartisan to partisan or from impartial to partial. Television continues to be the principal source of information about politics for most people in Britain, despite the enormous changes that have occurred in the country's broadcast media landscape in the past decade. Television news also continues to be the most trusted and most credible source of information at election time. Newspapers reach a much smaller audience, and they also offer a far more partisan perspective on politics. At election time, the tabloids in particular are known to be screamingly partisan. One of the most notorious examples of this was the front page of the *Sun,* the country's most popular tabloid, on election day in 1992. With the head of Labour Party leader Neil Kinnock pictured inside a light bulb, the *Sun* asked: "If Kinnock Wins Today, Will the Last Person to Leave Britain Please Turn Out the Lights?"

Developments in the 1990s may have signaled some movement away from both ends of this continuum toward the center. In the press, these developments include the remarkable flipping of newspaper partisanship from Conservative dominant to Labour dominant in the 1997 election. In addition, on television, viewers have many more channels nowadays, and this provides more opportunities for people either to tune out of politics altogether or to follow news continuously on dedicated news channels. News today also more often appears to involve journalists commenting on or evaluating politicians' activities than in the past. There also appears to be a heartier (and growing?) appetite for scandal across all media outlets. Whether these developments represent the first signs of an era of partisan dealignment in the press, a growing political assertiveness by journalists, or a general tabloidization of news remains an open question.

This chapter discusses developments in the British media landscape and their potential consequences for democratic political discussion and debate. In the first section, the basic characteristics of the British print and broadcast media and the regulatory framework in which they operate are discussed. The second section reviews research on the political impact of the media or, as some would have it, the lack of impact. The third section presents some data on the content and effects of political information in the press and on television during the most recent national election campaigns. The conclusion discusses the wider implications of these developments for political communication and electoral politics in Britain.

PARTISAN PRESS, IMPARTIAL BROADCASTING

Britain's national daily press has long been dominated by the mass-market tabloids, which have the highest circulation and reach and which are best known for their colorful coverage of sex, scandals, and sports. The broadsheet newspapers, by contrast, are known for their more serious public affairs news and have been struggling bravely to maintain readership amid damaging price wars. All have put color on the front page in the past decade and have redesigned their layouts to be more visually enticing.

The national daily press comprises "quality" newspapers (the long-standing *Daily Telegraph, Financial Times, The Guardian, The Times,* and *The Independent* launched in 1986); "middlebrow" tabloids (*Daily Mail, Daily Express,* and, from 1986 to 1994, *Today*); and mass, "popular" tabloids, the largest of which is the *Sun,* with a circulation of nearly 4 million and an estimated reach of 10 million per day (Norris 1998, 121). Newspaper readership acts as "a surrogate for the class composition of the electorate" – more professionals (ABs, on the Butler and Stokes scale) and the highly educated read the quality press, more skilled and semi-skilled workers (C1s and C2s) read the middlebrow tabloids, and more unskilled workers and those with little education (DEs) largely read the popular tabloids (Worcester 1994, 5).[2] Table 10.1 presents the British national daily press as of 1997.

The strength of press partisanship has fluctuated over the post–World war II period, declining during the 1960s and the early 1970s and becoming more intense thereafter until the mid-1990s (Seymour-Ure

Table 10.1   *Britain's National Daily Newspapers:*
Circulation, Partisanship, Editor, and Owner

Newspaper	Circulation (000s)	Preferred Winner	Editor	Owner
Sun	3,842	Labour	S. Higgins	New int./ R. Murdoch
Daily Mirror	3,084	Labour	P. Morgan	Mirror Group
Daily Star	648	Labour	P. Walker	MAI/ United/ Ld Hollick
Daily Mail	2,151	Conservative	P. Dacre	Associated Newspapers/ Ld Rothmere
Daily Express	1,220	Conservative	R. Addis	MAI/ United/ Ld Hollick
Guardian	401	Labour	A. Rusbriger	Scott Trust
Independent	251	Labour	A. Marr	Mirror Group
Daily Telegraph	1,134	Conservative	C. Moore	C. Black/ Hollinger
Financial Times	307	Labour	R. Lambert	Pearson/Ld/ Blakenham
The Times	719	Conservative	P. Stothard	News Int./ R. Murdoch

Source: C. Seymour-Ure, "Editorial Opinion in the National Press." In P. Norris and N.Gavin (Eds.), *Britain Votes 1997.* Oxford: Oxford University Press, 1997, 82–3.

1974, 165–8). For most of the postwar period, Labour suffered from being labeled by most of the pro-Tory tabloids as public enemy number one. Conservative support was the norm across the entire national daily press for most of the 1980s and early 1990s until a turning point after the 1992 election, culminating in the 1997 election.

Of the 17 national dailies existing in 1983, only 2 (the *Daily Mirror* and the *Sunday Mirror*) endorsed the Labour Party on election day, and none named the centrist Social Democratic Party (SDP)–Liberal Alliance as its unequivocal first choice. A similar situation prevailed in the 1987 general election. Although there were fewer press endorsements of the Conservatives in the 1992 general election, they still received a much larger number of endorsements than any other party. By 1997, however, the situation had changed completely. In response to widespread disillusionment with the Conservatives, who had been in power for 18 consecutive years and whose leader, John Major, had been the subject of largely negative news since the notorious Black Wednesday, when Britain's membership in the European Exchange Rate Mechanism was ignominiously suspended in fall 1992, Labour received the larger number of newspaper endorsements in the 1997 general election.

The intensity and form of the endorsements in the tabloids in particular are quite different from those found in the United States or, for example, in the Netherlands, where the newspapers are less partisan. In 1983 the *Sun*'s front page screamed "VOTE MAGGIE!" and in 1992 it was hardly less subtle, as noted in the introduction to this chapter. The *Sun*'s main competitor, the *Daily Mirror*, has long supported Labour, and on election day in 1992 ran a front page with Labour's red rose logo alongside a favorable photo of Neil Kinnock with the headline "THE TIME IS NOW – VOTE LABOUR." The most remarkable transformation in 1997 was the front page of the *Sun*: a flattering photo of a smiling Tony Blair as a golden boy being touched by a finger from the heavens. The *Sun*, owned by media mogul Rupert Murdoch, who had long been considered the darling of Margaret Thatcher, came down hard on John Major and urged its readers to support Tony Blair and the new Labour Party.

The coverage of the British tabloids is also heavily laden with partisan information at election time. In the 1983, 1987, and 1992 general election campaigns, for example, the *Sun* ran a series of articles critical of the Labour Party, while the *Daily Mirror* did the same with the Conservatives, as it did again in 1997. This is not to say that the tabloids' treatment of the election campaign was entirely devoid of substance, but rather that their coverage of substantive issues was often heavy with partisan overtones. On their front pages in 1992, for example, the many news stories that concerned social welfare issues were slanted to suit the newspapers' own partisan agenda (Semetko et al. 1994, 28). Although the *Sun* endorsed Labour in 1997, its "conversion" was far from complete. It still printed a slightly larger number of positive stories for the Tories than for Labour on the inside pages during the campaign (Golding et al. 1997).

The tabloids in the past 30 years have concentrated increasingly on the sensationalistic and the scandalous, often buying stories from insiders about, for example, the private lives of senior politicians and members of the royal family (Seymour-Ure 1991, 134–5). As the tabloids provided a steady diet of gossip about Fergie and Andrew or Charles and Di in the late 1980s and early 1990s, the broadsheets followed suit. The subsequent sex scandals involving senior members of the Conservative government, as well as those of less visible Tory backbenchers, were lapped up by the tabloids and hardly ignored by the broadsheets in the mid-1990s. This appetite for sex and scandal, described as the "tabloidization" of the British press, led one careful observer of British newspapers to conclude that, by the mid-1990s, "the journalism of scandal [had] trumped the journalism of partisanship hands down" (Norris 1998, 123).

Despite this "checkbook" journalism, there has been a decline in readership. The number of adults reading at least one national newspaper daily fell from four in five in 1969 to less than two-thirds (64 percent) in the mid-1990s. Moreover, "almost exactly half read either the *Sun* or the *Daily Mirror*" (Worcester 1994, 5). Much the same is true of the Sunday newspapers: of the two-thirds of adults who read these publications, almost half read either the *News of the World* or *People*. While the more sensationalist newspapers continue to capture the largest readership, only the *Sun* has escaped sharp declines in circulation. Its readership increased by 13 percent between 1969 and the mid-1990s, whereas that of the *Daily Express* and the *Daily Mirror* dropped by 18 and 22 percent, respectively. Readership of the *News of the World* and *People* also fell, by 11 and 23 percent, respectively (Worcester 1994, 4–5).

Radio and television are an entirely different story. The British broadcasting system has long been a hybrid of commercial and public-service elements. The public-service element came first as interwar governments chose to involve themselves closely in the development of the nascent broadcast media. After two committees of inquiry into the role of broadcasting, the British Broadcasting Corporation (BBC) was created by royal charter, and in 1935 the Ullswater Committee established the BBC's formal independence from the government in the daily management of its affairs. The principal aims of British broadcasting, as set forth in the BBC's charter, are "to inform, educate, and entertain." The public corporation has always been financed by an annual license fee paid originally by radio owners and now by all television owners. Some suggest that because of this form of financing, the BBC is of necessity more cautious in its coverage of government affairs, especially when a parliamentary vote on the license fee is approaching (Cockerell et al. 1984).

Independent Television (ITV), now officially known as Channel 3, was launched in the 1950s and, in contrast, is financed solely by advertising revenue (Blumler and Nossiter 1991). ITV was organized on a regional basis, in contrast to the BBC's more centralized structure. There were more than a dozen ITV regional companies, and each obtained an individual license to broadcast from the government. The ITV companies agreed to network most of their programming. For some 30 years, until the early 1980s, viewers in Britain turned to BBC1 and ITV for most of their news and entertainment programming. BBC2 was launched in the early 1960s as a second public-service channel under the direction of BBC1 and catered to a much smaller select audience. It did not aim to compete with BBC1 but instead offered a heavy diet of cultural programs.

The obligations of BBC and ITV are set forth by statute. The BBC is required to broadcast a daily, impartial account of the proceedings of Parliament, and both the BBC and ITV have an obligation to be impartial in reporting political affairs. This impartiality is largely self-imposed for the BBC but is set out in statute for commercial television in the various Broadcasting Acts passed since 1964 and their amendments.

In 1982, Channel Four was launched as a second national commercial channel, an alternative to BBC2, and did not seek to compete directly with ITV. Instead it aimed to cater to no more than about 10 percent of viewers, particularly those whose tastes were not catered to, or not represented in, the programming of the other channels. For example, Channel Four introduced independently produced evening sitcoms. One of them focused on the lives of an immigrant Asian restaurant owner and his family, speaking to the not insubstantial minority of immigrants from the Asian subcontinent. The new channel also introduced a series of films, identified by a pink triangle, dealing with gay and lesbian issues and carrying unusually explicit sexual material. It also offered special current affairs programs aimed specifically at Asian and African-Caribbean audiences. Channel Four News, broadcast in the early evening for nearly one hour, also catered to a small but elite audience in terms of their demographic characteristics and their appetite for in-depth coverage of current affairs.

From the 1950s to the early 1980s, when Channel 4 was launched, viewers had two options for television news – BBC and ITV. News on ITV was provided by Independent Television News (ITN), which contracted with all of the ITV regional companies to provide network coverage with three major news bulletins each day. For some 40 years, the country's flagship and widely respected main evening news programs were ITN's *News at Ten* and BBC's *Nine O'Clock News*. In recent years, audiences for ITN's evening program well exceeded the BBC's.

The most compelling evidence of the impact of the increasingly competitive television marketplace came just after the 1997 general election, when the possibility of adopting an American-style programming strategy on ITV evening schedules was seriously debated. After much discussion and deliberation in the press as well as within the organization, the Independent Television Commission, the regulatory body that oversees ITV, allowed the ITV companies to rearrange the network's evening program schedules in light of the many new channels coming on the market. The ITV regional companies wanted to end *News at Ten* and broadcast other, even more popular types of programming. In March 1999 *News at Ten* was replaced by a new early evening news program and a late evening news update. This is the same schedule found in most television news markets in the United States, and it gave the ITV (Channel 3) network the opportunity to air other programs during the prime-time viewing hours.

ITN's main evening bulletin is now broadcast at 6:30 P.M. for a half hour. The BBC also has a six o'clock news program. Channel 4 News is at 7 P.M. and has developed a loyal audience numbering more than 1 million. A new Channel Five covering two-thirds of the country was established just in time for the 1997 election campaign. Its news program, which is aired at 6 P.M., is aimed at younger adults, as well as those who would not normally watch TV news, with innovative formats and unusual political packages. BBC's half-hour *Nine O'Clock News* program remains firmly in place, for the time being at least, reaching several million. One hour after that main evening news program ends, every weekday evening, BBC2 broadcasts *Newsnight,* a special daily current affairs program with a more elite, loyal, and considerably smaller audience than the main evening news on BBC1.

Cable television in the form of SKYTV, owned by Rupert Murdoch, has a dedicated SkyNews channel. SKYTV first appeared on the election news scene in 1992, although only about 3 percent of homes had access to it. Many critics found SKYTV's coverage of the 1997 election to be much better (i.e., far more impartial) than expected, thanks to the expertise and hard work of its political editor, Adam Boulton, who was on the air almost 24 hours a day. Although *SkyNews* was watched in all the newsrooms during the 1992 and 1997 campaigns, its audience in the country remained small. By 1997, about 20 percent of homes could obtain dozens of satellite and cable channels, and during the 1997 election campaign, up to 15 percent of the audience watched cable or satellite programming. On the rare occasions when the terrestrial channels offered only political coverage, the 15 percent watching cable TV jumped to nearly 25 percent (Norris 1998, 125–6).

REGULATION

The 1990 Broadcasting Act continued to prohibit paid political advertising and to maintain the obligation of "due impartiality" in coverage of political affairs. At the same time, it recommended a more competitive broadcasting environment with a larger number of radio and television channels. It also changed the way in which the 15 regional ITV licenses were awarded. Although the 1990 act mandated a "quality threshold" to be met by applicants, the government's decision as to who would be awarded the license was now to be based entirely on financial considerations once that threshold was crossed. Victors in the competitive bidding process were obliged to pay a fixed amount annually to the Treasury, regardless of fluctuations in their advertising revenues. Thus, especially for those who had to bid high to win their license, making money was a primary goal and ITN, which provided a networked news service to each of the 15 regional companies, expressed concern in 1990 that as a result of this new procedure for awarding licenses, its clients would try to find cheaper ways of obtaining news programming, possibly reduce the amount of news programming they purchased, or perhaps even move the time the main evening news was broadcast to make way for high-revenue entertainment programming during peak viewing hours. As of the 1997 election, the worst fears of critics of the 1990 act had proved unfounded. The BBC and ITN main news broadcasts were still aired at their traditional time, and SKYTV had sought to emulate its established competitors in providing balanced coverage of both the 1992 and 1997 campaigns. But not long after the 1997 election, these concerns proved to be well founded. The change in the way the ITV licenses were awarded, mandated in the 1990 act, subsequently had a direct bearing on the move to end ITN's *News at Ten* in March 1999.

In anticipation of the renewal of its charter in 1996, the BBC sought to take advantage of the new financial calculus for commercial companies. Believing that "commercial pressures will force ITV, Sky and other privately-funded rivals to concentrate on easily-digestible, mass appeal entertainment shows and cheap imports," it identified one of its future key tasks to be the provision of "in-depth news and information coverage across a range of outlets to support a fair and informed national debate" (*Broadcast* 1992, 3). But fulfilling this public service role assumed that the BBC, traditionally funded by a compulsory license fee paid by all those with a television set, would not be subject to the same financial pressures as its commercial rivals, and that its maintaining a respectable audience share would be compatible with this mission when entertainment programming was increasingly the television norm.

The extent of government regulation of the print and electronic media is very different. Except on issues pertaining to libel and national security (May and Rowan 1982), the press is almost entirely unregulated and is free to report the news in heavily partisan terms, which it usually does.

Money, and hence the media, are playing an increasingly important role in British elections, although the level of spending remains much lower than in the United States. This is so for three reasons. First, election campaigns in Britain are relatively short. The postwar norm has been an official campaign period of 21 days. This was lengthened to 23 days after the October 1974 general election, and the 1997 campaign lasted for the unprecedentedly long period of 6 weeks.

Second, there are strict spending limits in the constituencies. In 1997, for example, each local candidate could spend £4,965 (approximately $7,950) on his or her campaign, plus an extra amount for each voter registered in the constituency. In towns, the amount per voter was 4.2 pence (about 6.7 cents) and in the country 5.6 pence (about 9 cents). These figures are adjusted from election to election to take account of inflation. Even at the level of central party expenditure, which has been on the increase and for which there are no strict limits, the overall amounts are still less than those in the United States. Central party headquarters election spending for all three major parties increased from £7.7 million in 1983 to £15.3 million in 1987 to £23.2 million in 1992 and to £56.4 million during the 12 months prior to May 1, 1997. In real terms, controlling for inflation (in 1997 constant pounds), campaign spending rose from £14.1 million in 1983 to £56.4 million in 1997 (Neill Report 1998). Labour headquarters spent £26 million, Conservative headquarters £28.3 million, and Liberal Democrat headquarters £2.1 million in 1997 (Norris et al. 1999, Tables 2.6 and 2.7). Regardless of the difference in the two countries' populations and surface areas, this is vastly less than the $2.2 *billion* that the 1996 presidential election in the United States is estimated to have cost.[3]

Finally, and most important, all broadcasting authorities are forbidden by law to make advertising time available for purchase by candidates or political parties. Political advertisements can be bought in newspapers, and spending on them, as well as on posters, has escalated in recent elections. This is part of the central party expenditure noted previously.

Television gives free air time (and studio time) to the major political parties to broadcast the political messages that they themselves want voters to see, although these messages are regulated by form, so that there is nothing like the 15- or 30-second spots in the United States. Party political broadcasts (PPBs) are aired throughout the year outside election campaigns. During campaigns, party election broadcasts (PEBs) are also aired free of charge. The criteria for allocating the number of PEBs to the parties have changed little over the past two decades. For those parties not represented in Parliament, there has been a long-standing practice of giving a five-minute slot to those contesting 50 or more seats. For those parties with parliamentary representation, their allocation has been based on their proportion of the vote in the previous general election. From 1964 to 1979, the Conservative, Labour, and Liberal parties received 5, 5 and 3 slots, respectively. The distribution changed to 5:5:4 in 1983, became 5:5:5 in 1987, and returned to 5:5:4 in 1992 and 1997. This distribution of PEBs among the three parties has meant that television has presented "a wider perspective on the election for the voters" than the press (Harrop 1987, 186). Television viewers saw PEBs from many parties, but newspaper readers saw ads only from the parties that could afford to buy space. The Liberal Democrats and the various other minor parties, as well as the nationalist parties, which have much smaller budgets than Labour or the Conservatives, cannot afford to spend huge amounts of money on press advertising and rely heavily on free PEB time to make their case to the voters.

Until the 1979 election, PEBS were broadcast on all channels simultaneously. The format of the PEB initially followed the public-service ethos and consisted largely of the serious discussion of policy issues as the "talking heads" of leading politicians explained, justified, and promoted party policy. More recently, however, PEBs have begun to look a little more like U.S.-style political ads as their content has become more visual, emotive, and negative. Parties have started to spend more time and money to film PEBs in the field, and the talking head format so common for many decades is now rarely seen. The parties are not permitted to break up the five ten-minute segments into a larger number of shorter broadcasts, however, although they are free to reduce the length of time each of their allocated broadcasts actually takes up. Thus, there is no British equivalent of the 30-second TV spot so often seen in the United States.

The 1970 election was the turning point with regard to negative advertising. One Tory PEB showed a pound note being attacked by a pair of scissors. With each chop, a voice-over announced the date and the reduced value of the pound due to inflation. The final proclamation was that the reelection of Labour would lead to the "Ten Bob Pound" (i.e., a "Fifty Cent Dollar"). A more recent development was the decision by both Conservative and Labour to devote at least one of their five PEBs to developing their leader's image. In 1987, the Conservatives reduced one ten-minute broadcast to a five-minute eulogy of Mrs. Thatcher as a world stateswoman. Labour's first PEB in the same election was used to portray Neil Kinnock, the new leader, as a strong family man from a humble background who was admired, trusted, and respected by his political colleagues. This seven-minute PEB was so popular that Labour chose to rebroadcast it as the fourth of its five PEBs later in the same campaign. In 1992, John Major's life was the focus of the Conservatives' first PEB. Following what by now seemed to have become a tradition, Labour's penultimate 1997 broadcast was a ten-minute portrait of the party's new leader, Tony Blair (Scammell and Semetko 1995). To the extent that the PEBs increasingly emphasize their political leaders, British politics can be described as increasingly presidential (Mughan 1998).

In sharp contrast to the partisanship of the press, television news in Britain does not and cannot systematically favor any political party because of the aforementioned requirement to provide fair and impartial coverage of politics that is set forth in statue. To guarantee balance, tradition has it that the coverage of each of the parties in the news is "stopwatched" during the election campaign to reflect the ratio of PEBs, which has been either 5:5:3 or 5:5:4 in the past decade. So, for example, every five minutes devoted to the Conservatives was matched somewhere in the bulletin with five minutes devoted to Labour and four minutes devoted to the Liberal Democrats. The broadcasters also kept a running tally of the amount of time devoted to the main parties each week and considered adjusting the balance independently only if there was a major gap, which rarely occurs. The parties also monitored this situation closely and quickly complained to the broadcasters if they believed they had not been treated fairly in the news. Broadcasters listened to these complaints and sometimes acted on them.

The SDP–Liberal Alliance, for example, complained to the BBC in 1987 that in one week its fair share of time appeared in a much later part of the bulletin in a campaign segment that ended the program after the sports news, while the battle between the Conservatives and Labour was covered at the top of the news program in the opening campaign segment. Although the Alliance was receiving its share of time, the placement of the story in the bulletin led campaign managers to voice their concerns that it was being marginalized, appearing "after the cricket, for

God's sake!" Although the BBC was explicit about not bowing to pressure, there was a noticeable change the following week. At least the Alliance no longer followed sports news, and sometimes the center parties even appeared in the opening campaign segment just after the story about the Conservative and Labour activities that day (Semetko 1987; 1989).

POLITICAL IMPACT OF THE MEDIA

Between 1945 and 1970, the British party system had two defining characteristics. The first was that it was dominated by the Conservative and Labour parties, between which there was a large area of agreement over the activities that governments should properly undertake in their management of society. It was an era, in other words, known for its consensus politics (Kavanagh and Morris 1994). The second characteristic was a social class underpinning of the party system that made for strong and stable links over time between the middle class and the Conservative Party, on the one hand, and the working class and the Labour Party, on the other. The result was that votes were cast primarily along class lines. As one famous aphorism of the time has it: "Class is the basis of British party politics; all else is embellishment and detail" (Pulzer 1967, 98). Moreover, the limited movement in the vote that did take place was largely uniform nationally, and was due less to conversion from one major party to the other and more to new voters entering the electorate, to movement into and out of abstention, and to the relative volatility of minor party supporters who might or might not have a constituency candidate to vote for from one election to the next (Crewe et al. 1977).

At the same time, there was a close fit between the configuration of the party system and the configuration of the media system. Until the end of the 1950s, the printed press was the clearly preeminent medium of political communication, and the Conservative-Labour duopoly in Parliament was matched in, and sustained by, the newspaper industry. Most of the national dailies supported one or the other major party, most preferring the Conservatives, and did not hesitate to propagate its cause in their news stories and editorial pages. Voters by and large chose to read the newspaper that reflected and reinforced their existing partisanship. As a result, the press reflected and reinforced the party status quo. "[O]ur evidence suggests that the national press, faithfully read by millions of partisans each morning, has helped conserve the established party alignments" (Butler and Stokes 1974, 119).

Television was only beginning to emerge as a political force in the 1950s. Part of the reason, of course, was that it was a new technology not widely available to ordinary people for most of the decade. In 1951, about 8 percent of adults had a television set in their own home, about 40 percent had one in 1955, and about 75 percent in 1959. In addition, self-imposed restrictions effectively limited television's role as an instrument of political communication in elections for most of the 1950s. It did not even provide campaign coverage for viewers until the 1959 election. Prior to this time, television authorities feared that such coverage would infringe on the law limiting spending on the promotion of candidates and so had opted, even in their news broadcasts, not to report the campaign from its onset until the close of polling (Seymour-Ure 1991, 159–69). Until 1959, the only political information on television during the official campaign was the PEBs from each of the parties. Public and commercial television were legally required to broadcast these PEBs.

Against a background of consensus politics, then, the 1959 contest may be regarded as the first television election. Three clear conclusions emerged from a study of that campaign in the constituencies. First, in 1959, newspaper readership had no effect on voters' level of political knowledge, but television exposure was directly and unequivocally associated with improving it. "There is a progression in the findings so that the more programmes people viewed the more they learned, and this was true whether we confine the comparison to Party election broadcasts, or to political news bulletins, or the whole output" (Trenaman and McQuail 1961, 188). The different effects of newspapers and television on knowledge levels were attributed to "the television situation" and its "atmosphere of restrained public debate, very different from the partisan campaigning so often associated with the popular Press" (Trenaman and McQuail 1961, 189).

Second, in 1959, the relative emphasis placed by the parties on the issues during the campaign had little effect on what voters considered to be important. In other words, television exposure did little to change voters' issue agendas during the campaign. "The remarkable thing is the stability of opinion on . . . issues, and the lack of any widespread reaction in the population as a whole to the mass of relevant material to which they were exposed during the election campaign" (Trenaman and McQuail 1961, 173; see also Milne and Mackenzie 1958, 111).

Finally, in 1959, the level and type of media exposure were associated marginally, at best, with the changes in political attitudes that did take place during the campaign. "With . . . incidental and slight exceptions, no medium or source of propaganda, or combination of sources, had any ascertainable effect upon any attitude changes. And attitude changes were certainly large enough to be susceptible of effect. . . . [W]hat is established here is not merely an absence of cause and effect but *a definite and consistent barrier between sources of communication and movements of attitude in the political field at the General Election*" (Trenaman and McQuail 1961, 191–2; emphasis in the original). Three reasons were adduced to explain this attitudinal stability. One, the "heat" of the campaign produced an intensification of political awareness and loyalties. Two, party propaganda and counter-propaganda tended to cancel each other out and therefore to have little effect on individuals' attitudes and loyalties. Three, group and social pressures intensified in the heat of the campaign and reinforced partisan loyalties even in cases where other considerations predisposed the voter to support the opposition (Trenaman and McQuail 1961, 234). These conclusions were much the same as those arrived at in similar studies in the United States at about the same time and were instrumental in establishing a conventional wisdom among psephologists (election researchers) about the political effects of the media, which was that they *reinforced* political attitudes and behavior but did *not change* them (Klapper 1960).

By the 1970s, however, a number of developments suggested the need to reconsider the continuing validity of this "reinforcement" thesis. For a start, the Conservatives and Labour abandoned the postwar consensus, and the ideological distance between them increased beginning in the late 1960s (Beer 1982). Second, the tabloid press in particular became even less balanced and more shrilly partisan in content and tone, reflecting this new lack of consensus between the major parties about the role of the state. In addition, television replaced newspapers in the mid-1960s as the most important source of political information for voters (Harrop 1987). Replacement was not that important in itself since television, being impartial, was not the partisan propaganda device that many newspapers were. It was important, however, when viewed in conjunction with two other developments in British political life that were also well underway by 1970. The first was the weakening of the traditionally strong relationship between social class and party support, and the associated weakening of identification with the major political parties, or "partisan dealignment" (Franklin and Mughan 1979; Sarlvik and Crewe 1983). The second was the gradual evolution of a new, more media-centered style of campaigning in British general elections as well as in parliamentary contests in other countries (Bowler and Farrell 1992;

Butler and Ranney 1992; Kavanagh 1995; Scammell 1995; Blumer et al. 1996; Swanson and Mancini 1996; Rosenbaum 1997).

Partisan dealignment represented a weakening of voters' psychological commitment to the Conservative and Labour parties in particular. It was rooted in a number of factors, including unpopular policies and both parties' repeated failure to halt, never mind reverse, the national decline. The electoral consequences of party dealignment have been numerous. The most relevant one was that it made voters more susceptible to short-term, campaign-specific forces in their behavior at the polls. This susceptibility has manifested itself in a number of ways, principally the growth of support for minor parties, arrival at voting decisions later in the campaign, greater electoral volatility between elections, and sharper fluctuations in party support in opinion polls. While television was not directly responsible for partisan dealignment in the first place, it may well bear some responsibility for translating this dealignment into election outcomes more heavily shaped by short-term forces than in the past. Crewe (1983, 190) has put it succinctly: "One possibility is that the emergence of television as the main mass medium of politics has made the short campaign period – and the issues, people and events it brings into prominence – a more powerful determinant of the vote."

Further increasing the likelihood that television began to play a qualitatively different role in influencing political attitudes and behavior than it did in the past is that political parties have made heavier and more innovative use of the medium for both mobilizing and converting support in the more volatile, post-1970s British electorate. The traditional image of parliamentary elections as being essentially a series of dour, largely discrete constituency battles waged by local party loyalists marshalled by professional party agents and made more resolute by the occasional fleeting visit from leading party figures was increasingly a thing of the past. More and more, campaigns nowadays are run and coordinated from the center, and voters are reached not through the door-to-door canvassing of party activists, but through the television sets in front of which a more atomized electorate spends a large part of its leisure time (over 26 hours per week in 1992). The greater resort to television by party strategists represents in part a necessary adaptation to changing social circumstances and habits. At the same time, one of its consequences has been to enhance the role of the party leader in election campaigns. The leader has become increasingly the vehicle by which the party projects and shapes its public image – an unavoidable development since television is a medium that lends itself far more readily to the projection of personalities than to the serious discussion of policy issues (Ranney 1983, 55–8).

The visual nature of television makes it a medium of communication that is most suitable to a strategy based on the projection of personality. The personality that parties have chosen to project, and the one in demand by television reporters and producers, is almost inevitably that of the single most important person in the party: its leader and the country's incumbent or potential prime minister. Thus, with television's ever more dominant role in the political communications process, party leaders have become one of the principal means by which parties project themselves and shape their popular image. Elections in which leaders have no implications for the way people vote are a thing of the past. Few observers would now accept the late 1950s conclusion that the leader "is not expected to transcend the party and he is not indispensable. . . . [H]e is to a large extent the embodiment of general political attitudes" (Trenaman and McQuail 1961, 60).

A study of campaigns in the postwar period has established that the media, and especially television, paid more attention to the Conservative and Labour leaders relative to their parties in the late 1980s and 1990s. This was interpreted as a "presidentialization of presentation." At the same time, there is weaker evidence of a "presidentialization of impact" insofar as their effect on the vote reached new, sustained heights (Mughan 1998; see also Foley 1993). Several studies have underlined this new-found importance for the way people vote. Cross-sectional analysis of the 1987 election, for example, has shown that party identification was the most important influence for each party; but leader images were second, and they were more important than issue priorities or evaluations of national and personal economic situations (Miller et al. 1990, 253; see also Bean and Mughan 1989; Stewart and Clarke 1992). Moreover, leaders do not make themselves felt in election campaigns alone; they are also potent predictors of support for government between elections. A sophisticated study of voting intention in monthly Gallup opinion polls between 1979 and 1992 concluded that "evaluations of prime ministerial performance have sizable short-run and long-run effects on Conservative support" (Clarke and Stewart 1995, 160).

The evidence suggests that voters respond above all to leaders' politically relevant character traits such as effectiveness (or competence) and ability to stick to principles. As one comparison of the electoral response to Australian and British party leaders concluded: "Nor is there much reason to believe that it is the trivial in leaders that appeals to voters. If it were, we would expect the highly personal quality of likability to have had a strong – if not the strongest – effect on voters. . . . Instead, perceived effectiveness dominates how voters respond to leaders, and few would deny that this quality is a key ingredient of successful political leadership, especially when viewed from the parliamentary perspective of implementing the manifesto on which the government was elected" (Bean and Mughan 1989, 1176; see also Stewart and Clarke 1992).

Party system change is perhaps television's most underappreciated political effect in Britain. Prior to the arrival of this medium on the political scene, minor parties were effectively denied access to the most important means of political communication: the national daily press. The Liberal Party in particular had difficulty getting its message across because it was largely ignored by a national press that concentrated its attention largely on the Conservatives and Labour. Television changed this situation, not least because of the need for it to remain impartial and to give air time to all parties with nontrivial electoral support. Unprecedented media exposure heightened voter awareness of a Liberal alternative that proved attractive to Conservative and Labour supporters disillusioned with their own party, but unwilling to go all the way and vote for the other class party (Butler and Stokes 1974, 272–5). In a spiral of good fortune, the increase in the Liberal vote with the arrival of political television in 1959, in turn, entitled the party to more air time.

This dynamic is suggested in the finding that the third party – the Liberals in the 1960s and 1970s, and the Liberal–SDP Alliance in the 1980s – won extra votes because it received exposure on television denied to it by newspapers (Semetko 1989). In 1964, for example, Blumler and McQuail (1968) found a positive and significant relationship between the use of television and improving attitudes toward the Liberal Party. Estimating what attitudinal gains meant in terms of votes, McAllister (1985) found that, in the 1979 and 1983 elections, television exposure accounted for 3 percent of the campaign-period votes gained by the Liberals and the Alliance. Finally, a long-term panel study, spanning six waves over three decades and several general election campaigns, based on 246 male subjects who participated in all waves, suggested that Liberal voters "tend to decide largely on the impression they form in the course of the electoral campaign itself." In particular, potential Liberal voters proved most sensitive to "the image, style and personalities" of the politicians in the campaign (Himmelweit et al. 1981, 171 and 173). In this regard, an added reason for the upturn in Liberal fortunes associated with political television may be that "[b]eyond the attractiveness to some voters of the Liberals' independent, apolitical image . . . the Liberals have been blessed throughout the television era with leaders able to communicate well on television" (Rasmussen 1981, 164).

But if having a telegenic leader had long been an electoral bonus for the Liberals, it became so in the 1980s and 1990s for Conservative and Labour as well, largely because all parties rely on television as their campaign medium of choice. There is even evidence that the Conservatives in 1992 gained an electoral bonus from the disproportionate popularity of their leader among those who perceived a pro-Labour bias in BBC television news (Mughan 1996).

In sum, voters' greater reliance on television for leisure as well as political information took place at much the same time that their partisan commitment weakened, and the political parties made more extensive and more creative use of television to reach and influence a more volatile voting public. The circumstances would seem to be ripe for a reassessment of the political role and effects of the media, particularly television, in British politics.

CONTINUITY AND CHANGE IN THE ROLE OF THE MEDIA IN ELECTIONS

In terms of political impact, little seems to have changed with the printed press over the last 20 years or so. It is still predominantly national in character and orientation, large sections of it continue to strongly favor the Conservative and Labour parties, and minor parties remain all but ignored. Politicians have long counted this bias important. Echoing Harold Wilson before him, the Labour leader, Neil Kinnock, reiterated the conviction that the Tory press was to blame for his party's electoral misfortunes in 1992. "[T]he Conservative supporting press has enabled the Conservative party to win yet again when the Conservative party could not have secured victory for itself on the basis of its record, its programme or its character" (quoted in Curtice and Semetko 1994, 43). But a study of the press in that same 1992 election found no evidence of a direct link between converting to a newspaper of a different partisan hue and vote switching to match the partisanship of the newspaper. "The message . . . is clear. Neither *The Sun* nor any other pro-Conservative tabloid newspaper were responsible for John Major's unexpected victory in 1992. There is no evidence in our panel that there was any relationship between vote switching during the election campaign and the partisanship of a voter's newspaper" (Curtice and Semetko 1994, 55). Press bias is unimportant because, armed with and protected by their partisanship, voters are largely able to discount discordant messages when making their voting decision.

Research on the impact of the press, and in particular the switch of the pro-Tory *Sun* to Labour in the 1997 election, did not reveal any decisive impact on readers. The authors concluded: "those who consistently read a Tory faithful newspaper were both less likely to defect from the Conservatives or switch to Labour;" meanwhile "those who started reading a traditionally pro-Labour newspaper were more likely to switch their support to Labour;" and "most importantly, we find neither significant nor consistent evidence that any of the papers that switched their support away from the Conservatives brought their readers with them. All that can be said is that the *Sun*'s defection meant the newspaper did not help to keep its Conservative supporters loyal" (Norris et al. 1999, 152–69).

When attention turned from the short-term campaign to a longer time period, however, newspapers were found to have political effects. Looking at the change between the 1987 and 1992 elections, for example, the same 1992 study found that those switching to a Labour tabloid between the two contests were heavily influenced, support for Labour rising in this group by 17 percent. Among those who had stopped reading a pro-Labour paper, support for Labour fell by 5 percent. Conservative support followed a similar pattern. It rose among those who read a pro-Tory quality or tabloid newspaper, and most sharply among tabloid readers. It fell among those who gave up reading a pro-Conservative tabloid and those who read pro-Labour tabloids. The Conservative press' success, however, "seems to have been not so much in dissuading people from voting Labour, but in winning over or maintaining in the Conservative camp electors who might otherwise have abstained or voted Liberal Democrat" (Curtice and Semetko 1994, 50). The next British Election Panel Study involving long-term (1992 to 1997) change concluded that reinforcement was the main effect of Britain's partisan newspapers: "Where they can make a difference is in mobilizing their more faithful readers by playing them a familiar tune, readers who indeed may well have chosen that paper precisely because it plays a tune they have long considered an old favorite. Like social class, the partisanship of British newspapers is clearly part of the structure of British voting behavior, but whether they can explain the flux is very much open to doubt" (Norris et al. 1999, 168–9).

Effects of press readership may also be defined more broadly, including both indirect and direct effects. Take perceptions of the economy as an example (see Gavin 1998). A study of the influence of newspaper coverage on economic perceptions and support for the government between 1979 and 1987 identified a weak link between press coverage of the economy and popular perceptions of performance. This, in turn, predicted government support. The study failed to find, however, any direct link between newspaper coverage of the economy and level of support for the government (Sanders et al. 1993).

Television also shows elements of strong continuity with the past. Recent studies have shown that, regardless of changes in both voters' exposure to and parties' use of television, it continues to have the effects it did in the 1950s and 1960s in two important respects. The first concerns levels of political knowledge, and the second concerns voters' issue agendas.

With regard to political knowledge, there is evidence that the PPBs broadcast between election campaigns educate the electorate. One study of viewers' responses to this type of political broadcast found that those who watched more of them knew more about politics. Thus, "for all their evident defects [of low popularity] . . . [PPBs] have some positive function in the process of political communication" (Wober and Svennevig 1981, 1). In the same vein, an analysis of the 1992 campaign found that media exposure was significantly related to political knowledge (measured on a ten-point political quiz scale) even after controlling for education, gender, age, class, and political interest, all of which also proved significant (Norris 1995). There is also some evidence of learning in the sense that television exposure helps viewers to crystallize their voting decision. In one 1983 study, for example, 21 percent of respondents said that television had helped them decide which party to vote for, and 39 percent of vote switchers and 36 percent of first-time voters said they were helped by television (Harrison 1984, 174). To the extent that the economy influences the vote, television may contribute indirectly to the vote choice. One study found that economic news on television had a modest but stable and significant relationship with public perceptions of government competence and that these perceptions were reflected in government approval ratings (Gavin and Sanders 1996).

Television, then, continues to provide people with information that may be instrumental in making their voting decision. Insofar as it does little to alter the issues voters think important, however, this information would seem to contribute more to the consolidation of voting decisions than to their conversion. One study of the 1987 general election campaign shows that while there may have been a small shift in the importance attached to unemployment and defense issues in response to the amount of television news coverage of these issues, the overall picture was one of a consistent gap between the public's issue agenda and television's. "The ebb and flow of controversy did *not* [emphasis in the original] produce any corresponding trends in public interest and discussion. . . . In the short span of a four- or five-week election campaign our conclusion must be that television failed to set the public agenda" (Miller et al. 1990, 231–2).

Drawing on the British Election Panel Study, content analysis, and experimental data, a study of the 1997 general election campaign addressed questions about the media's influence on civic engagement, the salience of issues in the minds of the public, and perceptions of political parties. Three findings are especially worth noting here. First, with respect to civic engagement, Norris et al. (1999) found that those who were more attentive to news in the press and on television, as well as regular viewers and readers, were significantly more knowledgeable about politics, policies, and candidates than the average person and were also more likely to vote. The authors concluded: "Far from producing cynicism and turning off voters, as critics charge, this evidence suggests that the British media largely succeeded in their public service role" (p. 113). Second, although in 1997 it was also found that the public's agenda (measured with survey data) and the media's agenda (measured with content data) diverged considerably, experiments testing the agenda-setting effects of television news found that "concern about foreign affairs did increase significantly when people were shown television news stories about Europe and developing countries" (p. 128). Third, and finally, additional experimental studies of television news provided "unambiguous evidence that exposure to positive news coverage of the Conservative and Labour parties can produce a clear and significant improvement in party support" (p. 149).

POLITICAL INFORMATION IN THE NEWS

The 1992 and 1997 general elections provide the most recent examples of the kinds of news available to audiences in Britain at election time. The first and clearest difference between the press and television was in the tone of the coverage. The tabloids were blatantly partisan, while television was comparatively speaking, largely impartial. Figure 10.1 shows that tabloid coverage was heavily partisan, with 1992 as the example. The vast majority of stories about Labour on the front page of the *Sun* and

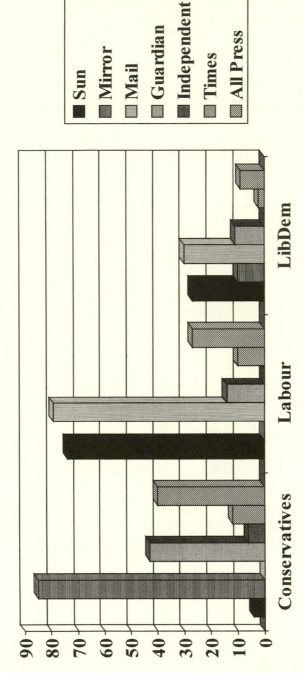

Figure 10.1 Proportion of negative news toward each party in the press, 1992.
Source: 1992 election party and media agenda content analysis by Margaret Scammell and Holli A. Semetko.

Daily Mail were negative, as were nearly one-third of the stories about the Liberal Democrats, whereas there was little or no negative coverage of the Conservatives in these two tabloids. The *Daily Mirror,* by contrast, carried no negative stories about Labour and few about the Liberal Democrats, but almost all of its front-page coverage of the Conservatives was negative. Such partisan bias was far less evident in the broadsheets. With the exception of *The Guardian,* in which more than 40 percent of front-page news about the Tories was negative, the percentage of negative news about each party on page one of other broadsheets in 1992 was quite low. The Liberal Democrats were less prominent here because little front-page attention, negative or otherwise, was paid to them in any of the newspapers.

The extent to which the press was capable of changing its tone on the front page can be seen in Figure 10.2. Overall, the press was far less negative than it had been in 1992. When there was negative news on the front page, the Conservatives bore the brunt of it in all the newspapers. Even the notoriously pro-Tory *Sun* carried considerably more negative stories about the Conservatives than about Labour on its front page in 1997 (see also Norris et al. 1999).

Television news was far less evaluative or negative than the press in 1997, as can be seen in Figure 10.3. In comparison with the press in 1997, there was very little negative news about the parties on BBC's *Nine O'- Clock News,* ITN's *News at Ten,* or SKYTV's main evening news hour. For the Conservatives, negative news accounted for more of their coverage on television than for Labour. The Liberal Democrats escaped negative news almost entirely.

Television news coverage of certain topics or issues shifted considerably from one election to the next. Figure 10.4 displays the extent to which the following four subjects were the main topic of news stories on BBC's *Nine O'Clock News* and ITN's *News at Ten* in 1992 and 1997: the conduct of the campaign, the polls, the party leaders, and the economy. This figures shows that on both news programs from 1992 to 1997 there was a considerable increase in the coverage of the conduct of the campaign, including the day-to-day activities of the parties on the campaign trail, at the morning press conferences, and at the evening rallies. There was also a notable and significant decline in the proportion of stories on both channels that had opinion polls as the main topic. In short, television news coverage in 1992 and 1997 became less focused on polls, more focused on the conduct of the campaign, and more concentrated on the important issue of the economy. News about party leaders declined

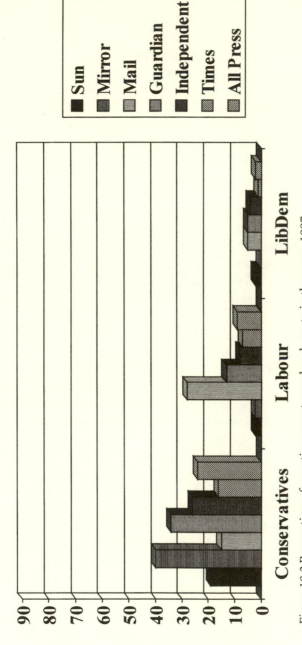

Figure 10.2 Proportion of negative news toward each party in the press, 1997.

Source: 1997 election party and media agenda content analysis by Margaret Scammell and Holli A. Semetko.

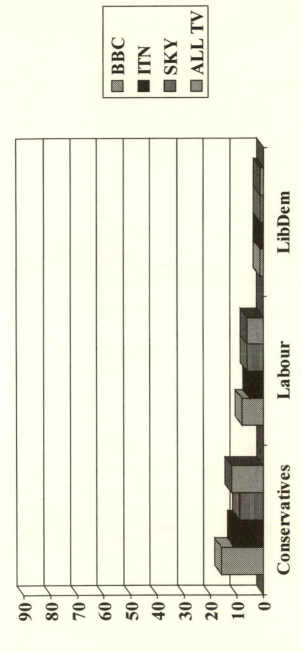

Figure 10.3 Proportion of negative news toward each party on TV news, 1997.
Source: 1997 election party and media agenda content analysis by Margaret Scammell and Holli A. Semetko.

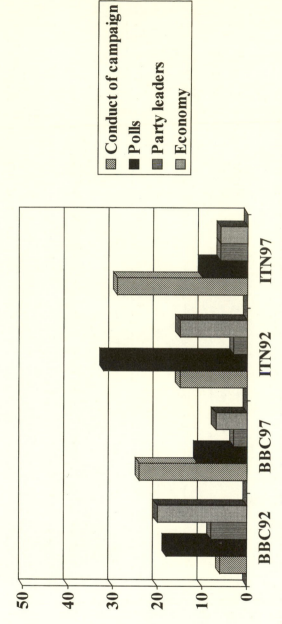

Figure 10.4 Main subject of BBC and ITV news stories, 1992 and 1997 (percentage of stories).
Source: 1997 election party and media agenda content analysis by Margaret Scammell and Holli A. Semetko.

slightly on BBC and increased slightly on ITN. The single biggest change over that period was in the number of stories derived from opinion polls. This was due partly to the closeness of the 1992 race – throughout the campaign the polls promised to end in a hung Parliament (i.e., one in which a single party was not in control of the majority of seats) – but it was also due partly to a change in BBC and ITN policy. ITN, for example, used polls it commissioned in 1992 to discuss the various demographic components of the electorate and the issues that mattered to them. Each Tuesday of the 1992 campaign, it led with the poll result and followed with a related story – for example, on how women would vote and what issues mattered most to them. The BBC took the opposite decision and, relatively speaking, downplayed the opinion polls, although its campaign coverage still included a higher proportion of polls-based stories than it had a decade earlier (see Semetko et al. 1991).

While *SKYNews,* on the cable channel, did provide full coverage of the 1992 campaign, analysis of its political content shows that it differed significantly from BBC and ITN coverage in at least two relevant respects. First, there were fewer stories devoted to the election campaign. Second, when the campaign was featured, substantially more attention was given to the horse race aspect than to coverage of the substantive issues (Stanyer and Nossiter 1993).

In the press, there was a similar increase between 1992 and 1997 in the coverage of the campaign and a decline in the coverage of opinion polls on page one. Figure 10.5 shows how these subjects emerged for six of the national newspapers taken together. News about the party leaders on page one declined slightly, and news about the economy declined considerably.

Figure 10.6 shows that there was some variation among the newspapers in 1997, however, in terms of the emphasis on these four subjects on the front page. With the notable exception of the *Daily Mail,* the front pages paid more attention to the campaign and the polls than to the important issue of the economy. The *Mail,* however, emphasized the economy on page one more than any other topic. The variation across the newspapers in putting poll news on page one shows that the editors, rather than the style of the newspaper (broadsheet or tabloid), largely determined how much the polls featured up front.

In sum, the evidence from content analysis of television and press coverage in the most recent general election campaigns shows that while emphasis on poll coverage declined, news about the daily activities on the campaign trail increased. This attention to campaigning meant a de-

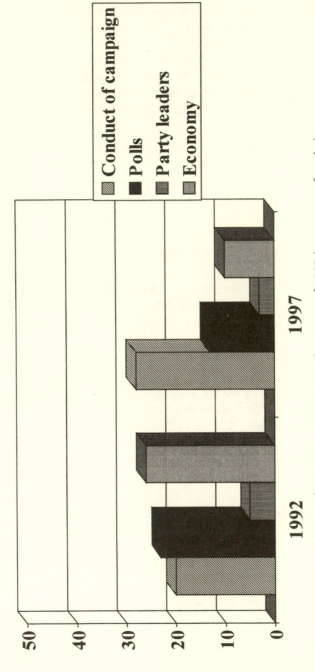

Figure 10.5 Main subject on front-page newspaper stories, 1992 and 1997 (percentage of stories).
Source: 1997 election party and media agenda Content analysis by Margaret Scammell and Holli A. Semetko. Newspapers include the *Sun, Daily Mirror, Daily Mail, The Times, The Independent,* and *The Guardian.*

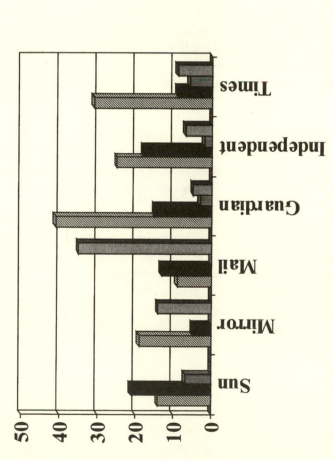

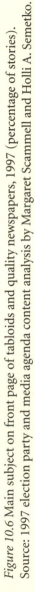

Figure 10.6 Main subject on front page of tabloids and quality newspapers, 1997 (percentage of stories).
Source: 1997 election party and media agenda content analysis by Margaret Scammell and Holli A. Semetko.

cline in the proportion of stories devoted primarily to substantive issues, such as the economy in both television news and the press. Although other substantive issues such as social welfare, education, or foreign affairs (which were largely European in the most recent election) received more attention on television in 1997 than in 1992, the overall amount of news devoted to substantive issues was smaller on both channels. The overall amount of substantive issue news on the front pages of the six newspapers also was down from 1992 (Norris et al. 1999, Chapter 5).

CONCLUSION

The decade of the 1990s in Britain was a watershed in terms of the dramatic changes in the media environment. The increase in the number of television channels was remarkable. Theoretically, this will mean more opportunities for the news junkies to find news, but it is more likely to result in more opportunities for the larger number of uninterested persons to avoid news. The most profound change was the end of one of the country's most popular evening news programs, ITN's *News at Ten*, in March 1999 after more than 40 years on the air, in response to pressures to open the network's prime-time schedule to other types of popular programming. This is a shift to an American-style evening schedule for one of the main television channels in Britain, with news now broadest at 6:30 P.M. and late headlines at 11 *p.m.* At this stage, it is only possible to speculate whether this major change could eventually lead the BBC to end its *Nine O'Clock News.*

Another development concerned the content of television news. In recent campaigns, there has been greater emphasis on the horse race and a corresponding decline in the coverage of substantive issues. British election news in the 1990s was less substantive than in the 1980s. A comparison of 1983 election news in Britain and 1984 news in the United States concluded that British election coverage on television was "more ample, more varied, more substantive, more party oriented, less free with unidirectional comment, and more respectful. By contrast, American election television is more terse, concentrated, horse-racist, guided by conventional news values, ready to pass judgment and ready to be occasionally disrespectful in passing such judgment" (Semetko et al. 142). More than a decade later, this cross-national comparative conclusion may still hold. Although British television news has moved further away from the substantive focus it once had, it remains more substantive than

U.S. election news, and British journalists remain more respectful and less negative about the politicians they cover.

Another remarkable change was the Conservative-to-Labour shift in the partisanship of the press between 1992 and 1997, especially in the mass-market tabloid the *Sun*. This shift was remarkable, first, because of the change in the number of newspapers actually endorsing the Labour Party. It was the first time Labour garnered more press endorsements than the Conservatives, with six of ten national newspapers backing Labour. There was also a dramatic decline in the negative news about the parties presented on the front pages of the newspapers. The screamingly partisan tabloids were simply not as negative on their front pages in 1997 as they had been in 1992. It is not clear whether these developments are unique to the 1997 contest, represent a long-term shift in the partisan preferences of British newspapers, or are the first signs of an era of partisan dealignment in the press.

Finally, research findings on the effects of the media on the vote in the elections of the 1990s are remarkable for their consistency with research findings from previous decades, which concluded that reinforcement, rather than change, was the main effect, if any, on vote choice. The dramatic shift in the partisanship of the *Sun*, for example, did not lead to a dramatic shift on the part of its readers to vote Labour.

The evidence in support of the agenda-setting hypothesis – that the issues in the news become the issues important in public opinion – was largely nonexistent in the 1987 general election based on a rolling cross section of the public (Miller et al. 1990). In 1997 the evidence was more mixed. Survey data showed a considerable distance between the agendas of the news media and the public perception of the most important issues. Panel data showed that those who had been exposed to the intense coverage of news about Europe in the early part of the campaign were not significantly more inclined to name Europe as the most important issue or problem facing the country. But experimental studies of television news found that there was a significant change in the public's issue priorities when they had been exposed to news about Europe and developing countries.

The most remarkable findings from research on Britain's most recent election campaign concern, first, the news media's role in promoting civic engagement and, second, in contributing to public perceptions of parties and politicians. Research over the 1992–7 period found that, in Britain, regular attention to news mobilized civic engagement, a finding that stands in contrast to claims regarding American political behavior: that the media are responsible for such negative developments as low turnout or political cynicism. The second conclusion is drawn from experimental studies of the effects of the tone of election news coverage and the balance of coverage between the main parties on television news. This showed that it was positive news, rather than negative news, that had a significant (and positive) effect on voters' perceptions of political parties and resulted in a significant improvement in party support. This is good news for political campaigners to the extent that they can succeed in bringing good news to the forefront in future election campaigns.

NOTES

1. I would like to thank the following people for valuable comments that contributed to the final version of this chapter: John Curtice, Anthony Mughan, Pippa Norris, David Sanders, and Margaret Scammell.
2. The occupational scale running from "A" (higher managerial or professional) to "E" (residual, on a pension, or receiving another state benefit) is a commonly used measure of objective social class in Britain. The top three categories (A, B, C1) have traditionally been equated with the middle class and the bottom three (C2, D, E) with the working class (Butler and Stokes 1974, 68–73).
3. This estimate, included in a report issued by the Center for Responsive Politics, was broadcast on National Public Radio's *The Morning Edition* on November 25, 1997, and published in *The New York Times* on that same day (p. A12).

CHAPTER 11

Germany: A Society and a Media System in Transition

Max Kaase[1]

The German case is of special interest in any study of the relationship between the mass media and democratic politics.[2] The idea of political reeducation after the period of totalitarian Nazi rule was a core element in the (Western) Allies' restructuring of Germany after 1945, and the mass media played a highly significant role in their resocialization program. Thus, this chapter will discuss to what extent and how the German mass media have contributed to what Conradt (1980, 263) has called a "remade political culture." Its basic theme is that the media are not a political force in their own right. Rather, their importance, especially that of the electronic media, is contingent on the pattern of their interaction with political institutions and the political process at large. The chapter is divided into three sections. The first describes the German mass media system, with its distinctive combination of external pluralism of the print media and internal pluralism of the monopolistic public radio and television systems (*Rundfunk*). The second section looks at the *dualization* of this system brought about by the emergence in the 1980s of privately owned and organized radio and television. Precisely because public radio and television had always taken their constitutionally prescribed role of providing political information for the public very seriously, the resultant changes in program offerings and, eventually, in audience behavior represent a highly significant development in German politics. The final section of the chapter builds on this information and examines the evidence available for mass media effects on the democratic political process at both the institutional (macro) and the individual (micro) level.

LEGAL AND INSTITUTIONAL CONTEXT

The basic structure of the German mass media system was determined by the four Allied powers in the immediate postwar years. The Russians were unique for wanting to create organizational and mass media structures that helped the Communist Party (Weber 1992). Despite following somewhat different licensing principles, at least initially, the three Western Allies, in contrast, were unanimous in their view that the mass media system should be independent of government influence and that structures should be created that were conducive to the democratic reeducation of the German citizenry. One objective was to guarantee external pluralism in the print media market. This did not mean that each party was to have its own newspaper. In fact, there was never a Communist press to speak of at this time, and Liberals (FDP) and Christians Democrats (CDU/CSU) indicated early on that they had little interest in developing a party press. The Social Democrats (SPD) did reestablish their party press, but found in the 1960s and 1970s that the market no longer supported this type of product and had to give up one party-controlled newspaper after the other (Ressmann 1991).

Instead, the notion of external pluralism in the daily newspaper market rests on the assumption that diversified ownership creates a competitive newspaper market that leaves the customer with choices, including political choices. This assumption became strained when a pervasive tendency toward the concentration of newspaper ownership developed in the late 1950s and 1960s (Roeper 1991). This trend has been watched carefully for many years to check that political pluralism has not been impaired. The belief is that oligopolistic concentration has not yet created a threat to external pluralism, although the range of political options voiced in the press may well have been reduced. An important reason for this conclusion is that the national quality newspapers have always represented, and continue to represent, a sufficiently wide range of political views (Schoenbach 1977, 62). These newspapers include most prominently the left-green, Berlin-based *Tageszeitung* (76,000 copies in 1991, or 5.4 percent of that market segment), the left *Frankfurter Rundschau* (195,300 copies, or 15.2 percent), the liberal, Munich-based *Süddeutsche Zeitung* (389,100 copies, or 30.3 percent), the liberal-conservative *Frankfurter Allgemeine Zeitung* (391,700 copies, or 30.6 percent), and the conservative, Bonn-based *Die Welt* of the Axel Springer Verlag chain (230,500, or 18 percent). The intense competition among these newspapers helps to create and maintain an open forum for political debate (Pfetsch 1986). In addition, of all the media, newspapers are by far the most frequently used information source for members of the national Parliament regardless of party (Herzog et al. 1990, 76).

The development of radio in Germany was also strongly shaped by the intervention of the Allied powers during the occupation period. Their initial response was to ban all radio broadcasting by German organizations and to establish their own networks, some of which, like the British and American Armed Forces Networks, are still in operation. Eventually, however, they agreed to the establishment of an indigenous radio system that, like newspapers, would be organized to guarantee maximum independence from government influence. After some disagreement, they created a public radio system fashioned after the British Broadcasting Corporation (BBC).

The Treaty on Germany (Deutschlandvertrag) of May 5, 1955, ended the authority of the Allied High Commission on the organization of the *Rundfunk* in West Germany, but the agreements between the Allies and German politicians reached in the late 1940s had profoundly shaped the future development of the electronic media system. By the mid-1950s, the public radio system in Germany had taken its first stable shape. It consisted of eight regional stations (BR, HR, NDR, SFB, SR, SWF, WDR, and Saar Radio – founded in 1956 after the Saarland's return from French to German rule), which were independent but cooperated under a 1950 arrangement named the *Arbeitsgemeinschaft öffentlich-rechtlicher Rundfunkanstalten der Bundesrepublik Deutschland* (ARD). With Germany receiving more broadcasting frequencies at the 1952 Stockholm conference, the ARD networks soon increased their output beyond the one radio program each had put out to that point. The next expansionary step for the ARD came with the advent of television in 1953, when it decided to produce a joint television program to which each network would contribute according to fixed quotas. This program came into being on November 1, 1954. It marks the last step in the initial development of the new West German *Rundfunk* system after the end of the war. Shaped by concepts originating from the three Western Allies, it was free from direct government intervention, public in structure, funded through viewer fees, and federalized according to central elements in the new German constitution (the *Grundgesetz*).

These principles reflected the concerns not only of the Allies, but also those of the Parliamentary Council (Parlamentarischer Rat) that prepared the 1949 West German constitution. Its constitutional deliberations were deeply influenced by the shortcomings of the constitution of the Weimar Republic and were significant not only for the high priority assigned to freedom of information (article 5), but also for the decision in favor of a federalized polity (article 20). While the authority over cultural affairs, including the electronic media, basically rests with the *Län-*

der (states) (articles 70–4), the *Grundgesetz* contains enough ambiguities not to exclude a priori the federal government completely from all *Rundfunk* affairs (for example, its authority over the postal and telephone systems laid down in article 72). As a consequence, the system of electronic media in Germany and its development over time have been shaped to a large degree by the structural tension between the federal and *Länder* governments.

An early manifestation of this tension was the federal government's creation of its own radio network in 1960, the Deutschland-Fernsehen-GmbH, an enterprise in which the *Länder* had declined to participate, with the result that it was completely under the control of the federal government. The SPD-ruled *Länder* governments of Hamburg, Hesse, Lower Saxony, and Bremen decided to contest this national network before the Constitutional Court (Bundesverfassungsgericht), which, in a noted verdict, declared the Deutschland-Fernsehen-GmbH unconstitutional. The court had felt that the *Bund* had impinged on the constitutional rights of the *Länder* regarding cultural affairs, and that the independence from government intervention essential for the free formation of public opinion in a democratic polity had been violated by the organizational structure planned for the new network. In sum, the Constitutional Court, with this first of its six major statements on the electronic mass media system, emphasized the role of the public organization of the *Rundfunk* in Germany, although the court itself had not a priori excluded the possibility that a network could also be privately organized (Gellner 1990, 39–42).

This legal and political defeat caused the national government to withdraw from *Rundfunk* politics for a while. It also triggered a quick decision by the *Länder* in 1961 to found, via a state treaty (*Staatsvertrag*), a new television network: the Zweites Deutsches Fernsehen (Second German Television Network – ZDF). It was centrally organized, located in Mainz, publicly organized, and funded by viewer fees, plus income from advertising sales. The ZDF started broadcasting on April 1, 1963. German viewers could now choose from two nationwide TV networks that, by state treaty regulation, had to be coordinated so that viewers could select from among different programs (the two networks had to avoid putting on the same type of program – sports, movies, information – in the same time slot). The coordination necessary to establish this goal was institutionalized in the form of a joint ARD-ZDF commission.

The partial, but still substantial, funding of the ZDF through advertising sales (37 percent in 1990) was not the first private element in the *Rund-*

funk system. Although only on an extremely limited scale and with the explicit intention of reinvesting returns in cultural activities outside the network, radio advertising had been introduced in the late 1940s. Then, in 1956, Bavarian Radio (BR) also decided to introduce a limited amount of advertising into its television programs. The result was a bitter conflict with the Association of Newspaper Editors, which was afraid of losing advertising revenue. The dispute was resolved legally in favor of the network so that, by April 1959, the other ARD networks had also introduced advertisements into their TV programs (Bausch 1980, 534–6). This was not the end of the dispute, however. Rather, it escalated so that the federal Parliament eventually became involved. A commission was established in 1963 to study the problem. Called the Michel Commission (after its president), it concluded some four years later that TV advertising did not harm fair competition between TV and the press, that a TV network owned by the publishers would be unconstitutional, and that a clause preventing TV advertising would impair the ability of the networks to fulfill their constitutional role of providing information to the public. In return for this favorable decision, the networks offered to limit advertising time to 20 minutes per day, to be placed into the regional segments of the general ARD program between 6 P.M. and 8 P.M. in blocks, excluding Saturdays and Sundays. Later, advertising was also permitted on Saturdays.

The next major development in the German media system was the government-sanctioned emergence of private television networks. Political events, like Elisabeth Noelle-Neumann's (1977) claim that left-wing journalists, particularly in the ARD networks, had cost the CDU/CSU the 1976 general election (Kaase 1989, 97–8), may well have contributed to this development. But more important was the emergence of new technologies of mass communication, like cable and communication satellites, and their increasing availability at reasonable cost. A crucial decision in opening up the German media market to these new technologies was taken in 1981, when the Constitutional Court determined (in the context of a media law in the Saarland meant to admit private radio) that private television was acceptable in principle as long as certain conditions were met – one of them being an obligation on the part of the states, even in case of a surplus of frequencies, to regulate the operation of private networks (Gellner 1990, 45). In the following years, every *Länd* passed a state media law creating an institution responsible for licensing private radio and television networks, controlling the content of the broadcasts, and deciding which programs are to be aired on cable networks (Kleinsteuber and Wilke 1992, 84).

This was not the end of the story, however. The emergence of privately owned national television networks, and the spread of new media technologies with their border-transcending qualities eventually forced the *Länder* governments to consider a new legal framework for the *Rundfunk* in Germany. The painstaking process of consensus-building among them had begun in 1982, accelerating in 1986 after the Constitutional Court laid out the principles under which a dual (public/private) system of electronic mass media had to be organized. One important element of the ruling was that the public elements of the system (ARD/ZDF) were assigned the function of providing society with all of the basic information necessary for a democratic polity (*Grundversorgung*) (Libertus 1991). To perform this task, the court accepted that both ARD and ZDF would continue to be funded by a mix of fees and advertising returns, whereas the private channels had to rely for their income only on advertising sales. With this ruling as a backdrop, the minister-presidents of the *Länder* agreed on a state treaty (DLM 1988, 307–15) that took effect on December 1, 1987.

But two new developments forced a revision of this treaty on August 31, 1991, which became effective on January 1, 1992. These were, first, German unification and the ensuing reorganization of the electronic media in East Germany (resulting in the creation of two new ARD regional networks – see Faul 1991) and, second, the need to adapt German regulation of the *Rundfunk* to European developments, especially those regarding the regulations of border-transcending broadcasts by the Council of Europe and the TV regulation (*Fernsehrichtlinie*) of the Commission of the European Communities (Siune and Truetzschler 1992). The 1991 treaty does not make any fundamental changes to its 1987 predecessor (Stock 1992), but it does represent the final seal of approval for the dual system of public and private electronic mass media in Germany.

GERMANS AND THE MASS MEDIA

The German "economic mirale" is manifest not only in the increased purchasing power of individual households, but also in the amount of time Germans have for leisure activities. In 1964 the average West German already had 5 hours and 40 minutes of free time per day, an amount that by 1990 had reached 8 hours, and 71 percent of this time was spent at home. This leisure time is more than that of any other industrialized nation in the world. Moreover, the consumption of mass media offerings is the most important leisure-time activity for Germans by a wide margin. To be more specific, on an average workday, about half of the West Germans (and even 68 percent of the East Germans) are in contact with all three media: newspapers, radio, and television. Each medium reaches about three-quarters of the adult population on a workday, and practically everyone has at least some mass media exposure. There have been some changes over time in these distributions, but by and large, the overall impression is one of stability (for details, see Berg and Kiefer 1992, 52).

The Germans' "love affair" with their media, however, does not necessarily translate into affect for them. The early 1980s, in fact, marks a break in their belief in the truthfulness and objectivity of the media. As indicated in Table 11.1, by 1990 only one-quarter of Germans definitely believed in the truthfulness and objectivity of the media, newspapers being the least trusted among the three. There is little reason to think that this loss of trust, particularly in television, is rooted in changes in the messages that the media communicate or in the way they communicate them. Since there are parallel findings for many other societal and political institutions, a more convincing argument is that declining trust is more the result of change in the subjective evaluation processes of Germans.

While trust in television has declined more than average for the media as a whole, it still outdistances radio and newspapers as the most trusted information source when the three media carry divergent information about the same event. This is probably because, while all three media would be greatly missed if hypothetically they were not available, television remains the medium of choice for about half of the population. When people were asked which program segments they would miss most, it was political information that ranked first, although its lead is greater in some media than others. The electronic media, for example, are also valued for the entertainment element in their programming, something that newspapers apparently cannot equally master. Instead, newspapers' strong point is local and regional information, which in Germany up to now, neither television nor radio has adequately provided (Berg and Kiefer 1992, 219, 230).

The dualization of Germany's *Rundfunk* system brought three major modes of access to television: terrestrial, through cable, and through satellite dish. By 1992, an average of 48 percent of the 25 million households in West Germany received television programs terrestrially, 44 percent through cable, and 8 percent via satellite dish. The matching figures for East Germany's 6 million households are 66, 17, and 17 percent, re-

Table 11.1   *Perceived Objectivity of the Mass Media, 1964 – 95*

Indicators of Objectivity	Year						
	1964 %	1970 %	1974 %	1980 %	1985 %	1990 %	1995[a] %
TV							
Is Truthful	47	56	43	51	27	28	20
Is objective	51	59	49	41	27	28	20
Is the most objective of the three media	—	75	70	68	62	63	56
Radio							
Is Truthful	45	47	38	32	25	24	19
Is objective	41	38	31	28	24	23	15
Is the most objective of the three media	—	13	13	14	17	15	15
Newspaper							
Is Truthful	32	23	22	21	18	19	20
Is objective	31	20	20	19	17	18	15
Is the most objective of the three media	—	12	14	15	21	22	31

[a]Germany, 1964–90: West Germany.
Source: Berg and Kiefer 1992, 255; Berg and Kiefer 1996, 252.

spectively. While these different modes of access are irrelevant for the comprehensively available ARD and ZDF public networks, the shortage of terrestrial frequencies has made private channels highly dependent on cable and satellite reception. By mid-1992, RTL and SAT 1 could reach about 80 percent of all households in East and West Germany, and the smaller PRO 7 and Tele 5 channels about 50 percent. This expansion of the private television sector has been accompanied by much concern, especially among the SPD, that high-quality programs would be replaced in viewer preference by low-quality progams. One fear was that the continuous education of the German people toward responsible citizenship (the *mündiger Bürger*) would be endangered. This fear revolved around what access to private channels would do to the program choices of the audience and, relatedly, what would be the effects of this changed pattern of viewing.

The effect on viewing patterns has certainly been dramatic. For a start, the availability of additional channels has increased the amount of time people spend watching television. Most of this increase has come from the extension of private channels into the daytime television hours, for a long time a definite "no-no" with the public networks. But since many households still have only limited access to cable TV, the average viewing time in TV households has increased only slightly over the last five years (Darschin and Frank 1992, 172–3). It is in the mix of programs people watch that cable TV has had its greatest impact, however. It has been able to satisfy the entertainment needs of viewers that the public channels could not because their governing bodies were wedded to the ideas of political education and cultural sophistication in TV programs. Thus, in 1992, viewers in cabled households devoted less of their time (44 percent) to the public than to the private channels. The national viewing averages, in contrast, are 53 to 47 percent in favor of the public networks, but this difference should vanish as more and more households obtain access to private channels. An even split between the two network types is about the best the public networks can hope for in the future. In fact, there is reason to believe that they will have a difficult time maintaining even a 50 percent share, thereby accentuating the financial strains ARD and ZDF are already feeling due to the financial ceiling on licence fees and at best stable nominal returns from an enormously increased budget for TV advertising. The public *Rundfunk*'s share of the 2,076 million DM (ca. $1,065 million) spent on television and radio advertising in 1986 was 94.8 percent. The same figure in 1991 was 47.6 percent of a 4,309 million DM ($2,210 million) total.

The attractiveness of the private networks derives almost exclusively from their attention to entertainment programming. A 1989–90 content analysis of the programs on the two large public and private networks (Krueger 1992, 138–76, 531–9) attests to the large role that fiction-based entertainment plays on the private channels compared to the public ones, especially in prime time (7 to 11 P.M.). The entertainment ratio is about two to one in the private networks' favor. The public channels correspondingly have about a three to one edge over the private ones in information. These data clearly corroborate all expectations that homogenization rather than diversification would result from the licencing of private networks. They also demonstrate how the Constitutional Court's assignment of the responsibility for providing programs satisfying all legitimate political information, culture, and entertainment needs to the public channels has to some extent relieved the private channels of this obligation.

MASS MEDIA AND THE STABILITY
OF GERMAN DEMOCRACY

The 1950s and early 1960s can, in retrospect, be viewed as the quiet years of economic recovery and democratic consolidation in Germany. A stable party system had emerged which by the 1961 election saw only the CDU/CSU, SPD, and FDP represented in the federal Parliament. The pluralistic press and the public system of electronic mass media were regarded at that time as the quasi-natural state of affairs, satisfying the need for a pluralistic information market (Rager and Weber 1992). Germans appeared to be politically interested, knowledgeable, and dutiful citizens who took their democratic obligation to vote very seriously. Indeed, their turnout at the polls was among the highest of any Western democracy (Almond and Verba 1963).

The mass media may well have contributed to this state of affairs. Article 5 of the German Constitution of 1949 had not only codified the right of every citizen to speak and be informed freely, but had also institutionalized freedom of the press as well as freedom of the *Rundfunk* and of film. Moreover, the organizational structure of the *Rundfunk* was evaluated from the outset by the Constitutional Court according to whether it adequately safeguarded the principles laid down in Article 5 of the Constitution, and the concept of internal pluralism was the normative yardstick that all corporate and individual actors inside and outside the *Rundfunk* system were expected to apply in producing and evaluating information in the *Rundfunk*.

Data are available, however, that allow us to speak with some degree of confidence about specific aspects of the interface between the mass media and democracy in postwar Germany. The first of them is political support. The 1959 Civic Culture Study had testified to a level of political information-seeking on the part of West German citizens that was high even when compared to the established democracies of the United States and Great Britain, but it also questioned how closely Germans identified with their new democratic political system. By the early 1970s, however, Germans had come to manifest substantial support for their political institutions, support that was independent of the system's economic performance (Conradt 1980; Fuchs 1989; Westle 1989). There is no empirical evidence available linking this development directly to the mass media, but the constitutional, legal, and political underpinnings of the media system were such that its strongly supportive role in developing the democratic creed after 1945 can be safely assumed, particularly given the widespread availability and use of media sources for political information. Taking television as an example, after a hesitant start with one network and one channel in the mid-1950s, practically every German household was receiving the two networks and three channels available by the early 1970s (Berg and Kiefer 1992, 173).

A second aspect of the media–democracy interface is the relationship between the mass media and political interest/political competence. Following World War II, both the Allied powers and Germany's own new political elites saw the mass media as playing a major role in creating a sense of popular involvement in the new political system after years of political apathy. It is also the case that one of the most pervasive trends in the political orientation of the German citizenry is the substantial rise in subjective political interest (Dalton 1988, 23; Noelle-Neumann 1988, 230; Berg and Kiefer 1992, 173). This development, which is not unique to Germany (Dalton 1988), took place mostly in the 1960s and coincided with the spread of television. It is not surprising that the above authors have posited a causal link between the two factors, television being regarded as the cause, and the surge in political interest the effect. This effect, however, may be more apparent than real since other important developments were taking place at the same time, and these provide equally credible explanations of the rising political interest. Prominent among them are the educational revolution, greater affluence, and the growth of leisure time through economic modernization, to name just three.

But even granting that the empirical evidence concerning the impact of television on political interest is inconclusive, one research finding deserves special mention. In 1966–7, Elisabeth Noelle-Neumann and her Allensbach Institut für Demoskopie were commissioned by the ARD to run a quasi-experimental field study to test media effects. In a before-after design covering a period of one year, 167 test group households and 169 control group households were interviewed before and after the test group purchased its first television set. By the end of the experiment, the test group showed a significant increase in political interest, thereby corroborating the suspected relationship between television exposure and politicization. Still more interestingly, however, the separation of test and control groups into strong and weak users of the print media showed that, in both groups, those with regular exposure to television *and* low exposure to newspapers changed their perception of politics: politics now appeared more entertaining, easy, active, and consensual – in essence, less political.[3]

One should be cautious about overinterpreting these findings. But bearing in mind that television is the most important and most trusted information source for most individuals, they should at least be noted. This would seem especially advisable since these findings identify a group in the media audience that time and again surfaces as being particularly vulnerable to television exposure: politically uninterested and uninformed people who receive almost all of whatever little information on politics they have from television.

A third aspect of the media–democracy interface concerns overall levels of political knowledge and sophistication in the public. The omnipresence of television and other mass media information sources raises the question of whether these levels have become higher with the spread of the media. While it is quite plausible to think that increased subjective interest in political matters also raises the level and quality of the public's political information and sophistication, this relationship cannot be studied empirically for want of appropriate data. Neuman (1986, 170–8) has concluded from his secondary analysis of American data that there seems to exist a stratified three-part public whose proportions remain stable over time: the apoliticals (20 percent), the middle mass (75 percent), and the activists (5 percent). Unfortunately, he does not deal explicitly and empirically with the question of whether the stability of this distribution of political competence is due to the fact that he considers only the relative, not the absolute, level of political knowledge and sophistication. One might well reason that even if the distribution of apoliticals, middle mass, and activists has remained stable over time, the public's absolute level of political information and sophistication has increased as a result of the availability of more diversified print and electronic media. More media, however, cannot be automatically equated with greater knowledge and sophistication because of the intervening variables of media content and audience behavior.

A similar argument would be that as more media sources become available, then, ceteris paribus, the probability of a better-informed public increases, and such a development would benefit democratic politics. But the opposite hypothesis is equally plausible. That is, greater availability might lead to more choice in media content, thereby further segmenting the public and reducing its overall level of political knowledge and sophistication. One could also speculate, as the knowledge gap hypothesis does, that as more and more sources of political information become available, the most privileged strata of society draw greatest profit from them, so that the overall distribution of political knowledge shifts, to the net disadvantage of those strata who were less knowledgeable to begin with. Unfortunately, there is presently no evidence that speaks authoritatively to the question of the relationship between increased media availability and the distribution of political knowledge and sophistication. Given Noelle-Neumann's (1988, 230) finding that surging levels of subjective political interest in Germany at least have not been associated with higher levels of political information, perhaps the wisest conclusion is the conservative one that, increased media availability notwithstanding, as the public becomes more interested in politics, it does not necessarily come to know more, and become more sophisticated, about politics.

A final aspect of the media–democracy interface is what has been termed the "video malaise" hypothesis (Robinson 1976). The media research dicussed to this point has suggested that long-term media effects may exist. A variation on this same theme is Robinson's observation that, in general, television consistently paints a negative picture of political actors and institutions in general, and this contributed, to say the least, to the widespread sense of political malaise in the United States in the 1970s. A more rigorous test of this hypothesis content analyzed newspaper and related survey respondents' usage of these newspapers to their political trust. By and large, the malaise hypothesis was supported. There proved to a stable and sizable positive relationship between negative newspaper evaluations of political actors and institutions, on the one hand, and respondents' newspaper exposure and their level of political distrust, on the other. This impact was found to be particularly strong among those with only elementary education (Miller et al. 1979).

A content analysis of the evaluative dimension in news and information programs was undertaken in Germany in the mid-1980s, and both types of television network were covered (Faul et al. 1988, 210–36). The researchers' initial step was to measure the extent to which evaluations were present at all in these programs, comparing especially the public and private networks. They came to a number of conclusions. First, there were only low levels of evaluative content, regardless of the program. Second, and reflecting the different missions of the two types of program, more evaluative content was found in magazine programs (32.7 percent on the average) than in news reports (12.8 percent on the average). Finally, evaluation was particularly prevalent in the magazine programs of the public channels. The private channels, especially RTL (at least in 1986), had almost no evaluative political content. Moreover, this difference persisted in the 1987 election campaign (Mathes and Freisens 1990, 557).

Table 11.2   *Evaluation of Political Institutions and Political Actors in News Programs and Political Magazines by Public and Private Channels, 1984–6 (Cable Pilot Project Ludwigshafen)*

Presence and Direction of Evaluation	Public Channels		Private Channels	
	ARD (%)	ZDF (%)	Sat 1 (%)	RTL Plus (%)
News programs				
Present	17	18	7	3
Not present	83	82	93	97
Political magazines				
Present	47	48	19	7
Not Present	53	52	81	93
Evaluation in news programs[a]				
Federal government	−.67	−.30	[b]	—
CDU/CSU	−1.29	−.95	—	—
SPD	−1.09	−.58	—	—
FDP	−.95	−1.00	—	—
Greens	−1.40	−1.60	—	—
Evaluation in political magazines				
Federal government	−.53	−.15	[b]	—
CDU/CSU	−.64	−.67	—	—
SPD	−1.04	−.85	—	—
FDP	−.62	−.83	—	—
Greens	−.85	−.29	—	—
Business Union	−.97	−.31	—	—
Trade Union	−1.60	−.52	—	—

[a]Coded on a + 3 to − 3 continuous scale.

[b]Not available because of the small number of evaluations.

Source: Faul et al. 1988, 215, 217, 233, 235.

More pertinent from the perspective of the video malaise hypothesis, however, is the finding that the television evaluation of political objects is consistently and quite sizably negative across government, parties, and intermediary organizations (see Table 11.2). Moreover, this finding was fully corroborated by a content analysis of public and private news and information programs during the 1990 election campaign (Kaase 1994).

However, Holtz-Bacha (1990), in a secondary analysis of a 1984 European election study and a 1984 Dortmund local study in the Robinson video malaise tradition, has embroidered the Noelle-Neumann idea that it is the specific interaction of reading and viewing that is important for media effects. In her study, Holtz-Bacha found that those scoring high on both television and newspaper information were low on political alienation, while those low on both television and newspaper information were high on alienation. Conversely, those high on television and newspaper entertainment were also high on alienation. When the impact of newspapers and television is compared, it appears that high newspaper exposure to information diminishes political alienation, whereas high television exposure to entertainment programs increases alienation. Once again, as in the American case, the effect is strongest for the low-education group (Holtz-Bacha 1990, 131–2).

This study not only emphasizes that types of media content matter, but also reinforces the need to look at the combinations of media people use in a holistic fashion. If, for reasons of media logic (Altheide and Snow 1979 and 1991), television encourages people to process political information in a way that cannot properly cope with the complexities of political reality, then it is necessary to take account of their reading habits as well as their television exposure. Noelle-Neumann (1988), for instance, argues that without learning to process political information sequentially, as is done in reading, people are not capable of fitting the many unconnected bits of political information from various sources into a meaningful picture. Thus, the argument continues, the disjointed bits of political information people get from television produce disproportionately strong effects, especially on depoliticized segments of the audience. When, as studies show (Franzmann 1989, 92), television also reduces the probability of reading, then the relationship between television and the political process might be much more complex than is usually believed.

POLITICAL INFORMATION AND THE DUALIZATION OF GERMAN TELEVISION

The emergence of private television (and radio) in the mid-1980s was undoubtedly a momentous change in the overall German mass media system. Its effect on audience viewing patterns was documented earlier in this chapter. When account is also taken of the argument that the abundance of political information on public television, to which there was no viewing alternative at the time, was at least partly responsible for the postwar rise in subjective political interest among Germans, then the new program options offered by the private networks have the potential to drive a wedge between the country's most and least resourceful citizens, in terms of their political information. This could happen through a cumulative twofold process: (1) the political information presented by the private networks has less quantity and richness of content than that offered by the public networks, and (2) less information, again in quantity and content, is consumed by groups already low in socio-economic status in particular.

Regarding the first stage in this potential process, the only relevant data presently available come from the early phase (1984–6) of dualization. Pfetsch (1991) has demonstrated a dramatic difference in the amount of political information in the news programs and magazine programs of the public and private networks. On the public channels, 74 percent of the news programs and 83 percent of the magazine programs have political content. The corresponding figures for the private channels are 34 and 47 percent, respectively. Clearly, the private channels are much less politicized (and at the same time, their political coverage avoids complexity; see Pfetsch 1991, 118–38). The outcome is to increase the tendency of many Germans to avoid political information altogether[4] (see Table 11.3).

The second stage in this process involves the potential differentiation of the German people into sub-publics, each with its distinctive media-exposure pattern. This outcome corresponds to concerns voiced against the dualization of the media system in the early phase of the debate. The essential argument was that "soft" pressure, in the sense of limiting program choices so as to enforce exposure to informational programs, was desirable for its contribution to maintaining a democratically oriented citizenry. While it says nothing about the democratic orientations of the different sub-publics, Table 11.4 does show that, in the West as well as in the East, those who favor private over public television channels do indeed tend to avoid political information. Moreover, this tendency embraces newspapers as well as television, but it is much less obvious with respect to radio.

To be sure, the differences between the two sub-publics are not breathtaking. It must be borne in mind, however, that private channels had been widely available for only about two years at the time of the study from which these results are taken (1990). Thus, this argument could be stood on its head, that is, that the effects are already surprisingly large given the short time span.

In sum, then, empirical evidence points to the fact that the dualization of the electronic mass media system has affected the flow of political information, since private networks provide less coverage of politics,

Table 11.3   *Centrality of Politics in TV News Programs*
and TV Political Magazines on Public and Private Channels:
1985/6 (Cable Pilot Project Ludwigshafen) and 1993

	Channels			
	Public Channels (ARD/ZDF)		Private Channels (SAT. 1/RTL)	
Centrality of	1985–6	1993	1985–6	1993
Politics in TV	(%)	(%)	(%)	(%)
New Programs				
Politics central	74	77	34	70
Domestic	54		58	
Foreign	25		22	
Both	21		20	
No political content	26	23	66	30
Political Magazines				
Politics central	83	n.a.	47	n.a.
Domestic	57		79	
Foreign	12		3	
Both	31		18	
No political content	17	n.a.	53	n.a.

Source: For 1985–6: Pfetsch 1991, 96 and 109; for 1993: Pfetsch 1996, 491.

convey information with substantially less political content, and, through their success in attracting a substantial fraction of the television audience, reduce the public's exposure to the high-level and high-quality political information provided by the public networks. There is some tentative evidence that dualization is producing audiences that are segmented according to the amount and content of political information to which they are exposed (see Table 11.4), but it is still too early to say whether this structural change in the media system will affect the future political orientations of Germans.

THE MASS MEDIA AND ELECTIONS

Electoral behavior in contemporary Western Europe can be characterized as an ongoing process of dealignment of long-established coalitions of social groups from political parties (Dalton et al. 1984; Crewe and Denver 1985; Bartolini and Mair 1990; Franklin et al. 1992). This dealignment, it is held, has weakened many voters' attachment to their political party of choice and has made them more susceptible to short-

Table 11.4 *Watching TV on Public or Private Channels and Using Specific Types of Political Information in the Mass Media: West Germany and East Germany, 1990 and 1995 (Percentages)*

Types of Political Communication in the Mass Media Used	West Germany				East Germany			
	Watched TV On . . .				Watched TV On . . .			
	Public Channel		Private Channel		Public Channel		Private Channel	
	1990	1995	1990	1995	1990	1995	1990	1995
TV								
Brief news	25	24	32	27	50	34	59	38
Extensive news	74	72	59	54	72	70	56	52
Other poplitical programs	16	15	11	10	24	15	17	10
TV, but no politics	16	19	25	32	12	19	19	30
Radio								
Brief news	51	42	51	41	71	57	70	56
Extensive news	34	34	29	31	52	47	42	40
Commentaries	10	8	9	7	24	13	19	11
Other poplitical programs	8	6	9	4	14	9	9	9
Radio, but no politics	15	20	17	20	8	13	9	14
Newspaper								
News	54	48	46	39	62	42	60	37
Commentaries	31	29	25	23	.5	23	29	19
Other poplitical news	31	26	24	22	.4	23	31	18
Newspapers, but no politics	14	18	16	19	14	24	14	26

Source: Berg and Kiefer 1996, 195.

term electoral forces like personalities and issues. Personality- or issue-based voting, however, is exactly the type of voting that is dependent on media information about the political agenda, the priority ranking of the various agenda items, and images of who is most competent to solve the problems in question. Strangely enough, this expanded role for the media in the electoral process has not resulted in more research attention being paid to it. In a survey of major German sociological and political science journals, Kaase (1986; 1989) found that mass communication is conspicuously absent from these fields. Most likely, the macro social sciences have shown so little interest in the mass media for a number of reasons. First, the media saturation of German society has been a slow process, and this has kept it below the threshold of scholarly and public attention. Second, as discussed previously, the effects of gradual changes resulting from complex macro–micro interactions are very difficult to estimate reliably through empirical research, not to mention, of course, that the use of appropriate research designs even in the present would be very expensive. Finally, the American dictum of the early 1960s that mass communications do not change existing attitudes, but rather reinforce them, created a highly durable consensus among political scientists (and politicians) in Germany that there was little point in studying media effects in the context of elections.

In retrospect, three partly interactive developments brought this consensus into question in Germany. First, there is the previously discussed public debate about the dualization of the electronic (mass) media market in the 1970s. Second, by the late 1960s, Elisabeth Noelle-Neumann and her followers had rejected the notion of a weak media and had established a new research agenda for German communication studies. Her revisionist claim was most powerfully made in her argument that ARD and ZDF coverage of the 1976 election had decisively influenced its outcome in favor of the SPD/FDP coalition already in power in Bonn (Kaase 1989). This was also the context in which she developed her concept of the "spiral of silence" (Noelle-Neumann 1977; 1989), which continues to have a major impact on politics as well as on research, despite recent empirical studies casting grave doubts on its validity (Scherer 1990; Fuchs et al. 1992). Third, some young social scientists trained in modern mass communication studies in the United States and working in political parties, especially in the CDU/CSU, came to a different understanding of the potentially potent role of television in election campaigning. Peter Radunski (1977; 1980; 1983) has been especially prominent among those helping to convince the CDU/CSU that elections in established democracies could be won on television.

In modern concepts of campaigning, the campaign itself remains the key element in the ongoing struggle to win or retain political power.[5] Television, however, has fundamentally changed the strategy of campaigning in Germany as well as in other countries. Party agendas are important elements in defining the framework by which actors are judged, particularly through priming processes. Thanks to television and the communication flexibility it offers party strategists, agendas are no longer permanently fixed in advance of the campaign, but are continually constructed and reconstructed to take account of developments beneficial or detrimental to the party's chances of victory. Furthermore, the parties deliberately stage campaign events for the media, so-called pseudo-events, to attract coverage and free publicity on popular television news and information programs in particuar. There also seems to be an increasing tendency to build campaigns around party leaders to suit the demands of television, a medium that lends itself better to the projection of personalities than to the discussion of issues or complex policy differences. The campaign strategies of political parties, in short, have adapted to the internal logic of television (Altheide and Snow 1979; 1991; Pfetsch 1991, 39–47).

The single most commonly noted consequence of television-based campaigning is personalization, or the thesis that mass publics have become more dependent on party leader images when choosing which party to vote for. It is difficult to assess the validity of this thesis in the particular context of Germany. It strongly reflects the influence of voting behavior research carried out in the United States, which, as a presidential system, embodies an institutional impetus for personalized campaigning. Findings from a large content analysis study of the 1990 German general election campaign point out that the type of political actor (individual or organizational) found in the German parliamentary system is far more organization-institutional than personal (Kaase 1994). This conclusion is buttressed by survey responses since 1969 to open-ended questions asking Germans what they think is good and bad about the major political parties. Table 11.5 shows that there has been no trend in the direction of increased personalization in popular evaluations of the parties. It indicates instead that people react to specific events and specific candidates (as, for example, in 1980, when Franz Josef Strauss was the CDU/CSU candidate for the chancellorship). The lesson would seem to be that institutional differences need to be taken into ac-

Table 11.5 *Percentage of Responses Naming Politicians When Asked about the Good and Bad Points of German Political Parties*

| Year | Political Parties | | | | | |
	SPD (%)	CDU/CSU (%)	FDP (%)	Greens[a] (%)	PDS[b] (%)	Number of Respondents
1969	23.6	19.3	—	—	—	939
1972	21.8	23.3	19.7	—	—	1,588
1976	24.0	32.2	16.7	—	—	2,076
1980	34.0	45.6	24.2	—	—	1,519
1983	25.3	32.7	22.0	5.9	—	1,197
1987	24.0	25.5	27.8	10.4	—	1,953
1990 (West)	27.8	29.7	44.4	7.0	—	1,476
1990 (East)	34.7	29.9	41.9	7.8	25.5	959
Mean value						
1969–1990 (West)	25.8	29.8	25.8	6.4	—	—

Note The author appreciates the support of Hans-Dieter Klingemann, who provided these data.

[a]The Greens were founded as a political party in 1980. They participated in the general election of 1980, but with 1.5 percent of the second vote (*Zweitstimme*), they did not make it into the Bundestag because of the 5 pecent threshold.

[b]The PDS *(Partei des Demokratischen Sozialismus)* is the follow-up party to the hegemonial *Sozialistische Einheitspartei Deutschlands* (SED) in the GDR.

count when generalizing about such phenomena as the personalization of politics.

Despite such conclusions, the mass media should not be dismissed. It must be remembered that politics, even at its most superficial, is hardly accessible to the individual citizen except through the mass media. Moreover, political authority in pluralist democracies is awarded to groups, usually parties, only for a constitutionally limited amount of time. It is this mutual dependency nexus that chains voters, parties, and the mass media inextricably to each other. Changes in the system of mass communications, therefore, invariably have a political impact. A shortcoming is that we know very little about the details of such interactions.

One element of it, though, is the effort of the political parties in Germany to control the *Rundfunk,* not only indirectly through its various boards (Rundfunkrat/Fernsehrat, Verwaltungsrat), but also directly by placing party-affiliated journalists on the ARD and ZDF staffs (Kutteroff

1984). It is doubtful, though, that this is why content analyses of the news programs of the public channels have always shown a strong preoccupation with established political actors and especially government institutions (Schatz et al. 1981; Faul et al. 1988, 195–210; Kepplinger et al. 1989, 56–64; Pfetsch 1991, 102–4). Since this preoccupation is far less apparent on the private channels, Pfetsch (1991, 133) plausibly explains this difference by arguing that the guiding principle of newscasting in public channels is elite orientation, whereas in private channels it is audience orientation. The two types of networks simply follow different internal operating logics.

In addition, despite objections in the 1970s from the (then) CDU/CSU opposition party that the public news programs favored the (then) governing SPD/FDP coalition parties, no bias to speak of has in fact been found. This is well summarized by Faul et al. (1988), who speak of an "almost book-keeping balance" in the political reports of the public channels on the major political parties.[6] Moreover, even if some parties had indeed been favored by ARD and/or ZDF in the 1970s, as Noelle-Neumann (1977) has claimed, no reliable evidence is available indicating that this imbalance had an impact on politics, such as by influencing voting decisions.

The truth of the matter is probably that West Germany's federal government structure, and the corresponding federalization of the public electronic media monopoly, have in the long run led not to pluralism but to an impasse – to an immobile balance between major political forces that has been jealously guarded by the established parties and the governing bodies of the public networks. The system of public licence fees, which is completely under political control, crucially underpinned this status quo and, although probably not deliberately, only the advent of private TV and radio networks was able breach it.

Given this kind of pillarized public *Rundfunk* structure, it is little wonder that campaign managers worked to develop campaign scenarios to take advantage of the characteristics of each medium and strategies (like creating pseudoevents) that apply news value theory and agenda building suited to the medium's effective exploitation for electoral purposes. Strangely enough, though, there is at present no study of continuity and change in the campaign strategies of the German parties over time (Kaase 1992). Even so, what cannot be doubted is that television has assumed a role in campaign planning (Radunski 1983) that extends far beyond the simple notion of obtaining television time for campaign advertisements, which are free of charge in Germany (Schoenbach 1987; 1991).

GERMAN UNIFICATION AND THE MASS MEDIA

After four months of political mobilization in the autumn of 1989, East German authorities opened their country's borders with West Germany on November 9. On March 18, 1990, East Germans for the first time voted in a free election for a national Parliament, and by October 3, German unity had been achieved. In the context of this chapter, two questions relating to German unification deserve special attention: (1) to what extent have the mass media contributed to the unification process? and (2) what is the potential mid- to long-range effect of regular exposure of substantial parts of the East German population to West German television and radio?

Before these questions can be addressed, a little information about the role of the West German mass media in the former German Democratic Republic (GDR) is necessary. As a totalitarian state, the GDR had always been concerned with controlling the flow of information to its citizens. However, other than with respect to the Central and Eastern European socialist countries, the GDR's geographical location made full control impossible. Except for the southeastern region of Dresden, West German radio and television could always be received relatively easily in the GDR. Geographical location was not the only important consideration, of course. West Germany also made a conscious effort to maintain, through the creation of powerful transmitter stations close to the East German border, a media linkage between the two countries. Hardly surprisingly, the East German authorities in the 1960s tried through various means, ranging from police controls to changing the program offerings of their own channels, to prevent their citizens from watching West German television. The East German government abandoned this policy in the 1970s, partly because it was causing a lot of animosity in its citizenry and partly because it felt that, with the construction of the Berlin Wall in 1961, it had stabilized the socialist system in the GDR. Indeed, access to West German television was even eased, in part because of the availability of technology like high-quality antenna systems.

The lack of routine large-scale audience research in the GDR and the unavailability, for political reasons, of whatever findings GDR audience research produced over the 40 years of its statehood make it difficult to assess how audience behavior developed in the GDR. However, results since 1989 indicate that young people exposed themselves more to West German than to East German radio and television since the mid-1980s and that this bias became stronger later that same decade (Stiehler 1990, 98–9). At least half of the apprentices, young workers, and students surveyed had been receiving political information from both the West German and East German electronic media by 1980. In addition, about three-quarters of all GDR families had relatives and/or friends in the West with whom they maintained regular contact (Friedrich and Griese 1991, 142). In sum, East Germans were regularly exposed to much the same kind of media world as the West Germans and, as such, were receiving a lot of manifest and latent countersystem information long before unification. This situation is aptly described by the dictum that "in Germany every evening, electronic reunification is happening in front of the tube" (cited by Hesse 1990, 334).

To return to the question of the West German media's contribution to the unification process, there can be no doubt that television in particular played an important role in accelerating the process of regime delegitimization in the GDR. The ARD and ZDF provided blanket coverage of developments in the GDR from the beginning of the exodus of GDR citizens to West Germany through Hungary, Poland, and Czechoslovakia in August–September 1989 (Krueger and Rinz 1990). This same coverage was also picked up by various citizen groups in East Germany, since their own media did not report fully on events until late October, when Erich Honecker resigned (Hesse 1990, 338). This was the signal that the East German Communist Party elite had totally lost its political control. Finally, the enormous increase in the number of participants in the Monday demonstrations before the opening of the Berlin Wall on November 9 undoubtedly was a result of a self-feeding, reflexive process by which media reporting and public involvement interacted so strongly that this outcome could no longer be prevented after a certain point. This is an example of strong media effects indeed.

As for the question of the long-term effects of East German exposure to West German radio and television, these effects are no more amenable to clear-cut demonstration than is the earlier example of television's responsibility for the surge in subjective political interest in West Germany. Nonetheless, there is consistent evidence (based on market research surveys) of a substantial impact of the mass media. Considering how long it took for democracy to become consolidated in West Germany after 1949, a question of immediate interest concerned the effects of 40 years of communism on the political values, attitudes, and beliefs of East Germans about to be absorbed into the West German political culture. As survey findings began to accumulate in 1990 and 1991, two basic and consistent conclusions emerged: (1) East Germans' sociopolitical beliefs in general seemed to resemble those of West Germans two decades earlier (delayed modernization), and (2) East and West German attitudes toward democracy were surprisingly similar. The anticipated totalitarian streak in East German political beliefs simply did not materialize (Bauer 1991a, b; Weil 1992). In addition, a study in the city of Jena in 1990 revealed that, when asked, people expressed a "virtual" identification with West German political parties reaching back to a time when the GDR still was an independent state (Bluck and Kreikenbom 1991). Kaase and Klingemann (1993) also discovered substantial knowledge about the West German parties among East Germans in 1990. All of these reports suggest that, over an extended period of time, East Germans absorbed to some extent the mores of another sociopolitical system in addition to their own, mostly through the electronic mass media.

To be sure, this type of evidence is at best circumstantial. Still, as German unification continues apace, it should be possible to determine more reliably than we can at present whether the West German electronic media have indeed performed the socialization function for East Germans that West Germany's statutes intended them to perform for its own citizens when they began the process of democratic consolidation decades earlier (Hesse 1990). However, it must still be kept in mind that for cultural and geopolitical reasons, the German case is a very special one indeed.

CONCLUSION

How the mass media contribute to democratic politics and how they influence the political process more generally are questions that go far beyond the simple media cause-and-effect models popular in the early days of communications research. While such models may still have something to contribute to the debate on media effects in the short term, they contribute little to the analysis of the long-term impact of the mass media on politics.

This is a crucial shortcoming since the mass media and politics are inextricably intertwined not only on the institutional (macro) and collective actor (meso) levels, but also in influencing the way individual citizens form their fundamental views on politics. The importance of the mass media in this regard stems from structurally based developments in modern societies as real nation-states. As the result of common factors guiding the internal logic of media systems, there are obvious regularities within and across nations in the way reality is defined and portrayed. It is these common news factors that help to create certain consistent and cumulative images of the political world. What is and what is not political, how opinion formation works, and how new information interacts with existing information are all questions that go far beyond the kind of problem one confronts when wanting to know whether and how a given bit of news has influenced somebody's voting decision. There is reliable evidence, it was shown, that the mass media have an impact on individual perceptions of political objects and on the way these objects are evaluated and imbued with emotional significance.

Postwar Germany had been deeply influenced by the historical experience of the Second World War. Its constitution and political institutions, as well as its foreign policy, were tailored so as to integrate the new Germany into the Western alliance and at the same time stabilize it politically so that a working democracy would eventually emerge. The occupying powers helped to shape a mass media system that has been conducive to those developments. When in 1961 the Constitutional Court issued its first ruling on the plans of the Adenauer government to create a central, federally controlled television network, the court emphasized in its definitive ruling the role pluralistic structures of mass communication play in a democratic polity. This remains to this day the consensus position in Germany. But as the Federal Republic became more and more of a normal democracy, some of the legacies of the past were overwhelmed by structural developments it shared with the other democracies. There can be no question that the rise of public television fulfilled the double function of, on the one hand, stimulating interest in politics and, on the other hand, altering the public perception of the "political" as something more simplistic and playful than in the days when newspapers were the most important source of political information for the mass public.

The same ambivalence is built into the new private television channels. Guided mainly by an economic rationale, they not only give a much smaller program share to political information than do the public channels, but they also further depoliticize the political. This entertainment emphasis may eventually end up differentiating the audience into politically informed and uninformed sub-publics. At the same time, the competitive challenge posed by the private channels is beginning to break up the cartel between the established parties and the public networks.

This situation once again points to the need to conceptualize the relationship between the mass media and politics as being dynamic and reciprocal. Since constitutional and institutional arrangements in a given polity usually remain fixed for an extended time, it is mostly dramatic changes in such arrangements that provide a fresh incentive to look at their impact, even from a within-country perspective. Germany is one of the few countries where far-reaching change in the electronic mass media system has recently taken place. The rarity of this situation highlights the need for those who study the relationship between mass communications and politics to take proper account of different macro arrangements in the organization of media systems when choosing their countries for analysis.

While it is too early to assess the political consequences of the changed landscape in *Rundfunk* organization in Germany, it is possible to say without reservation that the difference in programming and political content between the public and private television networks is substantial. Initial studies also indicate some depoliticization of the audience in the sense that Germans are exposing themselves less to political news and information programs. To follow these developments and their consequences in some detail will be a fascinating challenge to future research on the political effects of mass communications in Germany.

NOTES

1. The author appreciates critical comments on an earlier version of the chapter by Barbara Pfetsch.
2. German unification creates a problem of presentation in that there were two independent German states before 1990. For reasons of parsimony, the chapter uses only the term Germany. Before October 3, 1990, this term refers to the territory of the Federal Republic of Germany (West Germany), not to the German Democratic Republic (East Germany).
3. Noelle-Neumann 1988, 239–45. Also see Franzmann 1989 for similar results from a study in Switzerland. For a dissenting viewpoint, see Neuman 1986, 145.
4. A related finding is worth noting. In magazine programs, the share of nondomestic reports on the private channels is about half that on their public counterparts. This difference, though, may be partly a structural artifact. In the mid-1980s, the private channels simply lacked the technical and personnel infrastructure needed for the adequate coverage of foreign affairs. Their disadvantage in this regard may now have lessened as a result of the private networks' vastly improved economic health.
5. On the role of the mass media in German election campaigns see Schoenbach 1987; 1991. For the 1990 campaign, see Holtz-Bacha and Kaid 1993.
6. Faul et al. 1988, 207. The one bias that was found was that the small parties, the FDP and the Greens, were given far more attention on the public channels than their parliamentary strength warranted. The implications of this discrepancy have not been explored further.

CHAPTER 12

The Political Impact of the Media: A Reassessment

Richard Gunther and Anthony Mughan

This volume has presented an in-depth examination of the relationship between politics and the mass communications media in ten countries at different stages in their democratic evolution. Some have just made the transition to democracy; one, Italy, has undergone profound change in many of its most important political institutions; and the remainder have long-established democratic traditions and practices. Patterns in this relationship have emerged that are much too complex and varied to be captured satisfactorily by the conventional wisdoms that have held sway in this field of study for decades. Strongly and equally contradicted are the authoritarian/totalitarian image of the media as an all-powerful vehicles of manipulation that enable despotic politicians to mold public attitudes and behaviors, and the "minimal effects" thesis that emerged from the first individual-level studies of media impact in the 1940s and 1950s. Other notions are equally untenable: while all of the evidence presented in this volume reaffirms that media liberalization is a necessary prerequisite for successful democratization, for example, it would be unwarranted to jump to the conclusion that the freer the media from government regulation and the more they are embedded in a market economy, the stronger their contribution to the quality of democracy. Here, again, the picture that emerges is much more subtly nuanced and is conditional on a number of characteristics of individual countries.

Even our more modest and eclectic search for the "general" – patterns that apply in all social and political settings – has been frustrated by a reality that defies simple analysis. To be sure, some trends have emerged that appear to be universal. Everywhere, television has become the preeminent, if not overwhelmingly dominant, source of national and international political news for the majority of the population. Everywhere, even in authoritarian political systems where television is by far the most heavily censored and manipulated of the communications media, most people trust television more than any other medium as an objective and impartial source of political information. The notion of a "media logic" – according to which television is seen as privileging candidates over party, program, or policy-relevant issues – also receives considerable support, although this logic is not felt equally strong in all countries. Everywhere, in both democratic and nondemocratic systems, politicians have become increasingly aware of the growing importance of the media (especially television) and have sought to adapt its use to their varying political purposes, if only to take advantage of citizens' tendency to read newspapers less and spend more of their leisure time in front of the television set. Aside from such general tendencies, the political effects of the media that emerge from these studies are varied and highly conditional on other institutional, social-structural, and micro-level factors.

The basic explanation of why the aforementioned conventional wisdoms are largely unsupported by empirical evidence – and why our search for the general has produced such meager results – is that the causal processes linking politics and the media are not one-dimensional and are incompatible with some of the simplistic assumptions that guided the early research in this field. Instead, the nature of the political impact the media may have is strongly shaped by the interaction among a number of macro- and micro-level variables, and this interaction can take different forms in different countries. Among the important macro-level national (and often subnational) characteristics are political culture, the structure of society, the media and government institutions, the norms governing the relationship between journalists and politics, regulatory practices, and the level of technological development of the communications industry. Such characteristics help to shape media messages, as well as their patterns of circulation. Their political effects, however, are also a function of micro-level characteristics of their recipients. A number of characteristics of individuals themselves (e.g., their attitudinal or cultural proclivities, degree of exposure to each communications medium, and levels of education and cognitive complexity), as well as their degree of embeddedness in autonomous subcultures or networks of secondary associations, have profound implications for their receptivity to political communications. Variation from one country to another in the patterns of interaction among these macro- and micro-level factors profoundly influence the extent to which the media can be expected to have identifiable political effects. Thus, the proper focus for studies of the relationship between the media and politics is not the search for universal generalizations, but the search for more middle-level and contingent theoretical propositions.

THE MEDIA AND POLITICAL REGIME TYPE

The studies in this volume suggest that the institutional relationship between the media and the state does not vary substantially from one nondemocratic regime to another. Juan Linz was right: there is no qualitative difference in the manner in which authoritarian and totalitarian regimes seek to manage the dissemination of political communications. Be they totalitarian, posttotalitarian, or would-be totalitarian (e.g., the Soviet Union under Stalin, Hungary under Kádár, or East Germany under Ulbricht) or simply authoritarian (Franco's Spain or Pinochet's Chile), ruling elites sought to control the flow of politically relevant news to the general public in remarkably similar ways. State agencies oversaw the print media, encouraging self-censorship and occasionally imposing "directives" regarding the stories to be covered and the spin they should be given. News bureaus and the licensing of journalists were also subjected to state control. Television, however, was subjected to much stronger state control. Except in Chile (where the authoritarian regime came to power after independent television stations had already been established), television broadcasting was a state monopoly. Governments, moreover, were keenly interested in shaping the kind of television coverage they received and intervened heavyhandedly in the appointment of top broadcasting agency officials.

State control of the media in nondemocratic regimes can, at least for a time, contribute importantly to the relatively modest objective of maintaining the regime in power. In Chile, Hungary, the Soviet Union, and Spain, the great majority of citizens were successfully denied access to information that might have mobilized them in opposition to the regime, and no opposition group was given access to the broadcast media to articulate its grievances, to advance an alternative vision of the future, or to encourage political protest activity of any kind.

Despite their control over the media, the ability of nondemocratic regimes to shape the basic political attitudes and orientations of their subject populations was limited. There is no evidence, for example, that they succeeded in resocializing their populations to secure their legitimacy over the long term and to instill antidemocratic attitudes and values: eventually, all of these regimes collapsed, and most have been replaced by consolidated democracies. Interestingly, though, there is significant cross-national variation in the success of resocialization efforts. Failure was most complete in Chile and Spain. The brevity of the authoritarian interlude was probably a major reason for the inability of Pinochet to erase the prodemocratic values and even party loyalties of the Chilean people. At their first opportunity – a referendum whose wording stacked the deck in favor of continued authoritarianism – the majority of Chileans opted for democracy, and in subsequent elections cast ballots in favor of the same parties that had dominated political life prior to the Pinochet coup. By contrast, brevity cannot account for General Franco's failure to forge a popular consensus in support of his regime. Despite four decades of antiliberal, antidemocratic propaganda disseminated incessantly through the media and schools, the Spanish public quickly adopted attitudes that were as supportive of democracy as those in the average European Union country. And despite the monopoly status enjoyed by the National Movement (formerly the Falange), support for parties of the extreme right is virtually nonexistent, in sharp contrast with the situation in several other established European democracies, including France, Austria, and Belgium (Betz and Immerfall 1998).

At the other end of the continuum is Russia. Moderately high levels of electoral support for non- or antidemocratic parties of both the left (the Communist Party) and the ultra-nationalist right (Zhirinovsky), as well as public opinion data,[1] indicate that mass-level attitudinal support for democracy is by no means as widespread as it is in Western Europe. Still, the swift demise of the Soviet system and the rapid shift to electoral democracy are illustrative of the general lack of success of the regime's resocialization efforts.

The Central European cases are more complicated. On the one hand, Communist regimes were certainly not able to resocialize their populations effectively, as evidenced by the anti-Communist revolts in 1953 in East Germany, 1956 in Hungary, 1968 in Czechoslovakia, and 1976 and 1980–1 in Poland, as well as the ultimate success of the democratization process. On the other hand, historical evidence and current survey data indicate that censorship, propaganda, and efforts at formal socialization through the educational system have had some long-lasting effects. The aforementioned uprisings, for example, were not intended to eradicate socialism. Instead, nonauthoritarian forms of socialism received considerable support from intellectuals and organized workers. Workers' councils in Hungary took over all factories in 1956 in an attempt to resist privatization and promote a socialist economic system based on direct control by workers. During the Prague Spring in 1968, an alternative version of nonauthoritarian socialism was supported by intellectuals and workers' councils – "socialism with a human face." In Poland, during both the protests of 1980–1 and the subsequent years of underground resistance, the Solidarity trade union promoted a blend of ideas incorporating syndicalism, Polish Catholicism, and the notion of a self-organizing civil society. Survey data from the 1990s certainly point to the persistence of high levels of continuing support for an activist state in several policy areas, especially the provision of social welfare services. In short, one consequence of four decades of government censorship and propaganda was to inculcate a preference for some form of socialism to such an extent that it helped to establish the ideological framework of posttransition political and social attitudes. Such as it was, however, this success was no more than partial and proved to be incompatible with full democratization.

To be sure, resocialization of a population is a difficult task, so these failures are not entirely surprising. Nonetheless, variation from one country to another, and among subsets of the populations within them, point to certain variables that affect the success of the resocialization enterprise. It has been established that in all of these nondemocratic systems, state control over the broadcast media was rigid, more or less uniform, and remained intact until near the end of each regime's existence. Contrary opinions could be articulated (very cautiously!) only in certain print media with limited circulations. Thus, the explanation of this uneven pattern of resocialization failure cannot lie with variation in the nature, volume, or consistency of the messages disseminated by the regime-dominated media. Instead, it would seem to reside in the interaction between media system variables and other social-structural and individual-level factors.

Clearly pertinent is access to information contradicting the messages of the regime. If we can hypothesize that the more homogeneous the information flowing to individuals, the greater its credibility and likelihood of being accepted, then it follows that the more conflicting and inconsistent the available information, the more likely that the regime's resocialization effort will fail. The *permeability of national boundaries* enters directly into this equation, with East Germany standing out as the most noteworthy case. One of the most intolerant and repressive Communist regimes in the Soviet bloc, it failed miserably to legitimize itself in the eyes of its population. East Germans sought in droves to escape its oppressive political and social system, and virtually nobody aside from the party and the state administration sought to defend it in 1989. The unique geopolitical setting of West Berlin – in the very heart of East Germany – plays an important role in explaining this failure since as it meant that the overwhelming majority of East Germans had direct, unimpeded access to West German radio and television. Nightly, they could watch news broadcasts, public affairs programs, commercials for consumer goods, and entertainment programming, all of which contradicted the news and images coming from their own state media about the superiority of socialism and the crisis of capitalism. It also threw into sharp relief the bleakness of life in the dilapidated urban centers, polluted environment, and relative impoverishment that characterized East German society. A testament to the pervasiveness of exposure to the West German media is the high proportion of East Germans who, prior to 1989, identified with West German political parties and possessed a great deal of knowledge about daily politics in their neighbor to the west.

The Spanish case is somewhat similar since large segments of the population were regularly exposed to information inconsistent with the regime's general hostility toward liberalism and democracy. Since reporting about politics in other countries was largely uncensored, Spaniards who watched/read/listened to the news could experience the workings of democracy vicariously. One consequence of this learning process was that, even prior to the death of Franco, large numbers of them could correctly use the concepts of "left" and "right" and identify with one or another of Europe's "political families" (social democratic, Christian democratic, liberal, etc.), even though such terminology could not be used to discuss domestic politics in the broadcast or print media. At the same time, only about 15 percent of the population held authoritarian attitudes supportive of the regime.

Tourism also played a subversive role in several of these countries, particularly in Spain: the highly visible presence of up to 40 million relatively affluent and apparently happy tourists annually (in a country with a population of less than 40 million) undercut the credibility of the regime's propaganda condemning the evils of liberalism and democracy. Tourism was also a major source of exposure to inconsistent information in some Central and Eastern European countries. In Hungary each year, the number of foreign tourists approached the country's population of 10 million. High levels of tourism made it harder to seal borders and prevent the circulation of Western and emigré literature, including explicitly political materials (books, newspapers, magazines, and video- and audiotapes) aimed especially at the intelligentsia. The principal impact of exposure to tourism, however, stemmed from comparisons with the expendable incomes and high living standards of German, Austrian, and other foreign tourists, which gravely undermined the credibility of official propaganda.

In the case of the Soviet Union, contact with foreigners was sharply restricted, borders were far more effectively sealed, and most of the country was much too distant from regular radio and television stations in the West to be "contaminated" in the way that the East Germans were. Under Stalin especially, the degree of state control over the flow of information to the population was as close to total as one is likely to find. Nonetheless, by the 1980s, there were some 40 million shortwave radios in the country that could be used to pick up intentionally or unintentionally subversive broadcasts from the West. Still, the country's borders remained far less permeable than those of Spain or East Germany, which might help to explain the less than complete democratic transformation of Russian political culture following the collapse of the Communist regime. Indeed, the exception to this general pattern helps to prove the rule. The first regions in which mass mobilizations erupted to challenge the very existence of the Soviet Union were the Baltic republics, which are closest to the democratic West and most accessible to its broadcasts. Indeed, as Mickewicz points out in Chapter 3, Estonians regularly watched Finnish television. Similarly, although the case of China is not included in this volume, it is noteworthy that a recent study of the media in that country concluded that, despite the country's participation in the technological advances that have transformed the media everywhere, the level of exposure to (and the political impact of) broadcasts from the geographically distant, democratic West is much "less than in Eastern Europe during the 1980s" (Cullen and Hua 1998, 165). In general, then, it can be said that geographical isolation from discordant media messages from neighboring democratic countries helps authoritarian regimes to monopolize the flow of communications to their citizens.

A social-structural factor having implications for the effectiveness of media messages is the existence (or absence) of *social sectors or organized groups with some degree of subcultural autonomy* from the state and the rest of society. The importance of these groups is that they can maintain networks of face-to-face contacts able to serve as conduits of opinions, attitudes and values inconsistent with official propaganda, and therefore subversive of its credibility and acceptability. They may even exercise pressure to conform to subcultural norms that are diametrically opposed to those of the regime. Segments of the working class in heavily industrialized parts of Spain, for example, as well as students in university communities throughout the country, retained or developed varieties of socialist or Marxist orientations that were the very antithesis of the right-wing propaganda peddled by the Franco regime. These group networks and subcultural orientations led not only to the complete rejection of the regime's messages, but also to waves of protest activities in the 1960s. Subcultural autonomy also characterized the oppositions emerging in Central and Eastern Europe at about the same time. This argument is consistent with the "mass-society hypothesis," which asserts that populations are more malleable and responsive to media influences when parties and other secondary associations are weak and leaders communicate directly with followers (classic statements of which are Arendt 1951 and Kornhauser 1959).

If this finding is confirmed in studies of other nondemocratic regimes, it would suggest that the major difference between authoritarian and totalitarian political systems with regard to the effectiveness of state propaganda may derive from the presence or absence of autonomous groups or subcultures within which antiregime messages may circulate. As Linz and Stepan (1996) have pointed out, authoritarian regimes differ from totalitarian and posttotalitarian ones in that, in the former, a multitude of autonomous or semiautonomous secondary associations and a limited form of pluralism may exist, while the latter are characterized by "flattened landscapes" devoid of autonomous organized groups. In short, from the standpoint of media effects, neither the structure of the media themselves nor the consistency of the messages disseminated by them neatly distinguish authoritarian from totalitarian or posttotalitarian systems. Instead, differences in social-structural context may substantially affect the extent to which individuals are receptive to the regime's official propaganda.

Two contrasting vignettes from China at the time of the Tienanmen Square massacre provide particularly vivid illustrations of how social-structural and subcultural differences can affect the internalization of state propaganda. One of the authors happened to be in central China (lecturing on democratic theory, democratic institutions, and democratization, no less) at the time of the mobilizations and subsequent crackdown in May and early June 1989. On the morning after the massacre, there were absolutely no signs in the countryside that anything unusual had happened. Life in the villages carried on perfectly normally: there were no unusual clusters of individuals engaged in discussion or showing other evidence of curiosity, disquiet, or protest. Completely dependent on state-controlled radio and television stations, they may not have known about the events or, if they did, had not been exposed to messages casting doubt on the credibility of the official version of them. A walk around a university campus the following day could not have been more different: it was not necessary to have a shortwave radio of one's own because dozens of students in each dormitory building had their radios tuned at full volume to the British Broadcasting Corporation (BBC), effectively broadcasting the latest news about events in Beijing into the streets. In short, these differing social contexts, in interaction with individual-level factors (such as level of education, to be discussed later), greatly affected exposure to conflicting media messages and thereby the individual's susceptibility to the regime's efforts at propagandistic manipulation.

Individual-level factors also affect the predisposition to accept broadcast messages in nondemocratic regimes. The most important of these factors by far is education. A consistent research finding is that high levels of education make individuals less susceptible to antidemocratic propaganda, even though these same individuals are more exposed to these efforts at indoctrination by virtue of reading newspapers and listening to broadcast news more frequently. It is likely that several different causal factors underpin this relationship. First, education leads to the development of proto-participatory norms and expectations that clash with the "subject" role imposed on individuals in nondemocratic systems.[2] Second, the better educated are more likely to have traveled abroad or read about society and politics in other countries; hence, exposure to democratic life in other settings can provide an evidential basis for skepticism about propaganda claims. Third, the better educated are likely to be more cognitively complex and better able to "see through" the manipulative intent of regime propaganda. A paradox is thus created: the better educated are generally exposed to a greater volume of propaganda and resocialization efforts (especially through their more extensive exposure to formal socialization in state-operated educational institutions) but are, at the same time, less susceptible to their influence. This paradox helps to explain the anomaly noted in Chapter 1 of this book – that the "global resurgence of democracy" took place at precisely the same time that the emergence of television and other innovations in media technology should have increased the ability of ruling elites to manipulate their subjects. While this media-technology hypothesis accounts for the greater ability of the regime to reach its subjects, it fails to take into consideration that, following decades of socioeconomic development and increased education, this same population is better able to resist antidemocratic propaganda efforts.

Another individual-level factor concerns the *goodness of the fit* between the messages disseminated by governing elites and the attitudes or general cultural orientations of message recipients. The case of Chile is most instructive in this regard. Given the recency of most individuals' own experiences with democracy, the messages of the Pinochet regime were interpreted in light of long-standing beliefs and experiences that contradicted them. Spain provides a second example. The ultraconservative, traditionalist national Catholicism peddled by Franco's regime simply did not ring true in the increasingly urban, affluent, and secular society that was Spain in the 1970s. Finally, an old order of a different kind was also undermined in both Italy and Japan by a lack of fit. The major political parties of Italy's first republic had colonized their own sectors of the television system to secure their respective bases of popular support. The old guard's leading politicians, however, were unskilled in using television effectively, relying on an insider's vocabulary and self-referential rhetoric that may have been appropriate for bargaining behind closed doors but was largely unintelligible (or at least unappealing) to the majority of Italian voters. Similarly, in Japan (where, as in Italy, politicians rose to the top largely by being successful in factional infighting rather than by developing personal appeal to voters), old guard Liberal-Democratic politicians were by and large colorless, aged, and unable to connect with the public. While there were rare exceptions in both of these countries (e.g., Craxi and Nakasone), the established politicians of the old order generally were unable to master the use of television in order to mobilize popular support. The appearance of telegenic outsiders able to use television skillfully, as well as the media's exposure of corruption under the old regime, helped to bring the old order to an end or at least change it significantly.

Thus, the picture that is emerging from this examination of media effects on politics in nondemocratic settings is a highly conditional and interactive one involving both macro- and micro-level factors. An understanding of the political role and impact of the media must go beyond the study of the media themselves. Indeed, given the generally uniform institutions and practices of state control and manipulation of the broadcast media across both authoritarian and totalitarian regimes, a media-only focus could not explain either variations in media effectiveness among them or their failure to resist democratization. Message factors are important, but their impact can only be appreciated by taking careful account of their interaction with other kinds of social-structural and individual-level factors.

THE MEDIA IN THE TRANSITION TO DEMOCRACY

A number of common patterns have emerged from our case studies of the media in paving the way for, and eventually bringing about, the transition to democracy. In all cases, political communications through the media helped perpetuate the authoritarian/totalitarian elite in power in the short run, but over the long run they facilitated democratization in a number of ways. These involved erosion of the credibility and legitimacy of the nondemocratic regime; the development of pluralism in political attitudes, preferences, and partisan alternatives; and, eventually, resocialization of both masses and elites to the new democratic rules of the game. These contributions are especially evident in the Chilean case and in the late stages of the Spanish transition. Likewise in East Germany, extensive (West German) television coverage of the collapse of communism in Eastern Europe provided viewers with direct stimuli for mobilizing massive street protests against the regime that culminated in the storming of the Berlin Wall itself.

Before we discuss the role of the media in the transitional phase of the democratization process, it must be remembered that "media" is a plural noun – not only in the sense of including both print and broadcast channels of communication, but also insofar as individual television and radio stations, newspapers and magazines, and journalists have different, often conflicting, political objectives and play very different roles during the transition. Some continued their active support of the nondemocratic regime to the bitter end, others were advocates for change, and still others kept out of the fray altogether. Still, this diversity of responses represents a change from the status quo ante in which strict government controls led to monotonously uniform support for the regime, the exceptions being some small-scale print outlets for opposition viewpoints in Chile, to a lesser extent in Spain, and to a much lesser extent in Eastern Europe and the Soviet Union.

What brought about this alteration in the stance of the media in every case (except East Germany, where ready access to West German television and radio had always provided an alternative to the government's communications systems) was a process of *liberalization* – a relaxation of state controls over political communications through the media – initiated by the nondemocratic ruling elite. And in every case, the ultimate

412

story to emerge is one of "unintended consequences": in no case did the governing elite initiate this liberalization as the first step in a deliberate strategy of democratization, and yet that was the outcome in each of these cases.

Two distinctly different causal processes appear to have been at work in undermining nondemocratic regimes' direct control over the media and, eventually, support for the regime itself. The first involves the functionalist notion that changes in the structure of the media market or in media technology were initiated, and these changes had significant unintended implications for the regime's ability to manipulate the media. General Pinochet, for example, allowed the development of an extensive private sector of the communications industry as part of his regime's neoliberal economic development strategy. While he had no desire for *political* liberalization, the emergence of more autonomous media actors as a result of *economic* liberalization undermined the regime's capacity to control political communications. This loss of control was manifested most clearly on the occasion of the pope's visit to Chile. Pinochet had no choice but to allow relatively free television coverage of this religious event, particularly by the Catholic University's private television station. This created an opportunity for previously unheard opposition viewpoints to be voiced publicly for the first time in a decade and a half. (Similarly, Pope John Paul's visit to Poland in 1979 greatly contributed to the "ceremonial transformation" and development of non- and anti-Communist discourse in Poland [Kubik 1994]). It has often been argued that the greater liberties inherent in free-market economies, especially when accompanied by the emergence of new media technologies, facilitate the development of pluralism in political expression that can undercut support for authoritarian regimes and pave the way to full-fledged democratization.[3] The Chilean case provides partial support for this notion, particularly since it enabled opposition spokespersons to take advantage of such events as the pope's visit and Pinochet's plebiscite to articulate their dissenting views.

But while the greater pluralism inherent in market economies and the proliferation of new media outlets can open up new avenues for the expression of dissenting opinions, this functionalist argument is insufficient as an explanation of broader political liberalization. Even privately owned media in reasonably well-developed market economies can be censored and journalists intimidated into acquiescence by the threat of punitive sanctions. A recent study, for example, describes how the sophisticated authoritarian regimes of Malaysia and Singapore have succeeded in stifling internal dissent, and even in forcing journalists employed by the international press to modify or suppress news stories unflattering to the regime (Rodan 1998). More to the point, some of the techniques used to restrict press freedom involved the manipulation of incentives inherent in the market itself, including denial of access to the market through the suspension of publication rights, monetary fines, and protracted judicial proceedings relating to alleged "defamation" of the authoritarian regime or its leaders. This contrasts with the clumsy, ineffective censorship practices of other authoritarian regimes: to cite one example, while coverage of domestic politics was sharply restricted under General Franco, Spanish journalists were free to use their coverage of international political developments as a vehicle for criticizing their own regime; and while *Playboy* magazine was banned by this rightwing, traditionalist regime, the militant anti-Communism of its censors was insufficient to prevent an entire generation of Spanish economists from being educated using a textbook written by an individual who had been a member of the Communist Party's Central Committee since 1956! In short, the nature of the government's efforts to control the media – sophisticated and efficient, on the one hand, or crude, clumsy, and perhaps counterproductive, on the other – emerges as an important intervening variable between market liberalization and authoritarian control of political communications.

More direct in its impact on the emergence of media pluralism is the intentional relaxation of political controls in nondemocratic regimes. Two clear examples of such liberalization have been examined in this volume: Information and Tourism Minister Manuel Fraga introduced his 1966 Press Law in an explicit effort to increase freedom of expression in franquist Spain, and Mikhail Gorbachev loosened controls over the media in an effort to focus criticisms on the stultifying economic, social, and political institutions of the Soviet Union as part of a strategy designed to reform them. While both of these initiatives made crucial contributions to democratization over the long term, in neither case were they motivated by the desire to democratize. Rather, the franquist elite allowed Manuel Fraga to proceed with his Press Law only because they thought that the retention of some state regulation of the media would preclude a direct threat to the regime itself, and would be limited to stimulating some broader "contrast of opinions" within the fundamental framework of franquist authoritarianism. And Gorbachev, at no point in his incumbency, explicitly committed himself to democracy.

Each of these cases reveals that liberalization can set in motion processes of change that are difficult or impossible to control. This is largely a reflection of the unstable nature of partial liberalization. Both the nondemocratic, preliberalization regime and full-scale democracy can be characterized as "stable equilibria" within which behavior is constrained by clearly defined and widely understood rules. Partial liberalization of nondemocratic systems, however, invalidates some of the old rules underpinning authoritarianism, inadvertently calling into question the legitimacy of the remaining authoritarian constraints and giving rise to expectations of more sweeping changes. At the same time, the norms that constrain behavior in democratic systems are not set in place. Not only can this uncertain halfway situation stimulate mass mobilizations in favor of full democratization, but the ambiguities inherent in partial liberalization can give rise to considerable conflict between reformers and hardliners within the authoritarian elite itself, particularly regarding the question of how to deal with the opposition – that is, whether to crack down or tolerate (if not support) its existence. Such disagreement was apparent in Hungary in the late 1980s, when Prime Minister Karoly Grosz and the democratic socialist Imre Pozsgay publicly articulated diametrically opposed views on this question when both were still members of the Communist ruling elite. These disagreements, in turn, can contribute to a breakdown of consensus and collaboration within the ruling elite that further destabilizes the regime. In short, liberalization is a very slippery slope; the first step may lead to a destination far beyond that initially intended. Liberalization of the media speeds up this disintegrative process by publicizing and magnifying disagreements among the ruling elites.

Media liberalization in every nondemocratic regime surveyed in this book had two immediate outcomes that facilitated the transition to democracy. The first was that when some mild criticism of the shortcomings of the existing system was allowed, support for the regime began to erode. This was particularly true when the objectives of the governing elite were not clear. Hence, Gorbachev was criticized by both reformers, who were dissatisfied with the scope and pace of change, and hardline supporters of the old regime, who thought that he had betrayed their trust. To a lesser extent, the same situation occurred in Spain, particularly under the seemingly contradictory leadership of Carlos Arias Navarro. In the end, neither reformers nor regime loyalists were satisfied with the performance of the incumbents; at both the mass and elite levels of the polity, consensus broke down and support for the system declined precipitously.

The second consequence of media liberalization was its contribution to the development of pluralism – with regard to attitudes and beliefs, as well as visible alternative elites and partisan options. At the outset, this tended to involve the appearance in the broadcast and print media of representatives of the moderate opposition, as well as reformist forces from within the regime itself. Over time, however, access to the media was extended to a much wider range of opinionmakers. The public presentation of their respective visions of the future, programs, and symbols contributed to the pluralistic differentiation of the mass public that competitive party systems require. In short, following liberalization, the media helped to foster the kinds of pluralism that functioning democratic systems need.

Once the transition had proceeded to the point where opposing groups could organize and engage in institutionalized conflict with one another (which is the very essence of representative democracy), coverage of elite interactions implicitly served to socialize both mass and elite audiences to the new rules of the democratic game. In Spain, restrained, mutually respectful elite interactions not only helped to instill norms of tolerance among the actors themselves, but media coverage of these patterns of behavior played a key role in definitively laying to rest the old animosities of the civil war era. Indelible visual images (widely disseminated through the print and television media) provided emotionally powerful lessons in civility and respect for the new, democratic rules of the game.[4] In Chile, the disappearance from public discourse of the fiery rhetoric of the tumultuous period preceding Pinochet's violent coup of 1973, and its replacement by undramatic matter-of-fact treatment of the relatively mundane problems of everyday governance, reinforced the normalization of democratic politics. In Eastern Europe and the former Soviet Union, the picture is more differentiated. From about 1990 on, public discussion and media discourse in Central Europe steadily changed from general, symbolic, ideological, and nationalist in character to relatively concrete, practical, and policy oriented. In Russia, by contrast, implicit socialization through exposure to televised elite interactions was not so unambiguously favorable to future democratic consolidation. To be sure, the raucous clashes between opposing sides in televised parliamentary debates represented a decisive break from the uniformity (and monotony) of opinion previously disseminated by the state-dominated media, and this almost certainly encouraged the diversification of mass-level opinion. Those same rancorous conflicts, how-

ever, were hardly conducive to the elite-level consensus that characterizes consolidated democracies, let alone to conveying to the general
public the norms of restrained disagreement that underpin democratic
stability.

In general, then, we can conclude that, once liberalized, television, radio, and the press in transitions allow diverse elites unprecedented opportunities to communicate with the mass public. Whether or not the
style and content of their communications are conducive to democratic
consolidation appears, at least from the cases in this volume, to depend
on the decisions and behavior of the elites themselves. In this way, media effects during the transitions have contributed to the top-down, or
elitist, character of the democratization process.

THE MEDIA IN ESTABLISHED DEMOCRACIES

This overview of the impact of the media on politics in established
democracies must begin with a statement of one of the most significant
findings from some of the preceding chapters: media coverage, and especially television coverage, can have a substantial impact on politics at
the macro level, at the micro level, and at the intersection of the two. At
the macro level, for example, the emergence of political television has
helped to transform party systems by giving unprecedented publicity to
parties (such as the Liberals in Britain) that had previously been largely
ignored by a partisan press aligned with the governing Conservatives and
Labour, or to new parties, like Berlusconi's Forza Italia, which had just
recently been established to challenged the existing order. There is considerable evidence that television has had a marked impact on language
and political culture: regional television in Catalonia has played a major
role in the revival of the Catalan language, just as decades of television
broadcasting using standard Italian helped to homogenize linguistically
Italy by discouraging the use of regional and local dialects. More generally, in democracies worldwide, television is slowly but surely changing
the nature of electioneering and perhaps even the distribution of power
within parties: as political parties increasingly resort to this medium for
electoral campaigning, power has become concentrated at the center and
mass-party organizations have become less important; party leaders
have come to the fore as the principal foci of campaigns, raising the degree of personalization of elections to unprecedented levels; and the increasing electoral importance of party leaders has enhanced their au-

thority vis-à-vis their party colleagues,[5] encouraging a presidential-style concentration of political power even in ostensibly party-based parliamentary governments.

At the individual level as well, television matters insofar as it can subtly but significantly affect the attitudinal orientations of citizens, even to the point of shifting enough votes to determine the outcome of an election under certain circumstances. In Spain, for example, it was found that a shift to the Partido Socialista Obrero Español (PSOE) by formerly undecided voters who believed that Felipe González had won the second televised debate produced an overall net shift in the national vote of 4 percent, which was just enough to offset his rival's initial lead in the polls and reelect the prime minister to a fourth term. Even more convincing evidence (based on repeated polling of an Italian panel every 15 days throughout the 1994 campaign) found that 13.7 percent of these respondents changed their voting decisions in direct response to something they saw on television. Because media magnate Silvio Berlusconi shamelessly used his private television networks to advance his party's electoral prospects, while the public Radiotelevisione Italiana (RAI) channels were much more impartial, Berlusconi was able to benefit from a net shift of over 6 percent of all votes cast. One detailed study (Ricolfi 1994) flatly concluded that without this highly unbalanced coverage of the 1994 campaign, Berlusconi would not have become prime minister.

In sum, just as our earlier analysis of the roles of the media in nondemocratic settings effectively debunked the traditional stereotype of the media as the all-powerful accomplices of authoritarian despots, analysis of their role in established democracies just as roundly refutes the conventional wisdom of "minimal effects," especially with regard to television broadcasting. Instead, television coverage of political events can exert a moderate but sometimes highly significant impact on political structures, culture, and behavior.

The impact of the print media appears to be somewhat more modest, particularly since "selective exposure" tends to lead individuals to purchase or subscribe to newspapers and magazines that are compatible with their previously formed political preferences. Thus, what emerges from some studies as a strong zero-order correlation between the perceived biases of newspapers, on the one hand, and voting decisions of their readers, on the other, is substantially reduced once the individual's basic attitudinal orientation is introduced as a control. Even after this has been done (as in the Spanish study), however, some residual electoral impact of bias in the print media can be identified.

Unfortunately, there has been insufficient research on radio's political role to enable us to reach general conclusions concerning this medium. The few studies that we have encountered suggest that its impact is similar to that of the press: many channels are nonpartisan, and when this is not the case, listeners tend to follow programs whose political or ideological biases roughly accord with their own. As a result of this selective exposure, we speculate that its roles include increasing overall levels of political knowledge and (when relevant) reinforcing initial political orientations. The lack of comparative research (which is probably a product of the high level of fragmentation of radio, which consists of hundreds or thousands of local broadcasting stations in most countries) is unfortunate, since many radio stations provide the most voluminous and intensive flow of political communications of all the mass media. Some, such as BBC's Radio 4 and National Public Radio in the United States, provide hours of detailed coverage of political news each day, and do so in a way that provides a careful balance among competing viewpoints. Others, particularly with the massive expansion of talk radio in some countries, broadcast hours of one-sided political invective on a daily basis. Indeed, the audience for radio coverage of politics can be very large: in Spain, for example, 47 percent of those polled in 1993 said that they had followed political news on the radio three times per week or more often (which is less than the 79 percent who followed politics on television but significantly higher than the 32 percent who read political news in the press), and 27 percent of those same respondents said that it was the most credible and the most informative communications medium.[6] Given this prima facie evidence of its significance as a source of information about politics, it is hoped that more rigorous comparative studies of the political roles and impact of radio will be undertaken in the future.

Media effects are the product of multiple factors, sometimes in interaction with one another. Clearly, message factors are relevant: the study of Great Britain found no significant impact of television coverage on politics. This finding is attributable largely to the scrupulous impartiality of the two stations, the BBC and Independent Television News (ITN), that still command the lion's share of the news audience. In the absence of partisan bias, it is not surprising that no independent effects of television on electoral choice can be detected. This situation stands in sharp contrast with the powerful media effects observed in Italy in 1994, which resulted from Berlusconi's highly partisan manipulation of his private television networks.

The audience structures of the various media are also relevant. In some countries, television has secured a thoroughly dominant position as a source of information about politics, while in others (the clearest example being Japan), newspapers remain an important news source. The extent to which television-based media effects can influence electoral behavior is largely a function of whether viewers are completely dependent on the medium for information about politics or base their political opinions on information derived from a number of sources. As in the contrasting cases of Brazil and Argentina, referred to in Chapter 1, if multiple sources of information are utilized, the resulting pluralism of partisan messages can offset the influence exerted by one or another communications medium.

Individual-level characteristics of the audience also affect their receptiveness to media influences. As posited in the social-psychology literature cited in Chapter 1, the Spanish study found that individuals with strongly rooted opinions on either the left or the right are largely unfazed by the partisan biases of the media. Those near the middle of the ideological continuum (many of whom are presumably "false centrists," with weakly rooted or nonexistent attitudes on most issues), by contrast, can be significantly influenced by media biases, whether these biases are exerted by television, radio, or newspapers. Since these centrists are often the crucial swing voters in many elections, their susceptibility to media influences has considerable political significance.

The Media and the Quality of Democracy

The concerns of this volume go beyond the question of whether or not the media in democracies have partisan effects. We are also interested in the implications of differing media characteristics for the quality of democracy itself in each of these countries. The way in which the media, and especially television, now cover politics – functioning as the "connective tissue" linking elected officials to citizens – can affect the nature of the electoral process, the accountability of politicians to the general public, and hence the quality of democracy.

According to what standard should we assess the contribution of the media to the quality of democracy? Any answer to this question must be based on clearly stated criteria specifying the ideal role that the media should play. But these criteria are, in turn, closely related to which particular conceptualization of democracy is employed. Some scholars implicitly or explicitly base their analysis on "maximalist" notions of participatory democracy in which advanced, interactive communications technology can be used to allows citizens to make their views known directly to policy makers or even to allow them to set policy through initiatives, referenda, and the like, thereby (in their view) improving both the character and the quality of modern democracy (Abramson, et al. 1988, 164–89). This kind of electronic democracy, it has been argued, will "turn the United States into a nation of qualified citizens who are engaged not as isolated individuals pursuing their own ends but as public-spirited members who are dedicated to the common good" (Grossman 1995, 7).

The conception of democracy used throughout this book is the more modest "procedural" one that has become standard in the growing literature on transitions to democracy. Derived from Joseph Schumpeter, Robert Dahl, and Juan Linz, its focus is the relationship between citizens and elected officials and is perhaps most parsimoniously stated thus: "Modern political democracy is a system of governance in which rulers are held accountable for their actions in the public realm by citizens, acting indirectly through the competition and cooperation of their elected representatives" (Schmitter and Karl 1991, 76). The most important implication of this definition for our purposes is that, in an ideal representative democracy, plentiful and reliable political information should be readily available to allow citizens to make informed political decisions. As Delli Carpini and Keeter have noted, democracy "can be very responsive to the interests of civically engaged citizens. But to take even modest advantage of these opportunities, citizens need a number of political resources. Central among these resources is political information" (1996, 1). Accordingly, it is the responsibility of the media, as the major vehicle for communication between governors and governed, to convey to voters a considerable volume of accurate, policy-relevant information about politics in as impartial a manner as possible. More elaborately stated by Marletti and Roncarolo (in Chapter 6 of this volume), "This requires that politically significant parties and movements not be barred from access to the media so that their electoral options can be fairly presented to the general public. It also implies that the independent media ... should disseminate a variety of opinions without censorship and with a minimum of bias." The media, in other words, can improve the quality of representative democracy if they perform and provide "a number of functions and services for the political system ... [including] surveillance of the sociopolitical environment, ... meaningful agenda setting,

. . . dialogue across a diverse range of views, . . . and incentives for citizens to learn, choose and become involved" (Gurevitch and Blumler 1990, 270; also see Keane 1991 and Curran 1996).

Common to all such prescriptions is the view that the media are the principal carriers of the life blood of democracy: information. It is their responsibility, therefore, to maximize the opportunities for citizens to make political decisions and cast ballots on the basis of informed choice – retrospectively, about the extent to which the government has kept its promises in office, and prospectively, about how rival candidates will act if (re)elected to office. Accordingly, our normative standard for assessing the performance of the media in democratic systems includes two elements: one concerns their impartiality in presenting political information, and the other concerns the volume of policy-relevant information they disseminate to voters.

IMPARTIALITY: Impartiality involves essentially the balanced reporting of competing views. It can be achieved in two ways. The first is through media pluralism, and the second is through nonpartisan news coverage of politics.

Media pluralism is difficult to assess. If it is measured by ownership, then the recent trend toward the concentration of media ownership can be regarded as a negative development. In the United States, for example, "the number of controlling firms in all these media (daily newspapers, magazines, radio, television, books, and movies) has shrunk: from fifty corporations in 1984 to twenty-six in 1987, followed by twenty-three in 1990, and then, as the borders between the different media began to blur, to less than twenty in 1993. In 1996 the number of media corporations with dominant power in society is closer to ten" (Bagdikian 1997, xiii). Not only does this concentration span different media within countries, but it has also crossed national boundaries, so that such firms as Bertelsmann of Germany, Thomson of Canada, and News Corporation of Australia are global in their print and electronic press holdings. In this sense, a global media system may be said to have emerged (Herman and McChesney 1997; Albarran and Chan-Olmsted 1998; Demers 1999).

Concentration of ownership, however, need not necessarily impair the impartiality achieved through media pluralism since it is not incompatible with the articulation of divergent, sometimes conflicting, political views both within and between media empires. Rupert Murdoch's News Corporation holdings in Britain, for example, range from the most popular tabloid, the *Sun,* to the highbrow *Times.* Moreover, even though under Murdoch's ownership both newspapers have normally sided with the Conservatives, the *Sun* supported Labour in the 1997 general election, while *The Times* urged its readers to vote not for a particular party, but for candidates hostile to further European integration. More generally, Demers (1993) has shown that top editors at chain-owned newspapers enjoyed no less professional autonomy than those at independently owned ones, and that the corporatization and globalization of the media have not been associated with a shrinkage in the diversity of ideas available to mass publics (Demers 1999, Chapter 7). The bigger problem with media concentration, from our perspective, lies in the content of the political messages communicated. While there may have been isolated efforts, such as the editorial statutes in the Netherlands and government subsidization of newspapers there and in Sweden, to protect the substance and diversity of political communications, the commercialism of the global media system has been "associated [with a] marked decline in the relative importance of public broadcasting and the applicability of public service standards" (Herman and McChesney 1997, 1). In short, the impartiality pursued through media pluralism may not necessarily be threatened by the concentration of ownership, but the conveyance of adequate, policy-relevant information may. We shall return to this issue later.

The second way in which impartiality has been sought is through the avoidance of partisan bias in reporting the news. With the pillarization of the Dutch media as a particularly vivid example, "on the European continent, a great many newspapers and magazines began as the organs of political parties and remained closely affiliated with them. Others began as organs of the Catholic church" (Rothman 1992, 38). To the extent that these patterns of partisan favoritism are widespread, one of our normative criteria would be violated, thereby diminishing the quality of democracy.

Evidence of partisan bias on the part of the print media today reveals divergent patterns. In the United States, newspapers have traditionally shown less partisanship than their European counterparts. "Since the middle of the nineteenth century," Rothman writes, "most publishers have considered themselves free of any attachments other than those of profit, the expression of personal views, and the desire to report the news" (1992, 39). Certain exceptions (such as the *Manchester Union Leader*) notwithstanding, the American press remains generally nonpartisan (Patterson 1998, 19). The heavy reliance on news services (the Associated Press, Reuters, etc.) for coverage of national and international political developments further blurs the partisan distinctiveness of contemporary American newspapers. Japanese newspapers tend to be similarly nonpartisan in their political coverage. At the opposite end of the continuum stand the British tabloids – which dominate the national newspaper market in the United Kingdom. Strident partisanship and nasty attacks on rival parties and their leaders characterize what little attention they pay to political matters. Most newspapers in the other countries surveyed in this volume stand somewhere between these two extremes, and even when they have clear partisan preferences, most lack the rancor and scurrilousness of their British counterparts. Even in Britain, however, the impact of newspaper partisanship on mass-level political behavior is weak to nonexistent, since most readers purchase newspapers that are generally in accord with their existing political predilections. Thus, the main impact of the press has been to reinforce partisan political attitudes and behaviors rather than to change them.

Impartiality has never been as serious an issue regarding television. With few exceptions (e.g., Berlusconi's private networks in Italy, and television in the former Soviet Union), this medium is rarely partisan. When it is, there is evidence that voters' electoral preferences can be affected, as we saw in the chapters on Spain and Italy. But in most established democracies, television coverage of politics has remained above the partisan fray. This is so for a number of reasons. One is that, deregulation notwithstanding, in many countries rigorous impartiality is still commonly demanded (often by statute) of the major television channels. Second, and especially for commercial television enterprises, displays of partisan favoritism could undercut their efforts to maximize audience size and advertising revenue. Finally, journalistic norms often favor nonpartisan reporting. Indeed, even when Italian television channels were allocated to specific political parties (under the *lottizzazione* system), their biases in coverage of political news were quite restrained, especially in comparison with the parvenu Berlusconi networks.

While the chapters in this volume rarely indicate that partisan bias on the part of broadcast journalists is a serious problem in most democracies, this should not be interpreted as meaning that television always presents news about politics in a manner that enhances the quality of democracy. In the United States, there is good reason to believe that the reverse, journalistic cynicism toward politicians of all parties, *has* become a problem – that is, that television's style of political coverage has contributed substantially to the public's growing cynicism about politics and politicians in general, leading them to distance themselves attitudinally and behaviorally from political involvement.[7] In this respect, mass-level cynicism can become detrimental to the active and informed citizenry that lies at the heart of representative and responsible government. Moreover, as we shall argue, this pervasive cynicism is not neutral in its implications for deliberations over public policy and the future course of a country.

It must be made clear from the outset that we do not regard skepticism toward, or criticism of, politicians as inappropriate. A common journalistic role is that of watchdog, investigating improper behavior by politicians, checking abuses of power, and helping to put a stop to rampant corruption. Efficient execution of this role can – as exemplified by specific episodes in the histories of Japan, Hungary, Italy, and the United States – be important for preserving the integrity of democracy. If politicians are engaged in corrupt practices, or lie about their past performance in politics or the records of their opponents, it is the responsibility of journalists to aggressively seek out the truth and expose such malfeasance. We cannot emphasize too strongly, however, that there is a great difference between acting as a watchdog – a legitimate journalistic function that strengthens the basic democratic principle of holding elected officials accountable for their actions – and the pervasive and often completely unwarranted cynicism toward politics and politicians that has taken root in the United States and shows early signs of emerging elsewhere.

American journalists (on television, in particular) very rarely reveal their partisan preferences in covering the news, but they frequently exhibit disdain for politicians as a class, question their motives, and portray their policy proposals as little more than manipulations in a cynical game whose objective is nothing more than self-perpetuation in office. A perfect illustration of the extent to which journalistic cynicism can poison even those segments of the major networks' evening broadcasts normally devoted to highlighting the day's most noteworthy "hard news" developments is the opening segment of the June 4, 1996, broadcast of ABC's *World News Tonight* with Peter Jennings. Earlier that day, the president of the United States had announced a new proposal to give tax credits to help offset the cost of acquiring a college education. Jennings, one of the country's most respected news anchors, began his news broadcast as follows:

> Good Evening. We begin tonight with the latest giveaway in presidential politics, angling for the middle class. At a university gradu-

ation today, President Clinton called on all Americans to work for their own prosperity in the new economy by going to college for at least two years. And the President said that he would offer a tax credit so that everyone who wanted to go, could go. This is a subject that many people care very much about, and the Republicans think that Mr. Clinton is merely trying for political advantage. (ABC News Transcript #6111)

This lead hard news story comprised 22 sentences, only 4 of which provided a description (however skeletal) of the president's policy proposal. Fully seven sentences, by contrast, were devoted to interpreting the proposal as an election-year gimmick, to criticizing it more generally or to questioning the credibility of both the president and his opponent, Senator Bob Dole, who was briefly quoted in the story.

As noted by Patterson in Chapter 7 of this volume, there has been an increasing intrusion of pejorative editorializing into what should be straight news reporting by American journalists. There are also initial signs of its appearance in the most recent British and Dutch elections. Overall, however, this kind of politician-bashing bias is not the norm elsewhere. A common content-analysis protocol was applied to campaign news coverage in three of the countries discussed in this volume: the United States, Great Britain, and Spain. It showed that American journalists were clearly far more prone than their British and Spanish counterparts to inject editorial comments, most commonly of disdain, into news broadcasts.[8]

This pervasive cynicism has important implications for deliberations over public policy in the United States. While politicians of both major American parties have been objects of second-guessing and cynical barbs, this negativism on the part of television journalists is *not* neutral in its ideological and policy implications since it goes hand in hand with cynicism toward the federal government and the public sector in general. The evening news broadcasts of two of the three major networks, the National Broadcasting Company (NBC) and the American Broadcasting Company (ABC), include as regular features exposés of waste and corruption by government officials. NBC's "The Fleecing of America" and ABC's "It's Your Money" unrelentingly portray government programs as a waste of the taxpayers' money. They are almost never counterbalanced by reports on successful programs. Adding to this anti–public-sector bias is the seemingly invariant tendency of journalists in news stories to assume that public sector enterprises are almost

426

inevitably less efficient, more wasteful of the taxpayers' money, and more prone to corruption than activities undertaken by the private sector. (To cite one example, Peter Jennings began the July 15, 1996, edition of *World News Tonight* by proclaiming, "Yet another reason why you should be exercised about the way the government spends your money.") Rarely is such innuendo backed up by empirical evidence, and sometimes it is demonstrably incorrect. As such, these orientations hardly establish a level playing field for the conduct of public policy debates. They can have other, more seriously detrimental consequences as well.

Minimally, the public can become desensitized to actual instances of misbehavior by public officials. If one assumes that all politicians are crooks, why should one be surprised or outraged when evidence of misbehavior by a particular public official is unearthed? The notable lack of public outrage over the scandals surrounding the financing of the 1996 U.S. presidential election despite unrelenting media coverage of congressional hearings on the issue seems to provide prima facie support for this speculation. More seriously, trust in government and support for democratic institutions and practices can be undermined by the incessant and unwarranted drumbeat of negativism. As the data presented in Figure 12.1 clearly reveal, there has been a massive decrease in trust in government since the mid 1960s – a trend that corresponds perfectly with the change in self-perception and role definition by American journalists, which has shifted from being a neutral conduit of information between public officials and citizens to waging a tireless campaign to expose wrongdoing by an inherently self-serving political class.[9]

The Italian case illustrates the potential long-term political dangers of public cynicism. Unlike the American case, many prominent politicians of the Italian first republic were involved in corrupt practices on a massive scale (over 1,500 politicians were accused of crimes by magistrates, including two former prime ministers, one of whom, who served as head of government five times, was accused of having close ties to the Mafia). The result, not surprisingly, was widespread dissatisfaction with the performance of government and cynicism toward politics and politicians (Morlino and Montero 1995; Sani and Segatti 2000). The positive and negative implications of this pervasive distrust are two sides of the same coin: on one side, there was a wholesale replacement of most of the political class, removing those most deeply involved in corrupt practices from politics altogether; on the other side, it led to the election as prime minister of an individual who rejected some of the rules of the game that are essential for the functioning of democracy. Berlusconi was true to his

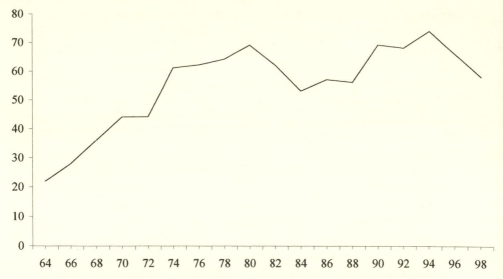

Figure 12.1 Percentage of Americans trusting the federal government "only some of the time," 1964–98. Source: U.S. National Election Study Web site.

word: he did, as promised, fundamentally change the game of politics in Italy, eliminating the *lottizzazione*'s allocation of television channels to different political parties. But he did not stop there. Unconstrained by a sense of fair play, he began to implement changes that would have complemented his near-monopolistic control over the private television sector with control over the public RAI networks as well. Such a monopoly of control by a single highly partisan individual over virtually all television broadcasting would have been without precedent among established Western democracies and would have threatened the informational pluralism that is integral to the democratic process. Fortunately for Italian democracy, Berlusconi's government coalition collapsed before his public-sector takeover could be completed and consolidated.

Politicians are the leading players in the game of democratic politics. Indiscriminate cynicism toward them carries with it a threat to the democratic rules of the game that keep officeholders and their opponents publicly accountable. Let us not forget that among those who most regularly expressed contempt for politics, politicians, and the game that they played are Francisco Franco and Benito Mussolini. There is an important distinction to be drawn between healthy skepticism and the journalistic watchdog role, on the one hand, and sweeping and unwarranted cynicism about democratic politics, on the other. The latter has often been articulated by authoritarian rulers as the rationale for their termination of democracy.

POLICY-RELEVANT INFORMATION: As in the case of impartiality, democracies manifest considerable differences in the extent to which their media convey policy-relevant information.[10] In general, the print medium continues to perform well in this regard, even if there is considerable variation in individual newspapers' performance within and between nations. At the low end on the continuum are Britain's already described daily tabloids, but this country also has a quality press (*The Independent, The Guardian, The Times, Financial Times*) that is as serious and informative as that found anywhere. Anchoring the other end of the continuum are countries like Spain – whose newspaper market completely lacks tabloid journals and is dominated by four major newspapers (*El País, ABC, El Mundo,* and, in Catalonia, *La Vanguardia*), all of which can be classified as high in quality and rich in informational content. The Dutch and Japanese newspapers also present a large volume of policy-relevant information to their readers.

Most other countries surveyed fall somewhere between these two extremes, with some newspapers (e.g., *The New York Times, The Washington Post, The Los Angeles Times, Frankfurter Algemeine Zeitung,* and *Süddeutsche Zeitung*) presenting readers with a large volume of policy-relevant news, others (e.g., *USA Today* and the *Bild Zeitung*) publishing relatively little such information, and most falling somewhere in the middle of this range. Studies of political-information levels among respondents in national surveys reflect these macro-level differences: in Spain, there is a very strong correlation between the frequency of newspaper reading and the respondent's score on a political-information test, while in Britain (where most citizens read tabloids), there is no similar association between knowledge of politics and newspaper reading (Trenaman and McQuail 1961, 188).[11] Somewhat offsetting the qualitative merits of the Spanish press, however, is the fact that very few Spaniards read newspapers.

There are disturbing signs, however, that even the most serious newspapers are "dumbing down" in their efforts to keep readers and market share. Apparent in European countries like Britain, Germany, and the Netherlands, these signs are already clearly in evidence in the United States, where even in newspapers like *The New York Times,* the serious discussion of political issues and candidates has progressively given way to coverage of the campaign as a "horse race," as a series of staged events, and as a trial by ordeal in which the avoidance of gaffes by candidates may be necessary for electoral survival (see Patterson 1993, 73–4). With the appearance of print media like *USA Today* and *People* magazine, market pressures have led publications with a tradition of serious and extensive coverage of policy issues to shift their attention to notable personalities and human interest stories. In comparison to television, however, the print media in the United States and elsewhere still convey, by and large, a reasonable volume of policy-relevant information.

Television coverage of political news shows a similarly broad pattern of variation from country to country and from one network to another within a given country. There is, however, pervasive evidence of some decline in the serious and substantive content of television political coverage. Seeking to entertain as well as inform viewers, television increasingly depicts politics as a game or personality contest, or reduces coverage of public policy issues, shifting attention to prominent personalities, human interest stories, and nonpolitical subjects in general. And when news articles deal with the substance of public policies at all, they convey little information to citizens. As with newspapers, this trend has progressed furthest in the United States, although it has not affected all broadcasting networks to the same extent. The Center for Media and Public Affairs (1993b), for example, found that 75 percent of all issue references in the news were communicated by a single sentence, and fewer than 10 percent of them contained enough substance to make their policy relevance readily apparent to even the most attentive members of the news audience. This trend has emerged at the expense of the central purposes of elections and citizen participation in representative democracies – establishing accountability for governance of the nation, and the adoption and implementation of policies that directly affect the lives of citizens.

With the move away from issues and toward entertainment, television news broadcasting has also shifted toward greater editorializing, with journalists emerging as the main protagonists on the television screen, and politicians being nearly crowded off altogether. Again, this trend is most pronounced in the United States, as evidenced by the dramatic reduction in the average soundbite in which politicians were allowed to speak for themselves, from 42 seconds in 1968 to less than 10 seconds in 1988. The real problem, however, is not the amount of time that journalists appear on the screen, but rather that they do not put this time to good account. As Steele and Barnhurst (1995, 16) concluded from a study of U.S. television news over a 20-year period, "rather than providing more information, journalists appear to provide less, and the context for the shrinking sound bite becomes not deeper, hidden fact, but a growing embroidery of journalistic opinion."

U.S. commercial television is unique in the extent to which its political coverage confounds news with entertainment. Democracies with strong public-service television traditions still present large volumes of serious, substantive information in their political programming. Japan's NHK is a world leader in this respect in that it devotes 40 percent of its broadcast time to news programs (60 percent of which deals with politics, government, and public affairs), and by far the most frequent subjects of these news articles are policy problems and responses by the government's administrative agencies. Britain's public and commercial television network is another stellar example of public-service-oriented journalism committed to providing citizens with a substantial and balanced amount of information and policy discussion.[12] The list could go on to include Germany, Italy, the Netherlands, and Spain, among others.

The chapters in this volume, however, have shown that, at the same time that television is playing an increasingly important electoral and political role, even countries with strong public-service broadcasting traditions are showing signs of following the trajectory of American television's "infotainment" style of political coverage. During the 1997 general election campaign, for example, the leader of the British Labour Party accused television of paying too little attention to the important issues in the campaign and too much to its transient and ephemeral epiphenomena. Indeed, there is much evidence that throughout Europe there is an increasing and unprecedented focus on the major personalities in parliamentary elections, as well as on the horse race aspect of the campaign, as reflected in the parties' standing in the opinion polls. Journalistic editorializing is also becoming more common: witness, for example, the rapid rise in popularity of the *News Show* in Japan, as well as British commercial television's decision in the 1997 campaign to give a more prominent role to popular television journalists to boost viewership.

TOWARD AN EXPLANATION

The preceding overview of media coverage of politics in a number of countries over time has revealed trends with clear implications for the quality of democracy. The first trend is a dilution of the substantive informational content of political communications disseminated by the media. The second is an increasingly rancorous relationship between journalists and politicians, ranging from struggle for control of the news agenda, as in Britain and the Netherlands, to pervasive negativity and cynicism about the actions and intentions of politicians, as in the United States. The first of these trends can be detrimental to the quality of democracy because its impact on the volume and content of political information reaching average citizens undermines their ability to assess the likely consequences for society of the electoral choices they make. The second can corrode both the ability and the desire of citizens to hold governments accountable for their (in)actions.

What factors can help to account for these trends and for cross-national differences in their progress in each country? We have argued in this volume that the causes of these phenomena are multiple and interactive. The nature of their political impact can best be clarified by ordering them within a "funnel of causality," with more distal and structural factors located at the broad base of this funnel and more contingent and elite-level variables at its tip. Moving from the more fundamental to the more specific and contingent, we would categorize these causal factors as *technological* (especially those pertaining to the emergence of new kinds of media); *economic* (pertaining both to the basic character of the country's economic system and to the location of the medium in question within the public or private sector); *subcultural norms* (such as journalists' professional ethics) and *regulatory structures* that constrain behavior; and, finally, short-term, conscious *choices* by journalists and politicians alike.

TECHNOLOGICAL FACTORS: The political impacts of some very recent technological advances, such as the proliferation of television channels resulting from new cable and satellite systems, not to mention the even more recent development of the Internet as an information source and a medium for the exchange of views, have not been adequately explored in this volume largely due to their novelty (and underdevelopment in some of the countries we have surveyed) and the resulting absence of comparative data. What little we do know paints a no more optimistic picture of the newest communication media's contribution to the quality of democracy than the one we have set forth. Despite the widely touted promise of greater citizen information and participation that these new channels of access make possible, preliminary data indicate that these new media are not filling the information gap created by changes in the longer-established broadcast media. Indeed, "narrowcasting" by highly specific sources of information has contributed to the emergence of a highly segmented media audience, ranging from "news junkies" to those who avoid coverage of politics altogether, as audiences for more traditional network news broadcasts continue to shrink.[13]

This volume has, however, thoroughly explored the political roles and impact of television as a national broadcast medium that emerged as the dominant medium for political communication in earlier decades. Like other investigations of the media and politics, we find some evidence of a "media logic," in which the inherent characteristics of television per se appear to be conducive to personalization and simplification in the presentation of political news. As Ranney (1983) noted, the television is poorly suited to conveying complex information but is well suited to the projection of the personal images of candidates. Accordingly, television journalism has shifted from the "talking heads" discussion of complex policy issues to a focus on the personal characteristics and behavior of candidates, thereby reducing what we would regard as the proper information content of television news programs. It is also widely believed that the visual image seems to have a stronger impact on most people than the spoken word. This has led parties and politicians themselves to reinforce this journalistic trend. They have taken great care to accommodate their "marketing" strategies to the needs of television, as typified by the British Conservative Party's abandonment in 1970 of the talking head format in its party election broadcasts in favor of a series of striking visual images that clearly and simply conveyed to viewers strong messages about, for example, inflation. Similarly, parties have placed unprecedented emphasis on telegenic leaders as the vehicle through which they communicate with the public and shape their popular image. Since television news is to a large extent dependent for its content on the raw material that the principal political actors supply, it is no surprise that leading political personalities in staged situations, surrounded by stock characters, loom larger in newscasts. This same trend is present in the print media as well. The appearance of *People* magazine and *USA Today*, for example, has led such time-honored publications as *Newsweek* and *Time* to dumb down in order to compete for market share by adopting the same entertainment-oriented and personality-focused formats.[14]

ECONOMIC FACTORS: To a considerable degree, these trends have been affected by the competitive pressure within a free-market system. Dependence on commercial advertising as a medium's only source of income can constitute a powerful incentive to stress entertainment at the expense of providing policy-relevant information to viewers or readers. In contrast, those media that receive subsidies from the state or charitable foundations, or derive all of their income from noncommercial sources (such as revenues from licensing fees or more general government taxation), are much less affected by these pressures. We have found, almost without exception among the cases surveyed in this volume, that private-sector broadcasters provide less policy-relevant information in their news programs than do their public-sector competitors. But it was also quite clear from these cases that commercial broadcasters have not all moved in the direction of personalizing or dumbing down the news to the same extent, even within the same country. What explains these variations across and within the countries in our sample after the media system's level of technological development and economic structure are taken into account?

PROFESSIONAL NORMS AND THE REGULATORY ROLE OF THE STATE: One variable is the set of norms that constrains the behavior of journalists in these countries. How journalists define their roles (conveyer of information between citizens and elected officials vs. protagonist in a struggle to reveal the shortcomings and foibles of politicians) has been shown in the American case study to play a significant role in accounting for changes in journalism since the 1960s. At the other end of the continuum are Japanese television journalists (even those in the commercial broadcasting sector), who closely associate with newspaper reporters and behave in much the same way as their print-media counterparts, presenting a considerable volume of policy-relevant information to their viewers. Unfortunately, there have been no systematic comparative studies of the norms, values, and role definitions of journalists in established democracies. We believe that empirical studies along these lines would enhance our understanding of the determinants of the trends identified in this volume. So, too, might studies of the academic preparation and professional training of journalists (see, for example, Gaunt 1988). Insofar as university education in mainstream liberal arts or scientific disciplines is displaced by narrow professional training in commercial advertising and visual-media techniques, one could speculate that journalists might themselves be less capable of reporting on the complexities of public policy, economics, and political life in general. Future research along these lines might help to explain the cross-national patterns and trends that we have observed.

Particularly significant in this regard is the extent to which a "public-service ethic" is pervasive within the journalistic subculture of a country. We have seen that where such norms are deeply rooted (e.g., Britain and Japan), news broadcasts by both public-sector and commercial networks adhere closely to the two sets of performance standards that have served as the leitmotif of this book: they tend to be objective and nonevaluative in their presentation of political information, and they present a high volume of policy-relevant information to their viewers. While a thorough exploration of the origins of these norms is beyond the scope of this volume, our ten country studies have consistently pointed to one actor that has greatly influenced the establishment of and adherence to these norms: the state. In most cases (e.g., Britain, Germany, Japan, Italy, and post-Franco Spain), the state played an active role in imposing "inform and educate" strictures on television broadcasters and in establishing regulatory bodies to guarantee that they are nonpartisan in their presentation of the news (or, in the Italian case, in making sure that the alternative views of the major parties are presented by one or another channel). In other cases, this was not done. The American government adopted a hands-off policy regarding the broadcast media from the very beginning. While the establishment of the Public Broadcasting System and National Public Radio in the late 1960s represented a modest effort to strengthen the inform and educate functions of the broadcast media, repeal of the Fairness Doctrine in the 1980s represented an abandonment of one of the key regulatory functions assumed by the state in most other democracies. In the cases of Russia and Hungary, the role played by the state in the predemocratic period – involving heavy-handed censorship and manipulation of the news – hardly presented an attractive model for emulation. The political transitions in these countries did not include an explicit redefinition of the role of the media in the positive sense of establishing professional norms or regulatory bodies. In the absence of such democratic controls, blatant partisan manipulation by incumbent governments resulted. It was only in the aftermath of the "media war" of the mid-1990s that the Hungarian Parliament drafted such norms and adopted appropriate regulatory practices. These findings regarding the positive functions performed by the state in democratic systems challenge the conventional wisdom prevalent in the free-market euphoria of the 1980s and 1990s and are therefore worthy of further discussion.

It has often been asserted that the interests of democracy are best served by a completely free, private-sector broadcasting system. Neuman, for example, has written: "All things considered, the open commercial systems of liberal democracies are probably the best that one is likely to find in the real world for maintaining an open, competitive and vibrant marketplace of ideas" (1991, 138). Our study of the role of the media in established democracies comes to a strikingly different conclusion. To be sure, outright government control of the media is highly subversive of the free flow of unbiased information that democracy requires. The most obvious (and overtly undemocratic) is the repressive kind of control exercised by rulers in authoritarian systems, as surveyed in the first several chapters of this book. Also undesirable are the manipulative interventions by governments in several of the democratic or semidemocratic regimes of the former Soviet bloc or even in the established democracies of Western Europe, such as France under De Gaulle (Kuhn 1998, 29). The Italian *lottizazzione* was based on some modest bias by each RAI channel in favor of its allied political party, but since channels were parceled out among the major parties, the public broadcasting system in the aggregate provided adequate informational pluralism to Italian citizens.

Far more typical of public-sector television networks is scrupulous impartiality regarding partisan matters. The public broadcasting systems of countries like Japan, Germany, and Britain have adhered to the strictest standards of objectivity and journalistic integrity. Indeed, the most common source of complaints of bias in the BBC's coverage of politics have been British government themselves, both Labour and Conservative. And even in the marginal cases of bias in Italy and Spain, far fewer explicit or implicit editorial remarks are made than on American commercial television or Berlusconi's private networks.

One reason for this strict impartiality is that, in recognition of the power and potential abuses of these crucial communications media, agencies were created to guarantee that public-sector networks would maintain strict neutrality in their political reporting. Two different approaches have been adopted. The first is exemplified by Britain: strictly nonpartisan regulatory and oversight bodies, independent of the government, were established to guarantee impartiality and balance in the way both public-service and commercial broadcast media cover politics. The second approach is illustrated by Spain, where an oversight committee, composed of representatives of all significant parliamentary parties, was established to closely monitor news broadcasts and public affairs programs on Radio Televisión Española (RTVE). In addition to the institutional roles performed by these bodies, this great sensitivity to the potential abuses of the public broadcast media has led to heightened vigilance by other key actors in the political system and society at large. News broadcasts during election campaigns in some countries are "stopwatched" (in Britain by the BBC and Independent Television (ITV) networks themselves) to ensure that equal time is given to the major parties, and in some countries the exact number of seconds devoted to each party and its candidates is published in the newspapers on a regular basis. Even modest departures from equal treatment are vigorously criticized and themselves become issues in the election campaign. In short, considerable pressures (institutionalized or manifested through mobilized public opinion) are exerted on public-sector broadcast journalists to keep their partisan preferences to themselves and to deal with politicians in as even-handed a manner as possible.

Commercial networks are not commonly subjected to these same constraints (with notable exceptions, such as Britain's ITV), and in practice they vary considerably with regard to the bias of their political news coverage. The naked partisanship of Berlusconi's channels appears to be the most extreme example among established democracies. At the other end of the continuum, American broadcast journalists reveal little overt partisan favoritism, except in the sense that their cynical disdain for politicians may vary in intensity from one individual to another, from one party to another, from one election campaign to another.

The issue of partisan balance and objectivity among private-sector broadcasters has become more salient in recent years as a result of the general trend toward the reduction of the state's role in regulating the broadcast media. Beginning in the 1980s, Western democracies generally deregulated their broadcast media, liberalizing governmental oversight and allowing the private, unregulated (largely cable and satellite) sector to expand. Deregulation has led to increased competition for ratings and audience share, and this has set in motion some of the same pressures that have helped to make American broadcasting what it is today. As is evident from British commercial television's increasing "reporter involvement" in newscasts to take advantage of the popular appeal of some of its reporters, journalists are functioning less as simple conveyors of information and more as actors involved centrally in the nation's political debate (White 1997). Whether in newscasts, documentaries, or the equivalent of the Japanese *News Show*, a "star system" is encouraged and journalists seek to work their way into the ranks of the favored few by doing battle with politicians and exposing their personal and political weaknesses – and the higher placed the victim, the more glorious the victory.

One form of regulation, however, remains in place in many other democracies and makes it unlikely that they will fully converge on the U.S. model. This is the legal framework within which journalists operate.

Grounded in the First Amendment's guarantee of free speech, deeply rooted in the country's political culture, and confirmed by a number of Supreme Court decisions, American journalists are relatively unfettered by fear of prosecution for inaccuracy or misrepresentation in what they write or say about politicians (Coliver 1993). The U.S. legal system distinguishes "defamation of a public figure from defamation of a private person, giving the press more room to err in its stories about the former so as to encourage press coverage of government and other powerful institutions" (Abramson et al. 1988, 240). Other democracies do not generally make this distinction, and they have stricter defamation and libel laws. Relatedly, the public service ethos is stronger and more strongly enforced in the mainstream media of democracies outside the United States.

A second obstacle that might help to discourage emulation of the American model might be labeled "cultural/institutional." Some present-day democracies have had checkered experiences with democracy or have experienced deep conflicts between segments of their populations. As a result, they go to great lengths to ensure that at least some significant portion of the media spreads and sustains democratic values like moderation, compromise, and mutual respect, and that they, as Kaase put it in Chapter 11, "provide society with all of the basic information necessary for a democratic polity." Dutch politicians, too, have learned the value of mutual restraint from their country's history of deep and divisive conflict among its pillarized communities prior to the 1917 "Pacification." While this style of politics is now a thing of the past, political parties still consciously avoid rancorous attacks to show respect for adversaries with whom they may have to cooperate to form and maintain an effective coalition government once elections are over. In short, highly salient political developments in the past can help forge norms that continue to influence the behavior of journalists. It is far from inevitable, however, that such formative experiences will encourage norms that reinforce objectivity in reporting political events. While American television and newspaper journalists have been admirably nonpartisan in their reporting of the news, their experiences with Watergate and the Vietnam War led them, as Patterson contends in Chapter 7, to adopt a more cynical and adversarial stance vis-à-vis politicians and government in general. And in the case of Russia, the "model" that helps to condition the behavior of journalists is that of the highly manipulative, government-dominated media of the Soviet era. In contrast, the strong public-service ethic present in Britain and Japan serves as a basis for norms strongly supportive of objectivity and partisan balance.

The presence or absence of a public-service ethic also affects how broadcasters perform on the second key criterion for assessing their respective contributions to the quality of democracy: the presentation of an adequate volume of policy-relevant information to citizens. Free-market, unregulated, commercial broadcasting differs significantly from public-sector broadcasting with regard to the volume and detail of policy-relevant information conveyed to viewers and listeners. Indeed, much of the cross-national variation in informational content noted in this volume is accounted for by the fact that the broadcast media of the United States were overwhelmingly commercial from the outset, while virtually everywhere else, public-sector broadcasting was initially dominant. Since an inform and educate stricture was explicit in the charters of most public-sector networks, it is not surprising that our contributing authors have consistently found that public television and radio stations present more policy-relevant information and public affairs programming than do their commercial rivals. But it is noteworthy that in those countries where this state-mandated commitment was strongest during the crucial formative stages of the broadcast-media systems, these norms have spread to journalists on commercial television as well. Clear evidence is provided in Ellis Krauss's chapter on Japan, where the high standards set by NHK eventually induced the private stations to upgrade their news and public affairs offerings as well.

With deregulation, however, the general trend has been a decline in the substantive informational content of political communications through the broadcast media. Opening up these media to market forces has induced the news divisions of television channels – even those bound by public-service requirements – to compete for ratings and audience share, and this has resulted in a decline in both the volume and the substantive, policy-relevant content of that information. This general trend notwithstanding, publicly subsidized channels like the BBC, RAI, RTVE, NPR, PBS, and NHK continue to provide a high volume of policy-relevant information, albeit often to a smaller share of the television audience. While this is in large part a reflection of their respective historical legacies, a fulfillment of the terms of their legal mandates, and a product of their journalists' norms and values, it can also be seen as part of an effort by public-sector broadcasters to justify their continued existence in the face of increasing criticism from governments newly converted to free-market doctrines and the associated view that the interests of democracy are best served by a private-sector broadcasting system characterized by weak to nonexistent government regulation.

Commercial broadcasters, however, have been more strongly buffeted by market pressures. Despite formal requirements that their broadcasts include public-service programs intended to inform and educate citizens, there is evidence that they are paying less attention to politics in their news broadcasts, and not only in the United States. In Britain, for example, BBC1 devoted 50 percent of its news space to coverage of the 1997 British election, while its principal commercial competitor, ITV, allocated only 29 percent of its news broadcasts to coverage of the campaign (Golding and Deacon 1997). At the extreme end of this continuum are cable and satellite channels that are under no legal obligation to provide political programming of any kind and that often do not bother to do so. They give citizens, in other words, the opportunity to avoid exposure to political news and information altogether. As these apolitical alternatives have grown, to cite one example, the U.S. networks have declined. "In the 1990–1991 season, the aggregate audience for ABC, CBS, and NBC dropped to 62.4 percent, down from 66 percent in the previous season and 85 percent in 1980" (Ansolabehere et al. 1993, 26).

What is most curious is that the evidence is mixed, at best, concerning whether the general public approves of this dumbing down of media coverage of politics. To be sure, if the media aim too high (as in the case of newspapers in Spain), they may leave behind the less well educated majority of the population for whom the language of macroeconomics or public policy making is unintelligible. But there is plentiful evidence that the media can lead and educate the general public to follow reliable factual information about politics and policies with interest, and that broadcasters have more freedom of *choice* in determining the style and content of their news coverage than an economic-reductionist or technologically driven explanatory model would suggest: in Chapter 8, Krauss pointed out that the heavy coverage of politics (with a strong emphasis on the bureaucracy, no less!) by NHK led Japan's commercial networks to increase their coverage in response; the introduction of half-hour network newscasts in the United States in the early 1960s, as Patterson showed in Chapter 7, led to an increase in audiences for news and public affairs programming during the brief "golden age" of American television journalism; and the BBC's extensive and information-rich coverage of British politics and world affairs led its principal private-sector competitor, ITV, to embrace without question the same approach to political broadcasting. Even in the United States in the 1990s, there was reason to believe that network-news audience shares declined in part as a reaction against the dumbing down and sensationalizing of television coverage of politics. As MacNeil (1996, 3) points out, "In 1993, the *Los Angeles Times* poll explored why Americans were less confident in the press than they used to be. The commonest answer, given by 28 percent, was that the press too often sensationalized or hyped events. Other common complaints were: failing to tell the whole story, biased or unfair reporting, and lack of accuracy" (see also Fallows 1996, 235–73, and Chapter 7 in this volume). Just et al. (1996, 240) found that participants in focus-group discussions provided strong evidence that "horse-race news is neither useful nor interesting to the public. . . . [H]orse-race news provoked little discussion, did not permit individuals to bring personal experience into their conversation, was difficult to build on as a topic for discussion, and was often perceived as biased. . . . [Conversely,] focus group participants responded quite differently to another form of news coverage: news analysis, a form represented in our study by the 'American Agenda' segment on ABC news," and by in-depth interviews with candidates on generally nonpolemical talk shows, such as *Larry King Live,* which they considered to be much more helpful and stimulating.[15] Fallows underscores this point by describing the great difference between the policy-relevant questions asked of American presidential candidates by ordinary citizens in a public meeting, on the one hand, and the political-game questions asked by professional journalists.[16]

Fortunately, it is unlikely that political programming or citizens' viewing patterns in other democracies will go the way of the United States, at least to the same degree. In the first place, the continuation of a strong commitment to public-service broadcasting – affirmed, for example, in the European Union's 1997 Amsterdam Treaty – will go a long way toward ensuring the continuation of a high volume of substantive political information in political programming. At the same time, it may be hoped to set and maintain standards that channels not subject to the same inform and educate strictures will feel obliged to mimic for fear of losing their more highly educated and affluent viewers who are potentially attractive to advertisers. This is because there is popular demand for plentiful and serious information about politics. The information-deprivation excesses of the United States, then, are unlikely to be replicated in other democracies where a public-service broadcasting ethos persists despite the deregulation of the 1980s and 1990s. In particular, it will be difficult for their citizens to avoid exposure to political information altogether when they watch television. In countries like Britain and Germany, for example, private-sector channels offer national news programs similar, albeit with less informational content, to those broadcast by their longer-established counterparts subject to inform and educate strictures. Nonetheless, it is undeniable that deregulation has diluted the volume of substantive political information on offer to viewers as entertainment, human interest stories, and the like have come to figure more prominently in the television newscasts of commercial channels that have been thrown into competition for ratings, audience share, and advertising revenue with the plethora of unregulated (and perhaps unregulatable) cable and satellite channels made possible by advances in communications technology.

At a minimum, the empirical studies presented in this volume debunk the current conventional wisdom that market forces and the minimization of the role of the state and public-sector entities will enhance the quality of democracy. Indeed, a clear pattern has emerged from this overview: in the established democracies of the West, the stronger the dominance of commercial broadcast media, the less the policy-relevant information content of television broadcasts and the more "news" programs tend to focus on the horse race, the game of politics, and the personalities, peccadillos, and pratfalls of politicians. Conversely, public-sector broadcasting in all of the established democracies surveyed here is characterized by more extensive coverage of public affairs, the conveyance of a greater volume of policy-relevant information, and a more scrupulous respect for journalistic norms of impartiality toward parties, politicians, and politics in general. Unfortunately, following the deregulatory trends set in motion in the 1980s, as more and more commercial broadcasting channels have been established, the public-service ethic has been progressively weakened and citizens exposed less to policy-relevant information. Indeed, most of them can now avoid television coverage of politics altogether. And as state regulation of the broadcast media is reduced – ranging from relaxation of inform and educate strictures to revocation of the Fairness Doctrine – these trends are exacerbated. In short, the more the deregulation of broadcasting spreads among established democracies, the more their media systems are likely to converge on the commercial American model.

ELECTION CAMPAIGN COVERAGE: The exceptional nature of the American case is nowhere more extreme than with regard to the commercialization of the electoral process itself. Unlike the situation in the other established democracies surveyed in this volume, free air time is not generally made available to candidates. In the era of the shrinking sound bite, the principal medium through which candidates can convey their messages to the voters is the privately funded commercial campaign advertisement. But while this format does enable candidates to inundate voters with campaign messages, it does so in a manner that is detrimental to the quality of democracy in two important respects. The first is that the overwhelming majority of the messages reaching American voters takes the form of highly simplistic symbol manipulation, personal-image mongering, and sometimes grotesque misrepresentations of the rival candidates' stands on the issues. These messages are typically 30 seconds in length, and convey very little reliable information (and much misinformation) about where the candidates and their rivals actually stand on key issues. The negativism and nasty personal attacks of many of these commercials, moreover, have been shown to turn off voters, and help contribute to their alienation from politicians and the game of electoral politics more broadly.

Second, television commercials are enormously expensive, requiring American politicians to devote an inordinate amount of time to campaign fund-raising. This not only distracts them from the business of government, it also opens up the political process to the risk of influence-buying on behalf of well-heeled contributors or Political Action Committees. It is estimated that the 1996 presidential election campaign, for example, cost $2.2 billion – a truly staggering sum – and that the great bulk of that money went for the purchase of television advertising.[17] This election campaign was followed by an unprecedented wave of accusations concerning illegal or improper fund-raising activities, as well as concerns over the extent to which various groups were able to "buy" favorable treatment in exchange for campaign contributions, further undermining public confidence in the political process. Moreover, despite naive assumptions about the "impartiality" of the market mechanism, the necessity of purchasing air time in order to broadcast political communications to voters diminishes the quality of democracy by giving well-organized and affluent interest groups a disproportionate ability to flood the airwaves with propaganda in support of their cause.

In sharp contrast, paid television advertising for parties and candidates is prohibited by law in countries like Spain and the United Kingdom and is not permitted on public television networks in countries like Italy. In the case of Japan, since only parties (not candidates) can purchase advertising time, there is greater stress on parties and programs than on personalities.

The United States stands alone among the established democracies in its wholesale commercialization of the electoral process. This survey of the relationship between democracy and the media has revealed that extreme dependence on commercial mechanisms in political campaigns is as detrimental to the quality of democracy as it is unnecessary. Elections are regularly and fairly held in other established democracies (with far higher voter turnout levels than in the United States) either wholly or predominantly in the absence of paid political commercials.

CONCLUDING OBSERVATIONS

The paradox of the contemporary political communications media is that they helped to sound the death knell of authoritarian or posttotalitarian regimes by fostering political pluralism, thereby helping to spread democracy, but within established democracies they have failed to live up to their potential to improve the quality of democracy. Despite the dramatic technological advances of the past few decades, which have moved in tandem with higher education levels in most countries, the richer political pluralism and the more active, better-informed citizenry that many observers predicted (e.g., Pool 1983) have failed to materialize. Indeed, in some countries (especially the United States), the trend has been toward ever lower levels of political participation and higher levels of cynicism toward democratic politics per se. The key to understanding this paradox is the recognition that the communications media are precisely that – a channel through which information flows to citizens. The political effects of this information are shaped by the interaction between its use by elites and the receptivity of individual citizens who are the target of political messages. While we have surveyed a number of technological, economic, and social-structural factors that influence the impact of the media on political behavior, we conclude that the most decisive determinants of media effects are the strategies and behavior of elites, particularly political elites. In nondemocratic systems, for example, mass publics retained an appetite for political messages subversive of the regime, but they were unable to act on these messages until authoritarian elites decided, for whatever reason, to relax their strict oversight of the media and allow them to disseminate alternative or opposition views. Similarly, broadcast deregulation in democratic systems, with all of its consequences for the polity, was not the product of an irresistible groundswell in public demand, but rather of an ideological commitment to free-market economics by governing elites in the 1980s. Even if some of them may, at the same time, have maintained their commitment to public-service broadcasting, their decision to increase competition over the airwaves established a context for commercialization and the dumbing down of the broadcast media. The technological innovation of remote-control channel selectors inadvertently reinforced the ability of viewers to avoid exposure to political information by enabling them to "surf" effortlessly in search of entertainment alternatives. In microcosm, this exemplifies the interaction between causal factors of very different kinds.

This collection of chapters points to the complexity of the explanation of media effects. At the same time, however, these country studies underline the centrality of human agency, especially at the elite level, in explaining the presence or absence of these media effects. Technological advances may increase the persuasive potential of the communications, assuming a receptive citizenry. But it is a political decision whether to take advantage of that potential (as in the United States, where personalization and commercialization of television have made it possible, for example, to inundate viewers with aggressive "attack ads") or to resist that temptation (as Dutch politicians have done, fearing the deleterious impact of negative campaigning on the postelection process of coalition building). In short, in democracies, both new and old, effective communication between governors and the governed is shaped more by political than by technological factors.

NOTES

1. For data on the disturbingly high levels of support for alternative regimes (ranging from restoration of the former Communist system to restoration of the tsar, as well as for government by "experts," "a strong leader," and the army), see White et al. 1997, 46.

2. For classic statements of the relationship between education and democratic participation, see Deutsch 1953; 1961; Lerner 1958; Nie et al. 1969; Milbrath and Goel 1977.

3. As Rodan (1998, 125) summarizes this conventional wisdom: "Try as they may, it is argued, authoritarian leaders will be unable to contain the social and political forces unleashed by the very economic transformation they have championed. In addition to social changes increasing the level and diversity of demand for news and information, there is also the difficulty of restricting the impact of new electronic technologies. Moreover, a free flow of information is depicted as a functional requirement, indeed, imperative, of further market development."

4. Among the most noteworthy are the following: (1) Prime Minister Adolfo Suárez (the last secretary general of Franco's National Movement), walked across the aisles from the government benches in the Cortes to greet the newly elected deputy, Dolores Ibárruri, the fiery Communist orator from the civil war era; bowing slightly, he shook her hand and said, "Madam, you are welcome in this house." (2) Communist Party Secretary General Santiago Carrillo, who just nine months before had been ar-

445

rested after his return to Spain following nearly four decades in exile, entering the prime minister's Moncloa Palace to negotiate an important interparty pact and received a formal salute from policemen who, just nine months earlier, had hunted him down and placed him under arrest. (3) Prime Minister Suárez, representative of the Spanish state that had repressed Catalan nationalism since the end of the civil war, stood before hundreds of thousands of people in Barcelona, hand in hand with the president of the Catalan government-in-exile, celebrating the Diada – the Catalan national day.

5. Wring (1998), for example, concludes that one of the reasons Tony Blair was successful in revoking Clause Four of the Labour Party's charter (which called for state ownership of the means of production), while several of his predecessors were unable to do so, is that the increasing reliance on mass media in election campaigns had strengthened the position of the top party leader at the expense of the mass base of party militants.

6. This is higher than the 17 percent who claimed that newspapers were the most credible, and the 20 percent who said they were the most informative, but less than the 33 and 44 percent, respectively, who said that television was the most credible and informative medium. (Source: Spanish 1993 CNEP data set.)

7. This concern was initially articulated by Robinson (1976 and 1977), Huntington (1975), Rothman (1980), Ranney (1983), and Putnam (1995). Iyengar and Kinder (1987, 130), however, rejected these claims, although without citing any empirical evidence.

8. For the British–American comparison, see Semetko et al. 1991, 142, and Chapter 10 of this volume. The American–Spanish comparison was based on the application of the U.S. media coding protocol to coverage of the Spanish 1993 election campaign (see Chapter 2 of this volume).

9. Many investigators have drawn attention to this apparent and complex relationship, but a causal relationship is difficult to establish definitively. See the discussion in Iyengar and Kinder (1987, 129–30).

10. Unfortunately, rigorous content analyses measuring the amount of information conveyed by the media have not been undertaken. Lacking reliable quantitative data, we must base cross-national assessments of this variable on more impressionistic evidence and the subjective assessments of contributing authors, as well as on our own experiences as long-time residents in several of the countries discussed in this volume.

11. Consistent with this argument concerning the relationship between the density of policy-relevant information conveyed by the media and political-information levels of the general public are the findings that in Britain, those who follow television news (which is of high quality) are better-informed citizens than those who do not, and that in Germany, those who read/view political news are more knowledgeable about politics than those who limit their exposure to entertainment articles and programming (see Chapters 10 and 11 in this volume).

12. Even in Britain, however, there are signs that the commercial television channel, ITV, is seriously reducing its commitment to public-service broadcasting. Amid great opposition, for example, it moved its flagship *News at Ten* from 10:00 P.M. to 6:30 P.M., so that prime-time entertainment programming would no longer have to be interrupted to air the news. In addition, its oversight body, the Independent Television

Commission, noted that its 1998 current affairs output stood at just 1 hour and 25 minutes per week, the lowest figure on record (*Observer,* April 4, 1999).

13. See the 1998 report issued by the Pew Research Center (www.people-press.org /med98rpt.htm).

14. The August 26, 1996, issue of *Time* magazine, for example, included four pages on "world" news (consisting of just two articles, one on Chechnya and the other on the Helms-Burton Act). The same issue devoted 13 pages to the movie actor Christopher Reeve, recently paralyzed in a horse-riding accident.

15. It should be noted that, consistent with the dumbing down of news coverage by some networks, ABC's *Evening News with Peter Jennings* has discontinued its "American Agenda" segment.

16. Fallows 1996, 24. Some have claimed, however, that the public journalism movement championed by Fallows is elitist and reactionary (see Schudson 1998).

17. The total amount of money spent on the 1996 campaign was included in a report issued by the Center for Responsive Politics, broadcast on National Pubic Radio's *The Morning Edition* on November 25, 1997, and published in *The New York Times* on that same day (p. A12). Estimates of the share of campaign contributions that are spent on commercial advertising range from two-thirds (Just et al. 1996, 63) to over three-quarters (the chairmen of both the Republican and Democratic parties of Ohio stated that 75 to 80 percent of their budgets were devoted to the purchase of television commercials [reported on WOSU AM radio's news program, *820 at 9:00,* on August 18, 1997]). It should be noted that a total of £56.4 million was spent in the 1997 British election (Neill Report 1998). With the British population in 1995 at 57.5 million, this worked out to 98 pence ($1.57) per person. The U.S. expenditure of $2.2 billion on 250 million people works out to $8.80 per person, or 5.6 times the amount spent per capita in the United Kingdom. When these rates are calculated on the basis of expenditures per voter, the ratio is much higher.

REFERENCES

Abellán, Manuel L. 1989. *Censura y creación literaria en España (1939–1976).* Barcelona: Ediciones Peninsula.

Abrams v. United States, 250 U.S. 216 (1919).

Abramson, Jeffrey B., F. Christopher Arterton, and Gary R. Orren. 1988. *The Electronic Commonwealth.* New York: Basic Books.

Adatto, Kiku. 1990. *Sound Bite Democracy: Network Evening News Presidential Campaign Coverage, 1968 and 1988.* Cambridge: Harvard University Press.

Aguilar, Miguel Angel. 1982. *El vértigo de la prensa.* Madrid: Editorial Mezquita.

Albarran, Alan B., and Sylvia M. Chan-Olmsted, eds. 1998. *Global Media Economics: Commercialization, Concentration and Integration of World Media Markets.* Ames: Iowa State University Press.

Aldrich, John. 1995. *Why Parties?* Chicago: University of Chicago Press.

Alexander, Herbert E. and Rei Shiratori, eds. 1994. *Comparative Political Finance among the Democracies.* Boulder: Westview.

Alférez, Antonio. 1986. *El cuarto poder en España.* Barcelona: Plaza y Janés.

Almond, Gabriel A., and Sidney Verba. 1963. *The Civic Culture.* Princeton: Princeton University Press.

Altheide, David L., and Robert P. Snow. 1979. *Media Logic.* Beverly Hills and London: Sage.

1991. *Media Worlds in the Postjournalism Era.* New York: Aldine de Gruyter.

Altman, Kristin Kyoko. 1996. "TV and Political Turmoil: Japan's Summer of 1993." In Pharr and Krauss, eds.

Andersen, Kristi and Stuart J. Thorson. 1989. "Public Discourse or Strategic Game? Changes in Our Conception of Elections." *Studies in American Political Development,* 3, 263–78.

Andras, Eduard. 1984. *Tevenezes Del-Szlovakiaban.* Budapest: Tomegkommunikacios Kutatokozpont.

Ansolabehere, Stephen, Roy Behr, and Shanto Iyengar. 1993. *The Media Game: American Politics in the Television Age.* New York: Macmillan.

Ansolabehere, Stephen, and Shanto Iyengar. 1995. *Going Negative: How Attack Ads Shrink and Polarize the Electorate.* New York: Free Press.

Anuario El País, 1988. 1988. Madrid: Ediciones El País.

Anuario El País, 1995. 1995. Madrid: Ediciones El País.

Arango, Joaquín, and Miguel Díez. 1993. "6-J: el sentido de una elección." *Claves de la Razón Práctica,* 36, 10–18.

Arato, Andrew. 1981. "Civil Society Against the State: Poland 1980–1981." *Telos,* 47, 23–47.

1982. "Empire vs. Civil Society: Poland 1981–1982." *Telos,* 50, 19–48.

Arendt, Hannah. 1951. *The Origins of Totalitarianism.* New York: Harcourt Brace.

Arzheimer, Kai, and Jürgen W. Falter. 1998. "'Annäherung durch Wandel?' Das Wahlverhalten bei der Bundestagswahl 1998 in Ost-West Perspektive." *Aus Politik und Zeitgeschichte. Beilage zur Wochenzeitung das Parlament,* 52/98, 33–43.

Asahi Shinbun. 1983. "Seiken hôsô mo 'seitô' PR," June 9, 22.

Aslund, Anders. 1991. *Gorbachev's Struggle for Economic Reform.* Ithaca: Cornell University Press.

Audiradio. 1988. *Indagine sull'ascolto radiofonico in Italia,* mimeo.

Avery, Robert K., ed. 1993. *Public Service Broadcasting in a Multichannel Environment: The History and Survival of an Ideal.* New York: Longman.

Baerwald, Hans. 1986. *Party Politics in Japan.* Boston: Allen & Unwin.

Bagdikian, Ben H. 1983. *The Media Monopoly,* 3rd ed. Boston: Beacon Press.

1992. *The Media Monopoly,* 4th ed. Boston: Beacon Press.

1997. *The Media Monopoly,* 5th ed. Boston: Beacon Press.

Bagnasco, Arnaldo. 1996. *L'Italia in tempi di cambiamento politico.* Bologna: Il Mulino.

Bakvis, Herman. 1981. *Catholic Power in the Netherlands.* Kingston: McGill-Queen's University Press.

Barbagli, Marzio, Piergiorgio Corbetta, Arturo Parisi, and Hans M. A. Schadee. 1979. *Fluidità elettorale e classi sociali in Italia.* Bologna: Il Mulino.

Barber, James David. 1978. "Characters in the Campaign: The Literary Problem." In James David Barber, ed., *Race for the Presidency.* Englewood Cliffs: Prentice-Hall.

1980. *The Pulse of Politics.* New York: W. W. Norton.

Barreiro, Belén, and Ignacio Sánchez-Cuenca. 1998. "Análisis del cambio de voto hacia el PSOE en las elecciones de 1993." *Revista Española de Investigaciones Sociológicas,* 82, 191–211.

Barrera, Carlos. 1995. *Periodismo y franquismo. De la censura a la apertura.* Pamplona: Ediciones Internacionales Universitarias.

Bartels, Larry M. 1993. "Messages Received: The Political Impact of Media Exposure." *American Political Science Review,* 87, 267–85.

Bartolini, Stefano, and Roberto D'Alimonte, eds. 1994. *Maggioritario ma non troppo. Le elezioni politiche del 1994.* Bologna: Il Mulino.

Bartolini, Stefano, and Peter Mair. 1990. *Identity, Competition and Electoral Availability. The Stabilisation of European Electorates 1885– 1985.* Cambridge: Cambridge University Press.

Bauer, Petra. 1991a. "Freiheit und Demokratie in der Wahrnehmung der Buerger in der Bundesrepublik und der ehemaligen DDR." In Rudolf Wildenmann, ed., *Nation und Demokratie. Politisch-strukturelle Gestaltungsprobleme im neuen Deutschland.* Baden-Baden: Nomos Verlagsgesellschaft.

1991b. "Politische Orientierungen im Uebergang. Eine Analyse politischer Einstellungen der Buerger in West- und Ostdeutschland 1990/91." *Kölner Zeitschrift fuer Soziologie und Sozialpsychologie,* 43, 433–55.

Bausch, Hans. 1980. *Rundfunkpolitik nach 1945.* Vol. 2. München: Deutscher Taschenbuch Verlag.

Bax, Erik. H. 1988. *Modernization and Cleavage in Dutch Society. A Study of Longterm Economic and Social Change.* Ph.D. dissertation, University of Gröningen.

Bean, Clive, and Anthony Mughan. 1989. "Leadership Effects in Parliamentary Elections in Australia and Great Britain." *American Political Science Review,* 83, 1165–79.

Bechelloni, Giovanni, and Milly Buonanno. 1981. "Un quotidiano di partito *sui generis: L'Unità.*" *Problemi dell'Informazione,* 2, 219–42.

Beer, Lawrence Ward. 1984. *Freedom of Expression in Japan.* Tokyo: Kodansha International.

1989. "Law and Liberty. In Takeshi Ishida and Ellis S. Krauss, eds., *Democracy in Japan.* Pittsburgh: University of Pittsburgh Press.

Beer, Samuel. H. 1982. *Britain Against Itself: The Political Contradictions of Collectivism.* New York: W. W. Norton.

Belligni, Silvano, ed. 1983. *La giraffa e il liocorno. Il Pci dagli anni '70 al nuovo decennio.* Milano: Angeli.

Beneyto, Juan. 1965. "Los diarios impresos españoles." *Revista Española de la Opinión Pública,* 1, 9–26.

Benkô, Zoltán. 1993a. "A Szabad Európa Rádió 1956-ban" [Radio Free Europe in 1956]. *Valóság,* 36, May, 63–9.

1993b. "A Szabad Európa Rádió 1956 után." *Valóság,* 36, August, 70–6.

Benn, David Wedgwood. 1989. *Persuasion and Soviet Politics.* Oxford: Basil Blackwell.

1992. *From Glasnost to Freedom of Speech: Russian Openness and International Relations.* London: Pinter.

Bennett, W. Lance. 1981. "Assessing Presidential Character: Degradation Rituals in the Political Campaigns." *Quarterly Journal of Speech,* 36, 64–76.

1988. *News: The Politics of Illusion,* 2nd ed. New York: Longman.

Bentivegna, Sara. 1988. *La televisione elettorale: un approccio empirico al caso italiano.* Torino: La Nuova Eri.

Berardinelli, Alfonso. 1994. "Il paese dei balocchi conquistato dalla televisione." *Micromega,* 1, 78–87.

Berelson, Bernard, Paul F. Lazarsfeld, and William N. McPhee. 1954. *Voting: A Study of Opinion Formation in a Presidential Campaign.* Chicago: University of Chicago Press.

Berg, Klaus, and Marie-Luise Kiefer, eds. 1992. *Massenkommunikation IV. Eine Langzeitstudie zur Mediennutzung und Medienbewertung 1964–1990.* Baden-Baden: Nomos Verlagsgesellschaft.

1996. *Massenkommunikation V. Eine Langzeitstudie zur Medienutzung und Medienbewertung 1964–1995.* Baden-Baden: Nomos Verlagsgesellschaft.

Berger, Paul M. 1995. "Exploring the Intersection of Government, Politics and the New Media in Japan: The *Tsubaki Hatsugen* Incident." Center for International Studies, Massachusetts Institute of Technology, MIT Japan Program Paper No. 95–04.

Berke, Richard L. 1992. "Why Candidates Like Public's Questions." *The New York Times,* June 5, A7.

Berruto, Gaetano. 1988. *Sociolinguistica dell'italiano contemporaneo.* Firenze: La Nuova Italia.

Bettinelli, Ernesto. 1995. *Par condicio: Regole, opinioni e fatti.* Torino: Einaudi.

Betz, Hans-Georg, and Stefan Immerfall. 1998. *The New Politics of the Right.* New York: St. Martin's Press.

Biorcio, Roberto, and Paolo Natale. 1986. "Mobilità e fedeltà elettorale negli anni ottanta: Un'analisi comparta su dati aggregati e di survey." *Quaderni dell'Osservatorio Elettorale,* 18, 43–87.

Blendon, Robert. 1996. Public opinion poll conducted for the *Washington Post* and the Kaiser Family Foundation.

Bluck, Carsten, and Henry Kreikenbom. 1991. "Die Waehler in der DDR: Nur issue-orientiert oder auch parteigebunden?" *Zeitschrift für Parlamentsfragen,* 22, 495–502.

Blumler, Jay G. 1982. "Political Communication. Democratic Theory and Broadcast Practice." In *Mass Communication Review Yearbook,* 3, 621–36.

Blumler, Jay G., Dennis Kavanagh, and T. J. Nossiter. 1996. "Modern Communications versus Traditional Politics in Britain: Unstable Marriage of Convenience." In Swanson and Mancini, eds.

Blumler, Jay G., and Denis McQuail. 1968. *Television in Politics: Its Uses and Influence.* London: Faber and Faber.

Blumler, Jay G., and T. J. Nossiter. 1991. *Broadcasting Finance in Transition.* Oxford: Oxford University Press.

Boddy, William. 1995. "The Beginnings of American Television." In Smith, ed.

Bonini, Francesco. 1990. *La grande contrapposizione. Aspetti delle elezioni del 1948 a Reggio Emilia.* Reggio Emilia: Tecnograph.

Bosetti, Gian Carlo. 1994. "Stampa Melassa: né élite né massa." *Reset,* 10, 3–13.

Bowler, Shaun, and David M. Farrell. 1992. *Electoral Strategies and Political Marketing.* New York: St. Martin's Press.

Bozóki, András, and Miklós Sükösd. 1993. "Civil Society and Populism in the East European Democratic Transitions." *Praxis International,* 13, 224–41.

Bradlee, Ben. 1995. *A Good Life: Newspapering and Other Adventures.* New York: Simon & Schuster.

Brants, Kees. 1985. "Broadcasting and Politics in the Netherlands: From Pillar to Post." *West European Politics,* 8, 104–21.

Brants, Kees, Walther J. P. Kok, and Philip van Praag, Jr. 1982. *De Strijd om de Kiezersgunst.* Amsterdam: Kobra.

Brants, Kees, and Philip van Praag, Jr., eds. 1995. *Verkoop van de Politiek. De Verkiezingscampagne van 1994.* Amsterdam: Het Spinhuis.

Brigida, Franco, Laura Francia, and Paolo Baudi di Vesme. 1993. *La pubblicità in Italia. Il mercato, i mezzi, le ricerche.* Milano: Lupetti.

Broadcast. 1992. "BBC's Secret Plans for Survival Revealed." September 4, 1.

Brody, Richard. 1991. *Assessing the President: The Media, Elite Opinion, and Public Support.* Stanford: Stanford University Press.

Brown, Archie. 1996. *The Gorbachev Factor.* New York: Oxford University Press.

Brunner, José Joaquín, Alicia Barrios, and Carlos Catalán. 1989. *Chile, Transformaciones Culturales y Modernidad.* Santiago: FLACSO.

Brunetta, Gian Pietro. 1978. *Mondo cattolics e organizzazione del consenso: la politica cinematoprofice.* In Isnenghi and Lanaro, eds.

Brunner, José Joaquín, and Carlos Catalán. 1989. *Industria y mercados culturales en Chile: descripción y cuantificacione.* Working Paper No. 359. Santiago: FLACSO.

Bruns, Thomas, and Frank Marcinkowski. 1998. "Konvergenz Revisited. Neue Befunde zu einter älteren Diskussion." *Rundfunk und Fernsehen,* 44, 461–78.

Bruszt, László. 1992. "1989: The Negotiated Revolution in Hungary." In András Bozóki,

András Körösényi, and George Schöpflin, eds., *Post-Communist Transition: Emerging Pluralism in Hungary*. London: Pinter.

Buckley, Mary. 1993. *Redefining Russian Society and Polity*. Boulder: Westview Press.

Budge, Ian. 1996. *The New Challenge of Direct Democracy*. Cambridge: Polity Press.

Budge, Ian, and Richard Hofferbert. 1990. "Mandates and Policy Outputs: U.S. Party Platforms and Federal Expenditures." *American Political Science Review*, 84, 111–31.

Budner, Stanley. 1992. "United States States and Japanese Newspaper Coverage of Frictions Between the Two Countries." In *Communicating Across the Pacific*. Report of the Mansfield Center for Pacific Affairs, Washington, D.C.

——— 1994. "Summary of Research Results." In *Creating Images: American and Japanese Television News Coverage of the Other*. Report of the Mansfield Center for Pacific Affairs, Washington, D.C.

Bugajski, Janusz. 1987. *Czechoslovakia: Charter 77's Decade of Dissent*. Washington, D.C.: Praeger and The Center for Strategic and International Studies.

Burgalassi Silvano. 1968. *Il comportamento religioso degli italiani*. Firenze: Vallecchi.

Burns, Tom. 1977. *The BBC: Public Institution and Private World*. London: Macmillan.

Burton, Michael, John Higley, and Richard Gunther. 1992. "Introduction: Elite Transformations and Democratic Regimes." In John Higley and Richard Gunther, eds., *Elites and Democratic Consolidation in Latin America and Southern Europe*. Cambridge: Cambridge University Press.

Butler, David, and Austin Ranney, eds. 1992. *Electioneering: A Comparative Study of Continuity and Change*. Oxford: Clarendon Press.

Butler, David, and Donald Stokes. 1974. *Political Change in Britain*, 2nd ed. London: Macmillan.

Caciagli Mario. 1977. *Democrazia cristiana e potere nel Mezzogiorno: Il sistema democristiano a Catania*. Rimini-Firenze: Guaraldi.

Cacioppo, John T., and Richard E. Petty. 1982. "The Need for Cognition." *Journal of Personality and Social Psychology*, 1, 116–31.

Calise, Mauro. 1978. *Il sistema Dc. Mediazione e conflitto nelle campagne democristiane*. Bari: De Domato.

——— 1994. "The Italian Particracy: Beyond President and Parliament." *Political Science Quarterly*, 3, 441–79.

——— 1994–5. "Dal partito dei media alla corporation multimediale." *Quaderni di sociologia*, 9, 19–32.

Calvaruso, Claudio, and Salvatore Abbruzzese. 1985. *Indagine sui valori in Italia*. Torino: SEI.

Campbell, John Creighton. 1996. "The Media and Policy Change in Japan." In Pharr and Krauss, eds.

Cappella, Joseph N., and Kathleen Hall Jamieson. 1997. *Spiral of Cynicism: The Press and the Public Good*. New York: Oxford University Press.

Carbonaro, Antonio. 1976. "Materiali per uno studio dei mutamenti elettorali in Italia." *Religione e politica. Il caso italiano*. Roma: COINES.

Cardini, Flaminia. 1994. "Stampa, 'sorella cieca' della TV." *Problemi dell'informazione*, 19(3), 317–25.

Cassano, Franco. 1979. *Il teorema democristiano: la mediazione della DC nella società e nel sistema politico italiani*. Bari: De Donato.

Catalán, Carlos. 1981. *El mercado de revistas de actualidad y la inversión publicitaria: el caso de Chile.* Santiago: CENECA.

Catalán, Carlos, and Guillermo Sunkel. 1990. *Consumo cultural en Chile: la elite, lo masivo y lo popular.* Documento de Trabajo No. 455. Santiago: FLACSO.

Catanzaro, Raimondo. 1993. "Teledemocrazia e partecipazione: molti interrogativi e prime risposte." *Problemi dell'informazione,* 4, 379–82.

Cavalli, Luciano. 1994. "The Personalization of Leadership in Italy." Firenze: Working Papers of the Centro Interuniversitario di Sociologia Politica, mimeo.

Cazzola, Franco. 1970. *Il partito come organizzazione. Studio di un caso: il Psi.* Roma: Edizioni del Tritone.

1985. "Struttura e potere del Partito Socialista Italiano." In Pasquino, ed.

Cebrián, Juan Luis. 1980. *La prensa y la calle.* Madrid: Editorial Nuestra Cultura.

Ceccanti, Stefano, Oreste Massari, and Gianfranco Pasquino. 1996. *Semipresidenzialismo: analisi delle esperienze europee.* Bologna: Il Mulino.

Center for Media and Public Affairs. 1992. "Clinton's the One." *Media Monitor,* November.

1993a. "The Honeymoon That Wasn't." *Media Monitor,* September–October.

1993b. "Report to the Markle Foundation's Commission on the Presidential Selection Process." Unpublished paper, Washington, D.C.

1994. "They're No Friends of Bill." *Media Monitor,* July–August.

1995. "No Newt Is Good Newt." *Media Monitor,* March–April.

1996. "Take This Campaign – Please." *Media Monitor,* September–October.

1998. "Sex, Lies and TV News." *Media Monitor,* September–October.

Centro de Estudios Públicos. 1988. *Estudios de Opinión.* Santiago.

Cheli, Enrico, Paolo Mancini, Gianpietro Mazzoleni, and Gilberto Tinacci Manneli. 1989. *Elezioni in TV: dalle Tribune alla pubblicità. La campagna elettorale del 1987.* Milano: Angeli.

Cheli, Enrico, and Gilberto Tinacci Mannelli. 1986. *L'immaginario del potere.* Milano: Angeli.

Cipriani, Ivo. 1962. "*Tribuna politica* in TV." *Il contemporaneo,* 5, 155–70.

Clancy, Maura, and Michael Robinson. 1985. "General Election Coverage: Part I." In Michael J. Robinson and Austin Ranney, eds., *The Mass Media in Campaign '84'.* Washington, D.C.: American Enterprise Institute.

Clarke, Harold D., and Marianne C. Stewart. 1995. "Economic Evaluations, Prime Ministerial Approval and Governing Party Support: Rival Models Reconsidered." *British Journal of Political Science,* 25, 145–70.

Cockerell, Michael, Michael Hennessy, and David Walker. 1984. *Sources Close to the Prime Minister: Inside the Hidden World of the News Manipulators.* London: Macmillan.

Coca, César, and Florencio Martínez, eds. 1993. *Los medios de comunicación en el País Vasco.* Bilbao: Universidad del País Vasco.

Cohen, Bernard. 1963. *The Press and Foreign Policy.* Princeton: Princeton University Press.

Cohen, Akiba, Hanna Adoni, and Charles R. Bantz. 1990. *Social Conflict and Television News.* Newbury Park: Sage.

1995. *Democracies and Foreign Policy. Public Participation in the United States and the Netherlands.* Madison: The University of Wisconsin Press.

Coliver, Sandra, ed. 1993. *Press Law and Practice: A Comparative Study of Press Freedom in European and Other Democracies.* London: Article 19 Publications.

Commission on Freedom of the Press. 1947. *A Free and Responsible Press.* Reprint 1974. Chicago: University of Chicago Press.

Committee of Concerned Journalists. 1998. "The Clinton Crisis and the Press." *Committee of Concerned Journalists' Report,* Washington, D.C.

Congressional Quarterly. 1994. "Presidential Support Scores." *Congressional Quarterly Weekly Report,* December 31, 3620.

Conradt, David P. 1980. "Changing German Political Culture." In Gabriel Almond and Sidney Verba, eds., *The Civic Culture Revisited.* Boston: Little, Brown.

Contreras, Marcelo. 1983. "Las revistas alternativas: expresiones democráticas en medio de los authoritarismos: éxitos y fracasos." In Fernando Reyes Matta, ed., *Comunicación alternativa y búsquedas democráticas,* Mexico, D.F.: ILET.

Contreras, Sergio. 1988. "Presentación." In Portales, Hirmas, Carlos Altamirano, and Egaña.

Converse, Philip E. 1964. "The Nature of Belief Systems Among Mass Publics." In David Apter, ed. *Ideology and Discontent.* New York: Free Press.

——— 1975. "Public Opinion and Voting Behavior." In Fred I. Greenstein and Nelson W. Polsby, eds., *Handbook of Political Science,* vol. 4. Reading: Addison-Wesley.

Converse, Philip E., and George Dupeux. 1962. "Politicization of the Electorate in France and the United States." *Public Opinion Quarterly,* 26, 1–23.

Corbetta, Piergiorgio, Arturo M. L. Parisi, and Hans M. A. Schadee. 1988. *Elezioni in Italia. Struttura e tipologia delle consultazioni politiche.* Bologna: Il Mulino.

Costantini, Costanzo, and Guido Moltedo. 1976. *Messaggi di fumo. Aldo Moro: i pensieri di un cavallo di razza.* Milano: Sugarco.

Couvret, Ellen, Cees van der Eijk, and Philip van Praag, Jr. 1995. "Effecten van de Campagne." In Brants and van Praag, eds.

Crewe, Ivor. 1983. "The Electorate: Partisan Dealignment Ten Years On." *West European Politics,* 4, 183–215.

Crewe, Ivor, and David Denver, eds. 1985. *Electoral Change in Western Democracies.* London: Croom Helm.

Crewe, Ivor, Tony Fox, and Jim Alt. 1977. "Non-Voting in British General Elections." In Colin Crouch, ed., *British Political Sociology Yearbook 3.* London: Croom Helm.

Crigler, Ann. 1996. "Political Ads Are Upbeat, It's the Press That's Gone Negative." *Public Affairs Report,* 37, July (Institute of Governmental Studies, University of California at Berkeley).

Crouse, Timothy. 1972. *Boys on the Bus.* New York: Bantam Books.

Cseh, Gabriella, and Miklós Sükösd. 1999. *Mediajog es mediapolitika Maygarorszagon.* Vol. I. Budapest: Uj Mandatum.

Csontos, Laszlo, Janos Kornai, and Istvan Gyorgy Toth. 1997. "Tax Awareness and the Reform of the Welfare State." Discussion Paper 37. Collegium Budapest/Institute for Advanced Study, Budapest.

Cullen, Richard, and Hua Ling Fu. 1998. "Seeking Theory from Experience: Media Regulation in China." *Democratization,* 5, Summer, 155–78.

Curran, James. 1996. "Mass Media and Democracy Revisited." In James Curran and Michael Gurevitch, eds. *Mass Media and Society.* London: Arnold.

Curry, Jane L. 1984. *The Black Book of Polish Censorship.* New York: Random House.

Curtice, John, and Holli A. Semetko. 1994. "Does It Matter What the Papers Say?" In Anthony Heath, Roger Jowell, and John Curtice, eds., *Labour's Last Chance? The 1992 Election and Beyond.* Aldershot: Dartmouth.

Curtis, Gerald L. 1970. "The 1969 General Election in Japan." *Asian Survey,* 10, 859–71. 1988. *The Japanese Way of Politics.* New York: Columbia University Press.

Daalder, Hans. 1966. "The Netherlands: Opposition in a Segmented Society." In Robert A. Dahl, ed., *Political Oppositions in Western Democracies.* New Haven: Yale University Press.

Daalder, Hans, and Galen Irwin, Eds. 1989. *Politics in the Netherlands–How Much Change?* London: Frank Cass.

Daalder, Hans, and Peter Mair, eds. 1983. *West European Party Systems.* London: Sage.

Daalder, Hans, and Cees Schuyt, eds. 1993. *Compendium voor Politiek en Samenleving in Nederland.* Houten: Bohn Stafleu van Loghum.

D'Alimonte, Roberto, and Stefano Bartolini. 1998. "How to Lose a Majority: The Competition in Single-Member Districts." *European Journal of Political Research,* 34, 63–103.

D'Alimonte, Roberto, and David Nelken. 1997. "L'anno del dialogo." In Roberto D'Alimonte and David Nelken, eds., *Politica in Italia. I fatti dell'anno e le interpretazioni.* Bologna: Il Mulino.

Dalton, Russel J. 1988 and 1996. *Citizen Politics: Public Opinion and Political Parties in Advanced Western Democracies,* 2nd ed. Chatham: Chatham House.

Dalton, Russell J., Paul A. Beck and Robert Huckfeldt. 1998. "Partisan Cues and the Media: Information Flows in the 1992 Presidential Election." *American Political Science Review,* 92, 111–26.

Dalton, Russel J., and Wilhelm Buerklin. 1995. "The Two German Electorates: The Social Bases of the Vote in 1990 and 1994." *German Politics and Society,* 13, 75–99.

Dalton, Russel J., Scott C. Flanagan, and Paul Allen Beck. 1984. *Electoral Change in Advanced Industrial Societies.* Princeton: Princeton University Press.

Dardano, Maurizio. 1994. "La lingua dei media." In Valerio Castronovo and Nicola Tranfaglia, eds., *La stampa italiana nell'era della TV.* Roma-Bari: Laterza.

Darschin, Wolfgang, and Bernward Frank. 1992. "Tendenzen im Zuschauerverhalten. Fernsehgewohnheiten und Fernsehreichweiten im Jahr 1991." *Media Perspektiven,* 172–87.

1998. "Tendenzen im Zuschauerverhalten. Fernsehgewohnheiten und Fernsehreichweiten im Jahre 1997." *Media Perspektiven,* 4, 154–66.

da Silva, Carlos Eduardo Lins, 1993. "The Brazilian Case: Manipulation by the Media?" In Skidmore, ed.

Davis, Richard. 1995. *The Press and American Politics.* Englewood Cliffs: Prentice-Hall.

Dayan, Daniel, and Elihu Katz. 1992. *Media Events: The Live Broadcasting of History.* Cambridge: Harvard University Press.

de Bergareche, Isabel. 1976. "Consumo, trabajo y ocio en el desarrollo económico." In *Estudios sociológicos sobre la situación social de España, 1975.* Madrid: Euroamérica.

De Lima, Venicio A. 1993. "Brazilian Television in the 1989 Presidential Election: Constructing a President." In Skidmore, ed.

de Vera, Jose M. 1970. "Television and the Japanese Elections of December 1969." Sophia University Faculty of Letters, *komyunike-shyon kenkyû,* No. 4.

Della Porta, Donatella, and Gianfranco Pasquino. 1983. *Terrorismo e violenza politica.* Bologna: Il Mulino.

Delli Carpini, Michael X., and Scott Keeter. 1996. *What Americans Know about Politics and Why It Matters.* New Haven: Yale University Press.

De Mauro, Tullio. 1973. "Il linguaggio politico e la sua influenza." In Gian Luigi Beccaria, ed., *I linguaggi settoriali della politica.* Milano: Bompiani.

Deemers, David. 1993. "Effect of Corporate Structure on Autonomy of Top Editors at U.S. Dailies." *Journalism Quarterly,* 70, 499–508.

1999. *Global Media: Menace or Messiah?* Cresskill: Hampton Press.

Dente, Bruno. 1985. *Governare la frammentazione. Stato, Regioni ed Enti locali in Italia.* Bologna: Il Mulino.

De Sandre, Paolo. 1965. "Religiosità e cultura di massa in Italia." *Il Mulino,* 14, 1181–98.

De Santis, Teresa, and Alberto Ferrigolo. 1990. "Dai primi passi sul cavo ai conforti della legge Mammì." *Problemi dell'informazione,* 4, 491–503.

Deutsch, Karl W. 1953. *Nationalism and Social Communication: An Inquiry into the Foundations of Nationality.* New York: Wiley.

1961. "Social Mobilization and Political Development." *American Political Science Review,* 55, 493–511.

Diagnos. 1986. "Preferencia de lectores de revistas e imagen de revista Apsi." Santiago, January.

Diamandouros, P. Nikiforos, and Richard Gunther, eds. 2000. *Parties, Politics and Democracy in the new Southern Europe.* Baltimore: Johns Hopkins University Press.

Diamanti Ilvo. 1992. "La mia patria è il Veneto: i valori e la proposta politica delle Leghe." *Polis,* 2, 225–55

1993. *La Lega. Geografia, storia e sociologia di un soggetto politico.* Roma: Donzelli.

1994a. "La politica come marketing." *Micromega,* 2, 60–7.

1994b. "Localismo." *Rassegna Italiana di Sociologia,* 3, 403–24 .

Diamanti, Ilvo, and Riccamboni Gianni. 1992. *La parabola del voto bianco. Elezioni e società in Veneto (1946–1992).* Vicenza: Neri Pozza.

Diamond, Edmond, and Robert A. Silverman. 1995. *White House to Your House: Media and Politics in Virtual America.* Cambridge: MIT Press.

Diamond, Larry, and Marc F. Plattner, eds. 1993. *The Global Resurgence of Democracy.* Baltimore: Johns Hopkins University Press.

Diani, Marco. 1995. "Voyage en Berlusconia identité nationale, mouvements sociaux et société civile en Italie." *Social Science: Information sur les sciences sociales,* 4, 539–66.

Díaz Nosty, Bernardo. 1994. *Comunicación social. Tendencias 1994.* Madrid: Fundesco.

Díez Nicolás, Juan, and Holli A. Semetko. 1995. "La televisión y las elecciones de 1993." In Alejandro Muñoz Alonso and Juan Ignacio Rospir, eds., *Comunicación política.* Madrid: Editorial Universitas.

Di Giovine, Alfonso, and Alfio Mastropaolo. 1993. "Verso la 'seconda Repubblica:' un abbozzo di dissenting opinion." *Politica del Diritto,* 1, 127–49.

DiPalma, Giuseppe. 1990. *To Craft Democracies: An Essay on Democratic Transitions.* Berkeley: University of California Press.

DLM (Direktorenkonferenz der Laendermedienanstalten), ed. 1988. *DLM Jahrbuch 88.* München.

Donahue, Hugh Carter. 1989. *The Battle to Control Broadcast News: Who Owns the First Amendment?* Cambridge: MIT Press.

Downs, Anthony. 1957. *An Economic Theory of Democracy.* New York: HarperCollins.

Dunleavy, Patrick, and Christopher T. Husbands. 1985. *British Democracy at the Cross-roads: Voting and Party Competition in the 1980s.* London: Allen & Unwin.

Duyvendak, Jan-Willem, Hein-Anton van der Heijden, Ruud Koopmans, and Luc Wijmans. 1992. *Tussen Verbeelding en Macht.* Amsterdam: SUA.

Dye, Thomas R. 1995. *Who's Running America? The Clinton Years,* 6th ed. Englewood Cliffs: Prentice-Hall.

Easton, David. 1965. *A Systems Analysis of Political Life.* New York: Wiley.

Eco, Umberto. 1973. "Il linguaggio politico." In Gian Luigi Beccaria, ed., *I linguaggi settoriali in Italia.* Milano: Bompiani.

Edelman, Murray. 1988. *Constructing the Political Spectacle.* Chicago: University of Chicago Press.

Edo, Concha. 1994. *La crisis de la prensa diaria. La línea editorial y la trayectoria de los periódicos de Madrid.* Barcelona: Editorial Ariel.

Efron, Edith. 1971. *The News Twisters.* Los Angeles: Nash.

Ellemers, Joop E. 1984. "Pillarization as a Process of Modernization." *Acta Politica,* 19, 129–44.

Emery, Edwin. 1977. *The Press and America: An Interpretive History of the Mass Media.* Englewood Cliffs: Prentice-Hall.

Entman, Robert. 1989. *Democracy Without Citizens: Media and the Decay of American Politics.* New York: Oxford University Press.

———. 1993. "Framing: Toward Clarification of a Fractured Paradigm." *Journal of Communication,* 43, 51–8.

Epstein, E. J. 1973. *News From Nowhere.* New York: Vintage Books.

Fabbrini, Sergio. 1994. "Personalization as Americanization? The Rise and Fall of Leader-Dominated Governmental Strategies in Western Europe in the 1980s." *American International Studies,* 2, 51–65.

———. 1995a. "Presidents, Parliaments and Good Government." *Journal of Democracy,* 3, 128–38.

———. 1995b. "Il compromesso storico." In Pasquino, ed.

———. 1996. "La transizione italiana e il governo di partito: un semipresidenzialismo alternante?" Paper presented at the meeting of AIS-Associazione Italiana di Sociologia-Sezione di Sociologia Politica, Torino.

Facchi, Paolo. 1960. *La propaganda politica in Italia.* Bologna: Il Mulino.

———. 1961. "La politica delle parole." *Comunità,* 15, 31–3.

Fallows, James. 1994. "Did You Have a Good Week?" *The Atlantic Monthly,* December, 32–3.

———. 1996. *Breaking the News: How the Media Undermine American Democracy.* New York. Pantheon Books.

Farley, Maggie. 1992. *The Politics of Scandal and the Japanese Media.* Master's thesis. Harvard University.

———. 1996. "Japan's Press and the Politics of Scandal." In Pharr and Krauss, eds.

Farneti, Paolo. 1976. "I partiti politici e il sistema di potere." In Valerio Castronovo, ed., *L'Italia contemporanea 1945–1975.* Torino: Einaudi.

———. 1983. *The Italian Party System.* London: Pinter

Faul, Erwin, in cooperation with Peter Behrens, Horst Grundheber, and Brigitte Willems. 1988. *Die Fernsehprogramme im dualen Rundfunksystem.* Berlin: VDE-Verlag.

Faul, Erwin. 1991. "Die Rundfunkordnung im vereinigten Deutschland: Ueberwuchern Interessendschungel die nationale Verfassungsaufgabe?" In Rudolf Wildenmann, ed., *Nation und Demokratie. Politisch-strukturelle Gestaltungsprobleme im neuen Deutschland.* Baden-Baden: Nomos Verlagsgesellschaft.

Fedele, Marcello. 1979. *Classi e partiti negli anni '70.* Roma: Editori Riuniti.

1994. *Democrazia referendaria.* Roma: Donzelli.

Feldman, Ofer. 1993. *Politics and the News Media in Japan.* Ann Arbor: University of Michigan Press.

Feldman, Ofer, and Kazuhisa Kawakami. 1989. "Leaders and Leadership in Japanese Politics: Images during a Campaign Period." *Comparative Political Studies,* 22, 225–43.

Fenati, Barbara. 1993. *Fare radio negli anni '90.* Torino: Nuova Eri.

Ferejohn, John A. 1990. "Introduction." In Ferejohn and Kuklinski, eds.

Ferejohn, John A., and James H. Kuklinski. 1990. *Information and Democratic Processes.* Urbana and Chicago: University of Illinois Press.

Fishel, Jeff. 1985. *Presidents and Promises.* Washington, D.C.: Congressional Quarterly Press.

Flanagan, Scott C. 1991. "Media Influences and Voting Behavior." In Flanagan, Kohei, Miyake, Richardson, and Watanuki, eds.

1996. "Media Exposure and the Quality of Political Participation in Japan." In Pharr and Krauss, eds.

Flanagan, Scott C., Shinsaku Kohei, Ichiro Miyake, Bradley M. Richardson, and Joji Watanuki, eds. 1991. *The Japanese Voter.* New Haven: Yale University Press.

Foley, Michael. 1993. *The Rise of the British Presidency.* Manchester: University of Manchester Press.

Follini, Marco. 1996. "Perché il Polo ha perso le elezioni." *Il Mulino,* 365, 468–77.

Foxley, Alejandro. 1983. *Latin American Experiments in Neo-Conservative Economics.* Berkeley: University of California Press.

Franklin, Bob. 1994. *Packaging Politics: Political Communications in Britain's Media Democracy.* London: Edward Arnold.

Franklin, Mark, Tom Mackie, and Henry Valen, eds. 1992. *Electoral Change: Responses to Evolving Social and Attitudinal Structures in Western Countries.* Cambridge: Cambridge University Press.

Franklin, Mark N., and Anthony Mughan. 1979. "The Decline of Class Voting in Britain." *American Political Science Review,* 72, 523–34.

Franzmann, Bodo. 1989. "Leseverhalten im Spiegel neuerer Untersuchungen. Ein Beitrag ueber Lesekultur und Medienkultur." *Media Perspektiven,* 86–98.

Freedom Forum Media Studies Center. 1992. "Covering the Primaries." New York: Freedom Forum Media Studies Center at Columbia University.

Fridli, Judit, Gábor Attila Toth, and Veronika Ujvari. 1997. *Data Protection and Freedom of Information.* Budapest: Hungarian Civil Liberties Union.

Friedrich, Carl J. 1964. "The Unique Character of Totalitarian Society." In Carl J. Friedrich, ed., *Totalitarianism.* New York: Grosset and Dunlap.

Friedrich, Walter, and Hartmut Griese, eds. 1991. *Jugend und Jugendforschung in der DDR. Gesellschaftspolitische Situationen, Sozialisation und Mentalitaetsbildung in den achtziger Jahren.* Opladen: Leske und Budrich.

Fuchs, Dieter. 1989. *Die Unterstüzung des politischen Systems der Bundesrepublik Deutschland.* Opladen: Westdeutscher Verlag.

1997. "Welche Demokratie wollen die Deutschen? Einstellungen zur Demokratie im vereinigten Deutschland." In Oscar W. Gabriel, ed., *Politische Orientierungen und Verhaltensweisen im vereinigten Deutschland.* Opladen: Leske und Budrich.

Fuchs, Dieter, Juergen Gerhards, and Friedhelm Neidhardt. 1992. "Öffentliche Kommunikationsbereitschaft. Ein Test zentraler Bestandteile der Theorie der Schweigespirale." *Zeitschrift für Soziologie* 21, 284–95.

Gábor, R. István. 1979. "The Second (Secondary) Economy. Earning Activity and Regrouping of Income Outside the Socially Organized Production and Distribution." *Acta Economica,* 22, 291–311.

Gaitán, Juan Antonio. 1992. "La opinión del diario *El País* en la transición española." *Revista Española de Investigaciones Sociológicas,* 57, 149–64.

Galasi, Peter, and Gyorgy Sziráczky, eds. 1985. *Labour Market and Second Economy in Hungary.* Frankfurt: Campus.

Gamaleri, Gian Piero. 1994. *Videodemocrzia. Convivere con la TV nel sistema maggioritario.* Roma: Armando.

Gans, Herbert J. 1980. *Deciding What's News: A Study of CBS Evening News, NBC Nightly News, Newsweek and Time.* New York: Vintage Books.

García Escudero, Juan Manuel. 1984. *"Ya:" Medio siglo de historia (1935–1985).* Madrid: Biblioteca de Autores Cristianos.

Garelli, Franco. 1991. *Religione e chiesa in Italia.* Bologna: Il Mulino.

Gaunt, Philip. 1988. "The Training of Journalists in France, Britain and the U.S." *Journalism Quarterly,* 68, 582–8.

Gavin, Neil T. 1998. *The Economy, Media and Public Knowledge.* London and New York: Leicester University Press.

Gavin, Neil T., and David Sanders. 1996. "The Impact of Television News on Public Perceptions of the Economy and Government, 1993–1994." In David M. Farrell, David Broughton, David Denver, and Justin Fisher, eds. *British Elections and Parties Yearbook 1996.* London: Frank Cass.

Gellner, Winand. 1990. *Ordnungspolitik im Fernsehwesen: Bundesrepublik Deutschland und Großbritannien.* Frankfurt am Main, Bern, New York, and Paris: Peter Lang.

Gibney, Frank. 1975. *Japan: The Fragile Super Power.* Rutland: Charles E. Tuttle.

Gitlin, Todd. 1980. *The Whole World Is Watching: Mass Media in the Making and Unmaking of the New Left.* Berkeley: University of California Press.

Goldfarb, J. C. 1991. *The Cynical Society: The Culture of Politics and the Politics of Culture.* Chicago: University of Chicago Press.

Golding, Peter, and David Deacon. 1997. "Campaign Fails to Hold the Front Page." *The Guardian,* April 14.

Golding, Peter, David Deacon, and Michael Billig. 1997. "Dominant Press Backs 'On-Message' Winner." *The Guardian,* May 5.

Gómez-Reino, Manuel, Francisco A. Orizo and Darío Vila. 1972. "Los medios de comunicación de masas y la formación de la opinión pública." In del Campo, ed.

1976. "Sociología política." In Fundación FOESSA, *Estudios sociológicos sobre la situación social de España, 1975.* Madrid: Euroamérica.

González Seara, Luis. 1967. "Los efectos de los medios de comunicación de masas y la opinión pública." *Revista Española de la Opinión Pública,* 8, 37–62.

1972. "Los medios de comunicación de masas y la formación de la opinión pública." In del Campo, ed.

Goodwin, Andrew. 1990. "TV News: Striking the Right Balance." In Goodwin and Whannel, eds.

Goodwin, Andrew, and Garry Whannel. 1990. *Understanding Television.* London: Routledge.

Gorbachev, Mikhail. 1995. *Erinnerungen.* Berlin: Siedler Verlag.

Gosman, Jan G. 1993a. "Massamedia: de Schrijvende Pers." In Daalder and Schuyt, eds. 1993b. "Massamedia: Radio en Televisie." In Daalder and Schuyt, eds.

Graber, Doris S. 1984 and 1988. *Processing the News: How People Tame the Information Tide,* 1st and 2nd eds. New York: Longman.

Graber, Doris, Denis McQuail, and Pippa Norris, eds. 1998. *The Politics of News: The News of Politics.* Washington, D.C.: Congressional Quarterly Press.

Graziano, Luigi. 1979. "Compromesso storico e democrazia consociativa: verso una 'nuova democrazia'?" In Luigi Graziano and Sidney Tarrow, eds. *La crisi italiana.* Vol. II Torino: Einaudi.

Gribaudi, Gabriella. 1980. *Mediatori. Antropologia del potere democristiano nel Mezzogiorno.* Torino: Rosemberg and Sellier.

Grossi, Giorgio, ed. 1976. *Informazione di massa e lotta sindacale.* Roma, Nuove Edizioni Operaie.

Grossi, Giorgio, Paolo Mancini, and Gianpiero Mazzoleni. 1985. *Giugno 1983: una campagna elettorale.* Torino: Eri.

Grossman, Lawrence K. 1995. *The Electronic Republic: Reshaping Democracy in the Information Age.* New York: Penguin Books.

Groth, David Earl. 1996. "Media and Political Protest: The Anti–Bullet Train Movement." In Pharr and Krauss, eds.

Gundle, Stephen, and Nöelleanne O'Sullivan. 1996. "The Mass Media and the Political Crisis." In Stephen Gundle and Simon Parker, eds., *The New Italian Republic. From the Fall of the Berlin Wall to Berlusconi.* London and New York: Routledge.

Gunther, Richard. 1980. *Public Policy in a No-Party State: Spanish Planning and Budgeting in the Twilight of the Franquist Era.* Berkeley: University of California Press. 1986. "El Colapso de UCD." In Linz and Montero, eds. 1988. *Culture and Politics in Spain.* Politics and Culture Series, Samuel H. Barnes Series, ed. Ann Arbor: Center for Political Studies, Institute for Social Research, University of Michigan. 1992a. "Spain: The Very Model of Modern Elite Settlement." In John Higley and R. Gunther, eds., *Elites and Democratic Consolidation in Latin America and Southern Europe.* Cambridge: Cambridge University Press. 1992b. *Política y cultura en España.* Madrid: Centro de Estudios Constitucionales. 2000. "The Anchors of the Partisanship: A Comparative Analysis of Voting Behavior in Four Southern European Democracies." In Richard Gunther and P. Nikiforos Diamandouros, eds.

Gunther, Richard, and Jonathan Hopkin. In press. "The Collapse of the UCD." In Richard Gunther, Juan J. Linz, and José Ramón Montero, eds., *The Changing Roles of Political Parties in Contemporary Democracies.* Oxford: Oxford University Press.

Gunther, Richard, and José Ramón Montero. 1994. "Los anclajes del partidismo: un análisis comparado del comportamiento electoral en cuatro democracias del sur de Europa." In Pilar del Castillo, ed. *Comportamiento político y electoral.* Madrid: Centro de Investigaciones Sociológicas.

461

Gunther, Richard, Hans-Jürgen Puhle, and Nikiforos Diamandouros. 1995. "Introduction." In Gunther, Diamandouros and Puhle, eds.

Gunther, Richard, Nikiforos Diamandouros, and Hans-Jürgen Puhle. 1995. *The Politics of Democratic Consolidation: Southern Europe in Comparative Perspective.* Baltimore: The Johns Hopkins University Press.

Gunther, Richard, Giacomo Sani, and Goldie Shabad. 1986. *Spain After Franco. The Making of a Competitive Party System.* Berkeley: University of California Press.

Gurevitch, Michael, and Jay E. Blumler. 1990. "Political Communications Systems and Democratic Values." In Lichtenberg, ed.

Habermas, Jürgen. 1989. *The Structural Change of the Public Sphere: An Inquiry into a Category of Bourgeois Society.* Cambridge: MIT Press.

Hallin, Daniel. 1992. "Sound Bite News: Television Coverage of Elections, 1968–1988." *Journal of Communication,* 42, 5–24.

Hamilton, James T. 1998. *Channeling Violence.* Princeton: Princeton University Press.

Hankiss, Elemér. 1987. "A Második Társadalom." *Diagnózisok/* Budapest: Magvető.

1992. *East European Alternatives.* Oxford: Oxford University Press.

1996. "The Hungarian Media War of Independence." In Andras Sajó, ed., *Rights of Access to the Media.* The Hague: Kluwer Law International.

Haraszti, Miklós. 1987. *The Velvet Prison: Artists Under State Socialism.* New York: Basic Books.

Hardacre, Helen. 1995. "Aum Shinrikyo and the Japanese Media: The Pied Piper Meets the Lamb of God." Institute Reports, East Asian Institute, Columbia University.

Harrison, Martin. 1984. "Broadcasting" In David Butler and Denis Kavanagh, eds., *The British General Election of 1983.* London: Macmillan.

Harrop, Martin. 1987. "Voters." In Jean Seaton and Ben Pimlott, eds., *The Media in British Politics.* Aldershot: Avebury.

Hellemans, Stef. 1990. *Strijd om de Moderniteit. Sociale Bewegingen en Verzuiling in Europa sinds 1800.* Leuven: UP/Kadoc Studies.

1993. "Zuilen en verzuiling in Europa." In U. Becker, ed., *Nederlandse Politiek in Historisch en Vergelijkend Perspectief.* Amsterdam: Het Spinhuis.

Hemels, Johan M. H. J. 1979. *De Nederlandse Krant 1618–1978, Van 'Nieuwstijdinghe' tot Dagblad.* Baarn: Ambo.

Herman, Edward S., and Robert W. McChesney. 1997. *The Global Media: The New Missionaries of Global Capitalism.* London: Cassell.

Hermet, Guy. 1985. *Los católicos en la España franquista.* Madrid: Centro de Investigaciones Scoiológicas.

Herzog, Dietrich, Hilke Rebenstorf, Camilla Werner, and Bernhard Wessels. 1990. *Abgeordnete und Bürger.* Opladen: Westdeutscher Verlag.

Hesse, Kurt R. 1990. "Fernsehen und Revolution: Zum Einfluß der Westmedien auf die politische Wende in der DDR." *Rundfunk und Fernsehen,* 38, 328–42.

Hetterich, Volker. 1998. *Die Längsschnittanalyse von Wahlkämpfen: Veränderung von Wahlkampfstrategien und -führung der Parteien?* Ph.D. dissertation, Universität Mannheim.

Himmelweit, Hilde T., Patrick Humphreys, Marianne Jaeger, and Michael Katz. 1981. *How Voters Decide: A Longitudinal Study of Political Attitudes and Voting Extending Over 15 Years.* London: Academic Press.

Hine, David. 1993. *Governing Italy. The Politics of Bargained Pluralism.* Oxford: Oxford University Press.

Hirmas, María Eugenia. 1989. "La franja: entre la alegría y el miedo." In Diego Portales and Sunkel, eds.

———. 1993. "The Chilean Case: Television in the 1988 Plebiscite." In Skidmore, ed.

Holtz-Bacha, Christina. 1990. *Ablenkung oder Abkehr von der Politik? Mediennutzung im Geflecht politischer Orientierungen.* Opladen: Westdeutscher Verlag.

Holtz-Bacha, Christina, and Lynda Lee Kaid, eds. 1993. *Die Massenmedien im Wahlkampf.* Opladen: Westdeutscher Verlag.

Hôsô Bunka Kenkyûjo. 1991. *Shichôritsu de tabukku 90.* Tokyo: Hôsô Bunka Kenkyûjo Yoron Chôsabu.

Hrebenar, Ronald J. 1986. *The Japanese Party System.* Boulder: Westview Press.

Huertas, Fernando, ed. 1994. *Televisión y política.* Madrid: Editorial Complutense.

Humphreys, Peter, and Matthias Lang. 1998. "Regulating for Media Pluralism and the Pitfalls of Standortpolitik: The Re-Regulation of German Broadcasting Ownership Rules." *German Politics,* 7, 2, 176–201.

Huntington, Samuel P. 1975. "The United States." In Michel Crozier, Samuel P. Huntington, and Joji Watanuki, eds., *The Crisis of Democracy.* New York: New York University Press.

Hurtado, María de la Luz. 1989. *Historia de la TV en Chile (1958–1973).* Santiago: Ediciones Documentas-CENECA.

Iglesias, Francisco. 1980. *Historia de una empresa periodística: Prensa Española, editora de "ABC" y "Blanco y Negro" (1891–1978).* Madrid: Prensa Española.

Ilardi, Massimo, and Aris Accornero, eds. 1982. *Il partito comunista italiano: struttura e storia dell'organizzazione: 1921–1979.* Milano: Feltrinelli.

Imbert, Gérard. 1988. *Le discours du journal. A propos de "El País." Pour une approach socio-sémiotique du discours de la presse.* Paris: Centre Nationale de la Recherche Scientifique.

"Interviu s rukovoditelem sluzhby sotsiologicheskogo analiza 'NTV-Kholdinga' Vsevolodom Vilchekom." 1998. *Teleskop,* 133, November 4.

IOP (Instituto de la Opinión Pública). 1964. *Estudios sobre los medios de comunicación en España.* Madrid: Instituto de la Opinión Pública.

———. 1965a. "Los medios de comunicación de masas en España." *Revista Española de la Opinión Pública,* 0, 145–51.

———. 1965b. "Encuesta sobre medios de comunicación de masas en España: prensa, radio, televisión, cine, teatro y libros." *Revista Española de la Opinión Pública,* 1, 181–296.

———. 1967. "Encuesta sobre la lectura de prensa diaria." *Revista Española de la Opinión Pública,* 7, 247–83.

———. 1969. "Opiniones sobre problemas nacionales e internacionales." *Revista Española de la Opinión Pública,* 17, 165–395.

———. 1970. "Encuesta sobre la radio." *Revista Española de la Opinión Pública,* 19, 167–216.

———. 1975a. "Informe sobre los medios de comunicación de masas en España." *Revista Española de la Opinión Pública,* 39, 297–329.

———. 1975b. "Informe sobre los medios de comunicación en España." *Revista Española de la Opinión Pública,* 40–1, 263–84.

———. 1976. "Medios de comunicación de masas." *Revista Española de la Opinión Pública,* 43, 399–410.

Irwin, Galen A., and Joop J. M. van Holsteyn. 1989. "Decline of the Structured Model of Electoral Competition." In Daalder and Irwin, eds.

Isaki, Kyôko. 1993. "Nihon no Seiji yo Kaware." *Aera,* August 10, 18–19.

Isnenghi, Mario, and Silvio Lanaro, eds. 1978. *La democrazia cristiana dal fascismo al 18 aprile.* Venezia: Marsilio Editori.

Iyengar, Shanto. 1991. *Is Anyone Responsible? How Television Frames Political Issues.* Chicago. University of Chicage Press.

Iyengar, Shanto, and Donald R. Kinder. 1987. *News That Matters: Television and American Opinion.* Chicago. University of Chicago Press.

Jacobelli, Jader, ed. 1971. *Dieci anni di Tribuna Politica, 1960–1970.* Roma: Rai.

Jamieson, Kathleen Hall. 1992. *Dirty Politics: Deception, Distraction, Democracy.* New York: Oxford University Press.

1994. "Newspaper and Television Coverage of the Health Care Reform Debate, January 16–July 25, 1994." A Report by the Annenberg Public Policy Center, funded by the Robert Wood Johnson Foundation.

Jamieson, Kathleen Hall, and Karlyn Kohrs Campbell. 1988. *The Interplay of Influence,* 2nd. ed. Belmont: Wadsworth.

Japan Times. 1997. "Newspapers in Japan and Trust in Them." October 19, 19.

Japan Times Weekly Internatonal Edition. 1993. "Ozawa Takes Swipe at the Press." November 15–21, 17. (Translation of excerpts from the November 11 issue of *Shukan Bunshun.*)

Jiménez Blanco, José, Eduardo López-Aranguren, and Miguel Beltrán Villalba. 1977. *La conciencia regional en España.* Madrid: Centro de Investigaciones Sociológicas.

Johnson, Chalmers. 1975. "Japan: Who Governs? An Essay on Official Bureaucracy." *The Journal of Japanese Studies,* 2, 1–28.

Jones, Philip, and John Hudson. 1996. "The Quality of Political Leadership: A Case Study of John Major." *British Journal of Political Science,* 26, 229–44.

Just, Marion R., Ann N. Crigler, Dean E. Alter, Timothy E. Cook, Montague Kern, and Derrell M. West. 1996. *Crosstalk: Citizens, Candidates and the Media in a Presidential Campaign.* Chicago: University of Chicago Press.

Kaase, Max. 1986. "Massenkommunikation und politischer Prozeß." In Max Kaase, ed., *Politische Wissenschaft und politische Ordnung – Analysen zu Theorie und Empirie demokratischer Regierungsweise.* Opladen: Westdeutscher Verlag.

1989. "Fernsehen, gesellschaftlicher Wandel und politischer Prozeß." In Max Kaase and Winfried Schultz, eds., *Massenkommunikation. Theorien, Methoden, Befunde, 30. Sonderheft der Kölner Zeitschrift für Soziologie und Sozialpsychologie.* Opladen: Westdeutscher Verlag.

1992. "Germany." In Butler and Ranney, eds.

1994. "Is there Personalization in Politics? Candidates and Voting Behavior in Germany." *International Political Science Review,* 15, 223–42.

1998. "Demokratisches System und die Mediatisierung von Politik." In Ulrich Sarcinelli, ed.

1999. "Deutschland als Informations- und Wissensgesellschaft-Konzepte, Probleme, Perspektiven." In Max Kaase and Günther Schmid, eds., *Fünfzig Jahre Bundesrepublik. WZB-Jahrbuch 1999.* Berlin: Edition Sigma.

Kaase, Max, and Petra Bauer-Kaase. 1998. "Deutsche Vereinigung und innere Einheit 1990–1997." In Heiner Meulemann, ed., *Werte und nationale Identität im vereinten Deutschland. Erklärungsansätze der Umfrageforschung.* Opladen: Leske und Budrich.

Kaase, Max, and Hans-Dieter Klingemann. 1993. "The Cumbersome Way to Partisan

Orientations in a 'New' Democracy: The Case of the Former GDR." In M. Kent Jennings and Thomas E. Mann, eds., *Festschrift for Warren E. Miller*. Ann Arbor: University of Michigan Press.

Kaase, Max, and Winfried Schulz, eds. 1989. *Massenkommunikation. Theorien, Methoden, Befunde*. 30. Sonderheft der Kölner Zeitschrift für Soziologie und Sozialpsychologie. Opladen: Westdeutscher Verlag.

Kabashima, Ikuo, and Jeffrey Broadbent. 1986. "Referent Pluralism: Mass Media and Politics in Japan." *The Journal of Japanese Studies*, 12, 329–61.

Kaid, Lynda Lee, and Christina Holtz-Bacha, eds. 1995. *Political Advertising in Western Democracies: Parties and Candidates on Television*. London: Sage.

Kalb, Marvin. 1992. "Too Much Talk and Not Enough Action." *Washington Journalism Review*, 14, 33–4.

——— 1999. "The Rise of the 'New News': A Case Study of Two Root Causes of the Modern Scandal Coverage." Joan Shorenstein Center Discussion Paper D-34, John F. Kennedy School of Government, Harvard University, Cambridge, MA.

Kampelman, Max. 1978. "The Power of the Press." *Policy Review*, 5, 7–41.

Kassof, A. 1964. "The Administered Society: Totalitarianism Without Terror." *World Politics*, 16, 558–75.

Katz, Elihu, and Paul F. Lazarsfeld. 1955. *Personal Influence*. New York: Free Press.

Katz, Helen. 1989. "The Future of Public Broadcasting in the US." *Media, Culture and Society*, 11, 195–205.

.Katz, Richard S., and Peter Mair. 1992. "The Membership of Political Parties in European Democracies, 1960–1990." *European Journal of Political Research*, 22, 329–45.

Kavanagh, Dennis. 1995. *Election Campaigning: The New Marketing of Politics*. Oxford: Blackwell.

Kavanagh, Dennis, and Peter Morris. 1994. *Consensus Politics from Atlee to Major*, 2nd ed. Oxford: Blackwell.

Kawai, Kazuo. 1960. *Japan's American Interlude*. Chicago: University of Chicago Press.

Keane, John. 1991. *The Media and Democracy*. Oxford: Polity Press.

Keizai Kôhô Center. 1992. *Japan 1993: An International Comparison*. Tokyo: Keizai Kôhô Center.

Kepplinger, Hans Mathias, Klaus Gotto, Hans-Bernd Brosius, and Dietmar Haak. 1989. *Der Einfluß der Fernsehnachrichten auf die politische Meinungsbildung*. Freiburg-Muenchen: Karl Alber.

Kim, Young C. 1981. *Japanese Journalists and their World*. Charlottesville: University Press of Virginia.

Kinder, Donald R., and David O. Sears. 1985. "Public Opinion and Political Action." In Gardner Lindzey and Elliot Aronson, eds., *Handbook of Social Psychology*, 3rd ed. Vol. II. New York: Random House.

Klapper, Joseph T. 1960. *The Effects of Mass Communication*. New York: Free Press.

Kleinnijenhuis Jan, Dirk Oegema, and Jan de Ridder. 1995a. "Dagbladen: Eenheid in verscheidenheid." In Brants and van Praag, eds.

——— 1995b. *De Democratie op Drift*. Amsterdam: VU Uitgeverij.

Kleinnijenhuis Jan, Dirk Oegema, Jan de Ridder, and Nel Ruigrok. 1998. *Paarse polarisatie: de slag om de kiezer in de media*. Alphen a.d. Rijn: Samson.

Kleinnijenhuis, Jan, and Otto Scholten. 1989. "Veranderende Verhoudingen tussen Dagbladen en Politieke Partijen." *Acta Politica*, 24, 433–60.

Kleinsteuber, Hans J., and Peter Wilke. 1992. "Germany." In Bernt Stubbe Ostergaard, ed., *The Media in Western Europe: The Euromedia Handbook.* London, Newbury Park, and New Delhi: Sage.

Klyamko, Eduard. 1993. "Komu prinedlezhit TV, tomu prinadlezhit strana." *Rossiiskaya gazeta,* April 21, 4.

Kobayashi, Yoshiaki. 1982. "Terebi no nyu-su hôdô ni kanasurunaiyô bunseki." *Keiô Daigaku Hôgaku Kenkyû,* 55, #9.

Kohei, Shinsaku, Ichiro Miyake, and Joji Watanuki. 1991. "Issues and Voting Behavior." In Flanagan, Miyake, Richardson, and Watanuki, eds.

Koitabashi, Jirô, and Onose Kenjin. 1986. "NHK vs. mimpô: shiretsu na hôdô sensô no jitai." *Tsukuru,* 6, 78–85.

Koole, Ruud A. 1992. *De Opkomst van de Moderne Kaderpartij. Veranderende partijorganisatie in Nederland 1960–1990.* Utrecht: Het Spectrum.

Kornhauser, William. 1959. *The Politics of Mass Society.* New York: Free Press.

Krauss, Ellis S. 1984. "Conflict in the Diet: Toward Conflict Management in Parliamentary Politics." In Ellis S. Krauss, Thomas P. Rohlen, and Patricia G. Steinhoff, eds., *Conflict in Japan.* Honolulu: University of Hawaii Press.

——— 1989. "Politics and the Policymaking Process." In Takeshi Ishida and Ellis S. Krauss, eds., *Democracy in Japan.* Pittsburgh: University of Pittsburgh Press.

——— 1991. *Competition among Japan, the U.S., and Europe over High-Definition Television.* Case Study, The Pew Charitable Trusts, Philadelphia.

——— 1992. "Going Under Coverage: Newspaper Structure in the United States and Japan." In *Communicating Across the Pacific.* Report of the Mansfield Center for Pacific Affairs, Washington, D.C.

——— 1994. "Explaining American and Japanese Coverage of the Other Nation." In *Creating Images: American and Japanese Television News Coverage of the Other.* Report of the Mansfield Center for Pacific Affairs, Washington, D.C.

——— 1996a. "Portraying the State in Japan: NHK Television News and Politics." In Pharr and Krauss, eds.

——— 1996b. "Media Coverage of U.S.–Japanese Relations." In Pharr and Krauss, eds.

——— 1998. "Changing Television News in Japan." *The Journal of Asian Studies,* 57, 663–92.

——— In Press. *NHK: Broadcasting Politics in Japan.* Ithaca: Cornell University Press.

Krauss, Ellis S., and Priscilla Lambert. 1999. "Japan's Press and the Issues of Reform." Unpublished manuscript.

Krauss, Ellis S., and Bradford L. Simcock. 1980. "Citizens' Movements: The Growth and Impact of Environmental Protest in Japan." In Kurt Steiner, Ellis S. Krauss, and Scott C. Flanagan, eds., *Political Opposition and Local Politics in Japan.* Princeton: Princeton University Press.

——— 1998. "Modernisierung bei stabilen Programmstrukturen. Programmanalyse 1997: ARD, ZDF, RTL, SAT.1 und PRO 7 im Vergleich." *Media Perspektiven,* 7, 314–30.

Krueger, Udo Michael. 1992. *Programmprofile im dualen Fernsehsystem 1985–1990.* Baden-Baden: Nomos Verlagsgesellschaft.

Krueger, Udo Michael, and Bodo Rinz. 1990. DDR-Berichterstattung – Renaissance der Information? *Media Perspektiven,* 104–21.

Krukones, Michael G. 1984. *Promises and Performance: Presidential Campaigns as Policy Predictors.* Lanham: University Press of America.

Kubik, Jan. 1994. *The Power of Symbols Against the Symbols of Power: The Rise of Solidar-*

ity and the Fall of State Socialism in Poland. University Park: Pennsylvania State University Press.

Kuchin, Valery. 1996. "Kogda kriveet zerkalo." *Obshchaya gazeta,* 11–18, December 12.

Kuhn, Raymond. 1998. "The Media and the Public Sphere in Fifth Republic France." *Democratization,* 5, 23–41.

Kuran, Timur. 1995. *Private Truths, Public Lies: The Social Consequences of Preference Falsification.* Cambridge: Harvard University Press.

Kuroda, Kiyoshi. 1985. *Shinbun kisha no genba.* Tokyo: Kodansha Gendai Shinsho.

Kurtz, Howard. 1992. "Media Circus." *Washington Post Magazine.* July 12, 34–8.

1996. *Hot Air: All Talk, All the Time.* New York: Times Books.

Kutteroff, Albrecht. 1984. "Politische Macht und Massenmedien. Veränderung der politischen Macht und des politischen Selbstverstaendnisses." In Jürgen W. Falter, Christian Fenner, and Michael Th. Greven, eds., *Politische Willensbildung und Interessenvermittlung.* Opladen: Westdeutscher Verlag.

Landi, Oscar. 1992. *Devórame otra vez,* Buenos Aires: Planeta-Espejo de la Argentina.

Lane, Christel. 1981. *The Rites of Rulers: Ritual in Industrial Society – The Soviet Case.* Cambridge: Cambridge University Press.

Lang, Kurt, and Gladys Engel Lang. 1968. *Politics and Television.* Chicago: Quadrangle.

LASA International Commission. 1989. "The Chilean Plebiscite: A First Step toward Redemocratization." *LASA Forum,* 11, Winter.

Lassagni, Cristina, and Paula Edwards. 1988. "La radio en Chile: historia, modelos, perspectivas." Working paper 64. Santiago: CENECA.

Lazar, Marc. 1995. "L'Italie à la veille de Berlusconi." *L'état de l'opinion.* Paris: Seuil.

Lazarsfeld, Paul F., Bernard Berelson, and Hazel Gaudet. 1948. *The People's Choice.* New York: Columbia University Press.

LeDuc, Lawrence, Richard G. Niemi, and Pippa Norris. 1996. "Introduction: The Present and Future of Democratic Elections." In Lawrence LeDuc, Richard G. Niemi, and Pippa Norris, eds., *Comparing Democracies: Elections and Voting in Global Perspective.* Thousand Oaks: Sage.

Lee, Jung Bock. 1985. *The Political Character of the Japanese Press.* Seoul: Seoul National University Press.

Lendvai, Paul. 1981. *The Bureaucracy of Truth: How Communist Governments Manage the News.* Boulder: Westview Press.

Lerner, Daniel. 1958. *The Passing of Traditional Society.* New York: Free Press.

Lerner, Max. 1943. *The Mind and Faith of Justice Holmes: His Speeches, Essays, Letters and Judicial Opinions.* Boston: Little, Brown.

Lévai, Béla. 1987. *A rádió és a televízió kronikaja 1979–85.* Budapest: Tömegkommunikációs Kutatóközpont.

Levin, Murray B. 1987. *Talk Radio and the American Dream.* Lexington: Lexington Books.

Levy, Michael. 1981. "Disdaining the News." *Journal of Communication,* 31, 24–31.

Libertus, Michael. 1991. "Der Grundversorgungsauftrag des öffentlich-rechtlichen Rundfunks und seine dogmatische Grundlegung." *Media Perspektiven,* 452–60.

Lichtenberg, Judith, ed. 1990. *Democracy and the Mass Media.* Cambridge: Cambridge University Press.

Lichter, S. Robert, and Richard E. Noyes. 1995. *Good Intentions Make Bad News: Why Americans Hate Campaign Journalism.* Lanham: Rowman & Littlefield.

Lichter, S. Robert, Stanley Rothman, and Linda S. Lichter. 1990. *The Media Elite: America's New Powerbrokers.* New York: Hastings House.

Liebling, A. J. 1961. *The Press.* New York: Ballantine Books.

Ligachev, Egor. 1991. *Speeches of Egor Ligachev at the Kennan Institute: Fall 1991.* Occasional Paper 247, the Kennan Institute of the Woodrow Wilson Center, Washington, D.C.

Lijphart, Arend. 1968. *The Politics of Accommodation, Pluralism and Democracy in the Netherlands.* Berkeley: University of California Press.

    1974. "The Netherlands: Continuity and Change in Voting Behavior." In Richard Rose, ed., *Electoral Behavior: A Comparative Handbook.* New York: Free Press.

    1984. *Democracies. Patterns of Majoritarian and Consensus Government in Twenty-One Countries.* London: Yale University Press.

    1989. "From the Politics of Accommodation to Adversarial Politics in the Netherlands: A Reassessment." In Daalder and Irwin, eds.

Likhina, Olga. 1998. "So skidkoi po zhizni." *Kommersant,* November 6, 5.

Linz, Juan J. 1974. "Una teoría del régimen autoritario: el caso de España." In Manuel Fraga, ed., *La España de los años setenta,* Vol. 3, *El Estado y la política.* Madrid: Editorial Moneda y Crédito.

    1975. "Totalitarian and Authoritarian Regimes." In Fred I. Greenstein and Nelson W. Polsby, eds., *Handbook of Political Science,* Vol. 3, *Macropolitical Theory.* Reading: Addison-Wesley.

    1982. "The Legacy of Franco and Democracy." In Horst Baier, Hans Mathias Kepplinger, and Kurt Reumann, eds., *Öffentliche Meinung und sozialer Wandel.* Westdeutscher Verlag.

    1985. "De la crisis de un Estado unitario al Estado de las Autonomías." In Fernando Fernández, ed., *La España de las Autonomías.* Madrid: Instituto de Estudios de Administración Local.

Linz, Juan J., Manuel Gómez-Reino, Francisco A. Orizo, and Darío Vila. 1981. *Informe sociológico sobre el cambio político en España.* Madrid: Euroamérica.

Linz, Juan J., and José Ramón Montero, eds. 1986. *Crisis y cambio: electores y partidos en la España de los años ochenta.* Madrid: Centro de Estudios Constitucionales.

Linz, Juan J., and Alfred Stepan. 1996. *Problems of Democratic Transition and Consolidation: Southern Europe, South America and Post-Communist Europe.* Baltimore: Johns Hopkins University Press.

Linz, Juan J., Alfred Stepan, and Richard Gunther. 1995. "Democratic Transition and Consolidation in Southern Europe, with Reflections on Latin America and Eastern Europe." In Gunther, Diamandouros, and Puhle, eds.

Lippman, Walter. 1922. *Public Opinion.* Reprint 1965. New York: Free Press.

Lipset, Seymour Martin, and Stein Rokkan, eds. 1967. *Party Systems and Voter Alignments.* New York: Free Press.

Livolsi, Marino, ed. 1986. *Almeno un libro. Gli italiani che (non) leggono.* Firenze: La Nuova Italia.

Livolsi, Marino, and Ugo Volli, eds. 1996. *La comunicazione politica tra prima e seconda Repubblica.* Milano: Angeli.

López Pina, Antonio, and Eduardo L. Aranguren. 1976. *La cultura política de la España de Franco.* Madrid: Taurus.

López Pintor, Rafael. 1974. "En torno a las conexiones entre opinión pública y decisión política: la actitud de los españoles ante la Comunidad Económica Europea." *Revista Española de la Opinión Pública*, 37, 7–22.

———. 1982. *La opinión pública española del franquismo a la democracia.* Madrid: Centro de Investigaciones Sociológicas.

López Pintor, Rafael, and Ricardo Buceta. 1975. *Los españoles de los años 70. Una versión sociológica.* Madrid. Editorial Tecnos.

López Pintor, Rafael, Miguel Beltrán, José Ignacio Wert, and José Juan Tohria. 1994. "El sistema político." In Miguel Juárez, ed., *V Informe sociológico sobre el cambio político en España.* Madrid: Euramérica.

Lorwin, Val R. 1971. "Segmented Pluralism: Ideological Cleavages and Political Cohesion in the Small European Democracies." *Comparative Politics*, 3, 141–75.

Losano, Mario. 1995. "La politica nell'era multimediale: verso il peronismomediatico?" *Teoria Politica*, 3, 3–14.

Lowi, Theodore, 1985. *The Personal President: Power Invested, Promise Unfulfilled.* Ithaca: Cornell University Press.

Luykx, Theo 1978. *Evolutie van de Communicatiemedia.* Brussel: Elsevier Sequoia.

Mammarella, Giuseppe. 1995. "Il Partito Comunista Italiano." In Pasquino, ed.

Mancini, Paolo. 1980. *Il manifesto politico: per una semiologia del consenso.* Torino: Eri.

———. 1987. "Rito, leader e mass media: Enrico Berlinguer." In Luciano Cavalli, ed., *Leadership e democrazia.* Padova: Cedam.

———. ed. 1993. *Persone sulla scena. La campagna elettorale 1992 in televisione.* Torino: Nuova Eri.

Mancini, Paolo, and Gianpietro Mazzoleni, eds. 1995. *I media scendono in campo. Le elezioni politiche 1994 in televisione.* Torino: Nuova Eri.

Mannheimer, Renato. 1987. "Electoral Trends and the Italian Communist Party in the 1970s." *European Journal of Political Research*, 15, 635–52.

———. 1991. *La Lega Lombarda.* Milano: Feltrinelli.

Mannheimer, Renato, Giuseppe Micheli, and Francesca Zajczyk. 1978. *Mutamento sociale e comportamento elettorale. Il caso del referendum sul divorzio.* Milano: Angeli.

Mannheimer, Renato, Mario Rodriguez, and Chiara Sebastiani. 1983. *Gli operai comunisti.* Roma: Editori Riuniti.

Mannheimer, Renato, and Giacomo Sani. 1987. "Electoral Trends and Political Subcultures." In Robert Leonardi and Raffaella Nanetti, eds., *Italian Politics.* London: Pinter.

———. 1994. *La rivoluzione elettorale: l'Italia tra la prima e la seconda repubblica.* Milano: Anabasi.

Mannheimer, Renato, and Chiara Sebastiani, eds. 1983. *L'identità comunista. I militanti, la struttura, la cultura del Pci.* Roma: Editori Riuniti.

Maraffi, Marco. 1995. "Forza Italia." In Pasquino, ed.

Maravall, José María. 1978. *Dictatorship and Political Dissent: Workers and Students in Franco's Spain.* London: Tavistock.

Maravall, José María, and Julián Santamaría. 1989. "Transición política y consolidación de la democracia en España." In José F. Tezanos, Ramón Cotarelo, and Andrés de Blas, eds., *La transición democrática en España.* Madrid: Sistema.

Marini, Rolando, and Franca Roncarolo. 1997. *I media come arena elettorale. Le elezioni politiche 1996 in tv e nei giornali.* Roma: RAI-Eri.

Marletti, Carlo. 1984. *Media e politica.* Milano: Angeli.

1985. *Prima e dopo. Tematizzezione e comunicazione politica.* Torino: Eri.

1988a. "Parties and Mass Communication: The RAI Controversy." In Raffaella Nanetti, Robert Leonardi, and Piergiorgio Corbetta, eds., *Italian Politics: A Review.* London: Pinter.

1988b. "L'informazione locale e il mercato della comunicazione nella prospettiva degli anni novanta." *Piccoli grandi media.* Torino: Edizioni Regione Piemonte.

1995a. "Media e comunicazione politica nelle democrazie." *Quaderni di Scienza Politica,* 2, 285–12.

1995b. "I media e la politica." In Pasquino, ed.

Martínez de las Heras, Agustín. 1989. "Las etapas españolas de la desreglamentación." In Jesús T. Alvarez, ed., *Historia de los medios de comunicación en España. Periodismo, imagen y publicidad (1900–1990).* Barcelona: Editorial Ariel.

Martinotti, Guido. 1978. "Le tendenze dell'elettorato italiano." In Alberto Martinelli and Gianfranco Pasquino, eds., *La politica nell'Italia che cambia.* Milano: Feltrinelli.

Massari, Oreste. 1987. "La leadership di Craxi e gli effetti sul partito (1976–1984)." In Luciano Cavalli, ed., *Leadership e democrazia.* Padova: Cedam.

Massey, Joseph A. 1976. *Youth and Politics in Japan.* Lexington: Lexington Books.

Mathes, Rainer, and Uwe Freisens. 1990. "Kommunikationsziele der Parteien und ihr Erfolg. Eine Analyse der aktuellen Berichterstattung in den Nachrichtenmagazinen der öffentlich-rechtlichen und privaten Rundfunkanstalten im Bundestagswahlkampf 1987." In Max Kaase and Hans-Dieter Klingemann, eds., *Wahlen und Wähler – Analysen aus Anlaß der Bundestagswahl, 1987.* Opladen: Westdeutscher Verlag.

Matsuda, Hiroshi. 1981. *Dokyumento – hôsô sengoshi II.* Kanagawa: Sôshisha.

Maxwell, Kenneth. 1983. "Introduction: The Transition to Democracy in Spain and Portugal." In Kenneth Masswell, ed., *The Press and the Rebirth of Iberian Democracy.* Westport: Greenwood Press.

Maxwell, Richard. 1995. *The Spectacle of Democracy: Spanish Television, Nationalism and Political Transition.* Minneapolis: University of Minnesota Press.

May, Annabelle, and Kathryn Rowan. 1982. *Inside Information: British Government and the Media.* London: Constable.

Mazzoleni, Giampietro. 1987a. "Media Logic and Party Logic in Campaign Coverage: The Italian Election of 1983." *European Journal of Communication,* 2, 95–103.

1987b. "The Role of Private Television Stations in Italian Elections." In David Paletz, ed., *Political Communication Research.* Norwood: Ablex.

1990. "Dal partito al candidato. Come cambia la comunicazione elettorale in Italia." *Polis,* 2, 249–73.

1991. "Emergence of the Candidate and Political Marketing: Television and Electoral Campaign in Italy in the 1980s." *Political Comminication and Persuasion,* 8, 201–12.

1992. *Comunicazione e potere. Mass media e politica in Italia.* Napoli: Liguori.

1993. "La comunicazione politica alla vigilia della seconda Repubblica." *Problemi dell'informazione,* 4, 383–92.

1995. "Toward a 'Videocracy?' Italian Political Communication at a Turning Point." *European Journal of Communication,* 3, 291–30.

1996. "La dinamica dell'ascolto." *Comunicazione Politica,* 1, 29–40.

McAllister, Ian. 1985. "Campaign Activities and Electoral Outcomes in Britain 1979 and 1983." *Public Opinion Quarterly,* 49, 489–503.

McCombs, Maxwell E., and Donald L. Shaw. 1972. "The Agenda-Setting Function of the Mass Media." *Public Opinion Quarterly,* 36, 176–87.

McGuire, William J. 1968. "Personality and Susceptibility to Social Influence." In E. V. Brogatta and W. W. Lambert, eds., *Handbook of Personality Theory and Research.* New York: Rand McNally.

1993. "The Evolution of Agenda-Setting Research: Twenty-Five Years in the Market-Place of Ideas." *Journal of Communication,* 43, 58–67.

McQuail, Denis. 1992. *Media Performance. Mass Communication and the Public Interest.* London: Sage.

Méndez, Roberto, Oscar Godoy, Enrique Barros, and Arturo Fontaine. 1989. "¿Por qué Ganó el No?," *Estudios Públicos,* 33. Santiago: Centro de Estudios Públicos.

Menduni, Enrico. 1994. *La radio nell'era della tv. Fine di un complesso di inferiorità.* Bologna: Il Mulino

1996. *La più amata dagli itliani. La televisione tra politicae comunicazione.* Bologna: Il Mulino.

Merkel, Walter. 1987. *Prima e dopo Craxi. Le trasformazioni del Psi.* Padova: Liviana.

Mervin, David. 1998. "The News Media and Democracy in the United States." *Democratization,* 5, 6–22.

Miami Herald Publishing Co. v. Tornillo, 418 U.S. 241 (1974).

Mickelson, Sig. 1972. *The Electronic Mirror.* New York: Dodd, Mead.

Mickiewicz, Ellen. 1981. *Media and the Russian Public.* New York: Praeger.

1988. *Split Signals: Television and Politics in the Soviet Union.* New York: Oxford University Press.

1998. "Transition and Democratization: The Role of Journalists in Eastern Europe and the Former Soviet Union." In Graber, McQuail, and Norris, eds.

1999. *Changing Channels: Television and the Struggle for Power in Russia,* revised and expanded ed. Durham: Duke University Press.

Milbrath, Lester, and M. L. Goel. 1977. *Political Participation,* 2nd ed. Chicago: Rand McNally.

Miliband, Ralph. 1962. *The State in Capitalist Society.* London: Merlin Books.

Miller, Arthur N., Edie N.Goldenberg, and Lutz Erbring. 1979. "Type-Set Politics: Impact of Newspapers on Public Confidence." *American Political Science Review,* 73, 67–84.

Miller, William L. 1991. *Media and Voters. The Audience, Content, and Influence of Press and Television at the 1987 General Elections.* Oxford: Clarendon Press.

Miller, William L., Harold D. Clarke, Martin Harrop, Lawrence Leduc, and Paul F. Whiteley. 1990. *How Voters Change: The 1987 British Election Campaign in Perspective.* Oxford: Clarendon Press.

Milne, R. S., and H. C. Mackenzie. 1958. *Marginal Seat 1955.* London: Hansard Society for Parliamentary Government.

Mondak, Jeffrey J. 1995. "Media Exposure and Political Discussion in U.S. Elections." *The Journal of Politics,* 57, 62–85.

Montabes, Juan. 1989. *La prensa del Estado durante la transición política española.* Madrid: Centro de Investigaciones Sociológicas.

1994. "Los parlamentos de papel en el caso español." In Carlos H. Filgueira and Dieter Nohlen, eds., *Prensa y transición democrática. Experiencias recientes en Europa y América Latina.* Madrid: Iberoamericana.

471

Monteleone, Franco. 1992. *Storia dell radio e della televisione in Italia.* Venezia, Marsilo.

Montero, José Ramón. 1988. "Las derechas en el sistema de partidos republicano del segundo bienio: algunos datos introductorios." In José L. García Delgado, ed., *La II República española. Bienio rectificador y Frente Popular, 1934–1936.* Madrid: Siglo XXI.

——— 1993. "Las dimensiones de la secularización: religiosidad y preferencias políticas en España." In Rafael Díaz-Salazar and Salvador Giner, eds., *Religión y sociedad en España.* Madrid: Centro de Investigaciones Sociológicas.

Montero, José Ramón, and Richard Gunther. 1994. "Democratic Legitimacy in Spain." Paper presented at the XVI IPSA World Congress, Berlin.

Montero José Ramón, Richard Gunther, and Mariano Torcal. 1998. "Sentimientos antipartidistas en el sur de Europa: una exploración preliminar." In Ángel Valencia Sáiz, ed., *Participación y representación políticas en las sociedades multiculturales.* Málaga: Servicio de Publicaciones de la Universidad de Málaga.

Montero, José Ramón, and Mariano Torcal. 1990. "La cultura política de los españoles: pautas de continuidad y cambio." *Sistema,* 99, 39–74.

Moral, Félix. 1989. *La opinión pública española ante Europa y los europeos.* Madrid: Centro de Investigaciones Sociológicas, Estudios y Encuestas.

Morcellini, Mario. 1986. *Lo spettacolo del consumo. Televisione e cultura di massa nella legittimazione sociale.* Milano: Angeli.

——— 1994. "La telepolitica: polifonia e rappresentazione." *Problemi dell'informazione,* 3, 261–85.

——— 1995. *Elezioni di TV. Televisione e pubblico nella campagna elettorale '94.* Genova: Costa e Nolan.

——— 1996. "La tv dell'incertezza." *Problemi dell'informazione,* 21, 301–13.

Morlino, Leonardo, ed. 1991. *Costruire la democrazia. Gruppi e partiti in Italia.* Bologna: Il Mulino.

——— 1995. "Parties and Democratic Consolidation in Southern Europe." In Gunther, Diamandouros, and Puhle, eds.

Morlino, Leonardo, and José Ramon Montero. 1994. "Legittimità, consolidamento e crisi nell'Europa meridionale." *Rivista italiana di Scienza Politica,* 1, 27–65.

——— 1995. "Legitimacy and Democracy in Southern Europe." In Gunther, Diamandouros, and Puhle, eds.

Mott, Frank Luther. 1962. *American Journalism, a History: 1690–1960.* New York: Macmillan.

Mughan, Anthony. 1993. "Party Leaders and Presidentialism in the 1992 Election: A Post-War Perspective." In David Denver, Pippa Norris, David Broughton, and Colin Rallings, eds., *British Elections and Politics Yearbook 1993.* London: Harvester Wheatsheaf.

——— 1995. "Television and Presidentialism: Australian and U.S. Legislative Elections Compared." *Political Communication,* 12, 327–42.

——— 1996. "Television Can Matter: Bias in the 1992 General Election." In David M. Farrell, David Broughton, David Denver, and Justin Fisher, eds., *British Elections and Parties Yearbook 1996.* London: Frank Cass.

——— 1998. "Party Leaders, Presidentialization and British Politics." Unpublished manuscript.

Multigner, Gilles. 1989. "La radio, de 1940 a 1960: ocios y negocios rigurosamente vigilados." In Jesús T. Alvarez, ed., *Historia de los medios de comunicación en España. Periodismo, imagen y publicidad (1900–1990)*. Barcelona: Editorial Ariel.

Munizaga, Giselle. 1981. "Marco jurídico legal del medio televisivo en Chile." Working Paper. Santiago: CENECA.

1984. "Revistas y espacio comunicativo." Working Paper. Santiago: CENECA.

Murialdi, Paolo. 1972. *La stampa italiana del dopoguerra: 1943–1972*. Bari: Laterza.

1986. *Storia del giornalismo italiano*. Torino: Gutemberg.

ed. 1990. *Dieci anni di televisione sotto il segno di Berlusconi*. Special issue of *Problemi dell'informazione*, 4.

Murialdi, Paolo, and Nicola Tranfaglia. 1994. "I quotidiani negli ultimi vent'anni. Crisi, sviluppo e concentrazione." In Valerio Castronovo and Nicola Tranfaglia, eds., *La stampa italiana nell'età della TV: 1975–1994*. Roma-Bari, Laterza.

Natale, Paolo. 1993. *Le tendenze elettorali degli anni Novanta*. In Marino Livolsi, ed., *L'Italia che cambia*. Firenze: La Nuova Italia.

Navarro, Arturo. 1985. "El sistema de prensa bajo el gobierno militar (1973–1984)." Working Paper. Santiago: CENECA, 1985.

Neijens, Peter, and Philip van Praag, Jr., eds. 1999. *De slag om IJburg – campagne, media en publiek*. Amsterdam: Het Spinhuis.

Neill Report. 1998. *5th Report of the Committee on Standards in Public Life: The Funding of Political Parties in the United Kingdom*. Chaired by Lord Neill of Blayden. London: Her Majesty's Stationary Office.

Neuman, W. Russell. 1986. *The Paradox of Politics. Knowledge and Opinion in the American Electorate*. Cambridge and London: Harvard University Press.

1991. *The Future of the Mass Audience*. Cambridge: Cambridge University Press.

Neuman, W. Russell, Marion R. Just, and Ann Crigler. 1992. *Common Knowledge: News and the Construction of Political Meaning*. Chicago: University of Chicago Press.

The New York Times v. Sullivan, 376 U.S. 259 (1964).

The New York Times v. United States, 403 U.S. 713 (1971).

Nie, Norman, G. Bingham Powell, Jr., and Kenneth Prewitt. 1969. "Social Structure and Political Participation: Developmental Relationships, Parts I and II." *American Political Science Review*, 63, 361–78 and 808–32.

Nihon Shimbun Kyokai. 1998. *Nihon Shimbun Nenkan, '98, '99*. Tokyo: Dentsu.

Nihon Shimbun Kyokai, ed. 1998. *Nihon Shimbun Nenkan*. Tokyo.

Nippon Hôsô Kyôkai. n.d.. *The Broadcast Law*. Tokyo: Nippon Hôsô Kyôkai.

1981. *Saikin Shicho Tokusei*. Tokyo: Nippon Hôsô Kyôkai.

1988. *NHK sekai no rajio to terebijyon 1988*. Tokyo: Nippon Hôsô Kyôkai.

1990. *NHK '90: poketto jiten*. Tokyo: Nippon Hôsô Kyôkai Shichôsha Kôhôshitsu.

Nippon Hôsô Kyôkai Yoronchôsajo. 1977. NHK Public Opinion Survey Research Institute internal memorandum.

Noczow, Aleksandar. 1982. *Black Book of Polish Censorship*. South Bend: AND Books.

Noelle-Neumann, Elisabeth. 1977. "Das doppelte Meinungsklima. Der Einfluß des Fernsehens im Wahlkampf 1976." In Max Kaase, ed., *Wahlsoziologie heute. Analysen aus Anlaß der Bundestagswahl 1976*. Special edition of *Politische Vierteljahresschrift*, 18, 2/3, 408–51.

1988. Das Fernsehen und die Zukunft der Lesekultur. In Werner D. Froehlich, Rolf Zitzlsperger, and Bodo Franzmann, eds., *Die verstellte Welt. Beitraege zur Medienoekologie*. Frankfurt am Main: Fischer Taschenbuch Verlag.

1989. *Öffentliche Meinung. Die Entdeckung der Schweigespirale.* Frankfurt am Main and Berlin: Ullstein.

Nomura, Tadao. 1981. "Freedom of Expression and Social Responsibility of Broadcasting." In *Summary Report: Symposium on Public Role and Systems of Broadcasting, September 30–October 2, 1981.* Tokyo: Hoso Bunka Foundation.

Norris, Pippa. 1995. "Political Communications in British Election Campaigns: Reconsidering Media Effects." In Colin Rallings, David M. Farrell, David Denver, and David Broughton, eds., *British Elections and Parties Yearbook 1995.* London: Frank Cass.

1998. "The Battle for the Campaign Agenda." In Anthony King, ed., *New Labour Triumphs: Britain at the Polls.* Chatham: Chatham House.

Norris, Pippa, John Curtice, David Sanders, Magaret Scammel, and Holli Semetko. 1999. *On Message: Communicating the Campaign.* London: Sage.

Notarnicola, Andrea. 1994. "La contesa delle immagini: gli spot televisivi dei partiti per le elezioni politiche del 1987 e 1992." *Quaderni di Scienza Politica,* 3, 395–488.

Novelli, Edoardo. 1995. *Dalla tv di partito al partito della tv.* Firenze: La Nuova Italia.

Novelli, Scipione. 1980. "Elezioni, stabilità e sistema politico in Italia. La stabilità elettorale." *Studi di sociologia,* 3, 233–52.

Oates, Sarah Ann. 1998. "Voting Behavior and Party Development in New Democracies: The Russian Duma Elections of 1993 and 1995." Ph.D. dissertation, Emory University.

O'Donnell, Guillermo, and Philippe C. Schmitter. 1986. *Transitions from Authoritarian Rule: Tentative Conclusions About Uncertain Democracies.* Baltimore: Johns Hopkins University Press.

Ooiwa, Yuri. 1991. "Nihon no kisha kurabu anke-to: gaikokujin kisha no kaiken shusseki jôken." *AERA,* October, 28.

Oppenhuis, Erik. 1996. "The Netherlands: Small Party Evolution." In van der Eijk and Franklin, eds.

Ossandón, Fernando, and Sandra Rojas. 1989. *La Epoca y Fortín Mapocho. El primer impacto.* Santiago: Eco-Cedal.

Owen, Diana Marie. 1991. *Media Messages in American Presidential Elections.* Westport: Greenwood Press.

Packard, George R., III. 1966. *Protest in Tokyo.* Princeton: Princeton University Press.

Page, Benjamin I., Robert Y. Shapiro, and Glenn R. Dempsey. 1987. "What Moves Public Opinion?" *American Political Science Review,* 81, 23–43.

Pallotta, Gino. 1991. *Dizionario del politichese.* Milano: Sugarco Edizioni.

Palmer, Michael, and Jeremy Tunstall. 1990. *Liberating Communications: Policy-Making in France and Britain.* Oxford: Blackwell.

Papa, Antonio. 1978. *Storia politica della radio in Italia.* 2 vols. Napoli: Guida.

Parisi, Arturo, ed. 1979. *Democristiani.* Bologna: Il Mulino.

Pasquino, Gianfranco. 1978. "La Democrazia cristiana: trasformazioni partitiche e mediazione politica." In Alberto Martinelli and Gianfranco Pasquino, eds., *La politica nell (Italia che cambia).* Milano: Feltrinelli.

1980. *Crisi dei partiti e governabilità.* Bologna: Il Mulino.

ed. 1985. *Il sistema politico italiano.* Roma-Bari: Laterza.

1988. *Istituzioni, partiti, lobbies.* Bari: Laterza.

1990. *"Persone non gratae?* Personalizzazione e spettacolarizzazione della politica." *Polis,* 2, 203–16.

ed. 1993. *Votare un solo candidato. Le conseguenze politiche della preferenza unica.* Bologna: Il Mulino.

ed. 1995. *La politica italiana.* Roma-Bari: Laterza.

Patterson, Thomas. 1980a. *The Mass Media Election: How Americans Choose Their President.* New York: Praeger.

1980b. "The Role of the Mass Media in Presidential Campaign:the Lessons of 1976 Elections." *Items,* 2, 25–30.

1987. "Television and Presidential Politics." In Alexander Heard and Michael Nelson, eds., *Presidential Selection.* Durham: Duke University Press.

1991. "More Style Than Substance: Television News in U.S. National Elections. *Political Communication and Persuasion,* 8, 145–61.

1992. "Irony of the Free Press." Paper presented at the American Political Science Association meeting, Washington, D.C.

1993. *Out of Order.* New York: Knopf.

1996. *The American Democracy.* New York: McGraw-Hill.

1998. "The Political Roles of the Journalist." In Graber, McQuail, and Norris, eds.

Patterson, Thomas, and Robert McClure. 1976. *The Unseeing Eye: The Myth of Television Power in National Elections.* New York: Putnam.

Pellegrino, Bruno. 1993. *Rai spa. Una holding della comunicazione per la terza fase del sistema audiovisivo italiano.* Milano: Il Sole 24 Ore.

Pempel, T. J. 1982. *Policy and Politics in Japan: Creative Conservatism.* Philadelphia: Temple University Press.

ed. 1990. *Uncommon Democracies: The One-Party Dominant Regimes.* Ithaca: Cornell University Press.

Pfetsch, Barbara. 1986. "Volkszählung '83: Ein Beispiel für die Thematisierung eines politischen Issues in den Massenmedien." In Hans-Dieter Klingemann and Max Kaase, eds., *Wahlen und politischer Prozeß. Analysen aus Anlaß der Bundestagswahl 1983.* Opladen: Westdeutscher Verlag.

1991. *Politische Folgen der Dualisierung des Rundfunksystems in der Bundesrepublik Deutschland – Konzepte und Analysen zum Fernsehangebot und zum Publikumsverhalten.* Baden-Baden: Nomos Verlagsgesellschaft.

1996. "Konvergente Fernsehformate von Politik? Eine vergleichende Analyse öffentlich-rechtlicher und privater Programme 1985/86 und 1993." *Rundfunk und Fernsehen,* 44, 1–20.

Pharr, Susan J. 1996. "Media as Trickster in Japan in Comparative Perspective." In Pharr and Krauss, eds.

2000. "Officials' Misconduct and Public Trust: Japan and the Trilateral Democracies." In Susan J. Pharr and Robert D. Putnam, eds., *What's Troubling the Trilateral Democracies?* Princeton: Princeton University Press.

Pharr, Susan J., and Ellis S. Krauss, eds. 1996. *Media and Politics in Japan.* Honolulu: University of Hawaii Press.

Pilati, Antonio. 1987. *Il nuovo sistema dei media.* Milano: Comunità.

Pinto, Francesco. 1980. *Il modello televisivo.* Milano: Feltrinelli.

Pizarroso, Alejandro. 1989. "Política informativa: información y propaganda (1939–1966)." In Jesús T. Alvarez, ed., *Historia de los medios de comunicación en España. Periodismo, imagen y publicidad (1900–1990).* Barcelona. Editorial Ariel.

Pizzorusso, Alessandro. 1995. "I nuovi sistemi elettorali per la Camera dei deputati e per il Senato della Repubblica." In Massimo Luciani and Mauro Volpi, eds., *Riforme elet-torali.* Roma-Bari: Laterza.

Poggi, Gianfranco. 1963. *Il clero di riserva. Studio sociologico dell'Azione Cattolica Italiana durante la presidenza Gedda.* Milano: Feltrinelli.

1974. "La Chiesa nella politica italiana dal 1945 al 1950." In Sidney J. Woolf, ed., *Italia 1943–1950. La ricostruzione.* Bari: Laterza.

Pomper, Gerald M., with Susan S. Lederman. 1980. *Elections in America: Control and Influence in Democratic Politics.* New York: Longman.

Pool, Ithiel de Sola. 1973a. *Talking Back: Citizen Feedback and Cable Technology.* Cambridge: MIT Press.

1973b. "Communication in Totalitarian Societies." In Ithiel de Sola Pool and Wilbur Schramm, eds., *Handbook of Communication.* Chicago: Rand McNally.

1983. *Technologies of Freedom.* Cambridge: Harvard University Press.

Popkin, Samuel. 1991. *The Reasoning Voter: Communication and Persuasion in Presidential Campaigns.* Chicago: University of Chicago Press.

Porro, Nicola. 1995. "L'innovazione conservatrice. Fininvest, Milan Club e Forza Italia." *Quaderni di Sociologia,* 9, 6–18.

Portales, Diego. 1981. *Poder económico y libertad de expresión. La Industria de la comunicación chilena en la democracia y el autoritarismo.* Mexico, DF: ILET, Editorial Nueva Imagen.

Portales, Diego, María Eugenia Hirmas, Juan Carlos Altamirano, and Juan Pablo Egaña. 1988.

Televisión chilena: Censura o Libertad. El caso de la visita de Juan Pablo II. Santiago: Editorial Pehuén, Estudios ILET.

Portales, Diego, and Guillermo Sunkel, eds. 1989. *La Política en pantalla.* Santiago: ILET-CESOC.

Postman, Neil. 1985. *Amusing Ourselves to Death: Public Discourse in the Age of Show Business.* New York: Penguin.

Prandi, Alfonso. 1968. "Le raccomandazioni dei Vescovi." In Mattei Dogan and Orazio M. Petracca, eds., *Partiti politici e strutture sociali in Italia.* Milano: Comunità.

Publimark. 1992. Revista de Marketing y Publicidad. Santiago.

Pucci, Emilio, ed. 1996. *L'industria dellla comunicazione in Italia.* Milano: Guerini e Associati.

Pulzer, Peter. 1967. *Political Representation and Election in Britain.* London: Allen & Unwin.

Putnam, Robert D. 1995. "Tuning In, Turning Out: The Strange Disappearance of Social Capital in America." *PS: Political Science and Politics,* 28, 664–83.

Radunski, Peter. 1977. "Wahlkampfentscheidung im Fernsehen." *Sonde,* 1(10), 51–74.

1980. *Wahlkämpfe. Moderne Wahlkampführung als politische Kommunikation.* München: Olzog.

1983. "Strategische Überlegungen zum Fernsehwahlkampf." In Winfried Schulz and Klaus Schoenbach, eds., *Massenmedien und Wahlen.* München: Oelschlaeger.

Rager, Guenther, and Bernd Weber. 1992. "Publizistische Vielfalt zwischen Markt und Politik." *Media Perspektiven,* 357–66.

Randall, Vicky. 1998. "Democratization and the Media." Special issue of *Democratization,* 5.

Ranney, Austin. 1983. *Channels of Power: The Impact of Television on American Politics.* New York: Basic Books.

Rasmussen, Jorgen. 1981. "David Steel's Liberals: Too Old to Cry, Too Hurt to Laugh." In Howard R. Penniman, ed., *Britain at the Polls, 1979.* Washington, D.C.: American Enterprise Institute.

Red Lion Broadcasting v. FCC, 395 U.S. 367 (1969).

Regonini, Gloria. 1994. "Partiti, reti, giochi, politiche pubbliche." In Mario Caciagli, Franco Cazzola, Leonardo Morlino, and Stefano Passigli, eds., *L'Italia fra crisi e transizione.* Roma-Bari: Laterza.

Reich, Michael R. 1984. "Crisis and Routine: Pollution Reporting by the Japanese Press." In George De Vos, ed., *Institutions for Change in Japanese Society.* Berkeley: Institute of East Asian Studies, University of California.

Reid, T. R. 1992. "In Japan, Socialists Air 'Negative,' if Innocuous, Political Ad." *Washington Post,* July 25, A16.

Ressmann, Wolfgang. 1991. *Strukturprobleme sozialdemokratischer Medienunternehmen.* Wiesbaden: Deutscher Universitäts Verlag.

Reston, James. 1975. "End of the Tunnel," *The New York Times,* April 30, 41.

Richardson, Bradley M. 1974. *Political Culture in Japan.* Berkeley: University of California Press.

———. 1988. "Constituency Candidates versus Parties in Japanese Voting Behavior." *American Political Science Review,* 82(3), 695–718.

Ricolfi, Luca. 1994. "Elezioni e mass media. Quanti voti ha spostato la Tv." *Il Mulino,* 13, 1031–46.

Righart, Hans. 1986. *De Katholieke Zuil in Europa. Het Ontstaan van Verzuiling onder Katholieken in Oostenrijk, Zwitserland, België en Nederland.* Meppel: Boom.

Roberts, Donald F., and Nathan Maccoby. 1985. "Effects of Mass Communication." In Gardner Lindzey and Elliot Aronson, *The Handbook of Social Psychology,* 3rd ed. Vol. II. New York: Random House.

Robinson, Michael J. 1976. "Public Affairs Television and the Growth of Political Malaise: The Case of 'The Selling of the Pentagon.'" *American Political Science Review,* 70, 409–32.

———. 1977. "Television and American Politics." *The Public Interest,* 48, 3–39.

———. 1981. "Television and American Politics: 1956–1976." In Morris Janowitz and Paul Hirsch, eds., *Reader in Public Opinion and Communication.* New York: Free Press.

———. 1983. "Improving Election Information in the Media." Paper presented at the Voting for Democracy Forum, Washington, D.C.

———. 1993. "The United States of America." Unpublished paper, Georgetown University, Washington, D.C.

Robinson, Michael J., and Margaret Sheehan. 1983. *Over the Wire and on TV.* New York: Russell Sage Foundation.

Roca, Miguel. 1989. "El desamparo político frente al periodista." In Ofa Bezunartea and Jesús Canga, eds., *Los límites de la información política. Las nuevas ofertas de TV privadas en el Estado español.* Bilbao: Universidad del País Vasco.

Rodan, Garry. 1998. "Asia and the International Press: The Political Significance of Expanding Markets." *Democratization,* 5, 125–54.

Rodotà, Stefano. 1994. "Berlusconi e la tecnopolitica." *Micromega,* 3, 85–94.

Roeder, Philip. 1993. *Red Sunset: The Failure of Soviet Politics.* Princeton: Princeton University Press.

Roeper, Horst. 1991. "Daten zur Konzentration der Tagespresse in der Bundesrepublik Deutschland im 1. Quartal 1991." *Media Perspektiven,* 431–44.

Roncarolo, Franca. 1993. "Il caso di Torino." In Paolo Mancini, ed., *Persone sulla scena. La campagna elettorale 1992.* Torino: ERI-VQPT.

1995. "Torino, più mercati che piazze elettroniche." In Mancini and Mazzoleni, eds.

Rosen, Jay. 1991. "Making Journalism More Public." *Communication,* 12, 267–84.

Rosenbaum, Martin. 1997. *From Soapbox to Soundbite: Party Political Campaigning in Britain since 1945.* New York: St. Martin's Press.

Rothman, Stanley. 1980. "The Mass Media in Post-Industrial Society." In Seymour Martin Lipset, ed., *The Third Century: America as a Post-Industrial Society.* Stanford: Hoover Institution Press.

ed. 1992. *The Mass Media in Liberal Democratic Societies.* New York: Paragon House.

Rusconi, Gian Enrico. 1969. *Giovani e secolarizzazione.* Firenze: Vallecchi.

Rustow, Dankwart A. 1970. "Transitions to Democracy." *Comparative Politics,* April, 337–63.

Sabato, Larry. 1991. *Feeding Frenzy: How Attack Journalism Has Transformed American Politics.* New York: Free Press.

Sabbatucci, Giovanni. 1995. "Il Partito Socialista Italiano." In Pasquino, ed.

Sanders, David, David Marsh, and Hugh Ward. 1993. "The Electoral Impact of Press Coverage of the British Economy, 1979–1987." *British Journal of Political Science,* 23, 175–210.

Sanger, David. 1993. "Japan's Old Guard Flails at the Talking Heads." *New York Times,* November 7, Section 4, 16.

Sani, Giacomo. 1980. "The Political Culture of Italy: Continuity and Change." In Gabriel A. Almond and Sidney Verba, eds., *The Civic Culture Revisited.* Boston: Little, Brown.

1993. "The Anatomy of Change." In Gianfranco Pasquino and Patrick McCarty, eds., *The End of Post-war Politics in Italy. The Landmark 1992 Elections.* Boulder: Westview Press.

1995. "Il Cavallo ed il Biscione: Italian Television in the Campaign of 1994 and 1995." Paper presented at the Annual Meeting of the American Political Science Association, Chicago, August 31–September 1.

1996. "I verdetti del 21 aprile." *Il Mulino,* 365, 451–8.

Sani, Giacomo, and Antonio Nizzoli. 1997. "L'offerta televisiva di politics elettorate (1994–1996)." *Quaderni di Scienza Politica,* 4, 465–81.

Sani, Giacomo, and Paolo Segatti. 2000. "Anti-Party Politics and the Restructuring of the Italian Party System. In Diamandouros and Gunther, eds.

Santos, Félix. 1995. *Periodistas. Polanquistas, sindicato del crimen, tertulianos y demás tribus.* Madrid: Ediciones Temas de Hoy.

Sarcinelli, Ulrich, ed. 1998. *Politikvermittlung und Demokratie in der Mediengesellschaft.* Opladen and Wiesbaden: Westdeutscher Verlag.

Sarlvik, Bo, and Ivor Crewe. 1983. *Decade of Dealignment: The Conservative Victory of 1979 and Electoral Trends in the 1970s.* Cambridge: Cambridge University Press.

Sartori, Giovanni. 1966. "European Political Parties: The Case of Polarized Pluralism." In Joseph LaPalombara and Myron Weiner, eds., *Political Parties and Political Development.* Princeton: Princeton University Press.

1998. *Homo videns: La sociedad teledirigida.* Madrid: Taurus.

Scalapino, Robert A., and Junnosuke Masumi. 1975. *Parties and Politics in Contemporary Japan.* Berkeley: University of California Press.

Scammell, Margaret. 1995. *Designer Politics: How Elections Are Won.* New York: St. Martin's Press.

Scammell, Margaret, and Holli A. Semetko. 1995. "Political Advertising on Television: The British Experience." In Lynda Lee Kaid and Christina Holtz-Bacha, eds., *Political Advertising in Western Democracies.* Thousand Oaks: Sage.

Scannell, Paddy. 1989. "Public Service Broadcasting and Modern Public Life." *Media, Culture and Society,* 11, 135–66.

1990. "Public Service Braodcasting: History of a Concept." In Goodwin and Whannel, eds.

Schatz, Heribert, Klaus Adamczewski, Klaus Lange, and Ferdinand Nuessen. 1981. *Fernsehen und Demokratie. Eine Inhaltsanalyse der Fernsehnachrichtensendungen von ARD und ZDF vom Frühjahr 1977.* Opladen: Westdeutscher Verlag.

Scherer, Helmut. 1990. *Massenmedien, Meinungsklima und Einstellung. Eine Untersuchung zur Theorie der Schweigespirale.* Opladen: Westdeutscher Verlag.

Scherer, Helmut, Winfried Schulz, Lutz M. Hagen, Theodor A. Zipfel, and Harald Berens. 1997. "Die Darstellung von Politik in ost- und westdeutschen Tageszeitungen. Ein inhaltsanalytischer Vergleich." *Publizistik,* 42(4), 413–38.

Schlesinger, Jacob M., and Masayoshi Kanabayashi. 1992. "TV Rabble-Rouser Helped to Topple One of Japan's Mightest Politicians." *Wall Street Journal,* October 16, A10.

Schmitt, Hermann, and Soeren Holmberg. 1995. "Political Parties in Decline?" In Hans-Dieter Klingemann and Dieter Fuchs, eds., *Citizens and the State,* Beliefs in Government Series, Vol. 1. Oxford: Oxford University Press.

Schmitt-Beck, Rüdiger. 1994a. "Intermediation Environments of West German and East German Voters: Interpersonal Communication and Mass Communication During the First All-German Election Campaign." *European Journal of Communication,* 9, 381–419.

1994b. "Vermittlungswelten westdeutscher und ostdeutscher Wähler: Interpersonale Kommunikation, Massenkommunikation und Parteipräferenzen vor der Bundestagswahl 1990." In Hans Rattinger, Oscar W. Gabriel, and Wolfgang Jagodzinski, eds., *Wahlen und politische Einstellungen im vereinigten Deutschland.* Frankfurt am Main: Peter Lang.

1998. "Of Readers, Viewers, and Cat-Dogs." In Jan W. van Deth, ed., *Comparative Politics. The Problem of Equivalence.* London: Routledge.

Schmitter, Philippe C., and Terry Lynn Karl. 1991. "What Democracy Is . . . and Is Not." *Journal of Democracy,* 2, 75–88.

Schoenbach, Klaus. 1977. *Trennung von Nachricht und Meinung. Empirische Untersuchung eines journalistischen Qualitätskriteriums.* Freiburg and München: Verlag Karl Alber.

1987. "The Role of Mass Media in West German Election Campaigns." *Legislative Studies Quarterly,* 12, 373–94.

1991. "Mass Media and Election Campaigns in Germany." In Frederick J. Fletcher, ed., *Media, Elections and Democracy.* Toronto and Oxford: Dundurn Press.

Scholl, Armin, and Siegfried Weischenberg. 1998. *Journalismus in der Gesellschaft.* Opladen and Wiesbaden: Westdeutscher Verlag.

Schöpflin, George. 1983. *Censorship and Political Communication in Eastern Europe: A Collection of Documents*. New York: St. Martin's Press.

Schudson, Michael. 1978. *Discovering the News*. New York: Basic Books.

1986. *What Time Means in a News Story*. New York: Freedom Forum Media Studies Center at Columbia University, Occasional Paper No. 4.

1998. "The Public Journalism Movement and Its Problems." In Graber, McQuail, and Norris, eds.

Schulz, Winfried. 1997a. *Politische Kommunikation. Theoretische Ansätze und Ergebnisse empirischer Forschung*. Opladen: Westdeutscher Verlag.

1997b. "Changes of Mass Media and the Public Sphere." *The Public*, 4(2), 57–69.

Scoppola, Pietro. 1995. "La Democrazia Cristiana." In Pasquino, ed.

Secretaría de Comunicación y Cultura. 1990. *La política de comunicaciones del Gobierno*. Santiago: Gobierno de Chile.

1991. "Consumo de periódicos en la transición democrática." Working Paper, Education and Culture Series 15. Santiago: FLACSO.

Semetko, Holli A. 1987. *Political Communication and Party Development in Britain: The Social Democratic Party*. Ph.D. thesis, London School of Economics and Political Science.

1989. "Television News and 'The Third Force' in British Politics: A Case Study of Election Communication." *European Journal of Communication*, 4(4), 453–81.

Semetko, Holli, Jay G. Blumler, Michael Gurevitch, and David H. Weaver, with Steve Barkin and G. Cleveland Wilhoit. 1991. *The Formation of Campaign Agendas: A Comparative Analysis of Party and Media Roles in Recent American and British Elections*. Hillsdale: Lawrence Earlbaum.

Semetko, Holli A., and María José Canel. 1997. "Agenda-Senders versus Agenda-Setters: Television in Spain's 1996 Election Campaign." *Political Communication*, 14, 459–79.

Semetko, Holli A., Margaret Scammell, and T. J. Nossiter. 1994. "Media Coverage of the 1992 British General Election Campaign." In Anthony Heath, Roger Jowell, and John Curtice, eds., *Labour's Last Chance? The 1992 Election and Beyond*. Aldershot: Dartmouth.

Semetko, Holli A., and Klaus Schoenbach. 1994. *Germany's Unity Election. Voters and the Media*. Cresshill: Hampton.

Senkyo to terebi kenkyûkai. 1980. "Senkyo ni okeru terebi no yakuwari ni kansuru kenkyû." Research Report of the Hôsô Bunka Foundation.

Seymour-Ure, Colin. 1974. *The Political Impact of the Mass Media*. London: Constable.

1991. *The British Press and Broadcasting since 1945*. Oxford: Blackwell.

Shigeru, Nozaki, Higashiyama Yoshiyuki, and Shinohara Toshiyuki. 1987. *Hôsô Gyôkai*. Tokyo: Kyôikusha.

Shimizu, Mikio. 1983. "30 years of Japanese TV in Figures and Tables." *Studies of Broadcasting, 1983*, 19, 120–9.

Shlapentokh, V. E. 1970a. *Problemy sotsiologii pechati*. Vols. 1 and 2. Novosibirsk: Nauka, Sibirskoe otdelenie.

1970b. *Sotsiologia dlya vsekh*. Moscow: Sovetskaya Rossia.

Siguán, Miguel. 1994. *Conocimiento y uso de las lenguas en España. (Investigación sobre el conocimiento y uso de las lenguas oficiales en las Comunidades Autónomas bilingües.)* Madrid: Centro de Investigaciones Sociológicas, Opiniones y Actitudes.

Silver, Brian. 1987. "Political Beliefs of the Soviet Citizen: Sources of Support for Regime Norms." In James R. Millar, ed., *Politics, Work, and Daily Life in the USSR*. Cambridge: Cambridge University Press.

Sinova, Justino. 1983. *La gran mentira*. Barcelona: Editorial Planeta.

　1989a. *La censura de prensa durante el franquismo (1936–1951)*. Madrid. Espasa Calpe.

　1989b. "La dificil evolución de la prensa no estatal." In Jesús T. Alvarez, ed., *Historia de los medios de comunicación en España. Periodismo, imagen y publicidad (1900–1990)*. Barcelona: Editorial Ariel.

　1993. *Un millón de votos. 6-J: la verdadera historia de las elecciones que alumbraron un nuevo orden político en España*. Madrid: Ediciones Temas de Hoy.

Siune, Karen, and Wolfgang Truetzschler. 1992. *Dynamics of Media Politics. Broadcast and Electronic Media in Western Europe*. London, Newbury Park, and New Delhi: Sage.

Sivini, Giordano. 1971. "Socialisti e cattolici in Italia dalla società allo Stato." In Giordano Sivini, ed., *Sociologia dei partiti*. Bologna: Il Mulino.

Skidmore, Thomas E., ed. 1993. *Television, Politics and the Transition to Democracy in Latin America*. Baltimore: Johns Hopkins University Press.

Smith, Anthony, ed. 1995. *Television: An International History*. New York: Oxford University Press.

Smoller, Fred. 1988. "Presidents and Their Critics: The Structure of Television News Coverage." *Congress and the Presidency*, 1, 75–89.

Sniderman, Paul, Richard A. Brody, and Philip E. Tetlock. 1991. *Reasoning and Choice: Explorations in Political Psychology*. Cambridge: Cambridge University Press.

Sofres, A. M. 1997. *Anuario de audiencias de televisión, 1997*. Madrid: Sofres.

Stanyer, James, and T. J. Nossiter. 1993. "The 1992 British General Election Campaign on Satellite Television News." Unpublished paper, Department of Government, London School of Economics.

Statera, Giovanni. 1986. *La politica spettacolo. Politici e mass media nell'era delll'immagine*. Milano: Mondadori.

　1987. *Il caso Craxi. Immagine di un Presidente*. Milano: Mondadori.

　1994. *Il volto seduttivo del potere. Berlusconi, i media, il consenso*. Roma: SEAM.

Steele, Catherine A., and Kevin G. Barnhurst. 1995. "The Growing Dominance of Opinionated Journalism in U.S. Presidential Campaign Television Coverage, 1968 and 1988." Paper delivered at the annual meeting of the International Communication Association, Albuquerque, New Mexico.

Sterngold, James. 1990. "In Newfound Focus on Issues, Japan's Parties Plan to Debate." *New York Times*, January 31, A4.

Stewart, Marianne C., and Harold D. Clarke. 1992. "The (Un)Importance of Party Leaders: Leader Images and Party Choice in the 1987 British Election." *Journal of Politics*, 54, 447–70.

Stiehler, Hans-Jörg. 1990. "Medienwelt im Umbruch. Ansätze und Ergebnisse empirischer Medienforschung in der DDR." *Media Perspektiven*, 91–103.

Stock, Martin. 1992. "Der neue Rundfunkstaatsvertrag." *Rundfunk und Fernsehen*, 40, 189–221.

Stock, Martin, Horst Roeper, and Bernd Holznagel. 1997. *Medienmarkt und Meinungsmacht. Zur Neuregelung der Konzentrationskontrolle in Deutschland und Großbritannien*. Berlin: Springer.

Straubhaar, Joseph, Organ Olsen, and Maria Cavaliari Nunes. 1993. "The Brazilian Case: Influencing the Voter." In Skidmore, ed.

Stronach, Bruce. 1989. "Japanese Television." In Richard G. Powers, Hidetoshi Kato, and Bruce Stronach, eds., *Handbook of Japanese Popular Culture.* New York: Greenwood Press.

Stuurman, Siep. 1983. *Verzuiling, Kapitalisme en Patriarchaat. Aspecten van de Ontwikkeling van de Moderne Staat in Nederland.* Nijmegen: Sun.

Sükösd, Miklós. 1990. "From Propaganda to Öffentlichkeit: Four Models of the Public Sphere Under State Socialism." *Praxis International,* 10, 39–63.

——— 1992. "The Media War in Hungary." *East European Reporter,* 5, 69–72.

Sunkel, Guillermo. 1991a. "Prensa y opinión pública en la transición." *Serie Educación y Cultura,* 15, Santiago: FLACSO.

——— 1991b. "Consumo de periódicos en la transición democrática." *Serie Educación y Cultura,* 8. Santiago: FLACSO.

——— 1992. "La prensa en la transición chilena." *Revista de Estudios Sociales,* 72, 155–72.

——— 1994. "La prensa en la transición chilena." In Carlos H. Filgueira and Dieter Nohlen, eds., *Prensa y transición democrática. Experiencias recientes en Europa y América Latina.* Madrid: Iberoamericana.

Swanson, David L., and Paolo Mancini. 1996. *Politics, Media and Modern Democracy: An International Study of Innovations in Electoral Campaigning and Their Consequences.* Westport: Praeger.

Szakadát, István. 1993. *A nómenklatúráról.* Ph.D. dissertation, Hungarian Academy of Sciences and Polytechnic University, Budapest.

Szczepanski, J. 1987. Public lecture at the Institute on East Central Europe, School of International Affairs, Columbia University.

Szelényi, Iván. 1988. *Socialist Entrepreneurs: Embourgeoisement in Rural Hungary.* Madison: University of Wisconsin Press.

Szûcs, Jenõ. 1988. "The Historical Regions of Europe." In John Keane, ed., *Civil Society and the State.* London: Verso.

Tahara, Sôichirô. 1993. "TV ga kimeru seiji: seiteki miryoku to seiji miryoku." *Bungeishunjû,* 71, 164–73.

Tamburrano, Giuseppe. 1990. *Storia del centrosinistra.* Milano: Rizzoli.

Tarrow, Sidney G. 1967. *Peasant Communism in Southern Italy.* New Haven and London: Yale University Press.

Taylor, Paul. 1990. *See How They Run: Electing the President in an Age of Mediacracy.* New York: Knopf.

Terebi Hôdô Kenkyûkai, ed. 1981. *Terebi Nyu-su Kenkyû.* Tokyo: Nippon Hôsô Kyôkai.

Terekhov, Alexander. 1991. "Zalozhnik." *Ogonyek,* November, 10–12.

Terrón, Javier. 1981. *La prensa en España durante el régimen de Franco. Un intento de análisis político.* Madrid: Centro de Investigaciones Sociológicas.

Thayer, Nathaniel. 1975. "Competition and Conformity: An Inquiry into the Structure of the Japanese Newspapers." In Ezra F. Vogel, ed., *Modern Japanese Organization and Decision-Making.* Berkeley: University of California Press.

Tillie, Jean. 1995. *Party Utility and Voting Behavior.* Amsterdam: Het Spinhuis.

Time-América Economía. 1991. *Chile. Marketing and Financial Statistics, 1990/1991.* Santiago: Time-America Economía.

Times-Mirror Center for the People and the Press. 1994. "Mixed Message about Press

Freedom on Both Sides of Atlantic." Eight-nation survey released on March 16, Washington, D.C.

Tinacci Mannelli, Gilberto, and Enrico Cheli. 1986. *L'immagine del potere. Comportamenti, atteggiamenti e strategie d'immagine dei leader politici Italiani.* Milano: Franco Angeli.

Tironi, Eugenio. 1990. *La invisible victoria. Campañas electorales y democracia en Chile,* Santiago: Sur.

1991. "La Nueva Epoca." *El Mercurio,* October 20,

1993. "Cultura, autoritarismo y redemocratización." In Saúl Sosnowski, Manuel Antonio Garretón, and Bernardo Subercaseaux, *Cultura, autoritarismo y redemocratización en Chile.* Santiago: Fondo de Cultura Económica.

Trenaman, Joseph, and Denis McQuail. 1961. *Television and the Political Image: A Study of the Impact of Television in the 1959 General Election.* London: Methuen.

Tuchman, G. 1978. *Making News: A Study in the Construction of Reality.* New York: Free Press.

Tusell, Javier. 1984. *Franco y los católicos. La política interior española entre 1945 y 1957.* Madrid: Alianza Editorial.

Ukhlin, Dmitry. 1998. "Pora pokazat narodu vino tabak." *Obshchaya gazeta,* 50, December 18–24.

Urettini, Luigi. 1978. "Propaganda anticomunista nella stampa cattolica dalla guerra di Spagna alle elezioni del '48." In Isnenghi and Lanaro, eds.

Valenzuela, Arturo. 1978. *The Breakdown of Democratic Regimes: Chile.* Baltimore: Johns Hopkins University Press.

Valenzuela, J. Samuel. 1992. "Democratic Consolidation in Post-Transitional Settings: Motion, Process and Facilitating Conditions." In Scott Mainwaring, Guillermo O'Donnell, and J. Samuel Valenzuela, eds., *Issues in Democratic Consolidation: The New South American Democracies in Comparative Perspective.* Notre Dame: University of Notre Dame Press.

van den Heuvel, Hans. 1976. *Nationaal of Verzuild – De strijd om het Nederlandse Omroepbestel in de periode 1923–1947.* Baarn: Ambo.

van der Eijk, Cees, and Mark N. Franklin. eds. 1996. *Choosing Europe? The European Electorate and National Politics in the Face of Union.* Ann Arbor: University of Michigan Press.

van der Eijk, Cees, Irene van Geest, Peter Kramer, and Lisette Tiddens. 1992. *Verkiezingen zonder Mandaat. Politieke Communicatie en Provinciale Verkiezingen.* The Hague: SDU.

van der Eijk, Cees, and Kees Niemöller 1983. *Electoral Change in the Netherlands.* Amsterdam: CT Press.

1984. "Het potentiele Electoraat van de Nederlandse Politieke Partijen." *Beleid en Maatschappij,* 11, 192–204.

1987. "Electoral Alignments in the Netherlands." *Electoral Studies,* 6, 17–30.

1992. "The Netherlands." In Franklin, Mackie, and Valen, eds.

van der Eijk, Cees, and E. Oppenhuis 1990. "Turnout and Second-Order Effects in the European Elections of June 1989. Evidence from the Netherlands." *Acta Politica,* 25, 67–94.

van der Eijk, Cees, and Philip van Praag, Jr. 1987. *De Strijd om de Meerderheid. De Verkiezingen van 1986.* Amsterdam: CT Press.

van Praag, Jr., Philip 1991. *Strategie en Illusie.* Amsterdam: Het Spinhuis.
 1992. "The Netherlands." In Bowler and Farrell, eds.
van Praag, Jr., Philip, and Kees Brants. 1999. "The 1998 Campaign: An Interaction Approach." *Acta Politica,* 34.
van Schendelen, Rinus, ed. 1984. *Consociationalism, Pillarization and Conflict-Management in the Low Countries.* Meppel: Boom.
Varshavchik, Sergei. 1997. "Drakulu zakazyvali?" *Obshchaya gazeta,* 50, 13.
Verba, Sydney. 1965. "Comparative Political Culture." In Lucian W. Pye and Sydney Verba, eds., *Political Culture and Political Development.* Princeton: Princeton University Press.
Vermeer, Jan P. 1995. *In Media Res: Readings in Mass Media and American Politics.* New York: McGraw-Hill.
Wall Street Journal. 1998. "Ex-Newsman Rebukes Media in His Run for Congress." August 10, A16.
Ward, Robert E. 1978. *Japan's Political System,* 2nd ed. Englewood Cliffs: Prentice-Hall.
Warner, Sidney, and Diego Gambetta. 1994. *La retorica della riforma. Fine del sistema proporzionale in Italia.* Torino: Einaudi.
Watanuki, Joji. 1967. "Patterns of Politics in Present-Day Japan." In Lipset and Rokkan, eds.
Weaver, Donald L., Doris A. Graber, Maxwell E. McCombs, and Chaim H. Eyal. 1981. *Media Agenda-Setting in a Presidential Election.* New York: Praeger.
Weaver, David H., and G. Cleveland Wilhoit. 1986. *The American Journalist.* Bloomington: University of Indiana Press.
Weaver, Paul. 1972. "Is Television News Biased?" *Public Interest,* 27, 57–74.
Weber, Hermann. 1992. "Gab es eine demokratische Vorgeschichte in der DDR?" *Gewerkschaftliche Monatshefte,* 43, 272–80.
Weil, Frederick David. 1992. "The Development of Democratic Attitudes in Eastern and Western Germany in a Comparative Perspective." In Frederick Weil, Mary L. Gautier, and Jeffrey S. Huffman, eds., *Democratization in Eastern and Western Europe.* Greenwich: JAI Press.
Weiss, Ignazio. 1961. *Politica dell'informazione.* Milano: Comunità.
Wert, José Ignacio. 1976. "Estructura y pautas de información en la España de hoy." *Revista Española de la Opinión Pública,* 43, 99–135.
 1980. *Política y medios de comunicación.* Madrid: Cuadernos de la Fundación Humanismo y Democracia.
 1986. "Los medios de comunicación en la década de la libertad." *Diez años en la vida de los españoles.* Barcelona: Plaza y Janés.
 1994. "Perspectivas de reforma del régimen electoral: campañas, medios de comunicación y encuestas electorales." In José Ramón Montero, Richard Gunther, José I. Wert, Julián Santamaría, and Miguel A. Abad, eds., *La reforma del régimen electoral.* Madrid: Centro de Estudios Constitucionales.
Wert, José Ignacio, Rafael López Pintor, and José Juan Toharia. 1993. "El regreso de la política. Una primera interpretación de los resultados del 6-J." *Claves de la Razón Práctica,* 34, 32–42.
Westle, Bettina. 1989. *Politische Legitimität – Theorien, Konzepte, empirische Befunde.* Baden-Baden: Nomos Verlagsgesellschaft.

Westney, D. Eleanor. 1996. "Mass Media as Business Organizations." In Pharr and Krauss, eds.

White, Michael. 1997. "Shoot the Messenger . . . From a Flattering Angle." *The Guardian,* April 28.

White, Stephen, Richard Rose, and Ian McAllister. 1997. *How Russia Votes.* Chatham: Chatham House.

White, Theodore. 1982. *America in Search of Itself: The Making of the President: 1956–1980.* New York: Harper & Row.

Whittemore, Edward P. 1961. *The Press in Japan Today – A Case Study.* Columbia: University of South Carolina Press.

Williams, Raymond. 1974. *Television: Technology and Cultural Form.* New York: Schocken Books.

Wober, Mallory, and B. Svennevig. 1981. *Viewers' Responses to Party Election Broadcasts.* London: IBA.

Worcester, Robert M. 1994. "Index of Partisanship: A Methodology for Determining Change in the Political Bias of Newspapers' Readers." Paper presented at the World Association for Public Opinion Research Asia-Pacific Rim Conference, Sydney, Australia.

Wring, Dominic. 1998. "The Media and Intra-Party Democracy: 'New' Labour and the Clause Four Debate in Britain." *Democratization,* 5, 42–61.

Yamamoto, Akira, and Fujitake Akira, eds. 1987. *Zusetsu – Nihon no masu-komyunike-shyon,* 2nd ed. Tokyo: NHK Books.

Yano Memorial Society, ed. 1991. *Sûji de miru: Nippon no hyakunen,* 3rd ed. Tokyo: Kokuseisha.

Yeltsin, Boris. 1994. *The Struggle for Russia.* New York: Times Books, Random House.

Yoshida, Jun. 1982. "Japanese TV Audiences as Seen from Surveys." *Studies of Broadcasting,* 18, 115–51.

Zaller, John R. 1992. *The Nature and Origins of Mass Opinion.* Cambridge: Cambridge University Press.

1996. "The Myth of Massive Media Effects Revived: New Support for a Discredited Idea." In Diana C. Mutz, Paul M. Sniderman, and Richard Brody, eds., *Political Persuasion and Attitude Change.* Ann Arbor: University of Michigan Press.

Zaller, John R., and Mark Hunt. 1994–5. "The Rise and Fall of Candidate Perot, Parts 1 and 2." *Political Communication,* 11(4), 357–91, and 12(1), 97–123.

Zaslavskaya, T. I. 1984. "The Novosibirsk Report." *Survey,* 28, 88–108.

1990. "Perestroika kak sotsialnaya revolyutsia," In V. A. Yadov, ed., *Sotsiologia perestroiki.* Moscow: Nauka.

Zollo, Antonio, ed. 1987. *Il villaggio di vetro.* Roma: Editori Riuniti.

Zuleta-Puceiro, Enrique. 1993. "The Argentine Case: Television in the 1989 Presidential Campaign." In Skidmore, ed.

Index